Da

The New Edinburgh Islamic Surveys
Series Editor: Carole Hillenbrand

Contemporary Issues in Islam Asma Asfaruddin
Astronomy and Astrology in the Islamic World Stephen P. Blake
The New Islamic Dynasties Clifford Edmund Bosworth
Media Arabic Julia Ashtiany Bray
An Introduction to the Hadith John Burton
A History of Islamic Law Noel Coulson
Medieval Islamic Political Thought Patricia Crone
A Short History of the Ismailis Farhad Daftary
Islam: An Historical Introduction (2nd Edition) Gerhard Endress
A History of Christian–Muslim Relations Hugh Goddard
Shi'ism (2nd Edition) Heinz Halm
Islamic Science and Engineering Donald Hill
Muslim Spain Reconsidered Richard Hitchcock
Islamic Law: From Historical Foundations to Contemporary Practice Mawil Izzi Dien
Sufism: The Formative Period Ahmet T. Karamustafa
A History of Islam in Indonesia Carool Kersten
Da'wa: *A Global History of Islamic Missionary Thought and Practice,* Matthew J. Kuiper
Islamic Aesthetics Oliver Leaman
Persian Historiography Julie Scott Meisami
The Muslims of Medieval Italy Alex Metcalfe
The Archaeology of the Islamic World Marcus Milwright
Twelver Shi'ism Andrew Newman
Muslims in Western Europe (4th Edition) Jørgen S. Nielsen and Jonas Otterbeck
Medieval Islamic Medicine Peter E. Pormann and Emilie Savage-Smith
Muslims in Eastern Europe Egdūnas Račius
Islamic Names Annemarie Schimmel
The Genesis of Literature in Islam Gregor Schoeler
Islam in Modern Turkey, Kim Shively
The Qur'an: A Historical-Critical Introduction Nicolai Sinai
Modern Arabic Literature Paul Starkey
Islamic Medicine Manfred Ullman
A History of Islamic Spain W. Montgomery Watt and Pierre Cachia
Introduction to the Qur'an W. Montgomery Watt
Islamic Creeds W. Montgomery Watt
Islamic Philosophy and Theology W. Montgomery Watt
Islamic Political Thought W. Montgomery Watt
The Influence of Islam on Medieval Europe W. Montgomery Watt
Muslims of Central Asia: An Introduction Galina M. Yemelianova

edinburghuniversitypress.com/series/isur

Da'wa

A global history of Islamic missionary thought and practice

Matthew J. Kuiper

EDINBURGH
University Press

For my parents

Edinburgh University Press is one of the leading university presses in the UK. We publish academic books and journals in our selected subject areas across the humanities and social sciences, combining cutting-edge scholarship with high editorial and production values to produce academic works of lasting importance. For more information visit our website: edinburghuniversitypress.com

© Matthew J. Kuiper, 2021

Edinburgh University Press Ltd
The Tun – Holyrood Road
12 (2f) Jackson's Entry
Edinburgh EH8 8PJ

Typeset in 11/13pt Baskerville MT Pro by
Servis Filmsetting Ltd, Stockport, Cheshire

A CIP record for this book is available from the British Library

ISBN 978 1 4744 5152 9 (hardback)
ISBN 978 1 4744 5153 6 (paperback)
ISBN 978 1 4744 5154 3 (webready PDF)
ISBN 978 1 4744 5155 0 (epub)

The right of Matthew J. Kuiper to be identified as author of this work has been asserted in accordance with the Copyright, Designs and Patents Act 1988 and the Copyright and Related Rights Regulations 2003 (SI No. 2498).

Published with the support of the University of Edinburgh Scholarly Publishing Initiatives Fund.

Contents

Expanded table of contents   vi
List of illustrations   ix
List of text boxes   x
Preface and acknowledgments   xi
Note on transliteration and dates   xiv

Introduction   1

Part I The pre-modern missionary history of Islam

1 The first invitation to Islam: *Daʿwa* in the Qur'an   19
2 The best inviter: *Daʿwa* in prophetic *sira* and hadith   39
3 *Daʿwa* after the Prophet, *circa* 632–1100 CE   65
4 *Daʿwa* in medieval and early modern Islamic history,
   circa 1100–1700 CE   91

Part II The modern missionary history of Islam

Introduction to Part II   133
5 Contextualising modern *daʿwa*, eighteenth to twentieth centuries 143
6 The first phase of modern *daʿwa*, *circa* 1850–1950: a survey   164
7 The second phase of modern *daʿwa*, *circa* 1950–2020: a survey   203

Conclusion   257
Epilogue: COVID-19 and *daʿwa*   258

Bibliography   261
Index   300

Expanded table of contents

List of illustrations	ix
List of text boxes	x
Preface and acknowledgements	xi
Note on transliteration and dates	xiv

Introduction	1
A look ahead	6
Defining key terms and anticipating key themes	8

Part I   The pre-modern missionary history of Islam

1 The first invitation to Islam: *da'wa* in the Qur'an	19
The Qur'an and its context: *da'wa* in the midst of other *da'wa*s	20
Da'wa to God and the *da'wa* of God in the Qur'an	22
The *da'wa* of God's Prophets in the Qur'an	25
Prophets and messengers before Muhammad	27
The Prophet Muhammad's *da'wa* in the Qur'an	28
The *da'wa* of the believing (Muslim) community	31
Summary and conclusions	34

2 The best inviter: *da'wa* in prophetic *sira* and hadith	39
Sira and hadith: a brief introduction	40
Mecca: *da'wa* from a position of weakness	42
Muhammad's first converts	44
The recitation of the Qur'an as a *da'wa* strategy	46
Da'wa, opposition and failure	47
Medina: *da'wa* from a position of rising strength	48
Continuing opposition and conversions	50
Da'wa and *jihad*	51
Da'wa, iconoclasm and the problems of success	53
Converting Arabia and beyond	55
Summary and conclusions	59

3   *Daʿwa* after the Prophet, *circa* 632–1100 CE   65
Daʿwa and the conquests   66
The emergence of Muslim disunity and the rise of religio-political *daʿwa*s   72
    The ʿAbbasid *daʿwa*   74
    The Ismaʿili/Fatimid *daʿwa*   75
Daʿwa and Islamic law and theology   78
Summary and conclusions   85

**4   *Daʿwa* in medieval and early modern Islamic history,
    circa 1100–1700 CE**   91
Turks, Mongols and other migratory peoples: Islamisation through
    in-migration   93
Muslim rulers and ruler-converts: Islamisation by royal example or
    expectation   99
    Muslim rulers and dynasties and the spread of Islam   101
The *ʿulama*: Islamisation through knowledge preservation and
    transmission   105
The Sufi brotherhoods: Islamisation through inspiration and
    indigenisation   109
Popular preachers and storytellers: Islamisation through popularisation   117
Merchants: Islamisation through networking and trade   119
Summary and conclusions   121

Part II   The modern missionary history of Islam

Introduction to Part II   133
Key terms and themes of Part II   135

**5   Contextualising modern *daʿwa*, eighteenth to twentieth
    centuries**   143
Contextualising modern *daʿwa* 1: early modern Islamic reform   143
Contextualising modern *daʿwa* 2: high modern colonialism   148
Conclusion: towards the first phase of modern *daʿwa*   158

6   The first phase of modern *daʿwa*, *circa* 1850–1950: a survey   164
The Indian subcontinent   164
Egypt   172
Turkey   176
Central Asia   178
Southeast Asia   179
Sub-Saharan Africa   181

North Africa   186
The Arab Fertile Crescent   187
Iran   191
Arabia   192
Muslim minority populations   195
Summary and conclusions   196

7   **The second phase of modern *da'wa*, *circa* 1950–2020:**
     a survey   203
Contextualising modern *da'wa* 3: post-colonial times to the present   203
Surveying the second phase of modern *da'wa*   212
    Non-state initiatives and actors in *da'wa*   212
        Non-state religio-political or militant *da'wa*s   226
    State-sponsored *da'wa* initiatives   229
        State-sponsored *da'wa* as domestic policy   230
        State-sponsored *da'wa* as foreign policy   236
    Non-state and state-sponsored *da'wa* organisations: conclusions   242
    Migration and the *da'wa* initiatives of Muslim minority populations 243
Summary and conclusions   249

Conclusion   257

Epilogue: COVID-19 and *da'wa*   258

Bibliography   261
Index   300

Illustrations

Figures

1.1	The Qur'an, the foundational wellspring of Islam	33
2.1	The Mosque of the Prophet, Medina	57
4.1	The Registan at night, Samarkand, Uzbekistan	97
4.2	Contemporary pilgrims at the Shrine (*dargah*) of Mu'inuddin Chishti, Ajmer, India	114
6.1	Mirza Ghulam Ahmad, 1835–1908, founder of the Ahmadiyya movement	169
6.2	Rashid Rida, 1865–1935, a pioneer in Islamic publishing and *da'wa*	172
6.3	Indonesian women of Muslimat NU, East Java, 2016	182
6.4	A participant in 'Shaykh Ahmadu Bamba International Day'	185
7.1	Fethullah Gulen (b. 1941), founder of the Gulen movement	215
7.2	The DVD cover of Ahmed Deedat's 'Great [1986] Debate' with Jimmy Swaggart	217
7.3	Yusuf al-Qaradawi (b. 1926)	220
7.4	The Shah Faisal Mosque in Islamabad, Pakistan	237
7.5	The cover of Dr Maurice Bucaille's 1976 book	239

Maps

I.1	World Muslim population distribution, 2020	3
3.1	The Arab-Islamic conquests, *circa* 622–750	67
4.1	The Mongol Khanates, *circa* thirteenth to fourteenth centuries	95
4.2	The Islamic gunpowder empires	104
4.3	The origins and spread of some major Sufi orders	112
5.1	The former Muslim ecumene under European and other non-Muslim powers, *circa* 1930	152
7.1	Post-colonial North and Central Africa, the Middle East, and Central, South and Southeast Asia, late twentieth to early twenty-first centuries	204

Text boxes

I.1 Some key terms in this book   13
1.1 Competing *da‘wa*s: the religiously contested world of the rise of
     Islam   23
1.2 The *da‘wa* of the Prophet Noah in the Qur’an   28
2.1 Modern *da‘wa* lessons from the Companion al-Tufayl   46
2.2 Ibn Ishaq’s description of the Mecca-to-Medina transformation in
     Muhammad’s *da‘wa* ministry   49
2.3 A modern Muslim scholar describes the ‘Year of Delegations’   56
2.4 Muhammad’s letter of *da‘wa* to Heraclius   58
3.1 Some examples of external *da‘wa* in the ‘Abbasid period   76
3.2 *Da‘wa* in al-Marghinani’s legal compendium *al-Hidaya*   80
4.1 The spread of Islam according to the *Kano Chronicle*   107
II.1 Some key terms in Part II   139
5.1 A monumental shift in the balance of Muslim piety   149
6.1 An excerpt from the most important text of the Tablighi Jama‘at   168
6.2 Two *da‘wa*-oriented English Qur’an translations from India   171
6.3 An early-twentieth-century excerpt from Rida’s *al-Manar*   174
7.1 Electronic media and *da‘wa*   216
7.2 A modern *da‘wa* lineage or *silsila*   218
7.3 The how-to of *da‘wa*: contemporary *da‘wa* manuals   222
7.4 Mainstream Salafi *da‘wa*logy   229
7.5 On *da‘wa*, from the Da‘wah Academy of the International Islamic
     University, Islamabad   233
7.6 Excerpt from IslamWeb.net’s article ‘Women in *Da‘wa*’   234
7.7 The ‘aims’ of Iran’s Islamic Culture and Religious Organisation
     (ICRO) and Ministry of Culture and Islamic Guidance (MCIG)   243
7.8 Women and *da‘wa*: the contrasting *da‘wa*s of Maryam Jameelah and
     Amina Wadud   247
7.9 A sermon to Muslims in the West   249

Preface and acknowledgements

Islam, in all its varieties, is the religion of nearly two billion people who live on every inhabited continent, speak hundreds of languages and dialects, represent countless of ethnicities and sectarian divisions, and make major impacts in most fields of human endeavour. Today, a majority of Muslims, or followers of Islam, and most Muslim-majority countries are found in the vast and historically rich swath of land stretching from Senegal and Morocco in the west all the way to Indonesia in the east. However, there are also growing Muslim populations in many other places, including western countries. The book in your hands surveys the story of how Islam became a 'world religion' of such immense scale. It does so by providing a global history of *da'wa*, or missionary thought and practice in Islam, from the Qur'an to the present (from *circa* 610 to 2020 CE) – but more on the book's purpose and plan in the Introduction, just a few pages ahead.

Anyone who sets out to study a major theme in history and then to write a 'global history' on that theme is either slightly crazy, or else blissfully unaware of what they are truly in for. I plead mostly the latter. Having already published a specialist monograph on Islamic mission or *da'wa* (Da'wa *and Other Religions*, Routledge, 2018), I believed that I had a decent head-start towards writing a second, more general, history of Islamic mission for a wider audience. I was only partially correct. While the earlier book gave me a foundation to build upon, writing this new book turned out to be a monumental undertaking which involved over two years of almost continuous research and reflection. Along the way, I ventured into many historical periods, regions of the world and subfields of Islamic Studies. While most of my earlier conclusions about *da'wa* were confirmed, in some cases I found myself refining my understandings. This book is the fruit of that process. In addition, writing this book enabled me to fill out several areas of the earlier book where I was only able to nod at certain phenomena or cover them thinly. I gratefully acknowledge the permission Routledge granted me to use material from Da'wa *and Other Religions* for this project. Although some aspects of Chapters 1, 2 and 3 bear similarity to corresponding material in the earlier book, each of these chapters was researched afresh and rewritten for this new book. The material from Chapter 4 to the end of Da'wa: *A Global History* is almost entirely new.

While this work – with its inevitable limitations and shortcomings – is mine alone, I gratefully acknowledge the help and support of multiple individuals and organisations. I thank Prof. Carole Hillenbrand, editor of the New Edinburgh Islamic Surveys series, and Nicola Ramsey and Kirsty Woods at Edinburgh University Press (EUP) for their expert guidance. I also thank the anonymous reviewers of the initial book proposal and the reviewer of the final manuscript. These scholars' comments and suggestions proved to be very helpful. I am grateful to Prof. John Voll, who invited me to write what would become two lengthy annotated bibliography articles, one on *Da'wa* and another on the Tablighi Jama'at, for *Oxford Bibliographies in Islamic Studies* in 2017–18. Writing these two articles was instrumental in preparing me for this project. I also thank Julian Millie and Dietrich Reetz who peer-reviewed these articles. I am indebted to my friend Gabriel Said Reynolds, with whom I initially floated my idea for this book and who provided encouragement and feedback along the way. So, too, Paul Kollman, who facilitated a week-long research retreat for me at the University of Notre Dame in May 2019 and who provided feedback on part of the manuscript. Appreciation is also due to the Holy Cross brothers who hosted me at Moreau Seminary at Notre Dame during that week. I am very grateful to Ermin Sinanović and the Center for Islam in the Contemporary World (CICW) at Shenandoah University for the generous research grant which enabled me to take additional research and writing retreats in July and November 2019.

Along with the scholars mentioned above (and in the bibliography), a few others who deserve special mention include Mun'im Sirry, Ebrahim Moosa, John Renard, Nile Green, Edward Curtis, Laury Silvers, SherAli Tareen, Fouad Naeem, Deborah Tor, Andrew McLaren, Heather Sharkey, Umar Ryad, Aaron Rock-Singer, Jan-Peter Hartung, Oguz Tan, Andrew O'Connor, Brannon Ingram, Gordon Nickel, Jason Welle, Thomas Gugler and Macodou Fall. I acknowledge my colleagues in the Midwest region of the American Academy of Religion (MAAR), where I have served as Islamic Studies section chair since 2017. I also acknowledge the help that Sam Thomas and Mourad Takawi provided at various stages. At Missouri State University, Steve Berkwitz, Jack Llewellyn and my other faculty colleagues in Religious Studies, along with Jane Terry, provided support and collegiality as I worked on the project. Victor Matthews, Dean of the College of Humanities and Public Affairs, offered input and provided generous research grants over two summers, in 2018 and 2019. Jonathan Bowman was my Graduate Assistant in 2018–19 and Tyler Cochran in 2019–20. Both provided invaluable help. I am grateful to Frank Einhellig, the Provost of Missouri State, along with the MSU Faculty Center for Teaching and Learning, for the regular faculty writing retreats I attended. The staff at MSU's Meyer Library helped me track down many books and articles. My students listened politely as I talked about this project, and many asked thoughtful questions.

I conclude with thanks to my family. First, my parents, Don and Lucille, have been my most unfailing and enthusiastic supporters over the years, and it is with gratitude and love that I dedicate the book to them. I also thank my brothers, Joel and Mark, and their families, for their interest and support. As it happened, in the summer of 2018, my family and I were visiting Uzbekistan, where Mark and his family were living at the time, when I learned that EUP had provisionally approved my book proposal. Days later, I was walking through the historic mosques and *madrasa*s of Bukhara and Samarkand and visited the tomb of the great hadith compiler al-Bukhari (d. 870). Finally, I owe thanks to my wife Laurie and my children Justin, John and Abby – you have lightened the load of writing this book in more ways than I can count. As I write these words, we have spent the past nearly two months together under a COVID-19 stay-at-home order. I cannot think of any others with whom I would rather 'shelter in place'. I am incredibly thankful for your love and support over the past two years, as your sometimes preoccupied husband and dad worked on this project.

Note on transliteration and dates

When I teach courses on Islam in my English-speaking university setting, I tell my students: 'This is not an Arabic course, but you cannot study Islam without learning some Arabic vocabulary along the way'. Similarly, although this book has been written in order to be accessible to general readers with no background in Arabic or Islam, it unavoidably cites Arabic sources and uses some Arabic terms – there is even an Arabic word in the book's title! A few terms from other 'Islamicate' languages, like Persian and Urdu, also make appearances. With respect to this book's approach to transliteration (how terms and phrases from languages using non-Roman alphabets are represented in English), the reader might find it helpful to keep two categories in mind. First, there are many Arabic and other non-English words which are not fully transliterated – they are written without diacritical marks and may not be italicised. Words which are well-known in English usage are unitalicised and follow normal conventions (for instance, Qur'an, Sufi, shaykh, Sunni, Shi'ite). Other common key words (words which are somewhat familiar to English speakers or which appear often in the book) may be written in italics but without diacritics (for instance, *da'wa*, *shari'a*, *'ulama*, *jihad*, *tawhid*). Proper names are written without any diacritics – for instance, Muhammad (not Muḥammad), 'Ali (not ʿAlī), Ishaq (not Isḥāq), Isma'il (not Ismāʿīl), Bukhara (not Bukhārā), Sa'ud (not Saʿūd) – although some names appear with diacritics in the endnotes and bibliography. In simplified transliterations and in proper names, the Arabic letters ʿayn (indicated by a forward apostrophe, as in 'Ali and *'ulama*) and sometimes *hamza* (represented by an apostrophe as in Qur'an) are still included. The more technical symbols for ʿayn (ʿ) and *hamza* (ʾ) are reserved for fully transliterated terms.

The second category consists of Arabic (and other) words and phrases which are fully transliterated (italicised with diacritics where applicable). My hope is that including these in various places adds richness to the text and benefits those who know some Arabic, without impeding general readers. To illustrate, in '*ḍarūra*' (Arabic for 'necessity'), 'ḍ' represents the 'thudding' 'd' of the Arabic alphabet (Arabic also has a softer, dental 'd'), 'a' is a short vowel, 'r' is pronounced like the English 'r', and 'ū' is a long vowel. When transliterating words which have the Arabic feminine singular ending (or *tāʾ marbūṭa*), I usually do not include a final 'h' (*da'wa* not *da'wah*, *hijra* not *hijrah*). Exceptions include words which are commonly represented in English with 'h', like *surah* and *ayah* (qur'anic chapter and verse). I write the Arabic definite article as 'al-' even when it is connected to the so-called solar letters. The Arabic dipthongs are generally '*ay*' and '*aw*'. For simplicity, certain Arabic plurals are represented by simply adding 's' to the singular form (*dā'īs* or *da'is* instead of *du'ā*). A few final pointers: (1) This book uses the English 'God' rather than the Arabic 'Allah' (or 'Allāh'), except in some quotations. (2) 'Middle East' (rather than 'Near East') is used throughout. (3) 'Qur'an' is capitalised, but the adjective 'qur'anic' is not. (4) For the Arabic letter *waw*, I generally prefer 'w' over 'v' (Ahmad Yasawi not Ahmad Yasavi, Mawlawiyya not Mevleviyya). (5) Names from Turkic and Mongol languages are represented in their familiar English forms (Genghis not Chinggis, Hulegu not Hülegü).

This book uses Gregorian, or common era, dates throughout. The reader should keep in mind, however, that the Islamic or *hijri* calendar is a lunar calendar that pivots on the Prophet's migration (*hijra*) to Medina in 622 CE. In a few cases, *hijri* dates are included when relevant. Finally, regarding English usage: this book follows British conventions, for instance, 'favour' instead of 'favor', 'Islamisation' instead of 'Islamization'. When I quote another author who uses American instead of British spelling, I retain that author's usage.

Introduction

Islam is a missionary religion. Like other missionary religions, it makes universal claims – claims which it holds to be true for all people everywhere – about God, the universe, revelation, the ethical life and human accountability. Muslims, or followers of Islam, ordinarily believe that God's word to Muhammad was, in some sense, a final word which completed all prior monotheistic revelation. In the Islamic reckoning, while earlier prophets were sent to limited groups of people, Muhammad's message was and is for the whole world. As such, from relatively early in its history, Islam has inspired its adherents to seek converts, and prospective converts to seek Islam. Intimately related to its universalism and sense of finality is the fact that Islam has always been a religion of preaching and persuasion. From the very start, in the Qur'an itself, one hears the voice of a preacher, urgently summoning his hearers to *islām*, submission to God, in light of the coming Day of Judgment. Not only do Muslims believe that the Qur'an contains a message for the whole world, several verses in the Qur'an also seem to assume that those who accept its message will themselves preach to others. Among the most well-known is the qur'anic command of Q 16:125, 'Invite [others] to the way of your Lord with wisdom'.

In the post-qur'anic Islamic sources, the Prophet Muhammad is presented, among other things, as a missionary preacher – *the* prototypical missionary preacher of Islam. Like the ancient prophets, he is depicted as one who persevered despite opposition and declared God's message faithfully. Gradually, according to the traditional sources, Muhammad's missionary preaching met with success. Multiple conversion narratives are found in the pages of the Prophet's biography. According to these narratives, several of the Prophet's early converts, such as Khadija, Abu Bakr, 'Ali and others were quickly transformed into missionary preachers in their own right. In the Qur'an and other formative Islamic sources, the Arabic word (and its variants) most often associated with missionary preaching is *da'wa* – 'invitation' or 'summons'. Five times a day across the Muslim world, from the loudspeakers of innumerable mosques or perhaps over their cell phones, believers (and often non-believers) hear a summons to true faith and piety in the *adhān*, the Islamic call to prayer. The call to prayer – which publicly declares the greatness of the One God and the prophethood of Muhammad, and which urges its hearers to prayer and salvation[1] – is, in many ways, a summons to Islam itself. In fact, throughout Islamic history, the *adhān* has been referred to as *da'wat al-tamma*, the complete or perfect *da'wa*.[2]

Following the death of Muhammad, there is substantial evidence that his followers initially thought of Islam as a 'religion' for Arabs only (see Chapter 3).[3] Yet, as they burst out of Arabia and conquered the late antique Middle East during the seventh and eighth centuries CE,[4] this idea was eventually cast aside, and Islam's latent universalism came to the fore. Slowly at first, but then picking up speed over time, Islam spread among the peoples of the Middle East, North Africa, Central Asia, Anatolia, southern Europe, India and western China. It won over Persians, Turkic peoples and Mongols. Eventually, it was established as far east as southeastern China and Indo-Malaysia. The spread of Islam to all these lands entailed the conversion of Jews, Christians, Zoroastrians, Manicheans, Hindus, Buddhists and followers of traditional religions to Islam. It also resulted in the emergence of classical Islamic civilisation with all its dazzling achievements. In more recent times, Islam has established an important presence outside of its traditional heartlands, including in western countries.

Today, roughly 25 percent, or one out of every four human beings on planet earth, self-identifies as 'Muslim', and that number is expected to rise to 30 percent by the year 2050.[5] The worldwide expansion of Islam from the seventh century to the present has resulted in a global religious community characterised by great ethnic, linguistic and theological diversity. What is commonly called today 'the Muslim World' – a term which refers collectively to those regions of the world where the faith of Islam predominates, or more broadly to the worldwide community of all Muslims[6] – came into being not only through the expansion of Islamic empires, natural demographic growth and the migration of Muslim peoples to new places, but also through the missionary endeavours of the Muslim community over the centuries (see Map I.1). These varied endeavours have been driven by a missionary impulse that can be said to emerge from Islam's universalism, its character as a religion of preaching and persuasion, the example of the Prophet Muhammad and his early followers, and the expansive momentum of Islamic history in general. This book has been written to provide an introduction to Islam *as a missionary religion*.

Talk of Islam's 'impulses' could be taken to imply that the missionary history of Islam is a story that emerges straightforwardly from the Qur'an and life of the Prophet. While these sources are the indispensable foundations for Muslim belief and practice, including missionary belief and practice, this book will show just how complicated and uneven the missionary history of Islam is. Historical context, as much as theological conviction, has often determined the ways in which Muslims have interpreted and implemented (or perhaps ignored) whatever missionary expectations and patterns are found in their sacred sources. In fact, as we will see, the sources themselves do not provide

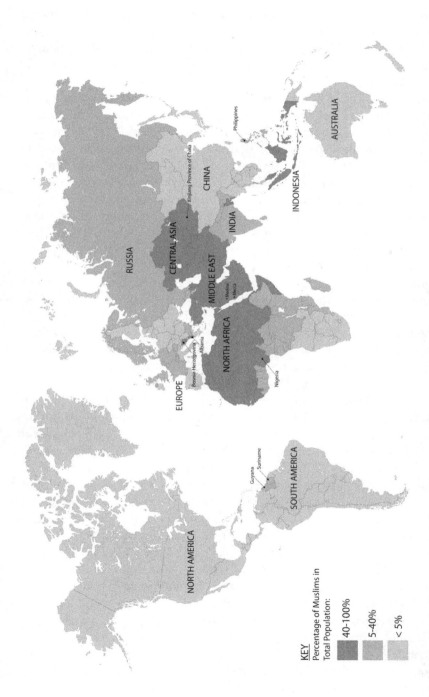

Map I.1 World Muslim population distribution, 2020. The world's nearly two billion Muslims live on every inhabited continent, represent countless ethnicities and languages, and make major impacts within most fields of human endeavour. Today, a majority of Muslims live in the vast swath of land stretching from Senegal and Morocco in the west all the way to Indonesia in the east, but there are also growing Muslim populations in many other places, including western countries.

a one-size-fits-all perspective on Islamic mission. The following chapters will show, therefore, that the 'missionary impulse' of Islam has both waxed and waned over time and exhibited itself in great diversity. Like any other phenomenon involving human beings, it has been subject to historical development and change. While the religious expansion of Islam was often intertwined with the political expansion of Islamic empires, at other times, it took place more or less independently of politics. In some regions of the world, Islamisation (or the spread of Islam, see below) has been stunningly successful. In others, it has been less so. While the expansion of Islam has sometimes been hindered by intra-Muslim rivalry and conflict (for instance, between Sunnis and Shi'ites), such conflict has also stimulated missionary outreach. For most of pre-modern Islamic history, missionary outreach was rarely carried out by centralised institutions or with organised intentionality. Nor was it thought to be a duty applicable to all Muslims. Instead, it was carried out through the relatively *ad hoc* and sporadic efforts of Muslim rulers, merchants, mystics, soldiers, scholars, preachers and others.

The situation, however, has changed dramatically over roughly the past century and a half. Since the late nineteenth and early twentieth centuries, and continuing to the present, there has been a remarkable upsurge in missionary commitment and activism among Muslims worldwide. This renewal of the missionary impulse of Islam has spawned a significant democratisation and diversification of the missionary task, so that more and more ordinary Muslims around the world see it as their personal responsibility to spread Islam and to do so with great creativity and variety. This renewal has also resulted in Muslim efforts to build countless local, regional and international organisations and institutions devoted to carrying out Islamic propagation in systematic ways. Coinciding with these trends has been the re-emergence of the term '*da'wa*' as a keynote concept among modern Muslims. An Arabic term which literally means 'calling', 'inviting', or 'summoning', *da'wa* is most frequently used by contemporary Muslims in reference to Islamic missionary activity – 'inviting' to Islam. Important variants of the word include the verb *da'ā* (to invite) and the participle *dā'ī* (one who invites). Among Muslims, regardless of their mother tongue, '*dā'ī*' (sometimes spelled 'daee' or other variations, hereafter *da'i*) is the word most often used for 'missionary'. While there are some in the Muslim community who are seen as professional or full-time *da'i*s, it is often argued by Muslim preachers today that every Muslim should think of him- or herself as *da'i*.

More or less obvious manifestations of contemporary *da'wa* range widely, from traditional sermons in mosques and *madrasa*s to newer modes of street or marketplace preaching; from Qur'an translation and distribution programs to the production of Islamic literature and films; from the founding of private (voluntary or non-governmental) *da'wa* societies and storefronts to departments of *da'wa* in Islamic universities; from the emergence of a distinct *fiqh al-da'wa*

(Islamic jurisprudence of *da'wa*) to the popularisation of the idea that the Qur'an anticipates the findings of modern science; from an array of *da'wa*-oriented Islamic websites to the emergence of Islamic televangelism; from the recruitment activities of political Islamist and Jihadi groups to the everyday religious witness of ordinary Muslim men, women and children. Contemporary *da'wa* is not limited to obvious examples such as these, however. Many other dynamics among modern Muslims may be more subtly oriented towards, or animated by *da'wa*: for instance, the myriad efforts of modern Muslims to promote modernisation or reform; the work of Muslim student groups on university campuses; the efforts of Muslim-majority states or inter-governmental organisations to showcase the achievements of Islamic civilisation; Muslim initiatives aimed at countering Islamophobic misinformation; a heightened emphasis in many communities on Islamic dress and comportment; initiatives in Islamic banking, finance and education; Muslim engagement in inter-religious dialogues and new ways of thinking about the place of Muslims in non-Muslim societies, to name just a few.

To put it simply, *da'wa* is a powerful and pervasive concept in contemporary Islamic thought and activism. Not only is the term itself instantly recognisable to many millions of Muslims worldwide, Muslims of nearly every background have had their lives touched by *da'wa* – both as agents and objects of *da'wa* – in recent times. Much as the concept of *jihad* has been used by modern Muslims to speak of a variety of contemporary 'struggles', *da'wa* has been drawn from the lexical repertoire of early and classical Islam as an organising term for a range of contemporary approaches to missionary outreach. In fact, as this book will show, significant numbers of Muslims have come to think of missionary *da'wa* as the most appropriate *jihad* for this moment in history.[7] Not surprisingly, Muslims are looking to the Qur'an and to the life of the Prophet Muhammad as perhaps never before to glean insights into what *da'wa* is, and how best to do it. All of this *da'wa* activity and ferment has resulted in the emergence of varieties of Islamic missiology or '*da'walogy*' (theological and practical reflection on *da'wa*). Following the lead of modern Muslims, therefore, this book's study of Islamic missionary history is organised around the concept of *da'wa*. Indeed, the contemporary resurgence of *da'wa* provides the starting point and ultimate rationale for the book.[8]

Few introductory books in English have been written on the subject of *da'wa* or the missionary aspect of Islam to which it refers. Unlike '*jihad*', '*shari'a*', or even '*hijab*' (classical Islamic concepts on which there are numerous introductory books), *da'wa* has attracted limited scholarly attention. Thomas Arnold's *The Preaching of Islam: A History of the Propagation of the Muslim Faith*, first published in 1896 and republished in 1913, is a still influential work which covers Islamic missionary propagation from the beginning of Islam to the dawn of the twentieth century.[9] It should come as no surprise, however, that Arnold's work has significant limitations, the most important being that its narrative ended just before the twentieth-century *da'wa* resurgence got underway.[10] Since the early 1990s, numerous scholars have begun to take notice of *da'wa*, and several fine studies have been published. These, however, tend to be technical – written by scholars for other scholars, or focused narrowly on particular case-studies of *da'wa*.[11] Other, popular writings on *da'wa* tend to be apologetic or polemical in nature – written in praise of *da'wa*, or to warn of the alleged menace of *da'wa*.

This book is an attempt to meet the need for an up-to-date historical survey of *da'wa*, or missionary thought and practice in Islam, from the Qur'an to the present. Drawing on the author's own research, as well as on the findings of others, it surveys the scriptural roots, pre-modern history and contemporary practice of *da'wa*. One of the book's core arguments is that that there is a discernible story of *da'wa* in Islam from the Qur'an to the present, even if it is a story marked by considerable variation over time. It is, in other words, a story characterised by continuity and change. For all the novelty of modern styles *da'wa* in the Muslim world (see Part II), these should still be understood within the context of the older missionary history of Islam. If nothing else, it is hoped that this book contributes something fresh to our understanding of what Ignaz Goldziher once called the 'vast historical effect of the *call to Islam*'.[12]

A look ahead

Da'wa: *A Global History of Islamic Missionary Thought and Practice* is divided into two parts. Part I (Chapters 1 to 4) examines the scriptural roots and pre-modern history of *da'wa*, while Part II surveys *da'wa* in the modern world. Since the modern resurgence of *da'wa* provides the starting point for the book as a whole, Part I frequently draws attention to the ways in which pre-modern developments are related to modern trends. Depending on their interests, readers can profitably focus on Part I or Part II, or proceed directly to individual chapters. However, readers will benefit most by following the book's narrative and arguments through from beginning to end.

Chapter 1 provides an original introduction to and analysis of Islam's foundational scripture, the Qur'an, from the perspective of *da'wa*. It introduces readers to the Qur'an and examines in detail the Qur'an's missionary theology or *da'wa*logy, along with the ways in which the Qur'an itself seems to do, and to encourage its followers to do, *da'wa*. Chapter 2 turns to the major post-qur'anic Islamic sources, the *sira* (traditional biography of the Prophet Muhammad) and hadith literatures. Following a general introduction to these literatures and their place in the Islamic tradition, the chapter examines the ways they might be said to present Muhammad and his Companions (*ṣaḥāba*) as *da'is* or missionary preachers, and it gives special attention to the distinction between Muhammad's 'Meccan *da'wa*' and his 'Medinan *da'wa*'. This contrast provides a thematic frame which will reappear throughout the book. By beginning with the scriptural and formative sources of Islam in Chapters 1 and 2, it should be stressed that this book is not implying that all subsequent developments in Islamic missionary history can somehow be traced to scriptural teachings and precedents – far from it. As much as Muslim preachers and apologists might wish it were so, Islamic history does not flow in an unbroken and uncomplicated fashion from the faith's sources. In fact, the story is full of unexpected twists. Nevertheless, inasmuch as Islam is self-consciously a 'religion of the book' (or books) and inasmuch as Muslims, for most of Islamic history, have looked to the Qur'an and hadith as central touchstones of belief and piety, this book considers it necessary to examine critically what these sources might say, or might be interpreted as saying, about *da'wa* and Islamisation.

Part I of this book is rounded out by Chapters 3 and 4. Together, these chapters survey the long period from the death of Muhammad (632 CE) to the dawn of modern times (roughly 1700 CE). Chapter 3 provides a thematic overview of the history of *da'wa* from the death of the Prophet and the establishment of the early caliphate (*circa* 632 CE) to approximately 1100 CE. It traces Islamic missionary history in relation to three major developments: (1) the Arab-Islamic conquests (*circa* 632–750 CE); (2) the rise of Muslim disunity and the internal *da'wa*s of Muslim religio-political movements such as the 'Abbasids and Fatimids; and (3) the place that *da'wa* would come to occupy in Islamic law and theology. Chapter 4, covering the period from roughly 1100 to 1700, focuses on what it calls 'agents and patterns of Islamisation' during these centuries. The chapter begins with an overview of what it calls the 'Muslim ecumene', stretching from Morocco in the west to Indo-Malaysia in the east, which was stabilised during these centuries. It then introduces and analyses the *da'wa* contributions made by migratory peoples, Muslim rulers and ruler-converts, *'ulama* (Muslim scholars), Sufis (members of Islamic mystical orders), popular preachers and traders. It also highlights the patterns of Islamisation that these actors represent. Taken together, Chapters 1 to 4 illustrate the continuity and diversity of *da'wa* and Islamisation in pre-modern Islamic history.

Part II of the book pivots to *da'wa* in the modern world. Following a stand-alone Introduction, Chapter 5 examines key historical factors which paved the way for a renewed emphasis on missionary *da'wa* among Muslims in modernity. Along with several eighteenth-century Islamic renewal movements, it highlights the transformations associated with the high modern or colonial age (*circa* nineteenth to mid-twentieth centuries). While the former played a preparatory role, the latter ushered in what this book is calling the *first phase* of modern *da'wa*. This phase (*circa* 1850–1950), the subject of Chapter 6, witnessed the early stirrings of a turn towards *da'wa* among modern Muslims, and then, in the early twentieth century in particular, a surge in the creation of new *da'wa*-oriented movements and organisations. Chapter 7 turns to a *second phase* of modern *da'wa*, a phase which coincides with the post-colonial history of the Muslim world (*circa* 1950–2020). To make sense of this second phase, Chapter 7 first explores some key features of Muslim societies in post-colonial times, before providing a global survey of the widespread and highly diverse world of *da'wa* from *circa* 1950 to 2020. Chapter 7 is followed by a brief conclusion to the book as a whole, and an epilogue on *da'wa* and the COVID-19 pandemic of 2019–21.

Defining key terms and anticipating key themes

Before we proceed further, several key terms and themes which will be encountered in the following pages should be defined and explained. Let us begin by making our use and definition of '*da'wa*' more explicit, and perhaps a bit more complicated. In this book, following the lead of contemporary Muslims, *da'wa* will most frequently refer to missionary efforts on behalf of Islam (or particular versions of Islam), and/or efforts to encourage Muslims towards a more devoted practice of their faith. This broad definition of *da'wa*, which we might label '*da'wa* as missionary invitation', will ordinarily refer to efforts that are focused on propagating Islam among diverse populations at the grassroots level. Terms that are roughly synonymous with *da'wa* in this sense include 'missionary preaching', 'missionary efforts', 'outreach' and so on.[13] 'External *da'wa*' (efforts to invite non-Muslims to conversion) and 'internal *da'wa*' (efforts to instruct or revive fellow Muslims) are both included in this definition. While this book remains attentive to varied Muslim uses of the actual term *da'wa* throughout history, it should be kept in mind that it also uses '*da'wa*' as shorthand for Muslim missionary activity in general. As we will see, usage of the terminology of *da'wa* has ebbed and flowed in Islamic history, and Muslim missionary efforts have sometimes taken place without recourse to the term. For the purpose of this study, it is assumed that missionary activity on behalf of Islam (or particular versions of Islam) can justifiably be referred to as '*da'wa*', even if in different historical periods the word itself lacked widespread currency. It should also be noted that *da'wa* has been closely associated with other classical concepts, such as *jihad* (struggle), *al-amr bi'l-ma'rūf* (commanding the right and forbidding the wrong) and *tablīgh* (conveying, communicating, or preaching Islam). Popularised today by the Tablighi Jama'at (Preaching Congregation), one of the world's largest *da'wa* movements (see Chapter 6), the word *tablīgh* (hereafter *tabligh*) is sometimes used synonymously with *da'wa* today.[14]

In relation to '*da'wa* as missionary invitation', a few additional words should be said about the neologism '*da'wa*logy'.[15] This term, which is analogous to the term 'missiology' used in Christian Studies, will be used in this book for various Islamic missionary theologies – perspectives on, or beliefs and principles that undergird Muslim missionary practice. We will speak, for instance, of the *da'wa*logy of the Qur'an and of the *da'wa*logies of various Muslim thinkers throughout history. In general, modern *da'wa*logies seek to normatively describe *da'wa* with reference to the Islamic sources and to explore how it ought to be carried out. One's *da'wa*logy may be explicit – as when a text or thinker intentionally formulates a theology of *da'wa* – or implicit – as when *da'wa* is carried out based on unarticulated principles. A related category, recently studied by Jamal Malik and more legal in its framing, is *fiqh al-da'wa* (the Islamic jurisprudence of *da'wa*). While *fiqh al-da'wa*, as Malik shows, is an important category among some modern Muslims, this book proceeds on the assumption that the category '*da'wa*logy' allows us to speak of a broader range of Islamic missionary theologies – articulated and unarticulated, formal and informal. One cannot properly speak, for instance, of the Qur'an's *fiqh al-da'wa*, but one can speak of its *da'wa*logy.[16]

'*Da'wa* as missionary invitation' may be the major focus of this book, but since political uses of the concept are well-attested in Islamic history and continue up to the present, the book also maintains a focus on '*da'wa* as religio-political summons'. In this sense, it refers to efforts to call others to join Islamic political movements or give loyalty to particular parties, rulers, or states. Such efforts, sometimes labelled 'Islamist' today,[17] have been animated by the assumption that the capture of political power in the name of Islam and the top-down establishment of public 'Islamic ambiences' are necessary components of the spread of Islam. Movements that follow this understanding have combined grassroots preaching with political engagement and, occasionally, armed struggle. When they have gained power, such movements have sometimes used the instruments of the state to enforce Islamic norms. By taking '*da'wa* as religio-political summons' into its purview alongside '*da'wa* as missionary invitation', this book attempts not only to be true to the historical evidence, but also to maintain a balance that is largely missing from Arnold's *The Preaching of Islam* and subsequent studies. Since, in Arnold's view, most nineteenth-century European scholars had overstated the role of military conquest in their studies of Islamic expansion, Arnold focused almost exclusively on peaceful preaching as the means by which Islam spread around the world. This useful correction for the late nineteenth and early twentieth century, however, has proven to be something of an overcorrection given the longevity of Arnold's book.

Both of these tendencies – '*da'wa* as missionary invitation' and '*da'wa* as religio-political summons' (or what I called in an earlier publication 'bottom-up' and 'top-down' *da'wa*)[18] – have ample precedents in early and pre-modern Islam. As Chapter 2 will show, both can be seen in the traditional life of the Prophet Muhammad. The former corresponds (roughly) to the sources' depiction of Muhammad's *da'wa* in the city of Mecca, during the first twelve years of his prophetic ministry, while the latter corresponds (roughly) to Muhammad's *da'wa* in the city of Medina, during the last ten years of his ministry. As noted above, the tension between these two broad varieties of *da'wa* constitutes an important theme in the missionary history of Islam. In fact, for much of pre-modern Islamic history, the word *da'wa* – when it was used at all – was more 'political' than 'missionary' in its connotation. However, a significant shift has occurred in the last century or so: While the religio-political usage of the concept ('Medinan *da'wa*') has certainly not disappeared, it is *da'wa* as grassroots missionary activism ('Meccan *da'wa*') which has arguably gained wider popularity and had a more significant impact among Muslims worldwide. Although religio-political 'Medinan' movements, especially militant ones, persist and attract significant media attention today, among the major purposes of Part II of this book is to account for the more widespread popularity of less conspicuous 'Meccan' styles of *da'wa*.

Another important set of concepts are 'Islamisation' and 'conversion'. For our purposes, Islamisation will be used in this book to speak of the processes by which peoples and societies have embraced Islam and/or become more self-consciously 'Muslim' over time.[19] Roughly synonymous concepts include the 'spread of Islam' and 'expansion of Islam'. Processes of Islamisation have varied greatly, depending on historical context, and have often coincided with other transformations, such as linguistic change (for example, Arabisation, the spread of the Arabic language) and the transformations of public spaces and soundscapes. Islamisation, that is, refers not only to the spread of the religion of Islam, but also to the 'dissemination of a distinctively Islamic way of doing things' in the social, political, aesthetic, architectural and even auditory realms.[20] Closely related to Islamisation, 'conversion', for our purposes, will refer to the movement of individuals or groups from one religion to another.[21] This definition of conversion is meant to be broad enough to include a range of phenomena. For instance, while conversion can be sudden, it can also be the result of gradual, sometimes drawn-out processes. Conversion can involve profound changes in cognitive belief, but it might also begin with almost imperceptible changes on the levels of language and practice. In terms of the relationship between the convert's old religion and the new, conversion involves varying levels of renunciation and demarcation, on one hand, and retention and syncretism, on the other.[22] Sometimes scholars use 'acculturation' for the idea that, as non-Muslims slowly accommodate to an Islamic environment, for example, by adding Arabic-Islamic vocabulary to their speech or by participating peripherally in Islamic rituals, they are slowly acculturated to Islam and may eventually come to self-identify as Muslims.[23] In this model, a specific moment of 'conversion' might be all but impossible to discern. Generally, however, this book sticks to the term 'conversion', using it in a way that allows for both sudden and gradual, consciuous and subliminal religious change.

As should already be clear, this book refrains from making judgments about what constitutes 'genuine' conversion. This is especially important to underscore with respect to Islam, a religion which has often been criticised by non-Muslims for inducing conversions by 'worldly' means and motivations. Not only does such a critique perhaps give too much weight to Protestant Christian sensibilities regarding what 'genuine' conversion is, it also fails to see that many Muslims from the time of the Prophet Muhammad on have, without much ado, accepted and even encouraged 'superficial' conversions as a first step towards a deeper Islamisation of the heart.[24] When we speak of conversion, readers should also keep in mind the twin concepts of *transmission* (how a religion is spread by agents acting on behalf of the religion) and *reception* (how a religion is embraced and appropriated by recipients and converts). It has often been the case that the 'religion' converts received, or the way they received it, was not quite what its transmitters intended. A final note on conversion: Some *da'wa*-minded Muslims today prefer the word 'reversion' to 'conversion'. In this way of thinking, one does not 'convert' to Islam, one 'reverts' to Islam, which is conceived of as the primordial religion of humankind and the 'natural' religion of every baby born into the world. Although this book seeks to accurately represent insider Muslim perspectives on *da'wa*, given the theological assumptions with which the term 'reversion' is laden, it would be inappropriate for us to adopt this usage. In addition, although many *da'wa* movements have been animated by the desire to spread a 'true Islam' in competition with other versions of the faith, this book deliberately casts a wide net. Provided that particular practitioners of *da'wa* or *da'wa* movements self-identify as 'Muslim' and claim to represent the religious tradition bound to the Qur'an and the Prophet Muhammad, it reckons them to be part of Islamic missionary history. This does not mean, of course, that this book is exhaustive. As an introductory survey, it is necessarily selective. Yet, it is hoped that it will prove to be broadly representative. Text boxes, illustrations and endnotes are provided throughout the book for those who want to explore particular topics further.

This book also touches on the themes of 'inter-religious relations' and 'intra-religious relations'. While 'inter-religious' has to do with encounters and interactions *across different religions* (for instance, Muslim-Christian or Muslim-Buddhist relations),[25] 'intra-religious' speaks to relations *within a religion*, or between different sects of the same religion (for example, Sunni-Shi'ite relations within Islam, or Catholic-Protestant relations within Christianity). It goes without saying that missionary activism on behalf of any religion impacts inter-religious relations in a variety of ways. Missionaries of whatever religion, by definition, find themselves on the front lines of inter-religious encounter. Their activities may provoke inter-religious tension and conflict, but sometimes also understanding and cooperation. Similarly, missionary effort can be a consequence of, or serve as a stimulus to, *intra*-religious rivalry or collaboration.[26] As a missionary religion which began in contexts of religious diversity, Islam has always been in contact with and concerned about religious and theological rivals. Put another way,

Islam exemplifies the general point that 'any attempt to configure a "same" [a coherent group] is always dependent on . . . a series of "others." '[27] Or as sociologist Martin Riesebrodt put it: 'Every religion needs a perception of difference . . . in order to see itself and represent itself . . . Religions constitute themselves in relation to each other. On the one hand, religions often become conscious of themselves by demarcating themselves from . . . other religions. On the other hand, interacting religions also borrow [from] . . . one another'.[28] *Da'wa*, as we will see, has served as an important mechanism in catalysing the inter- and intra-religious encounters by which Islam has come to define and constitute itself as a religious tradition.

This brings us to what is sometimes called 'enculturation' or 'indigenisation'. Used in reference to religions, these terms denote the processes by which religions adapt to or acquire characteristics of new social, cultural and linguistic contexts. In short, how do religions change when they cross cultural or historical frontiers? It is sometimes said that Islam, because of the priority it places on its Arab origins and the Arabic language, is limited in its translatability or adaptability to new contexts. While there may be a kernel of truth in this, the following chapters will nevertheless show that, in its own way, Islam has exhibited an indigenising tendency. As we will see, the missionary impulse of Islam and the historical practice of *da'wa* help to explain why. Lastly, some readers – especially scholars of religion – may have noticed that this Introduction has used the terms 'religion', 'missionary religion' and 'Islam' with little explanation. While this is not the place for a detailed discussion or defence of such terms, it is important to make explicit what is implicit above – namely, that this book regards these terms as useful and meaningful, provided they are used thoughtfully and understood within specific contexts. As we will see, not only have the concepts of 'religion' and 'missionary' had shifting meanings throughout history, so too 'Islam' today is quite different (although certainly not disconnected from) what it was to its earliest adherents. To call the 'Islam' of the Qur'an a 'missionary religion' means something rather different from calling Islam today a 'missionary religion.'[29] This book takes it for granted, therefore, that while the terms may be the same, the realities to which they point have been anything but static. Context is key. While other terms and themes will be encountered in the following pages, those covered above are particularly important for the reader to keep in mind for now. Another important cluster of concepts related to Chapters 5 to 7 will be discussed and defined in the Introduction to Part II.

I.1 Some key terms in this book

__Da'wa__ – Literally, 'inviting', 'calling', or 'summoning'. Used by many Muslims today for Islamic missionary activity.

   -*__Da'i__* (*Dā'ī*) – One who calls others to Islam.

   -*__Tabligh__* (*Tablīgh*) – Communicating, conveying (the message of Islam).

__Da'wa__ as missionary invitation – Missionary efforts on behalf of Islam or particular varieties of Islam. Includes both 'external *da'wa*' (efforts to invite non-Muslims) and 'internal *da'wa*' (efforts to revive fellow Muslims).

   -'__Meccan *Da'wa*__' – *Da'wa* from a position of (political) weakness. Often non-political, focused on grassroots outreach and religious persuasion. Roughly synonymous with '*da'wa* as missionary invitation' (see Ch. 2).

__Da'wa__ as religio-political summons – Efforts to call others to join Islamic political movements or give loyalty to particular parties, rulers, or states which claim to represent 'true' Islam.

   -'__Medinan *Da'wa*__' – *Da'wa* from a position of (political) strength, or aiming at the attainment of power. Roughly synonymous with '*da'wa* as religio-political summons' (see Ch. 2).

__Da'walogy__ – Islamic missionary theology; reflection on, or beliefs and principles that undergird, *da'wa* practice. May be formal or informal, articulated or unarticulated.

__Islamisation__ – Processes by which peoples and societies embrace varieties of Islam and/or become more self-consciously 'Muslim' over time.

__Conversion__ – The sudden or gradual movement of individuals or groups from one religion to another. May involve major changes in belief but may also begin with small changes on the levels of language and practice.

__Transmission__ – How a religion such as Islam is spread by agents acting on behalf of the religion.

__Reception__ – How a religion such as Islam is embraced and appropriated by recipients and converts.

__Inter-religious__ – Encounters and interactions across different religions.

__Intra-religious__ – Encounters and interactions within a religion, or between different sects of the same religion.

__Enculturation__ or __Indigenisation__ – Processes by which religions adapt to or acquire characteristics of new social, cultural and linguistic contexts.

Notes

1. The *adhān* in English reads: 'God is most great! (four times). I bear witness that there is no god except God (twice). I bear witness that Muhammad is the messenger of God (twice). Hurry to prayer (twice). Hurry to salvation (twice). God is most great! (twice). There is no god except God'.
2. As seen, for example, in al-Bukhari's *Ṣaḥīḥ*. Al-Bukhari 1420/1999, no. 614. On how this book cites hadith, see Chapter 2.
3. As discussed below, to call earliest 'Islam' a 'religion' is not quite the same thing as calling it a 'religion' today.
4. For an introduction to 'Late Antiquity', see Pregill 2018.
5. Pew Research 2015.
6. On the notion of the 'Islamic world' or 'Muslim world', see Gelvin and Green 2014a, p. 4.
7. As reflected in the phrase '*jihad al-da'wa*' (the struggle to spread Islam).
8. Some might contest the words 'resurgence' and 'renewal'. The rise of modern *da'wa*, they might argue, represents not so much a renewal, but something entirely new. While, in agreement, this book stresses the novelty of modern *da'wa*, it also takes seriously the logic of seeing modern *da'wa* as the continuation of an older story.
9. Arnold 1896/1913/2012. Arnold rarely used the term *da'wa*, reflecting that the book was published before the twentieth-century re-popularisation of the term.
10. To this day, one finds Arnold's book quoted by leading Muslim scholars.
11. A comprehensive bibliography covering recent works on *da'wa* is Kuiper 2018c.
12. Goldziher 1981, p. 6. Italics added.
13. Although 'proselytisation' captures something of this nuance, it will rarely be used in this book.
14. *Da'wa* carries something of a centripetal thrust (calling into or towards Islam), while *tablīgh* is more centrifugal (conveying Islam outward). They come together in the Arabic phrase *tablīgh al-da'wa* (communication of the call). Masud 1995b, pp. 162–5. See also Masud 2000, pp. xii–lx.
15. In my 2018 book Da'wa *and Other Religions*, I used the term '*da'waology*' (*da'wa* + ology). In this book, I have dropped the 'o' and made the word – more accurately – *da'walogy* (*da'wa* + logy). I thank Thomas Gugler for alerting me to this.
16. Malik 2018.
17. This book follows Euben and Qasim Zaman regarding the term 'Islamism'. For these authors, Islamism struggles in ways that are 'explicitly and intentionally political'. Euben and Zaman 2009.
18. Kuiper 2018a.
19. See Peacock 2017b, pp. 1–20; DeWeese 1994, pp. 17–27.
20. Hoyland 2015, p. 219. Hoyland distinguishes between Islam as religion and Islamic civilisation: 'Certainly the religion of Islam was a major part of Islamic civilization, but it was never all there was to it . . .'
21. Peacock 2017b, p. 5. See also Hermansen 2014, pp. 632–66. I concur with Bulliet 2010, p. 530, that 'no general history of . . . conversion [to Islam] is possible'. In this book, we will look at cases, patterns and themes without offering any grand theory.
22. See Riesebrodt 2010, ch. 2.
23. See Chrysostomides 2017, pp. 118–21. Chrysostomides also suggests that, while the process of acculturation is ongoing, individuals might maintain more than one religious identity (for instance, 'Christian' and 'Muslim'), 'enacting one . . . or another as is socially expedient'.

She calls this 'religious code-switching'. Green uses the term 'acculturation' to refer to initial 'nominal' conversions followed by a gradual process in which converts 'acquire the wider cultural trappings of Islam'. Green 2015b, p. 370.

24. See Chapter 2. See also DeWeese 1994, pp. 24–5, 56–7. This point also applies in cases of 'mass conversion', in which a group embraces Islam together.

25. Although 'inter-religious relations' is sometimes used prescriptively (how *should* religions interact?), this book uses the phrase descriptively.

26. For example, a *daʻi* seeking to spread a Sunni version of Islam might be motivated, in part, by a desire to outpace rival Shiʻite preachers. However, faced with an external competitor, Sunnis and Shiʻites might find common cause.

27. Norton 2004, p. 65. Nealon and Giroux 2012, p. 58.

28. Riesebrodt 2010, pp. 23–4.

29. For defences of the concept of 'religion', see Riesebrodt 2010, ch. 2; Tweed 2006, chs 2–3. On 'Islam', see Brown 2017, ch. 1. On 'missionary religion', see Sharma 2011, pp. 175–96.

PART I

The pre-modern missionary history of Islam

CHAPTER 1

The first invitation to Islam: *da'wa* in the Qur'an

An important consequence of the modern renewal of Islam's missionary impulse is that Muslims are turning to their faith's scriptural sources as never before to discern the what, why and how of missionary outreach or *da'wa*. That Muslim believers have unprecedented access to these sources today is, of course, another contributing cause and consequence to which we will return in Part II. For many modern *da'wa*-minded Muslims, particularly those with 'scripturalist' or 'Salafi' proclivities,[1] the most pressing question is not, what did classical and medieval scholars, mystics, or rulers think about *da'wa*, but what does the Qur'an say and what did Muhammad and his Companions do? In this chapter, we examine *da'wa* in the Qur'an. We are seeking to answer the following questions: Does the Qur'an have a missionary theology or *da'wa*logy, and if so, what are its main features? What does the Qur'an tell us, if anything, about the *da'wa* of the Prophet Muhammad? Does the Qur'an command Muslims to do missionary *da'wa*, and if so, how?

In addressing these questions we are seeking primarily to describe the qur'anic raw materials upon which contemporary Muslims draw, or might draw, when formulating their own approaches to *da'wa*. In other words, our concern is less with critical questions about the sources and history of the Qur'an, as important as these questions are, but more with the Qur'an as a theological 'given' within Islamic thought and activism. In Chapter 2, we turn to *da'wa* in the *sira* (biography of the Prophet Muhammad) and hadith literature. To repeat a key point, by starting with Islam's scriptural sources, this book is not implying that all later developments in Islamic missionary history can somehow be explained by or traced back to these sources. Nevertheless, given the central roles that these sources have played in the Islamic tradition from very early on, this book considers it necessary to examine critically what they say, or might be interpreted as saying, about *da'wa*.

There are several ways in which we could approach the topic of *da'wa* in the Qur'an. One option would be to collect and analyse key qur'anic verses or 'proof texts' that seem to enjoin upon Muslims the duty to propagate their faith. Thomas Arnold followed this approach in the few pages he devoted to the Qur'an in *The Preaching of Islam*, and many writers on *da'wa* since have followed suit. Such an approach, however, misses the subtle texture of the Qur'an's missionary thought. As such, the approach followed here is to consider how the Qur'an, as a whole, conceives of *da'wa*. Although we remain attentive to actual occurrences of the word *da'wa* (and its variants), we assume that the Qur'an's *da'wa*logy transcends the term. In terms of structure, the chapter first provides an introduction to the Qur'an and its historical context. Then, it studies the Qur'an's *da'wa*logy under three main headings: (1) *da'wa* to God and the *da'wa* of God, (2) the *da'wa* of God's prophets, and (3) the *da'wa* of God's (Muslim) community. The chapter shows that, although the Qur'an has its enigmas, looking at it through the lens of *da'wa* provides a compelling pathway into its overarching message and purpose.

The Qur'an and its context: *da'wa* in the midst of other *da'was*

The Qur'an is the foundational wellspring of Islamic belief, practice and piety. For the majority of Muslims past and present, the Qur'an is the very speech of God, sublime in its style and perfect in what it communicates. Whenever they are seeking guidance – whether on missionary endeavour or some other topic – pious Muslims begin with the Qur'an. Readers who are unfamiliar with the Qur'an would do well to get a feel for the text by reading a good translation of several of its chapters or *surahs* before proceeding.[2] Contrary to the expectations of many first-time readers, the Qur'an *does not* narrate the story of the Prophet Muhammad and his early followers – it provides no chronological account of their trials and triumphs in seventh-century Arabia. Although some things may be gleaned from the Qur'an about Muhammad, his context and his *da'wa* (see below), the more detailed life of the Prophet and story of the early Muslims would come later with the *sira* and hadith literatures, the subject of Chapter 2. Instead of a chronological narrative, the Qur'an contains a series of revelations or speeches, which, according to Islamic belief, were sent down by God, via the angel Gabriel, to Muhammad between 610 and 632 CE. That is to say, the revelations were not sent down all at once, but rather in piece-meal fashion over a twenty-two-year period in the early seventh century. They were first delivered as oral recitations ('*al-qur'ān*' means 'the recitation'), and many have a poetic quality which can only be appreciated when heard in their original Arabic.

Evidence for the Islamic account of how the Qur'an was revealed is found in its generally unsystematic, indeed piece-meal, quality. Back-to-back chapters (*surahs*) or verses (*ayahs*) may or may not have a discernible relationship to each other. In addition, the Qur'an rarely provides the reader with context. One is often unable to determine – from the Qur'an by itself – who is speaking and to whom, or where and when particular qur'anic events took place. In contrast to later readers like ourselves, the first audience(s) of the Qur'an apparently knew the context and background of these revelations. It is for this reason that the Qur'an rarely explains itself, but rather seems to assume that the audience already 'gets' what it is talking about. In order to make sense of the Qur'an and provide it with context, Muslims have traditionally read its revelations through the lens of Muhammad's later biography, understanding some revelations to be from the 'Meccan' period (from 610 to 622 CE) and some to be from the 'Medinan' period of the Prophet's ministry (from 622 to 632 CE). For many historians, however, the relationship between the Qur'an and the Prophet's biography is not at all straightforward. Since this chapter is taking the Qur'an as a 'given' within Islamic thought, it follows the traditional understanding for the sake of argument.

Despite these uncertainties, there are some things that are unmistakably lucid in the Qur'an. For one thing, as Fazlur Rahman showed in a classic study, the Qur'an has major recurring themes that bind the whole together and give it a stunning religious message and vision.[3] Closely related to this, the Qur'an as a whole has a strongly sermonic and persuasive style. When hearing the Qur'an, one hears above all the urgent and insistent voice of a preacher.[4] In many cases, this preacher is said to be God himself,[5] calling or summoning the world to repentance and submission (*islām* means submission) in light of the coming Final Judgment. Although the context and identity of other qur'anic preachers may sometimes be difficult to discern, the import of their messages is not: There is one God, this God has no associates, he created and has supreme power over all things and he demands that the world give him exclusive devotion and unhesitating obedience. In stark contrast to the divine 'Unmoved Mover' of ancient philosophy, the God of the Qur'an cares about human action and will hold humans accountable for their deeds. However, because he is 'merciful and compassionate', according to the Qur'an's repeated refrain, the God of the Qur'an also reaches out to humanity. He communicates in a variety of ways in order to call people back to correct belief, worship and conduct. In light of all this, one of the most helpful ways of approaching the Qur'an is to see it as a series of sermons which add up to one grand sermon. As we will see, this grand qur'anic sermon can reasonably be called a *missionary sermon*. In other words, the Qur'an not only *contains* but *is* the first *da'wa* of Islam.

Something else that emerges quite clearly from the Qur'an is that its *da'wa* was originally proclaimed in a context of inter-religious diversity and debate, or in a 'sectarian milieu', as John Wansbrough memorably described it.[6] This was a context in which religious 'groups of numerous different persuasions devoted a considerable amount of time to defining their own doctrinal stance and refuting that of others'.[7] The Qur'an shows a persistent awareness of such religious interlocutors and often addresses them by name, with phrases such as 'Oh People of the Book . . .', 'Oh Polytheists (or Pagans) . . .', 'Oh Jews . . .' and 'Oh Christians . . .' It also frequently addresses its own followers ('Oh believers . . .') with an internal *da'wa* of warning and exhortation. The Qur'an's *da'wa*, we might say, is proclaimed in the midst of competing *da'wa*s. Although scholars disagree about the precise identities of the audiences the Qur'an addresses, it is sufficient for our purposes to note that the Qur'an is indicative of a context of religious rivalry that is consistent with what we know of the Middle East in the seventh century CE and late antiquity more generally (see Text Box 1.1).[8] This fact underscores the value of seeing the Qur'an through the lens of *da'wa*. As noted above, missionary activity on behalf of any religion has inherent inter- and intra-religious ramifications. If indeed one of the Qur'an's major themes and purposes is *da'wa*, it should not surprise us that the Qur'an is concerned about other religions and their *da'wa*s. Also worth mentioning here is the fact that aspects of the Qur'an's *da'wa* seem to reflect a context – again, generally consistent with what we know of Arabia and the Middle East in late antiquity – of social change and of the exploitation of the poor and powerless by the rich and powerful. The Qur'an, then, not only summons its hearers to God in competition with other religions, it also summons them to ethical social behaviour.[9] These facts – that *da'wa* is central to the Qur'an, that the Qur'an's *da'wa* is concerned about religions and that the Qur'an speaks to a context of perceived social injustice – only enhance its relevance to *da'wa*-minded Muslims living in today's pluralistic global contexts.

Da'wa to God and the *da'wa* of God in the Qur'an

In the Qur'an, variants of the word *da'wa* occur over 200 times.[10] The term's connotations include calling, inviting, summoning, invoking and exhorting. It sometimes has a 'secular' meaning, such as an invitation to someone's house (Q 28:25, 33:53), calling witnesses to observe a financial transaction (Q 2:282), or being called to battle (Q 8:24, 48:16).[11] Perhaps most frequently, *da'wa* and its variants are used in the Qur'an for prayer (*du'ā'*): calling to God.[12] In Q 2:186, the Qur'an quotes God as saying: 'When My servants ask you about Me, [tell them that] I am indeed nearmost. I answer the supplicant's call (*da'wa al-dā'i*) when he calls (*da'ā*) Me . . .'[13] Intrinsic to the Qur'an's understanding of prayer is its assumption that there can be true and false prayer. Reflecting its inter-religious context, the Qur'an divides its hearers into two broad groups: those who acknowledge the one God and call on God alone, and those who call on what the Qur'an deems to be false gods (for example, Q 26:213, 40:65–6).[14] Q 40:65 clarifies the connection between faith in the one God and calling on God correctly: '[Allah] is the Living One, there is no god except Him. So supplicate Him (*ad'ūhu*), putting exclusive faith in Him. All praise belongs to Allah, Lord of all the worlds'. Similarly, Q 13:14 contrasts true prayer (*da'wa al-ḥaqq*) with the prayers of the faithless (*du'ā' al-kāfirīn*) (see also Q 46:5). Q 4:117 goes even further, warning that it is possible to be so misled that one's prayers are actually directed to Satan. Many similar verses challenge the Qur'an's hearers to try, and

1.1 Competing *da'was*:
the religiously contested world of the rise of Islam

While scholars debate the precise audiences to which the qura'anic *da'wa* was first addressed, we do know that the late antique Middle Eastern context of the rise of Islam (and the setting into which the Islamic tradition places the life of Muahmmad, see Chapter 2) was a colourful world of significant religious diversity. Arabia at the dawn of Islam was bounded to the northwest by the officially Chalcedonian (Greek Orthodox) Christian Byzantine Empire (*circa* 400–1453 CE) and to the northeast by the officially Zoroastrian Sassanian Empire (*circa* 224–651 CE) (see Map 3.1). These two 'confessional empires' were the 'super powers' of the late sixth and early-to-mid-seventh centuries, and both had religiously diverse populations, including various sects of Christianity, Judaism, Zoroastrianism, movements like Manichaeism and Mazdakism and a series of Gnostic sects. Christians made up the largest single religious group across the region, but they were divided – sometimes bitterly – into Chalcedonian (or Melchite), Miaphysite (still sometimes called 'Monophysite') and Nestorian (or East Syrian) churches, as well as into sects like the Marcionites, so-called Jewish Christians and others. Closer to Mecca and Medina, the Arab Lakhmids were a Nestorian client kingdom of the Sassanians, while the Arab Ghassanids were a Miaphysite client kingdom of the Byzantines. Just across the Red Sea from Arabia was Abyssinia or Axum (Ethiopia), whose king presided over a distinctive version of Miaphysite Christianity as his state religion. There were also old and internally diverse Jewish and Christian communities in Egypt, Syria and Palestine. Preachers and writers representing all these groups argued (or did '*da'wa*') for their doctrines against their religious competitors. Throughout the region, Christian monasticism was an important phenomenon. For its part, Yemen, according to traditional sources, had changed hands between Jews and Christians in the century before Muhammad. Everywhere, popular religiosity – with shrines to saints, fascination with relics and other popular practices – was prominent. Within Arabia itself were several Jewish communities and some Christians as well, along with the traditionally polytheistic Arab religions famously depicted in the traditional biography of Muhammad (see Chapter 2). It is no wonder that, in presenting its own *da'wa*, the Islamic scriptures show a keen awareness of competing religious *da'wa*s.

presumably find useless, *da'wa* to other gods (for instance, Q 6:56, 6:71, 7:194–7, 10:66, 16:20, 17:56, 34:22).[15]

In piecing together the Qur'an's missionary thought or *da'wa*logy, therefore, we might begin with the observation that the Qur'an's *da'wa* to humans aims to produce true *da'wa* to God. Like most everything else in the Qur'an, it is oriented in a God-ward direction. In other words, in a religiously competitive setting, the Qur'an's missionary *da'wa* summons its hearers to give proper *da'wa* to the one God. This in turn provides the ultimate basis for the ethical and social conduct that the Qur'an expects of its hearers. In the Qur'an's appeals on this theme, we hear its sermonic quality. For the Qur'an, the choice before people is an urgent one, since on the Day of Judgment it will be too late for humans to offer true *da'wa* to God (Q 14:44, 40:10–14, 40:49–50).[16] Indeed, on the Day of Judgment, those who waited too long will offer the only *da'wa* that remains: 'they will call out (*da'aw*) for annihilation' in order to put an end to their torment in Hell (Q 25:13).[17] What all of this indicates is that prayer itself is a site of inter-religious contrast in the Qur'an. A corollary of this is the Qur'an's expectation that those who perform true *da'wa* will dissociate themselves from non-believers in order to form a distinct religious community (Q 3:118, 19:48).

So far, we have seen that orienting one's life towards God and calling upon the true God correctly is a serious concern for the Qur'an. Before one can offer true *da'wa* to God, however, one must hear and respond to God's own *da'wa* to humanity. In the Qur'an, God is the first and ultimate missionary preacher or *da'i*. In the age leading up to God's climactic *da'wa* on Judgment Day (another nuance of the term), when God will 'summon' the dead from their graves (Q 30:25),[18] he holds out a *da'wa* of repentance and guidance for humanity. Through his *da'wa*, God gives people a chance to escape before a 'painful punishment' overtakes them (for instance, Q 31:7). As Q 10:25 puts it, 'Allah invites (*yad'ū*) to the abode of peace, and He guides whomever He wishes to a straight path'. From the perspective of Islamic theology, the very existence of the Qur'an is the result of God's own *da'wa*. This is somewhat reminiscent of the concept of *missio Dei* (the mission of God) in Christian theology – wherein God takes the initiative to communicate with humans and provide for human salvation.[19] Here, then, we encounter the ultimate starting point of the Qur'an's *da'wa*logy: the idea that God himself is a missionary preacher.

Implicit in the concept of call, invitation, or summons is the concept of response. In human affairs, if one is invited or summoned to something, especially by a person of authority, one is expected to respond. This brings us to another aspect of the Qur'an's *da'wa*logy, an aspect that is linked to the Qur'an's anthropology (its assumptions about human personhood). In the Qur'an, variants of *da'wa* very often appear together with variants of the Arabic word '*jawāb*' (reply, response, answer), and the point of this seems to be that the Qur'an expects its hearers to respond to God's *da'wa* with faith and obedience (e.g.,

Q 2:186, 11:13–14, 14:44, 17:52, 46:31–2).[20] In the words of Q 8:24, 'O you who believe, answer (*istajībū*) Allah and the Apostle when he calls you (*daʿākum*) . . .' Underlying this expectation is the Qur'an's assumption that humans are reasonable actors who can be motivated by self-interest.[21] In the Qur'an's way of thinking, who would not rather be rewarded by God than punished by God? Indeed, the Qur'an relates several anecdotes of people who did in fact respond rightly to God's *daʿwa*.[22]

Despite the Qur'an's hopefulness about human nature, there is abundant qur'anic evidence which points in the opposite direction. The Qur'an routinely speaks of individuals and groups of people who resisted God's *daʿwa* and went their own way (for instance, Q 7:64, 7:72, 7:78, 7:82, 7:90, 36:15). The Qur'an seems to assume, in other words, that God's *daʿwa* can be, and regularly is, ignored or refused by humans. In fact, the Qur'an's tone is often rather gloomy when it speaks of human responses to God's initiative. In several places, the Qur'an says of human beings that 'most of them do not apply reason' (Q 5:103, 8:22). In Q 36:10, the divine voice says to the qur'anic prophet: 'It is the same to them whether you warn them or do not warn them, they will not have faith'. This human ability to either accept or resist God's *daʿwa* is something of a mystery, given that, overall, the Qur'an (and later Islamic theology) views God's sovereign will as irresistible – God's will cannot be thwarted.[23] A further mystery in the Qur'an is the fact that God allows the misleading *daʿwas* of Satan and of other false preachers to coexist in the world with his own *daʿwa*, perhaps as a way to test humans. In fact, it may be mentioned briefly that 'spiritual warfare' is another aspect of the Qur'an's *daʿwa*logy: God's *daʿwa* does battle, not only with the 'false' *daʿwas* of other religions, but also with what we might call the anti-*daʿwa* Satan and his hosts.[24] In any event, the most important point for our purposes is that the Qur'an's *daʿwa*logy holds in tension an optimism regarding human reason in the face of God's *daʿwa* on the one hand, and a pessimism regarding human responsiveness on the other. Although it paints a bleak picture of human obstinacy, it persists in proclaiming God's *daʿwa* in the hope that at least some will respond rightly.

The *da'wa* of God's prophets in the Qur'an

The God of the Qur'an cares deeply about human belief and behaviour, and many qur'anic verses indicate that God is actively observing human beings in order to reward or punish them (for instance, Q 2:39, 24:39, 35:36, 47:12). However, since he is 'merciful and compassionate', God appeals to the world through his *daʿwa* of repentance and submission. That God is the ultimate *dāʿī* in the Qur'an, therefore, is clear. But it is also clear that God usually communicates his *daʿwa* through human prophets or messengers.[25] While God also communicates through the 'signs' of nature (*ayāt*),[26] it is primarily *through the prophets* that his *da'wa* reaches humanity. One cannot overstate the importance of prophets and messengers in the Qur'an's *da'wa*logy. According to the Qur'an, each prophet communicates God's *da'wa* and faces a number of typical responses from his audiences. The Qur'an's discourse on prophets often includes the ideas of sending (*irsāl*) and sending down (*inzāl*) – God *sends* prophets and *sends down* 'books' of revelation with or through them. Their mission is spoken of in terms of warning (*nadhar*), giving guidance (*hūdā*), arguing (*jidāl*), commanding (*amr*), bearing witness (*shahāda*), communicating or preaching (*balāgh*, from the same root as *tabligh*)[27] and, of course, inviting (*da'wa*) – all words that refer to verbal communication.[28] Kate Zebiri lists thirteen elements of the preaching of the Qur'an's prophets and messengers, all of which underscore its specifically missionary character: exhortation, rebuke, arguments, challenges, refutations, threats or warnings, declarations of woe, curses, satire, rhetorical questions, exclamations and emphatic denials.[29] The use of illustrations and parables is another aspect of the repertoire of prophets and messengers in the Qur'an (Q 39:27). Qur'anic messengers use all these rhetorical strategies in order to call people back to true monotheism and a 'straight path' (*ṣirāṭ mustaqīm*). In short, although prophetic ministry may involve non-verbal action,[30] central to the qur'anic notion of prophethood is the obligation to verbally *communicate* God's *da'wa* in a variety of ways.

In fact, according to a number of passages in the Qur'an, a prophet's or messenger's calling is *simply* to communicate (Arabic: *balāgh*). That is to say, preaching, not conversion, is the duty of the Qur'an's prophets and messengers. For example, in Q 3:20 the divine voice instructs the qur'anic prophet: 'And say to those who were given the Book and the uninstructed ones, "Do you submit (*aslamtum*)?" If they submit, they will certainly be guided; but if they turn away, then your duty is only to communicate (*al-balāgh*) . . .' Similarly, in the context of a debate with 'polytheists', Q 16:35 asks rhetorically: 'Is the apostles' duty anything but to communicate (*al-balāgh*) in clear terms?'[31] Returning to an earlier discussion, one apparent reason for the Qur'an's insistence that preaching alone is the duty of the prophets and messengers is its pessimism about the human ability or willingness to respond to God. At times, the Qur'an's prophets are even depicted enduring hostility from their audiences. Prophets are often portrayed in the Qur'an, therefore, as lonely figures who persevere despite the incomprehension and antagonism of their hearers. For their part, modern *da'wa* activists may take comfort in this portrayal when they encounter similar responses.

Be that as it may, a central component of the Qur'an's *da'wa*logy is that God repeatedly sends prophets to communicate his *da'wa* to humanity. Each prophet is sent to his own people or nation at a particular point in history, and this process culminates with the sending of the Qur'an's own prophet – identified by the Islamic tradition as Muhammad. As Q 10:47 puts it: 'There is a messenger for every nation; so when their messenger comes, judgment is made between them with justice, and they are not wronged'.[32] Linguistic affinity with his audience is another hallmark of a prophet's *da'wa*: 'We did not send any apostle except with the language of his people, so that he might make [Our messages] clear to them' (Q 14:4). Speaking to its own Arab prophet (Muhammad), the Qur'an says, 'This is indeed [a Book] sent down by the Lord of all the worlds . . . in a clear Arabic language' (Q 26:192–5). Just as the Qur'an's prophets spoke the languages of their people, modern *da'wa* theorists insist that Muslim preachers today should know their audiences – culturally, linguistically and so on – and tailor their efforts accordingly.

Prophets and messengers before Muhammad

Before we turn to what the Qur'an says about the *da'wa* of Muhammad, it is important to say something about earlier prophets and messengers (those who preceded the coming of Muhammad) in the Qur'an. The qur'anic Noah may be taken to illustrate the functions of a typical qur'anic prophet and the nature of a prophet's *da'wa* (see Text Box 1.2). True to its sermonic style, the Qur'an shapes its narratives of earlier prophets and their *da'wa*s in line with its own concerns. Partly for this reason, prophets and messengers of the past are portrayed in extraordinarily similar terms, a dynamic some have labelled 'monoprophetism'. Along with Noah, other qur'anic prophets who deliver God's *da'wa* include Abraham (Ibrahim), who is portrayed in the Qur'an as rejecting polytheism and giving *da'wa* to 'his father and his people' to worship the one God (Q 6:74–83, 19:41–5, 37:83–98), and Ishmael (Isma'il), who is commended as one who summoned his family to maintain prayer and give alms (Q 19:54–5). The Qur'an also includes many retellings of the *da'wa* of Moses (Musa) (Q 7:103–41, 26:11–66). Other qur'anic prophets include Elijah (Ilyas) (Q 37:123–32), Hud (Q 7:65–72), Salih (Q 7:73–9), Shu'ayb (Q 7:85–93), Joseph (Yusuf) (Q 12:35–41) and Jesus ('Isa) (Q 3:49–57, 61:6). The case of the qur'anic Solomon (Sulayman) is distinctive; he sends a letter of *da'wa* to the ruler of Sheba (Q 27:22–44).[33]

Beyond the prophets, the Qur'an also narrates the *da'wa* of several 'ordinary believers'. Q 40, for instance, speaks at length of an unnamed 'man of faith from Pharaoh's clan' who tries to persuade his people to listen to Moses and believe in God (Q 40:28). His words sum up the Qur'an's concern to separate its *da'wa* from false *da'wa*s: 'O my people! [Think,] what makes me invite you (*ad'ūkum*) to deliverance, while you invite me (*tad'ūnanī*) towards the Fire? You invite me (*tad'ūnanī*) to defy Allah . . ., while I call you (*ad'ūkum*) to the All-mighty, the All-forgiver' (Q 40:41–3).[34] The fact that 'ordinary believers' are depicted doing *da'wa* in the Qur'an is significant for contemporary *da'wa* thinkers and activists. Presumably, if the only people in the Qur'an who did *da'wa* were the great prophets, then ordinary Muslims might reasonably feel excused from the

1.2 The *da'wa* of the Prophet Noah in the Qur'an

According to Q 7 and Q 71, Noah was sent by God to warn his people of a 'painful punishment', but the people rejected his *da'wa*. The qur'anic Noah says: 'I have summoned (*da'awtu*) my people night and day, but my summons (*du'ā'ī*) only increases their evasion. Indeed whenever I have summoned them (*da'awtuhum*) so that [God] might forgive them, they would put their fingers into their ears' (71:5–7). Noah is also portrayed as engaging in inter-religious debate with his hearers. After calling them to worship God, his audience responds, 'you are in manifest error' (7:59–60). Noah's rejoinder is found on the lips of other qur'anic prophets: 'I communicate (*uballigh*) to you the messages of my Lord . . . Do you consider it odd that a reminder from your Lord should come to you through a man from among yourselves . . . ?' (7:62–3). In short, the qur'anic Noah delivers God's *da'wa* to an ungodly people and is vindicated when his hearers suffer divine punishment (in this case, they are drowned). These are prominent themes in the Qur'an's prophetic *da'wa* narratives: (1) the messenger's obligation to communicate God's *da'wa*, (2) the hearers' unresponsiveness, and (3) the final destruction of the obstinant (see also Q 11:25–48, 37:75–82).

duty. For those *da'wa* mobilisers today who want to persuade every Muslim to be a missionary, the Qur'an's examples of ordinary missionary preachers must seem like Godsends.

The Prophet Muhammad's *da'wa* in the Qur'an

The Qur'an discusses earlier prophets, in large part, in order to confirm the genuineness of Muhammad's prophethood and the legitimacy of his *da'wa* (Q 17:90–3, 23:25, 42:24, 43:30–1, 52:30, 53:2–3, 69:24).[35] What we have said about prophets and messengers so far, therefore, has been in preparation for our discussion of Muhammad. The name 'Muhammad' is found four times in the Qur'an (Q 3:144; 33:40; 47:2, 48:29). Most often he is simply addressed in the second person or quoted directly. This has led some scholars to note that, when the Qur'an speaks of or addresses 'the Prophet' or simply 'you', it is not obvious that it is referring to Muhammad.[36] This chapter sets this question aside and, for the sake of argument, adopts the stance of the Islamic tradition and of most modern *da'wa* movements: that the Qur'an's prophet is Muhammad. At this stage, however, we are seeking to discern what the Qur'an alone can tell us about Muhammad's *da'wa*. The later Islamic tradition's more elaborate picture of Muhammad and his *da'wa* is covered in Chapter 2. Among the titles that the Qur'an applies to Muhammad are *rasūl* (messenger), *nabī* (prophet), *bashīr* (announcer), *nadhīr* (warner), *mubashshir* (preacher of good news), *shahīd* or *shāhid* (witness) and, of course, *dā'ī* (or *da'i*, missionary preacher, caller). Q 33:45–6 gives Muhammad several titles, including *da'i*: 'O Prophet! Indeed We have sent you as a witness, as a bearer of good news and as a warner and as a summoner (*da'i*) to Allah by His permission, and as a radiant lamp'. Q 46:31–2 also speaks of Muhammad as 'God's summoner (*da'i Allah*)' (see also Q 12:108).[37] For the Qur'an, the *da'wa*s of God and Muhammad are virtually inseparable: 'O you who have faith! Obey Allah and His Apostle, and do not turn away from him . . . O you who have faith! Answer (*istajībū*) Allah and the Apostle when he summons you (*da'ākum*) . . .' (Q 8:20–4).[38] Like the other qur'anic prophets, the purpose of Muhammad's *da'wa* is to call people to God in a context of religious competition (see Q 61:7–9, 9:33, 48:28). Also like the other prophets, at a basic level, the call of Muhammad is simply 'to communicate in clear terms' (Q 3:20, 24:54, 64:12).[39] All of this indicates that in the Qur'an's view of things, God's *da'wa* is now made decisively through Muhammad, the 'seal of the prophets' (Q 33:40).[40] This is another major component of the Qur'an's *da'wa*logy. The remainder of this section surveys several additional facets of Muhammad's *da'wa* that are relevant to our exploration of the Qur'an's *da'wa*logy.

First, as presented in the Qur'an, Muhammad's *da'wa* is both local and universal. On one hand, he is an Arab messenger (Q 2:151, 9:128), and he brings an *Arabic* Qur'an so that he may warn Arabs (Q 42:7, 6:92). On the other hand, he has been sent to the People of the Book (Q 5:15) and seemingly to all of humanity (Q 4:79, 7:158).[41] Some, who follow the traditional Mecca/ Medina division of the Qur'an, suggest that it is in the earlier, 'Meccan' chapters that a more local or parochial understanding of Muhammad's mission seems to predominate, while in the later, 'Medinan' chapters, Muhammad's mission begins to be thought of as universal. This has led them to wonder whether early qur'anic 'Islam' was in fact a universal missionary religion.[42] However one answers this question, the Qur'an does seem to suggest something of an evolution from the local to the universal in Muhammad's *da'wa*. Chapter 3 will chart a similar development in the first century after the death of Muhammad (632 CE).

Second, in another indication of the Qur'an's inter-religious context, Muhammad's *da'wa* includes significant debate and argument. One of the dominant images of Muhammad in the Qur'an is that of a preacher constantly having to respond to critical counterpoints from his audiences. Because of this, Muhammad is encouraged to engage in *da'wa* in a particular manner. In Q 16:125, the divine voice instructs Muhammad to 'Invite (*ad'u*) to the way of your Lord with wisdom and good advice and dispute with them (*jādilhum*) in a manner that is best'. Here *da'wa* and argumentation (*jidāl*) are explicitly paired. Although debating and arguing are sometimes condemned in the Qur'an (Q 2:197, 6:25, 8:6, 40:4), this verse and others show that there is a legitimate place for disputation in communicating God's *da'wa* – provided one does it 'in a manner that is best'. It is not surprising that the Qur'an allows room for disputation and debate in *da'wa*, since in the Qur'an's view, 'man is the most disputatious of creatures' (Q 18:54).[43] As we will see in later chapters, many *da'wa* movements today still consider debate and argument to be important *da'wa* strategies, and several major *da'wa* preachers have earned their reputations by engaging in high-profile inter-religious debates.

Third, Muhammad's qur'anic *da'wa* is both inter- and intra-religious.[44] We have already observed that the Qur'an's and Muhammad's *da'wa* is often addressed to unbelievers (external *da'wa*). When it is addressed to believers (internal *da'wa*), it is often preceded by the form of address 'O you who have faith' (*yā ayuhā aladhīna āmanū*). For instance, Q 22:77 reads, 'O you who have faith! Bow down and prostrate yourselves, and worship your Lord, and do good . . .' Similarly, Q 57:28 warns: 'O you who have faith! Be wary of Allah and have faith in His Apostle'. In stronger terms, the Prophet urges his community in Q 9:38–9, 'O you who have faith . . . Are you pleased with the life of this world instead of the Hereafter? . . . If you do not go forth [in *jihad*], He will punish you . . .' (see also Q 4:72–4). Muhammad's qur'anic *da'wa* thus had a double effect: It called unbelievers to repentance and conversion, and it served to call believers to solidify and deepen their devotion. This dynamic – *da'wa* earnestly directed both to non-Muslims (external *da'wa*) and Muslims (internal *da'wa*) – continues today.

Finally, there is a tension in Muhammad's *da'wa* between a gradualist and inclusive approach one hand, and a more confrontational and exclusive approach on the other. One of the most famous verses of the Qur'an (in modern times anyway) is Q 2:256. The verse begins, 'There is no compulsion in religion (*lā ikrāha fī al-dīn*)'. This has been taken by many to teach something like freedom of religion: No one should be compelled to embrace a religion except on the basis of personal conviction and choice. Complementary to this is the above-mentioned idea that the duty of a prophet or messenger is simply to communicate God's *da'wa*, leaving results with God.[45] The upshot seems to be that the qur'anic Muhammad is called to preach and persuade, but never to compel. Indeed, as already noted, many verses of the Qur'an seem to assume that peaceful, if vigorous, debate and dialogue are the most appropriate approaches to winning over non-believers. In theological terms, 'inclusivism' refers to a position of openness to the possibility of truth, goodness and even salvation in religions other than one's own; at times, this too can be detected in Muhammad's qur'anic *da'wa*. The Qur'an, for instance, counts some of the People of the Book 'among the righteous' (Q 3:114). Other verses seem to encourage Muhammad (and his followers) to approach the People of Book in a friendly spirit (for instance, Q 29:46) and even to seek their insights on religious or scriptural questions (for instance, Q 10:94). Finally, in several places the Qur'an seems to defer to the Last Day the question of which religious group is ultimately right (Q 5:48, 22:17).

While religious liberals might find such data attractive, the Qur'an also indicates that Muhammad's *da'wa* had an exclusive and confrontational side. In contrast to 'inclusivism', 'exclusivism' refers to the position that there is only one true religion and that all others are ultimately false. Qur'anic exclusivism is seen, for instance, in the repeatedly stated purpose of Muhammad's *da'wa*: to make God's religion, 'the religion of truth' prevail over all others (see Q 9:33, 48:28, 61:7–9). It is also seen in the fact that Muhammad's *da'wa* in the Qur'an is marked by urgency; it is delivered in light of the coming Day of Judgment and the horrors of hell.[46] If it assumed that multiple religions were equally valid paths to God (or in the modern cliché, that 'all paths lead to the top of the mountain'), the Qur'an, presumably, would not assert that the only way to escape hellfire is to heed the *da'wa* of Muhammad. In addition, the Qur'an sees almost nothing of religious value among those it labels 'polytheists' or 'associators' (*mushrikūn*). As far as 'People of the Book' are concerned, those who follow a Meccan/Medina reading of the Qur'an cannot avoid the conclusion that, over time, Muhammad's *da'wa* seems to have become increasingly hostile towards the beliefs of Jews and Christians. In the Medinan chapters of the Qur'an, the Jews are accused of 'rejecting Allah's signs' and 'killing the prophets' (Q 3:21, 112, 5:13), and Christians, whose central beliefs are strongly rejected (Q 4:157, 5:17, 5:116–17, 19:35, 9:30), are grouped with 'the faithless' whose eternal abode is Hell (Q 5:14–18, 5:72–4). Notably, Medinan chapters like Q 4 and Q 9 (the latter is often considered to be the last to be revealed) inject something of a political and militant dynamic into this overall tone of religious exclusivism. Q 4:72–4 and Q 9:36–9, mentioned above, call the Muslims to 'go forth' and 'fight' non-Muslims, Q 9:5 seems to imply for polytheists a choice to either repent or be killed and Q 9:29–31 features a call to fight and subdue the People of the Book, in part because of their theological errors. While there is more that may be said, our purpose here is to note the Qur'an's ambiguity on this point: Is Muhammad's qur'anic *da'wa* gradualist and inclusive, or confrontational and exclusive? Is it strictly religious, or is it religious *and* political? We will see that these ambiguities continue to characterise *da'wa* up to the present.

The *da'wa* of the believing (Muslim) community

The Qur'an portrays God as the ultimate *da'i*, and it considers God's prophets and messengers (especially Muhammad) to be the primary means by which God communicates his *da'wa* to the world. But what about Muhammad's followers, those who have accepted his *da'wa* and become 'Muslims'?[47] Does the Qur'an expect them to engage in *da'wa* too? The foregoing has made it clear that the

Qur'an 'imagines' in its discourse a Muslim community that is endowed with certain responsibilities. We have already mentioned duties like embracing God's oneness, dissociating from unbelief, calling on God rightly, fasting, struggling (*jihad*) and so on. Along with these things, it is reasonable to infer from certain texts that *da'wa*, or calling people to 'Islam', is also among the expectations the Qur'an holds for Muslims in general.[48] This is the final aspect of the Qur'an's *da'wa*logy to be considered in this chapter.

We begin with Q 22:78, which assumes that just as Muhammad was a witness, so his community should also witness to the rest of humanity: 'And wage *jihad* for the sake of Allah . . . He named you 'Muslims' before, and in this, so that the Apostle may be a witness (*shahīd*) to you, and that you may be witnesses (*shuhadā'*) to mankind . . .' In the Qur'an, witnessing to the truth may be taken as one kind of communication that is related to missionary *da'wa*. Another verse which seems to indicate that Muslims in general are called to do *da'wa* is Q 41:33: 'Who has a better call than him who summons (*da'ā*) to Allah and acts righteously and says, "Indeed I am one of the Muslims"?' Q 29:46 provides further evidence. Speaking to the believers, it says, 'Do not argue (*lā tujādilū*) with the People of the Book except in a manner which is best . . . and say, "We believe in what has been sent down to us and in what has been sent down to you; our God and your God is one [and the same], and to Him do we submit" '. We noted above a relationship between *da'wa* and arguing (*jidāl*) in the Qur'an, and in this verse it is the believers who are called to argue while engaging in missionary outreach. Importantly, the language of Q 29:46 recalls that of Q 16:125: 'Invite (*ad'u*) to the way of your Lord with wisdom and good advice and dispute with them (*jādilhum*) in a manner that is best'. While 16:125 was originally spoken to Muhammad (see above), many thinkers and activists today apply this verse to all Muslims. In fact, Q 16:125 is one of the popular and frequently-quoted verses today among the *da'wa*-minded (see Figure 1.1). It is cited repeatedly in *da'wa* manuals and training workshops as something like an Islamic version of what mission-minded Christians call 'the Great Commission'.[49]

After Q 16:125, arguably the most important qur'anic texts concerning the *da'wa* of the believing community are Q 3:104 and Q 3:110. Q 3:104 says: 'There has to be a nation (*umma*) among you summoning (*yad'ūna*) to the good, bidding what is right, and forbidding what is wrong. It is they who are the felicitous'. Just a few verses later, Q 3:110 begins: 'You are the best nation (*umma*) [ever] brought forth for mankind: you bid what is right and forbid what is wrong, and have faith in Allah'. In both verses, the Muslims are called a 'nation' or *umma*, and in 3:110 they are said to be the 'best nation brought forth for mankind'. This language is reminiscent of the 'chosen people' motif found in the Hebrew Bible (Old Testament) and New Testament (see, for example, Exodus 19:5–6, I Peter 2:9–10). As the chosen people of God in the Bible are blessed in a special way, but also given special responsibilities and assignments by God, so too are

Figure 1.1 The Qur'an is the foundational wellspring of Islamic belief and practice. In Q 16:125 and other places, the Qur'an seems to command Muslims to do *da'wa*: 'Invite to the way of your Lord with wisdom and good advice and dispute with [non-believers] in a manner that is best'. However, the Qur'an as a whole can reasonably be called a missionary sermon given in the divine and prophetic voices. From this perspective, the Qur'an not only contains but *is* the first *da'wa* of Islam. Photo: Mira Pavlakovic, from freeimages.com.

the qur'anic Muslims.[50] In Q 3:104, they are first said to summon, or make *da'wa*, 'to the good' (*al-khayr*). While the verse does not specify what 'the good' is, the standard viewpoint among Muslims is that 'the good' refers to the religion of Islam and all that flows from its establishment.[51] Q 3:104 is thus taken to mean that Muslims should do missionary *da'wa*. The second aspect we learn from 3:104 and 3:110 about the mission of the believers is that their *da'wa* is related to the duty to 'bid what is right and forbid what is wrong' (*al-amr b'il-ma'rūf*). The idea of commanding right and forbidding wrong is found in eight verses in the Qur'an.[52] In Q 3:104, 3:110 and 9:71 it is a duty that believers undertake in contrast to other religious communities, but it is not clear towards whom the duty is directed. Q 3:114 speaks of the duty being carried out by People of the Book, but it does not specify how they did it. In two places, the duty is that of an individual: In Q 7:157 it is carried out by the Prophet Muhammad, and in Q 31:17 the prophet Luqman advises his son to command and forbid. In Q 5:79, the Jews are condemned for failing to carry out the duty. Q 9:112 and 22:41 seem to suggest that only those who are engaged in *jihad* or those who exercise leadership should fulfill the duty. Finally, Q 9:71 includes believing men *and women* among those who carry out this duty: 'But the faithful, men and women, are comrades of one another: they bid what is right and forbid what is wrong . . .' Modern *da'wa* activists appeal to this final verse in order to encourage women's participation in *da'wa*.

Thus, while the Qur'an clearly expects Muslims to command and forbid, the Qur'an provides little by way of specifics on who is to carry out the duty, and towards whom. The Qur'an is also not very specific on *how* Muslims should command and forbid. While the duty is in some way connected to *da'wa*, the specific activities it entails would have to be spelled out by the later Islamic tradition.[53] Indeed, while the content of *what* Muslims are to command and forbid can be assumed, from the Qur'an's perspective, to be synonymous with what the Qur'an itself commands and forbids (regarding worship, belief, ethics and so on), the later Islamic tradition would greatly expand and elaborate on those things which must be commanded and forbidden. To conclude this section, although there are lingering ambiguities, it seems safe to say that there is ample qur'anic evidence to support the idea that *da'wa* is not merely the prerogative of God and the prophets, but also of the Muslim community in general.

Summary and conclusions

In the course of this chapter, we have made the following observations about the *da'wa*logy of the Qur'an: First, God in the Qur'an is the first and ultimate *da'i* or missionary preacher. In Islamic thought, the Qur'an itself is the result of God's *da'wa*; indeed, the Qur'an reads like an extended missionary appeal to humanity, delivered from the divine perspective. Because of this, not only does *da'wa* happen to be a major theme in the Qur'an, one might truly say that the Qur'an *is* the original *da'wa* of Islam. Among the Qur'an's major overall purposes is to urgently persuade its audience to heed God's *da'wa* in light of the Last Day. Second, God's *da'wa* in the Qur'an calls for a human response of worship and obedience. That is to say, in a religiously competitive setting, the Qur'an's *da'wa* (missionary call) to humans aims to produce true *da'wa* (prayer and worship) to God. Yet, third, there is a tension in the Qur'an's *da'wa*logy between hopefulness on the one hand, and pessimism on the other, regarding human nature in the face of God's *da'wa*. The human response to God's *da'wa* is complicated, according to what we have seen in this chapter, not only by deeply conflicted human nature, but also by the presence of false, satanic *da'wa*s in the world. The Qur'an's *da'wa*logy, in other words, considers it normal that God's true *da'wa* has to contend with other *da'wa*s in spiritually fraught settings.

Fourth, although the Qur'ans *da'wa*logy allows that God communicates something about himself through the 'signs' of nature, it is primarily through human prophets and messengers that God's *daʿwa* reaches humanity. In the Qur'an's *daʿwa*logy, God sends a succession of prophets and messengers, including some ordinary believers, who use a number of rhetorical strategies to call humans to true monotheism. These emissaries are tasked only with communicating God's *daʿwa* and enduring hardship; they are not responsible for the results. Fifth, the succession of messengers and their *daʿwa*s culminates in the coming of the Qur'an's own Arab prophet, identified by the Islamic tradition as the Prophet Muhammad. In the Qur'an's view, the *daʿwa*s of God and Muhammad are inseparable, which is to say that God's *daʿwa* is now made definitively through Muhammad, the 'seal of the prophets'. Muhammad's *daʿwa* epitomises the overall qur'anic *daʿwa*logy we have described in this chapter: It is urgent, it is delivered in light of the coming Day of Judgment, it is both inter- and intra-religious, and it involves a great deal of debate and argumentation. Finally, according to the Qur'an, *daʿwa* is an obligation, not only of God's prophets and messengers, but also of the entire Muslim community. In the Qur'an, the community of Muslims is spoken of as 'the best nation', which is entrusted with the related tasks of *daʿwa* and *al-amr bʾil-maʿrūf* (commanding and forbidding).

So far so good, but it is important to emphasise several additional points as we conclude this chapter. First, while the Qur'an clearly has a *daʿwa*logy, the lineaments of which we have just summarised, it should be kept in mind that its *daʿwa*logy is more implicit than explicit. Overall, as we have seen, the Qur'an is more interested in doing *daʿwa* than in analysing or systematising it. In later chapters, we will see other examples of implicit *daʿwa*logies, in contrast to explicit or articulated ones. Second, and closely related, it should be kept in mind that there are a number of lingering ambiguities in the Qur'an's *daʿwa*logy. For one thing, we observed tensions in Muhammad's qur'anic *daʿwa* between the local and the universal, and between an inclusive, gradualist approach and an exclusive, confrontational approach. In other words, the Qur'an leaves open the question of whether *daʿwa* is chiefly a polemical exercise, driven by an exclusivist theology of religions, or an exercise in finding common ground, driven by an inclusivist theology of religions.[54] The Qur'an is also ambiguous regarding the relationship of *daʿwa* to politics. While the qur'anic *daʿwa* tends to be mostly religious in nature, there are some instances, observed above, in which it seems to have a political undertone.[55]

Thus, while the Qur'an provides the undisputed starting point for any pious Muslim seeking to know God's will regarding missionary activity, one would be hard pressed to derive a full-fledged, systematic guide to *daʿwa* from the Qur'an alone. Although the Qur'an provides the crucial theological underpinnings of *daʿwa*, Muslims seeking more specific and comprehensive direction on *daʿwa* would seem to require additional sources of guidance. For most Muslims, it is the life and sayings (or *sunna*) of the Prophet Muhammad – as recorded in books of *sira* (biographies of Muhammad) and collections of hadith (reports of his words and deeds) – that meet this need. It is to these sources that we now turn.

Notes

1. 'Scripturalism' refers to stances that are oriented towards scripture, as opposed to later tradition, in determining what is authentic in a religion. See Loimeier 2005, pp, 216–54. Although most modern Muslims are not Salafis, it is nevertheless true that the Salafi insistence on the Qur'an and hadith (that is, scripture) as the only valid proof in religious matters has had a widespread impact. See Ingram 2018, p. 213. See also the Introduction to Part II.
2. The English translations of Yusuf 'Ali, Quli Qara'i, Pickthall and Itani are all useful. One can access multiple English translations on Qur'an websites, such as tanzil.net and quran.com.
3. Rahman 1994.
4. '. . . the style of the Qur'an more closely resembles Christian . . . sermons . . . Like a good preacher, the Qur'an presents its audience with reasons to repent and believe in God'. Reynolds 2012, p. 102.
5. This book follows the general practice of the Islamic tradition in using the male pronoun for God.
6. Wansbrough 1978.
7. Hoyland 2012, p. 1061.
8. Late antiquity refers to the 'half-millennium between the mid-third and the mid-eighth century [CE] in Europe, North Africa, [the Middle East], and Central Asia'. See Nicholson 2018, p. vi.
9. For a few examples of passages on the Qur'an's social injunctions relative to wealth and poverty, orphans and so on, see Q 2:271, 4:9–10, 90:11–20.
10. For the various nuances of the Arabic root *d-ᶜ-w*, see Lane 1867/1997, vol. 3, pp. 882–5.
11. In classical Arabic, *daᶜwa* can refer to the invitation to a feast, and *ṣāḥib al-daᶜwa* is the host. See Walker 1995, pp. 343–6.
12. *Nādā* (to call) sometimes has a synonymous meaning (for examle, Q 11:45, 19:3–4, 21:76, 37:75).
13. The original Arabic of the standard 1924 Egyptian edition of the Qur'an is this chapter's primary reference, but English quotations come from Quli Qara'i 2011. For *daᶜwa* as prayer, see also Q 3:38, 6:52, 40:60.
14. These other gods or 'associates' (*shurakāʾ*) can take the form of idols (Q 29:17, 22:30), intercessors (*shufaᶜāʾ*; Q 6:51, 10:18), offspring of God (Q 19:88–92, 21:26), or even angels or jinn (Q 37:58, 43:19). Ascribing associates to God arises from *ẓann* (conjecture, speculation) rather than from knowledge (*ᶜilm*; Q 2:78, 10:66, 35:28–9). See Zebiri 2004, p. 270.
15. As Walker writes, 'a primary lesson in the Qur'an is that to make *daᶜwa* to other gods is vain . . . and to persist in it once apprised of its uselessness is a wickedness'. Walker 1995, p. 343. Along with its warnings against calling on false gods, the Qur'an also rebukes those who make *daᶜwa* to God only when they face hardships (Q 7:134–5, 10:12, 17:67, 29:65, 30:33, 39:49, 42:51).
16. According to Q 40:59–60, 'Indeed the Hour is bound to come; there is no doubt in it . . . Your Lord has said, 'Call Me (*adᶜūnī*), and I will hear you!' Indeed those who are disdainful of My worship will enter hell in utter humiliation'. See also Q 41:48.
17. See also Q 7:5.

18. The Day of Judgment is called 'the day when the Caller calls' (*yawm yadʿū al-dāʿī* – 54:6). See also Q 30:25.
19. For one attempt to read the entire Bible through the lens of the *missio Dei*, see Wright 2006.
20. Q 24:51 makes this explicit: 'All the response (*qawl*) of the faithful, when they are summoned (*duʿū*) to God and His Apostle . . . is to say, "We hear and obey"'.
21. Zebiri 2004, p. 267. A common refrain in Qur'an is: 'Do you not exercise your reason (*lā taʿqilūna*)?'
22. It assumes that there are genuine 'believers' (*muʾminūn*) and that there is authentic faith among 'People of the Book' (Q 3:110, 3:113–14).
23. God in the Qur'an is said to guide and harden whomever God wishes (Q 2:284, 4:88, 6:125, 114:4). Later Islamic theology enshrines *qadr*, or divine predestination, as one of the six core beliefs of Islam.
24. On Satan's *daʿwa*, see Q 14:22, 35:6, 31:21, 22:52. See also Q 7:200–1. The Qur'an also refers to Pharaoh and his hosts as false callers in the time of Moses. See Q 2:221, 28:41.
25. For prophets and messengers in the Qur'an, see Rubin 2001a, p. 289f.
26. For signs (*ayāt*), see for instance, Q 2:118, 2:164, 3:190, 10:6, 31:20–32.
27. '*Tablīgh*' is not found in the Qur'an, but *balāgh*, which derives from the same root, has a roughly synonymous meaning.
28. *Nadā* (to invite, summon, convene) is sometimes used synonymously with *daʿā* (for example, Q 3:193; 11:45, 21:76, 37:75).
29. Zebiri 2001, pp. 115–17.
30. Such as fighting (*qitāl*) and struggle (*jihad*). See Q 3:146. For *jihad*, see Q 66:9.
31. See also Q 5:99, 13:40, 16:82, 24:54, 34:27, 42:48, 64:12. In Q 7, the refrain of prophetic figures like Noah, Hud, Salih and Shu'ayb is roughly the same: 'I communicate (*uballigh* or *ablaghtu*) to you the messages of my Lord' (Q 7:62, 68, 79, 93).
32. See also Q 2:213.
33. Zahniser 2001, p. 558.
34. Q 36:20–7 tells of another man 'from the city outskirts' (presumably Sodom, although it is not mentioned by name) who called his people to heed the warning of three unnamed 'apostles'.
35. See Zebiri's comments in Zebiri 2004, p. 274.
36. These qur'anic texts *may* be taken to refer to Muhammad as we know him from later Islamic literature, but other readings are also possible. See, for instance, Rippin 2000, pp. 298–309; Hoyland 2007, pp. 1–22; Reynolds 2011, pp. 188–206; Sinai 2017, pp. 12–4. For a spirited defence that the Qur'an's prophet is indeed Muhammad, see Saleh 2008.
37. See also Q 12:108.
38. In this verse 'Allah and His Apostle' are treated in singular terms. 'Him' ('do not turn away from him') and 'he' ('when he summons you') are singular pronouns. See also Q 33:36.
39. Qur'anic prophets sometimes fought unbelievers. See Q 3:146, 48:16, 24:63.
40. Although other prophets, notably Abraham, are presented by the Qur'an as having been 'Muslims', the Qur'an stresses the idea that Muhammad was the first Muslim from among his own people. See Q 6:14, 6:162–3.
41. Even the *jinn* listen to the message of the Qur'an (Q 72:1–2). On the local and universal in the Qur'an's presentation of Muhammad, see Rubin 2001b, p. 443.
42. One must remember that the 'Islam' of the Qur'an was a basic, primitive form of the religion. The 'Islam' of the Qur'an may be the basis of, but is not at all synonymous with, the 'Islam' that developed in later times. Racius, who follows the Mecca/Medina typology, writes: 'It is hardly possible that the spreading of Islam beyond the confines of Arabia was of any concern for Muhammad while he was still in Mecca . . . But once he relocated to

Yathrib [Medina], his attention, even if only partially, turned to non- Arabs . . .' Racius 2004, p. 32.

43. Muhammad's debate partners include associators or polytheists (*mushrikūn*), unbelievers (*kāfirūn*), People of the Book (*ahl al-kitāb*), Christians (*naṣāra*), Jews (*banū Isrā'īl, yahūd*) and others. For more on each of these groups, see Zebiri 2004, and Zebiri 2001. See also Sirry 2014, ch. 2.

44. I thus differ from Racius, who writes: '. . . in no Quranic verse are Muhammad, or Muslims in general, commanded to exercise *da'wa* (invitation) towards fellow Muslims . . .' Racius 2004, p. 37.

45. It has been suggested by Zebiri, moreover, that Muhammad's preaching is meant to *gradually* induct its hearers into its way of thinking. See Zebiri 2004, pp. 279–81.

46. The Day of Judgment is called 'the day when the Caller calls' (*yawm yad'ū al-dā'ī* – Q 54:6). See also Q 14:44, 30:25, 40:10–14, 40:49–50, 41:48.

47. It should be remembered that to be a 'Muslim' in basic, qur'anic terms is not the same thing as being a Muslim in terms of the more elaborate later Islamic tradition.

48. Again, what the Qur'an means by 'Islam' is something much more basic than the full-blown 'Islam' of later centuries.

49. This refers to Matthew 28:18–20 in the New Testament, in which Jesus is depicted telling his followers to 'go and make disciples of all nations'.

50. An issue arising from Q 3:104 and 3:110 is whether the duties of *da'wa* and *al-amr b'il-ma'rūf* are incumbent on each individual member of the community (*farḍ al-'ayn*), or only on some members of the community (*farḍ al-kifāya*). The use of the preposition *min* in 3:104 seems to indicate that there is to be a special group from the broader community. This is one interpretation. On the other hand, the whole community may be implied: 'You are a community, summoning . . .' The medieval Qur'an commentary of the Jalalayn (the two Jalals) prefers the first reading for 3:104: '. . . the particle *min*, 'of', [in *minkum*, 'of you'] is partitive, since what is mentioned is a collective obligation [*farḍ kifāya*], and is not incumbent upon every individual of the community, for not every person . . . is up to it'. Jalāl al-Dīn al-Maḥallī and Jalāl al-Dīn al-Suyūṭī 1410/1995, p. 60.

51. See, for example, the comments of the Jalalayn on this verse: 'Let there be one community of you calling to good, *to Islam*, and enjoining decency, and forbidding indecency'. Jalāl al-Dīn al-Maḥallī and Jalāl al-Dīn al-Suyūṭī 1410/1995, p. 60. Italics added.

52. Cook 2000.

53. 'In short, [the Qur'an] on its own has relatively little to tell us about the duty of forbidding wrong'. Cook 2000, pp. 13–17.

54. In seeking to resolve these tensions, it may help, or perhaps further complicate matters, to appeal to the traditional Islamic approach to Qur'an. Following Muhammad's *hijra*, it might be observed that there is a movement from the local to the universal, and from a more inclusive view of religious others to a more exclusive view. Then, if we think in terms of the doctrine of abrogation (*naskh*), we might have to conclude that the Qur'an's universalism and exclusivism take precedence.

55. Additionally, the Qur'an presents 'other religions' obliquely. Precisely which Jews, Christians, or polytheists the Qur'an debates is unclear. See, for instance, Waardenburg 1999, pp. 8–9; Watt 1967, pp. 197–201.

CHAPTER 2

The best inviter: *da'wa* in prophetic *sira* and hadith

In his late nineteenth-century book *The Preaching of Islam*, Thomas Arnold included a chapter on the Prophet Muhammad's traditional biography, in which he focused on 'one of its aspects only . . . that in which the Prophet is presented to us as a preacher . . . of a new religion'. In keeping with the times in which he lived, Arnold provided the following, somewhat essentialist, rationale for studying Muhammad specifically as a missionary preacher: 'The life of the founder of Islam and the inaugurator of its propaganda may naturally be expected to exhibit to us the true character of the missionary activity of this religion . . . For the missionary spirit of Islam is no after-thought in its history . . . [and] Muhammad the Prophet is the [prototypical] missionary of Islam'.[1] When Arnold wrote these words, he could not have foreseen the extent to which Muslims over the course of the twentieth century and into the twenty-first would come to embrace this very sentiment. Prompted by what this book is calling the modern renewal of Islam's missionary impulse, *da'wa*-minded Muslims have turned not only to the Qur'an, but also to the life of Muhammad, whom they have indeed come to see as the archetypal Muslim *da'i*.

That they have done so follows a well-established pattern. Alongside the Qur'an, Muslims throughout history (or, at least, since roughly the late eighth century CE) have made it their practice to look to the life and sayings of the Prophet Muhammad as a second source of divine guidance. In classical Islamic thought, if the Qur'an is the eternal word of God, then the *sunna* (customs, habits, sayings) of Muhammad, preserved in books of *sira* (biographies of Muhammad) and in collections of hadith (reports of his words and deeds), provides the practical illustration of how that word is to be implemented.[2] In other words, the Muhammad of the *sunna* is viewed as the very embodiment of the Qur'an's message. Thus, returning to our main theme, if the Qur'an provides the foundation for an Islamic *da'wa*logy (Chapter 1), it is the example of the Prophet Muhammad that, theoretically, should make the Qur'an's *da'wa*logy concrete and actionable for would-be *da'wa* practitioners.

Building on Chapter 1, the present chapter provides an original study of the ways in which the *sira* and hadith literatures portray Muhammad and his Companions (*ṣaḥāba*) as missionary *da'i*s, giving special attention the various *da'wa* strategies that these literatures attribute to them. In terms of structure, the chapter turns on the distinction between what it calls the 'Meccan pattern' of Muhammad's *da'wa* on one hand, and the 'Medinan pattern' on the other. Muslims remember the life of the Prophet as a story with a certain progress and logic: The Prophet's years in Mecca led to the *hijra* (migration) to Medina, and his years in Medina, in turn, led to the political and spiritual conquest of Arabia and the wider Middle East. The approach of this chapter allows us to trace *da'wa* in relation to this progress and logic. First, however, a few words should be said about the origins of the *sira* and hadith literatures, their place in Islam and the manner in which this chapter draws upon them.

Sira and hadith: a brief introduction

Sira and hadith emerged against the backdrop, first, of the dramatic conquests of the first century of Islam after the Prophet's death (*circa* 632–750 CE; see Chapter 3) and, second, the above-mentioned silence or ambiguity of the Qur'an on topics of concern to later Muslims. These factors, among others, combined to produce a state of affairs in which the first generations of Muslims after the Prophet's death in 632 CE were driven to seek out and develop extra-qur'anic sources of religious guidance.[3] Mindful of this historical background, Tarif Khalidi compares the development of the *sira* and hadith literatures to the disentangling of a 'ball of many colored threads'. After the Prophet's death, oral traditions containing 'legal injunctions, ritual practice, ethical conduct, correct manners, admonitions, homilies, fragments of Muhammad's biography' and so on proliferated among Muslims. This 'vast sea' of material had initially been transmitted orally,[4] but began to be sorted out, categorised and written down in the centuries after the Prophet. In the process, two strands that became central to the emerging Islamic tradition were *sira* and hadith.[5]

Although *sira* and hadith are not the only types of literature Muslims produced in this formative, post-qur'anic period (*circa* 661–900 CE),[6] they are indispensable for anyone seeking to understand Islamic faith and history.[7] Hadith tend to portray Muhammad as a legislator who makes timeless legal pronouncements, whereas works of *sira* provide chronological accounts of Muhammad's life. Leading figures who collected and popularised hadith include Malik Ibn Anas (d. 795), al-Shafi'i (d. 820) and Ibn Hanbal (d. 855), as well as the canonical (*ṣaḥīḥ* – correct or authentic) compilers al-Bukhari (d. 870) and Muslim Ibn al-Hajjaj (d. 875).[8] As for *sira*, the main compilers were Ibn Ishaq (d. 767) (whose work was edited and preserved by Ibn Hisham, d. 833), Ibn Sa'd (d. 845) and al-Tabari (d. 923). In this chapter, we primarily rely on the *sira* of Ibn Ishaq/Ibn Hisham and secondarily on the hadith collections of al-Bukhari and Muslim.[9]

As with the study of the Qur'an provided in Chapter 1, this chapter is less concerned with questions about the compilation history and reception or historical reliability of the narratives contained in *sira* and hadith, as important as such questions are, but more with these literatures as 'givens' within

Islamic thought.[10] From a historical-critical perspective, what we know with certainty about the historical Muhammad, and especially about Muhammad's years in Mecca, is very limited.[11] These literatures, then, tell us more about the 'Muhammad of faith' than the 'Muhammad of history'. However, since the traditional Islamic view is that these sources faithfully recount the facts of Muhammad's life and constitute an authoritative guide for Muslim practice, the goal of the remainder of this chapter is to survey the raw materials in the *sira* and hadith upon which contemporary Muslims draw, or might draw, when formulating *da'wa*logies and *da'wa* strategies.[12] This way of putting things underscores an important point: This chapter is not suggesting that Muslims of the past normally read *sira* and hadith in order to discern or copy the Prophet's 'missionary methods'. The fact is that Muslims in different times and places have used these literatures to construct 'images' of Muhammad in keeping with their own needs and agendas, and the image of 'Muhammad-as-missionary' has rarely been one of them – until relatively recently.[13] Nor is it to suggest that later developments in Islamic missionary history can be straightforwardly traced back to the example of the Prophet and his Companions as depicted in *sira* and hadith. Instead, it is precisely because of the contemporary preoccupation of *da'wa*-minded Muslims to elevate the specifically missionary elements of the Prophet's biography that this chapter, like Chapter 1 *vis-à-vis* the Qur'an, seeks to elaborate on what these sources communicate about mission or *da'wa*.

In short, faced with new challenges sparked by Muhammad's death and the ensuing conquests, most Muslim communities came to look to the extra-qur'anic words and deeds of the Prophet and his Companions, as contained in hadith and *sira,* as essential sources of divine guidance alongside the Qur'an. A final note: Chapter 1 highlighted the fact that the Qur'an's *da'wa* reflects contexts of inter-religious rivalry and debate. This is also true of the *sira* and hadith. An important effect of the early expansion of Islam after the time of Muhammad was that it amplified the early Muslims' experience of and confrontation with religious pluralism. As noted in Chapter 1, the late antique Middle East (a world the Muslims inherited through the conquests and the world reflected in the Qur'an and hadith) was a world dominated religiously by older and larger religious communities, including diverse communities of Jews and Christians, as well as varieties of Zoroastrianism, Manichaeism and other religious movements (see Text Box 1.1). One of the original purposes of the *sira*, therefore, was to establish 'the place of Muhammad among the prophets, and that of Islam among the other religions'.[14] Many of the anecdotes we examine below, therefore, underscore the point that there is an unavoidable relationship between *da'wa* and inter-religious relations.

Mecca: *da'wa* from a position of weakness

Ibn Ishaq begins his *sira* with pre-Islamic Arabia. Despite their acknowledgement of the virtues and poetic abilities of pre-Islamic Arabs, Muslims have customarily thought of Arabia before 'Islam' in terms of the word *jahiliyya* (ignorance).[15] The application of a single, seemingly uncomplicated label to this period might be taken to mean that Arabia before Muhammad was somehow a religious vacuum. In fact, in keeping with what was noted in the previous paragraph, Ibn Ishaq portrays pre-Islamic Arabia as a highly religious context and, indeed, as a site of competing missionary *da'was*.[16] For one thing, in the context of reports about the Arabs' pre-Islamic gods and pagan practices,[17] he introduces a character named 'Amr b. Luhayy. 'Amr, who is said to have lived sometime in the centuries before Muhammad, is presented as a false *da'i* who was 'the first to change the religion of Ishmael' and to introduce idol worship to the Arabs.[18] The underlying idea here is that the Arabs' primitive faith was monotheism, a monotheism which had been passed on to them by Abraham and Ishmael in ancient times. This monotheism, in turn, had been lost or corrupted by the Arabs through the influence of figures such as 'Amr.[19] Still today, as later chapters show, Islamic *da'wa* is often conceived of as a struggle against the perpetual human tendency to listen to false *da'was* and stray from true monotheism. Indeed, there are prominent modern Muslims who think of *da'wa* as Islam's never-ending struggle against *jahiliyya* in all its forms.[20]

Ibn Ishaq also relates multiple reports of fortune-tellers, Jews and Christians in the pre-Islamic context.[21] Prominent among these is Bahira, a Christian monk who discovered the 'seal of prophethood' on the boy Muhammad. Another is the Christian Waraqa b. Naufal, the cousin of Muhammad's first wife Khadija, who assured the adult Muhammad that he was, indeed, a prophet.[22] In some reports, we encounter a phenomenon in which non-Muslims, particularly Jews, unintentionally do *da'wa* for the coming Prophet. Several times, for example, the conversion of a particular Arab tribe to Islam is credited to the Jews and their predictions.[23] Another example is the story of Salman the Persian, a Zoroastrian who converted to Islam in part because Christian leaders told him that 'a prophet was about to arise'.[24] Two additional reports of pre-Islamic *da'wa* are those, first, of Faymiyun, a wandering Christian holy man who allegedly introduced Christianity to the southwestern Arabian city of Najran, in part by performing a dramatic miracle,[25] and second, of the Jewish warlord Dhu Nuwas who is depicted attacking Najran, but not before he 'invited' (*da'āhum*) the city's people to convert to Judaism.[26] The ideas of *da'wa* being delivered through a miracle-working holy man, and of *da'wa* being given prior to battle will be encountered again in this book.

Muhammad's prophetic ministry, according to the *sira*, began in this context of competing *da'was*. At the age of forty, in 610 CE, Muhammad is reported to

have had a fateful encounter with the angel Gabriel, in which he was commanded to 'recite' a divine revelation – a revelation Muslims believe is found in
Q 96. Despite Muhammad's initial self-doubt, this was the defining moment that
began his ministry as God's *daʿi*. Ibn Ishaq tells us that Muhammad went public
with his *daʿwa* three years later, in 613 CE. He explains: 'When [Muhammad]
openly displayed Islam as God ordered him, his people did not withdraw or turn
against him . . . until he spoke disparagingly of their gods'.[27] What we see here is
that Muhammad began his public *daʿwa* ministry not only by positively preaching his own message, but also by preaching negatively *against* other gods. In
response to this affront, Muhammad's tribesmen, the Quraysh, 'stirred up . . .
foolish men who . . . insulted [Muhammad], and accused him of being a poet,
a sorcerer, a diviner and of being possessed'.[28] The beginning of Muhammad's
public *daʿwa* is reported in slightly different terms in the hadith collection of
Muslim: After Muhammad waited for three years, he climbed a nearby mountain and announced God's coming judgment to the people of Mecca.[29] While
we are not told precisely how the crowd responded, we learn that they honoured
Muhammad as a man of good character, and that Abu Lahab – the Prophet's
uncle and one of his most intransigent foes – cursed Muhammad.[30] In both versions, therefore, the theme of opposition is prominent.

From here, the *sira*'s portrayal of the Meccan period of Muhammad's ministry may be summarised straightforwardly. Over the next nine years, from 613
to 622 CE, Muhammad proclaimed his message in the midst of the constant
antagonism of his tribe, the Meccan Quraysh. In the Meccan phase, therefore, we find Muhammad presented as faithful missionary in a hostile society.
Bereft of worldly power, he is depicted relying chiefly on the power of persuasion to win converts. According to Ibn Ishaq, despite the persecution of his
tribe, the Prophet 'was continually giving them counsel and preaching salvation
from their evil state'.[31] Along with perseverance and persuasion, the Meccan
Muhammad also relied on his character. Many reports in *sira* and hadith concerning this period stress that people were attracted to Muhammad on account
of his wisdom and fair dealing. Muhammad's nickname, in fact, was *al-amīn* (the
trustworthy).[32] Similarly, *daʿwa* manuals today argue that every Muslim who
aspires to do *daʿwa* should live an upright life that will attract non-Muslims (see
Chapter 7).

Another aspect of Muhammad's ministry in Mecca – an aspect which continues into the Medinan period – is what we might call *daʿwa* through signs and
miracles. In general, this chapter focuses on the ordinary human *daʿwa* strategies ascribed to Muhammad and his Companions. This is in keeping, to some
extent, with the Qur'an's insistence that Muhammad's only miracle was the
Qur'an itself (Q 13:38, 17:90–6, 29:50–1, 41:6). It is a striking and curious fact,
however, that the *sira* and hadith ascribe many spectacular signs and wonders
to Muhammad – signs attending his birth, an angelic cleansing of his heart, his

'night journey' to Jerusalem, his ascent into heaven, his splitting of the moon, his miraculous feeding of a multitude of people and his power over nature, to name a few.[33] In reports on the Meccan period, these miracles serve not only to confirm Muhammad's status as a true prophet, but also to accentuate the hard-heartedness and guilt of the Quraysh for refusing to accept his *da'wa*. Another helpful way of understanding the miracles of Muhammad in these literatures, however, is with reference to the inter-religious context in which the *sira* and hadith emerged. Muhammad's miracles, as it were, represent an effort on the part of these literatures and their compilers to persuade Jews and Christians to believe in Muhammad. Why would miracle stories be relevant to late antique Jews and Christians, among others? For one thing, both groups have founders – Moses and Jesus – who are believed to have performed many miracles. For another, appealing to miracles was a standard feature of religious apologetics in the late antique period.

In short, this overall pattern – the pattern of Muhammad's Meccan *da'wa* – might be called '*da'wa* from a position of weakness'. Even if he occasionally performed powerful miracles and even if his message had latent political implications,[34] ultimately the only style of *da'wa* available to Muhammad in the challenging Meccan situation from 613 to 622 CE was what this book is calling '*da'wa* as missionary invitation' (in contrast to '*da'wa* as religio-political summons'). Related to this, it is important to stress that, as far as the sources are concerned, *religious* issues – Muhammad's preaching, his attack on pagan gods and so on – were at the root of the hostility that Muhammad faced in Mecca, even if political and economic issues also played a part.[35] This image of Muhammad as a powerless but noble and basically religious *da'i* should be kept in mind because, as Part II argues, many Muslims today can identify with the Meccan Muhammad perhaps more easily than with the Medinan Muhammad. Before we turn to the Medinan period, three additional aspects of *da'wa* in the Meccan period deserve our attention: (1) narratives of Muhammad's first converts, (2) the recitation of the Qur'an as a *da'wa* strategy, and (3) opposition and failure in *da'wa*.

Muhammad's first converts

By definition, missionaries seek converts. If, therefore, part of the purpose of the *sira* and hadith is to present Muhammad as a faithful missionary preacher, we should expect conversion narratives to be an important sub-genre within these literatures – and that is precisely what we find. Muhammad's first convert was his wife Khadija, a fact that carries significance for contemporary Muslims who seek to encourage women's participation in *da'wa*. One contemporary Islamic website, for instance, makes much of Khadija's conversion and notes that she gave considerably from her own wealth to support the early *da'wa* of Islam.[36] Soon after the conversion account of Khadija, the *sira* narrates the conversions of the Companions 'Ali, Zayd and Abu Bakr. Reflecting an aspect

of the Qur'an's *da*ʿ*walogy* – that *da*ʿ*wa* is a duty of the prophets as well as of
Muslim believers in general – the *sira* frequently depicts the transformation of
Muhammad's converts into dynamic preachers in their own right. Ibn Ishaq
reports at length, for instance, on Abu Bakr's speedy transformation into an
energetic missionary for Islam.[37] After becoming a Muslim, he 'began to call
(*ja*ʿ*ala yad*ʿ*ū*) . . . to Islam all . . . those who came to him'. We are told further that
among those who accepted Islam at Abu Bakr's *da*ʿ*wa* were the Companions
'Uthman (later the third caliph), al-Zubayr, Sa'd b. Abu Waqqas and Talha b.
'Ubaydallah.[38] The case of Abu Bakr, a respected Qurayshi businessman and
later Islam's first caliph, highlights the focus that the *sira* often puts on the conversion of elite members of society.[39] Following from this, some *da*ʿ*wa* activists
today hope to bring about the conversion of contemporary 'Abu Bakrs', people
who can translate their social standing into trickle-down missionary impact.[40]
Another important conversion narrative is that of 'Umar (later, the second
caliph), a story – like that of Saul of Tarsus in the New Testament – in which a
one-time enemy is transformed into a zealous believer.[41]

Not long after the conversion of 'Umar, we learn of the conversion of al-
Tufayl of the Arab Banu Daus Tribe.[42] Although al-Tufayl is perhaps less well-
known today than other Companions of Muhammad, his story is worth a closer
look for a number of reasons. First, it further illustrates the theme of opposition
in *da*ʿ*wa*, insofar as the story opens with the Quraysh trying to prevent Tufayl
from giving Muhammad's *da*ʿ*wa* a fair hearing. Second, like the story of Abu
Bakr, it illustrates the transformation of a called one into a caller, insofar as
the Prophet commissioned Tufayl to return to his own people in order to bring
them the *da*ʿ*wa* of Islam. Third, it illustrates Muhammad as a master tactician
of *da*ʿ*wa*, insofar as his advice to Tufayl to 'preach to your people gently' gave
Tufayl greater success. It illustrates, fourth, a connection between *da*ʿ*wa* and
prayer. When Muhammad sent Tufayl back to the Banu Daus, he prayed for a
sign that would help Tufayl in his *da*ʿ*wa*, and he asked God to guide the Banu
Daus to the truth. Still today, *da*ʿ*wa* groups such as the Tablighi Jama'at (see
Chapter 6), begin and end their *da*ʿ*wa* outreaches with fervent prayers for God's
help. In short, like that of Abu Bakr, the conversion story of Tufayl provides
contemporary Muslims with a treasure house of potential lessons on how best to
do *da*ʿ*wa* (see Text Box 2.1).

A final, noteworthy example of this genre is the story of the Ansar or
'helpers' from the town of Medina. After the deaths of Khadija and Abu Talib
(Muhammad's uncle who had raised Muhammad after the deaths of his parents
and grandfather), a group of men from Medina are said to have come to Mecca
for a festival. While in Mecca, they met the Prophet, heard his *da*ʿ*wa* and
embraced Islam. Then, significantly, they returned to Medina as *da*ʿ*ī*s themselves: 'When they came to Medina they told their people about the apostle and
invited them to Islam until . . . there was no home [in Medina] . . . but Islam and

2.1 Modern *da'wa* lessons from the Companion al-Tufayl

The following excerpt is taken from an online article in which the author draws contemporary *da'wa* lessons from the conversion story of Tufayl as found in the *sira*:

The story shows us a technique of the media war waged against the Prophet Muhammad (peace be upon him) during the early days of his [da'wa]. The chieftains of Arab tribes would ask their people not to listen or meet the Prophet Muhammad because [they said] he is a sorcerer, liar, troublemaker, etc. or a terrorist . . . despite the fact that Muhammad is completely free of all of this. He was a rational person who [sowed] peace, love . . . and noble manners . . . The same conditions of [al-]Tufayl are true for the current reality as people are now influenced by media makers who spread false rumors about Islam and its Prophet day and night and manipulate the minds of people [with] fabricated and unjust . . . knowledge (Source: Editorial Staff 2018.

the apostle had been mentioned therein'.[43] The following year, these residents of Medina are said to have returned to Mecca, along with others, in order to pledge themselves to the Prophet. This has been called the 'first pledge of 'Aqaba' because it took place at 'Aqaba near Mecca.[44] When the Medinans left, the apostle sent a trusted Companion, Mus'ab b. 'Umayr, along with them as *da'i*.[45] Ibn Ishaq gives considerable space to Mus'ab's *da'wa* outreach in Medina. Here, then, is an example of Muhammad delegating missionary outreach to a chosen agent. Later, Mus'ab returned with about seventy Ansar from Medina, who made the so-called 'second pledge of 'Aqaba' to the Prophet. Mus'ab's *da'wa*, which not only won people religiously but also prepared Medina for its eventual political take-over by the Prophet, thus straddled the line between *da'wa* as missionary invitation and *da'wa* as religio-political summons. We will return to Muhammad's use of religio-political missionary agents later.

The recitation of the Qur'an as *da'wa* strategy

When the *sira* summarises Mus'ab's *da'wa* strategy, it says simply: 'He explained Islam . . . and read the Qur'an'.[46] Testifying to his own conversion, Muhammad's Companion al-Tufayl is reported to have said: 'The apostle explained Islam to me and recited the Qur'an to me. By God I never heard anything finer . . . So I became a Muslim'.[47] An encounter with the recited Qur'an was also an important factor in the conversion of 'Umar.[48] Another story which illustrates Qur'an recitation as *da'wa* strategy is the story of the Negus, the Christian king of Abyssinia, who is reported to have welcomed a group of Muslim refugees from Mecca during the so-called 'first *hijra*' (migration) of Islam around 615 CE. At one point, the leader of the Muslims in Abyssinia, Ja'far b. Abu Talib, was called in to speak to the Negus. In this context, Ja'far recited a chapter of the Qur'an known as *sūrat Maryam* (Surah of Mary, Q 19) – a shrewd choice for a Christian audience, since this chapter speaks much of Jesus and his mother Mary. Upon hearing the Qur'an, the Negus 'wept until his beard was wet'.[49] A similar story is told of a delegation of Christians from Abyssinia which came to Mecca to meet the Prophet. Muhammad 'invited them (*da'āhum*) to Allah and recited (*talā*) the Qur'an to them. When they heard the Qur'an their eyes flowed with tears and they accepted his call . . . '[50] Still today, *da'wa*-minded Muslims employ Qur'an recitation as *da'wa* strategy, something I have experienced personally on a number of occasions.[51] As these stories are meant to illustrate, the hearing of the Qur'an is believed to soften hearts and smooth the way for conversion to Islam.

In these episodes we see Muhammad sharing Islam with those who happened to come to him, a phenomenon we might call centripetal *da'wa*, and we also see him sending envoys to other regions to preach, a dynamic we might call centrifugal *da'wa*. The efforts of some Muslims today, particularly in the West, to welcome curious non-Muslims into mosques for the sake of *da'wa* (on 'visit a mosque day', or mosque open houses) might be seen as an example of the former. The Meccan period also provides a number of instances in which the Prophet is portrayed answering questions about Islam as a means of *da'wa*. Ibn Ishaq reports, for instance, that the above-mentioned delegation from Abyssinia asked the Prophet many questions before they embraced Islam. As we will see in Chapter 7, *da'wa* through questions and answers is also a prominent phenomenon today.

Da'wa, opposition and failure

We have already noted that opposition and adversity were significant features of Muhammad's *da'wa* in Mecca. We have thus spoken of Muhammad's Meccan ministry as '*da'wa* from a position of weakness'. Reports from the Meccan period also contain several stories of failure. In fact, looking at the Meccan period as a whole, Saleh contends that 'there is no escaping the conclusion that Muhammad's mission in Mecca was a failure'.[52] In contrast to the overwhelmingly successful Muhammad of the Medinan period, stories of a struggling Muhammad provide resources for later Muslims who find themselves in challenging circumstances – circumstances more like Mecca than Medina. A significant sub-theme that emerges from stories of persecution and failure recalls a qur'anic theme we discussed earlier: God's true *da'wa* exists in the midst of, and may be threatened by, 'false' *da'was* and their promoters. In a typical summary statement, Ibn Ishaq reports, 'the Quraysh showed their enmity to all those who followed the apostle; every clan which contained Muslims attacked them . . . so as to seduce them from their religion'.[53] In this context, we are introduced to Bilal, a slave of mixed Arab and African descent who had converted to Islam. Although viciously persecuted, he refused to deny his faith, and thus he is still remembered as a hero of early Islam.[54]

Among the most important stories from the Meccan period on the theme of opposition and failure is the story of Muhammad's first mission to Ta'if. After the deaths of Abu Talib and Khadija, and as a consequence of the growing hostility he was facing, Muhammad set out for Ta'if, a small town to the east of Mecca, in order to preach to and seek the aid of the Banu Thaqif tribe.[55] When he arrived at Ta'if, Muhammad 'invited them to Islam and asked them to help him against his opponents at home'.[56] In Ta'if, therefore, Muhammad's *da'wa* to Islam was joined with an invitation to enter into a sort of mutual-help alliance. In the end, however, Muhammad's *da'wa* in Ta'if was a dismal failure. The people not only rejected his message (only a Christian slave responded positively), they also abused him verbally and physically. The response of Muhammad was not to seek vengeance, but to pray. His prayer, recorded by Ibn Ishaq, provides an illustration of a Muslim missionary seeking God's comfort and strength in the midst of trials: 'O God, to thee I complain of my weakness . . . O Most Merciful, Thou art the Lord of the weak, and Thou art my Lord'.[57] Upon his return to Mecca, Muhammad continued to practise the kind of *da'wa* he had attempted at Ta'if. He began to 'offer himself to the tribes of the Arabs . . . whenever the opportunity came, summoning them (*yadᶜūhum*) to Allah'.[58] In general, like the Banu Thaqif, the tribes declined Muhammad's invitation.[59] According to the traditional account, it was not long after these moments of failure, however, that Muhammad's situation began to improve. The stories which appear next are those of the pledges of 'Aqaba, discussed earlier.

Medina: *da'wa* from a position of rising strength

The *hijra*, Muhammad's 'migration' from Mecca to Medina in 622 CE, was a major turning point, not only in the life of the Prophet, but also in Islamic and world history. It is no coincidence that the *hijra* provides the pivot and starting point of the Islamic calendar. Following the pledges of 'Aqaba and the successful *da'was* of the Ansar and Mus'ab, the Arabs of Medina invited Muhammad to relocate to their town. They assured him that his religious message and leadership would be welcome among them. Muhammad and his followers thus made plans to set up a new base of operations in Medina, and Muhammad himself arrived in the city in 622 CE. This constituted a shift, not only to a new geographic location, but also to an important new phase in the Prophet's *da'wa* ministry.

One cannot overstate the importance of the memory of the Medinan period

– the ten-year period of the Prophet's ministry from the *hijra* in 622 CE to his death in 632 CE – to the formation of the Islamic tradition. About three-quarters of the material in the *sira* of Ibn Ishaq and most of what is found in the hadith literature purport to be from the Medinan period.[60] While many of the styles of *da'wa* we observed in the Meccan period continue into the Medinan period, *da'wa* nevertheless undergoes a significant transformation in Medina.[61] Whereas in Mecca Muhammad and the Muslims had responded to opposition by persevering in their preaching and trusting in God, in Medina they set out to establish an Islamic society and political order. *Da'wa* was no longer merely about quietist (non-political) preaching aimed at winning religious converts, but also about establishing a cohesive state: 'When the apostle was firmly settled in Medina and his brethren the emigrants were gathered to him . . . Islam became firmly established. Prayer was instituted, the alms tax and fasting were prescribed, legal punishments fixed, the forbidden and permitted described, and Islam took up its abode with them'.[62] With the *hijra*, therefore, Muhammad and the early Muslims moved from *da'wa* from a position of weakness to *da'wa* from a position of rising strength. Not surprisingly, in Medinan reports, *da'wa* takes on an increasingly political connotation. To accept the invitation 'to God and the Prophet and Islam' increasingly meant to enter an alliance with, or submit to, Medina as an emerging city-state.[63]

2.2 Ibn Ishaq's description of the Mecca-to-Medina transformation in Muhammad's *da'wa* ministry

[In Mecca] The apostle had not been given permission to fight or allowed to shed blood before the second [pledge of] 'Aqaba. He had simply been ordered to call men to God (daʿāʾ ilā Allah) and to endure insult and forgive the ignorant . . . When the Quraysh became insolent towards God and rejected his gracious purpose . . . he gave permission to his prophet to fight and to protect himself against those who wronged [the Muslims] and treated them badly . . . When God gave permission to fight . . . the apostle commanded his companions, the emigrants of his people and those Muslims who were with him in Mecca, to migrate to Medina and to link up with their brethren the Ansar.

According to this passage, in Mecca, Muhammad was only commanded to 'call [people] to God and to endure insult and forgive the ignorant'. This underscores our characterisation of 'Meccan *da'wa*' as '*da'wa* from a position of weakness'. However, after the second pledge of 'Aqaba, and especially after the *hijra*, this pattern of ministry came to be augmented with 'fighting' and political alliance making. This underscores the idea of 'Medinan *da'wa*' as '*da'wa* from a position of (rising) strength' (Source: Ibn Ishaq 1955/2012, pp. 212–13 [Ibn Hisham 1858–60, pp. 313–14]).

This general transformation in *da'wa* can be seen from another angle, from the perspective of the duty to command the right and forbid the wrong – discussed at the end of Chapter 1 (Q 3:104, 3:110). A well-known hadith regarding this duty has the Prophet say: 'He who amongst you sees something abominable (*munkar*) should modify it with the help of his hand (*bi yadihi*); and if he has not the strength . . . then he should do it with his tongue (*bi lisānihi*), and if he has not the strength . . . then he should (abhor it) from his heart (*bi qalbihi*)'.[64] Relating this tradition to the Prophet's biography, we might say that, whereas in Mecca the Prophet and his Companions could command the right and forbid the wrong *only* with the heart and the tongue (personal commitment to God's will and verbal persuasion), in Medina they were increasingly able to do so with the hand as well (enforcing obedience to God using state power). Having examined the overall character of the Prophet's Medinan *da'wa* – '*da'wa* from a position of rising strength' – as above, this section continues by highlighting several additional aspects of the Prophet's Medinan *da'wa* as depicted in *sira* and hadith: (1) continuing conversions and opposition, (2) the relationship between *da'wa* and *jihad*, (3) *da'wa*, iconoclasm and the problems of success, and (4) converting Arabia and beyond.

Continuing opposition and conversions

Our characterisation of the Medinan *da'wa* as '*da'wa* from a position of rising strength' should not be taken to indicate that the Prophet's *hijra* brought opposition to an end. Ibn Ishaq reports on two groups that proved to be a thorn in the Prophet's side in Medina: the 'Jewish adversaries' and 'the hypocrites'. In addition, there was continuing hostility from the Meccan Quraysh, albeit now from a distance. Initially, Muhammad's response to Jewish opposition in Medina was peaceful *da'wa*: 'The apostle summoned (*da'ā*) the [Jews] to Islam and made it attractive to them and warned them of God's punishment'.[65] However, over time, the relationship between Muhammad and the Medinan Jews became increasingly hostile and violent.

In the midst of stories of conflict with the Jews and others, there are numerous additional stories of conversion. For instance, there is the conversion story of the Jewish rabbi 'Abd Allah b. Salam. Despite the mutual hostility between Muhammad and many of the Jews, 'Abd Allah, we are told, 'became a Muslim . . . and ordered [his] family to do the same'.[66] Another conversion story is that of the Qurayshi nobles, 'Amr b. al-'As and Khalid b. al-Walid.[67] Both of these men, who later became famous warriors for Islam, embraced Islam after the so-called Treaty of Hudaybiyya (usually dated to six years after the *hijra*, or 628 CE). For 'Amr and Khalid, the appropriate consequence of their acceptance of Islam was to relocate to Medina. This provides further insight into the Medinan transformation of *da'wa*: To become a Muslim now apparently meant to migrate to Islamic territory governed by a Muslim ruler rather than to remain among unbelievers. We thus find here an early pointer to that aspect of classical Islamic thought which divides the world into *dar al-Islam* ('the house of Islam', territory in which Muslims and their faith are dominant) and *dar al-harb* ('the house of war', territory where non-Muslims and their faiths are dominant). Following the precedent provided by the stories of 'Amr and Khalid, over time, Muslim scholars would teach that Muslims who find themselves living in the latter should, ideally, migrate to the former.

An extension of this principle relates to the general bias seen in Muhammad's ministry towards settled, as opposed to nomadic, life. Islam, with its rhythms of frequent prayer and other communal rituals, and its social, commercial and political ethics is ideally practised by settled people in urban settings. Therefore, 'the Prophet placed great emphasis on the importance of settlement and the abandonment of the nomadic life for those embracing Islam; it was considered impossible to remain a nomad and to be a Muslim in the true sense of the word'. Settlement of nomadic groups was thus 'a conscious policy of Muhammad's' – a policy which facilitated the integration of the nomads into Muhammad's emerging state.[68] In other words, in Medina, Muhammad's *da'wa* was increasingly aimed not only at religious conversion, but also at political submission, settlement and integration.

A final conversion tale from the Medinan period worth mentioning is that of Jabbar b. Salma. In this case we discover *da'wa* taking place through martyrdom.[69] Given the prominence of warfare in the Medinan phase of the Prophet's ministry (see the following section), it is not surprising that martyrdom itself emerges as a major motif in reports on this period. Several months after the Battle of Uhud, Jabbar fought on the non-Muslim side in a skirmish against the Muslims. According to Ibn Ishaq, Jabbar later reported concerning Haram b. Milhan, a Muslim warrior whom Jabbar had killed in the battle: 'What led me to become a Muslim was that I stabbed [Haram] between the shoulders . . . I saw the point of the spear come out of his chest, and I heard him say, "I have won, by God!" '[70] Haram's joyful response to martyrdom so impressed Jabbar that he converted to Islam. *Da'wa* through martyrdom is a theme that has reappeared in modern times among some militant Jihadi groups (see Chapter 7 for more on these groups and their *da'was*). Such groups hope that their willingness to sacrifice their lives for the cause of Islam will not only win them a place in paradise, but also bear witness to a watching world.

Da'wa and *jihad*

Mention of the Prophet's battles and the emergence of an ideology of martyrdom among his earliest followers raises the question of the relationship between *da'wa* and *jihad* in the *sira* and hadith literatures. The Arabic word *jihad* ('struggle') has had several connotations in the Islamic tradition over the centuries. It has been taken to refer, first, to the spiritual struggle to be a devout Muslim and to overcome one's lower, sinful inclinations. This is *jihad* as *taqwa* (piety), sometimes called *jihad al-akbar* (the 'greater jihad'). Second, it has been taken to refer to military struggle in the cause of Islam. This is *jihad* as *qitāl* (fighting), sometimes called *jihad al-asghar* (the 'lesser jihad'). In keeping with the theme of this book, we may add a third connotation to which we will return in Chapter 5: *jihad* as *da'wa* (struggle for the missionary spread of Islam). In the major hadith collections and in the *sira*, however, it is overwhelmingly the second of these connotations – *jihad* as military struggle – which predominates.[71]

How, then, might we characterise the relationship between *da'wa* and military *jihad* in *sira* and hadith? Reports of the Prophet's battles – for instance, the famous Battles of Badr (624 CE), Uhud (625 CE), the Trench (627 CE), Khaybar (628 CE), Mu'ta (629 CE) and Hunayn (630 CE), as well as other battles and raids in which the Prophet participated or sent out[72] – take up a significant proportion of the materials depicting the Medinan period. The sources portray these battles as more firmly establishing Muhammad as a leader and Medina as an Islamic centre, which in turn increased his prospects for *da'wa*. Because of the Prophet's military successes and growing strength, the Arab tribes could no longer ignore or dismiss him, as the city of Ta'if had done in the Meccan period.[73] From this evidence, we might conclude that, on a descriptive level, *jihad* precedes *da'wa* insofar as it creates conditions beneficial to *da'wa*. There is, however, ample precedent in *sira* and hadith for the reverse – that *da'wa* precedes *jihad*. This can be seen first in the chronology of the Prophet's ministry: Had it not been for the success of his Meccan *da'wa* among individuals like 'Ali, Abu Bakr and 'Umar, as well as groups such as the Medinan Ansar, military conquest would have proven impossible. In fact, the logic of *da'wa* before *jihad* is enshrined in an important hadith that records a dialogue between Muhammad and 'Ali during the Battle of Khaybar: "Ali said "O Allah's Messenger! I will fight with [our opponents] till they become [Muslims] like us." Allah's Messenger said, ". . . When you enter their territory, invite them to embrace Islam (*adᶜuhum ilā al-Islām*) . . . for by Allah, even if a single man is led on the right path by Allah through you, then that will be better for you . . ."[74] In other words, 'Ali is directed by the Prophet to do *da'wa before* he wages *jihad*.[75] Another example comes from the so-called 'Year of Delegations'. When the Prophet sent his Companion Khalid b. al-Walid to the Banu al-Harith tribe, 'he ordered him to invite them to Islam for three days before he attacked them'. As it turned out, the tribe accepted Khalid's *da'wa*. Thus, instead of playing the warrior, Khalid played the missionary. He 'stayed with them, teaching them Islam . . .' [76] Later on, the idea that one should give missionary *da'wa* before initiating military hostilities became an established point of Islamic law (see Chapter 3). Thus, as far as the Medinan example of the Prophet is concerned, there seems to be a circular relationship at play: *Da'wa* enabled *jihad*, which in turn expedited *da'wa*.[77] *Da'wa* and military *jihad*, in short, reinforced each other in the Medina period.

Da'wa, iconoclasm and the problems of success

By 630 CE, Muhammad was thoroughly in control of Medina and poised to become the dominant power on the Arabian Peninsula. First, however, he had to conquer Mecca. As the Prophet and his army marched towards Mecca in that same year, the city's leaders recognised that the tide had turned, and they surrendered without a fight. The Prophet, in turn, is reported to have treated his one-time Meccan opponents magnanimously. While the people of Mecca were treated fairly well under the circumstances, the same cannot be said for their idols. Bukhari reports: 'When the Prophet entered Mecca on the day of the Conquest, there were 360 idols around the Ka'ba. The Prophet started striking them with a stick he had in his hand and was saying, "Truth has come and Falsehood will neither start nor will it reappear"' (Q 17:81).[78] If the sources are to be believed, this was the start of a general campaign to wipe out idol worship among the Arabs. After the fall of Mecca, we are told that 'the apostle sent out troops in the district around Mecca inviting (*tad'ū*) men to God: he did not order them to fight. Among those he sent was Khalid b. al-Walid whom he ordered to go . . . as a missionary (*dā'ī*)'.[79] Besides communicating Muhammad's *da'wa* to the area around Mecca, Khalid was also sent to destroy idols.[80] The account of Ibn Sa'd contains several other accounts of Muhammad sending out agents to destroy idols in the region around Mecca.[81] This joining of *da'wa* with iconoclasm provides another example of commanding right and forbidding wrong with the hand.

The conquest of Mecca was followed by the Battle of Hunayn, a battle fought against a coalition of Arab tribes who remained resistant to Muhammad's *da'wa*, and to the siege of Ta'if. Not long after, the *sira* reports on the Tabuk expedition, in which Muhammad led an army against a Byzantine garrison to the northwest of Medina. Several implications of these battles may be highlighted. First, these stories illustrate the fact that, in the sources' depiction of the Medinan period, *da'wa* and fighting were both aspects of the Prophet's overall program. Those Arab tribes who resisted his religious *da'wa* could be fought until they submitted. While submission as a consequence of peaceful preaching seems to have been preferred, fighting could be used in case preaching failed. Second, these battle tales provide more illustrations of the relationship between *da'wa* and the character of the *da'ī*. Repeatedly, Muhammad is portrayed dealing kindly with those he has defeated as well as being scrupulous in the distribution of booty. Finally, the outcomes of these battles further illustrate the relationship between *da'wa* and political alliance-making. After the Battle of Hunayn, Muhammad is portrayed as using booty to win over certain elite Qurayshi tribesmen. Known in Arabic as *ta'līf al-qulūb* (conciliation of hearts), this was a policy Muhammad and his successors, the early caliphs, utilised in order to ensure the allegiance of former rivals.[82] As Ibn Ishaq reports, Muhammad 'gave gifts to those whose hearts were to be won over (*mu'allafat qulūbuhum*), notably the chiefs of the army, to win them and through them their people'.[83] Among these were Abu Sufyan b. Harb, his son Mu'awiyya (later the founder of the Umayyad Dynasty) and Safwan b. Umayya.

This practice, which is particularly evident during the 'Year of Delegations', introduced a seeming dilemma into the enterprise of *da'wa*. Although Muhammad's political and military success added greatly to the Muslims' power and influence, the question arose: How could the Muslims be sure that the new converts were motivated by religious conviction and not merely by thoughts of worldly advantage? This situation is somewhat reminiscent of the effects of Constantine's Edict of Toleration (313 CE) on fourth-century Christianity. In the words of Stephen Neill, 'the favourable attitude of [Constantine] produced a complete change in the situation of the Christian Church . . . Crowds pressed into it, and the Church was in danger of being submerged under the flood of new believers . . . In all this there were great dangers. Faith became superficial . . .'[84] Similarly, the worldly success of Muhammad, symbolised by the conquest of Mecca and subsequent victories, brought a wave of new converts into Islam. This is apparently one reason why *sira* and hadith devote special attention to those Quraysh who converted at this time. What was to be made, for instance, of the conversion of al-'Abbas (the Prophet's uncle and namesake of the later 'Abbasid dynasty who converted late and somewhat reluctantly), or the conversions of the two Abu Sufyans (one-time opponents who converted only when it became clear that Muhammad's victory was irresistible)?[85]

For his part, Muhammad took a liberal stance in accepting these converts and even incentivising their conversions. For those who had been with the Prophet from the beginning and who had suffered as a result of their conversions, however, it must have been irksome to find their one-time persecutors not only welcomed into the Islamic fold, but also bestowed with gifts and positions of influence. Yet, the distinction we are tracing between the Prophet's Meccan *da'wa* and his Medinan *da'wa* helps make sense of his actions. By the later Medinan period, Muhammad was no longer merely seeking religious converts, but also political allies and collaborators, and he wanted the best and brightest among the Quraysh on his side. Muhammad's acceptance of these converts might also be interpreted as an illustration of Muhammad's commitment to gradualism in *da'wa*. As depicted, Muhammad seems to have been clear-eyed about that fact that these 'conversions' were statements less of religious faith and more of political submission, but he also seems to have believed that one could lead to the other. That is to say, he welcomed these converts, because, no matter how seemingly superficial, self-serving, or 'political' their motives might have been at first, he expected that they could become 'excellent Muslims' over time.[86] Evidence for this may be seen in the fact that, in several instances, the Prophet is portrayed as making arrangements for new converts to receive further instruction. When he returned to Medina after the conquest of Mecca, for instance, 'He left 'Attab b. Asid in charge . . . He also left behind with him Mu'adh b. Jabal to instruct the people in religion and teach them the Qur'an'.[87] Some modern *da'wa* groups follow this pattern when they do what they call 'follow-up' with the recently converted.[88] Most missionary religions recognise the need for such follow-up efforts, since new converts cannot be expected to immediately grasp the full implications of what conversion entails.[89]

Converting Arabia and beyond
The cascade of victories which followed the 'conquest' of Mecca led to the above-mentioned 'Year of Delegations' – a period in which the tribes from all over Arabia sent delegations to offer submission to Muhammad. The Year of Delegations provides what is undoubtedly the most stunning picture of cen-tripetal *da'wa* in the life of Muhammad. Several important aspects of the Year of Delegations may be highlighted. First, although the sources emphasise that the delegations experienced religious conversion, it seems clear that political submission was the primary point. As seen in the later 'wars of *ridda* (apostasy)' during the caliphate of Abu Bakr, many of the tribes are reported to have gone back on these 'conversions' after the Prophet's death, meaning that they rebelled politically.[90] Second, we can detect an element of lingering religious competition in several of these stories. We learn, for instance, that Muhammad was not the only 'prophet' preaching in Arabia at this time. His most prominent competitor was Musaylima b. Habib al-Hanafi. By saying yes to Muhammad, the tribes which came to offer submission were also saying – or were expected to say – no to Islam's religio-political rivals such as Musaylima. This is another instance of the theme we observed in Chapter 1 of competition between the 'true' *da'wa* and 'false' *da'wa*s.[91] A final, related theme in the delegation stories is that loyalty to Muhammad and Islam now takes precedence over other loyal-ties. This may be observed, for instance, in the story of 'Amr b. Ma'dikarib, a man who broke with his tribe in order to embrace Islam.[92] 'Amr's story and others like it illustrate the idea that conversion to Islam embeds converts in a new 'tribe', formed by religio-political, rather than physical ties. Today *da'wa* also often implies the call to dissociate oneself from traditional ties of family and locality and to identify oneself primarily with the community of 'true Muslims' worldwide. In this way of thinking, one's true 'brothers and sisters' are no longer from one's family of origin, but fellow believers of whatever background.

We observed several examples from the Meccan period in which the Prophet sent out specially chosen agents or missionary envoys to do *da'wa* in new places. During the Year of Delegations, he sent out many more (see Figure 2.1). In these examples, however, the envoy's role changes consistent with the overall Medinan transformation of *da'wa* we are studying. These envoys not only have a religious role, a duty to preach Islam, but they are also commissioned to tear

2.3 A modern Muslim scholar describes the 'Year of Delegations'

Paraphrasing Ibn Ishaq, twentieth-century Muslim writer Abu'l-Hasan 'Ali Nadwi describes the Year of Delegations in such a way as to empha-sise the spiritual attractions of Islam and the Prophet, the religious char-acter of the Arabian tribes' conversions and the transformation of the tribesmen into missionaries:

After Mecca had been conquered and the Prophet had returned victorious from [the battle of] Tabuk, Arab delegations [from each Arab tribe] began to pour into the heart-land of Islam. They learned about Islam, saw the character of the Messenger of Allah, and the lifestyle of his Companions. Tents were erected for them in the courtyard of the mosque; they heard the Qur'an recited; watched the Muslims praying and asked the messenger of Allah to explain the faith to them. He impressed them with his eloquence and wisdom and he constantly quoted versus from the Qur'an. They believed what they heard and were well satisfied. They returned to their homes full of zeal, calling other people to accept Islam and decrying paganism and its negative effects (Source: Nadwi 1993, p. 171).

down idols, collect taxes, raise armies and ensure ongoing loyalty to the Islamic proto-state. They move beyond commanding and forbidding with the heart and tongue to doing so with the hand as well. In his classic study of Muhammad's life, Watt devotes considerable attention to these 'agents' (*ʿummāl*) who func-tioned as Muhammad's personal representatives in the areas of Arabia newly brought under his rule.[93] Donner, building on Watt, also studies what he calls Muhammad's 'network of administrative agents', most of whom were elites from among the Quraysh or Medinan Ansar.[94] While both authors are right to emphasise the administrative duties of Muhammad's agents, particularly their role as tax collectors, they have little to say about their missionary functions. As portrayed in the sources, however, many of these agents were expected to do religious *da'wa* alongside their administrative tasks. They thus constitute an important aspect not only of the political, but also of the missionary history of Islam.[95]

A good illustration of Muhammad's use of such politico-missionary agents in this period is the story of the Companions Abu Musa and Muʿadh b. Jabal, whom Muhammad sent to Yemen. Many traditions speak of the missions of Abu Musa and especially of Muʿadh, and from these, several points are worth highlighting. First, Abu Musa and Muʿadh were expected to combine religious and political functions in their *da'wa* – they were to spread Islam, administer

Figure 2.1 The mosque of the Prophet Muhammad in Medina in 2018. After the surrender of Mecca and the Tabuk expedition, Muhammad is portrayed as receiving Arab delegations at his mosque in Medina and summoning them to Islam (the 'Year of Delegations', an example of centripetal mission). He is also portrayed sending out envoys from Medina to do religio-political *da'wa* in other regions (an example of centrifugal mission). Photo: Konevi, from pexels.com, cropped from original.

justice and collect taxes. Second, they were to tailor their *da'wa* to their specific audiences. The Prophet told these two envoys: 'Call (*ad'ū*) people and give good tidings to the (people), and do not repel them, make things easy for them and do not make things difficult'.[96] In recognition of the fact that Yemen at this time was populated largely by Christians and Jews, he also is reported to have told them: 'You will soon find yourself . . . among the people of the Book, so first call them (*ad'uhum*) to testify that there is no God but Allah, that I am the messenger of Allah, and if they accept this, then tell them Allah has enjoined upon them five prayers . . . and if they accept it, then tell them that Allah has made Zakat obligatory for them'.[97] The *da'is*, that is, were to start with the basics of Islam (the confession of faith or *shahāda*) and then proceed to the 'harder' teachings, like daily prayers and the giving of alms.[98]

Not all of the envoys sent out by Muhammad in the late Medinan period were formal envoys, of the kind described above. A good illustration of an informal envoy who engaged in *da'wa* is the story of Dimam b. Tha'laba. After visiting Muhammad during the Year of Delegations and responding favourably to his *da'wa,* he returned to his own tribe (the Banu Sa'd b. Bakr) full of zeal to spread Islam. Here then is another example of a convert to Islam quickly transformed into a missionary preacher. Gathering his people together, he approached them with a strongly polemical *da'wa*: 'the first thing he said to them was, "How evil are al-Lat and al-'Uzza! . . . They can neither hurt nor heal." '[99] Although conventional wisdom would suggest that a missionary should first seek friendly relations and common ground with his or her audience, in this case Dimam's polemical approach is portrayed as being wonderfully effective: 'Before the night was over, there was not a man or woman in the tribe that had not become a Muslim'.[100]

With the submission of Arabia well underway, the sources indicate that Muhammad began to think about religio-political outreach beyond Arabia. This can be seen in the final *da'wa* strategy we will highlight in this chapter – the Prophet's use of written letters. In the Qur'an, it may be recalled, Solomon is reported to have sent a letter of *da'wa* to the queen of Sheba (Q 27:22–44). Similarly, the *sira* and hadith portray the Prophet using letter-writing as a means of *da'wa* in the later Medinan period. These letters were directed to rulers outside Arabia such as the Byzantine Emperor Heraclius (r. 610–41 CE), 'the Khosrau' (the Sassanian Emperor), 'Muqauqis' (the governor of Egypt) and to the Negus of Abyssinia, among others.[101] While these letters did not contain explicit threats of war, it is clear, taking the sources at face value, that Muhammad was thinking of more than peaceful *da'wa* when he sent them. In fact, these letters may be taken as illustrations of the principle, discussed above, that Muslims should give *da'wa* before they initiate military hostilities (see Text Box 2.4). Although

---

2.4 Muhammad's letter of *da'wa* to Heraclius

While of doubtful authenticity, *sira* and hadith report that Muhammad wrote or dictated the following:

*In the name of Allah the Beneficent, the Merciful (This letter is) from Muhammad the slave of Allah and His Apostle, to Heraclius the ruler of Byzant[ium]. Peace be upon him who follows the right path. Furthermore I invite you to Islam (*ad'ūka bi di'āyat al-Islām*), and if you become a Muslim you will be safe, and Allah will double your reward, and if you reject this invitation of Islam you will be committing a sin by misguiding your [people]. And I recite to you Allah's Statement: 'O people of the Book! Come to a word common to you and us that we worship none but Allah and that we associate nothing in worship with Him, and that none of us shall take others as Lords beside Allah. Then, if they turn away, say: Bear witness that we are Muslims'* (Q 3:64) (Source: al-Bukhari 1420/1999, no. 7 [1997, 1:50-5]).

the historicity of these letters is doubtful,[102] for modern *da'wa* activists, they may yet communicate important lessons. They may be taken as precedents, for example, for the use of literature and other media in *da'wa* – a major trend in contemporary times (see Chapter 7). More importantly, they may be (and have been) taken to signal that the Prophet anticipated the religio-political expansion of Islam beyond Arabia.

Summary and conclusions

Like the Qur'an, the *sira* and hadith literatures are more readily available to Muslims than ever before in history. This, combined with a renewed emphasis on *da'wa* and a 'scripturalist' mood among many contemporary Muslims, means that these sources are being mined as never before for insights into missionary outreach. Guided by the chronology of Ibn Ishaq's *sira* and drawing on several major hadith collections and other early sources, this chapter has illustrated some of the extra-qur'anic materials upon which contemporary Muslims draw when formulating missionary thought and practice. As they study the life of the Prophet, 'the best inviter', and his Companions, modern Muslims can find precedents for many kinds of *da'wa*. In this chapter, we have encountered, for instance, *da'wa* through religious dialogue and debate, *da'wa* through noble Islamic character, *da'wa* through Qur'an recitation, *da'wa* through miracles, trickle-down *da'wa* through elite converts, *da'wa* preceding military engagement, *da'wa* through questions and answers, centripetal and centrifugal *da'wa*, delegated *da'wa* through agents and envoys, gradualist *da'wa*, *da'wa* as religious call, *da'wa* as political summons, *da'wa* through martyrdom and *da'wa* through letters. In all this, I have argued that one of the (implicit) purposes of *sira* and hadith is to develop the *da'wa*logy of the Qur'an and to differentiate emergent Islam and its *da'wa* from religious rivals and their *da'wa*s. On balance, like the Qur'an, the *sira* and hadith reflect a stance of religious exclusivism – they overwhelmingly assume the universality and superiority of Islam, the ultimate falsehood of other religions and the urgent necessity of conversion to Islam.

Our final task is to reemphasise this chapter's distinction between the Meccan and Medinan patterns of the Prophet's *da'wa*. Although there is continuity in the ways *da'wa* is portrayed in these two phases – in both Mecca and Medina, Muhammad is portrayed as preaching, debating, winning converts, enduring opposition and so on – there is nevertheless an important change in the Prophet's approach after the *hijra*. From a primarily religious and largely apolitical (or pre-political) *da'wa* carried out from a position of weakness (the Meccan pattern), the narrative shifts to a religio-political *da'wa* carried out from a position of increasing strength (the Medinan pattern). In other words, recalling terms defined in the Introduction, we see the Prophet moving from '*da'wa* as missionary invitation' to '*da'wa* as religio-political summons'. As we will see, these two fundamental orientations to *da'wa* – and the tensions between them – continue to the present.

Notes

1. Arnold 1896/1913/2012, p. 11.
2. This two-source model (Qur'an and *sunna*) seems to be modelled on the relationship between the Written and Oral Torahs in Rabbinic Judaism.
3. See Goldziher 1981, pp. 28–30. There were other options besides prophetic hadith. For a time, Muslims looked to the caliph and his *sunna*, to Islamic judges, or local custom. See Crone and Hinds 1986.
4. Lecker 2010, p. 68.
5. Khalidi 2009, pp.15, 37–9, 58–9. For the relationship between *sira* and hadith, see Raven 1960–2007; Kister 1983; and Hinds 1983, pp. 57–66.
6. This book follows the periodisation in Robinson 2003, pp. xix–xx.
7. In the classical formulation, hadith constitutes the second root of Islamic law.
8. Melchert 2002b.
9. Raven writes of 'The fame of Ibn Hisham, whose *sira* is . . . the most prominent'. Raven 1960-2007. See also Fiazer and Rippin 2011; Guillaume 1955/2012, p. xvi.
10. For critical issues, see Chapter 3; see also, Kister 1983, p. 367; Hoyland 2007; and Lecker 2010, pp. 61–81.
11. These literatures were compiled in the post-conquest period and reflect that era's concerns. 'The narratives of the *Sirah* have to be carefully . . . sifted in order to get at the . . . historically valid information, which is in fact meagre'. Kister 1983, p. 367.
12. Contemporary Muslims may not have first-hand acquaintance with hadith or *sira*. However, to the extent that the outline of the Prophet's life preserved in these sources are continually recycled in books, sermons and other media, they remain widely known. For an example, see Nadwi 1993.
13. Kecia Ali has shown how Muslims throughout history have drawn on the *sira* and hadith to portray Muhammad in line with their own needs: Muhammad has been portrayed as ideal husband and father, warrior, statesman, legislator, paradigm of etiquette, miracle-worker, mystic and, in modern times, great reformer. Ali 2014. See also Khalidi 2009; and Brockopp 2010.
14. Raven 1960–2007, pp. 661–2.
15. As noted in Chapter 1 regarding the 'Islam' of the Qur'an, the 'Islam' that Ibn Ishaq knew was a faith in development. It was not yet the 'Islam' of later centuries.
16. Citations from the *sira* are from Ibn Ishaq's *The Life of Muhammad*, translated by Guillaume; hereafter Ibn Ishaq 1955/2012. Arabic citations from the *sira* are from Ibn Hisham's *Sīrat Rasūl Allāh*, edited by Wüstenfeld; hereafter Ibn Hisham 1858–60.
17. For a complication of Ibn Ishaq's portrayal, see Hawting 1999.
18. Ibn Ishaq 1955/2012, p. 35.
19. See Rubin 2016, pp. 141–2.
20. One even finds 'Amr referenced in intra-Muslim polemics. See, for instance, Gift2Sufis 2011.
21. Ibn Ishaq 1955/2012, p. 90f (Ibn Hisham 1858–60, p. 130f.).
22. Ibn Ishaq 1955/2012, p. 79f (Ibn Hisham 1858–60, p. 115f.).
23. Ibid., p. 93f. (pp. 134–6).
24. Ibid., p. 96 (p. 139).

25. The *sira* depicts Faymiyun confronting the people with the claims of the one God and, in an episode resembling the Christian legend of St. Boniface, cursing their sacred palm tree, which was promptly uprooted. Thereafter, we are told that Najran adopted Faymiyun's religion, 'the law of 'Isa Ibn Maryam'. Ibid., pp. 14–17 (pp. 22–5).

26. Upon their refusal, he slaughtered some 20,000 of them. Ibid., p. 17 (p. 24).

27. Ibn Ishaq 1955/2012, p. 118 (Ibn Hisham 1858–60, pp. 166–7). Italics added.

28. Ibid., p. 130 (p. 183).

29. God is said to have revealed two qur'anic verses regarding this event: Q 15:94, 26: 214–15.

30. This is said to have resulted in the revelation of Q 111:1. Muslim ibn al-Hajjaj (1433/2012), no. 406 (vol. 1, p. 138). I cite the hadith number with Siddiqi's volume and page number in parentheses. See further the comments on this incident in Rubin 1995, pp. 127–48.

31. Ibn Ishaq 1955/2012, p. 175.

32. The Meccan Muhammad is portrayed as forgiving and concerned above all with the welfare of his people. Muhammad's nickname, *al-amīn* (the trustworthy), is another example. Ibn Ishaq 1955/2012, p. 128 (Ibn Hisham 1858–60, p. 178).

33. On the miracles ascribed to Muhammad in the *sira*, see Rubin 2010.

34. Donner notes that '[a]lready in the Meccan phase of Muhammad's career', Muhammad's teaching provided the underpinnings for the emergence of a cohesive and expansionist state. See Donner 2008, pp. 55–62.

35. For example, Shaban 1979, pp. 25–7. Lecker 2010, pp. 73–4, notes that the sources tend to 'marginalise' the political and economic interests which contributed to Muhammad's rise to power.

36. Islamweb 2018b. Mainstream Islamic websites like Islamweb are cited in Part I of the book for illustrative purposes. More will be said about *da'wa* and the internet in Chapter 7.

37. 'Ali, the Prophet's cousin and later son in law , was the first male convert. Upon becoming a Muslim, 'Ali 'declared [Muhammad's] truth'. Ibn Ishaq gives more space, however, to Abu Bakr. Ibn Ishaq 1955/2012, pp. 114–15 (Ibn Hisham 1858–60, pp. 158–61).

38. Ibid., p. 115 (p. 161).

39. There are later political motives behind the portrayal of Abu Bakr. In Ibn Ishaq's time proto-Sunnis and proto-Shi'ites were battling over the legitimacy of Abu Bakr against the claims of 'Ali.

40. See, for example, the discussions of Abu Bakr in these online articles: Alim.org [n. d.]; Qassem [n. d.].

41. Ibn Ishaq 1955/2012, pp. 155–9 (Ibn Hisham 1858–60, pp. 224–30). On Saul of Tarsus, see Acts of the Apostles 9.

42. Ibn Ishaq 1955/2012, pp. 175–7.

43. Ibn Ishaq 1955/2012, pp. 197–8 (Ibn Hisham 1858–60, pp. 285–7).

44. On the 'Aqaba meetings, see Rubin 1995, pp. 169–85.

45. Ibn Ishaq 1955/2012, p. 199 (Ibn Hisham 1858–60, pp. 289–90).

46. Ibid., p. 200 (p. 291).

47. Ibid., p. 176 (p. 235).

48. Ibid., pp. 155–9 (pp. 224–30). For another example, see Ibid., p. 197 (pp. 285–6).

49. Ibid., pp. 150–5 (pp. 217–24).

50. Ibid., p. 179 (p. 259). These stories have a clear exegetical function related to Q 5:83.

51. Kuiper 2018a, p. 32.

52. Saleh 2010, p. 34.

53. Ibn Ishaq 1955/2012, p. 143 (Ibn Hisham 1858–60, p. 205), italics added. In another

place, we read, 'the Quraysh incited the people against [those] who had become Muslims. Every tribe fell upon the Muslims . . . beating them and seducing them from their religion'. Ibid., p. 120 (p. 170).

54. Abu Bakr is said to have freed him from slavery; later, he became the first *mu'adhdhin* (one who calls to prayer) of Islam.

55. The death of Abu Talib provides another interesting example of failure in *da'wa*. See al-Bukhari 1420/1999, no. 1360 (vol. 2, p. 254). Citations from al-Bukhari are from the *Ṣaḥīḥ*. An English translation is *Sahih al-Bukhari: Arabic-English*, trans. Muhsin Khan (1997). This book cites the hadith number with Muhsin Khan's volume and page number in parentheses.

56. Ibn Ishaq 1955/2012, p. 192 (Ibn Hisham 1858–60, p. 279).

57. Ibid., p. 193 (p. 280)

58. Ibid., p. 194 (p. 282).

59. Ibid., p. 195 (pp. 282–3).

60. Khalidi 2009, pp. 38, 86. Not only is the material from the Medinan period considered to be more reliable, the Medinan Muhammad would come to provide the lens through which the rest of his life would be viewed. Saleh 2010, p. 25; Rubin 2010, p. 54. Other *sira* compilers, such as Ibn Sa'd (d. 845) and al-Baladhuri (d. 892), practically omit Mecca from their accounts.

61. On this continuity, see Arnold 1896/1913/2012, pp. 34–5. Arnold notes that 'it is false to suppose that Muhammad in Medina laid aside his role of missionary and preacher'. This may be correct, but the shift to Medina still transformed Muhammad's *modus operandi* in important ways.

62. Ibn Ishaq 1955/2012, p. 235 (Ibn Hisham 1858–60, p. 346). A hadith from Bukhari notes: 'The apostle of Allah said, "I was ordered to migrate to a town which will swallow (conquer) other towns . . . and that is Medina"'. Al Bukhari 1997, no. 1871 (vol. 3, pp. 69–70).

63. Some of these dynamics may be seen in the so-called 'Constitution of Medina', a document which Ibn Ishaq tells us governed the relationships between the Prophet and the Muslim and non-Muslim residents of Medina. See Lecker 2010, pp. 67–8. Some modern Muslims use this document to argue that Muhammad endorsed democracy and freedom of religion. See, for instance, Shah 2012.

64. Muslim ibn al-Hajjaj 1433/2012, no. 79 (vol. 1, p. 33).

65. Ibn Ishaq 1955/2012, p. 259 (Ibn Hisham 1858–60, p. 382).

66. Ibid., pp. 240–1 (p. 353).

67. Ibid., pp. 484–5 (pp. 716–18).

68. Donner 1981, pp. 263–7, 79–81.

69. There are also some 'almost-conversion' tales. These are stories in which people would not convert despite knowing the truth, for example, a group of Christians from Najran. See Ibn Ishaq 1955/2012, pp. 271–2 (Ibn Hisham 1858–60, pp. 401–3).

70. Ibid., p. 435 (p. 650).

71. In Bukhari and Muslim, most of the material on *jihad* relates to military *jihad*. Racius 2004, pp. 49–52. The idea of a spiritual 'greater *jihad*' is a Sufi idea which originated no earlier than the ninth century CE. Cook 2005, pp. 35–6.

72. According to Ibn Sa'd, Muhammad participated in twenty-seven raids and battles, and he sent out forty-seven. Ibn Sa'd 1986, pp. 1–2.

73. We are told several times by Ibn Ishaq that, because of the Prophet's victories, 'Allah cast terror' into the hearts of unbelievers (see Q 8:12, 8:57, 59:2). See Ibn Ishaq 1955/2012, p. 438 (Ibn Hisham 1858–60, p. 654).

74. Al-Bukhari 1420/1999, no. 4210 (vol. 5, p. 321); see also no. 2942 (vol. 4, p. 125).
75. At the Battle of the Trench, 'Ali followed the same principle. Ibn Ishaq 1955/2012, p. 455 (Ibn Hisham 1858–60, p. 677).
76. Ibid., p. 645 (p. 959). The Prophet told his warriors: 'When you meet your enemies . . . invite them (ad'uhum) to Islam; if they respond . . . desist from fighting against them . . .' Muslim ibn al-Hajjaj 1433/2012, no. 4294 (vol. 3, p. 943).
77. The Treaty of Hudaybiyya is another illustration. Ibn Ishaq 1955/2012, p. 507 (Ibn Hisham 1858–60, p. 751). See also Peters 1994, pp. 224–8.
78. Al-Bukhari 1420/1999, no. 4287 (vol. 5, p. 353). See also Ibn Ishaq 1955/2012, p. 552 (Ibn Hisham 1858–60, p. 821).
79. Ibid., p. 561 (p. 833).
80. Because Khalid's efforts at peaceful da'wa were marred by his warrior's instincts – he ended up killing several – the Prophet sent 'Ali to pay compensation. Ibid., p. 561 (pp. 834–5). Later, when the Banu Thaqif of Ta'if finally embraced Islam, Muhammad sent Abu Sufyan b. Harb to destroy their idol of al-Lat. Ibid., p. 616 (pp. 916–17).
81. Ibn Sa'd 1986, pp. 180–3.
82. Donner 1981, pp. 65, 77, 260–1.
83. Ibn Ishaq 1955/2012, p. 594 (Ibn Hisham 1858–60, p. 880). See also Ibid., p. 593 (p. 879); Watt 1956, pp. 73–4.
84. Neill 1991, p. 41.
85. The two Abu Sufyans are Abu Sufyan b. al-Harith, Muhammad's cousin, and Abu Sufyan b. Harb, the ancestor of the Umayyads. Ibn Ishaq 1955/2012, p. 547 (p. 813). Abu Sufyan's wife, Hind d. 'Utba also converted. Ibid., p. 553. The problem was mitigated by series of 'tests' which appear later in the sira. For instance, did prominent converts obey the Prophet during unpopular campaigns such as Tabuk?
86. Abu Sufyan is said to have become an 'excellent Muslim' after Hunayn. Ibn Ishaq 1955/2012, p. 570 (Ibn Hisham 1858–60, p. 847).
87. Ibn Ishaq 1955/2012, p. 597 (Ibn Hisham 1858–60, pp. 886–7).
88. See, for instance, Dawah Institute [n. d.].
89. Devin DeWeese writes: 'From the Muslim perspective . . . there is nothing inherently base in conversion to Islam for economic or . . . political benefit . . . [F]rom the early days of Islam the promise of participating in the material benefits enjoyed by . . . the Muslim community by joining it was recognized as a legitimate . . . inducement . . .' DeWeese 1994, pp. 25, 56–7. See also Hodgson 1974, vol. 2, pp. 535–6.
90. Ibn Ishaq 1955/2012, p. 689.
91. Ibn Ishaq 1955/2012, pp. 648–9 (Ibn Hisham 1858–60, pp. 964–5); al-Bukhari 1420/1999, no. 4378 (vol. 5, pp. 404–5). See also no. 3606 (vol. 4, pp. 484–5): 'Narrated Hudhaifa bin Al-Yaman: Once I said, "O Allah's Messenger! We were in ignorance . . . and Allah has bestowed upon us the present good; will there be any evil after this good?" He said, "Yes . . . there will be some people who will invite others to the doors of Hell (du'ātun ilā abwāb jahannam) . . ."'
92. Ibn Ishaq 1955/2012, p. 640 (Ibn Hisham 1858–60, pp. 951–2).
93. Watt 1956, pp. 235–8, 366–8.
94. Donner 1981, pp. 73–5, 251–3.
95. For a partial list of Muhammad's agents, see Watt 1956, pp. 366–8. From the time of the Prophet's death, Tabari informs us that Muhammad 'sent out some of his companions . . . to the kings of the Arabs and the non-Arabs inviting them to Islam'. In a twist that seems to echo the New Testament's account of Pentecost (Acts 2), in which Jesus' followers were enabled to speak new languages, the account continues: 'every one of [Muhammad's

envoys] was able to speak the language of the people to whom he was sent'. Ibn Ishaq, *Life*, pp. 652–3; Arnold 1896/1913/2012, p. 30.
96. Muslim ibn al-Ḥajjaj 1433/2012, no. 4298 (vol. 3, p. 944).
97. Ibid., no. 27 (vol. 1, pp. 14–15).
98. An interpretation of this episode is found, for example, in Elias 2012.
99. Ibn Ishaq 1955/2012, p. 635 (Ibn Hisham 1858–60, pp. 943–4).
100. Ibid.
101. Al-Bukhari 1420/1999, no. 4424 (vol. 5, p. 436).
102. See Serjeant 1983, pp. 141–2.

CHAPTER 3

Da'wa after the Prophet, *circa* 632–1100 CE

Now that we have examined *da'wa* in the Qur'an, *sira* and hadith (in Chapters 1 and 2, respectively), it might seem tempting to skip ahead to the modern period. After all, the starting point of this book is the contemporary resurgence of *da'wa*, a resurgence that has been characterised by a pervasive orientation towards scripture (or 'scripturalism'). That is to say, many modern *da'wa*-minded Muslims go directly from the scriptural sources to contemporary *da'wa* practice and back again, passing over much of what happened in between. This, however, is a temptation we should resist. Modern Muslims are heirs to their faith's entire legal, political, theological, mystical *and missionary* legacy, and this legacy continues to influence *da'wa* practice today. In any case, no serious study of Islamic missionary history can overlook the crucial pre-modern centuries which followed the death of Muhammad – centuries which witnessed the massive spread of Islam and establishment of the general boundaries of what we now call 'the Muslim world'. Chapters 3 and 4, which survey almost eleven centuries between the death of Muhammad and the dawn of modern times, constitute a vital bridge between *da'wa* in the Islamic sources (Chapters 1–2) and *da'wa* in modernity (Chapters 5–7). Taking a thematic approach in approximate chronological order, Chapter 3 considers the period from 632 to roughly 1100 CE, and Chapter 4 surveys the period from roughly 1100 to about 1700 CE.[1] If Chapters 1 and 2 discussed 'early' or 'scriptural' Islam, then Chapter 3 is devoted to 'formative' or 'classical' Islam, and Chapter 4 to 'medieval' and 'early modern' Islam.

There is much that may be said about *da'wa* or Islamic missionary thought and practice in the period from 632 to 1100 CE; far too much, in fact. This chapter, like the next one, therefore, looks at *da'wa* and Islamic missionary history in relation to several key developments: (1) the Arab-Islamic conquests which continued for about a century after Muhammad's death; (2) the emergence of Muslim disunity and the internal *da'wa*s of Muslim religio-political movements; and (3) the emergence of Islamic law and theology. While the year 1100 serves to bracket this chapter in a general chronological sense, it should be kept in mind that these three developments have had far-reaching effects, effects that continue into the present. A further word of orientation to Chapters 3 and 4 is in order: Muslim uses of the word *da'wa* were far from uniform during the periods surveyed in these chapters. In some phases, '*da'wa*' took on strongly political connotations, and in others it seems to have dropped out of usage altogether. Whatever the status of the term, we will see that examples of '*da'wa* as missionary invitation' and '*da'wa* as religio-political summons' are still observable.

Da'wa and the conquests

One reason for the importance of this chapter is that it helps bridge Islam's early and modern periods. Another is that it complicates several stereotypes regarding Islamic expansion, including the notion that Islam was spread chiefly 'by the sword'. This misunderstanding very often emerges from an insufficient understanding of the Arab-Islamic conquests, the subject of this section. The Arab-Islamic conquests[2] constitute a major watershed in world history, as seen in the permanence of their effects. In the Middle Eastern and North African lands in which the initial conquests took place, the dominant religion remains Islam, and the dominant language remains Arabic to this day. That is to say, the conquests catalysed the decisive Islamisation and Arabisation of the wider Middle East.[3] Yet, as we will see, it is not true that these changes were imposed on the region instantaneously or primarily through the threat of violence.

Following the Islamic sources, Muslims in later times would overwhelmingly assume that the Arab-Muslim conquest of the Middle East was a development that the Prophet himself set in motion during his years in Medina. Since the traditional life and *da'wa* of Muhammad was discussed in Chapter 2, this section is concerned with what happened from the Prophet's death in 632 CE roughly up to the rise of the 'Abbasid caliphate in 750 CE.[4] This is not the place for a detailed examination of the conquests.[5] Suffice it to say that, in just under 120 years, Muslims, under a series of Arab regimes, conquered and established rule over territories and peoples stretching from North Africa and Spain in the west to the Indus River in the east (see Map 3.1).[6] In the first three decades of the conquests (632–61 CE), the Arabs subdued what had been the Byzantine Empire's Syrian and Egyptian territories to the north and west of Arabia, and the entirety of the erstwhile Sassanian Empire to the north and east of Arabia. After the defeat of the Byzantines at the Battle of Yarmuk in 636 CE, the Syrian cities of Damascus, Jerusalem and Caesarea fell to the Arabs in short order, in 636, 638 and 640 CE, respectively. Egypt came under Arab-Muslim rule shortly thereafter, during the 640s. Similarly, following the defeat of the Sassanians at the Battle of Qadisiyya around the year 637 CE, most of Iraq and Iran fell to the Arabs by around 650 CE. While the Byzantine Empire (within diminished borders) survived as the principal rival to a succession of Islamic empires until 1453, the Sassanian Empire ceased to exist altogether by the mid-seventh century. Following on the heels of these early successes, the Muslims would go on in the following decades

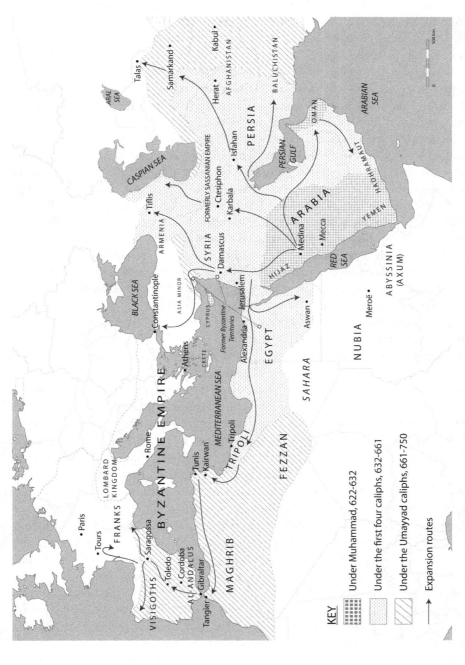

Map 3.1 The Arab-Islamic Conquests, *circa* 622–750 CE

KEY

Under Muhammad, 622-632

Under the first four caliphs, 632-661

Under the Umayyad caliphs, 661-750

Expansion routes

to establish beachheads in eastern Anatolia and Armenia, and to conquer most of North Africa (by 711 CE) and Spain (by 759 CE). They would also subdue much of Central Asia (or Transoxania) and present-day Afghanistan, with the great Silk Road cities of Balkh, Bukhara and Samarkand falling in 705, 712 and 713 CE. Although the westward advance of the Muslims would be checked in the eighth century by the Byzantines in eastern Anatolia (and at the walls of Constantinople) and by the Franks in southern Europe, they would score an important victory over the Chinese T'ang dynasty on the eastern frontier of Central Asia, at the Battle of Talas in 751 CE.

As with the life of the Prophet discussed in Chapter 2, the narrative of the conquests most familiar to Muslims (and many historians) is based on Arabic histories which were compiled considerably later than the events. Two of the most important are the histories of al-Baladhuri (d. *circa* 892) and al-Tabari (d. 923). While these histories contain valuable information, in general, they are marked by a tendency to project later conditions onto the past.[7] There is thus a distinction to be kept in mind between the history of the conquests in terms of 'what actually happened' and the place the conquests have occupied as a 'given' in the pious memory of the Muslim community.[8] Mindful of both ends of this continuum, this section offers four reflections on the conquests from the perspective of the missionary history of Islam.

In the first place, over the centuries, the conquests have served to buttress Muslim confidence in the ultimate truth and triumph of Islam. Such confidence has, in turn, resulted in efforts to spread Islam. Much as Christians have tradi- tionally seen the dramatic spread of Christianity in its first three centuries as a confirmatory miracle, so have Muslims seen the rapid advance of Islam in late antiquity as validation that it is God's final religion for humankind. As with the 'manifest success' of Muhammad at Medina, so now the manifest success of the early community in the conquests came to be seen as a vindication of Islam.[9] The centrality of the conquests in Islam can also be seen in the fact that, after the Prophet himself, the generation of Muslims who initiated them have traditionally been seen as the best and most-to-be-imitated Muslims.[10] Because of this, for most of Islamic history, Muslim scholars and preachers felt little need to explain or defend the militant expansionism of early Islam. Indeed, follow- ing the precedent set by the conquests, a host of Muslim thinkers and regimes throughout history believed that expanding the borders of Islam through mili- tary *jihad* was one of the chief duties of a Muslim ruler. As we will see, this idea is also enshrined in classical Islamic law. It is in roughly the past two centuries, in which the manifest success of Islam seems to have been checked and in which Islam has come under withering critique for its alleged militancy, that Muslims have felt the need to defend and in some cases rethink the conquests.

Second, many of the missionary or *da'wa* patterns observed in Chapter 2 also appear in the traditional narrative of the conquests. This is not entirely surprising, since the traditional account of Muhammad's life and *da'wa* was compiled in and reflects conquest and post-conquest circumstances. From a historical-critical perspective, in fact, it is not so much that the conquests followed precedents actually set forth by Muhammad, but rather that Muslim beliefs and practices which developed during the conquest period were back-projected onto the life of the Prophet in order to lend them legitimacy.[11] Be that as it may, for most Muslims, the Arab-Islamic conquests followed seamlessly from the ministry of the Prophet, because the early successors of the Prophet (or caliphs) faithfully implemented the Prophet's religious, political and *da'wa* strategies. This is particularly true with respect to the way in which the first four caliphs, revered by Sunni Muslims as the 'Rightly Guided' (or *rāshidūn*), have been remembered. Thus, according to the traditional narratives, in imitation of the Prophet, the early caliphs and Muslim military commanders sometimes issued a *da'wa* to Islam before attacking new territories or cities.[12] Like Muhammad, they are portrayed utilising the strategy of *ta'līf al-qulūb* (conciliation of hearts), in which gifts of plunder or influence were used to encourage conversion to Islam and ensure allegiance.[13] One also encounters in these narratives a theology of martyrdom, in which those killed in the cause of Islam were promised direct admission into Paradise. In tune with the Medinan Muhammad, the early caliphs are portrayed sending out agents (*'ummāl*) – who combined political and missionary functions – to newly conquered territories.[14] Thus, taking the traditional narratives at face value, one sees in them a general continuation of the Medinan pattern of the Prophet's *da'wa*.

Third, although these examples could be taken to indicate that fostering conversions to Islam must have been a major motivation for the conquests, and although this motivation is sometimes put into the mouths of the heroes of the conquest narratives,[15] the preponderance of evidence suggests that the conquests were chiefly concerned with territorial expansion, not religious conversion. In Chapter 2, we noted the Prophet's apparent preference for settled over nomadic life. Following Muhammad's death, the early caliphs are portrayed as continuing to encourage the nomads to settle – except that now they were encouraged to do so in the conquered territories of Syria, Egypt and Iraq. Once settled, these Arabs could be more effectively controlled and, when necessary, mustered for battle by the emerging Arab-Muslim ruling elite.[16] One of the most interesting aspects of this policy was that the early Arab conquerors and settlers were generally expected to keep their distance from conquered populations. During the first half-century of the conquests, 'the Arab-Muslim elite assumed that they would form a dual society in which the conquerors would constitute an aristocracy and the conquered peoples a subject population'.[17] The former would serve 'as military elite and the latter as producers and taxpayers'.[18] Given their need to fund the expanding Islamic empire, it is clear that the Arab rulers were less than eager to seek the conversion of non-Muslims who, at least in theory, could be more heavily taxed so long as they remained non-Muslims.[19] Indeed, following Sassanian more than Byzantine administrative precedent, the early Muslim conquest rulers seem to have calculated that peace and stability would be best promoted in their emerging empire by leaving non-Muslim communities to manage their own affairs, as long as they remained loyal and paid their taxes.[20] To keep Arabs separate from natives, the rulers went so far as to establish separate *amṣār* (Arab garrison towns) during the early conquest period. In addition, early on, conversion to Islam for non-Arabs required that they first be made honorary Arabs, as it were. That is, non-Arab converts, or *mawālī*, were not welcomed as full members of the Islamic community without qualification, and even after their conversion did they not enjoy full equality with Arabs until the later Umayyad period (early 700s CE).[21]

Based on this and other evidence, it seems clear that, early on, the Arab conquerors and settlers thought of 'Islam' primarily as a tribal religion (a religion for Arabs), and not as a universal missionary religion. 'Islam' had enabled the heretofore divided Arabs to embark on the conquests,[22] yet it was *their* religion, the expansionist ideology of *their* empire, not something they felt was important to share with non-Arabs. If this conclusion seems jarring, given the emphasis we have placed so far on the idea that Islam is a missionary religion, it must be remembered that, into the ninth century, the expansion of Islam and emergence of Islam were taking place simultaneously. It is certainly the case, as argued above, that there is a latent universalism and missionary thrust in the Qur'an and preaching of Muhammad. Yet, it is not so much that the conquests were activated by the missionary impulse of early Islam, but rather that the missionary impulse of early Islam was activated by the conquests. Put differently, one might say that early Islam had the potential to develop in one of two directions: It could have become (or remained) a predominantly Arab tribal religion or a universal/missionary religion (a religion for all). Even though Islam still enshrines its Arab roots in a variety of ways, it was the conquests that firmly decided the matter in favour of the latter.

Non-Arab conversion to Islam was a significant factor in catalysing this development, and this brings us to our fourth reflection on the conquests. During the conquests, and especially in the centuries that followed, more and more non-Arab inhabitants of the Middle East sought conversion to Islam. Although the Arabs had initially tried to keep their distance from the conquered populations, intermingling between Muslims and non-Muslims increased over time. The garrison towns (*amṣār*), originally meant to keep Arabs separate, became 'bustling heterogeneous' settings 'where one was exposed to contact with persons from very diverse origin, creed, and status'.[23] None of this is surprising, given that communities of Jews and especially of Christians dominated the conquered regions demographically and given that the Arabs brought back captives from their battles and raids 'from all the peoples under the heavens'.[24] Here we see an early example of a Muslim 'diaspora' – those Arabs who migrated outside the Arabian Peninsula to participate in the conquests – contributing to inter-religious contact and eventually to *da'wa* and Islamisation. Additionally, in the Arabs' importation of slaves taken in frontier battles (many of whom would eventually convert to Islam), we see an early example of what Chapter 4 calls 'Islamisation through in-migration'.

Along with increased intermingling, state-sponsored programs of Arabisation and Islamisation also helped foster conversion to Islam in the conquest period. The Umayyad caliph 'Umar II (r. 717–20 CE) continued the policies initiated by his predecessor 'Abd al-Malik (r. 685–705 CE) in promoting Arabic as the official language of the empire and in making Islam, not Arab ethnicity, the basis of the empire.[25] 'Abd al-Malik's magnificent Dome of the Rock, built on the Temple Mount in Jerusalem around the year 692 CE, illustrates a self-confident Islam which by that time had come to see itself as an independent religion able to compete on equal terms with Christianity. The building itself, which contains some of our earliest Qur'an inscriptions, can be interpreted as a *da'wa* to Islam in brick and mortar addressed to Christians, and as a political challenge to the Byzantine Empire. Other factors which incentivised conversion included the slow erosion of non-Muslim cultural influence and the disabilities attached to being non-Muslim *dhimmi*s – 'protected' or tolerated peoples under Muslim rule.[26] In the immediate wake of the conquests, therefore, it was not so much that Muslims organised centrifugal *da'wa* initiatives, in which they specifically went out and tried to convert non-Arabs – although there are some examples of this in the traditional sources[27] – but rather that more and more non-Arabs sought out conversion centripetally. The point we are making is that the conquests contributed to the long-term spread of Islam in the Middle East, North Africa and Central Asia by creating an Islamic environment (or Islamdom)[28] within which widespread conversion became a viable possibility over the long term. Because of the conquests, it would not be long before Persians, Turks, Berbers, Kurds, Mongols and others would embrace Islam, vie with the Arabs for leadership and add their own distinctive spice to what would become classical Islamic civilisation.

Bringing all this together, it is important to emphasise a distinction one must keep in mind when studying the expansion of Islam: that between 'conversion under Muslim rule established by conquest', on one hand, and 'conversion beyond the military expansion of Islam', on the other. Under the former, a further distinction is that between conversion to Islam as the *immediate* result of conquest and conversion to Islam as a *gradual process* once conquest has established an 'Islamic ambience'. While conversion immediately upon conquest – one can think of the 'conversion' of Arabia beginning in the time of the Prophet – tended to produce tenuous conversions and happened rarely in Islamic history,[29] gradual long-term processes of conversion within an overall

Islamic ambience tended to result in more stable conversions and have been more common historically. Whether we look to the Byzantine or Sassanian territories conquered early on, or to contexts like Central Asia which were conquered slightly later, the long-term pattern was the same: first came Islamic rule and Islamic domination of public spaces, soundscapes and positions of influence, then came decades- and centuries-long processes of conversion to Islam through *da'wa* and other means. Although it is difficult to determine with precision, scholars generally agree that the point at which the population of the Middle East and North Africa became predominantly Muslim was only reached three to five centuries after the conquests began.[30] The key point is that the conquests contributed to the spread of Islam, not through *da'wa* at the point of a sword, but by creating conditions which would prove conducive to widespread conversion over time.[31] The conquests, in short, created a context in which the missionary spread of Islam became possible and even probable. *Jihad* preceded *da'wa*. Islamdom preceded Islamisation.[32]

Before we move on from this topic, a further point should be made explicit – namely, that the gradual embrace of Islam among the conquered peoples opened up Islam to internal cultural diversity. That is, as a result these developments, 'Islam' would develop in such a way that it would simultaneously hold on to its Arab roots (by giving priority to the Arab Prophet, the Arabic language and the sacred geography of Arabia) *and* come to absorb the religio-cultural-political traditions and values of non-Arabs.[33] In other words, the non-Arabs of the Middle East – both those who converted and those who did not – were not passive recipients of an Islam exported fully-formed from seventh-century Arabia, but active contributors to what would become classical Islam. Many of the leading Muslim thinkers of the 'Abbasid period and beyond, for instance, hailed from Persian and Central Asian backgrounds and 'oversaw a large-scale Persianization' of the Muslim world.[34] Later on, the conversion and rise of Turkic peoples led to the 'Turkification' of the Muslim world (see Chapter 4). The ingredients of what would become classical Islamic civilisation, in short, derived from both the Arab conquerors and the conquered populations.[35]

The emergence of Muslim disunity and the rise of religio-political *da'was*

When I teach 'Introduction to Islam' to undergraduate students, I devote several sessions to what I call 'The Arab-Islamic conquests and consequences'. One cannot hope to understand Islam, I tell my students, unless one understands something about the conquests and all that flowed from them. In the preceding section, we looked at the conquests and several of their consequences, but in some ways the remaining sections of this chapter – and even the remaining chapters of this book – are a continuation of this discussion. Directly or indi-

rectly, the conditions created by the conquests led to and shaped the development of everything we customarily mean by the terms 'formative' or 'classical'
Islam. The legacy of the conquests has also informed many developments and
debates in modern Islam. Closer to our immediate purpose, the conquests set
the stage not only for external *da'wa*, the spread of Islam among non-Muslims,
but also for a host of internal *da'wa*s, efforts to reform or recruit fellow Muslims.

The political subjugation and gradual conversion of the Middle East, combined with the sharp eschatological divide presupposed in the Qur'an between
the saved and the damned, raised for many Muslims in the post-conquest situation the vexing question of who was a genuine Muslim believer. This question,
which appears again and again in Islamic history and which seems to be peren-
nial in what A. D. Nock called 'prophetic religions',[36] was in part responsible
for the division of Muslims during and after the conquest period into distinct
'piety-minded' camps or orientations.[37] On one end of the spectrum, rigorists
like the Khawarij (or Kharijites) thought that many 'Muslims' had not been
genuinely converted. Convinced that they alone constituted the remnant of
true Muslims, they were quick to practise *takfir* – declaring other Muslims to
be *kafir*s or unbelievers. They thus advocated separation from, and sometimes
violence against those whom they judged to be false Muslims. Even caliphs
could fall under the Kharijites' condemning gaze (the fourth caliph, 'Ali, was
assassinated by a Kharijite). In passing, we might note that some observers see a
contemporary renewal of the Kharijite orientation in Sunni Jihadi groups such
as ISIS (which are sometimes labelled by their opoonents as *takfir*s, or those
who practise *takfir*). On the other side of the spectrum were the Murji'ites, who
were champions, one might say, of gradualism. They believed that half-hearted
Muslims or less-than-sincere converts could still be considered believers, since
anyone had the potential to become a genuine Muslim over time. In any case,
the Murji'ites believed that only God knows who the genuine believers are; it is
not for fellow humans to judge.

The impulse to ask who was a true believer also had profound implications
for politics. If the faith of ordinary Muslims could be called into question,
what about the caliph or sultan? What should Muslims do if the ruler fails to
meet Islamic criteria for leadership? What about a situation in which different
Muslims have different criteria for who may serve as caliph in the first place? In
the centuries after the death of the Prophet, these questions, among others, led
not only to the main Sunni-Shi'ite sectarian division of Islam, but also to a series
of Islamic political movements which used internal *da'wa*s to recruit Muslims
to their causes and, in some cases, foment revolution. To illustrate this trend,
this section discusses two of the most important of such movements: the Sunni
'Abbasid and the Shi'ite (Isma'ili) Fatimid movements.

The 'Abbasid *da'wa*

Despite a tendency in Islamic historiography to idealise the early period of Islamic history as a period of pious and triumphant expansion, the sources admit that it was also a period of widespread disagreement and bloodshed. The so-called First Fitna (intra-Muslim civil war, 656–61 CE) was one of the first, but certainly not the last time Muslims would turn on each other. It brought an end to the period of the 'Rightly Guided' caliphs and ushered in the rule of the Syria-based Umayyad caliphate. It also confirmed among some Muslims a radical commitment to 'Ali, Muhammad's cousin and son-in-law, and the belief that he alone should have been chosen as the first caliph (or Imam) after the death of the Prophet. This orientation would blossom, over time, into the various branches of Shi'ite Islam (from *shī'at 'Alī*, the party of 'Ali). By contrast, what would become Sunni Islam was represented by those Muslims who regarded as legitimate the selection of Abu Bakr as the first caliph and who rejected the standpoint of 'Ali's partisans. It was also during the First Fitna that the above-mentioned Kharijite movement emerged. Less than twenty years later, the so-called Second Fitna (680–92 CE) witnessed more Kharijite and Shi'ite (or proto-Shi'ite) restlessness, particularly in Iraq and Khurasan,[38] and for over a decade the existence of two rival caliphs. This brings us to the so-called Third Fitna or 'Abbasid Revolution (744–50 CE).

As with the earlier Fitnas, the 'Abbasid Revolution was driven by intra-Muslim disputes over political legitimacy.[39] In the later Umayyad period, the 'Abbasids – a party named after the Prophet's uncle 'Abbas, whom we met briefly in Chapter 2 as an example of a late and somewhat reluctant convert – skilfully played on simmering proto-Sunni and proto-Shi'ite tensions and, with proto-Shi'ite support, eventually overthrew the Umayyads in 750 CE. In the roughly half-decade before they took up arms against the Umayyads, however, they utilised a religio-political *da'wa* which proved to be highly effective in preparing the way for their revolution.[40] The 'Abbasid *da'wa*, facilitated by specially appointed religio-political missionary agents,[41] was particularly active in Khurasan. Interestingly, having come to power through proto-Shi'ite support, the 'Abbasids, once in power, turned against the Shi'ites, eventually patronising Sunni Islam as their official religion.[42] Several aspects of the 'Abbasid *da'wa* may be highlighted here.

First, the 'Abbasids represent what was perhaps the first Muslim mass movement in history to put *da'wa* on an organisational footing. The 'Abbasids were very deliberate in the way in which they communicated their *da'wa*, in their selection of *da'is* (missionaries/propagandists) and in their choice of Khurasan, a 'field' which proved to be receptive to their message. 'The 'Abbasid movement was the first to use the term *da'wa* extensively within the framework of Islam and to develop a systematic institution around it'.[43] Second, and more importantly, underlying the 'Abbasid *da'wa* was the premise that the strife within the Muslim community was 'the outcome of abandoning the Prophet's original teachings'.[44] What the 'Abbasids prescribed, therefore, was a restoration of the pure Islam of Muhammad under divinely sanctioned leadership. Fundamentally, therefore, the 'Abbasid *da'wa* was a restorationist or reformist *da'wa*, a summons to Muslims to return to 'true Islam' by overthrowing the allegedly compromised Umayyads and installing a true caliph or Imam.[45] This 'Abbasid style of *da'wa* – a reformist, internal religio-political *da'wa* – set a precedent that would be repeated many times in Islamic history.

Indeed, following the 'Abbasids' example, in subsequent centuries, many would-be founders of Islamic states or dynasties 'used the same tactics and had [their] *da'wa*[s]'.[46] In a remarkably matter-of-fact fashion, the great fourteenth-century Arab historian Ibn Khaldun wrote as if *da'wa* was one of the normal means of founding a new Islamic empire or dynasty.[47] This reflects the world in which he lived: From the eleventh century on, the myth of the political unity of the Muslim world under a single caliphate, symbolised by the Rightly Guided caliphs, had given way to 'a multiplicity of sultans, amirs (or emirs), maliks, and so on',[48] many of whom founded dynasties, in part, through religio-political *da'was*. To give but a few of many possible examples, the tenth-century founder of the Shi'ite (Zaydi) state of the Rassids in Yemen, al-Hadi ila al-Haqq Yahya, spoke of his religio-revolutionary activities in terms of *da'wa*,[49] as did the movement of the Almohads (*al-muwaḥḥidūn*), founded by the religious preacher and political revolutionary Ibn Tumart (d. 1130) in twelfth- and thirteenth-century North Africa and Spain.[50] The reformist nature of the Almohad *da'wa* (calling for a radical return to the doctrine of *tawhid* or God's Oneness), its tribal (Berber) context and the fact that it eventually succeeded in forming a state (in Maghrib and southern Spain) at the expense of what it deemed to be impure Muslim rivals give it an eerie similarity to the later Wahhabi movement and *da'wa* of eighteenth-century Arabia (see Chapter 5).[51] Above all, this pattern of *da'wa* was exemplified by the Isma'ili Fatimid movement, which we will revisit in a moment. Today, too, there are multiple groups which claim to represent authentic Muslim religio-political leadership and which use the language of *da'wa* to rally Muslims to their causes. In short, by using '*da'wa*' in the sense of a restorationist religio-political summons to Muslims, the 'Abbasids let the cat out of the bag.

The Isma'ili/Fatimid *da'wa*

The origins of Shi'ism, as already noted, go back to the succession crisis which followed the death of Muhammad. In contrast to those who supported the selection of Abu Bakr, and after him the second and third caliphs 'Umar and 'Uthman, the Shi'ites or *shī'at 'Alī* held that 'Ali alone was qualified to lead the Muslims. In time, the *shī'at 'Alī* came to believe in a line of infallible descendants

3.1 Some examples of external *da'wa* in the 'Abbasid period

In discussing the 'Abbasids, we focused on the religio-political *da'wa* which brought them to power, but there are fascinating examples of external missionary *da'wa* taking place at elite levels during the 'Abbasid period as well. One example is the dialogue between the Christian (Nestorian or East Syrian) Patriarch Timothy I (d. 823 CE) and the 'Abbasid Caliph al-Mahdi (r. 775–85 CE), in which the two men sought to win the other over to their respective faiths (see Mingana 1928). Another example is the written dialogue between al-Hashimi, a Muslim scholar at the court of the Caliph al-Ma'mun (r. 813–33 CE), and al-Kindi, an educated Arab Christian. Although there is doubt about their authenticity, we have versions of al-Hashimi's letter of *da'wa*, along with al-Kindi's response, contained in what is known as al-Kindi's *Apology*. The following are excerpts from al-Hashimi's letter of *da'wa*:

So, now . . . I invite you to accept the religion that God has chosen for me and I for myself, assuring you entrance into Paradise and deliverance from Hell . . . I invite you . . . to bear witness and acknowledge the prophetic mission of my lord and the lord of the sons of Adam . . . and the seal of the Prophets, Muhammad . . . sent by God with glad tidings and warnings to all mankind. 'He it is who hath sent His Apostle with the guidance and the religion of truth, that He may make it victorious over every other religion . . .' (Q 9:33). [Muhammad] invited all men from the east and from the west, from the land and sea, from mountain and from plain, with compassion and pity and good words, with kindly manners and gentleness. Then all these people accepted his invitation, bearing witness that he is the apostle of God . . . They entered into his religion and accepted his authority without being forced and without unwillingness . . . and in his name becoming victorious over those who denied his divine mission and rejected his message . . . So God set them up in the cities and subjected to them the necks of the nations of men, except those who hearkened to them and accepted their religion and bore witness to their faith, whereby their blood, their property and their honour were safe and they were exempt from humbly paying jizya *. . . [Since] 'there is no compulsion in religion' (Q 2:256), I have only invited you to accept our faith willingly and of your own accord and have pointed out the hideousness of your present belief. Peace be with you and the mercy and blessings of God!* (Source: al-Kindi, *Apology*. English trans. in Arnold 1896/1913/2012, pp. 428–35).

of 'Ali, designated Imams, who were thought to be the true leaders of the Muslim world. It did not take long, however, before the early Shi'ites began to disagree among themselves and to form sectarian subdivisions.[52] Among the most important were the Imamiyya (or Imamis), the Zaydiyya (or Zaydis) and the Isma'iliyya (or Isma'ilis). While each of these groups would develop their own distinctive *da'wa*s in the battle for Muslim hearts and minds of the eighth to tenth centuries and beyond, the term '*da'wa*' itself would come to be most strongly associated with the Isma'ilis.

The crisis that produced the Isma'ili movement was the death of the sixth Shi'ite Imam, Ja'far, in 765 CE. Ja'far had five sons, and while the group that would become the Twelver Imamis (because they would accept twelve Imams in the line of 'Ali) declared Ja'far's son Musa to be the seventh Imam, the group that would come to be called the Isma'ilis supported the line of Ja'far's oldest son Isma'il. During the late eighth and early ninth century, little is known of the Isma'ilis, but in the middle of the ninth century, a unified Isma'ili movement burst onto the scene ready to challenge the 'Abbasids, just as the 'Abbasids had challenged the Umayyads in the eighth century. One of the weapons that the Isma'ili movement employed was its *da'wa*: 'In a mere twenty-five years, from *circa* 875 to 900, the Isma'ili *da'wa* had formed a network of cells and communities which spanned the whole Islamic world from North Africa to Pakistan, from the Caspian Sea to . . . Yemen'.[53]

Owing to the success of the Isma'ili *da'wa*, Isma'ili states were established in the tenth century, including the Fatimid Empire, which was founded by 'Ubaydallah al-Mahdi in North Africa in 909 CE.[54] 'Ubaydallah's successors, who took the title of caliph, would eventually conquer Egypt and establish the city of Cairo and the famed mosque of al-Azhar in the late tenth century. It was the Fatimids who were in control of Jerusalem (they had wrested the city from the Sunni Saljuqs) when the Crusaders arrived in 1099, and it was Saladin, the Sunni hero who drove the Crusaders out of Jerusalem in 1187, who brought the Fatimid dynasty to an end in 1171. *Da'wa* remained an important element in the Fatimids' *modus operandi* throughout their reign: 'In line with their universal claims, the Fatimids did not abandon *da'wa* activities on assuming power . . . they in fact retained a network of *dā'īs* operating on their behalf as religio-political missionaries both within and outside Fatimid dominions'.[55] From the perspective of the 'Abbasid caliphate and the Sunni establishment which had come to support it, the Isma'ili *da'wa* was bad enough. However, the rise of the Fatimid state was even worse. Unlike other Islamic dynasties that emerged in the ninth and tenth centuries, many of which gave at least nominal recognition to the 'Abbasid caliph in Baghdad, the Fatimids' aim was to overthrow the 'Abbasid caliphate altogether and claim leadership of the entire Muslim world. Even the Fatimid's famed *Dar al-'Ilm* (House of Knowledge, founded in 1005) in Cairo was no mere *madrasa* and library, but also a centre for Isma'ili *da'wa*, perhaps meant to rival and counter the 'Abbasid's *Bayt al-Hikma* (House of Wisdom, founded in the eighth/ninth century) in Baghdad.[56] The remainder of this section focuses on several important aspects of the Isma'ili/Fatimid *da'wa*.

First, the Isma'ili/Fatimid *da'wa* was extraordinarily well-organised and cohesive given the times in which it operated. Today, modern technologies facilitate the activities of *da'wa* movements on a global level. Without air travel, mass printing, or the internet, the Isma'ilis maintained an impressive transregional *da'wa* in the ninth and tenth centuries. Their *da'wa*, moreover, was adapted to specific audiences and contexts. '[T]he Isma'ili missions tended to adapt to the prior religious convictions . . . of the persons being proselytized. [They] initiated their converts step by step, so that the true teachings of the faith were not fully presented to everyone'.[57] According to some sources, Isma'ili missionaries who made it to India went so far as to present 'Ali as an Avatar of Vishnu in an effort to make their teachings attractive to Hindus.[58] Second, although many have stressed the political nature of the Isma'ili/Fatimid *da'wa*, it also had a significant religious basis. For the Fatimids, the *da'wa* of the Imams continued that of the Prophet and gave further revelation. It offered, in other words, another 'true Islam' to a now crowded market of competitors for that title. Like the 'Abbasid *da'wa*, the Fatimid *da'wa* was strongly restorationist: Their 'immediate goal was to return Islam to its true and proper form by bringing those who most loved the family of the prophet back into positions of authority'.[59] Third, the Isma'ili/Fatimid *da'wa* had important ramifications for Sunni self-awareness and Sunni-Shi'ite relations. As is often the case in the history of religions, the presence of a menacing inter- or intra-religious 'other' can cause competing groups to confirm and harden their own identities and communal boundaries. Similarly, the Isma'ili *da'wa* and establishment of the Fatimid empire proved to be a significant factor that led to the strengthening of Sunni identity and unity in the eleventh and twelfth centuries.[60] The Isma'ili/Fatimid threat may also partially explain the apparent decrease in the use of the word '*da'wa*' among Sunnis during medieval times. To the extent that the word became strongly associated with the Isma'ilis/Fatimids, it might have lost popularity among other Muslims.[61]

In sum, the 'Abbasids and Fatimids are emblematic of an important tendency in the missionary history of Islam: *da'wa* as religio-political summons to fellow Muslims. As we will see, even when it is carried out in the name of reaching non-Muslims, the realm of *da'wa* today remains a site where intra-Islamic rivalries and competing restorationist agendas are played out. Building on the Medinan legacy of the Prophet, the 'Abbasid and Fatimid movements solidified in Islamic history a connection between *da'wa* and revolutionary politics.

Da'wa and Islamic law and theology

In the previous two sections we discussed the religiously fluid world of early and classical Islam. Despite the sectarian division of Islam and the rise of competing *da'wa*s in the post-conquest context, Muslim empires nevertheless provided reasonably stable settings within which Islamic thought could develop and mature.

This final section of Chapter 3 considers two important categories of Islamic thought – law and theology – and their relationship to *da'wa*. First, Islamic jurisprudence or *fiqh* is the scholarly discipline (*'ilm*) that seeks to discern God's law (*shari'a*) and apply it to human life. Since *fiqh* emerged in the same conquest and post-conquest milieu which this chapter has been describing, it is not surprising that various groups of Muslims developed different systems of law, not only to guide the faithful, but also to differentiate themselves from one another.[62] There were also inter-religious impulses behind the development of Islamic law.[63] Gradually, the main Sunni schools of law came to agree on four sources of *fiqh*: (1) the Qur'an, (2) the *sunna* of the Prophet (derived from hadith), (3) consensus (*ijmā'*, and (4) analogical reasoning (*qiyās*).[64] Based on these four sources, the vast Islamic *fiqh* literature – which truly constitutes 'one of the great achievements of Islamic civilisation'[65] – establishes rules that are meant to regulate acts of worship (*'ibādāt*) and dealings between people (*mu'āmalāt*).[66]

Like the hadith collections discussed in the previous chapter, major *fiqh* manuals do not have sections devoted to missionary *da'wa* per se. Rather, explicit material on *da'wa* in legal texts is usually found in discussions of *jihad* (expansionist warfare in the cause of Islam) or *siyar* (relations with non-Muslims, or Islamic international law). In these contexts, *da'wa* serves a fairly straightforward function: Muslims are to give *da'wa* to non-Muslims – or more precisely, to the rulers of non-Muslim territories – before fighting them or attacking their lands. Those pagans or non-monotheists (the Qur'an's *mushrikūn* – 'polytheists' or 'associators') who refuse the *da'wa* of Islam in such contexts are subject to attempted conquest by the Muslims and, should that conquest succeed, to the confiscation of their land and property, as well as the slaughter or enslavement of their persons. In the case of monotheists or People of the Book, before commencing hostilities, Muslims are to call them to conversion to Islam or alternatively to willingly submit to Islamic rule without conversion and thus become *dhimmi*s (protected or tolerated peoples under Muslim rule) who render to the Muslim authorities a special tax known as the *jizya* (Q 9:29). In Islamic law, therefore, '[t]he infidels' familiarity with, or ignorance of [the *da'wa* of Islam] determined the way in which the Muslims should fight against them. Those to whom the *da'wa* had not yet penetrated had to be invited to embrace Islam before fighting could take place'.[67] Islamic legal manuals – for instance, al-Shaybani's eighth-century *Kitab al-Siyar al-Kabir* (Great Book of International Law) and al-Marghinani's twelfth-century century *al-Hidaya* (The Guidance, see Text Box 3.2), which are both considered Sunni works, as well as al-Tusi's eleventh-century Shi'ite legal compendium *al-Nihaya* (Concise Legal Rulings) – discuss the *da'wa*-before-*jihad* rule in fairly similar terms, sometimes citing the very hadiths discussed in Chapter 2 which establish this precedent.[68] Sometimes Q 17:15 is also cited. This verse quotes God as saying: 'We do not punish [any community] until we have sent [it] an apostle' (Q 17:15).[69]

3.2 *Da'wa* in al-Marghinani's legal compendium *al-Hidaya*

*When the Muslims commence battle, and they have surrounded a city or a fort, they are to invite the inhabitants to accept Islam (*da°ūhum ilā al-Islām*), due to what is related by Ibn 'Abbas 'that the Prophet (SAWS) did not commence combat with a people without first inviting them to Islam' (*da°āhum ilā al-Islām*). He said: If they respond positively, they are to refrain from fighting them, due to the attainment of the purpose. If they refuse, they are to invite them to the payment of jizya, and this is what the Prophet (SAWS) ordered the commanders of the armies to do . . . This applies to those among them who are eligible to accept the payment of the* jizya [that is, People of the Book]. *Those from whom* jizya *is not acceptable like the apostates or the idol worshipers from among the Arabs, there is no benefit in inviting them to accept* jizya, *because only [conversion to] Islam is acceptable from them . . .*

*It is not permitted to engage in battle those whom the invitation to accept Islam (*al-da°wa ilā al-Islām*) has not reached without first inviting them. This is based on the saying of the Prophet (SAWS) when he gave advice to the commanders of the detachments, 'Invite them then to witness that there is no god, but God'. The reason is that through the invitation (*bi'l-da°wa*), they come to know that we engage them in battle on account of our* dīn *[religion], and not for purloining their wealth or the enslavement of their families. Perhaps, they will respond positively so that the burden of battle is avoided. If the commander engages them in battle before communicating the invitation, he commits a sin . . . It is recommended that even those whom the invitation has reached already, be invited, so that there is an enhanced warning for them* [the Hanafi school of fiqh, which Marghinani followed, recommended a second da'wa] . . . *If they reject the invitation, the [Muslims] are to seek the help of Allah and engage them in combat, due to the saying of the Prophet (SAWS) . . . 'If they refuse this then invite them to accept the* jizya . . . *[and] if they refuse that, then seek the help of Allah and engage them in combat'* (Source: al-Marghinani 2006, pp. 291–2, and al-Marghinani 1720 (Arabic), pp. 434–5).

Behind this use of *da'wa* is an important assumption of classical Islamic law – namely, that the world is divided into two spheres: *dar al-Islam* (the sphere in which Islam is dominant and ruled by Muslims) and *dar al-harb* (the sphere in which non-Muslim peoples and rulers predominate).[70] This *dar al-Islam/dar al-harb* distinction, which does not appear explicitly in the Qur'an, but is implicit in *sira* and hadith (see Chapter 2), is a clear consequence of the Arab-Islamic conquests discussed earlier.[71] Because of the conquests (and the model of the Prophet at Medina), Islamic law would proceed on the assumption that the ideal Islamic state should be expansionist and that its expansionism should have 'an ultimate religious objective, the proselytization of [humankind]'.[72] Since *jihad* was the means by which this transformation would be achieved, the theory of the two spheres became 'an essential part of the doctrine of *jihad*' in legal literature.[73] Thus, as far as classical Islamic law is concerned, the rulers of *dar al-harb*, especially non-monotheists and/or those who do not have a treaty with the Muslims,[74] are to be invited to convert to Islam or face military conquest. In turn, territory that is conquered in the name of Islam becomes part of *dar al-Islam*. It is, of course, considered preferable if non-Muslim rulers accept the *da'wa* of Islam voluntarily and thus avoid – at least in theory – military hostilities. It might also be noted here that, in general, Islamic law has little to say about Muslims living outside *dar al-Islam*. The expectation is that Muslims living in *dar al-harb* should migrate (or make *hijra*) to a proper Islamic environment. This point is worth keeping in mind because, as we will see in Part II, as Muslim migration picked up speed in modern times, more and more Muslims either had to, or chose to, take up residence outside of traditional *dar al-Islam*. As a result, new kinds of Muslim thinking developed, some of it oriented towards missionary *da'wa*.

It is important to emphasise that, like many things in Islamic law, these regulations represent an ideal. Such a clear-cut division of the world and image of the expansion of Islam it envisions have rarely been realised in the untidy contingency of the real world. In fact, when one digs a little deeper, one finds that Muslim legal scholars themselves differed over the precise meaning of the *dar al-Islam/dar al-harb* distinction and sometimes discussed ambiguous situations which were not easily assigned to either side of this continuum.[75] Indeed, since the conquests eventually petered out and *dar al-Islam* did not, in fact, encompass the whole world, legal scholars necessarily adapted the *siyar* legislation 'to include peaceful as well as hostile relationships' with the nations of *dar al-harb*: 'Rules . . . governing the termination or suspension of hostilities, the making of treaties, and the movement of individuals from one territory to another . . . developed from necessity'.[76] Still, as far as the *ideal* of classical Islamic law is concerned, one of the normal ways in which Islam spreads is by means of the *da'wa* offered to, and/or the conquest of non-Muslim territories and peoples by expansionist Islamic governments. Islamic law, one might say, enshrines as normative the Medinan pattern of *da'wa* discussed in Chapter 2.

If we focus narrowly on the term, Islamic law seems to restrict its discussion of *da'wa* to this single case – the obligation to invite others to conversion as an alternative or prelude to conquest. Yet, are there other ways in which we might relate Islamic law to broader missionary aims within Islam? Indeed, there are, and we might mention just a few here. To begin with, since Islamic law imagines a social order *within dar al-Islam* in which Muslims and Islam are ascendant and since, to that end, it codifies rules which favour Muslims and put non-Muslim *dhimmi*s under a range of disadvantages, one can say that a significant objective of the law is to foster conversions to and prevent defections from Islam. In a detailed study, Friedmann speaks of the overwhelming presupposition in Islamic law of 'the exaltedness of Islam'. That is, the Islamic legal tradition assumes a hierarchy of religions in which Islam stands alone at the apex. In earlier chapters, we spoke of the general stance of theological exclusivism found in the Qur'an and *sira*/hadith literatures. This provides the background for numerous legal provisions – for instance, involving taxation, dress, protection of property and person, inheritance, marriage and so on – which preserve Muslim superiority and give Muslims certain rights and freedoms not enjoyed by non-Muslims and which thus, at least indirectly, incentivise conversion to Islam.[77]

By the same token, Islamic law strongly disincentivises apostasy or conversion *from* Islam. Although the 'law of apostasy' in Islam is more nuanced than has often been portrayed by western writers, the fact remains that 'most classical jurists consider that the execution of the unrepentant apostate is the proper punishment for [apostasy]'. The assumption of Islamic law, in short, is that 'conversion to Islam ought to be irreversible'.[78] While one cannot draw a straight line of causation between the incentives to conversion and disincentives to apostasy in Islamic legal texts on the one hand, and the contingencies of history on the other, it is still a striking fact that Islam has never suffered the kinds of mass defections in the lands where it attained majority status – Spain notwithstanding – as were experienced, for instance, by Christianity and Manichaeism in the Middle East and North Africa, or Buddhism in India and Central Asia. In short, developed as it was in the conquest and post-conquest situation, the regulations of Islamic law seem to reflect and support the logic of gradual and permanent Islamisation in ambiences of Islamic domination.

Intersecting with this discussion at several points is the question of slavery (Arabic: *riqq*, *ʿubūdiyya*). Following normal pre-Islamic Middle Eastern custom as well as the Qur'an and hadith literature, the institution of slavery is taken for granted within classical Islamic law.[79] Questions about what kinds of people can be legitimately enslaved by Muslims and under what circumstances, about the treatment of slaves and about the freeing (or manumission) of slaves are among the concerns of classical legal manuals.[80] While Islamic law mitigates some of the worst aspects of this ancient institution,[81] it is nevertheless the case that Islamic law, reflecting the post-conquest situation in which thousands of slaves were brought into the cities of the emerging empire, allows certain forms of slavery, including the taking of female slaves as concubines.[82] In general, wars of conquest against non-Muslims served as 'the theoretical justification for the acquisition of slaves'.[83] Islamic law prohibits the enslavement of Muslims and People of the Book within the borders of *dar al-Islam*. By contrast, in contexts of *jihad* against pagan territories, it permits the capture of slaves and their forcible importation into *dar al-Islam*. In Islamic law, slavery is generally not inherent in any particular race or ethnicity, but is a consequence of unbelief: 'According to some jurists, slavery originally had a punitive aspect, in that the non-Muslim enemy by failing to use his intelligence to perceive the truth of Islam had assimilated himself to nonrational beings and therefore deserved to be treated as such'.[84] Thus it is that discussions of slavery in Islamic law overlap with discussions of *da'wa*, conversion and Islamisation. The enslavement of pagans by Muslims was sometimes seen as a mercy to the former, insofar as it exposed them to Islam and might lead to their conversion. Slavery, in this view, was a lesser evil than remaining an unbeliever. In addition, Islamic law provides incentives for slaves to convert and assumes that many will do so.[85] We will return to the actual practice of slavery in pre-modern Islamic history and its relation to Islamisation in Chapter 4.

It is worth examining the relationship between *da'wa* and the legal heritage of Islam from one more angle. In Islamic legal theory, *maqāṣid al-sharīᶜa* (the purposes of the law) 'refers to the idea that . . . God intends to bring about a certain state of affairs by instituting particular laws'.[86] While missionary *da'wa* is not included in formal lists of *maqāṣid*, to the extent that the enterprise of Islamic jurisprudence is intended to help Muslims order their lives on the basis of God's revelation, one can say that it performs a kind of internal *da'wa*. Such an end can be observed in the venerable Muslim practice of 'commanding right and forbidding wrong', a practice rooted in the Qur'an (see Chapter 1) and developed in legal texts.[87] Before one can command and forbid others or even oneself, one must know the demands of the law, and this is precisely what *fiqh* clarifies. Thus, when a Muslim preacher calls other Muslims to be more observant, or when grassroots '*sharīᶜa* patrols' attempt to see that God's law is obeyed in diverse contexts, they are doing internal *da'wa* by commanding the right and forbidding the wrong. Similarly, *fiqh* may be said to assist external *da'wa*. As already noted, specific rulings of *fiqh* can be said to incentivise conversion to Islam. Likewise, to the extent that, from a believing perspective, it helps to bring about a state of affairs that is aligned with God's will, the implementation of Islamic law may be thought to make Islam attractive to non-believers. As modern *da'wa* thinkers frequently argue, the first step in winning the world to Islam is that Muslims should make their own lives and societies authentically and attractively Islamic under God's law. Before we move on to Islamic theology, we should point out that, although this section has presented Islamic law as a somewhat unified phenomenon (an approach that is justified by the many commonalities between the main Sunni, and even Shi'ite, law schools), in fact, the various law schools within Islam have jostled with one another and engaged in mutual competition in order to establish their superiority and justify their approaches – another example of internal *da'wa*.[88] Sometimes, this could involve alliances with rulers or states, but perhaps most often the legal scholars battled it out discursively, in their writings and debates.[89]

If Islamic law seeks to clarify what Muslims are supposed to *do*, Islamic theology (*kalām*) seeks to clarify what they are supposed to *believe*. It is sometimes asserted that Islam is a religion of *orthopraxis* (right action) more than it is a religion of *orthodoxy* (right belief). Although this statement accurately captures where the accent falls in Islam, in fact, Islam cares about both action and belief. As in the first few centuries of Christian history, in the religiously contested world of early and classical Islam, heresy and orthodoxy were major concerns. Muslims not only debated law and politics, but also wrestled with issues such as the relationship between God and God's Word, divine sovereignty and human responsibility, faith and works, human reason and divine revelation, the nature of true monotheism, the question of who is a true believer (see above) and other theological puzzles. Muslim debates over these issues led to the rise of numerous 'schools' of theology in the classical and medieval periods, such as the above-mentioned Kharijites and Murji'ites.[90] For a time, the theological school of the Mu'tazilites also flourished. The Mu'tazilites' doctrines – for instance, that the Qur'an is created, not uncreated, and that God's justice is only meaningful if humans have genuine free will – were spread by Mu'tazilite missionaries and even became briefly ascendant at the court of the 'Abbasid caliph al-Ma'mun (r. 813–33 CE).[91] In addition to these, there were Shi'ite schools and the school of theology that would come to be considered 'orthodox' by most Sunnis, the Ash'arite school.

Members of these schools sparred with one another and engaged in mutually competitive *da'wa*. They also sparred with Christian and Jewish rivals.[92] These dynamics can be seen in Muslim works of heresiography – a genre in which particular heresies or sects (*firāq*) are named and refuted. The famous medieval Sunni scholar Ibn Taymiyya (d. 1328), for instance, wrote voluminously against what he deemed to be heresies and false religions. Theology, in other words, was another area in which Muslims engaged in internal and external *da'wa*. Indeed, the word '*kalām*' refers not only to the enterprise of Islamic theology itself, but also to efforts to dismantle false views and to establish the truth about any given point of belief. It is, in other words, 'apologetic theology'.[93] According to the Muslim philosopher al-Farabi (d. 950 CE), *kalām* is 'a science which enables a man to procure the victory of [God's] dogmas and actions . . . and to refute all opinions contradicting them'.[94] *Kalām* sometimes took the form of public debates or disputations called *munāẓara*s. In a *munāẓara* debate, Muslim scholars would debate Jews, Christians, or representatives of competing Islamic schools of thought before an audience which might include the Muslim ruler. Such public debates were 'executed in the form of questions and answers'; in general, it was expected that the loser would convert.[95] Chapter 1 discussed the place given to argumentation (*jadal*) in the *da'wa*logy of the Qur'an. Chapter 2 presented examples of religious debate in the *da'wa* repertoire of the Prophet. Building on these precedents, *kalām* elevates religious debate to an Islamic science in its own right.[96] Like other missionary religions, Islam is 'argumentative' – it makes exclusive and universal claims which necessarily stand in opposition to the universal and exclusive claims of others. In the modern period, as we will see, there has been something of a revival of Muslims engaging in inter- and intra-religious argumentation and debate as forms of *da'wa*.

Summary and conclusions

This chapter examined several key developments and themes related to *da'wa* or Islamic missionary thought and practice in the formative period from roughly 632 to 1100 CE. We considered, first, the Arab-Islamic conquests (*circa* 632–750 CE) and their relation to *da'wa* and the spread of Islam. We noted that the conquests were not, in the first place, about converting the world to Islam, but about securing the territorial expansion of the emerging Arab-Islamic Empire. Within the 'Islamic ambience' (or *dar al-Islam*) created by the conquests from Morocco in the west to Afghanistan in the east, conversion to Islam would prove to be a gradual, centuries-long process. To repeat a key point, although the earliest conquerors seem to have assumed that 'Islam' was a religion for Arabs only, the conditions created by the conquests, including the rising (and somewhat unexpected) phenomenon of non-Muslim conversion to Islam, activated or unleashed, as it were, the universal or missionary impulse of the Qur'an and early Islam. Far from the polemical image of Muslim conquerors converting people 'by the sword', Islam usually spread in the post-conquest world in more prosaic, if complex, ways. We will explore several additional ways in the next chapter. Yet, although it was not the immediate cause of conversion, inasmuch as the conquests paved the way for eventual widespread Islamisation and inasmuch as the conquests and their heroes have had paradigmatic status within the Islamic tradition, 'the sword' remains an undeniable part of the missionary history of Islam.

Second, we considered the organised, restorationist *da'wa*s of the 'Abbasids and Isma'ilis/Fatimids. Both of these movements, as well as the sectarian division of the Muslims they represent, point to an important nuance of *da'wa* in Islamic history: *da'wa* as internal summons to wayward, wavering, or undecided Muslims to help restore 'true Islam' by returning to the practice of the Prophet and installing a true Islamic ruler. To put it more broadly, these movements point to the fact that *da'wa* is not merely about the missionary propagation of Islam to non-Muslims, but also about active efforts to persuade or compete with other Muslims in the religious (and sometimes also political) sphere. Third, we explored the missionary thought and implications of Islamic law and theology. We saw that Islamic law enshrines the principle, also observed in the Medinan period of the Prophet's life, that Muslims must give non-Muslims a *da'wa* to Islam before making war on their territories. We also examined some of the less explicit ways in which the Islamic legal heritage relates to the missionary aims of Islam; for instance, the ways in which Islamic law incentivises conversion and disincentivises apostasy, and the ways in which *da'wa* may be seen as one of the goals (*maqāsid*) of Islamic law. We finally analysed a few of the ways in which Islamic theology represents the struggle of Islam (or versions thereof) against internal and external rivals, a struggle that takes place in the realms of written argument, denunciation of heresy and false belief, and public debate.

Notes

1. Chapter 3 includes some material that takes us slightly beyond 1100, while Chapter 4 includes some material from before 1100. As to the approximate year 1100 as a natural place to divide these chapters, and roughly the 1700s as a place to bring them to an end, see Morgan and Reid 2010, pp. 1–2.
2. It is roughly correct that the 'Arab' conquests evolved into 'Islamic' conquests. Hoyland 2015, p. 5.
3. In general, 'Middle East' will refer to the region from Persia in the east through North Africa in the west, and from Arabia in the south to Central Asia in the north.
4. Islamic political history to the 1200s is divided as follows: (1) the period of the four 'Rightly Guided' caliphs from 632–61 CE, based in Medina and briefly in Kufa; (2) the Umayyad caliphate from 661–750 CE, based in Damascus; and (3) the 'Abbasid caliphate from roughly 750 to 1258 CE, based in Baghdad. Although the expansion of Islamic empires continued after 750 CE, this date provides an appropriate bookend for the initial wave of conquests. Kennedy 2007, p. 363.
5. On this, readers may consult Kennedy 2007 and Hoyland 2015. See also Donner 1981. In addition, see Donner 2008. Most introductions to Islam provide useful summaries of the conquests; see, for instance, Brown 2017, 3rd ed., ch. 7; Lapidus 2014, pp. 31–4.
6. Blankenship 1994 outlines four waves of expansion.
7. Kennedy 2007, pp. 12–33. According to Hoyland, 'The 9th-century historians wanted to create a distinctively Arab Muslim history, which meant downplaying the role of non-Arabs and non-Muslims and placing God, Muhammad and the Muslims center stage'. Hoyland 2015, p. 3.
8. One should note, however, that there is no straight line from the ninth-century Muslim histories to later Muslim views of the conquests. Ayman Ibrahim argues that later Muslim views cannot be substantiated from these sources. See Ibrahim 2018.
9. Kirk 2010, pp. 240–1. 'Manifest success' is the idea that Islam is destined (by God) to rule.
10. Muslims have traditionally interpreted the motivations of the conquests to have been pious and altruistic, but Ibrahim shows that the reality was more complicated. Ibrahim 2018, pp. 1–8, 145, 236–40.
11. A classic statement of this perspective is Crone and Cook 1976, followed up by Crone 1980. See also Hoyland 2015, pp. 231–9.
12. For an example, see Arnold 1896/1913/2012, pp. 50–1. See also Ibrahim 2018, pp. 143, 155–6, where the author notes (with scepticism) that Khalid b. al-Walid seems to have given *da'wa* to Islam before attacking.
13. For examples, see Donner 1981, pp. 65, 77, 260–1. In such contexts 'conversion' very often denotes political submission more than change of religion. Further, see Hoyland 2015, pp. 60–5.
14. See, for example, Arnold 1896/1913/2012, p. 51.

15. Kennedy 2007, pp. 62–3. For Ibrahim, examples like these put a religious veneer over the conquests' political/economic motives. Ibrahim 2018, pp. 155–6, 166.
16. Crone 1960–2007.
17. Lapidus 2014, p. 61.
18. Lapidus 1988, p. 48.
19. On taxation in the early Islamic state, see Donner 1981, pp. 69–75, 251–5.
20. According to Hoyland, 'The [unbelievers] were generally left . . . to manage their own affairs . . . The only major demand made of them was that they pay a special tax (*jizya*) to demonstrate their twin shame of having been conquered and having rejected the true religion'. Hoyland 2004, pp. xiii–xiv.
21. Crone 1960–2007, pp. 874–82. An intriguing example of the desire to keep Arabs and non-Arabs separate is the story of Arab governor al-Hajjaj driving non-Arabs out of the *amsar* of Iraq. Hawting 1987, p. 77.
22. As argued by Donner 1981, pp. 256, 269–71. See also Kennedy 2007, pp. 363–76, Hoyland 2015, pp. 57–8, 197–8. For additional examples, see Arnold 1896/1913/2012, pp. 47–50.
23. Hoyland 2015, p. 220.
24. On captured slaves, see Hoyland 2015, pp. 221, 229. On demographics, see Bulliet 1979; Levtzion 1979c, pp. 1–23; Griffith 2008; Berkey 2003, ch. 10. Chrysostomides summarises: 'Throughout the Umayyad and early Abbasid eras, Islam was the minority religion amongst a majority of Christians, Jews and Zoroastrians. Yet . . . in terms of cultural capital identifying as Muslim provided social . . . benefits'. Chrysostomides 2017, p. 118.
25. Lapidus 2002, p. 52.
26. On *dhimmi* status, see Griffith 2008, pp. 14–20; Hoyland 2015, pp. 195–201; and Humphreys 1991, ch. 11. Griffith notes that 'Christians of all communities unanimously regarded the [Arab] conquests as a disaster'. Griffith 2008, p. 28. Arnold 1896/1913/2012, pp. 47–55, puts a positive spin on it.
27. See, for instance, Hoyland 2015, p. 202. For another example see Al-Tabari's *Tarikh*, 'Ashras and the affair of the people of Samarqand and those who followed them in it', cited and translated in Levi and Sela 2010, pp. 19–21.
28. Hodgson defines 'Islamdom' as 'the society in which the Muslims and their faith are recognized as prevalent and socially dominant . . . a society in which . . . non-Muslims have always played an integral, if subordinate, element, as have Jews in Christendom'. Hodgson 1974, vol. 1, p. 58. See also Hoyland 2015, p. 209.
29. Levtzion 1979c, pp. 6–7, cites the conquest of Arabia and the conquest of the Berbers. In both cases, immediate 'conversion' was symbolic of political submission, and it was often followed by political rebellion. Levtzion cites Ibn Khaldun and Ibn 'Idhari as saying that the Berbers rebelled twelve times before their Islam was finally 'made good'. See also Lapidus 2002, p. 202.
30. See Bulliet 1979; Levtzion 1979c, pp. 1–23; Peacock 2017b, pp. 6–7; Berkey 2003, ch. 17.
31. Poston 1992 calls this 'external-institutional missiology' (structural Islamisation precedes mass conversion), which he contrasts with 'internal-personal missiology' (conversion of the masses precedes structural Islamisation).
32. As Rahman notes, 'What was spread by the sword was not the religion of Islam, but the political domain of Islam'. Rahman 1994, p. 63.
33. A fact that is evident in the hadith collections. 'Whatever Islam produced on its own or borrowed from outside was dressed up as hadith . . .' Goldziher 1981, pp. 36–40.
34. Hoyland 2015, p. 221; see also Starr 2013.
35. Hoyland 2015, pp. 213–19.
36. That is, exclusivist religions which require unqualified commitment. In his 1933 study of

conversion, Nock distinguished between 'prophetic' religions and 'nonprophetic' religions. The latter are more pragmatic in seeking to satisfy local and natural needs. Quoted in Levtzion 1979c, p. 21.

37. Hodgson 1974, vol. 1, p. 250.

38. Khurasan corresponds to eastern Iran and parts of Central Asia and Afghanistan

39. Sharon 1991, pp. 115–52.

40. 'In the politico-religious sense, *da'wa* is the invitation to adopt the cause of some individual or family claiming the right to [rule] over the Muslims . . . Such was the 'Abbasid *da'wa* . . .' Canard 1960–2007. See also Daniel 2007.

41. Such as Abu Muslim and Abu Salama. See Moscati 1960–2007a and 1960–2007b. Abu Salama was a 'freed slave from Kufa, [who] was sent in 127/744–5 to Khurasan as one of the chief 'Abbasid emissaries'. Abu Muslim, 'probably a slave of Persian origin', was sent 'in AH 128/745–6 CE to Khurasan with the mission of directing the movement . . . in that province'.

42. Daftary 1998, p. 28.

43. '[F]or the first time in the history of Islam a . . . well-organized opposition movement accomplished a total change in government through armed rebellion which itself was the violent climax of prolonged . . . propaganda'. Sharon 1983, p. 19.

44. Sharon 1983, p. 20.

45. Composed or redacted in the 'Abbasid period, the classical sources portray the Umayyads as innovators who perverted the Islam of the Prophet. See Madelung 1997, p. 88f.

46. Canard 1960–2007a.

47. For examples, see Ibn Khaldun 1958, vol. 1, pp. 318–19 (I, 283), 322–9 (I, 288–92), vol. 2, pp. 121–2 (II, 110–11), 128–30 (II, 118–19). For Ibn Khaldun, a would-be ruler's *da'wa* is one strategy that produces the "*asabiyyah*' (group feeling) which makes new dynasties possible. Interestingly, in vol 1, p. 476 (I, 418), Ibn Khaldun speaks of Christian mission.

48. Morgan and Reid 2010, p. 1.

49. Cook 2000, pp. 233–7.

50. Fierro 2010b, pp. 66–9.

51. The Almohads overthrew the Almoravids in Maghrib and Spain. The Almoravid movement, too, began with a religio-political *da'wa* in the early eleventh century. This *da'wa* featured the alliance of a local African tribal chief with the Maliki religious scholar and 'missionary of orthodox Islam', 'Abd Allah Ibn Yasin (d. 1059). See Viguera-Molins 2010, pp. 36–9.

52. Daftary 1998, p. 24.

53. Halm, *Shi'ism*, p. 168. Daftary 1998, pp. 39–41.

54. 'Ubaydallah claimed that after Muhammad b. Isma'il, the true believers had adopted a policy of *taqiyya* (concealing their true beliefs and identities) so as to spread their *da'wa* effectively. With the success of their *da'wa*, however, 'Ubaydallah said that the time was right to come out into the open. While many Isma'ilis accepted this, others rejected 'Ubaydallah's claim and formed their own sect, later to be called Qarmati. A Qarmati state was established in Bahrayn 899 and lasted until 1077. Daftary 1998, pp. 45–7.

55. Ibid., p. 64.

56. Irwin 2011, pp. 9–10.

57. Lapidus 2002, p. 107.

58. Arnold 1896/1913/2012, pp. 211–12.

59. Walker 1998, p. 120. An Isma'ili law school or *madhhab* came into being during the early Fatimid period. Cook 2000, pp. 301–4.

60. Also stoking Sunni fears was a break-off group of Isma'ilis, known as Nizaris, who became

infamous in the eleventh and twelfth centuries for assassinations. Berkey 2003, pp. 141, 189f.

61. Janson speaks of a 'recession' in the use of the word *da'wa* from roughly the thirteenth century on. Along with the reasons Janson offers – for instance, that the Sufis did not use the word *da'wa* for their preaching – it is likely that the Isma'ili/Fatimid use also played a role. See Janson 2003, pp. 73–7; Janson [n. d.], p. 31.

62. For example, Stewart 1998.

63. '. . . it is widely accepted that the Jewish model . . . influenced the development of Islamic law by the Muslim jurists'. Berkey 2003, pp. 143–4. Scholars also detect the influence of Byzantine law, the canon law of the Eastern churches and Persian Sassanian law on Islamic law. Schacht 1960–2007, pp. 886–91.

64. Chapter 2 mentioned the sending of Muhammad's companion Mu'adh as a religio-political *da'i* to Yemen. Interestingly, the rudiments of this four-source theory of Islamic law are embedded in the missionary instructions Muhammad is said to have addressed to Mu'adh. See Abu Dawud 2008, no. 3592 (vol. 4, p. 104).

65. Brown 2017, p. 189.

66. The law is not so much a fixed or static code, but a collection of living texts in which Muslim jurists express educated opinions. *Fiqh* as we now understand it took a long time to develop – the main Sunni schools of law (Shafi'i, Maliki, Hanbali, Hanafi) were formed only by the late ninth and early tenth centuries. Shi'ite sects also developed their own law schools. Melchert 1997; Picken 2011.

67. Canard 1960–2007. See also Janson 2003, p. 67, Masud 2000, pp. xxiii–xxiv.

68. Compare Khadduri 1966, pp. 75–6, 95–6; al-Marghinani 2006, pp. 291–2; al-Tusi 2008, pp. 216–18.

69. Khadduri 1955, p. 97.

70. According to Friedmann, the concepts of the two *dars* 'were so well known that [classical] jurisprudents did not deem it necessary to elaborate on their meaning'. Friedmann 2017, pp. 341–2.

71. Bonner and Hagen 2010, p. 475.

72. Khadduri 1966, pp. 11–14.

73. Ibid., pp. 10–17; Peters 2009, p. 27.

74. Such territories were sometimes designated '*dār al-ahad*' or '*dār al-ṣulḥ*', the sphere of truce or treaty.

75. Abou Ramadan 2018, pp. 219–35. The medieval scholar Ibn Taymiyya classified some territories as composite spheres (*dār murakaba*). For more, see Algar 1993/2011.

76. Khadduri 1966, pp. 5–6.

77. Friedmann 2003, esp. chs 2, 5.

78. Ibid., pp. 124–6.

79. For general introductions, see Lewis 1990, pp. 3–15; Marmon 1999, pp. 1–8.

80. Hamid Algar writes: 'All schools of [*fiqh*] tended, before modern times, to regard slavery as a permanent feature of Muslim society; the ethical emphasis of the Koran and Sunna on the desirability of emancipation never became fully reflected in law'. Algar 1988/2000.

81. For instance, by presupposing that freedom is humanity's natural state, by calling masters to follow Muhammad, by treating slaves with compassion and by underscoring the rewards of freeing slaves. See, for example, al-Marghinani 2006, vol. 2, pp. 105–11; Brunschvig 1960–2007, pp. 24–40.

82. Some modern Muslims argue that classical law departs from the Qur'an and *sunna* regarding slavery. According to this argument, the Qur'an and Muhammad took slavery for granted, but intended its elimination. Brockopp 2001, pp. 58–60.

83. '. . . but the war was often fictive and consisted of little more than raids . . . by professional slavers. The jurists never condemned this degeneration of [*jihad*] . . .' Algar 1988/2000.
84. 'Heresy and rebellion might also lead to enslavement. *Fatwa*s issued by the Ottomans . . . occasionally provided for enslavement of the wives and children of Shi'ites . . . and Shi'ites kidnapped from Khorasan were routinely sold as slaves in Bukhara'. Ibid.
85. Legal texts include material on the status of converted slaves. Slaves who converted post-enslavement were to remain slaves. Yet, conversion did bring advantages, including the greater possibility of being freed.
86. Gleave 1960–2007, pp. 569–70.
87. See Cook 2000, chs 1–2.
88. Green 2015b, pp. 378–9.
89. See Lapidus 2014, pp. 217–20, 277–8.
90. Morewedge 2009.
91. Cook 2000, p. 196. Commanding and forbidding is 'one of the celebrated 'five principles' of Mu'tazilism'. Reynolds 2004, pp. 38–9.
92. See Reynolds 2004, p. 24.
93. Chittick 2009, p. 207.
94. Gardet 1960–2007, pp. 1141–2.
95. Wagner 1960–2007, p. 565. Along with narratives of debates, such debates led to a genre called *adab al-jadal* (manners of argumentation). Examples of debates that reflect this *adab* come from the courts of the 'Abbasid caliphs al-Mahdi (r. 775–85 CE) and al-Ma'mun (r. 813–33 CE). See Text Box 3.2 above.
96. *Kalam* 'always postulates the existence of an opponent who is to be won over'. Gardet, 1960–2007.

CHAPTER 4

Da'wa in medieval and early modern Islamic history, circa 1100–1700 CE

The centuries after the Arab-Islamic conquests – the same centuries which witnessed the rise of the 'Abbasids and Fatimids, and the emergence of Islamic law and theology – witnessed the continuing expansion of Islam, politically and religiously.[1] Until about the eleventh century, that expansion was mostly confined – if 'confined' is the right word – to the Middle East, North Africa and Spain, as well as some of Central Asia. In these territories, moreover, majorities in some places, and respectable minorities in others, remained non-Muslim. Conversion to Islam continued in these core areas, until most of the Middle East and North Africa were decisively Muslim (and Arabic-speaking) by the fourteenth and fifteenth centuries. Looking beyond these regions, beginning roughly in the eleventh century, Islam advanced deeper into Central Asia and India, as well as into western China, and it expanded along maritime trade routes to Southeast Asia and southern China. The religion also spread into Anatolia (modern-day Turkey), the Balkans and sub-Saharan Africa. In some of these places Islamisation turned out to be fairly thorough (as in the Middle East and Southeast Asia), whereas in others it remained partial (as in India and the Balkans). Despite the eventual territorial loss of Spain and parts of southern Europe to Muslim rule, by around the year 1700 (and continuing beyond 1800), a trans-regional Muslim ecumene[2] had been established from Senegal in the west to Indo-Malaysia in the east.

Travelling from one end of this vast Muslim ecumene to the other, one would have encountered dazzling diversity and striking familiarity. If one travelled in the western Islamic lands (from the Atlantic Ocean to eastern Iran), one would have encountered an Islam that was shaped by its long encounter with Christianity, Judaism, the Greco-Roman heritage and Persian civilisation. By contrast, if one travelled in the eastern Islamic lands (from eastern Iran to southeast Asia), one would have seen a younger Islam that was being forged through the interaction of its Middle Eastern heritage with eastern cultures and religions, including Hinduism, Buddhism, Daoism, Confucianism and others.[3] Increasingly over these centuries, one would have also seen ethnic diversity: Arab, Berber, Turkic, Mongol, sub-Saharan African, Indian, Chinese, Indo-Malaysian and other peoples would come to make up the fabric of the Muslim ecumene. In both east and west, however, there would have been sufficient continuity to allow Muslims from one area to feel at least somewhat 'at home' in others. In most places, for instance, one would have encountered sound-scapes in which the *adhān* (Islamic call to prayer) in Arabic would have been an important feature. One also would have seen recognisable Muslim rituals, like the five daily prayers, or fasting during the month of Ramadan. One would have met Sufi holy men and Muslim scholars (*'ulama*), who were regarded as the religious guides of Muslim communities. In addition, even though the styles of their architecture might differ from one place to another,[4] one would have seen mosques, *madrasa*s and Sufi convents – a number of which are still standing today.[5] We are given glimpses of this world of diversity and familiarity in the writings of the Muslim scholar Ibn Battuta (d. 1369), who visited nearly every corner of the Muslim ecumene (as it existed in his day) in the 1300s, and in the seventeenth-century scholarly career of Nur al-Din Raniri (d. 1658), who spent time in his native India, as well as in Egypt, Arabia and Aceh.[6]

Adding to a sense of familiarity, in most places, one would have found oneself under the auspices of a Muslim ruler who oversaw warfare and trade, and selec-tively patronised scholars and Sufis, as well as perhaps philosophy, science and art. Yet, the politics of these centuries also underscored diversity. After the 1100s (and even as early as the 900s) there was never again a unified Islamic empire or caliphate such as the one that the Rightly Guided caliphs, the Umayyads and the early 'Abbasids had ruled; instead, a series of diverse Muslim states were organised across this vast territory. Bosworth's handbook, *The New Islamic Dynasties*, covers some 186 Islamic empires and statelets that ruled parts of the Muslim ecumene over these centuries, often in competition with one another.[7] Between roughly the fifteenth and eighteenth centuries, despite the persistence of smaller states, a significant portion of the Muslim world came to be domi-nated by the Ottoman, Safavid and Mughal empires. Whether long- or short-lived, to one degree or another most of these states sought to style themselves as defenders of Islam and extenders of *dar al-Islam*.

In the midst of frequent political change, Islam became a stabilising factor: 'While conquerors and regimes came and went, Islam became ever more firmly and widely entrenched as the basis of the social . . . order'. Thus, 'by the eight-eenth century *a global system of Islamic societies* had come into being . . . Although each society was unique, they resembled each other in form and were intercon-nected by political and religious contacts and shared values'.[8] While the seeds were planted earlier (see Chapters 1–3), it is between about 1100 and 1700 CE, therefore, that Islam became a global phenomenon.[9] How did this 'global system' come into being? By what mechanisms did Islam spread, and how is it that so many varied peoples from southwestern Europe to southeastern China came to identify themselves as 'Muslim' during these centuries? Once the conquests had set the stage, the spread of Islam was spearheaded by several classes of Muslim actors and followed several interrelated patterns of Islamisation. Seeking to be broadly representative, this chapter highlights six sets of 'agents and patterns' which, taken together, provide a window into *da'wa* and the spread of Islam in this long period: (1) Turks, Mongols and other migratory peoples: Islamisation through in-migration; (2) Muslim rulers and ruler-converts: Islamisation by royal example or expectation; (3) The *'ulama*: Islamisation through knowledge preservation and transmission; (4) The Sufis: Islamisation through inspiration and indigenisation; (5) Popular preachers and storytellers: Islamisation through popularisation; and (6) Merchants: Islamisation through networking and trade. As noted in the Introduction, Islamisation, like the spread of any religion, has two sides: transmission and reception. In the following, the focus will be mostly, and unavoidably, on the former.[10]

Turks, Mongols and other migratory peoples: Islamisation through in-migration

'Islamisation through in-migration' refers to a pattern in which migratory peoples' entry into the Muslim ecumene or *dar al-Islam* led to the gradual conversion of the newcomers. Two particularly consequential examples stand out. The first is seen in the migrations of the Turkic peoples of Inner Asia[11] into the Islamic heartlands beginning in the tenth century, and their eventual conversion to Islam. The Turkic embrace of Islam constitutes another major turning point in Islamic and world history.[12] In recognition of this fact, Sunni writers from the eleventh century to the present have celebrated the conversion of the Turks, a number of whom have been remembered as zealous defenders and promoters of Sunni Islam.[13] Turkic peoples first appear in Islamic history as slave-soldiers in the army of the 'Abbasid caliphs in the ninth century. The conscription of Turks by the 'Abbasids heralded more widespread Turkic people movements and conversions to come. Leaving aside the question of what prompted Turkic peoples to migrate westward into Central Asia and the Middle East as other peoples had done in previous millennia,[14] we are mainly concerned here with the results of their movements. Over time, the Turks' migrations (*circa* ninth to twelfth centuries CE) exposed them to the ambience and attractions of *dar al-Islam*. It also brought Turks into contact with Sufi orders. As we will see below, Sufis helped facilitate the transition of the Turks from their ancestral suite of 'shamanistic' religions to Islam. The main point for now is that 'The Turkic encounter with, and subsequent integration into, the Muslim world occurred *largely through migrations* . . . Many of the Turks who made their way out of the steppe did so as conquerors, many others did so as slaves, *but the majority eventually embraced Sunni Islam*'.[15] Before long, the migrants would become the rulers; Turkic-Muslim states would emerge and come to dominate the political order of a sizable portion of the Muslim world (with interruptions) for nearly a thousand years, from the establishment of the

Qarakhanid dynasty in 999 CE to the collapse of the Ottoman Empire in the early twentieth century.

In turn, as these Turkic-Muslim states engaged in expansionist conquest in the name of Islam – something they were known for – the conquest-followed-by-gradual-conversion pattern which we first encountered in the aftermath of the conquest period (post-750 CE) repeated itself in new places. For instance, Islamic rule was gradually established in Anatolia at the expense of the Byzantine Empire through Turkic conquest regimes (the Saljuqs and Ottomans) between the eleventh and fourteenth centuries. Following the Battle of Manzikert in 1071 CE, during which the Byzantines suffered a devastating defeat at the hands of the Saljuqs, Anatolia was flooded with Turkic settlers.[16] This set the stage for the rise of the Ottomans in the period after the Mongol invasions. By the time the Ottomans brought the Byzantine Empire to an end at Constantinople in 1453 CE, an expansive Turkic Sunni Islamdom had been established. Within that ambience, in turn, the Islamisation (and Turkification) of native populations became a viable result. Anatolia itself, which had been predominantly Christian for centuries, was converted to Islam and remains predominantly Muslim and Turkish to this day.[17] Meanwhile, the Turkic-Uzbek Shaybanids inherited the territories of the great Turko-Mongol conqueror Timur (d. 1405 CE); their rule marked the beginning of Uzbek domination of Central Asia. Under a series of Uzbek regimes, Central Asia's identification with Sunni Islam would increase and prove resilient enough to persist through later periods of Russian imperial and Soviet domination. Interestingly, while Turkic peoples were Islamised, they were never fully Arabised (in the sense of adopting the Arabic language). At elite levels, many Turkic rulers adopted the Persian language and Persianate court culture, while others, notably the Ottomans, adopted a (Persianised and Arabised) variant of Turkish. Among ordinary Turks, Turkic languages persisted.

A second example of Islamisation through in-migration may be seen in the Mongol conquests and migrations of the thirteenth and fourteenth centuries. The Mongol conquests were initiated by Genghis (or Chinggis) Khan, a non-Muslim warlord who had established leadership over a number of Inner Asian peoples during the late twelfth and early thirteenth centuries, and who had, somewhat like Muhammad in the seventh century, mobilised these peoples into a potent conquest force. With legendary ferocity, Genghis and his descendants conquered territory stretching from China to the Mediterranean, thus creating the largest continuous territorial empire the world has ever seen. For the Muslims of the Middle East, the Mongol invasions were a disaster. The Mongol sack of the city of Baghdad under Genghis's grandson Hulegu Khan (d. 1265 CE) and the final destruction of the line of 'Abbasid caliphs in 1258 CE was indicative of the catastrophic threat that the Mongols posed. At the time, especially in the eastern parts of the Muslim ecumene, the Crusades (*circa* 1095–1291 CE) would have seemed insignificant by comparison.

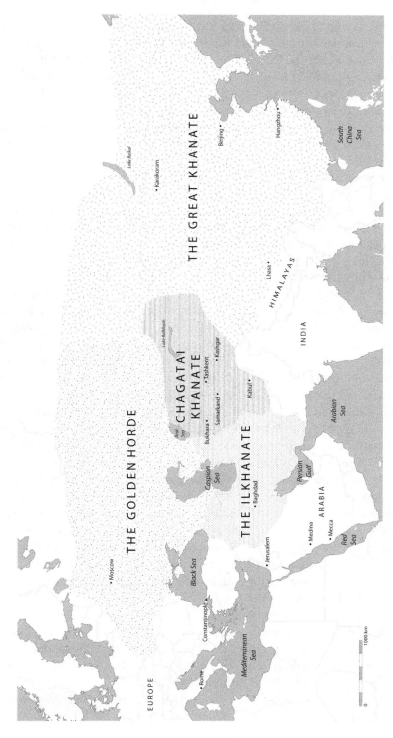

Map 4.1 The Mongol Khanates, *circa* thirteenth to fourteenth centuries.

Following Genghis' death in 1227 CE, his sons and grandsons divided the empire into four kingdoms or Khanates: the Golden Horde to the north of the Black and Caspian Seas, the Ilkhanate from Iran to the Mediterranean, the Chagatai Khanate in Central Asia and the Great Khanate in China and Mongolia (see Map 4.1). Although the process was uneven in each case, the ruling elites of three out of the four – excluding the Great Khanate – would come to embrace Islam. A common factor contributing to Islamisation in these three Khanates was the fact that each of them had come to rule territories 'with a substantial Muslim presence in pre-Mongol times'.[18] While there were additional 'vectors of Islamisation' at play, the Mongol experience in the three western Khanates, therefore, constitutes another example of Islamisation through in-migration. Even though he generally takes a dim view of the Mongols, the modern writer Abu'l-Hasan 'Ali Nadwi, writing from a pious Muslim perspective, says of their conversion: '[W]hen all seemed lost . . . a few unknown and sincere Muslim preachers . . . commenced the work of the propagation of Islam among the ruling circles of the [Mongols] and Islam's magic did the rest. The conquerors . . . became the captives of Islam'.[19] In contrast to Nadwi, Fletcher provides an academic analysis of why the Mongols converted to Islam. In line with our idea of Islamisation through in-migration, Fletcher suggests, first, that the western lands that the Mongols conquered were already substantially Islamised; the Mongols' presence in and rule over Islamic ambiences thus made their conversion more likely. He also suggests, second, that Islam, as a religion of the nomad and the townsman, and as a religion that gives an honoured place in its early tradition to military conquest, provided a particularly good fit for the nomadic, militant Mongols who now found themselves ruling settled peoples.[20]

Following their gradual embrace of Islam, in subsequent centuries Mongol and Turko-Mongol rulers (Timur's descendants in Central Asia and India are good examples of the latter) would expand the borders of Islamdom. Once again, the gradual-conversion-within-Islamic-ambiences pattern would repeat itself. Mongol and Turko-Mongol rulers would also foster inter-regional links along which goods and ideas could spread, and they would sponsor Islamic scholarship, architecture and art.[21] Landmarks such as the mosques and *madrasas* of Samarkand, Bukhara and Kashgar, as well as the magnificent Taj Mahal in India, all bear witness to the Turko-Mongol legacy in the Islamic world (see Figure 4.1). Thus, unlike the seventh- and eighth-century Arabs, who had resisted conversion to the previously dominant monotheisms of the lands they conquered (Christianity, Judaism and Zoroastrianism), the Turks and Mongols were won over by Islam. In this way, the Islamisation of the Turks and Mongols resembles the Christianisation of the Vandals, Goths and other Germanic peoples beginning in fourth- and fifth-century Europe.[22]

Turks and Mongols are not the only peoples who exemplify the pattern we are calling Islamisation through in-migration, but they have been highlighted

Figure 4.1 The Registan (three *madrasa*s facing a common courtyard, fifteenth to seventeenth centuries) at night, in Samarkand, Uzbekistan. Magnificent landmarks such as the mosques and *madrasa*s of Samarkand, Bukhara and Kashgar, as well as the Taj Mahal in India, all bear witness to the Turko-Mongol legacy in the Islamic world. Photo: Matthew J. Kuiper.

because of the scale of their migrations and their influence on Islamic history. Across the Muslim ecumene, other peoples would come into contact with Islam, sometimes in the course of their own migrations or sometimes through the establishment of Islamic ambiences near them. A key point is that Islam has often exhibited a centripetal pull. Whatever the reasons migratory peoples first came into contact with the Muslim ecumene, Islam (both the religion and the civilisation) proved attractive to them. This attractiveness certainly would have included the everyday lives of ordinary Muslims, although we sadly have little documentation of this in the available sources. To put Islam's centripetal attraction in terms of a general principle, where Muslims reached a critical mass of the overall population and where Islamic ambiences had been established, newcomers (and indigenous populations) tended to convert sooner or later.[23]

A final variation of Islamisation through in-migration should be mentioned before we move on. Migration can be voluntary or forced,[24] and historically the significant forced migrations caused by the worldwide slave trade have proven to be catalysts for religious change.[25] As observed in Chapter 3, Islamic scripture and law assume the validity of slavery and seek to regulate its practice.[26] In practical terms, slavery got its major start in the Muslim ecumene with the conquests, during the course of which hundreds of thousands of slaves were captured and brought into the Islamic empire. Most of these were fairly rapidly absorbed into the general population by conversion and/or emancipation.[27] With the slowing of the conquests, the supply of slaves was met through wars beyond the frontiers and by professional slavers who made forays into frontier regions. Eventually, there would be a 'network of trade routes and markets extending all over the Islamic world' involving 'commercial relations with suppliers in Christian Europe, in the Turkish steppe-lands, and in black Africa. In every important [Muslim] city there was a slave market, usually called *sūq al-raqīq*'.[28]

The breadth of the phenomenon may be seen through a few examples. First, in medieval times, 'slaves represented one of the most important exports from Europe to the Muslim world', and European slaves would continue to play a role in Muslim societies at least until the eighteenth century.[29] The Ottoman *devshirme*, a system of conscripting military slaves from Christian families in the Balkans, continued into the seventeenth century, and the Tatar Khanate supplied the Ottomans with slaves of Georgian and Circassian backgrounds into the eighteenth. Second, between the eleventh and fifteenth centuries, hundreds of thousands of captives from India were taken to the slave markets of Ghazna, Samarkand, Bukhara, Khiva and elsewhere. Muslim states in Central Asia would continue to participate in the slave trade until the nineteenth century.[30] Third, sub-Saharan Africa proved to be a major source of slaves for the Muslim world, with some African slaves being sent as tribute to Muslim overlords (as in a well-known case from Nubia),[31] others being transported across the Sahara to North Africa, and yet others being transported across the Red Sea and the Indian Ocean. In the course of the nineteenth century, Africa 'came to provide the overwhelming majority of slaves used in Muslim countries'.[32] A fourth source of slaves were the Turkic peoples of Inner Asia. As noted above, while many Turkic peoples migrated into the Muslim ecumene voluntarily, others did so as slaves. Military slaves (*mamlūks*), which were mostly taken from Inner and Central Asia but also from southern Europe, were converted to Islam and given education and military training in exchange for service. The institution reached its apogee with the Mamluk sultanate of Egypt (r. 1254–1517 CE).[33] According to Ayalon, military slaves 'were the determining military factor in Islam during the greatest part of its existence . . . Without that factor Islam's geographical boundaries would have been much narrower'.[34]

In short, whether as 'ordinary' (domestic and agricultural) slaves, or as military slaves, millions of persons were brought into *dar al-Islam* through slavery from the time of the Arab-Islamic conquests to the late nineteenth century, when slavery began to be repudiated and suppressed across the Muslim world.[35] Although in some instances Muslim rulers and masters tried *not* to convert their slaves, in many others, they encouraged conversion.[36] Either way, it can be assumed that the majority of these often nameless, subaltern groups of men and women ultimately converted to Islam, even if the process took generations. While our information on slave converts is scarce (with the exception of a few who achieved notoriety), we know that they were not only influenced by Islam, but that they also influenced Islam, for instance, by introducing their ancestral religious practices into Muslim communities.[37] Like the Arab-Islamic conquests discussed in Chapter 3, slavery in Islamic history has been, unavoidably, on the apologetic agenda of modern Muslim thinkers and *da'wa* activists.[38]

Muslim rulers and ruler-converts: Islamisation by royal example or expectation

The conversion of the Turks and Mongols to Islam were gradual and multi-faceted processes, but from the perspective of Turkic and Mongol legend, it was often the conversion of key rulers or chieftains which proved most decisive in bringing about their Islamisation. Indeed, what we are calling Islamisation through royal example or expectation is a prominent theme in the missionary history of Islam, particularly from the time the Turks and Mongols enter the scene. 'The first great expansion of Islam owed little to the conversion of rulers but instead followed, albeit slowly, in the footsteps of . . . military conquest'. Yet, in later centuries, Islam 'expanded further and faster by means of ruler conversions than its proselytising rivals, Christianity and Buddhism'.[39] Although we should read the accounts (or panegyrics) of the Muslim ruler-converts which have come down to us with a grain of salt, there is no reason to doubt that they should still be included among our agents of Islamisation. Here we see interesting parallels to the medieval Christianisation of Europe. In Christian legend, Europe's conversion saw instances of kings or chieftains embracing Christianity and leading their peoples or armies into the new religion – for instance, Clovis of the Franks in the sixth century, Oswald of Northumbria in the seventh century, Harald of Denmark in the ninth century and Vladimir, 'Baptiser of Russia', in the tenth century.[40] Building on the previous section, a few representative examples of Turkic and Mongol ruler-coverts are provided here, followed by reflections on the importance of Muslim rulers and dynasties in general in contributing to the spread of Islam.

First, in the middle of the tenth century, according to Arab historian Ibn al-Athir, '20,000 tents of the Turks converted' to Islam.[41] This mass conversion, apparently of the Qarakhanid Turks, seems to have been initiated by the Turkic leader Satuq Bugra Khan (d. 955 CE). The Qarakhanids would go on to establish 'the first Turkic-Muslim dynasty in Central Asia'.[42] Bughra Khan's conversion is reported in several sources.[43] In one account, he was converted at the age of twelve, after observing Muslims at their prayers and after coming under the influence of a Muslim scholar from Bukhara. After his conversion, from his base at Kashgar (in far western China), he is said to have 'brought about a wholesale conversion of his people' and to have spread Islam to surrounding areas.[44] Another significant ruler-convert among the Turkic peoples was Saljuq, a chieftain of the Oghuz confederation, who converted to Islam around the year 985 CE. Within seventy years, the Saljuq dynasty, named for this ruler-convert, would become the dominant force in the Islamic world, famed for their expansionist commitment to Sunni Islam. Surveying the 'Turkification' of the Muslim world which these events represent, Golden writes: 'The Turks had not only adopted [Sunni] Islam, but had also become its champions in the Islamic heartlands as well as in Central Asia'.[45]

Turning to the Mongols, two ruler-converts stand out: Uzbek Khan of the Golden Horde and Ghazan Khan of the Ilkhanate (see Map 4.1). Following the death of Genghis in 1227 CE, Mongol leaders seem to have abided by Genghis's instructions that his successors were to uphold indigenous Mongol religious customs and rule diverse peoples even-handedly. As such, the Mongols 'took some time to succumb to Islam'.[46] With the ascension of Berke, who ruled from 1257 to 1266 CE, the Golden Horde was the first of the Mongol states to have a Muslim ruler. The somewhat hazy details of Berke's conversion need not concern us here, but we should note that a Sufi, Sayf al-Din al-Bakharzi of Bukhara, was said to have been instrumental in Berke's conversion. The decisive turning point in the Islamisation of the Golden Horde, however, came with the conversion of Uzbek Khan (r. 1313–41 CE). While it may be that the conversion of prominent families among the Golden Horde was the cause of Uzbek's conversion and not *vice versa*, Uzbek Khan was nevertheless mythologised as the decisive 'Islamiser' of the Golden Horde. In the version of Uzbek's conversion story that became most popular, Uzbek embraced Islam after four Sufi holy men boldly approached the khan with a *da'wa* to Islam. In the ensuing discussion, a literal trial by fire was proposed between the Muslim missionaries and the shamans of Uzbek's entourage. In this account, a Sufi by the name of Baba Tukles passed through a fiery oven unscathed. By contrast, the Mongol shaman who attempted the same feat was burnt to a crisp.[47] Demonstrations of the superior power of the new God and new religion are common motifs in accounts of Muslim ruler-converts.[48] Once converted, Uzbek is portrayed as a zealous Muslim ruler who actively promoted the spread of Islam in his realm and beyond. The conversion of Uzbek Khan and of the Golden Horde would prove to be far-reaching. Uzbek, for instance, would later be seen as the forefather of the (now predominantly Muslim) Uzbek people.[49]

Turning to the south and east of the Golden Horde, the ruler-convert Ghazan Khan is credited with bringing about the conversion of the Mongols of the Ilkhanate. The main source for what we know about the conversion of Ghazan Khan (r. 1295–1304 CE) comes from an account written by Rashid al-Din, who has been described as Ghazan Khan's 'vizier, and . . . his apologist'. Although Rashid al-Din seems at pains to stress the religious character of Ghazan's conversion, it still comes off as a largely political act, calculated to help him win support in his own struggle for power.[50] We should note that a Muslim military leader, Nawruz, and a Muslim scholar-Sufi, Shaykh Sadr al-Din, are both portrayed as playing prominent roles in Ghazan's conversion. Among the reported results of his embrace of Islam was that 'the whole army adopted Islam as well'.[51] Despite the weight that was retrospectively given to Ghazan's actions, we know that the sincerity of his conversion (and that of the Ilkhanids in general) was contested. The well-known Muslim scholar of the Hanbali school of law and contemporary of Ghazan Khan, Ibn Taymiyya (d. 1328 CE), famously issued *fatwa*s in which he ruled that Ghazan's conversion was inauthentic or insufficient, and thus, that *jihad* against the Mongols was justified. Ibn Taymiyya's *fatwa*s have had a long shelf life; they have been used in recent times to justify the actions of militant Muslims against the leaders of Muslim-majority states whom the militants consider to be insufficiently Islamic.

Muslim rulers and dynasties and the spread of Islam
We have highlighted just a few Turkic and Mongol ruler-converts in this section, but it must be stressed that these examples are representative of a widespread trend in the period covered in this chapter.[52] In fact, one cannot overstate the importance of Muslim rulers and dynasties in general in contributing to the spread of Islam. While Islam often arrived in new locations independent of political expansion or conquest, few places would attain Muslim-majority populations that were not at some point conquered and/or ruled by Muslim dynasties. For instance, while Islam initially reached Indo-Malaysia through the activities of Muslim merchants and Sufis (see below), beginning in the late thirteenth century, parts of Southeast Asia came to be ruled by Muslim sultans or ruler-converts, such as Malik al-Salih (d. 1297 CE) in northern Sumatra, Iskandar Shah (d. 1424 CE) in Malacca and a whole series of local kings who embraced Islam in Java beginning in the fifteenth century. Similarly, although Islam first reached sub-Saharan Africa through Arab and Berber merchants, the Islamisation of Mali, Songhay and Hausaland in West Africa was given substantial impetus by the conversion of African rulers. Examples could be multiplied. While Spain, India and the Balkans provide counter-examples where Islamic rule did not lead to Muslim-majority societies, in general, Islamic rule was a crucial component of *da'wa* and Islamisation up to the modern period.

This brings to the fore an issue which should be addressed at this point: Islamisation through state-sponsored persecution or violence. As discussed earlier, although Islamic scripture and law provide precedents for peaceful relations with and the tolerant treatment of non-Muslims, there are also precedents for a less tolerant attitude. Reflecting this tension, Islamic history has witnessed many periods of tolerant and amicable relations with non-Muslims, but also episodes in which religious minorities suffered persecution at the hands of Muslim governments and societies. Among the latter, some resulted in movements of conversion to Islam. For example, historians highlight the thirteenth and fourteenth centuries as a decisive turning point marking the eclipse of Christianity in the Middle East, North Africa and Anatolia, as well as a concomitant surge in conversions to Islam.[53] Into the twelfth and thirteenth centuries, respectable Christian minorities survived in these regions. During the thirteenth and fourteenth centuries and continuing into the fifteenth, however, several historical factors led to outbreaks of anti-Christian violence by Muslim regimes and, sometimes, mobs. Such factors included the above-mentioned Mongol invasions,[54] along with the Crusades (*circa* 1095–1291 CE) in which militant Latin Catholics sought to conquer (or reclaim, as they saw it) parts of Syria, the Levant and Egypt. In the face of such dangers, there seems to have been a general Muslim hardening against Christians and other *dhimmi* minorities. This can be seen in the writings of Ibn Taymiyya (d. 1328 CE), whose life was lived in the shadow of these threats. Adding to these factors the 'Little Ice Age', which began in the twelfth and thirteenth centuries, and the 'Black Death' of the fourteenth century, the stage was set for a perfect storm of hostility towards 'the other' – that is, religious minorities and other marginalised peoples. It is worth pausing here to note that some observers have drawn tentative parallels (and emphasised major differences) between the 'Black Death' of the fourteenth century and the more recent COVID-19 pandemic. Although the focus of most governments, NGOs and religious groups today has been on educating and urging people around the world to follow public health guidance in order to contain the disease (science-based 'public health' was a concept that did not exist in the fourteenth century), as in the fourteenth century the tendency and temptation of some groups to scapegoat 'others' is once again rearing its ugly head (for more on COVID-19, see the Epilogue).[55]

Returning to our narrative, beginning under sultan Baybars (d. 1277 CE) and continuing throughout the fifteenth century, the Mamluk dynasty in Egypt took severe measures against Christians and Jews, including state-directed violence, confiscation of Christian and Jewish property and unusually harsh application of the *dhimmi* regulations of Islamic law.[56] These developments, among others, led to a mass conversion of Coptic Christians to Islam, a change which altered the Egyptian religious landscape forever.[57] Similar measures were employed on and off to comparable effect by Muslim regimes in Mesopotamia and Syria under the recently converted Mongols and their successors, in North Africa by the Almoravids and Almohads, and in Anatolia and beyond by the Seljuqs and Ottomans. Ultimately, these persecutions played a part in speeding up Islamisation. Even so, conversion did not always resolve the tensions faced by minorities, since the genuineness of their conversions could always be questioned.[58] In this way, the situation faced by Christians and others under Islamic rule during these centuries bears similarity to that faced by Jews and Muslims in Catholic post-Reconquista Spain.[59]

Chapter 3 discussed the disadvantages stipulated in Islamic law for *dhimmi*s under Islamic rule as constituting one precondition favouring or incentivising (gradual) conversion to Islam. It is as if, during the thirteenth to fifteenth centuries and beyond, political and economic circumstances caused these stipulations to be applied with a new literalism and ferocity. To give another example, in the late fifteenth century, the legal scholar and member of the Qadiriyya Sufi brotherhood 'Abd al-Karim ibn Muhammad al-Maghili (d. 1505 CE) insisted that the law's *dhimmi* regulations, heretofore applied with apparent laxity by local rulers, should be strictly applied to the Jews of the Tuwat oasis towns of central Algeria. After attracting support from some rulers and scholars, but opposition from others, he stirred up a crowd of Tuwati Muslims which tore down the synagogue in the town of Tamantit and killed several Jews. As a result, 'Many Tuwati Jews evidently fled to other oases, while those who remained behind in Tuwat were obliged to convert to Islam, as also happened to Jews . . . over the centuries'.[60] What is important to stress in this context is not that Islam is inherently violent or that it spreads chiefly through persecution; rather, it is to underscore the complex historical factors – factors which include periodic episodes of persecution against non-Muslims – that have contributed to Islamisation.[61]

Finally, we should not lose sight of the *intra*-Islamic forms that ruler-prompted Islamisation could sometimes take. An important example of a Muslim ruler who engaged in top-down *da'wa* directed to other Muslims was Shah Isma'il I, the founder of the Safavid Empire. As noted earlier, the Safavids, Ottomans and Mughals formed a trio of Islamic empires that dominated much of the Muslim ecumene beginning in the fifteenth and sixteenth centuries (see Map 4.2). Although the Safavid movement began as a Sunni Sufi brotherhood in the fourteenth century (the Safawiyya), Shah Isma'il declared Twelver Shi'ite Islam to be the state religion of the Iranian and Iraqi territories which he and the Safavids had conquered (Isma'il's rule began in 1501 CE). Beginning with Isma'il and continuing through a succession of Safavid rulers, the state vigorously promoted Twelver Shi'ism and embarked on a program 'to eliminate all rival forms of Islam'.[62] This Safavid *da'wa* included the import of Shi'ite *'ulama* to replace Sunni *'ulama* and the founding of a state bureaucracy to oversee religion. The chief official of this bureaucracy, the *sadr*, was responsible for forcefully directing the country towards Shi'ite Islam. Mosques were placed under government control, and the cursing of the first three caliphs (revered by Sunnis) was enforced. Shrines to Sunni saints were suppressed, while shrines to Shi'ite heroes were made the focus of popular devotion. As for the consequences of all this, the Safavid era not only led to the 'Shi'ite-isation' of Persia, it also reinforced the Sunni identity of their main rivals, the Ottomans, and led to the hardening of the sectarian (or Sunni-Shi'ite) boundaries of the Middle East. To this day, the former Ottoman lands remain predominantly Sunni, whereas the former Safavid lands remain predominantly Shi'ite.

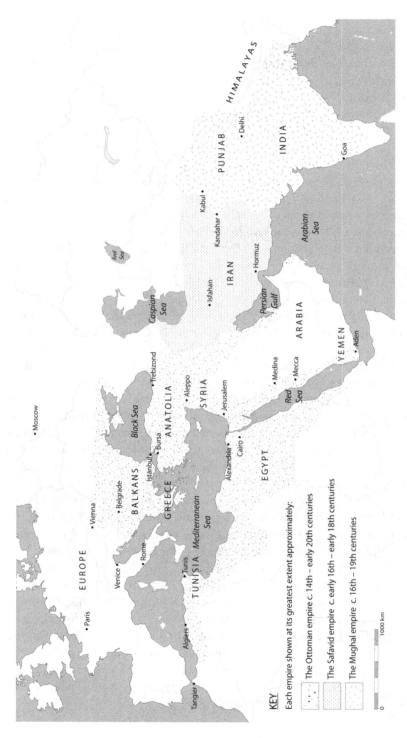

Map 4.2 The Islamic gunpowder empires. This trio of great empires (the last of their kind in Islamic history) dominated the Islamic world from the fifteenth and sixteenth centuries to the dawn of modernity and beyond. That Sunni Islam was the official religion of the Ottomans and Twelver Shi'ite Islam the official religion of the Safavids helped determine the sectarian make-up of today's Middle East.

The *'ulama*: Islamisation through knowledge preservation and transmission

From early on in Islamic history, Islam's scholarly class, the *'ulama* (plural of *ᶜālim*, one who knows), has been indispensable to the formation, preservation and dissemination of Islam. Muslim scholars of Qur'an, hadith, law, theology and Arabic grammar played significant roles in defining and advocating for Islam both within and beyond *dar al-Islam*.[63] In the early decades after the Prophet's death, the caliphs were thought to combine political and religious leadership in one person. During and after the conquests, however, a gradual separation of roles between political and would-be religious leaders took effect.[64] This separation was confirmed after the short-lived *miḥna* (or inquisition) of the 'Abbasid ruler al-Ma'mun (r. 813–33 CE).[65] From that point on, by whatever title he was called (caliph, sultan, amir and the like), the Muslim ruler was left with a more limited portfolio – such as responsibility for statecraft and warfare – while the *'ulama* took up responsibility for the religious leadership of Muslim communities.[66] Although we are treating the *'ulama* and Sufis (two categories of Muslim religious leaders) separately in this chapter, it should be kept in mind that for much of pre-modern Islamic history 'Sufis and *'ulama* were frequently the same persons'.[67]

The *'ulama* were generally urban men whose religious authority derived primarily from their *'ilm* (knowledge) of Islamic texts and practices. Since Islam was destined to become a textual and literary tradition, at least in its 'high' forms, education in Islamic literature, lore and law has always been a highly regarded activity. Those who mastered and transmitted this knowledge, in turn, 'constituted perhaps the most important . . . group in most traditional Islamic societies'.[68] Indeed, not only have we already observed several instances in which Muslim scholars played important roles in the conversion of key rulers, we should also remember that our ability to study the Qur'an, hadith and *sira* (see Chapters 1 and 2), as well as Islamic law and theology would not be possible in the first place without the labours of the *'ulama*. In addition, in the midst of the political fluidity of the Muslim ecumene after the 900s, the *'ulama* proved to be a resilient, stabilising force. The *'ulama* helped create 'an enormous common pool of knowledge' that was shared across the Muslim ecumene.[69] The relationship between the *'ulama* and the plethora of Muslim governments that ruled the Muslim world between the eleventh and eighteenth centuries cannot be captured in a soundbite. Nevertheless, it is worth pointing out that, while the *'ulama* in some periods and places kept aloof from politics or played the role of government critics, others maintained close ties to Muslim dynasties. In some cases, *'ulama* filled official positions as legal advisors, judges in Islamic courts and so on. Either way, there is evidence that, in general, *'ulama* tried to maintain some critical distance from the various Muslim states under which they lived.[70]

As insiders or outsiders to the state, the *'ulama* – Sunni and Shi'ite – have contributed to external and internal *da'wa* throughout Islamic history. Whether through writing legal manuals (as *faqīhs*), giving *fatwas* (as *muftīs*), leading prayers and preaching in the mosque (as *imāms* or *khāṭibs*), engaging in intra- and inter-religious debate, advising Muslim rulers, serving as judges (as *qāḍīs*), memorising or commenting on the Qur'an (as *ḥāfizs* or *mufassirs*), preserving and teaching hadith (as *muḥaddiths*), or providing spiritual direction (as Sufis), the *'ulama* are responsible for much of what we customarily recognise as Islam. Particularly in their capacity as legal guides and preachers, the *'ulama* have been on the frontlines of fulfilling the twin qur'anic duties of calling the world to God and Islam (*da'wa*) and commanding the right and forbidding the wrong (*al-amr bi'l-ma'rūf*). For this reason, I think it is appropriate to speak of '*'ulama da'wa*' as a phenomenon that is comparable with 'Sufi *da'wa*' (the subject of the next section). 'For the *'ulama*, it was the active process of transmitting knowledge that was critical'.[71] As to how they transmitted knowledge among themselves or to the next generation, the *'ulama* have followed a pattern that has been called the '*isnād* paradigm'. Based on the chains of transmitters found in hadith reports, this refers to the idea that '*ilm* should be passed on from teacher to disciple in genealogical lines traced back to the Prophet.[72] A student's authorisation to speak for Islam was validated through certificates or *ijāzas* stating that a student had studied under a recognised authority within a recognised lineage. In many cases, earning an *ijāza* involved going on *riḥla*, a journey undertaken to study under a leading scholar.[73] Through their participation in such lineages and through their extensive travels, Muslim scholars forged links and shared their ideas and practices widely, thus contributing significantly to a sense of coherence across the Muslim ecumene.[74] Muslim rulers and dynasties might come and go, but the *'ulama*, a trans-regional guild which represented an Islam of timeless texts and universal norms, was not going to be suddenly overthrown.

Another important means by which the *'ulama* have preserved and repro-duced '*ilm* has been through one of Islam's most distinctive institutions, the *madrasa* (religious school or seminary). The *madrasa* had its origins in Khurasan in the tenth century, and by the eleventh century it had become a fixture throughout much of the Muslim east.[75] Through *madrasas*, the *'ulama* were able to pass on their knowledge and develop cadres of men who would be authorised to teach others. In other words, the transmission of '*ilm* through education and mentorship has always been among the central roles of the *'ulama*. Although, in comparison to the titles listed above (*muftī*, *faqīh*, *qāḍī* and the like), the title 'missionary' (*da'ī*) has been uncommon for members of the *'ulama*, one can still relate the educational goals of the *'ulama* to mission-ary preaching, particularly to internal *da'wa*: 'Winning over new followers presuppose[s] the formation of a system of transfer of religious knowledge. To a large extent, Islamic education has therefore been synonymous with preaching. Converting the world to "true religion" was inseparable from educating others in the way of Islam'.[76]

Having said all this, it is difficult to discern the extent to which the *'ulama*'s knowledge trickled down to ordinary Muslims in pre-modern times. We do know that in all regions of the Muslim ecumene up to the nineteenth century, a minority of the population would have been literate, 'with men being far more likely to be literate than women and town-dwellers than agrarian or pastoral peoples'.[77] We also know that the knowledge of the *'ulama*, usually transmitted in the Arabic language – which in many places was not the native language of the population – 'served as the cultural capital of the self-replicating clerical families'.[78] In other words, even though there existed some opportunity for social advancement through joining circles of *'ulama*, in fact, access to those circles was limited. In addition, the Muslim world's printing and translation revolutions, which would begin the process of making the Islamic scriptures available to common people, would not get underway until the early nineteenth century. It is safe to say, in general, that ordinary Muslims had limited access to *'ilm* and that the *'ulama* were less concerned about ordinary Muslims than they would prove to be in modern times. If this was true for ordinary Muslims in general, it was particularly so for women. Despite the roles played by noteworthy women (such as Muhammad's wife 'Aisha) in transmitting hadith, and although there is evidence that some women achieved the status of scholar-teachers in medieval times, for the most part, the exceptions prove the rule: Women were mostly excluded from formal education in *madrasas* and from the male-dominated ranks of the *'ulama*.[79] Chapters 5 through 7 will speak of the *'ulama*'s 'turn to the masses' (including women) in modernity, and several consequences of this. If, then, we want to find the agents of *da'wa* and Islamisation perhaps most responsible for diffusing Islam among ordinary people in pre-modern times, we should turn our attention to Sufis and popular preachers.

4.1 The spread of Islam according to the *Kano Chronicle*

'Ulama travelled to gain knowledge or perform the *hajj*; yet, there are also some records of medieval missionary journeys undertaken by *'ulama*. In such narratives, there is often overlap with the roles of Muslim rulers in Islamisation (see above), as well as with the roles of Sufis and merchants (see below). All of this can be seen in the *Kano Chronicle*, a collection of stories written in Arabic about the medieval rulers (*sarki*s) of the Hausa people of Kano, part of today's northern Nigeria. The account (in its present form dating from the late 1800s) includes several tales of *da'wa* and conversion involving *'ulama* or *'ulama-Sufis*. In the first excerpt, we learn that in the days of the Hausa chief Yaji (*circa* 1349–85 CE) 'the

Wongarawa', identified by scholars as a merchant people from already Islamised Mali, arrived in Kano under the leadership of one Abdurahaman Zaite, a Muslim scholar/trader. With Yaji's blessing, Islamic rituals were introduced and a mosque was built by these merchant-missionaries:

The eleventh Sarki was Yaji, called Ali. His mother was Maganarku. In Yajis's time the Wongarawa came from Melle [Mali], bringing the Muhammadan religion. The name of their leader was Abdurahaman Zaite . . . When they came they commanded the Sarki to observe the [Islamic] times of prayer. He complied . . . The Sarki commanded every town in Kano country to observe the times of prayer. So they all did so. A mosque was built beneath the sacred tree facing east, and prayers were made at the five appointed times in it.

In a second excerpt, set in the days of the Hausa chief Rimfa (or Rumfa), we read of the arrival of a Muslim named 'Abdu Rahaman' or 'Abdu Karimi', whom scholars identify as 'Abd al-Karim ibn Muhammad al-Maghili (d. 1505 CE). Al-Maghili is also identified in the *Chronicle* as a 'Sherif'. After the incident with the Jews in Tuwat (discussed earlier in this chapter), al-Maghili traveled into Sudanic Africa, where he is depicted introducing or shoring up Islamic beliefs and practices in Kano with the cooperation of Rimfa. He is also depicted as fulfilling an old prophecy (mentioned in the *Chronicle*) about a visitor who would cut down Kano's sacred tree. According to Hiskett, in Hausaland, 'all things Islamic are said to go back to al-Maghili'.

The twentieth Sarki was Mohamma, son of Yakubu, commonly called Rimfa [Rumfa] . . . In his time the Sherifs came to Kano. They were Abdu Rahaman and his people. There is a story that the Prophet appeared to Abdu Rahaman in a dream and said to him, 'Get up and go west and establish Islam'. Abdu Rahaman got up and took a handful of the soil of Medina, and put it in a cloth, and brought it to Hausaland. Whenever he came to a town, he took a handful of the soil of the country and put it beside that of Medina. If they did not correspond he passed that town. So he journeyed until he came to Kano. And when he compared the soil of Kano with Medina soil they resembled one another . . . So he said, 'This is the country that I saw in in my dream' . . . The Sarki [of] Kano Rimfa went out . . . and escorted Abdu Rahaman back to the city . . . Abdu Rahaman lived in Kano and established Islam. He brought with him many books. He ordered Rimfa to build a mosque for Friday, and to cut down the sacred tree and build a minaret on the site. And when he had established the Faith of Islam, and learned men had grown numerous in Kano, and all the country round had accepted the Faith, Abdu Karirmi returned to Massar, leaving Sidi Fari as his deputy to carry on his work (Source: Palmer 1908. Background: Hunwick 1985, ch. 2; Hunwick 1960–2007, pp. 1165–6; Hiskett 1960–2007; Gilliand 1979; Smith 1983).

The Sufi brotherhoods: Islamisation through inspiration and indigenisation

'Sufism' refers to devotional or mystical pathways within Islam, as well as to the orders or brotherhoods which developed them. As Christian mysticism and institutionalised monasticism are overlapping but not synonymous, so with Islamic mysticism and the Sufi orders. When thinking of Sufism, the image of the lone Muslim mystic or wandering dervish must be held together with institutionalised Sufism, and even with a land-owning, politically-connected Sufism.[80] In general, Sufi pathways combine the beliefs and practices of ordinary (exoteric) Islam with special (esoteric) teachings passed down through lineages (*silsilas*) of teachers and disciples. Central to Sufi thought and discipline is the idea that each Muslim must train his or her innermost self (*nafs*) towards God-consciousness. Practices like *dhikr* (remembrance of the names of God), obedience to one's Sufi master, and perhaps dancing, singing, listening to mystical poetry, celebrating the Prophet's birthday and visiting saints' shrines are among the techniques which aid in this process. As classically understood, therefore, Sufism was thought to supplement or intensify, not replace, the ordinary practices of Islam, such as the 'Five Pillars'.[81] Sufi masters or saints, known as the 'friends of God' (*awliyāʾ Allah*), taught that there were the stages (*maqāmāt*) on the Sufi path, and they developed reputations for making progress through these stages. Sufi masters and saints – both living and dead – have also sometimes been viewed as mediators between humans and God, and they have been understood to have special powers, such as the ability to perform miracles and defend against evil spirits. The saints' lodges or convents (Persian: *khānqāh*s; Arabic: *ribāṭ* or *zāwiyya*), along with their tombs, became places not only of Islamic learning (an instance of overlap between Sufis and *ʿulama*), but also of power and pilgrimage.

This is not the place to delve deeply into the rich history of Sufism.[82] Suffice it to say that for the Sufis themselves, the origins of Sufism go back to Muhammad himself. Muhammad is depicted in the hadith and *sira* literature, after all, not only as a prophet or preacher of God's *daʿwa*, but also as a devotional master upon whom God bestowed numinous experiences and supernatural powers. In this view of things, the Qurʾan itself is the result and proof of Muhammad's nearness to God, not to mention a treasury of mystical teachings. Like the *ʿulama*, the Sufi orders have usually traced their lineages back to the Prophet (often via ʿAli), and over the centuries the Sufis regarded themselves (and came to be regarded by others) as legitimate heirs of the Prophet's charisma. In contrast to the Sufis' internal perspective, one might also locate the origins of Sufism in the post-conquest encounter between emergent Islam and the late antique Middle Eastern context. In this milieu, Neoplatonic, Jewish and especially Christian forms of monasticism and devotionalism were already well developed, and the resonances between Sufism and these earlier traditions are well-documented.[83]

Whatever account of 'Sufi origins' one leans towards (and the two just mentioned are not mutually exclusive), it is not until the late eighth and early ninth centuries that one can speak of the emergence of 'Sufism' proper. Beginning with these centuries' piety-minded orientations and movements of Islamic asceticism (*zuhd*), Sufism developed gradually and, from the eleventh to fourteenth centuries, came to be regarded as a form of Islamic knowledge and practice comparable to Qur'an and hadith study, law and theology.[84] The great Muslim theologian al-Ghazali (d. 1111 CE) both reacted and contributed to the popularity of Sufism in making it integral to his thought.[85] Along with the emergence of Sufi thought, other major trends of the eleventh to fourteenth centuries were (1) the formation of Sufi orders (*tarīqas*), and (2) the proliferation of Sufi lodges throughout the Muslim ecumene. Some of the best-known orders, often named retrospectively after their founding figures, include the Suhrawardiyya, Rifa'iyya, Qadiriyya, Badawiyya, Kubrawiyya, Yasawiyya, Mawlawiyya, Naqshbandiyya, Chishtiyya and others. As these orders spread out over space and time, they in turn gave rise to new branches and sub-orders.[86] While there are tantalising parallels between the formation of the Sufi orders and the monastic orders of late antique and medieval Christianity, a major difference is that the Sufis did not have to seek formal recognition by a central authority. Their legitimation came through their ability to generate popular followings and, in some cases, to cultivate the patronage of rulers.

While no typology of Sufi 'orientations' can do justice to the complexity and fluidity of Sufism as it has been practised across such vast geography, scholars of Sufism, adapting distinctions made by Sufi themselves,[87] often differentiate between a sober 'Shari'a-Sufism', on one hand, and an intoxicated 'Visionary Sufism', on the other. The former combines commitment to the ordinary injunctions of Islam with an embrace, in moderation, of Sufi practices such as *dhikr*. The latter emphasises a direct encounter with God through mystical knowledge (gnosis) and practices such as dance and singing – all things that *shari'a*-Sufis might consider dangerous.[88] Another important variation has been called 'Shrine-Sufism', a kind of Islamic popular religion focused on the veneration of Muslim saints and visits to their tomb-shrines.[89] What Peter Brown writes of the cult of saints and martyrs in late antique and medieval Christianity could just as well have been written of its counterpart in medieval Islam: 'The graves of the saints . . . were privileged places . . . [T]he saint in Heaven was believed to be 'present' at his tomb on earth . . . [The saints'] intimacy with God was the *sine qua non* of their ability to intercede for . . . fellow mortals. The martyr was the "friend of God" '.[90]

Taking all this together, the key point for our purposes is that 'from the thirteenth to eighteenth centuries . . . Sufism *in all its forms* became the most widespread and popular form of Islam'.[91] Traveling across the Muslim ecumene, one would have increasingly observed a world that was 'Muslim' largely because it was 'Sufi'.[92] It was one thing for Muslim conquerors to establish Islamic rule over far-flung territories, but quite another for the peoples of those territories to begin to think of themselves as 'Muslim' in any meaningful sense. Owing to their roles in expanding *dar al-Islam* and in facilitating the identification of the masses with Islam, it is reasonable to conclude that the Sufis were the preeminent agents of *da'wa* and Islamisation, particularly at the grassroots level, in medieval and early modern history.

How, then, did Sufis contribute to Islamisation, or what was the nature of 'Sufi *da'wa*?[93] We will sketch the beginnings of an answer to this question from two perspectives: (1) an insider perspective (that of Muslim memory and hagiography,) and (2) an outsider (scholarly) perspective. First, there are countless examples in the collective memory of Muslim communities of Sufi preachers who set out on successful missions to convert non-Muslims (as well as to instruct and revive Muslims). Along with classical Sufi manuals and theological works, one of our most important sources for understanding the Sufis of the past – or at least how they have been remembered – are hagiographies (sacred legends) about the 'Friends of God'. One scholar speaks of the 'immense wealth of this vast tradition and the host of characters it enshrines'.[94] An important theme in this literature is constituted by stories in which Sufi saints are depicted doing *da'wa* and spearheading Islamisation.[95] In one indication of the ongoing salience of these stories, throughout parts of the Muslim world still today, if one asks local people about the saints to whom many old, sometimes crumbling, tomb-shrines are dedicated, one will often be told, 'He brought Islam here'.[96]

It is true that one must take these stories with a grain of salt. Modern understandings of the word 'missionary' should not be imposed on pre-modern Sufis, and one should be sensitive to the agendas lurking behind the hagiographies.[97] Yet, regardless of whether or not we can uncover 'what actually happened', it is striking just how prominent the theme of Sufis-as-missionaries is. Furthermore, the ways Muslims have remembered Islamisation constitute an important aspect of Islamic missionary history in its own right. Perhaps we can see this more clearly if we consider a few examples from other missionary religions: Whether or not King Ashoka actually sent Buddhist missionaries to Sri Lanka in the third century BCE, or whether or not St Patrick actually won the 'Irish' to Christianity in fifth-century CE Ireland, later Buddhists and later Christians would cherish stories like these as integral to their faiths' missionary heritages. So, too, Sufis have been remembered as significant players in the spread of Islam, and even as primogenitors of entire peoples.[98]

Because of the vast number of Sufis remembered as successful *da'is*, only a few will be mentioned here. We might begin with Ibrahim al-Kazaruni (d. 1033 CE, founder and namesake of the Kazaruniyya order, also called the Ishaqiyya and Murshidiyya). In sources such as Farid al-Din Attar's *Tadhkirat al-Awliya* (Biographies of the Friends), he is reported to have converted thousands

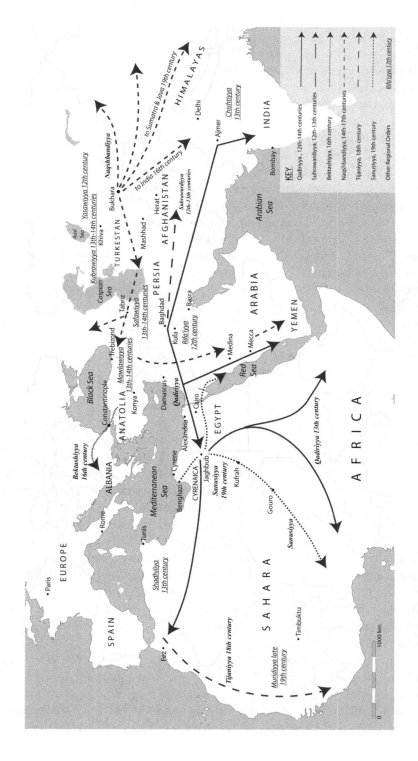

Map 4.3 The origins and spread of some major Sufi orders. Travelling across the Muslim ecumene from the thirteenth to the eighteenth centuries, one would have observed a world that was 'Muslim' largely because it was 'Sufi'.

of Zoroastrians and Jews in western Persia in the late tenth and early eleventh centuries and to have initiated the establishment of numerous mosques and *khānqāhs* (hereafter *khanqah*).[99] Another is 'Abd al-Qadir Jilani (d. 1166 CE, founder and namesake of the Qadiririyya order), 'probably the most popular saint in the Muslim world'.[100] Around the age of fifty, this Hanbali scholar and ascetic had vivid dreams which were interpreted to mean that Jilani was called by God to preach in public. His resulting 'sermons were said to have powerfully affected persons at all levels of twelfth-century Iraqi society. Not only Muslims but also Jews and Christians . . . allegedly altered their lives in response' to his preaching.[101] His *madrasa-khanqah* became a centre from which 'Abd al-Qadir trained others, and in subsequent centuries, followers of the Qadiriyya spread Islam to many new places.[102] Another example is a contemporary of 'Abd al-Qadir, Shaykh Ahmad Yasawi (d. 1166 CE, founder and namesake of the Yasawiyya), who is sometimes said to have spread Islam, through preaching and miracles, among the Turkic peoples of Central Asia.[103] From the fourteenth century, we learn of Shaykh Sayyid 'Ali Hamadani (1314–85 CE), who would later be considered a master of the Kubrawiyya order. In the midst of his travels throughout Asia, he is said to have visited Kashmir, according to some accounts, in response to dreams in which he was called to be a missionary to the region. He is still remembered as the decisive Islamiser of Kashmir.[104] Looking to the south of Kashmir, Sufis from several orders are remembered as successful missionaries, for instance, Abu'l-Hasan 'Ali Hujwiri (d. *circa* 1070s),[105] who is believed to have spread Islam in the region around Lahore. His shrine in that city, the Data Darbar, remains very popular to this day. Also noteworthy is Mu'inuddin Chishti (d. 1236; founder of the Chishtiyya brotherhood in India), who is believed to have been a successful missionary of Islam in his day, and whose tomb-shrine at Ajmer (in today's Rajasthan state of India) still welcomes hundreds of thousands of pilgrims every year (see Figure 4.2). In India and Pakistan, the many Sufi shrines which dot the landscape are often remembered for *da'wa* and Islamisation.

Turning to Anatolia, in a hagiography known as the *Vilayetname* (or *Wilayetname*) many *da'wa* exploits are attributed to Haji Bektash Wali (d. 1271, namesake of the Bektashiyya order). In turn, the Bektashi brotherhood would come to be known for its indigenisation of and consequent success in spreading Islam, particularly in Anatolia and southern Europe.[106] Also in medieval Anatolia, the great Sufi master and poet Rumi (d. 1273 CE), the founding figure of the Mawlawiyya (or Mevleviyya) brotherhood, is depicted in the fourteenth-century hagiography of Aflaki (d. 1360 CE) as a successful missionary among Jews and Christians in south-central Anatolia.[107] Along with numerous anecdotes of Rumi converting individuals,[108] Aflaki reports that 'from the time of Rumi's appearance until the day of his death, eighteen thousand infidels found the faith [of Islam] and became disciples'.[109] Looking to Southeast Asia, Muslims there cherish

Figure 4.2 Contemporary pilgrims at the Shrine (*dargah*) of Mu'inuddin Chishti (d. 1236) in Ajmer, India. Photo: Matthew J. Kuiper.

memories of the legendary Wali Songo, or 'Nine Saints'. The Wali Songo, about whom numerous legends are told, are credited with spreading Islam on the island of Java in the fifteenth century. Today, the tomb-shrines of the Wali Songo remain popular pilgrimage sites.[110] Examples could be multiplied.[111] In sum, in written hagiographies and in the memory of Muslims worldwide, Sufis are remembered as integral to the missionary spread of Islam from the eleventh to eighteenth centuries.

Turning to our second, more academic perspective, we have already mentioned the resonances between early forms of Sufism and varieties of late antique Judaism, Neoplatonism and especially Christianity.[112] In Chapter 3 we analysed several factors that fostered gradual non-Muslim conversion to Islam in the post-conquest situation. Now it is time to highlight another: the Sufis' ability to introduce Islam to new peoples gradually, in part through their apparent genius for 'indigenising' or 'localising' Islam. This was true initially in the Middle East, but as Sufi Islam spread into Sub-Saharan Africa, India, Southeast Asia and elsewhere, resonances between Sufism and so-called tribal religions, Hinduism and Buddhism would also prove to be factors in the Sufis' popularity in these contexts. Whether as part of intentional missionary strategies or not, many Sufis exhibited a pragmatic willingness to adapt to local customs. Sufis, in fact, often spearheaded processes of linguistic indigenisation (or 'vernacularisation'). According to Green, 'by the 1400s the Sufis were vernacularizing their teachings [into Persian, Indic, Turkic and Malay languages] to an extraordinary degree'.[113]

Rumi serves as an example. He is quoted as saying that he introduced (Sufi) Islam to the natives of Anatolia in a gradualist fashion, likening himself to a skilful doctor who uses a sweetener to help a child take her medicine. He taught non-Muslim Anatolians 'in a way that suited them', using music and dance to draw them to God.[114] In this context, Green points out how Rumi (as seen in his famous poem, the *Mathnawi*) and other Sufi poets adopted the genre of the Persian narrative poem as a means for spreading Islamic ideas to the masses. Laced with 'the folklore, idioms and humour of the people', but also with qur'anic verses, hadith and Islamic stories, narrative poems like Rumi's served a double function. Since they could be recited in markets and village squares as forms of popular entertainment, such poems (and other forms of popular preaching or storytelling) gave the Sufis access to the masses in a way that that legal and doctrinal writings and sermons of the *'ulama* could not. At the same time, they served as vehicles for subtly instructing the people and increasing their identification with Islam.[115] Taking a somewhat more whimsical example, it has been suggested that the 'sawing' *dhikr* associated with Central Asian brotherhoods – so named because of the heavy sounds made in the throat – was perhaps 'the Yasawiyya answer to the ecstatic shamanistic dances' of pre-Islamic Turkic or Mongol religion.[116] Indeed, there are records of 'wilder, charismatic [Sufis] more likely to be seen wearing the skins and horns of animals than the plain cloak and turban of the scholar' – figures whose 'shamanised Islam' was suitable for the peoples of Inner and Central Asia in their earliest encounters with Islam.[117] Returning to the Bektashi brotherhood: As 'energetic missionaries' with a seeming willingness to accommodate Islam to pre-Islamic beliefs and practices,[118] Bektashis are thought to have facilitated the conversion of both pagans and Christians to Islam, particularly in Ottoman Anatolia, Albania and the Balkans.[119] Bektashis also accompanied the Ottoman military into the Balkans; perhaps not surprisingly, their blended version of Islam became popular among the Janissaries – the elite military slaves who came from Christian backgrounds.[120] In Africa and India, some Sufis took on roles as traditional healers or purveyors of Islamic charms and amulets. Whether their efforts at indigenisation were intentional or not, the Sufis' Islam often appealed to local tastes.[121]

For ordinary people from West Africa to Southeast Asia, in other words, Sufism, and especially the ubiquitous Sufi shrines, often served as first ports of entry into the Islamic tradition.[122] An important consequence of the Sufis' indigenising activities was that, by 1600, the Sufi tradition, and thus Islam itself, had significantly diversified: 'Different Sufis did different things, sometimes spectacularly so, and this range of doctrine and practice begged the question as to whether all of them could possibly be the true tradition of the Prophet'.[123] In turn, as we will see later, in the seventeenth and eighteenth centuries numerous reform movements arose in the Muslim world, some from within Sufism and some from without; they began to criticise Sufi ideas and practices which, from the reformers' perspectives, seemed out of tune with 'true' Islam.

Not only did the Sufis indigenise or vernacularise Islam, thus fostering diversity, they also served as 'agents of inter-connection between Muslims', thus fostering 'recognizability'.[124] One way in which they did this was by making Islam tangible for those who could not travel to Arabia or imagine the world of the Prophet. In the medieval world,

> . . . mass illiteracy meant that knowledge was sought through persons rather than books . . . In embodying the charisma and teachings of Muhammad . . . and in providing shrines . . . which were infinitely closer than Mecca, the local representatives of the Sufi brotherhoods were able to bridge the distance of time, space and culture that separated the Muslims of the middle ages from the distant age and homeland of the Prophet.[125]

Thus, even as they adapted Islam to new contexts, the brotherhoods also helped local Muslims feel that they were part of the macro-phenomenon of Islam. This last point makes it clear that our focus on the indigenising 'genius' of Sufism should not be taken to imply a simplistic binary between a culture-assimilating Islam (represented by visionary Sufis) and a culture-imposing or exclusivist Islam (represented by *shari'a*-minded Sufis or the *'ulama*). Sufis in general were orthodox Muslims. As such, they should not be anachronistically thought of as liberal proponents of benign inter-faith relations. Even Rumi, so often imagined today as an all-roads-lead-to-God inclusivist, 'was first and foremost a Muslim who viewed Islam as the perfect religion' and who sometimes had disparaging things to say about other religions.[126] Although the notion of a peaceful, spiritual *jihad* (the 'greater *jihad*') is often associated with Sufism, members of Sufi brotherhoods generally believed that non-Muslims were infidels and, as a result, many Sufis fought in military *jihad*s (the 'lesser jihad').[127]

Furthermore, although there have always been some Sufi orders – such as the early Naqshbandiyya – which maintained aloofness from Muslim rulers and states, others – such as the Chishtiyya in India – availed themselves of government patronage and even served as government agents. In several telling cases – for instance, on the Mughal frontier of Bengal, the Ottoman Balkans and areas of Sub-Saharan Africa – Sufis were granted land and/or financial endowments in exchange for their efforts to extend the state's reach into these places. By building mosques, shrines and caravanserais, by transforming jungle into farmland, or by serving as middlemen in the 'global trade in gold, spice and slaves', Sufis helped create territorial 'outposts of Islamic civilization'. As with the Arab-Islamic conquests, the Sufis' 'conversion of places' into Islamic ambiences would lead to the gradual 'conversion of peoples'.[128] In short, like

Christian missionaries in nineteenth-century Africa, whose mission stations sometimes served the interests of the colonial powers, some Sufis (and *'ulama* and merchants) were missionary 'frontiersmen',[129] who both spread Islam and served the interests of Muslim states.

It is worth emphasising again the importance of Sufi lodges (*khanqahs*) in this story. Not entirely unlike Christian monasteries in medieval Europe, Buddhist monasteries along the Silk Road, or Christian mission stations in later times,[130] Sufi *khanqahs* served as centres of both internal and external *da'wa*.[131] As we have seen, Sufi convents and shrines were launching points for centrifugal mission, but insofar as they housed local Muslim 'communities of grace', they also drew people to Islam centripetally.[132] Indeed, it is important to note that *khanqahs*, and Sufism in general, contributed to the spread of Islam by and among women. Not only do the ranks of pre-modern Sufis include some noteworthy women, such as Rabi'a al-'Adawiyya (d. 801 CE) or the women Sufis mentioned in Attar's *Tadhkirat al-Awliya*, unlike many mosques and *madrasas* in pre-modern times, Sufi shrines were religious spaces that were welcoming of women.[133] In light of all this, one would think that *da'wa*-minded Muslims today would universally line up to celebrate the Sufis' missionary heritage. Yet, ironically, this has not been the case. Since the eighteenth century (and in some cases going as far back as the late sixteenth), many Muslims have been galvanised for *da'wa*, in part, by a shared critique of Sufism. Yet, as we will also see, Sufism itself continues to be a major player in *da'wa* today.

Popular preachers and storytellers: Islamisation through popularisation

The Sufis were not alone in spreading Islam to ordinary people. In many pre-modern Islamic societies, there were also popular Muslim preachers (*wuᶜᶜāẓ*) and storytellers (*quṣṣāṣ*) who took it upon themselves to transmit basic religious knowledge to and sometimes simply entertain common people. These figures, who could be self-taught, stood in contrast to the men who preached the sermon in the mosque or who taught in the *madrasa* or *khanqah*. Two factors seem to have fed into the proliferation of popular, non-authorised preachers and storytellers in Islam. First, with its urgent eschatology, demand for ethical self-improvement and stock of entertaining and edifying stories, Islam is a 'preacher's religion' *par excellence*. Listening to preaching – preaching infused with moralistic stories about Muhammad and his Companions, great scholars and/or miracle-working Sufis – has been a major feature of the historical experience of Muslims in most times and places. Second, while the *'ulama* and members of the Sufi brotherhoods held the keys to religious knowledge, their power was never absolute. More like Protestant than Catholic Christianity, Sunni Islam lacks a hierarchy of religious officials to determine correct belief and practice. In other words, the informal nature of Islamic (particularly Sunni) religious leadership has always created spaces for alternative purveyors of *'ilm* and *da'wa*. If they lacked the credentials of the *'ulama* or Sufis, the popular preachers and storytellers could at least point to their popularity to justify their claim to speak for Islam. As with many Sufis, moreover, they could always claim to have been called to preach through a dream or vision.[134]

Popular preachers and storytellers, however, also engendered controversy. Indeed, we know about these figures not from their own records, but almost exclusively from the polemics inveighed against them by medieval and early modern *'ulama*. Having examined the writings of several major critics (including Ibn Taymiyya) of popular preachers, Berkey comments that 'the polemic over preachers and storytellers was ultimately a question of knowledge. The [storytellers and preachers] served the role *of transmitting basic religious knowledge and instruction to the common people*; the controversy that their activities engendered was in the final analysis about how the common people were to understand Islam'.[135] Not only were popular preachers and storytellers accused of promoting questionable practices such as seeking the intercession of saints, or of blurring the lines between Islam and other religions (they would sometimes mix in Christian or Jewish legends or other folk tales), critics were also scandalised that the ranks of popular preachers even included women, 'who would recite hadith and religious tales and expound upon them to groups of women, or even to mixed groups of men and women'. As one medieval Muslim scholar asked, how could women, who are 'crooked, root and branch', be trusted to pass on reliable knowledge?[136] For our purposes, although we know sadly too little about the roles women played in the spread of Islam in pre-modern times, it is noteworthy that there were at least some who spoke publicly for Islam. In any event, we should remember that, while the focus of this book has been on public manifestations of Islamic mission, *da'wa* also takes place in the domestic realm, and it is in this 'popular' or 'private' realm of the family and the home that pre-modern women had perhaps their greatest impact in spreading Islam.[137]

With respect to *da'wa*, whatever their gender and in whatever realm they operated, popular preachers and storytellers spread Islamic knowledge – although their critics maintained that it was faulty knowledge – by popularising it for common people. In doing so, they directly and indirectly increased people's identification with Islam. The rationale for including this (brief) discussion of popular preachers and storytellers in medieval and early modern Islam ultimately lies in the modern period. Recent decades have witnessed a dramatic increase in the number of ordinary Muslims acting as preachers and spokespersons for Islam, as well as a resurgence of the debate about who may speak for Islam. Many of today's new spokespersons lack *madrasa* training. Like pre-modern Sufis and popular preachers, their claim to legitimacy may come through the popular followings they generate (online and in other spaces), as well as from their ability to communicate Islam to ordinary people in effective ways. Despite their popularity, they thus attract criticism from other Muslims, *'ulama* in particular. As we will see in Part II of this book, many of these popular spokespersons – television preachers, tract and pamphlet writers and developers of Islamic websites – act in the name of *da'wa*.

Merchants: Islamisation through networking and trade

Muslim merchants were also important to the spread of Islam in the centuries covered by this chapter and, in fact, from the beginnings of Islam. Muhammad and several of the Companions are portrayed in the sources as having been merchants, and many *'ulama* and Sufis combined the roles of men of religion and men of business (Arabic: *tijāra*). One might say, in fact, that Islam is a religion particularly well-suited to the inclinations of traders, even as it seeks to curtail greed, dishonesty and injustice among the merchant class.[138] 'In Islam, migration to the town is considered meritorious because it is in the urban milieu that one can fully practise the Islamic way of life'.[139] As we saw in Chapter 2, Muhammad is depicted as encouraging the settlement of nomads as an aspect of his *da'wa*, a practice followed by the early caliphs. From the perspective of a Muslim merchant, not only is the town or city the ideal place to practise Islam, it is also an ideal place to conduct business. Cities, like commerce, run on predictability and stability, and they bring different kinds of people into close proximity with each other.

Like cities, regions can also be united into coordinated trade zones. It should be remembered that the lands conquered in the Arab-Islamic conquests – North Africa, the Middle East and Central Asia – had served as trading centres and crossroads from before the Common Era.[140] Despite interruptions (such as the Mongol conquests), from medieval to early modern times, Muslims played major roles in (and often controlled) the lucrative trade which passed through these regions. For many Muslim states, maintaining the flow of trade was a key objective, so much so that they built or widened roads, dug wells and constructed caravanserais at regular intervals, and even went to war when trade was threatened.[141] Needless to say, within the Muslim ecumene, trade was facilitated by shared Islamic commitments and symbols, the very things rulers, *'ulama*, Sufis and popular preachers were spreading during these centuries. It certainly helped that in many places Arabic, and in other places Persian served as *lingua francas* (as pointed out before, Arabisation and Persianisation often coincided with or followed from Islamisation). Since Muslim merchants often preferred doing business with fellow Muslims, there are cases in which non-Muslims are reported to have converted to Islam in order to improve their business prospects.[142] In short, not unlike the Pax Romana in an earlier time, a restless Pax Islamica facilitated trade across the Muslim ecumene.

Among the commodities traded in Muslim lands were slaves (see above), horses, salt, textiles, spices, timber and foodstuffs, often in exchange for precious metals.[143] The demands of trade sometimes led to compromises towards non-Muslims. As much as they might be objects of conquest, conversion, or co-existence, non-Muslims – for instance, the merchants of medieval Italy – could also be valued partners in trade. In this way, as it does today, trade created inter-religious contacts and encounters. Trade also rendered the distinction between *dar al-Islam* and *dar al-harb* murky at times. In part because of trade, Muslims formed alliances with non-Muslims and created spaces within Islamic cities for non-Muslim businesspeople (although such visitors were sometimes confined to separate enclaves and forbidden from proselytising). Overall, trade was a vibrant aspect of life in the Muslim ecumene in medieval and early modern times. While the conventional narrative suggests that Muslim trade precipitously declined once Portugal and Spain 'took to sea' in the fifteenth and sixteenth centuries, in fact, lively trade continued in the Muslim world until modern times.[144] The riches generated by conquest and trade – one can think of the fabulously rich Muslim ruler of Mali, Mansa Musa (d. 1337 CE) – and the civilisational achievements in art, architecture and Islamic scholarship which flowed from this wealth, helped enrich Islamic societies and increase that much more the attractiveness of Islam to potential converts. We might reasonably speak, therefore, of a centripetal attraction to Islam and *dar al-Islam* which was fostered, in part, by trade.

Traders, however, can also be driven by centrifugal impulses to leave stable environments and seek opportunity in new places.[145] We alluded earlier to a Muslim 'diaspora' consisting of the Arab soldiers and nomads who left their homelands to seek fame and fortune in the Arab-Islamic conquests. In due course, this diaspora settled down and in numerous ways contributed to the spread of Islam. We also looked at the peregrinations of *'ulama* and Sufis. Historically, another kind of Muslim diaspora has been generated by trade, and this 'merchant diaspora' has also played important roles in introducing Islam to new places: 'If nomads carried the burden of the militant expansion of Islam, traders served as vehicles for the propagation of Islam beyond the boundaries of the military expansion'.[146] A common pattern saw Muslim traders arrive on the coastlands of territories where Muslim armies had never set foot, such as the southern coasts of India and China, the northern coast of Java, the coasts of East and West Africa, or the southern inland 'shores' of the Sahara.[147] From there, Muslim merchants would learn local languages, seek business contacts and introduce their wares. Like European traders in colonial times, they would often establish settlements which might, over time, become major urban centres. Oftentimes, intrepid merchants would seek out local rulers for permission to trade, or even set themselves up as local rulers. Since Muslim traders represented a doorway to the wider world and, thus, to greater wealth and power, it is well-established that numerous local rulers (and their peoples) found their way to Islam through the Muslim merchants who arrived in their territories in pre-modern times.

A major impetus for these ruler-conversions, in other words, was the ability (or claim) of Muslim merchants to integrate new lands into the vast networks and 'world system' represented by *dar al-Islam*.[148] Rulers who converted to Islam were attracted not only by trade opportunities, but also by the possibility of gaining an advantage over nearby rivals. Whatever the case, this seems to have been the general pattern by which Islam was adopted in several territories. Beginning in the fifteenth century, for instance, Southeast Asia hosted Muslim merchants from Arab lands, Persia, India and elsewhere, but it has recently been shown that it was most likely Chinese Muslim merchants who were most responsible for initiating the Islamisation of Java – perhaps in concert with the famed Wali Songo.[149] This points to a dynamic which has been called the transmission of Islam 'in relay' – Islam was first brought to coastal China by Muslims from elsewhere and, in turn, Chinese Muslims brought it to Java. To give another example, Arab Muslims brought Islam (through conquest) to North Africa, leading to the eventual conversion of the Berbers. They in turn 'carried Islam across the Sahara to hand it over to the Soninke in the Sahel . . . The Soninke brought Islam to the Malinke, their neighbours to the south, and Malinke-speaking traders . . . spread Islam as far as the fringes of the forest'.[150]

In sum, in many regions beyond the borders of *dar al-Islam*, the initial spread of Islam was due to the efforts of Muslim merchants (alongside Sufis and others) who founded outposts of Islam and persuaded 'local elites interested in state formation, trade, or political legitimation to accept their religion'.[151] It goes without saying that, had Muslim merchants been interested in nothing more than trade and profit, we would have had little reason to include them in this book. And to be sure, there were certainly Muslim merchants who gave little thought to spreading their religion. Yet, the fact that so many Muslim merchants played vital roles in the pre-modern spread of Islam shows the extent to which they were committed to their faith and even to *da'wa* (although they may not have used that term). As we will see in Part II, Muslim merchant and other professional classes have continued to play major roles in facilitating *da'wa* up to the present.

Summary and conclusions

By the eighteenth century, a 'global system of Islamic societies' or Muslim ecumene had been established from the Atlantic coast of Africa to the Pacific coastlands of Asia. How did this Muslim ecumene come into being, and by what mechanisms did so many peoples embrace Islam between the eleventh and eighteenth centuries? In this chapter we examined several 'agents and patterns of Islamisation' as one way to begin answering these questions. We considered, first, Islamisation through the migration of new peoples into *dar al-Islam*, such as Turkic peoples, Mongols and slaves. With respect to the Turks and Mongols, we saw that their conversions led to reprises of a pattern we first discerned in the Arab-Islamic conquests: that of gradual conversion within Islamic ambiences established through conquest. Second, we explored the roles of Muslim rulers and ruler-converts in stimulating conversion to Islam, along with the place of Muslim states in Islamisation. We dealt next with the ways in which the *'ulama* in their varied roles as hadith scholars, legal guides, mentors to future *'ulama* and travellers in international circuits made contributions to internal and external *da'wa*. The Sufis and Sufi orders took up a somewhat larger proportion of the chapter, in part because their missionary achievements – in fact as well as in legend – were so substantial. As loners on the fringes of society or power-brokers in elite circles, as miracle-working holy men or sober-minded scholars, Sufis did *da'wa* by preaching, offering spiritual protection, developing key institutions, opening up new territories and serving as heroes of the faith. Fifth, we looked at the ways in which pre-modern popular preachers disseminated Islam to common people (and engendered controversy), thus foreshadowing today's popular Muslim spokespersons. Finally, we saw that the activities of Muslim merchants contributed not only to the centripetal attraction of Islamic civilisation, but also to the centrifugal spread of Islam to new frontiers.

This chapter makes no claim that these 'agents and patterns' provide an all-encompassing portrait of *da'wa* and Islamisation in medieval and early modern times. Yet, when taken together, they provide a useful way of thinking about the spread of Islam in these centuries. While the *'ulama* and Sufis probably come nearest to embodying what many today understand by the word 'missionary', it should now be clear that this period of Islamic history furnishes few examples of organised, centrally-directed missionary outreaches of the kind that are so common in the history of Christianity. The pre-modern spread of Islam usually took place, in other words, in informal ways. In many cases, missionary outreach does not seem to have been a primary aim of the actors involved. Rather, *da'wa* and Islamisation usually followed in the wake of other dynamics, such as empire-building, the search for knowledge, mystical quests for God and trade. It is perhaps in part for this reason that the word '*da'wa*' was rarely used by Muslims in these centuries for missionary outreach. To be sure, internal and external *da'wa* were still happening, but rarely in association with the term.[152] As we will see in Part II, the place of the word *da'wa* among Muslims, and many other things related to Islamic missionary thought and practice, would change dramatically in modern times. Yet, we will also see instances of continuity. Indeed, the agents and patterns studied here (along with the content of Chapters 1 to 3) foreshadow important aspects of *da'wa* today, even as they serve to highlight major transformations.

As we transition to Part II of this book, a final comment should be made about so-called ordinary, or non-elite Muslims up to the dawn of modernity. Although some basic knowledge of the Qur'an and Islamic thought filtered down to common people through the agents and activities studied in this chapter, and although we can assume that common people contributed in some ways to the spread of Islam (as discussed above), in general the Muslim masses in pre-modern times had very limited access to and very limited personal knowledge of Islamic scripture and law. For many ordinary people, if it meant anything intellectually substantive at all, 'Islam' simply meant participation in Islamic rituals or celebrations, such as those associated with mosques or Sufi shrines, or the use of Islamic symbols with varying levels of understanding. In addition, as far as pre-modern Muslim rulers were concerned, the 'religion' of the population, particularly of peasants, was often considered quite irrelevant. What mattered was the loyalty of intermediaries – such as clan leaders, regional notables and other elites – in ensuring allegiance to (or non-rebellion against) the ruler or dynasty.[153] As such, while Muslims rulers patronised Islamic institutions and deployed Islam's symbols for their own legitimacy, they rarely concerned themselves with *daʿwa* efforts among the masses. This was not entirely unlike the situation in medieval, pre-Reformation Europe *vis-à-vis* ordinary people's knowledge of the Bible and Christian theology. This points us forward to Part II. As we will see in Chapters 5, 6 and 7, the modern period has witnessed a major democratisation of access to Islamic knowledge. Closely related, there has been an increasing demand that all Muslims, including ordinary Muslim men, women and even children, should participate in *daʿwa* on behalf of Islam.

Notes

1. 'The expansion of Islam . . . embraces two phenomena. The first is the expansion of Islamic states . . . The second phenomenon is the spread of Islam as a religion or faith'. Although the two are related, they are not the same. Donner 2004, p. 239.
2. The term 'ecumene' refers to a large territory bound together by common elements, in this case 'Islam'. The word 'civilisation' is also sometimes used. On 'Islamic civilisation', see Irwin 2011, pp. 1–7.
3. Morgan and Reid 2010, pp. 3, 8–13; Fierro 2010, pp. 1–2.
4. Compare, for instance, the fourteenth-century Djingguereber Mosque in Timbuktu, made largely of mud and earth, with the fourteenth-century Kashmiri-style Chaqchan Mosque in today's far northern Pakistan.
5. On the great mosques of this era as 'symbols of imperial and Islamic might', see Green 2015b, p. 358.
6. Ibn Battuta 2010; Irwin 2011, p. 5; Zaman 2010, p. 598; Green 2015b, p. 369.
7. Bosworth 1996.
8. Lapidus 2014, pp. 226, 490. Italics added. In Hodgson's words, '. . . after 945, the . . . caliphate was replaced by a . . . linguistically and culturally international society . . . Yet . . .

it was held together in virtue of a common Islamicate social pattern . . .' Hodgson 1974, vol. 2, pp. 3, 9.

9. An important consequence is that Islam became an 'Asian religion'. Today, nearly 60 percent of Muslims live in Asia.

10. The historian's reconstruction of pre-modern Islamisation is 'bound to be somewhat uneven because of the nature of the sources . . . In general . . . one can say that the process of [Islamic] state expansion is much better documented than is the process of Islam's adoption by new "converts"'. Donner 2004, p. 240.

11. 'Inner Asia' refers to areas that are now part of western China, Mongolia and eastern Russia. Despite overlap, Inner Asia should be distinguished from 'Central Asia', the region made up of today's 'stan' countries.

12. See Findley 2005, pp. 56–7.

13. For Mahmud al-Kashgari's take on the Turks, see Findley 2005, pp. 56, 77. For the view of Ibn Khaldun, who saw the rise of Turks as a mercy from God, see Brown 2017, p. 249. More recently, 'Ali Nadwi celebrated the Turks in his influential *Islam and the World*; Nadwi 1977, pp. 92–4.

14. The Turkic migrations were part of an old pattern of population movements from east to west and west to east going back millennia. One might recall, for instance, the migrations of the so-called Indo-Aryans.

15. Levi and Sela 2010, p. 48. Italics added.

16. Findley 2005, pp. 14–15.

17. Lapidus 2014, p. 274. Peacock 2017c, pp. 134–55. See also Garcia-Arenal 2010, pp. 590–3.

18. DeWeese 2009, p. 122.

19. Nadwi 1977, p. 91.

20. Fletcher 1986, p. 45. See the summary in Brown 2017, p. 260.

21. Allsen 2009, pp. 135–54.

22. In both cases, the migrants initially posed a threat, but over time they were won by, and became champions of, the monotheisms of the conquered lands. Kennedy 2007, p. 375.

23. 'The greater the proportion of Muslims in the population, the steeper the conversion curve' among non-Muslims. Garcia-Arenal 2010, p. 588, citing Bulliet.

24. Koser 2007, Ch. 1.

25. Less western scholarly attention has been paid to slavery in the Muslim world than to the horrific trans-Atlantic slave trade. Among the secondary works cited in this chapter, the theme of slavery and Islamisation receives limited attention. For one study, see Levtzion 1985, pp. 182–98.

26. Brunschvig 1960–2007, pp. 24–40.

27. Hoyland 2015, pp. 93, 159; Lewis 1990, p. 11.

28. Lewis 1990, pp. 12–13.

29. Constable 2010, p. 640.

30. Levi 2010, pp. 568–9.

31. In 652, the King of Nubia avoided conquest by agreeing to an annual tribute of black slaves to the Arabs. This continued until the twelfth century. Brunschvig 1960–2007; Lewis 1990, pp. 9–10.

32. Lewis 1990, p. 12. See also Willis 1985, p. vii.

33. Ze'evi 2009, p. 173.

34. Ayalon 1999, pp. 89–90.

35. This occurred partly through European abolitionist pressures, partly through internal reform. Nevertheless, slavery continued in parts of the Muslim world into the late twentieth century. Ze'evi 2009, p. 174.

36. Converting or educating the slave carried the risk of undermining his/her inferiority. Levtzion 1985, pp. 192–5.
37. See Levtzion 1985. See also Green 2012, pp. 172–4. This dynamic has also been studied with respect to Afro-Caribbean religions which combine African religions with Christianity.
38. Apologetic arguments include, first, the idea that Islam actually improved the lives of many slaves and, second, that in any case 'true Islam' tends towards the abolishment of slavery. Brunschvig 1960–2007 cites works by Ameer 'Ali, Sayyid Ahmad Khan and others on the subject.
39. Strathern 2017, p. 21.
40. See Neill 1991, ch. 3. See also Berend 2007.
41. See Golden 2011, p. 70; Golden 1992, pp. 212–13; Soucek 2000, pp. 83–4.
42. Levi and Sela 2010, p. 47. The rise of the Qarakhanids came at the expense of the Persianate Samanids.
43. The thirteenth-century account of Jamal Qarshi is included in Levi and Sela 2010, pp. 73–6.
44. Soucek 2000, p. 84; Golden 1992, pp. 214–15.
45. Golden 2011, p. 75.
46. Jackson 2009, p. 44.
47. See DeWeese 1994; Findley 2005, pp. 61–4.
48. Strathern 2017, pp. 21–7. A successful fire ordeal story is also part of a conversion story regarding Genghis's grandson, Hulegu. This late (fourteenth-century) story is fictitious – Hulegu never converted to Islam – but the fact that the story came into circulation shows the prominence of this motif. See Biran 2016, pp. 79–88.
49. '[A] remarkable range of modern Turkic 'national' and ethnic groups owe their origins . . . to the era of the [Islamisation of] the Golden Horde', among them the Tatars, Bashkirs, Kazakhs and, of course, the Uzbeks. DeWeese 2009, pp. 125–6.
50. See Melville 1990, pp. 159–77. See also Manz 2010, pp. 150–4.
51. Melville 1990, p. 160.
52. For other examples, see Strathern 2017.
53. See, for example, Moffett 1992/2009, vol. 1, chs 21–22; Browne 1933.
54. And, for a time before their conversion, a concern that the Mongols actually favoured Christianity. See Moffatt 1992/2009, ch. 18.
55. For examples of scapegoating in the wake of COVID-19 (which, fortunately, has risen nowhere near the level of anti-minority blame and violence unleashed in the fourteenth century), see, for instance, Fisk 2020; Frayer 2020, Al-Jazeera English 2020; Bartholomew 2020; Mondschein 2020.
56. The Mamluks inherited Egypt from the Isma'ili Fatimids and the Sunni Ayyubids (of Saladin fame). Under these earlier dynasties, religious minorities were treated fairly.
57. el-Leithy 2005; Lapidus 2014, pp. 159–60.
58. Lapidus 2014, p. 160.
59. On which see ibid., pp. 304–7, 311–14. These centuries also had negative consequences for Christian states like Armenia, Georgia, Ethiopia and Nubia. Each of them was pressured or was conquered by Muslim regimes.
60. Hunwick 1985, pp. 35–8. See also Hunwick 1960–2007, pp. 1165–6.
61. Jenkins 2009, ch. 4. Jenkins writes (p. 100): 'Persecution [was] not integral to Islamic rule; but such conditions could and did develop at particular times, and when they did, they could be devastating. At their worst, we can legitimately compare the conditions of Christians under Islam with that of Jews in . . . Christian Europe'. It is also worth noting that persecution against 'the other' on the basis of religion should be distinguished from

punishment for disloyalty. The Mughals in India, for instance, patronised Hindu shrines and had Hindu and Sikh collaborators, but would at times destroy non-Muslim religious shrines as punishment for disloyalty.

62. Lapidus 2014, p. 381.
63. See Zaman 2010, pp. 582–610.
64. Crone and Hinds 1986, p. 109.
65. Hinds 1960–2007. The *miḥna* (inquisition) was an effort by the caliph to enforce religious uniformity. The issue was whether the Qur'an is created or uncreated. Ibn Hanbal (the namesake of Hanbali *fiqh*) resisted the caliph's effort, declaring that he would follow the Qur'an literally, which seemed to him to teach the uncreatedness of the Qur'an. Scripture, for the *'ulama*, became a higher authority than the caliph. See Melchert 2006; Lapidus 2014, pp. 104–5.
66. Lapidus 1975, p. 369.
67. Green 2015b, p. 361. Both traditions emerged out of the same eighth- and ninth-century piety-minded circles which stressed hadith study. Lapidus provides a helpful typology of Muslim religious guides in medieval times: *'ulama*, *'ulama*-cum-Sufis and mystical Sufis. Lapidus 2002, pp. 207–10.
68. Berkey 2004, p. 203.
69. Irwin 2011, p. 4.
70. Marin 2010, pp. 696–701. The *'ulama* were co-opted into the state machinery of the Ottomans and Safavids.
71. Berkey 2003, p. 224. See also Berkey 2001, ch. 4.
72. Graham 1993, pp. 495–522.
73. Vajda, Goldziher and Bonebakker 1960–2007, pp. 1020–2.
74. Islam encourages travel: the *hajj* (pilgrimage to Mecca) and *hijra* (the obligation to migrate to *dar al-Islam* from non-Muslim lands). The *'ulama* travelled widely in search of knowledge. See Eickelman and Piscatori 1990. For the *'ulama*'s cosmopolitanism, see Zaman 2010.
75. Berkey 2003, p. 226. See also Marin 2010, pp. 682–92.
76. Reetz 2010, p. 107.
77. Green 2015b, p. 361.
78. Ibid., p. 360.
79. Keddie 2007, pp. 29–47.
80. Green 2012, pp. 1–13.
81. In a famous hadith, the angel Gabriel appears in disguise to Muhammad and asks him to define *imān* (belief), *islām* (practice) and *iḥsān* (beauty, excellence). To the first, Muhammad gives the six points of Islamic belief; to the second, the Five Pillars; to the third, apparently referring to Sufism, he says, '*iḥsān* is to worship Allah as if you see him'. Al-Bukhari 1420/1999, p. 65, 4777.
82. See Green 2012. See also Ernst 1997. For short introductions, see Renard 2005, pp. 1–15, and Chittick 2009, pp. 207–16. Classic works, such as Nicholson 1989 and Schimmel 1975 are still well worth reading.
83. Green 2012, pp. 16–23, provides a good review, but is somewhat exaggerated in his critique of the idea that Sufism 'borrowed' from earlier traditions – something it clearly did. On this theme, see Nicholson 1989, pp. 1–27. For resonances between Sufism and Shi'ism, see Schimmel 1975, pp. 41–2, 82–3.
84. Ernst 2004, p. 5; Gobillot 1960–2007, pp. 559–62; Melchert 1996, p. 54.
85. 'While the basic literatures of Quran commentary, hadith, law, theology and mysticism had originated in an earlier era, in the tenth to thirteenth centuries these literatures and mentalities were merged into the forms that we still recognise as classical Islam. The Sunni-

scripturalist-Sufi orientation became the most commonly accepted form of Islam'. Lapidus 2002, p. 156.

86. Trimingham 1971, ch. 2.
87. Such as Sarraj (d. 988), Kalabadhi (d. 990/995), Qushayri (d. 1072) and Hujwiri (d. 1072).
88. The former is sometimes associated with al-Junayd (d. 910) and with sober branches of the Naqshbandiyya, the latter with Ibn al-'Arabi (d. 1240) or various 'drunken' Sufi orders. For a complication, see Mojaddedi 2003, pp. 1–13. For another useful typology, see Ingram 2018, pp. 12–13.
89. Lapidus 2014, pp. 279–80. These orientations reflected tensions between those who favoured versions of spirituality appropriate to the city-dwellers and those who seemed to promote the spiritual elitism of a few. Melchert 2002b, p. 429.
90. Brown 1981. See also Cunningham 2005, ch. 6. To call this version of Sufism 'popular' might be misleading, since Sufi shrines were also frequented by rulers and elites. See Ingram 2018, p. 81.
91. Lapidus 2002, pp. 207–10, italics added. Sufism was 'institutionalized mass religion' in the Islamic world. Berkey 2003, p. 239, quoting Hodgson.
92. '[T]o a very large extent, Sufism was Islam in its medieval form'. Green 2012, pp. 126, 154.
93. On 'Sufi da'wa', see Masud 2000, p. xxvi; Kuiper 2018a, p. 64.
94. Renard 2008, p. 7. On Sufi hagiographies, see pp. 1–9.
95. Ibid., p. 256.
96. DeWeese 2017, p. 336. Writing of post-Soviet Central Asia, DeWeese notes, 'any . . . shrine may be linked with a saint who tends to be identified as a bringer of Islam'. While he is speaking of the haziness of such memories, the fact that these shrines are so identified is telling. This echoes my experience in India.
97. See Ernst 2004, pp. 157–60, and Ernst 1997, pp. 138–41. Lawrence, 1982/2011 pp. 132–3.
98. This was the case, for instance, with the above-mentioned Baba Tukles, whom the peoples of the Golden Horde would remember as their 'collective convertor or . . . ancestor'. Green 2015b, pp. 372–3. The Tukles legend illustrates common motifs: Sufis are portrayed approaching non-Muslim rulers with missionary motives; often, miracles prove to be more decisive than arguments; Sufis are often portrayed doing da'wa in response to a dream or vision. See Renard 2008, chs 1–3.
99. "'Attār gives the total of his converts to Islam as 24,000 . . . The ḵānaqāh at Kāzarūn was the center of [his] activity; from there he directed his disciples to establish other ḵānaqāhs, perhaps . . . sixty-five throughout Fārs'. Lawrence 1983/2011, pp. 274–5.
100. Schimmel 1975, p. 247.
101. Lawrence 1982/2011. See also Chabbi 2007.
102. For examples of Qadiriyya da'wa in India and Africa, see Arnold 1896/1913/2012, pp. 271, 274, 328–30.
103. Lapidus 2014, pp. 418, 425. See, however, DeWeese 2017, pp. 336–52.
104. DeWeese 1999, pp. 149–53; Rowe 2007.
105. An Iranian, he was author of the earliest Persian treatise on Sufism, Kashf al-Maḥjūb (Revelation of the Hidden).
106. Vryonis 1971, pp. 384–90.
107. Ibid. Vryonis argues for the historicity of Aflaki's account. Turan 1959, pp. 141–3, presents Rumi's success in winning converts as a (unintended) consequence of his reputation and power, while Vryonis presents Rumi as if he were missionising intentionally. For a critique of the idea of Rumi as missionary, see Peacock 2017c, pp. 144–5.
108. Vryonis 1971, pp. 387–91, gives multiple examples.

109. Aflaki 2002, pp. 418–19. Aflaki quotes Rumi as saying, 'Drawing us from Khorasan to the country of Rūm, God gave my descendants refuge in this pure land so that we might scatter gifts . . . on . . . Rūm's inhabitants and thus they would be entirely transformed . . .' Aflaki 2002, pp. 143–4.
110. See Gade 2009, pp. 341–58. Wain 2017, pp. 419–43; van Bruinessen 2007.
111. For further examples, see Arnold 1896/1913/2012; Levtzion 1979a; Peacock 2017a.
112. Nicholson 1989, pp. 1–27. Some Sufi practices are also close to Shi'ism. Sufi devotion to specially inspired individuals, for instance, bears similarity to Shi'ite devotion to the family of 'Ali. See Schimmel 1975, pp. 41–2, 82–3; Berkey 2003, pp. 234–5.
113. Green 2012, ch. 2. The quote is from p. 111.
114. Ibid.
115. Green 2012, pp. 108–9.
116. See Schimmel 1975, p. 176.
117. Green 2012, p. 101. Findley suggests that discussions of the Turks' conversion suffer from a tendency to portray 'the Islamization of the early Turkic converts as "nominal" . . . classifying everything nonstandard . . . as residues of "shamanism."' Findley 2005, p. 59. On 'Shamanism', see DeWeese 1994, pp. 32–9.
118. Vryonis 1971, p. 376.
119. Ibid., pp. 368–81.
120. Trix 2009, pp. 332–3.
121. See, for isntance, Dargah Quli Khan's eighteenth-century *Muraqqa-yi Dihli* (Delhi Scrapbook), in which Khan speaks of Hindus frequenting Sufi shrines. Cited in Ingram, *Revival*, pp. 81–2.
122. Identification with 'a living tradition requires at least some *preliminary* participation . . . especially at Sufi *khānqāhs* . . . the inquiring [non-Muslim] could begin to participate enough in Islam to . . . commit himself to it'. Hodgson 1974, vol. 2, pp. 535–6. In Green's words, '. . . conversion to Islam to Islam was a multi-tiered process in which there existed many points of negotiation between former custom and wholesale sharia'. Green 2015b, p. 374.
123. Green 2012, pp. 154–5.
124. Green 2015b, pp. 368–9.
125. Green 2012, pp. 87–9.
126. Such as Christianity, a religion in his Anatolian context with which he was familiar. Ridgeon 2001, pp. 99–126. For Ridgeon, Rumi did say inclusive things, yet he concludes that this was a 'veneer'.
127. Renard 2008, pp. 146–9; Lapidus 2002, p. 203; Schimmel 1975, p. 346.
128. Green 2012, pp. 89–91, 127. For a good case-study, see Eaton 1993.
129. Green 2015b, pp. 371–3.
130. See, for example, Robert 2009.
131. See Chabbi 1960–2007.
132. Abun-Nasr 2007.
133. Keddie 2007, pp. 43–4; Hoffman-Ladd 2009a, pp. 539–41. See also Silvers 2015, pp. 24–52.
134. Berkey 2001, pp. 80–5.
135. Ibid., p. 21. Italics added.
136. Berkey 2003, p. 254.
137. In traditional Muslim societies, public spaces are (mostly) male spaces, and domestic spaces are mostly female spaces. Evidence for the *da'wa* in the domestic sphere can be seen in Islamic writings in which pious Muslim mothers are favourably remembered or, conversely, in which women may be blamed for passing on defective beliefs. See Silvers 2015, pp. 40–1, 45–51.

138. Bosworth, Heffening and Shatzmiller 1960–2007.
139. Berkey 2001, p. 15.
140. '[T]hat Islam should take shape in a largely urban milieu . . . is hardly surprising, given the long history of urban life and culture of those lands which . . . formed the heart of Islamdom'. Berkey 2003, p. 120. See also Levi 2010, pp. 561–2.
141. Levi 2010, pp. 562–4; Constable 2010, pp. 632–5.
142. Green 2015b, pp. 375–6; Irwin 2011, p. 6.
143. Constable 2010, pp. 636–40.
144. Levi 2010, pp. 565, 573–4, Irwin 2011, pp. 12–13. Ch. 5 discusses Europe's economic surge.
145. They were also sent by trading families and companies. Parker 2015, pp. 190–212.
146. Levtzion 1979c, p. 15.
147. 'On the coasts . . . Muslim communities took root in innumerable locations, from Gujarat . . . to the Indo-Malaysian archipelago and China; and everywhere their raison d'être was trade'. Wink 2010, p. 80.
148. Acceptance of Islam won princes 'an entrée into extensive trading networks'. Lapidus 2014, p. 275. On a pre-modern world system in which Muslims were major players, see Abu-Lughod 1991.
149. Wain 2017; for West Africa, see Levtzion 1979b, pp. 207–16.
150. Levtzion 1979b, p. 208.
151. Lapidus 2014, pp. 274–5.
152. See Chapter 3.
153. See Humphreys 1991, pp. 273–83, ch. 12.

PART II

The modern missionary history of Islam

Introduction to Part II

We began this book with the observation that there has been a remarkable surge in missionary commitment and activism among Muslims worldwide over the past 150 years or so. We noted further that, for all its vibrancy and diversity, much of this surge has coalesced under the term '*da'wa*' (and, to some extent, '*tabligh*'), a concept whose sundry pre-modern fortunes and uses, among other matters, we traced in Chapters 1 to 4. Indeed, not only are '*da'wa*' and variants like '*da'i*' now household words for many millions of Muslims worldwide regardless of their mother tongues (alternative renderings include *dawah* and *dakwah*), but contemporary Muslims of nearly every background have also been personally impacted by *da'wa*, both as doers and as objects of Islamic outreach. Underneath the big tent of modern *da'wa*, new kinds of Muslim actors have been empowered and new stars born, but older Islamic traditions too, such as Sufism and the scholarly traditions of the *'ulama*, have been transformed and renewed. As *da'wa* discourses and activities have increasingly proven their ability to mobilise Muslims on a mass scale, most contemporary denominations and movements of Islam have taken up the challenge of *da'wa* in one way or another.[1] At a basic level Sunnis and Shi'ites, and at a more specific level Salafis, Wahhabis, Imamis (or Twelvers), Isma'ilis, Barelvis, Deobandis, Gulenists, Tablighis, Muhammadis, Mourides, Ahmadis and followers of the Nation of Islam – along with modernists, reformists, Islamists and a host of other Islamic movements and sects – have organised for *da'wa*, very often in rivalry with one another. Indeed, a number of these movements were launched specifically with *da'wa* in mind. In organising for *da'wa*, Islamic movements have facilitated the involvement of Muslim laymen, women and children in Islamic preaching and other forms of activism. One of the most characteristic aspects of contemporary *da'wa* discourse is the idea that all Muslims should see themselves as missionaries for Islam, missionaries who are tasked with exhorting fellow Muslims and reaching out to non-Muslims. In contrast to pre-modern assumptions, modern Muslims have widely concluded that missionary *da'wa* is not simply a 'collective obligation' or *fard al-kifaya* undertaken by some (*'ulama*, Sufis, Muslim rulers and so on) on behalf of the rest, but that it is an 'individual obligation' or *fard al-'ayn*, binding for every believer.[2] An orientation towards *da'wa* is also among the major reasons Muslims have taken up modern technologies and embraced or innovated novel techniques for defending and commending their faith. It is truly no exaggeration to say that *da'wa* is ubiquitous in the contemporary Muslim world.

While *da'wa* is certainly not the only scriptural or classical Islamic concept to have been energetically recovered (and debated) by Muslims in the modern age – one can think of concepts such as *jihad, shari'a* or *ijtihad,* for instance – the extent to which missionary *da'wa* has proven to be uniquely appealing to modern Muslims is among the most arresting facts of modern Islamic history, and all the more so in light of what we learned about *da'wa* and Islamisation in pre-modern times. To repeat several points from Chapters 1 to 4: until the 1700s, the tasks associated with internal and external *da'wa* were primarily carried out by Muslim elites in fairly *ad hoc* ways, and the term '*da'wa*' itself was used irregularly. In addition, we observed that *da'wa* and Islamisation were often linked to the expansion of Islamic political power and presupposed the establishment of public Islamic ambiences by Muslim rulers and states. Indeed, as seen in classical Islamic law, what we have been calling the 'Medinan pattern' of *da'wa* (*da'wa* or Islamisation from a position strength or aiming at the attainment of power) seems to have been the norm and expectation for much of pre-modern Islamic history. Against this backdrop, the appeal and prevalence of *da'wa* (both the term and the phenomena) in the modern era, and in particular the rebirth and democratisation of variations of the 'Meccan pattern' of *da'wa* (*da'wa* or Islamisation from a position of relative powerlessness), are dynamics that call for explanation and elucidation. This is what Part II of this book aims to provide.[3]

In continuation of our study of *da'wa* and Islamisation in Part I, Part II contextualises and describes *da'wa* in the modern period by reflecting on the 'where', 'why' and 'what' of modern *da'wa*: *Where* did the modern surge in *da'wa* come from (or what are its historical roots and contexts)? *Why* has involvement in *da'wa* proven to be such a significant avenue of Muslim engagement with modernity? And *what* are some of the most important *da'wa* actors, movements and trends over the past 150 years? In answering these questions, we will see that there is not only continuity with the pre-modern history of *da'wa*, but also significant rupture – *da'wa* has been recovered *and* reinvented in modernity.

Part II follows a chronological and thematic structure. Chapter 5 provides necessary context and background for Chapters 6 and 7 by examining several eighteenth- to mid-twentieth-century historical developments which paved the way for a renewed emphasis among modern Muslims on missionary *da'wa*: (1) the emergence of reform and renewal movements within Islam, and (2) the transformations associated with the high modern or colonial age (*circa* nineteenth to mid-twentieth centuries). While the former played an anticipatory and preparatory role, the latter ushered in what we will call the *first phase* of modern *da'wa*. This phase (*circa* 1850–1950), the subject of Chapter 6, witnessed the early stirrings of a turn towards *da'wa* among modern Muslims and, in the early twentieth century in particular, a surge in the creation of new *da'wa*-oriented movements and organisations. Chapter 6 examines this phase by providing a global survey of colonial-era *da'wa* movements up to about 1950. We will see that *da'wa* in this period was largely, though not exclusively, a matter of *internal da'wa* (it was directed towards Muslims). Another striking feature of this phase was the widespread embrace of 'Meccan' (quietist, voluntary) *da'wa* approaches.

Chapter 7 turns to a *second phase* of modern *da'wa* thought and activism, a phase which coincides with the post-colonial history of the Muslim world (*circa* 1950–2020). To make sense of this second phase, Chapter 7 first explores a few key features of the experience of Muslim societies in post-colonial times: for instance, the formation of modern-style nation-states across the former Muslim ecumene, the eventual (real and perceived) failures of those states, the continuing migrations of Muslims to new parts of the globe, the impacts of technological change, the ongoing geopolitical domination of the West and so on. Building on earlier patterns, Muslims have generated a range of lively responses to these post-colonial dynamics, and, as with the colonial era, *da'wa* has proven to be a major element in many of them. Thus, if the colonial era gave rise to the first stage of modern *da'wa*, the post-colonial era produced a second, even more dynamic phase of *da'wa*. After outlining the context, Chapter 7 provides a global survey of *da'wa*-oriented activists and movements in the period of *circa* 1950–2020. We will see that in this second phase quietist, grassroots versions of *da'wa* continue to thrive, but that there has also been a resurgence of varieties of religio-political *da'wa*. We will see additionally that, while internal *da'wa* remains the primary thrust of *da'wa* activism worldwide, the second phase has witnessed an expansion of *external da'wa* (efforts towards non-Muslims).

Key terms and themes of Part II

Before we turn to Chapters 5, 6 and 7, it is important to explain a few key concepts which are specific to Part II. In the first place, 'modernity' in these chapters serves as a placeholder for the effects and dilemmas produced by the gargantuan changes in technology, human knowledge and consciousness, as well as social, economic and political organisation that have swept the globe over the past two and a half centuries. As an 'ideal type' or heuristic abstraction,[4] modernity refers to a world and ways of living shaped by the rise and prestige of science and a scientific outlook; industrialisation and mass consumption; the modern nation-state; constitutionalism (and its alternatives); capitalism (and its opponents); globe-integrating travel and communication technologies; increased migration and urbanisation; and a trend towards individualism,[5] among other things. It might be convenient to think of it in terms of three broad periods which have given us 'modernity': *early modern* (roughly 1500–1800), *high modern* (1800–1950) and *late modern* (1950–present). The early modern period set the stage, so to speak, for modernity,[6] the high modern period witnessed major changes in political, economic and social life typically associated with modernity,[7] and the late modern period has witnessed an intensification of the tendencies and tensions of modernity.[8] Part II will sometimes use the phrase 'colonial modernity' as an approximate synonym for the high modern period *as experienced by* (or *from the perspective of*) the non-western world. The phrase colonial modernity, in other words, draws attention to the fact that the high modern period coincides with an era in which expansionist European powers established colonial rule or other forms of economic and political domination over vast stretches of the globe, including much of the former *dar al-Islam*. While the rise of modernity was often experienced in Europe and North America as a set of 'internally generated' transformations, in the Muslim world modernity was often experienced as something imposed from outside, by foreign powers.[9] An important result of these dynamics was that many Muslims around the world were subject to varied processes of 'minoritisation' in the high modern or colonial period – they were reduced to the experience of living as a marginalised or minority people or group of peoples, literally in some cases and more symbolically in others.[10] In keeping with the perspective implied in the phrase colonial modernity, the term 'post-colonial' will sometimes be used as a synonym for late modern (the period from 1950 to the present). It was in this period, after all, that most of the non-western world came out from under colonial rule – although not entirely, as we will see, from under western domination.

Also useful is the concept of 'multiple modernities' – the idea that various communities around the world have experienced, configured and embodied modernity differently.[11] While the development of multiple modernities was in some ways an unconscious, subliminal process, in other ways it was intentional. In the nineteenth and twentieth centuries, under the circumstances of colonial modernity, some non-western intellectuals argued for 'modernity, but in our own way'.[12] Religion has often played a key role in efforts such as this, which is to say that people around the world have turned to religion in order to creatively preserve or reinvent their distinctiveness and authenticity in the face of modernity's westernising and secularising pressures.[13] It is as if many in the non-western world were saying: The West may have given us printing presses and steam engines, automobiles and airplanes, cell phones and satellites, but we still have our own traditions and beliefs which are worth preserving, protecting, and promoting. We can selectively embrace modernity while remaining true to ourselves. We can be *modern* without becoming *western*.[14]

That Muslims have developed plural and mutually competitive Islamic modernities can be seen in the now familiar typology of Muslim orientations towards the modern world: 'modernist' (attempts to reshape or 'update' Islam and Islamic faith or practise in line with scientific or liberal values), 'reformist' (attempts to remove 'un-Islamic' innovations from Muslim communities and make Muslims more devout through a return to the Qur'an and *sunna* of the Prophet) and 'Islamist' (attempts to bring all of life under the control of Islamic revelation through grassroots activism and the capture of state power in the name of Islam).[15] Although there are good reasons to have reservations about this typology (none of these orientations are static, and positions often overlap or morph into new ones), we will use it in Part II for quick reference. The primary points to remember for now are, first, that Muslims have developed *plural* responses to modern conditions and, second, that *da'wa* has proven to be a vital ingredient in nearly all of them. The lively internal diversity and energetic debates which characterise Muslim communities in modernity are on full display in the wide world of *da'wa*.

In addition to this basic three-fold typology, it is important to say something about another category of Muslim response to modernity: 'Salafism'.[16] A subset of Sunni reformism which sometimes draws on modernism and at other times shades into Islamism, Salafism has become, over the course of the twentieth century and into the twenty-first, 'one of the most high profile tendencies in contemporary Islam'.[17] Salafism is particularly important for our purposes because it has been a major driver of *da'wa* activism in the late modern period. If they are anything, Salafis are zealous missionaries for their version(s) of Islam.[18] The word 'Salafism' derives from *salaf al-ṣāliḥ*, an Arabic phrase which, in Islamic thought, refers to the pious original three generations of Islam. These are said by Salafis to have been the best and most pure Muslims who ever lived; therefore, Salafis want to imitate the *salaf* down to the minutest details. Although Salafism is sometimes thought to have begun with seminal modernist-reformist thinkers such as Muhammad 'Abduh and Rashid Rida (see Chapter 6), in fact, Salafism in its current manifestations is woven together from several sources of influence: (1) the scripturalist reformism of the medieval scholar Ibn Taymiyya (d. 1328, see Chapter 4); (2) the radical 'Najdi *da'wa*' of Muhammad Ibn 'Abd al-Wahhab (d. 1792, see Chapter 5); and (3) the hadith-centred belief and practice of the Indian Ahl-i Hadith movement (founded in the mid-nineteenth century). The term 'Salafi' itself burst into global consciousness especially in the second half of the twentieth century.[19]

Despite significant internal fragmentation – which is only to be expected of a movement whose existence is premised on being the only true 'saved' sect of Islam – there is a family resemblance that binds Salafi movements together. Salafism is scripturalist (scripture is consulted directly and is acted upon literally), rigorist (in keeping to literal hadith-based piety) and purist (in terms of rejecting everything which is considered to be an un-Islamic 'innovation'). Salafis can often be recognised by the distinctive ways they dress and pray, and if one digs a little deeper, one will usually discover the influence of Salafi scholars such as Shaykh Nasir al-Din al-Albani (1914–99) and 'Abd al-Aziz b. Baz (1910–99).[20] For the sake of clarity, we will consider Wahhabism (the variety of Sunni Islam that prevails in contemporary Saudi Arabia) to be a type of Salafism. Scholars have developed a useful categorisation of three major types of Salafism. First is 'quietist' (generally non-political, non-militant) Salafism,[21] a tendency which is close in emphasis to the Saudi Arabian religious establishment. Quietist Salafis shy away from overt politics and focus on 'purification and education', as well as on missionary *da'wa*. Second, on the opposite end of the spectrum are 'Jihadi-Salafis' who call for violent action to overthrow what they consider to be un-Islamic regimes and to set up Islamic states or restore an Islamic caliphate. Jihadi-Salafis share much in common with, and have sometimes been mutually influenced by, Islamist movements. Third, somewhere in the middle are so-called Salafi 'activists'.[22] These share the quietists' orientation towards education and *da'wa*, but also participate in political activism (usually of a non-violent kind), which may include electoral politics.[23] Even though these categories are imperfect, they will help to facilitate our analysis in the pages that follow. Finally, it should be stressed that, while Salafism shares much in common with Sunni reformism more broadly, there are many reform-minded Sunnis – for instance, those who continue to identify with the schools of law and commentarial traditions of the pre-modern era – who should not be (and would not want to be) grouped under the umbrella of Salafism. The Sunni reformist Deoband tradition and the Tablighi Jama'at of South Asia, for instance, are examples of movements which are sometimes wrongly labelled 'Salafi'.

A final set of key concepts in Part II are 'disestablishment' and 'religious marketplace'. Among the most important consequences of modernity for our purposes has been the formation of global marketplaces, not only of goods, but also of ideas and religions.[24] Modernity, that is, has tended towards disestablishment – situations in which religions lose or lack official government (or assumed societal) backing and are forced to compete with one another for influence, converts and so on on a more level playing field. This is somewhat analogous to situations in the realm of global business in which previously nationalised corporations – corporations which held state-backed monopolies – are privatised and find themselves having to compete in the open marketplace. So, too, in the realm of religion: Contrary to the expectations of some twentieth-century thinkers, the advance of modernity has not led to the demise of religions in the face of unstoppable secularisation, but it arguably has led to their widespread disestablishment, as well as to a corresponding acceptance of 'religious marketplace mentalities' among the world's peoples.[25] As Peter Berger put it, 'Modernity is not necessarily secularizing; it is necessarily pluralizing . . . Each [religious tradition] must cope with the fact that there are "all these others," not just in a faraway country but right next door'.[26] Indeed, the manifestly modern notion that there are discreet 'world religions' which one may line up side-by-side and from which one may choose one's favourite (or blend of several, or reject them all), much like a consumer might choose among different brands of toothpaste or automobiles, is a cause and symptom of this mentality. Combined with technological change, advances in education and literacy, as well as widespread urbanisation, this trend towards disestablishment has corresponded with a trend towards 'democratisation' or 'laicisation' in the world's religions. That is, ordinary believers (the laity or lay people) have been empowered as never before to weigh their own options in the religious marketplace, to interpret religious texts for themselves and, in some cases, to innovate entirely new religious movements. This laicisation of religions in disestablishment, marketplace contexts is a key global trend in modernity.

Bringing this last set of concepts together, one of the major arguments of Part II is that, from the late eighteenth century onwards, 'situations of disestablishment' (the plural is intentional) progressively constituted a new normal for many Muslims around the world. While some have responded by taking up variations of political or militant activism in order to resist disestablishment, and while there are multiple countries today that aspire to be 'Islamic' states (countries in which Islam enjoys a religious monopoly or some measure of state support), missionary *da'wa*, often of a 'Meccan' variety, has proven to be an even more significant response to these circumstances. In fact, Part II suggests that it is in part *owing to* disestablishment circumstances and the emergence of religious marketplace mentalities that missionary *da'wa* has become so popular among modern Muslims as a form of activism and mobilisation.

II.1 Some key terms in Part II

Modernity – An 'ideal type' which helps us think about the massive changes in science, technology, governance, mobility and consciousness that have swept the globe and altered human experience since the mid-eighteenth century.

Periodisation of Modernity
   -*Early Modern Period* – approximately 1500–1800
   -*High Modern or Colonial Period* – approximately 1800–1950
   -*Late Modern* – approximately 1950–present

Colonial Modernity – A rough synonym for the high modern period *as experienced by* the non-western world facing the challenge of western imperialism and colonialism.

Minoritisation – The literal or felt experience of being reduced to a marginalised or minority people or group of peoples under the domination of others.

Post-Colonial – A rough synonym for 'late modern' (the period from 1950 to the present). It was in this period that most of the non-western world shook off colonial rule.

*Multiple Modernities – The idea that various communities around the world have consciously and unconsciously experienced, configured and embodied modernity differently.

*Basic Typology of Muslim Orientations towards the Modern World

  -*Modernism* – Attempts to reshape or 'update' Islam and Islamic faith or practice in line with scientific or 'modern' liberal values

  -*Reformism* – Attempts to remove 'un-Islamic' innovations from Muslim communities and make Muslims more devout through a return to the Qur'an and *sunna* of the Prophet.

  -*Islamism* – Attempts to bring all of life under the control Islamic revelation through grassroots activism and the capture of state power in the name of Islam.

*Salafism – A subset of Sunni reformism; a scripturalist, rigorist and purist group of movements which aim to restore 'true' Islam by imitating the practice of the original three generations of Islam.

  -*Wahhabism* – Founded by Muhammad Ibn 'Abd al-Wahhab (d. 1792), a variety of Salafism which prevails in contemporary Saudi Arabia.

*Basic Typology of Salafism

  -*Quietist Salafism* – Avoids overt politics and focuses on education and missionary *da'wa*.

  -*Jihadi-Salafism* – Calls for violent action to overthrow 'un-Islamic' regimes and to set up Islamic states or restore an Islamic caliphate.

  -*Activist Salafism* – Shares the quietists' orientation towards education and *da'wa*, but also engages in (usually non-violent) political activism.

*Disestablishment – Situations in which religions lose or lack official government (or assumed societal) backing and are forced to compete with one another for influence, converts and so on on a more level playing field.

*Religious Marketplace – A major consequence of modernity's trend towards disestablishment has been the formation of global marketplaces of ideas and religions somewhat analogous to global marketplaces of goods.

*Democratisation or *Laicisation* – The empowerment of ordinary believers (lay people) to weigh their own options in the religious marketplace, to interpret religious texts for themselves and, in some cases, to innovate entirely new religious movements.

Notes

1. Hedin, Janson and Westerlund speak of *daʿwa* as a widespread 'discourse of mobilization'. See Hedin, Janson and Westerlund 2004, p. 170.
2. The terms *farḍ al-kifāya* and *farḍ al-ʿayn* come from the Islamic legal tradition.
3. While all studies of modern Islam rightly speak to the ferment within Muslim communities in response to modernity, fewer have given attention to *daʿwa*. Perhaps this is because, unlike the political/militant movements which attract media attention and unlike Muslim intellectuals who attract the attention of academics, *daʿwa* activism has often taken place on the popular level.
4. For Max Weber, ideal types facilitate analysis and are 'good to think with'. Weber 1963.
5. In modernity, the individual becomes a bearer of 'rights' and an agent of choice. One's identity is not 'conferred' (by place of origin or family), but it is 'chosen' and 'constructed' by the migratory individual.
6. Early modern movements such as the Renaissance, Reformation and Enlightenment entailed major challenges to 'tradition'. The boundary-shattering encounters of the Age of Exploration also took place in early modern times.
7. In the high modern period a 'clutch of global developments' – including European imperial expansion, industrial capitalism, political/constitutional revolutions, the rise of the modern state and the like – 'created a step-change forward in human organization and experience'. Bayly 2004, pp. 9–12.
8. Late modernity is marked by globalisation, new information technologies and increasing movement. Zygmunt Bauman speaks of late modernity as a 'light and liquid' continuation of modernity, characterised by impermanence and nomadism. Bauman 2000.
9. 'Modernity' can refer to the historical transformations described above, or to a particular attitude towards the past. In the latter sense, 'modernity' equals rationality and progress, while pre-modern 'tradition' equals backwardness. Colonial rule was sometimes legitimised by viewing the world through this lens. Schulze 2000, pp. 21–32. Salvatore 2009, pp. 3–35. Nevertheless, modernity should not be thought of as 'something which some people or some regions did to others less favored . . . but as a series of transformations in which most of the people of the world participated and to which most of them contributed'. Moore 2004, p. xxi.
10. There is a growing literature which draws on the concept of 'minoritisation'. For instance, it is used in socio-linguistics to refer to the marginalisation or stigmatisation of indigenous languages as dominant languages like English spread around the world, or in nationalistic demands for linguistic conformity ('newcomers or migrants must learn *our* language and conform to *our* ways'). For a thoughtful use of the term, see Mufti 2007.
11. Eistenstadt 2000, pp. 1–29. See also Robinson 2008.
12. Bayly 2004, p. 10.
13. Chatterjee 1993, pp. 3–13. See also Woodhead 2002, p. 8, and Martin 2005.
14. On becoming modern without becoming western, see Kenney and Moosa 2013, p. 3. In emphasising the creative choices that Muslims made in this scenario, we should not forget that there was also a good dose of compulsion at play. As we will see, colonial rule created structures that *required* identification as 'Muslim' for political participation, education and so on.
15. Robinson 2008, pp. 259–60. For a more complex five-fold typology see, Shepard 1987, pp. 307–36. See also Kuiper 2018a, pp. 77–8. To borrow a useful oversimplification: While some Muslims seek to modernise Islam, others seek to Islamise modernity. Shepard 2004, pp. 61–103.
16. On 'Salafi' and 'Salafism', Part II follows Meijer 2009. See also Wiktorowicz 2006, pp. 207–39. For a summary of scholarship on Salafism, see Brown 2017, ch. 17.

17. Brown 2017, p. 318.
18. Salafism is 'vast educational network', in which followers 'spend most of their time learning about Islam . . .'. In turn, Salafis preach what they have learned through *da'wa*. Wiktorowicz 2006, p. 212.
19. 'Before the twentieth century the term ['Salafi'] was used, but not widely . . . But by the 1920s, in part through the influence of the Salafiyya bookstore [in Cairo], use of the term spread . . . The original founders of the Salafiyya bookstore began printing books for the new Saudi state in 1924, and in 1927 they set up a printing press and a branch of the store in Mecca. In the 1930s a Salafi Association formed in Egypt'. Brown 2017, pp. 320–1, summarising Lauziere 2010, pp. 369–89.
20. Al-Albani used the term Salafi to denote those who strictly follow Qur'an and hadith. See Lacroix 2009, pp. 58–80. Lacroix traces Indian Ahl-i Hadith influence on al-Albani via Sa'd ibn 'Atiq (1850–1930) and his student 'Abd al-'Aziz ibn Baz, later the grand *mufti* of Saudi Arabia.
21. Also called 'scholastic Salafism' (*al-salafiyya al-'ilmiyya*), or *Jāmī* or *Madkhalī* Salafism.
22. Also known as *ḥarakī*, *ṣaḥwī*, or *Surūrī* Salafis.
23. On these three types, see Haykal 2009, pp. 48–50. See Lacroix 2009, pp. 74–7; Wiktorowicz 2006, pp. 207–39. For a critique, see Hegghammer 2009, pp. 251–7.
24. On the concept of 'religious marketplace', see Finke and Stark 2000, pp. 193–8, 283–4; Green 2011, pp. 8–23, 240–3. Green, quoting Stark, defends the 'religious economy model'. See also Kuiper 2018a, p. 14 n. 25, p. 132 n. 17; for yet another extension of the concept, see Farquhar 2017, pp. 10–18.
25. Esposito 2000, pp. 1–12.
26. Berger 2008, p. 23.

CHAPTER 5

Contextualising modern *da'wa*, eighteenth to twentieth centuries

This chapter examines key historical contexts and transformations which paved the way for a renewed accent on *da'wa* among Muslims in the modern period. We consider, first, a trend towards renewal and reform among eighteenth-century Muslims and, second, the transformations associated with the high modern or colonial age (*circa* nineteenth to mid-twentieth centuries). This provides the necessary backdrop for Chapter 6, a survey of Islamic *da'wa* movements which emerged around the world in the shadow of colonialism, *circa* 1850–1950.[1] This is what we are calling the *first phase* of modern *da'wa*. Chapter 7 covers a *second phase, circa* 1950–2020.

Contextualising modern *da'wa* 1: early modern Islamic reform

As far as many *da'wa*-minded Muslims today are concerned, modern missionary thought and practice in Islam emerge, or should emerge, directly from the Qur'an and life of the Prophet (see Chapters 1 and 2) and perhaps secondarily from the antecedents of pre-modern Islamic history (see Chapters 3 and 4). Muslim communities over the past century and more have indeed pored over their sacred sources for guidance on how to be Muslim and do *da'wa*, but there is clearly more to the story than that. After all, what prompts religious communities in the first place to return to foundational sources or to recover old concepts in the face of new challenges? The usual answer consists of historical transformations or crises of various kinds; not long ago, many observers viewed the crisis of the Muslim world's encounter with modernity and the West as the most significant factor behind the lively ferment of modern Islam. Albert Hourani, for instance, in his seminal 1962 book *Arabic Thought in the Liberal Age, 1798–1939* began with Napoleon's entry into Egypt (1798) and spent much of his book on the ways in which modern Muslims reacted to or appropriated western thought. While Napoleon's short-lived colonisation of Egypt was indeed a symbolic turning point, and while western thought has undeniably served as a challenge and inspiration to Muslim thinkers, Hourani later concluded that the massive renovations of modern Islamic thought were already stirring prior to the Muslim world's fateful encounter with Europe and that, to a significant extent, they grew out of dynamics that are indigenous to Islam.[2] In agreement with Hourani's later judgment, this section argues that, while the crises of western colonialism and modernity were very significant in prompting and shaping modern *da'wa*, our starting point in this chapter should be Islam's latent impulse towards renewal and reform, an impulse that, as we have already seen, has appeared again and again (in diverse guises) in the missionary history of Islam. That is to say, modern *da'wa* is not in the first place a reaction to external factors, but something produced from within.

One of the 'most characteristic traits of the Islamic vision of history [is] the idea . . . that this history was said to have begun with a golden age, which was said to have been inevitably followed by a period of . . . deviation and finally of division'.[3] Not only Salafis (see Introduction to Part II), but Muslims in general have identified the Islamic 'golden age' with the time of Islam's first three generations –the Prophet and his Companions, the Successors of the Companions and the Successors of the Successors – the same generations which are credited with the founding and early expansion of Islam. With such idealised models to live up to, it has not been difficult for subsequent periods of Islamic history to be judged as falling woefully short. Among the consequences of this way of thinking is a 'restless disposition' towards renewal (*tajdīd*, hereafter *tajdid*) and reform (*iṣlāḥ*, hereafter *islah*) in Islam.[4] In a well-known hadith, the Prophet is quoted as saying that there will be a 'renewer' (*mujaddid*, one who does *tajdid*) for each Islamic century.[5] It is expected, in other words, that Islamic history will be marked by periods of corruption and waywardness, but that *mujaddid*s will come from time to time in order to restore the pristine Islam of the Prophet. In light of this, it is not surprising that, as Part I demonstrated, reform-minded preachers have appeared throughout Islamic history, beginning with the Prophet Muhammad himself, whose *da'wa* (as examined in Chapters 1 and 2) was a summons to *renew* or *return* to a pure and primordial monotheism. We might also recall the strongly restorationist *da'wa*s of the 'Abbasids and the Fatimids (see Chapter 3). And who can forget the reformist preaching of the likes of Ibn Taymiyya (see Chapter 4) and others throughout the centuries?

Coming nearer to the period covered in this chapter, the centuries from *circa* 1600–1800 witnessed the rise of numerous *tajdid* movements across the Muslim ecumene. It has recently been argued that the nearly simultaneous emergence of so many *tajdid*-oriented movements in the early modern period can be traced to a '"crisis of conscience" that surrounded the turning of the Islamic millennium in 1591'.[6] As we saw in Chapter 4, the background for the rising critique of Sufism in the seventeenth and eighteenth centuries was in fact the success of the Sufis in indigenising Islam and thus facilitating its spread to new places. As of the eighteenth century, it was still the case that Sufism was largely 'indistinguishable from Islam in general'.[7] But while the indigenising diversity of Sufism was a key to the success of Islamisation in pre-modern times, that same diversity would energise the *da'wa* preaching of Muslim reformers – some from within Sufism and some from without – who preached that there was but one true Islam, an Islam from which Muslims had allegedly strayed in a variety of ways. Most importantly for our purposes, these reform movements foreshadowed and prepared the way for the twentieth- and twenty-first-century *da'wa* efflorescence.[8] Let us consider three examples from different parts of the Muslim world.

First, among the most important examples of pre-colonial Islamic renewal (in retrospect) was the movement of Muhammad Ibn 'Abd al-Wahhab (1703–92) in eighteenth-century Arabia.[9] 'Abd al-Wahhab sought to purify Islam of what he considered to be unscriptural innovations and restore what he believed to be the true practice of Islam based on the proto-Salafi thought of none other than Ibn Taymiyya. He was distressed by what he saw as the idolatry of popular Sufi piety, and he was committed to a radical return to *tawhid* – the central Islamic belief in One God and rejection of all God-substitutes. The trigger for the reformist preaching of 'Abd al-Wahhab, in other words, was not primarily an encounter with the West, but his perception that Muslim practice in his own time had departed from the sources. 'Abd al-Wahhab was a *da'i* insofar as he sought to persuade others and eventually gained a respectable following.[10] In fact, his movement was known as the 'Najdi *da'wa*' (*al-da'wa al-najdiyya*, from Najd, Abd al-Wahhab's home region).[11] 'Wherever ['Abd al-Wahhab] went, he found that [Muslims] had lapsed into religious ignorance, *jahiliyya* . . . His call (*da'wa*), the essence of the Wahhabi mission, was to revive pure devotion of worship to God alone'.[12] 'Abd al-Wahhab's model for *da'wa* was not only the Muhammad of Mecca, however, but also the Muhammad of Medina.[13] Although he relied on missionary preaching and education as central aspects of his strategy, 'Abd al-Wahhab also seems to have accepted that godly Muslim rulers were necessary to fully carry out the qur'anic duty to 'command the right and forbid the wrong' (see Chapter 1). Thus, he ultimately hoped to form an alliance with an Arab ruler who would help him establish his vision of an Islamic society built on *tawhid*.[14] In the mid-eighteenth century, he won over just such a ruler, the chieftain of Dar'iyya, Muhammad b. Sa'ud, and several members of his family (at the time, the interior of Arabia was ruled by competing chieftains, with the western littoral and the holy cities controlled by the Ottomans).[15]

From these beginnings, the consolidation of Ibn Sa'ud's power in Najd and military expansion throughout Arabia went hand in hand with the Wahhabi *da'wa* – a pattern which would be repeated in the early twentieth century with the second major rise of the Saudi state (see Chapter 6). In order to justify militant expansionism, 'Abd al-Wahhab drew on the hadiths and legal precedents mentioned in Chapters 2 and 3 regarding the necessity of extending *da'wa* to unbelievers prior to fighting them, and he argued that this principle could also be applied to wayward or false Muslims. So long as one invited them to true Islam (meaning true *tawhid*, as understood by 'Abd al-Wahhab), and so long as a military *jihad* had been declared by a legitimate Muslim ruler, one could, if wayward Muslims resisted, attack them, confiscate their property, enforce proper Islam among them and so on.[16]

In fact, there is an interesting parallelism, also noted in Wahhabi hagiographies, between the trajectory of the Prophet's own seventh-century *da'wa* and that of 'Abd al-Wahhab in eighteenth-century Arabia. As discussed *vis-à-vis* the Prophet in Chapter 2 and as seen in the eighteenth-century Wahhabi movement, there was a transition from *da'wa* from a position of weakness (or Meccan *da'wa*) to *da'wa* from a position of growing strength (or Medinan *da'wa*). Moreover, just as the Prophet, once he had attained sufficient political strength, is portrayed as having sent agents (*'ummāl*) to call the tribes of Arabia to Islam as well as to political submission, Ibn Sa'ud and 'Abd al-Wahhab sent agents and letters of religio-political *da'wa* to the towns of Arabia in their time.[17] Even though 'Abd al-Wahhab and later Wahhabis faced considerable Muslim opposition (on both theological and political grounds), his teachings would, from this time on, serve as the official doctrine of the Saudi state in its various iterations.[18] In turn, especially after the 1950s Saudi Arabia would use its oil wealth and position of regional leadership to fund Salafi-Wahhabi *da'wa* efforts around the world. In other words, the conversion of the Sa'ud family to 'Abd al-Wahhab's teachings combined with the eventual wealth of the Saudi state ensured that the Najdi *da'wa* would not fade from historical memory (in his own time, Abd al-Wahhab's movement was an outlier in terms of mainstream Islam), but would become one of the most consequential in modern Islam.

It is important to note, however, that well before Saudi Arabia became an established, wealthy Middle Eastern power in the twentieth century, 'Abd al-Wahhab's ideas were already making a global impact. For instance, the revivalist Padri movement of nineteenth-century Sumatra was spearheaded by men who had had embraced Wahhabi ideas while in Arabia for the *hajj*. Similarly, the Fara'idi movement in Bengal was initiated by Haji Shariatullah (1781–1840), a scholar who carried Wahhabi teachings and zeal back home after spending nearly twenty years in Arabia in the late eighteenth and early nineteenth centuries. Wahhabi *da'wa*, in other words, was already 'going global' to some extent before the Saudi discovery of oil. We will return to the role that oil-generated wealth has played in the Wahhabi *da'wa* in Chapter 7.

A second example is Shah Wali Allah of Delhi (1703–62), a contemporary of 'Abd al-Wahhab, who came to be widely regarded as a *mujaddid*.[19] A member of the Naqshbandi Sufi order, Wali Allah built on the sober, reformist Sufism (or Shari'a-Sufism) for which the Naqshbandis had become famous beginning in fourteenth-century Central Asia.[20] A century prior to Wali Allah's own time, Shaykh Ahmad Sirhindi (d. 1624), who was celebrated (by himself among others) as a *mujaddid*, became the eponymous founder of the Mujaddidi branch of the Naqshbandi order, a branch which was very active in the missionary expansion of Islam throughout South Asia, the Ottoman lands and Central Asia.[21] The continuing activity of the Naqshbandis provides an indicator that, far from being swept away in modern times, many Sufi orders were actually revived and have played major roles in modern Islam.[22] Unlike Sirhindi who lived at the height of Mughal power in India, Wali Allah witnessed the steady eighteenth-century disintegration of Muslim political power following the time of the Mughal emperor Aurangzeb (d. 1707).[23] While European power had appeared on the horizon in Wali Allah's time, the eighteenth-century decline of the Mughal Empire owed more to fellow 'Indians' like the Jats, Marathas and Sikhs, as well as fellow Muslims like the Persian and Afghan warlords who invaded Delhi throughout the eighteenth century.[24] At any rate, Wali Allah came to believe that the political disorder he saw around him was a result of religious deviation among Muslims. Thus, Wali Allah felt that the *'ulama* and *'ulama*-Sufis had a responsibility to restore correct Islamic belief and practice as a prelude to the restoration of Muslim political power. This was to be done through direct engagement with the Qur'an and especially with hadith, legal creativity (*ijtihad*)[25] and efforts to curb Sufi 'excesses', along with Shi'ite and Hindu influences on India's Muslims. Wali Allah's efforts were primarily concentrated on fellow and future *'ulama*. What we might call Wali Allah's *da'wa*, therefore, was not yet a grassroots, to-the-ordinary-people *da'wa*. Nevertheless, in the decades and centuries to come, Wali Allah's legacy would be claimed and built upon by several major *da'wa*-minded groups in South Asia and beyond.

A third example of eighteenth/nineteenth-century reform from yet another region of the world was the movement led by 'Uthman Dan Fodio (or 'Uthman b. Fudi; 1754–1817) in what today is northern Nigeria. Dan Fodio founded the Sokoto Caliphate (which was eventually to become the largest independent state of nineteenth-century Africa) through the so-called 'Fulani *jihad*'.[26] This brought an end to the Hausa states in northern Nigeria, some of the rulers of which are memorialised in the *Kano Chronicle* (see Chapter 4). Prior to his founding of the Sokoto Caliphate, Dan Fodio had already established himself as a reformist scholar and preacher calling for a return to a less 'superstitious' practice of Islam. A shaykh of the Qadiri Sufi order, Dan Fodio 'inspired a reform movement that transformed the role of Islam in West Africa: What had been the profession mainly of religious specialists became the everyday religion of ordinary people'.[27] It is important to note that Dan Fodio was not alone in his activities: 'By the late 1700s, all across Saharan Africa Sufis' – such as Ahmad al-Tijani (d. 1815, namesake of the Tijaniyya Sufi order), Ahmad ibn Idris (d. 1837, namesake of the Idrisiyya or Muhammadiyya) and others – were calling Muslims back to "true" Islam'.[28] Religio-political reform movements also took place in Futa Jalon, Niger and along the Gambia River. We will see that Dan Fodio and several of his contemporaries remain inspirations for African *da'wa* movements today.

These three examples (among others we might have chosen) show that a trend towards Islamic renewal and reform, in line with earlier precedents, was already stirring in the early modern world before the rise of full-blown European colonialism. In their own ways, each anticipated important trends in twentieth- and twenty-first-century *da'wa*. For instance, all were united in preaching against the supposedly wayward condition of Muslims, and all emphasised a return to scripture (especially hadith) and independent legal thought (*ijtihad*).[29] In the name of banishing unacceptable innovations, they were united in calling for an end to Sufi practices – shrine-centred Sufism was attacked with particular force – which they believed had no basis in the sources.[30] Although to differing degrees and to a lesser extent than would be seen later, each was concerned about ordinary Muslims, whom they wanted to see brought back to more authentic versions of Islam. In their relentless critique of accommodationist or popular versions of Islam, early modern renewal movements, then, were moving in the direction of the de-localised, scripturalist, one might even say 'Protestant' brands of Islam, such as Salafism, that would become the rallying cry of many later *da'wa* movements. However, of the three, the Wahhabi movement has been by far the most willing to practise *takfir* (labelling other Muslims unbelievers) and to justify the use of coercion against wayward Muslims. Indeed, these movements anticipate the diversity of contemporary *da'wa* with respect to politics. Abd al-Wahhab and Dan Fodio saw state-formation and the use of state power, alongside grassroots preaching, as vital to their projects, while Wali Allah remained mostly apolitical and focused on the training of reform-minded *'ulama*. Therefore, while it might be said that 'Abd al-Wahhab and Dan Fodio operated under Medinan *da'wa*logies (Islamisation or renewal through preaching and state power), it is possible to interpret Wali Allah as trending, at least subtly, in the direction of a Meccan *da'wa*logy (Islamisation or renewal through preaching and education alone). These movements also anticipate modern *da'wa* in terms of the varied ways in which they related to Sufism. While the preaching of 'Abd al-Wahhab was thoroughly anti-Sufi (although he apparently never used the word 'Sufi' in his polemics),[31] the examples of Sirhindi, Wali Allah, Dan Fodio and others show that, into the 1800s, it was often the Sufis themselves preaching a *da'wa* of renewal and reform.[32] Still today, Sufis are among the most successful purveyors of *da'wa*; at the same time, attacks on 'Sufism' constitute a major aspect of the *da'wa*s of their rivals.

Contextualising modern *da'wa* 2: high modern colonialism

While early modern renewal movements within Islam anticipated the twentieth and twenty-first century *da'wa* upsurge, the rise of European colonialism and colonial modernity would give further impetus and urgency to modern *da'wa*. If there was a growing feeling among seventeenth- and eighteenth-century

5.1 A monumental shift in the balance of Muslim piety

Whatever their precise relationship to Sufism, at the heart of eighteenth-century reform movements were the beginnings of 'a shift in the balance of Muslim piety from an other-worldly to a this-worldly Islam' – a shift Francis Robinson considers to be 'the most important development in Muslim piety of the past thousand years'. This shift would powerfully feed into an emphasis on *da'wa* in the nineteenth and twentieth centuries. According to Robinson, . . .

[A] shift in the balance of Muslim piety from an other-worldly to a this-worldly Islam . . . meant a devaluing of a faith of contemplation of God's mysteries and of belief in His will to intercede for man on earth, and a valuing instead of a faith in which Muslims were increasingly aware that it was they, and only they, who could act to create a just society on earth . . . The Prophet and his companions had promulgated a this-worldly activist socio-political ethic, but as the Muslim community expanded . . . an other-worldly . . . strand developed in their piety . . . Moved, more often than not, by political decay and corruption in their worlds, the 'ulama and Sufis, and later on the lay folk who led the movements of Muslim revival, were concerned to renew the faith of their societies by removing all practices that compromised the sovereignty of God . . . and by promoting the requirement to act on earth to achieve salvation . . . The expansion of this-worldly piety, and the activism it demands, has released a great surge of energy through Muslim societies . . . It is a process that bears many similarities to the Protestant Reformation in Christianity: the attack on intercession; the emphasis on personal responsibility; the emphasis on literacy and the study of the sources; the role of print; the empowering of individual believers, etc. Indeed, some leaders of the revival drew specific comparisons (Source: Robinson 2011, pp. 13–16, italics added).

Muslims that things were not right in the Muslim world and that reform was needed, that feeling would become much more intense and widespread – at all levels of society – during the high modern or colonial period (early nineteenth to mid-twentieth centuries). During this fateful period, Europe – spurred on by major scientific, industrial, political and religious developments at home – asserted itself in the Muslim ecumene, eventually taking control of vast areas. While pre-modern Muslims, confident in the superiority of their faith and civilisation, took limited notice of the goings-on in what seemed to them the barely-civilised northwestern fringes of the known world, Europe's early modern Renaissance, Reformation and Age of Discovery, and advances in science, seafaring and military technology were building towards 'a revolution in world history'.[33] On the heels of the Wars of Religion, the Enlightenment and the American and French Revolutions, the old European model of Christendom began to give way to nationalist societies in which religion was increasingly seen as properly belonging to the realm of private devotion and/or privately organised (that is, not state-sponsored) activism.[34] As science and a scientific mentality grew in prominence, human society and the world of nature were disenchanted; now they were seen to be amenable to scientific analysis and control. It is in this context that the Industrial Revolution and Europe's commercial and imperialist expansion should be placed. These dynamics 'would profoundly change the conditions of life not only for Muslims but for all the world's peoples'.[35]

As far as the Muslim ecumene was concerned, the major colonial powers were the British (who to varying degrees would come to control India, Egypt, Nigeria, Sudan, Kenya, South Africa, Malaysia, Singapore, Jordan, Palestine and Iraq), the French (who to varying degrees would come to control Algeria, Tunisia, Morocco, Senegal, Mali, Chad, Niger, Syria and Lebanon), the Dutch (who would come to control much of what is now Indonesia) and the Russians (who to varying degrees would come to control the Crimea, the Caucasus and Central Asia).[36] While British, French and Dutch rule of their colonies mostly came to an end by the 1950s, under the Soviets, Russian rule would carry on in Central Asia until the early 1990s. Additionally, during the colonial era the Austro-Hungarians and the Spanish would come to rule Muslim communities in parts of the Balkans and North Africa, respectively.[37] While the primary narrative of this era is one of western advance, it is also worth noting that the Chinese Qing Empire expanded into the Xinjiang region of western China and absorbed the region's Muslim communities beginning in the mid-eighteenth century. Non-Muslim Chinese rule of Xinjiang continues to the present under the People's Republic.[38] A final example of Muslims coming under 'alien rule' was prompted by the significant labour migrations (and other kinds of voluntary and forced migration) that colonialism engendered. Owing to new waves of Muslim migration, more and more Muslims found themselves living as minorities outside traditional *dar al-Islam*. Muslims in these diasporic situations would turn out to be major innovators in *da'wa*.

In short, in about 120 years, from the early nineteenth century to the end of World War I, almost all of the world's Muslim peoples, in one way or another, came under European (or other non-Muslim) rule.[39] While the great early modern Islamic empires were already in decline by the seventeenth and eighteenth centuries, European gains hastened their permanent collapse: the Mughal Empire by 1858 and the Ottoman Empire by the early 1920s (the Safavid Empire had come to an end in 1736). Many smaller Islamic states, when not smothered altogether, were forced to come to terms with European dominance. Only a few areas – Afghanistan, Yemen, Iran and parts of Arabia – could claim to have maintained a tenuous independence. The upshot of all this was a massive disruption of the Islamic world system described in Chapters 3 and 4.[40] There are few analogues to this situation in Islamic history, although perhaps the Mongol depredations of the thirteenth and fourteenth centuries come closest.[41] But unlike the Mongols who eventually converted to Islam, and unlike the Crusaders who had threatened a relatively small area of the Muslim ecumene, 'here were Crusaders who could not be laughed off, Mongols who refused to be converted' (see Map 5.1).[42]

The loss of Muslim political power was far from the only consequence of Europe's rise. Other consequences included the introduction of western ideas about progress and science, along with new western styles of schooling. Enlightenment ideas about 'the rights of man' (and eventually, European abolitionism) would challenge the traditional acceptance of slavery and the inferior position of women and minorities in Islamic societies. In colonial settings, the roles of old-style elites – such as Sufis, *'ulama* and Muslim ruling families – were challenged by foreign administrators and soldiers, along with indigenous but western-educated military officers, journalists, lawyers and bureaucrats. Traditional systems of exchange gave way before a Euro-centric global economy.[43] Colonies were increasingly made to serve the raw materials needs of this economy, a fact which shook up traditional industries and farming practices. The introduction of European technologies – such as the steam engine, the printing press and the telegraph – not only changed how Muslims travelled, moved goods and communicated, but also how they thought about their place in the world.[44] New technologies also facilitated the activities of a growing number of western missionaries, orientalist scholars and others, many of whom arrived in the former Muslim ecumene confident of the superiority of *their* religion(s) and civilisation(s). While the colonial age produced some outstanding western scholarship on Islam, colonial-era studies of Islam tended to fluctuate between romanticising and demonising tendencies.[45] Facts like these underscore the point, noted earlier, that while the rise of modernity was experienced in Europe and North America as a set of internally generated changes, in the Muslim world, the onslaught of modernity was often experienced as something externally imposed, in the context of foreign domination.[46] It is for this reason that the term 'colonial modernity' is entirely appropriate when speaking of the impact of this era among the world's Muslims.

In the midst of this turbulent cauldron of change, one of the most important developments as far as this book is concerned was the widespread *disestablishment* (or at least *felt* disestablishment) of Islam and an accompanying intensification of inter- and intra-religious competition. The Muslim ecumene – governed for centuries by rulers who could be counted on to champion Islam to one degree or another, to maintain public Islamic ambiences and/or to support or provide the contexts within which Chapter 4's 'agents of Islamisation' could operate – was

Map 5.1 The former Muslim ecumene under European and other non-Muslim powers, *circa* 1930.

now largely in the hands of non-Muslims. Of course, one should not exaggerate the extent to which Islam was 'established' in pre-modern times. The policies of pre-modern Muslim rulers differed widely, and sometimes their support for Islam was merely symbolic.[47] Nevertheless, it is still generally the case that Islam enjoyed official support, or at least presumed societal backing and prominence throughout *dar al-Islam* in pre-modern times. With the arrival of direct and indirect foreign control, that support and privilege was endangered or brought to an end.

Although it is natural enough to assume that European colonial policy must have not only disestablished Islam, but also favoured Christianity, it is important to note that a more significant long-term effect of European colonialism was to foster pluralistic environments in which each religion had to make a case for itself in the open marketplace, since none held a monopoly.[48] While the earliest European colonial ventures, such as the Spanish conquest of Latin and South America (*circa* fifteenth and sixteenth centuries), had included efforts to extend Christendom in a heavy-handed manner, subsequent colonial powers generally abandoned the pretence that their enterprises had much to do with religion.[49] Particularly from the eighteenth and nineteenth centuries onwards, colonial authorities came to see religion as a factor to be managed, not promoted. While there were, of course, colonial officials who sympathised with Christian mission and missionaries who collaborated with and benefited from colonial regimes, the fact is that the aims of the two groups were often distinct and, at times, directly at odds.[50] In fact, in their quest to avoid the appearance of religious favouritism, the European powers sometimes discouraged or prohibited missionaries from entering Muslim areas. The British East India Company, for instance, kept missionaries out of India until 1813 and even after that time tried to maintain a stance of religious neutrality so as not to upset the Hindus and Muslims upon whose collaboration British rule depended.[51] In northern Nigeria, the British colonial authorities similarly restricted Christian missionary access 'on the grounds that it might arouse Muslim animosity'.[52] In Egypt after the 1880s, *de facto* British colonialism might have encouraged Christian missionaries to begin directly evangelising Muslims, but in general the British authorities themselves maintained a policy of non-interference which was calculated to avoid arousing 'Muslim popular sentiment against British colonialism'.[53] In colonial West Africa, the French authorities, influenced by *laïcité* (a distinctively French form of secularism) at home, tried with varying degrees of success to maintain a secular stance which favoured neither Christians, nor Muslims, nor practitioners of indigenous religions.

As for the Dutch in the East Indies (today's Indonesia), although there were Dutch Christians and politicians, such as Abraham Kuyper, who felt that God had 'given' Indonesia to the Dutch partly for the purpose of spreading Christianity,[54] the ultimate purpose of the colonial regime was commercial, not religious. Around the turn of the twentieth century, the Dutch government of Indonesia embraced a distinction, made by the orientalist scholar and colonial advisor Christiaan Snouck Hurgronje, between Islam as religion and Islam as political ideology. It decided to take a hands-off approach to the former while keeping a watchful eye on the latter.[55] In late-nineteenth-century Central Asia and the Caucasus, the Russian authorities, adapting the relatively tolerant policies that Catherine the Great (r. 1762–96) had applied to her Muslim-majority territories, did not actively suppress Islam but rather left the religion to fend for itself.[56] This, of course, would change drastically under the Soviets, as we will see. At any rate, this general pattern of leaving Islam to itself in its own 'religious' sphere, so long as Muslim actors did not turn 'political' or threaten the colonial order, was repeated in varied ways across the former Muslim ecumene. In general, then, it is not that the colonial authorities tried to impose Christianity or Christendom on colonised territories, but rather that they more often 'advanced policies of *disestablishment* . . . facilitating the emergence of "religion" as a private domain of conscience'[57] and as an unregulated (or selectively regulated) marketplace of choice.

A few complications to this overall picture should be noted at this point. For one thing, colonialism was never complete; there were some areas, noted above, which never came under direct colonial rule. The Ottoman state, for instance, continued to style itself an Islamic Empire and to patronise Islamic institutions into the early twentieth century. In other places the colonial powers exercised 'indirect rule' through Muslim (and other indigenous) princely states. Examples include the states of Hyderabad and Awadh in India, Bukhara and Khiva in Central Asia, and parts of East and West Africa. In these settings, the colonial powers tended to leave religious affairs in the hands of their Muslim vassals; therefore, Islam was not disestablished to the same degree as in other areas (most of these Muslim principalities would give way to non-Muslim rule in the end). In still other cases – whether in areas of direct or indirect rule – the colonial powers favoured or formed alliances with certain 'cooperative' Muslim actors or groups. The British and French, for instance, tended to cultivate collaborative relations with Sufis, even while jailing or exiling Muslims they considered threatening. By contrast, the Russians in Central Asia harboured a long-standing suspicion of Sufism and tended to look upon anti-Sufi reformers as favoured collaborators.[58] In fact, both the Russian Empire and the later Soviets (after World War II) would maintain government-sponsored Islamic institutions in Central Asia precisely to prevent the rise of underground Islamic movements.

Policies such as these should not, of course, be taken as an indication that only a few western missionaries arrived in the Muslim world during the colonial period. On the contrary, the years from 1793 to 1914 have been called the 'great century' of Protestant missionary endeavour.[59] During these years, Protestant (and eventually also Catholic) Christians fanned out all over the non-western world, bent on extending Christianity, and in many ways it was the colonial order which enabled them to do so.[60] The high modern period in the West has been called the 'age of the voluntary society'. The growing ease of travel and communication, along with Euro-American ideas about the separation of the political and religious spheres, were responsible in part for the nineteenth-century burgeoning of *non-state* voluntary societies and associations devoted to religious and non-religious causes.[61] As it turned out, western Christians were among the most active in forming humanitarian, temperance, abolition, education *and* missionary societies throughout the nineteenth century. Responding in part to the plea of William Carey (1761–1834) that Christians should organise themselves and 'use means' for the conversion of the non-Christian world, the Baptist Missionary Society was formed in England in 1792, the London Missionary Society in 1795, the Scottish and Glasgow Missionary Society in 1796, the Netherlands Missionary Society in 1797, the (Anglican) Church Missionary Society in 1799, the British and Foreign Bible Society in 1804, the American Board of Foreign Missions in 1812 and the American Bible Society in 1816.[62] Dozens of similar denominational and inter-denominational missionary societies were set up in subsequent decades. Of special note was the founding of the China Inland Mission by Hudson Taylor in 1865, an early example of a 'faith mission', of which there would be many imitators. Among Catholics, the Society of Missionaries of Africa (or 'White Fathers') was established in 1868 by Cardinal Charles Lavigerie, who was persuaded that French rule of Algeria had opened a door for Catholic mission to all of Africa. Once they reached their fields of service, western missionaries built churches, schools, orphanages, hospitals and publishing houses. As members of non-state voluntary associations, then, many of the missionaries who planted themselves in the Muslim world took for granted a disestablishment, marketplace model of religious advocacy.[63]

In fact, missionary actors and organisations would not only challenge, but also provide models to Muslims (and members of other religions) who would develop missionary organisations, training centres and presses of their own in the late nineteenth and early twentieth centuries. The activities of colonial-era Christian missionaries, in other words, resulted in a widespread phenomenon of 'counter-proselytism' – the idea that colonised peoples were stirred to missionary activism on behalf of their own (newly reified) religions not only in response to their political subjugation, but also in response to the activities of western missionaries (and over time, by the missionary activities of Hindus, Buddhists, Baha'is and Ahmadis, among others).[64] The nineteenth-century Muslim embrace of the printing press, western education models, steamship and rail travel, Qur'an translation and distribution, as well as efforts to reach and empower lay Muslims (all developments of epochal significance) were owing in part to the presence and modelling of Christian missionaries and other religious competitors.[65] Moreover, the fact that Muslims began to gather in large-scale international conferences or congresses to plan for the advancement of Islam in the modern age, was anticipated by the many missionary meetings and gatherings held by Christians into the twentieth century.[66] Contrary to the western missionaries' hopes, therefore, one of the most enduring 'unexpected consequences' of Christian mission in the colonial era was to stir up an urgent Muslim defence of Islam, a dynamic which in turn generated a host of 'new [Muslim] religious entrepreneurs, firms, products, and communities' often patterned on those of the missionaries.[67] That is to say, although Christian missionaries in the former Muslim ecumene 'gained relatively few Muslim converts', their impact in prompting movements of counter-proselytism was immense.[68] Evidence for this can be seen in the ways Christian missionaries are referenced in a wide range of Muslim writings from the colonial period.[69] As we will see in Chapter 6, everywhere in the colonial Muslim world, Muslim writers and preachers spoke about the twin menaces of western imperialism and Christian mission, and such ideas have continued to reverberate right down to the present.[70] A final note: while our focus here has been on places where Christian missionaries were active, in Russian Central Asia and the Caucasus, in Chinese-ruled Xinjiang, in French Algeria and eventually in British Palestine, Muslim alarm was heightened by the added dynamic of Russian, (Han) Chinese, French and Jewish mass immigration and land appropriation.[71]

Contributing yet further to the emergence of religious marketplace environments and mentalities in the colonial Muslim world was the fact that colonial regimes began to count their populations and to classify them by race, language *and religion*. In the British census of 1871, for example, communities in India were counted on the basis of religion for the first time.[72] As religions came to be reified as discreet 'systems', and as Europeans began to enumerate people on the basis of such differences, the strength of Islam came to be regarded as a function of the numerical strength of the worldwide Muslim community. As opposed to the pre-modern scenario in which the identification of ordinary people with Islam might have been little more than a matter of visits to Sufi shrines or occasional participation in Islamic rituals, ordinary people now had to be made conscious that they were 'Muslims', adherents of the 'world religion' called 'Islam'. This in turn required mass outreach efforts. In addition, the perception that religious competitors, especially Christian missionaries, focused their proselytising on the 'ignorant masses' led to a race for numbers. In other words, a new concern with the numerical strength of Islam combined with a heightened awareness of religious competitors in disestablishment situations prompted Muslim religious leaders (and leaders of other religions) to turn their attention towards ordinary people. This *turn to the masses* is among the most important features of modern Islamic thought and activism, a feature which would feed all the more into (and be fed by) a new emphasis on *da'wa*.[73]

A final piece of the colonial puzzle is the fact that in the late nineteenth and early twentieth centuries, western power and influence seemed to 'embrace Muslim societies ever more tightly'.[74] Throughout colonial times, up to the early years of the twentieth century, there were multiple militant *jihad* movements which attempted to preserve or re-instate Islam's establishment status by confronting European encroachment through force of arms.[75] For instance, there was the *jihad* of Sayyid Ahmad of Bareilly (d. 1831) in early-nineteenth-century India (a *jihad* that was preceded by village-to-village *da'wa* preaching and a ground-breaking use of the printing press),[76] the above-mentioned Padri movement of Sumatra (1821–38), the Java *jihad* of 1825–30, the anti-Russian *jihad*s of the Naqshbandi followers of Ghazi Muhammad (d. 1832) and Imam Shamil (d. 1871) in the Caucasus, the 1832–47 anti-French *jihad* in Algeria led by the religious scholar 'Abd al-Qader (d. 1883), the 1857 anti-British uprising (or 'Mutiny') in India, the Aceh war of 1873–1904 (which provided the context for some of the activities of the above-mentioned Christiaan Snouck Hurgronje), the anti-French Algerian uprising of 1870–1, the anti-Ottoman, French, British and Italian activities of the Sanussiyya Sufi order in North Africa in the late nineteenth and early twentieth centuries, the 1898 Andijan uprising against the Russians led by the Naqshbandi Sufi Shaykh Dukchi Ishan (or Ihsan Madali), the anti-Turkish, Egyptian and British *jihad* of the Mahdist state of Sudan (1881–99) and the anti-Soviet *basmachi jihad*s of the early 1920s. While some of these movements achieved short-term success, perhaps their most notable feature is that they all ultimately failed, with most of them being crushed or 'pacified' by the colonial powers. It is also notable that the same general period witnessed the failure of the most recent major attempt in Islamic history at an 'Abbasid- and Fatimid-style *da'wa* (see Chapter 3), that of the Ottoman Sultan Abdulhamid II (r. 1876–1909). On the heels of the Russian defeat of the Ottomans in the war of 1877–8, a defeat which discredited the modernising Ottoman reform movement known as the *Tanzimat*, Abdulhamid made an attempt to shore up the Ottoman state along more traditional lines, through a pan-Islamic, religio-political *da'wa* centred on himself as the 'caliph' of all Muslims.[77] Among others, the sultan employed the Muslim scholar-activist Jamal al-Din al-Afghani (d. 1897) as a *da'i*. In the end, however, Abdulhamid's *da'wa* was not able to arrest the advance of the European powers, the dismemberment of the Ottoman Empire, nor the eventual abolishment of the caliphate by the new Turkish nationalist state in the early 1920s. In short, by the turn of the twentieth century across the Muslim ecumene, western power – whether in the form of the European powers themselves or of westernising influences – seemed entrenched and, in the eyes of many, irresistible.

Conclusion: towards the first phase of modern *da'wa*

Among the consequences of this apparent tightening of the western grip on power and, indeed, in consequence of all we have discussed in this chapter, there was a growing recognition among Muslims around the turn of the twentieth century that open resistance to the new rulers was no longer a practical or realistic option. There was also a clear-eyed recognition that there would be no going back to the way things had been in pre-modern times. Western technological modernity was here to stay. Later in the twentieth century, especially after World War II, diverse independence movements across the Muslim world (and the non-western world in general) would in fact succeed in throwing off European rule, sometimes assisted by force of arms. Many of these, however, had little more than an Islamic veneer to them. As we will see later, moreover, the independence struggles did not ultimately dislodge the feeling among many Muslims that they were living in the modern world on terms set by (non-Muslim) others. Nevertheless, as of the dawn of the twentieth century, following on the heels of so many unsuccessful *jihad*s, restoration of Islamic rule seemed a long way off.

Many Muslims, one might say, came to realise that they were no longer in 'Medina', but back in 'Mecca' – under alien rule, largely deprived of worldly power, and faced with unprecedented threats to their religion. Put differently, one might say that Muslims around the world were subject to a process of minoritisation: They were reduced to the experience of living as a minority people or group of peoples (see Introduction to Part II). This minoritisation could be quite literal – for instance, in cases where Muslims who had been minorities, but under Islamic rule, suddenly found themselves under non-Muslim rule. This happened, as we will see, in India in the eighteenth and nineteenth centuries and in parts of the Caucasus and the Balkans in the nineteenth century. Minoritisation was also literal for those millions of Muslims who began to live outside of *dar al-Islam*, for instance, in western countries, during the colonial period and beyond. But minoritisation could also be figurative or experiential. That is, even in Muslim majority contexts, there could be a *felt* minority experience prompted by the rise of foreign domination, the disestablishment of Islam and the rising prestige of western ways of thinking and living. Minoritisation could also result from the diversification of Muslim communities, if, for example, secular-minded Muslims gained power and tried to marginalise more conservative brands of Islam, or *vice versa*. The key point is that, whatever their specific circumstances, Muslims worldwide were confronted with the realisation they were living in a world not of their own making.

In response to these circumstances, while there were some who continued to call for political and militant *jihad*, another very important trend was that of making an uneasy peace with the new realities. Whether they set aside political and military *jihad* at this time as a matter of principle or merely out of pragmatism, the fact is that many Muslim leaders did precisely that, adopting a range of quietist (non-political) positions which would simultaneously allow them to pursue their programs of reform and outreach and avoid overt conflict with the new rulers. It is in this overall colonial context that Muslims, drawing on the rich Islamic traditions of reform and renewal, began to seriously excavate missionary *da'wa* from the Islamic past. If the strength of the colonial order seemed to foreclose explicit military or political resistance in the short term, if Islam was no longer in an established place of privilege and if Muslims had been minoritised in one way or another, they could still do *jihad* or 'struggle in the way of God' through educational and missionary *da'wa* in the religious marketplace. Indeed, in an indirect way, this could constitute a powerful form of resistance to colonial domination in its own right.[78] Perhaps, many Muslim leaders thought, God has allowed infidels to rule over us because of our waywardness and in order to test us. Perhaps it is not our job to re-establish the political or territorial greatness of Islam immediately, but rather to struggle through *da'wa* – to do *jihad*-as-*da'wa* – for the incremental reform and purification of the Muslim masses and the defence of Islam here in our 'Mecca'. Perhaps, if we are persistent in this, God will intervene in time to restore 'Medina'. In fact, not only does such thinking permeate Muslim writings from the late nineteenth and early twentieth centuries, this era also witnessed a burgeoning of new Islamic movements oriented towards missionary *da'wa* – movements which, having pragmatically accepted the realities of the colonial situation and having learned from competitors like Christian missionaries, got to work spreading and defending Islam. Yet, as we will see, they did so from diverse perspectives and on behalf of alternative versions of Islam and visions of the future. We now turn to a survey of *da'wa*-oriented movements up to *circa* 1950.

Notes

1. 1950 is an approximation for the point in the mid-twentieth century when many territories of the Muslim world entered their post-colonial histories.
2. Hourani 1962/1983. For his later view, see Hourani 1991, pp. 125–36. He writes of *Arabic Thought*: 'It now seems to me to have been wrong [to lay] too much emphasis upon ideas which were taken from Europe, and not enough upon what was retained, even if in a changed form, from an older tradition . . .'
3. Chaumont 1960–2007.
4. Hefner 2011b, p. 8.
5. Abu Dawud 2008, no. 4291 (vol. 5, p. 16). See Voll 1983.
6. Green 2012, pp. 128–9, 154–7.
7. Ibid., pp. 154–5.
8. Despite their similarities, these movements diverged in important ways. See Commins 2006, pp. 11, 218 (n. 13); see also Farquhar 2017, pp. 31–2.
9. Commins 2006, ch. 1. This chapter provides a useful summary of 'Abd al-Wahhab's *Kitāb*

al-Tawḥīd (or Book of God's Unity). See also DeLong-Bas 2004, ch. 2; Hodgson 1974, vol. 3, pp. 158–61.

10.   Thus, al-Fiqī (1358/1935) entitled his study *Āthār al-daʿwa al-wahhābiyya*. ʿAbd al-Wahhab not only wrote theological and legal works, but also *daʿwa* letters inviting others to his cause.

11.   Commins 2006, p. 47; Crawford 2011, pp. 147–61; Qadhi 2014. 'In order to ensure proper missionary work, Ibn Abd al-Wahhab wrote the treatise *Kitab Kashf al-Shubhat* as a 'how-to' guide for his followers in matters of conversation and debate'. DeLong-Bas 2004, p. 199.

12.   Commins 2006, p. 3

13.   I generally agree with DeLong-Bas: 'Although many have claimed that Wahhabis believe that jihad is the appropriate means of proselytization, Ibn Abd al-Wahhab's writings make it clear that he believed that daʿwah, or missionary work, was the preferred method for gaining true adherents'. DeLong-Bas 2004, p. 194. This book's Meccan/Medinan distinction provides a way to see ʿAbd al-Wahhab's mission in both terms.

14.   Crawford 2011 usefully nuances the usual way in which the story of the *daʿwa* of early Wahhabism is told.

15.   'In AH 1157/1744 CE, the *amīr* and the theologian swore an oath of mutual loyalty (*bayʿa*) to strive, by force if necessary, to make . . . God's word prevail. This pact . . . marked the true beginning of the Wahhābī state . . .' Laoust 1960–2007.

16.   On ʿAbd al-Wahhab theory of jihad, see Commins 2006, pp. 24–6. For an alternative reading, see DeLong-Bas 2004, ch. 5. DeLong-Bas writes: 'Rather than proclaiming the responsibility of Muslims to fight permanently and continuously . . . against . . . all non-Wahhabis . . . ʿAbd al- Wahhab's writings reveal a worldview in which education and dialogue play [an] important role in winning converts . . . than does violence'.

17.   Commins 2006, pp. 24–30.

18.   On the fierce opposition the Wahhabis faced, see Commins 2006, pp. 19–30.

19.   Interestingly, Wali Allah studied hadith with a Medinese scholar who also taught ʿAbd al-Wahhab, Muhammad Haya al-Sindi (d. 1750). Dallal 1993, p. 342.

20.   The Naqshbandiyya began in Central Asia, in the region around Bukhara with Khwaja Baha' al-Din (d. 1318). See Algar 1960–2007; Weismann2007.

21.   Richards 2007, pp. 98–100; Weismann 2007, ch. 4; see also Metcalf 1982, pp. 21–2.

22.   See Green 2012, ch. 4.

23.   On the imperial 'overreach' of Aurangzeb resulting in increasing loss of power to regional powers, see Hardy 1972, pp. 19–23.

24.   The invasion of Delhi by the Persian Nadir Shah in 1739 was felt to be particularly devastating to Mughal power.

25.   Metcalf 1982, pp. 36–8; Dallal 1993, p. 343f.

26.   The *daʿwa*s of both ʿAbd al-Wahhab and Dan Fodio included a role for *jihad*: for both, '*hijra*, migration to a true community, and *jihad* . . . were . . . overriding obligations'. Lapidus 2002, p. 419. Dan Fodio's caliphate lasted until the British Protectorate in 1903. Sanneh 2003, pp. 232–44.

27.   Last 1960–2007.

28.   Green 2012, p. 172.

29.   Hodgson 1974, vol. 3, p. 161.

30.   Green 2012, p. 172.

31.   Ibid., p. 160

32.   Ibid., p. 157; Robinson 2011, pp. 16–17. We have mentioned the Naqshbandiyya, Tijaniyya and Idrisiyya, but others, like the Khalwatiyya, were also active.

33.   For a good summary, see Lapidus 2014, pp. 501–7.

34. For an account of the rise and collapse of Christendom in Europe, see Walls 1997, pp. 68–94. Although national churches persisted in parts of Europe, western political leaders came to see themselves not primarily as defenders of Christianity, but of national interest. One exception was the Russian Empire, which retained a confessional identity. See also McLeod 2007, pp. 6–29 (see the definition of 'Christendom' on p. 18).

35. Lapidus 2014, p. 501.

36. On the Russian occupation of Central Asia, see Khalid 2007, ch. 2. Unlike the maritime powers, Russia's expansion into Central Asia, like that of China into Xinjiang and Tibet, took place in 'territories contiguous with the imperial homelands'. Thus, from the Russian and Chinese points of view, 'the "colonial" problem was a "minority" problem'. Lapidus 2014, pp. 667, 696–7.

37. For useful summaries, see Robinson 2011, pp. 1–13; Green 2012, pp. 187–91.

38. '[I]n areas beyond Western control Muslim communities were coming to feel the weight of alien rule'. Robinson 2011, p. 3.

39. Robinson 2011, p. 3.

40. For centuries, 'Muslims had grown accustomed to regarding their civilization as foremost in trade, science, and the arts', as well as in religion. Hefner 2011b, p. 2.

41. The fifteenth-century Catholic Reconquista of Spain is another example, although it was more localised in its effects.

42. Brown 2017, p. 284

43. While Silk Road trade continued, Europe's maritime trading would surpass it. So, too, Europeans would dominate maritime routes, such as Indian Ocean routes, which had once been dominated by Muslim traders.

44. See Gelvin and Green 2014b, pp. 1–23.

45. In turn, the 'Islams' as portrayed by western writers would inform the ways some Muslims would come to understand their own tradition. For example, some Europeans would convert to Sufi versions of Islam celebrated by romanticising authors, while some Muslims, such as Muhammad Iqbal (1877–1938) and 'Salafi' thinkers, would echo western critics in decrying the supposed decadence of Sufism. See, for instance, Green 2012, pp. 200–1, 214–15.

46. Nevertheless, modernity should be thought of as 'a series of transformations in which most of the people of the world participated and to which most of them contributed'. Moore 2004, p. xxi.

47. Sometimes, too, what was privileged by Muslim states was a 'courtly-cosmopolitan' Islam of art, philosophy, or science, not 'urban religious' Islam. Lapidus 2002, p. 67. Also, despite the ideal union of religious and political in scripture and law, pre-modern Islamic societies generally observed a pragmatic separation of the two. Lapidus 1975, pp. 363–85. See also Hefner 2011b, p. 8.

48. The experience of the Muslim world under colonialism illustrates a sociological principle: 'To the degree that a religious economy is *unregulated*, it will tend to be[come] very pluralistic' (and we might add, competitive). Stark and Finke 2000, pp. 193–8, 283–4; Green 2011, pp. 8–23, 240–3; Farquhar 2017, pp. 10–18. I am stressing the point that 'situations of disestablishment' favour voluntarist forms of religious propagation.

49. As the Portuguese had already learned in sixteenth-century Asia, Islam, Hinduism and Buddhism, as well as the civilisations built upon them, proved much more resistant to Christianisation than the indigenous religions of the Americas. See Walls 1997, pp. 57–163. See also Walls 2002, pp. 27–48.

50. Over time, an 'ideological rift' emerged between missionaries and 'British officialdom' over colonial policies. 'But this rift was not visible to many Muslims . . . who instead saw missions

and empire as allies'. Sharkey 2005, pp. 43–60. From a long-term perspective, missions can be seen as undermining colonialism, as seen, for example, in Sanneh 2009.

51. In light of nineteenth-century British sensitivity to the religious concerns of Hindu elites upon whose collaboration they depended, Frykenberg goes so far as to call the British Raj a 'Hindu Raj'. He speaks elsewhere of the 'fragility of British rule', since it depended on 200,000 to 300,000 Indian civil servants and comparable numbers of Indian infantry. See Frykenberg 2008, chs 7, 11.
52. Launay 2011, p. 259.
53. See Sharkey 2008, p. 142.
54. Goddard 2001, p. 127.
55. Lapidus 2014, p. 733.
56. The Russians took the approach that 'Islam was to be ignored, not destroyed'. Khalid 2007, p. 39.
57. Ingram 2018, p. 32, italics added.
58. This was traceable to their hard-won victory over the Caucasian *jihad* state of the Naqshbandi Sufi Imam Shamil in 1859. See Green 2012, p. 205 and, more generally, pp. 191–206.
59. Latourette wrote: 'Never before in a period of equal length had Christianity or any other religion penetrated . . . as large an area as it had in the nineteenth century . . . Never before had so many hundreds of thousands contributed voluntarily of their means to assist the spread of Christianity or any other religion'. These lines, taken from various volumes of Latourette's *Expansion* are brought together in Hudson 1973, p. 157.
60. Even though 'the high period of the European empires in the later nineteenth century provided a degree of security for [Christian] missionaries by comparison with earlier periods, the official policy of the colonial powers had other goals, which often involved the conciliation or furtherance of Islam'. Walls 1997, p. 84.
61. Many of the associations formed at this time crossed international boundaries, in part through what Benedict Anderson called 'print capitalism' – the production of printed literature which gave people access to 'imagined communities' of common interest. While nationalism was on the rise in this period, participation in voluntary associations allowed people to transcend the confines of their nationalities and work for larger causes (such as 'world religions'). Anderson 1991. See also, Metcalf 1992, pp. 229–31; Bayly 2004, pp. 71–6, 325–63.
62. Carey, who arrived in India in 1793 wrote his 'Enquiry into the Obligations of Christians to use Means for the Conversion of the Heathens' in 1792. See Goddard 2001, p. 122.
63. Fuelled by pietism and the evangelical revivals, many of these activists were committed to the necessity of personal conversion, an experience that made one a member of a global community of believers, independent of any political order.
64. The spur to 'contre-prosélystisme' was the arrival of 'missionnaires protestants évangéliques beaucoup plus systématiques et agressifs que les prêtres catholiques qui les avaient précédés . . .' Gaborieau 2011, p. 5.
65. Robinson 2000b, pp. 66–104. See also Gelvin and Green 2014b, pp. 1–23. Green 2015a, pp. 281–2.
66. Kramer 1986, p. ix.
67. For a useful synopsis of colonial Christian missions' consequences, see Sharkey 2013b, pp. 1–14. On the burgeoning of Islamic 'firms' see Green 2015a, pp. 281–8.
68. Sharkey 2005, p. 47.
69. Thinkers as diverse as Jamal al-Din al-Afghani, Rehmatullah Kairanawi, Rashid Ahmad Gangohi, Muhammad Qasim Nanautawi, Muhammad Zakariyya, Muhammad 'Abduh, Rashid Rida, Sayyid Ahmad Khan, Ahmad Dahlan, Muhammad Iqbal, Muhammad

Husayn Haykal and many others made frequent mention of Christian missions as a way of motivating Muslims to take up the defence of Islam.

70. For further examples, see Sharkey 2005, pp. 54–6; Goddard 2001, pp. 133–5.
71. For example, Lapidus 2014, pp. 668–9.
72. The census forced people to identify themselves as 'Hindu' or 'Muslim'. This contributed to the creation of 'the pan-Indian "Muslim" and "Hindu" communities'. Sikand 2002, p. 25. A reification of the various communities of Sri Lanka was also a result of British policies in that context. See Berkwitz 2008, pp. 202–3.
73. A closely related dynamic was a growing pan-Islamic sentiment among Muslims fostered by an increase in Muslim travels (for instance, to Mecca for the pilgrimage or *hajj*), as well as by the availability of printed literature such as newspapers. These factors made it possible for Muslims in one place to take an interest in events involving Muslims thousands of miles away. For instance, Muslims in India took to the streets in the early twentieth century to protest the abolishment of the Ottoman caliphate by the emerging modern state of Turkey.
74. Robinson 2011, p. 21.
75. On 'anti-colonial *jihad*', see Sedgwick 2007, pp. 10–11.
76. Kuiper 2018a, pp. 116–19; Green 2012, pp. 192–3.
77. 'Abdulhamid pursued a "policy of the caliphate," aimed at strengthening his legitimacy, adding a religious dimension to his power, and resacralizing the office of sultan after the secularization processes triggered by the Tanzimat'. Georgeon 2007. Green 2012, pp. 208–9.
78. If one could not contest the power of the colonial state or dispute the superiority of western technology, one could at least defend one's religion and assert its spiritual superiority. Chatterjee 1993, pp. 3–13; van der Veer 2002, pp. 173–87.

CHAPTER 6

The first phase of modern *da'wa*, *circa* 1850–1950: a survey

Let it be repeated at the outset of this chapter that 'colonialism' was not a mono-lithic or static reality, nor was it experienced uniformly across the Muslim world. It is for this reason that we have deliberately spoken in the plural of Muslim *responses* to *situations* of disestablishment. Nevertheless, in the midst of colonial-ism's complexities, there are still larger trends to be observed, including a trend among Muslims towards missionary *da'wa*. Building on Chapter 5, the purpose of this chapter is to survey some significant *da'wa*-oriented thinkers and move-ments which emerged across the Muslim world from roughly 1850 to 1950. This constitutes what we are calling the *first phase* of modern *da'wa*. Following from this survey, the chapter's concluding section draws out some major themes of modern *da'wa*'s first phase.

The Indian subcontinent

In an earlier publication, I argued that, in the aftermath of the British defeat of the 1857 Uprising and partly in response to increased Christian (and Hindu) missionary activity, India's Muslims played trend-setting roles among Muslims worldwide in developing 'bottom-up' *jihad*-as-*da'wa* styles of activism well-suited to colonial (and post-colonial) conditions.[1] Here, I follow that insight and begin with India before turning to other areas. Although sometimes considered to be on the 'periphery' of the Muslim world, in fact, India's Muslims (which today include those of India, Pakistan and Bangladesh) have had an enormous influ-ence on global Islam in the modern period. Nowhere is this more observable than in the realm of *da'wa/tabligh*. Perhaps this may be partly explained by the fact that India's Muslims faced the crises of disestablishment and minoritisa-tion relatively early and that they developed particularly creative and fitting responses.[2] To illustrate this, we might begin with Rehmatullah Kairanawi (1818–91), a pivotal Muslim scholar whose life and work embodies much of what we mean by the modern Muslim turn to *da'wa* in situations of disestablish-ment. Troubled by British domination of his native Hindustan (northern India), as well as by the activities of Christian missionaries – activities which provoked a number of well-publicised 'conversion scares'[3] – Kairanawi engaged in a literal marketplace debate with the German missionary Karl Pfander (d. 1865) in

Agra in 1854.[4] A decade later, he published a Muslim critique of the Bible and defence of the Islamic scriptures entitled *Izhar al-Haqq* (Revelation of the Truth). Kairanawi's book, which was in many ways the first of its kind in Islamic history, would go on to become a bestseller. As Muslims in other places came face to face with the same kinds of colonial dilemmas (how to live as devoted Muslims in a disestablishment situation marked by competitive pluralism), it is not surprising that Kairanawi's efforts would resonate. After fleeing India in the wake of the 1857 Uprising, Kairanawi was invited to Istanbul by the Ottoman Sultan 'Abd al-Aziz.[5] Through the support of 'Abd al-Aziz and later rulers of the fading empire, Kairanawi would have *Izhar al-Haqq* translated into multiple languages and widely published. The book became a sensation. Traveling in Damascus in 1877, the Hungarian Islamicist Ignaz Goldziher (d. 1921) reported that everyone was talking about Kairanawi's book.[6] Rashid Rida endorsed Kairanawi's work in his own *da'wa* efforts in early-twentieth-century Cairo, and it continues to be widely available up to the present. Kairanawi's model of confronting other religions peacefully, but head-on, would serve as a model for many later imitators, including South Africa's Ahmed Deedat and India's Zakir Naik. In short, Kairanawi was a pioneer of a kind of *da'wa* ideally suited to religious marketplace conditions: a *da'wa* that engaged non-Muslim religions and scriptures in order to 'prove' the superiority of Islam. That news of Kairanawi's debate and copies of his book spread around the Muslim world illustrates both a rising sense of interconnectedness among Muslims in the colonial era and a growing Muslim use of technologies such as the printing press.

In fact, this is a good place to say a few more words about the printing press in the colonial Muslim world and its relationship to *da'wa*. In an important article, Francis Robinson asks why Muslims adopted print in a widespread fashion only in the nineteenth century, nearly four centuries after print culture swept Europe (the Gutenberg press was invented in the fifteenth century). In reply, he notes that print threatened traditional Islamic forms of knowledge preservation and transmission. Because of this, Muslims 'came to adopt printing only when they felt Islam itself was at stake and print was a necessary weapon in the defence of the faith'.[7] In other words, the Muslim adoption of print was spurred, in part, by threats posed to Islam in colonial contexts, including the threats posed by other religions. Because Christian missionaries were using the printing press effectively, Muslim elites felt compelled to begin mass-producing Islamic texts. The fact that printing was in widespread use within many of the institutions of colonial rule – colleges, bureaucracies, courts, the military and so on – added further pressure. The Muslim adoption of print, that is, goes hand in hand with what we are calling the spread of religious marketplace mentalities among Muslims. Indian Muslims, as it turned out, played pioneering roles: 'By the 1820s in the Indian sub-continent Muslim reformist leaders were busily printing tracts . . . By the 1870s editions of the Quran, and other religious books, were selling in tens of thousands'.[8] As Nile Green demonstrates, this general pattern was repeated across the Muslim world in the early decades of the nineteenth century. In fact, it was often Muslim or religiously hybrid middlemen – such as Iran's Mirza Salih (d. *circa* 1841), Egypt's Niqula al-Massabiki (d. 1830) and Lebanon's Ahmad Faris al-Shidyaq (d. 1887) – who played instrumental roles in transferring print technology and know-how from Christian missionaries or other Europeans to Muslim societies.[9] Not surprisingly, the Muslim embrace of print would herald further transformations. It would pave the way, for instance, for the subsequent embrace of technologies such as audio and video cassettes, television and the internet as *da'wa* tools.

Another Indian example of *da'wa* in the first phase is the now world-famous Muslim seminary of Deoband which was founded in 1867, ten years after the 1857 Uprising. Largely setting aside politics, the early founders of Deoband quietly adapted British and Christian missionary educational models in order to equip a new generation of Muslim scholars to bring Islamic reform to the masses. Today, there are thousands of Deoband-affiliated schools and seminaries all over the world, most of which adhere to the original pattern of 'Deobandi *da'wa*' – namely, avoiding overt politics but instead educating future *'ulama*, mosque leaders and missionaries, producing *fatwa*s (or Islamic legal advice) and providing literature to help ordinary Muslims follow 'true' Islam and resist the allurements of other religions. While it is sometimes mistakenly identified as such, the Deoband movement is not Salafi. Deobandi scholars follow the Hanafi legal school and promote a reformed Shari'a-Sufism. In its own historiography, the religious marketplace context of colonial India plays a central role: Deobandi histories make much of the role of the school's founding *'ulama* in defending Islam against Christian mission, as well as against the proselytising activities of the Hindu Arya Samaj (founded 1875) and the Ahmadiyya sect of Islam (see below).[10] Although the Afghan Taliban later grew out of Deobandi schools in Pakistan, its activities are exceptional within the movement (we will discuss the '*da'wa*' of militant Islamist or Jihadi groups in Chapter 7). In fact, arguably the most important offshoot of Deoband, and one truer to Deoband's original pattern of *da'wa*, is the Tablighi Jama'at (TJ), likely the largest *da'wa* movement in the world today.

Founded in early twentieth-century north India by Muhammad Ilyas (d. 1944), the TJ – which eschews politics, focuses on grassroots spiritual formation and house-to-house preaching, and operates on a 'faith mission' model – is now active in well over 150 countries. Although he harboured dreams of the restoration of Islamic political power, Ilyas largely modelled his *da'wa* on the Prophet's Meccan ministry, which he saw as analogous to the situation he faced in colonial India.[11] More than any other organisation, the TJ has been responsible for spreading reformist Islam (a reformed Shari'a-Sufism) to the masses through peaceful preaching-oriented *da'wa/tabligh*. The TJ's *modus operandi* and the movement's eventual global popularity are powerful indicators of both the pioneering role of India's Muslims in developing these modes of activism and the spread of religious marketplace mentalities across the Muslim world in the early twentieth century. Among Ilyas's most important disciples was his biographer Abu'l-Hasan 'Ali Nadwi (d. 1999), an important theologian of *da'wa* to whom we will return to in Chapter 7. The TJ has trained and mobilised millions of Muslim laymen as missionaries for Islam, in part through its spectacular annual *ijtima's* (mass congregations or missionary conferences), especially those held at Bhopal in India, Raiwind in Pakistan and Tongi in Bangladesh (see the cover image of this book). In fact, some observers believe that these TJ *ijtima's* constitute the second-largest recurrent Muslim religious gatherings in the world after the *hajj*. There are also large annual *ijtima's* in Europe, North America and elsewhere. Along with its mobilisation of men, the TJ has also been active among women. Underscoring this effort has been a conviction that women – in their God-given role of raising the next generation – are on the frontline of the battle for Islam in colonial and post-colonial religious marketplaces.[12]

Like the TJ, a number of other *da'wa* movements emerged in the shadow of British colonialism in early-twentieth-century India.[13] These movements, some of which were associated with the Deobandis' main Sunni rivals, the Barelvis and Ahl-i Hadith,[14] as well as with Shi'ite groups in India, were also reacting to the presence of Christian missionaries, the rise of Hindu proselytising efforts and the *da'wa* activities of the Ahmadiyya movement. In fact, the Ahmadiyya movement, founded decades earlier than the TJ (in 1889) by Mirza Ghulam Ahmad (d. 1908; see Figure 6.1), was among the first Islamic movements in the world to make *da'wa* an explicit focus. Reckoning with the realities of British power, disestablishment and competitive missionisation (as a young man, he had been active debating Christian missionaries in the Panjab), Ghulam Ahmad declared that military *jihad* had ended with his appearing (he claimed to be the Islamic Mahdi and Messiah) and that now the true *jihad* would be that of peaceful *da'wa*. Here, in a late-nineteenth-century Islamic movement, a Meccan *da'wa*logy is made a central point of belief and practice. Ghulam Ahmad called for non-conflict with the British authorities, even while he strongly advocated for his version of Islam in the colonial religious marketplace. In fact, the Ahmadiyya movement's embrace of these emphases is certainly among the reasons it has proven attractive to potential converts. Not only does Ahmadiyya teaching make distinctive claims which sets it apart in the modern marketplace of religions (it sees itself as transcending or bringing about the fulfillment of earlier Islamic and non-Islamic religious paths), it also empowers its followers to do peaceful, if vigorous, *da'wa* in that very marketplace. In short, it is not despite, but because of its core teachings that the Ahmadiyya movement embraces peaceful persuasion-oriented styles of mission well-suited to the modern marketplace of religions. By the time of

6.1 An excerpt from the most important text of the Tablighi Jama'at

The main textbook of the TJ is *Faza'il-i Amal* (or *Faḍā'il-i A'māl*; The Merits of Acts of Piety), written over several years by the primary theologian of the movement and Ilyas's nephew, Muhammad Zakariyya (d. 1982). Like Ilyas, Zakariyya was a scholar-Sufi and exemplar of the Deobandi-pattern *da'wa*. *Faza'il-i Amal* is expected reading for anyone involved with the TJ. Given the size of the TJ, it has been suggested that this text may be today 'the most widely read book in the Muslim world after the Qur'an' (Sikand 2002, p. 73). Most editions of *Faza'il-i Amal* begin with *Hikayat Sahaba* (Stories of the Prophet's Companions) and interestingly, on the very first page, Zakariyya addresses Muslim women and mothers. 'The lap of the mother', he writes, 'is . . . the best field of instruction . . . Alas! Our children are brought up in surroundings that draw them away from Islam . . .' (Zakariyya [n. d.], p. 174). The following lines are taken from a section of the work entitled '*Faza'il-i Tabligh*' (The Virtues of Missionary Propagation). Zakariyya is commenting on Q 3:104:

> *In this noble verse (Qur'an 3:104), [God] has given an important command: that from the* umma *a* jama'at *should be set apart for the work of* tabligh *– calling people to Islam. This command was given for all the Muslims, but regrettably, we have completely neglected it. Other communities, by contrast, have taken up preaching their religions in the most organised manner. Permanent* jama'ats *of Christians have been set apart for Christian* tabligh *throughout the world. Other communities have made similar arrangements. But is there any such* jama'at *among the Muslims?* (Zakariyya [n. d.], *Faza'il-i Tabligh*).

Ghulam Ahmad's death in 1908, his movement had well-organised missionary programs and was spreading rapidly. Although most Muslim leaders consider the Ahmadiyya movement (which they sometimes call 'Qadianism', from the name of Ahmad's hometown) heretical, it would, like Christian mission, serve as a challenge and model for Islamic *da'wa* movements the world over. Despite enduring severe persecution in Pakistan and elsewhere, the Ahmadiyya movement today has tens of millions of followers in over 200 countries. Its importance in the history of modern *da'wa* cannot be overstated.[15]

An additional example of the trend-setting role of Indian Muslims in turning to a Meccan style of *da'wa* in colonial conditions was Sayyid Ahmad Khan (1817–98), the notable nineteenth-century Muslim modernist reformer and founder of what is today Aligarh Muslim University. 'The *da'wa* that Khan

Figure 6.1 Mirza Ghulam Ahmad, 1835–1908, founder of the Ahmadiyya movement. Loved or reviled, Ghulam Ahmad founded a movement which is of great significance in the history of modern *da'wa*. Photo: Public Domain.

presented to his contemporaries was to modernise their outlook . . . Muslim civilization(s) would be restored to former greatness by shunning customs that had resulted in the denigration of Islam'.[16] Khan also wanted to help Indian Muslims come to terms with British rule and the presence of Christianity in nineteenth-century India. To that end, he wrote *The Muhammadan Commentary on the Holy Bible*. Despite drawing on some of the same sources as the Kairanawi, Sayyid Ahmad adopted a less polemical approach, going so far as to write of the Bible as a repository of true revelation. He also wrote a life of Muhammad in part to counter missionary attacks and present a more irenic face of the Prophet. Although Sayyid Ahmad has had a significant impact, the polemical style of Kairanawi's *Izhar al-Haqq* has arguably a made a deeper impression on modern *da'wa*.

Yet another important South Asian example is seen in the activism and scholarship of Abul A'la Mawdudi (1903–79) in India and what was to become Pakistan. By the early 1940s, and especially as the Partition of British India approached, Mawdudi would move in a political, Islamist direction. Until that time, however, although he chafed under western rule and railed against 'godless' western thought, he found missionary *da'wa* to be the most suitable outlet for his considerable intellectual and activist energies. Taking a cue from Christian missionaries, Mawdudi poured out his revivalist *da'wa* through print, in his monthly journal *Tarjuman al-Qur'an* and in numerous books and pamphlets. In fact, Mawdudi's rise to prominence would have been unthinkable without the printing press.[17] In 1941, he founded the Jama'at-i Islami (Islamic Society, JI), an organisation which seeks to directly influence politics but which has also maintained a focus on grassroots *da'wa*.[18] Like the Muslim Brotherhood in Egypt (see below), Mawdudi's JI championed the use of not only the printed word, but also modern forms of organisation. It is important to stress the extent to which Mawdudi's and the JI's emphasis on the total transformation of society (encompassing the religious and political) is distinctly modern and therefore quite novel within Islamic history as a whole.[19] Mawdudi also wanted to mobilise women. As seen in his *Purdah and the Status of Women in Islam*, Mawdudi maintained a traditional Islamic view on the proper roles of women. He argued that Islam alone (not western ideas) provided the true basis for women's freedom and empowerment, and he instructed women to make the home their primary sphere of activity. In doing so, he argued, they would serve important functions in protecting and passing on 'true' Islam. The Jama'at started a women's wing in the 1940s to engage women in the organisation's objectives. Interestingly, Mawdudi was not a classically trained member of the *'ulama*, but a self-taught Muslim with a background in journalism. His life and activism are emblematic of the ways *da'wa* has facilitated the rise of new kinds of Muslim actors, sometimes called 'new religious intellectuals', in the modern age.[20]

Finally, while not an example of missionary outreach *per se*, we might say something here about the '*da'wa*' of the Indian Muslim League, an organisation established in 1906, which by 1940 had emerged as the main political representative of India's Muslims (at least as far as the British were concerned). Over time, the League advocated for the 'Two Nation Theory'. In the face of the disestablishment of Islam and the minoritisation of India's Muslims, this theory asserted that the Muslims of India were a single nation – inexorably distinct from Hindus and Hinduism – which required a separate homeland. This dream was ultimately realised in 1947 with the Partition of British India and the formation of the nation-state of Pakistan (from which Bangladesh seceded in 1971). The activities of the League leading up to Partition reflected and contributed to a rising mood of religious nationalism among India's Muslims. While India's Muslims had heretofore been internally divided by region and language, and while for generations many ordinary Muslims had lived in ways that were largely indistinguishable from their non-Muslim neighbours, the League encouraged Muslims to identify themselves more fully with 'Islam'. This was also a result, to

6.2 Two *da'wa*-oriented English Qur'an translations from India

The Meaning of the Holy Qur'an by Yusuf 'Ali (1872–1953): 'Ali, who was born in Gujarat in 1872, combined a deep Islamic piety and love for the Qur'an with a knowledge of the West and western scholarship. He spoke of the unity of religions and viewed the Qur'an primarily as a source of personal inspiration. 'Ali's English translation of the Qur'an, published in India in the 1930s, gained worldwide popularity among English-speaking Muslims through a revised Saudi-sponsored edition published in the 1980s. It has been called 'by far the best known, most studied, and most respected English translation of the Qur'an'. 'Ali's translation features a monumental commentary, including over 6,000 notes and poetic intro-ductions to each Surah. Although written in a contemporary idiom (as of the 1930s), 'Ali's commentary is traditional. It takes a decidedly exclusiv-ist stance on the relationship of Islam to other religions. For 'Ali, Islam is the only true religion and 'the perfect light of Truth', and it 'is bound to prevail . . . [it] will outshine all else' and 'conquer with the help of God' (Sources: 'Ali 1989; Troll 1998, pp. 77–101).

Tafsir-ul-Qur'an by 'Abd al-Majid Daryabadi (1892–1977): Daryabadi's English Qur'an translation and commentary *Tafsir-ul-Qur'an* (Karachi: Darul Ishaat, 1991) was published in four volumes in 1957. Written in the context of late colonial India, *Tafsir-ul-Qur'an* carries on a dialogue with western scholars and other religions, particularly Christianity and Judaism, but also Hinduism and ancient paganism. As in 'Ali's transla-tion/commentary, an exclusivist stance and expectation of the missionary triumph of Islam pervade the work. According to Abu'l-Hasan 'Ali Nadwi, who recommends the work, Daryabadi has provided Muslims with a valuable *da'wa* tool and is to be appreciated for his firm belief in the Qur'an and in Islam as the solution to the world's problems. Nadwi also praises Daryabadi for taking the 'findings of modern Biblical researches' into account, something Kairanawi had done in his *da'wa* years earlier. It is likely, in fact, that Daryabadi drew on Kairanawi's *Izhar al-Haqq* (Sources: Daryabadi 1957/1991, Nadwi 1957/1991).

some extent, of colonial policies and the rhetoric of emerging Hindu nationalist organisations. The main point is that, while several important leaders of the Muslim League were secularists, their agitation ultimately encouraged, at least indirectly, the further identification of India's Muslim masses with 'Islam' which was now seen as utterly distinct from 'Hinduism'.

Egypt

While these pioneering developments were underway in colonial India, similar trend-setting *da'wa* currents were emerging in Egypt. This may be seen in the first place in the influential thought and activism of Rashid Rida (1865–1935). Rida was a committed protégé of earlier thinkers such as Jamal al-Din al-Afghani and Muhammad 'Abduh. In light of the realities of British power in Egypt (and British and French power over much of the Middle East) from the 1880s onward, 'Abduh (1849–1905) himself had made a decidedly 'Meccan' shift away from the politically activist *da'wa* of al-Afghani and towards quietism.[21] 'Abduh's approach to modernist Islamic renewal would have a tremendous impact, not only on Rida, but on modern Islam and *da'wa* activism in general around the world. So too, alarmed by but also somewhat resigned to the rise of the West, Rida would edit (from Cairo) the popular journal *al-Manar* (The Lighthouse) from 1898 to 1935. *Al-Manar* was published, partially on the model of Christian missionary journals, in order to advocate for Islam and for the reform and modernisation of Islamic thought.[22] The journal made a particular point of responding to Christianity; as noted above, Rida made use of Kairanawi's *Izhar al-Haqq* in formulating his response.[23] In 1908, Rida translated into Arabic the *Gospel of Barnabas*, a late apocryphal work which had been translated into English from a medieval Italian manuscript in 1907. The work narrates the life of Jesus following the New Testament storyline, except that it 'Islamises' key details, so that the Jesus of *Barnabas* ends up confirming Islamic doctrines.[24] Since that time, owing in part to Rida's efforts, the *Gospel of Barnabas* has become very popular in Islamic *da'wa* around the world.

The pages of *al-Manar* and numerous other Muslim periodicals reflect a strong current of anti-missionary panic among segments of the Egyptian Muslim population in the early decades of the twentieth century – not unlike what was being felt in India. Until the late nineteenth century, Christian missionaries in Egypt had confined their proselytising activities to indigenous Christian groups, like the Copts. This was in part because

Figure 6.2 Rashid Rida, 1865–1935, a pioneer in Islamic publishing and *da'wa*. Photo: Public Domain.

the still-ruling 'Ottoman authorities made it clear to missionaries that evangelization among Muslims was off-bounds'.[25] Encouraged by the rise of *de facto* British rule after 1882, however, missionaries turned to the direct evangelisation of Muslims. This led to a full blown 'anti-missionary agitation' in early-twentieth-century Egypt.[26] In this context, it was alleged that missionaries were enticing Muslim conversions to Christianity through unsavoury methods and that they were publicly abusing the Prophet and burning copies of the Qur'an.[27] There were also, as in India, several well-publicised 'conversion scares'.[28] In this fraught setting, Rida not only took up the pen and printing press in defence of Islam, but he also established an organisation and school for training Muslim missionaries. His school, founded in Cairo in 1911, was named the *Dar al-Da'wa wa'l Irshad* (House of *Da'wa* and Guidance). Interestingly enough, when Thomas Arnold published the second (1913) edition of *The Preaching of Islam*, he included a new appendix on what he called 'a recent development in the missionary history of Islam' – namely, the founding of Protestant-style Muslim missionary organisations. Among the handful of organisations Arnold listed was Rida's *Dar al-Da'wa*. Even though the school did not survive the outbreak of World War I, it set a precedent for many subsequent *da'wa* training efforts in the Muslim world.[29] Indeed, as seen in Rida's life, *tarbiyya* (education or training) has been closely related to *da'wa* in modern Islamic thought and activism. Rida was also active in a number of international Muslim conferences or congresses which were convened in the late nineteenth and early twentieth centuries. These congresses, which bear resemblance to Christian missionary congresses of the same period (such as the world missionary conference held at Edinburgh in 1910,[30] or 'The Second General Conference of Missions among Muslims' held in Lucknow in 1911),[31] brought together Muslims 'of common conviction who shared . . . a vision of a revitalised Islam'.[32] While, according to Kramer, these meetings did not produce much of a lasting impact, they served as a precedent for a burgeoning of Muslim conferences focused on *da'wa* in the later twentieth and twenty-first centuries.[33]

Also worth mentioning is the life and activism of the noted Egyptian modernist Muhammad Husayn Haykal. Educated in both Egypt and Paris, Haykal promoted a modern, liberal version of Islam, as seen in his 1935 biography of Muhammad.[34] In this influential work, Haykal used the traditional *sira* (see Chapter 2) to cast Muhammad as paving the way for the triumph of reason and science over blind adherence to tradition.[35] Haykal also accentuated the tolerant nature of the Prophet's rule over Medina. In this effort to 'modernise' the Prophet, Haykal was explicitly motivated by what he saw as the anti-Islamic attacks of European missionaries and orientalists. In the preface to his first edition of *The Life of Muhammad*, Haykal stated his desire to correct Christian missionaries 'who continue their attacks against Islam and Muhammad with the same ferocity as their predecessors . . .', as well as to enlighten uniformed

6.3 An early-twentieth-century excerpt from Rida's *al-Manar*

In the following early-twentieth-century excerpt from *al-Manar*, Rida is addressing a situation in which a Muslim reader of the journal has expressed some doubts about Islam after reading Christian missionary literature. Note especially his statement of *al-Manar*'s purpose and his recommendation of Kairanawi:

It is imperative that we address [this reader's] doubts, because the defence of the religion of Islam is the most important task for which al-Manar *was established . . . We desire that no one slanders the religion of the other . . . But the Christians do not agree with us about this . . . Hence we see them making gatherings in order to hurt Islam verbally, publishing newspapers . . . and writing books to attack its scripture . . . Truly, we are astonished by this Muslim reader of the Christian books, by his being satisfied with reading them without reading the Islamic books that confront them . . . and oppose against them that which cannot be repelled, such as [Kairanawi's]* Izhar al-Haqq *. . . and other such books. Our first response to the reader is that it is incumbent upon him to read those Islamic books . . .* (Source: Rida 2009, pp. 71–7).

Muslims as to the true nature of Islam.[36] As a journalist, Haykal served as the editor of the newspaper *Al-Siyasa*; this gave him another platform, along with his books, for communicating what one might reasonably call his modernist *da'wa* to a mass audience.

In the same period in which Rida and Haykal were active and during the same decade in which the TJ was founded in India, the year 1928 witnessed a particularly momentous event in the history of modern *da'wa*: the founding of the Muslim Brotherhood (MB) in Egypt by Hasan al-Banna (1906–49). Al-Banna, like Rida who influenced him, was inspired to counteract the activities of Christian missionaries by adapting their tools and techniques for Islamic revivalist ends. As a youth, al-Banna had been involved in a Sufi order, the Hasafiyya, which at that time aimed to 'fight for the preservation of Islamic morality and resist the work of Christian missionaries' through grassroots *da'wa*.[37] He hoped to restore the lost glory of Islam and wanted to unite Muslims under the banner of Islam, rather than under alternative banners such as secularism or Arab nationalism. He believed that this could best be accomplished by reaching the masses through a private organisation made up of committed volunteers.[38] Regarding the early movement, we are told that

[MB] Missionaries . . . preached in the mosques and other public places; the Brethren founded schools of various grades, organized courses of religious instruction, taught the illiterate, set up hospitals and dispensaries, undertook various enterprises to raise the standard of living in the villages, built mosques and even launched industrial and commercial enterprises.[39]

The Brotherhood's weekly magazine[40] reported on the 'efforts of the Brothers all over Egypt . . . The Muslim Brothers' resistance against [Christian] missions was one of the factors that earned [them] . . . credibility . . . among the Muslim public'.[41] We might note in passing that his was also true of the Young Men's Muslim Association (YMMA), founded around the same time as the Muslim Brotherhood as an alternative to the Christian-mission-affiliated Young Men's Christian Association (YMCA) of Cairo.[42] Most of the Brotherhood's 'early activities in its formative years', therefore, 'were devoted to the incremental reform of society from the bottom up'.[43] In other words, despite its evolution in subsequent decades in an Islamist direction, like Mawdudi's JI, the Brotherhood began as a grassroots da'wa movement in a colonial milieu. As we will see further in Chapter 7, with affiliates and sympathisers in many nations, the Muslim Brotherhood has had a tremendous influence on modern da'wa.[44]

In 1932, the Brotherhood set up a women's wing called the Muslim Sisters Group. At a time when some colonial officials and missionaries were speaking out against the alleged oppression of Muslim women, when Muslim secularists were pushing for greater freedoms for women and when one could witness an emerging feminist movement in Egypt (represented by Huda Sha'rawi's Egyptian Feminist Union, founded in 1923), the women who took up da'wa alongside the Brotherhood tended to reject western-style feminism and argue that 'true' Islam, properly understood, provides remarkable rights to women. They argued, in short, that if women are mistreated in Muslim societies, the blame does not lie with 'Islam', but with non-Muslim customs which persist among the uneducated. Views like these found perhaps their ablest spokes-person in Zaynab al-Ghazali (d. 2005), who established the Muslim Women's Association in Egypt in 1936. Al-Ghazali's life illustrates the fact that by the early twentieth century the field of da'wa was opening up new opportunities for those (men and women) who may not have had formal Islamic training, but who had 'moral uprightness and practical knowledge of [Islam]' and who felt a per-sonal calling to preach.[45] In Egypt, many da'wa actors of this kind would become influential in the sphere of private, voluntary da'wa activism. Al-Ghazali kept her organisation independent from the Muslim Brotherhood, but she shared al-Banna's basic worldview and pledged loyalty to him in 1949. She was known, in fact, as the 'mother of the Muslim Brotherhood'.[46]

Finally, a word should be said about Cairo's Al-Azhar madrasa and its response to the colonial situation. Although founded by the Fatimids over a thousand years ago (in the late tenth century) to support the pre-modern Isma'ili da'wa (see Chapter 3), Al-Azhar is often considered today to be the world's most important centre of Sunni learning.[47] Unsurprisingly, an important theme in the history of Al-Azhar from the mid-nineteenth century to the present is the *madrasa*'s checkered efforts to navigate colonial and post-colonial modernity. For instance, beginning in the late nineteenth century, the school began a process of modernising its curriculum and educational approach.[48] The school has also struggled to maintain its independence in the midst of the efforts of the Egyptian state(s) to control it. With respect to *da'wa*, Al-Azhar did not establish a stand-alone Department of *Da'wa* until 1961.[49] Nevertheless, one can discern among Al-Azhar's leadership a growing orientation towards *da'wa* and towards reaching ordinary Muslims already in the early twentieth century.[50] This was spurred, as with Rida, Haykal, al-Banna and al-Ghazali, by the rise of colonial modernity and the threat of Christian mission. In one particularly notorious incident, in 1926 the American missionary Samuel Zwemer (1867–1952) entered Al-Azhar itself and handed out Christian tracts. In response to provocations of this sort, *'ulama* associated with Al-Azhar formed the Society for the Defense of Islam which 'lashed out against missionaries' in the following decade.[51] The *madrasa*'s High Council of Ulama (formed in 1911) published several works in the early 1930s, in which they appealed to Muslims to resist Christian missionary efforts. They also published *fatwa*s against Christian mission in their periodical *Nur al-Islam* (Light of Islam). The *'ulama* of Al-Azhar sought to call the Muslim masses to stand firm for Islam, but through these efforts they also sought to demonstrate their own ongoing relevance. There were, after all, not only inter-religious threats, but also newer Islamic movements, such as the Muslim Brotherhood, which claimed to authoritatively speak for Islam. The latter asserted that the *'ulama* were out of touch with the needs of changing times and that the *'ulama*'s response to the missionary threat was feeble at best.[52] This, then, is another illustration of the fact that the colonial situation not only prompted Muslims towards *da'wa* in general, but also fostered intra-Muslim competition in *da'wa*.

Turkey

Turning to early-twentieth-century Turkey, we find yet more examples of the rise of 'Meccan' *da'wa* in disestablishment conditions. The Ottoman Empire had always based its legitimacy, in part, on its status as a patron of Sunni Islam and on its successful military expansion in the name of Islam. In the seventeenth and eighteenth centuries, however, the Ottoman juggernaut began losing ground to the European powers, and over the course of the nineteenth century the empire was progressively dismantled and partitioned, particularly by the Russian and Austro-Hungarian Empires, but also by Britain and France.[53] By the end of World War I, the Ottoman Empire, for all intents and purposes, had ceased to exist. The disestablishment of Islam, however, began in the nineteenth century, in the context of the Ottomans' somewhat haphazard efforts to reform and reorganise and thus save the empire. Under a series of Ottoman regimes, power was shifted away from the traditional *'ulama*, institutions which were considered barriers to progress (such as the Bektashi Sufi order and the Janissary, or elite slave-soldier corps) were abolished, and new rights were granted to non-Muslim subjects. European-style legal codes were adopted, European military technology imported, and a new modernising elite came to prominence, represented first by the Young Ottomans and then the Young Turks. These elites would eventually commit themselves to forming a modern nation-state as a homeland for the Turkish people.[54] While the Young Turks were united on many points, they differed regarding the role Islam would play in the new nation they envisioned. In the end, it was a faction associated with Mustafa Kemal Ataturk (1881–1938), which came to power after World War I and which brought the terminally-ill Ottoman Empire to its ultimate end.

Until the middle of the twentieth century, under Ataturk's presidency and that of his successor, the new Turkish state embraced aggressively secularising and westernising policies. Religious affairs came under a powerful state bureaucracy, Sufi orders were outlawed, modern European law codes were enacted and 'People's Houses' were set up to disseminate the state ideology. It might be said that the government of independent Turkey was engaging in its own top-down secularist *'da'wa'* of sorts. This *da'wa* might have occasionally used the symbolism of Islam, but ultimately it aimed to undermine traditional piety and to keep religion out of public life. It was also Ataturk who famously abolished the caliphate in 1924, prompting vehement protests among Muslims as far away as India. Although many among the educated, urban population in Turkey embraced Ataturk's ideology, in rural areas the Sufi traditions and the piety of the ordinary people survived.[55] Be that as it may, in the early decades of the new Republic, reform-minded Muslims had to find ways to cope with the new situation of aggressive disestablishment. Once again, quietist missionary *da'wa* proved to be a go-to resource. This can be seen, for instance, in the life and activism of Bediuzzaman Said Nursi (1877–1960), founder of the 'most powerful faith movement in contemporary Turkey'.[56]

As a child and young man, Said Nursi was influenced both by the reformism of the Naqshbandi brotherhood and by western learning, and he would become convinced that western scientific thought and traditional Islam could be combined.[57] In fact, part of the appeal of Nursi's thought has been its claim to resolve major tensions thrown up by colonial modernity: for instance, between faith and science, belief and doubt, Islam and the West.[58] In the waning years of the empire, Nursi became an enthusiastic political activist and spokesman for political reform, and during World War I he fought for the Ottomans and was briefly taken prisoner by Russia. Following the rise of the new Turkish Republic, however, Nursi made a definite 'Meccan' turn: 'From 1918–1922, Nursi went through an internal transformation, relinquishing his active involvement in politics ... and moving towards a mystically charged life of asceticism and piety'.[59] From then until the 1950s, although constantly watched by the authorities and jailed several times, Nursi persisted in dictating *Risale-i Nur*, a compendium of his teachings in the form of a six-thousand-page mystical-modernist commentary on the Qur'an. He also gathered a growing cadre of committed disciples. Nursi believed that the best way to overcome top-down secularism was through a *jihad* of peaceful preaching and writing.[60] 'I seek refuge in God from politics and satan' became a mantra of Nursi's students.[61] Living under a regime that had banned Sufi orders in 1925, Nursi developed what was for all intents and purposes a *da'wa*-oriented Sufi movement, without using the word 'Sufi'.

This strategy of avoiding explicit identification with the Sufi tradition in the face of anti-Sufi sentiments has been common across the Muslim world since the high modern period. Sufism has operated under 'new guises', including as *da'wa* or educational movements.[62] In sum, faced with aggressive disestablishment in early-twentieth-century Turkey, Nursi developed an approach comparable to that of Muhammad Ilyas and the TJ in India. He embraced, that is, a Meccan *da'wa*logy. Nursi's significant legacy has been carried on by the Nur (or Nurcu) movement which, since the 1950s, has experienced greater freedom in Turkey and abroad.[63] A particularly important offshoot of the Nurcu movment is the Gulen movement, which we will meet again in Chapter 7.

Central Asia

Turning to Central Asia under Russian imperial and Soviet rule, we see a similar turn to quietist activism in varying disestablishment conditions. According to Adeeb Khalid, as Russian power tightened in Central Asia in the late nineteenth and early twentieth centuries, '[t]he *'ulama* fell back on a long tradition of quietism well-articulated in the local Hanafi tradition . . . [in] the generation following the Russian conquest . . . the *'ulama* . . . accommodated themselves to the new order'. In this situation, 'Muslim institutions flourished' under the *'ulama*'s leadership.[64] Another Muslim response to Russian rule around the turn of the twentieth century was Jadidism. The *da'wa* of Jadidism called on Muslims to embrace modernist reform, along the same lines as Sayyid Ahmad Khan in India and the Young Ottomans in Turkey. As seen in the advocacy of the Crimean intellectual Isma'il Gasprinski (d. 1914), perhaps the most famous of the Jadid leaders, the Jadidists' *da'wa* argued that the 'acquisition of modern knowledge . . . was mandated by Islam itself. In common with other modernists . . . the Jadids ascribed the . . . "degeneration" of their community to its departure from the true path of Islam . . . The solution was a return to "true Islam"'.[65] Gasprinski and other Jadidists took advantage of the printed word, disseminating their ideas through newspapers, books and pamphlets.

The rise of the Soviet Union after 1917 initially brought to Muslims of the former Russian Empire hope that independence might be imminent (since the

Bolsheviks were supposed to be anti-imperialists). However, it soon became clear that the Soviets had no intention of letting go of Central Asia or the Caucasus.[66] To win Muslim support, the Soviets initially allowed for some religious freedom. An interesting case in this context is that of the purist Sunni preacher Shami Damullah (d. 1932). While the Soviets generally opposed Sufism, since it seemed to them reactionary and superstitious, they allowed some limited freedom for Wahhabi-style reformers like Shami Damullah in the early 1920s. Damullah, who was originally from Syria (like Rashid Rida) and who had studied at Al-Azhar, settled in Tashkent in 1919 and saw some success in winning converts. His followers became known as 'Ahl-i Hadith' (not to be confused with the Indian group of the same name); for a time, they cooperated with the Soviets in the destruction of Sufi shrines and in opposing customary practices. However, as the Soviets' repression of Islam became more systematic, Damullah's movement parted ways with the Soviets.[67]

Beginning in the mid-1920s, the Soviets closed countless mosques and *madrasa*s across these regions, outlawed veiling and engaged in the aggressive promotion of Leninist ideology. Many Muslim leaders were killed or removed from positions of influence. Soviet educational initiatives attempted to inculcate anti-religious perspectives.[68] This state of affairs, which has been characterised as 'The Soviet Assault on Islam', lasted at least until the outbreak of World War II, when the Soviets softened their stance somewhat. Whether aggressively or less so, the Soviets' program in the long term aimed at nothing less than the 'Sovietisation' of Central Asia's Muslims.[69] Here, then, was disestablishment with a vengeance, a development that was in keeping with the totalising vision of Soviet ideology.[70] Thus, unlike Muslims in British India or other places where 'softer' versions of disestablishment often prevailed, Muslims under the Soviet Union prior to World War II were tasked in the first place simply with survival. But survive they did, albeit in diminished form. Direct political opposition to the Soviets might have been out of the question, and most of the mosques and *madrasa*s might have been turned into museums or centres of Soviet propaganda, but one could still engage in quietist and quiet (perhaps secret) *da'wa*. An example of the latter can be seen in the secret religious 'cells' (or *hujras*) which met illegally in Muslim homes during the Soviet era. These *hujras* allowed a small number of devoted Muslims 'to be engaged in [*da'wa*]. While this system . . . represented an obvious decline from even the [Russian Imperial] era . . . it did represent sufficient . . . vitality to keep Islam alive' in Central Asia.[71]

Southeast Asia

Continuing our tour of the Muslim world, Southeast Asia also witnessed the birth of important *da'wa* movements in the shadow of colonialism. Over the nineteenth century, the Dutch progressively established control over diverse ethno-linguistic populations ruled heretofore by a cluster of indigenous states – first Java, then Sumatra and eventually the outer islands. By 1911, the Dutch had taken control of most of what was then called 'the Indies'.[72] Meanwhile, Muslim populations in what is today Malaysia and Singapore were brought under British rule. As in other colonial situations, a pressing question was how Southeast Asian Muslims, traditionally divided into many *aliran* (religious/ ethnic communities or orientations), would frame their response to colonialism. If their response was to be 'Islamic' in some way, then which Islam would they draw from – the locally-flavoured Sufi-inflected versions of Islam traditional to Indo-Malaysia, or more 'orthodox' reformist versions of Islam? Through the modalities of the *hajj* (which Southeast Asians were then making in record numbers) and improved communications with other parts of the Islamic world, reformist, modernist and secularist currents emerging from Egypt, Arabia, India, Turkey and elsewhere were making themselves felt. As in other areas, then, it is not surprising that colonialism in Southeast Asia provoked an array of responses, and that each of these had their related '*da'was*'. As we will see in Chapter 7, Indonesia, like other emerging Muslim nation-states, would begin its post-colonial history under a nationalist leader (Sukarno, in office 1945–67) who, like Ataturk, envisioned Indonesia as a secular state.

Of the various Southeast Asian movements which emerged in the colonial period, two of the most important from the perspective of *da'wa* are the Muhammadiyah and the Nahdlatul Ulama. Founded by Ahmad Dahlan (1868–1923) in Yogyakarta in 1912, the Muhammadiyah is the 'most powerful [modern] reformist movement in Muslim Southeast Asia'.[73] Dahlan, who was from a pious Muslim family, spent several years in Mecca as a young man. While there, he was exposed to reformist and modernist ideas, including the thought of Muhammad 'Abduh. Returning to Indonesia, he was troubled by what he saw as the syncretistic religiosity of the Indonesian people, as well as by the activities of Christian missionaries – particularly missionary efforts in building schools. At the same time, he wanted to see Muslims engage constructively with scientific modernity. From the time he established the Muhammadiyah until his death, Dahlan engaged tirelessly in advocacy for reformist-modernist Islam. Notably, like Ilyas in India and Nursi in Turkey, Dahlan eschewed politics and focused instead on the bottom-up *jihad* of *da'wa* in a disestablishment milieu.[74] Like Dahlan himself, the organisation he founded has generally avoided explicit political involvements (after Indonesian independence, the movement has occasionally participated in electoral politics). Instead, it has primarily concentrated on *da'wa* through education, preaching and social welfare. By all accounts, this apolitical stance is among the reasons for its success. Recalling our discussion in Chapter 5 of nineteenth-century Christian missionary societies, the Muhammadiyah movement (like the TJ, the early MB, the Muslim Women's Association, the early JI and the Nurcu movement, among others) is a *voluntary* organisation – it is not state-sponsored, but runs on the labour of volunteers. Over the decades, the Muhammadiyah has established countless local branches with tens of millions of members. Along with orphanages, clinics and book-shops, the movement has also established thousands of schools. In contrast to the traditional religious schools of Indonesia (*pesantren*),[75] Muhammadiyah schools were explicitly modelled on western missionary-run schools. They teach reformist Islam alongside modern subjects. Although the movement stresses traditional gender roles, it has been a champion for women's education; indeed, the Muhammadiyah's women's branch, Aisyiyah, is one of the largest women's *da'wa* organisations in the world.[76]

The second major Southeast Asian *da'wa*-oriented movement is Nahdlatul Ulama (NU), founded in 1926. If the Muhammadiyah has combined reform-ism and modernism in its *da'wa*, NU has championed the traditional Islam of Indonesia, as taught in the rural *pesantren*. Somewhat akin to the Barelvi movement of India, NU is traditionalist in that it holds to the traditional Sunni schools of law (especially the Shafi'i school) and in that it defends practices such as visits to saints' shrines and seeking the guidance of Sufi masters. While reformists and modernists attacked traditional Sufi Islam, NU preached the virtues of traditional Islam – moderation, flexibility, obedience to one's Sufi master and remembrance of God. At the same time, NU leaders supported a limited reformism. Through the extensive network of *pesantren* which came to be affiliated with NU, the movement channelled traditional spirituality into a pow-erful movement of renewal. It did so in part, however, by embracing modern techniques of missionary mobilisation and by quietly updating the *pesantren*. Like the Muhammadiyah, until Indonesian independence NU mostly functioned as a voluntary, grassroots movement guided by the *'ulama* and *'ulama*-Sufis (or *kyais*). Although NU would indeed become politically active as Indonesian independ-ence approached and thereafter, it has always maintained its core character as a grassroots *da'wa* movement. Along with educational work, NU sponsors mission-ary outreaches, social projects and programs for women, children and students. Founded in 1938 but made official in 1946, Muslimat NU is a NU-affiliated women's movement which has successfully mobilised and organised women for *da'wa*, education and other initiatives across Indonesia (see Figure 6.3).[77] Today, it is estimated that there are over forty million participants in NU, making it the largest *da'wa*-oriented movement in Indonesia, and one of the largest anywhere in the world.[78]

Sub-Saharan Africa

Sub-Saharan Africa in the colonial era also witnessed the emergence of numer-ous *da'wa*-oriented movements. As in other places, the colonial powers – chiefly the British and the French – cultivated African secular elites as preferred

Figure 6.3 Indonesian women of the Muslimat NU gather in East Java in 2016 to celebrate the seventieth anniversary of the founding of the Nahdlatul Ulama-affiliated organisation. Photo: Nownaufal from Wikimedia Commons, CC BY-SA.

collaborators; indeed, as independence movements gathered momentum across Africa towards the mid-twentieth century, they tended to be led by western-educated secularists. Somewhat paradoxically, however, among the major results of European rule in Africa was the significant spread of Islam.[79] In numerous areas of colonial East and West Africa, there were major movements of conversion, particularly among traditional indigenous or 'tribal' peoples. Thus, while many of the cases of *da'wa* we have examined in this chapter exemplify internal *da'wa* (efforts to revive or instruct Muslims), Sub-Saharan Africa in the colonial era saw significant successes in external *da'wa* (efforts to convert non-Muslims). 'The establishment of colonial rule [in Africa] . . . facilitated the diffusion of Islam by providing political security and expanded commercial opportunities, and by stimulating urbanisation . . . and the migration of merchants and workers'.[80] In numerous cases, the colonial powers also indirectly fostered Islamisation by barring Christian missionaries from Muslim areas. This was the case, for instance, in northern Nigeria. This does not mean, therefore, that Muslims were unaware of the growing presence of Christian missions throughout sub-Saharan Africa – for instance, in southern Nigeria or in those numerous contexts (such as today's Ivory Coast, Ghana, Ethiopia, Uganda, Kenya and Tanzania) where Muslims were a minority of the total population. To the contrary, as in India, Egypt, Indonesia and elsewhere, both foreign political domination *and* the threat of Christianisation stimulated African Muslim leaders to take action. However, as we have seen again and again, it is not surprising that the political and social realities of colonialism would end up shaping the kinds of action they took.

In general, as Europeans consolidated their power over Africa, Muslims were forced to 'abandon their eighteenth- and nineteenth-century political aspirations' (recall the *jihad* states of 'Uthman Dan Fodio and others discussed earlier) 'and to accept foreign domination'.[81] Although there would continue to be scattered anti-colonial *jihad*s, by the turn of the twentieth century African Muslims from Zanzibar to Senegal had pragmatically (if grudgingly) accepted the realities of the colonial situation and had thus taken up variations of grassroots missionary activism as an appropriate '*jihad*' for these conditions. While many *da'wa*-minded actors were indigenous to the regions in which they worked, there were also Sufis and traders from North Africa who made fresh inroads south of the Sahara and fostered new rounds of Islamisation. Other Africans returned to their homelands from sojourns in Arabia or Egypt eager to spread newly acquired reformist or modernist ideas. In West Africa (today's Chad, Niger, Nigeria, Mali, Mauritania, Senegal, the Gambia, Guinea, Sierra Leone, Liberia, Ivory Coast, Ghana, Togo, Benin, Burkina Faso and Cameroon), the new emphasis on missionary *da'wa* resulted in a 'phenomenal surge in conversions to Islam among [African] populations who had heretofore been indifferent if not resistant'.[82] As a result, between 1900 and 1960 the Muslim population of West Africa grew massively; by some estimates, it more than doubled. As with mass movements of conversion to Christianity among 'marginal' peoples in the colonial age, conversion to Islam in this context can be interpreted as providing a mechanism for coping with the profound dislocations unleashed by modernity. To some peoples, that is, Islam felt credible 'because it was able to fill the gap caused by the collapse of the old structures and ideas'.[83]

While colonial Africa saw the emergence of the same variety of Muslim movements observed elsewhere – secularist, modernist, reformist and so on – some of the most dynamic colonial-era *da'wa*-oriented movements were led by Sufi brotherhoods. In Africa, the Sufis were under comparatively less pressure and, in some cases, were able to continue pre-modern patterns of Sufi-prompted Islamisation (see Chapter 4). Sufis, that is, continued to form alliances with and/ or foster the conversions of rulers and chieftains, to offer themselves as mediators in various conflicts and to be sought after as spiritual healers and purveyors of power-objects like charms and amulets. This is comparable to India and Indonesia, where Sufi orders and practices continued to thrive into the modern age, even if under new guises. As Green has shown, a number of the Sufi brotherhoods in Africa weathered the colonial storm by shifting 'from resistance to

accommodation' and by using the opportunities afforded by colonialism to re-
assert their leadership of ordinary Muslims and propagate Islam among them.[84]
Indeed, not only did the older Sufi brotherhoods, like the Qadiriyya, creatively
adapt to colonialism, the period also witnessed the emergence of entirely new
Sufi brotherhoods or new offshoots of older brotherhoods which would make
major impacts.[85] A particularly interesting example of the latter is the West
African Muridiyya order.

Founded in 1886 by Ahmadu Bamba (1850–1927), the Muridiyya has been
instrumental in spreading Islam in the Senegambia region (today's Senegal and
the Gambia). Coming of age in a time of rapid change – a time marked by the
rise of French colonialism and the disintegration of the traditional Wolof states
or chieftancies – Bamba, who had been affiliated with the Qadiriyya order,
developed a reputation as Muslim scholar and Sufi of considerable spiritual
power. In the year 1886 he founded both his new movement and the city of
Touba (Senegal) as a centre for the movement. Also in 1886, Shaykh Ibrahima
Fall (1858–1930), a descendant of a powerful Wolof family, pledged allegiance
to Bamba and led his followers into the movement. Fearing his growing influence and in a moment of anti-Sufi paranoia, the French captured Bamba and
sent him into exile for what turned out to be the better part of seventeen years,
from 1895 to 1912. As stories spread of Bamba's patient suffering and miraculous exploits while in captivity, his following only increased. During his exile, his
deputies (including Ibrahima Fall) continued to spread his *da'wa* and encouraged members of the movement to buy land and take up the communal cultivation of peanuts. This provided a practical means of supporting the movement
and practically living out the teachings of Islam. In an era in which Christian
missionaries were engaged in similar experiments – creating settlements or
villages where practical (farming and other) work and Christian instruction
went hand-in-hand – this provides an Islamic example of the same phenomenon. Settlements of this sort (Christian and Muslim) also provided refuge for
former or runaway slaves and facilitated the 'evangelization of slaves'.[86] These
Muridiyya activities were in keeping with Bamba's conviction that 'war against
the French was futile' and that Muslims should turn 'from war to work' in the
changing world of colonial modernity.[87]

Returning from exile in 1912, Bamba gave his blessings to these policies and
efforts. For the Mourides (followers of the Muridiyya movement), therefore, *jihad*
was not understood as holy war against the French, but as the 'greater *jihad*' of
hard work, obedience and missionary outreach. Through the Mourides' successful peanut cultivation and creative use of colonial markets, Touba became
a prosperous city as well as a centre of Muridi *da'wa*. Before and after Bamba's
death in 1927, the movement continued to spread. It may be that part of the
reason for the success of the movement has been its indigenisation to traditional
African cultures. For instance, the role of Bamba in the movement reflects that

of traditional religious practitioners, and the veneration of his tomb and memory
(since his death) reflects African ancestor veneration. In fact, Bamba bears more
than a passing resemblance to his almost exact contemporary William Wadé
Harris (1860–1929), the African 'prophet' who, after turning from politics,
preached an indigenous, African form of Christianity in today's Liberia, Ivory
Coast and Ghana, and baptised hundreds of thousands of converts.[88] Today,
Bamba's movement boasts millions of members in Senegal, the Gambia and in
the Senegalese and Gambian diasporas around the world. Like other African
movements of the same period, the Muridiyya thus serves as another (uniquely
African) example of a turn to quietist, grassroots *da'wa* under colonial conditions
(see Figure 6.4).[89]

Figure 6.4 A participant in 'Shaykh Ahmadu Bamba International Day' carries an
iconic image of Bamba (1853–1927), Dakar, Senegal, 2019. Photo: Macodou Fall.

North Africa

To the north of Senegal, by the early twentieth century, much of North Africa (west of Egypt), formerly under the Ottoman Empire, had come under European colonial rule. The French established a protectorate over Tunisia in 1881, the French and Spanish over Morocco in 1912, and the Italians invaded Libya in 1911. The most dramatic example of colonial rule in North Africa, however, was seen in Algeria, which was first invaded by the French in 1830 and which would not attain independence until 1962. Throughout North Africa, colonialism meant different things, and disestablishment proceeded at different rates. For instance, despite colonial tinkering with and modernist calls for the reform of education and law in Morocco, traditional Islam remained central to Moroccan society, and the Moroccan sultans retained their Islamic legitimacy even under colonial rule. Traditional Algerian society, by contrast, was virtually destroyed under the aggressive brand of colonialism the French imposed in that context.[90] In spite of these differences, as across the wider Muslim world, a similar mix of secularist, modernist, Islamist and reformist *da'wa*s emerged throughout colonial North Africa during the late nineteenth and early twentieth centuries. In Tunisia, for instance, there were the efforts of the French-educated Young Tunisians to modernise Islam and Tunisian society, as well as to restore pride in Arabic literature and culture. Meanwhile, reformist currents – of the sort associated with 'Abduh and Rida – were making themselves felt. By the 1930s, as in so many other areas, a secular nationalist party rose to the fore in Tunisia, a party which would lead the independence struggle and rule Tunisia until 2011.

In Algeria, after the French put down the 1870–1 uprising, colonial rule was tightened, and French colonisation began in earnest. Many Islamic schools were closed, and the leadership and institutions of the Sufis and *'ulama* fell into disarray. The Catholic Church was also active in Algeria in the late nineteenth century, at first primarily catering to the religious needs of the growing numbers of French and other European settlers. The situation changed, however, with the arrival of missionary-minded Catholics such as Charles Lavigerie (1825–92, founder of the Society of Missionaries of Africa, or 'White Fathers'). From their first base of operations in Algiers, the White Fathers would lay the foundations for the Catholic Church in what were to become fifteen African nations.[91] In addition, Catholic orphanages and schools were established across Algeria. Thus, as in other places, the fact of political subjugation was combined with the perceived threat of Christianisation in the minds of many Algerian Muslims. In response to this situation, some, such as the French-educated Young Algerians, urged the acceptance of French rule, even as they called for the modernisation of Islam and the equal treatment of Arabs. Other movements took secularist or socialist stances, including those which would dominate the formation of post-colonial Algeria. Of special note for our purposes is that in the 1920s and 1930s, Algeria witnessed the emergence of a significant reformist *da'wa* movement, that associated with 'Abd al-Hamid b. Badis (or Ben Badis).

While completing his Islamic education at the famous Zaytuna *madrasa* (founded in the eighth century CE) in Tunisia, Ben Badis was exposed to the modernist-reformism of 'Abduh. Zaytuna, it might be noted in passing, underwent a similar process of responding to colonial modernity as seen in the case of Al-Azhar. In the early years of the twentieth century, it played a significant part in the Tunisian and Algerian independence movements, by producing a number of important reformist thinkers, such as Ben Badis.[92] Returning home to Algeria in 1913, Ben Badis found his vocation in spreading a *da'wa* of reform. He wanted Islam, as opposed to secular alternatives, to become the basis of Algerian nationhood. As with the other examples we have seen in this chapter, Ben Badis used the printed word as a major vehicle for spreading his *da'wa*. In 1925, he began publishing *Al-Muntaqid* (The Critic), which was banned after just eighteen issues. As a result, Ben Badis toned down his politics and tried again with *Al-Shihab* (The Meteor), which was published from 1925 to 1939. He also took a largely apolitical stance in the activities he pursued through the Association of Algerian Ulama, which he founded with like-minded colleagues in 1931. The association promoted reformed Islam and attacked popular Sufi practices. It also opened hundreds of schools which sought to educate Algerians in 'true' Islam. As independence approached, Ben Badis was drawn more and more into politics. Nevertheless, his early movement serves as another example of a turn towards grassroots *da'wa* and education in a colonial context. The *da'wa* associated with Ben Badis has been called 'the most energetic and widespread cultural force in Algeria' in the era of French rule.[93]

The Arab Fertile Crescent

The colonial history of the 'Arab Fertile Crescent', those lands which had been the eastern provinces of the Ottoman Empire, or today's Iraq, Syria, Jordan, Lebanon and Palestine parallels the history of colonial North Africa. Divided under British and French protectorates after World War I, the peoples of these territories would develop a similar range of responses to colonial modernity. Initially under declining Ottoman rule and then under European rule, reformists of various stripes would develop outreach programs alongside and in competition with the promoters of modernism or secularism. As elsewhere, not only the reform-minded or western-educated, but also traditional religious leaders like the *'ulama* and Sufi brotherhoods continued to disseminate their ideas. As colonial rule wound down, secular-nationalist military and/or family regimes would take up the reins of power in this region. Several developments in the

Arab Fertile Crescent deserve special mention in relation to the first phase of modern *da'wa*.

First, we have already mentioned the rise of Arab nationalism in colonial Egypt and North Africa in the waning years of the Ottoman Empire. Interestingly, some of the foundational thinkers of this trend were Arab Christians from Syria and Lebanon, who, along with their Arab Muslim counterparts, called for Arab self-determination and a revival of the splendours of the Arab past. Arab nationalism was focused on independence, not only from European imperialism, but also from Ottoman/Turkish imperialism. Arab Christians, for obvious reasons, favoured the idea of secular, pluralist states. For them, Arab-ness was more of an ethno-linguistic than religious matter. By contrast, numerous Arab Muslims framed Arab nationalism in religious terms. For them, Arab greatness was inseparably bound up with Islam. The '*da'wa*' of Arab nationalism, then, could easily shade into Islamic modernism or reformism or some combination of the two – Arabs would become great again, not only by throwing off imperialism, but by returning to Islam. A good example of the latter trend is 'Abd al-Rahman al-Kawakibi (d. 1902), the son of a prominent Muslim family from Aleppo. Like 'Abduh and Rida (whose views Kawakibi generally shared), he called for a return to the purity of original Islam and spoke out against the corruptions caused by wayward Sufism, the alleged stagnation of the law schools and the 'despotism' of the Ottomans. For Kawakibi, part and parcel of the revival he envisioned was the restoration of the caliphate to the Arabs. To accomplish this, he floated the idea of establishing an Islamic missionary society which would educate Muslims around the world on the need for reform and on the necessity of Arab leadership.[94]

Standing in contrast to Arab nationalism – along with other emerging nationalisms (such as Turkish, Iranian, Indonesian and Indian) among Muslim peoples – was pan-Islamism, the idea that Muslims should not divide themselves on ethno-linguistic or geographic grounds, but that they should unite under the common banner of 'Islam'. While pan-Islamism held considerable appeal, it would gain little headway against the nationalistic zeitgeist of the early twentieth century. In fact, because of the strength of nationalistic sentiments across the Muslim world, numerous would-be pan-Islamists pragmatically accepted the temporary division of the world's Muslims by 'nation'. For instance, despite his sympathy with pan-Islamism, Indian thinker Muhammad Iqbal (d. 1938) wrote: '[T]he trend of modern Islam . . . for the present [is that] . . . every Muslim nation must sink into her own deeper self, temporarily focus her vision on herself alone'. Iqbal would even become an advocate for a distinctly Indian Islamic version of nationalism, and his ideas would contribute to the formation of Pakistan. Yet, Iqbal also foresaw a time when Muslim nations would come together 'to form a living family of republics'.[95]

At any rate, the rising mood of Arab nationalism actually contributed to a short-lived religio-political *da'wa*, when Husayn Ibn 'Ali al-Hashimi (1854–1931), an Arab notable who had been appointed to be the ruler and custodian of Mecca by the Ottomans, attempted to rally Arab support to himself before revolting against the Ottomans and declaring himself king of the Arabs in 1916. For a time, Husayn's movement achieved some success, with tacit British support. Around the same time, however, the British and the French entered the Sykes-Picot Agreement in 1916. Effectively ignoring Husayn's claims, Sykes-Picot became the basis for the somewhat arbitrary carving up of the Arab east into several new semi-autonomous states: Syria and Lebanon under French Mandate, and Iraq and Palestine under British Mandate (Palestine was later divided to create a fifth state, Transjordan, in the early 1920s). Husayn's sons Faisal and 'Abdullah were made the kings of Iraq and Transjordan, both under British supervision. Descendants of Husayn would rule Iraq until 1958 and Transjordan (or Jordan) to the present. Meanwhile, during World War I, the British had also entered into an agreement with the Arabian chieftain 'Abd al-Aziz b. Sa'ud, the founder of modern Saudi Arabia. In a region that had no history of independent states, with competing visions of the future and with important non-Arab (for example, the Kurds) and non-Muslim (for instance, the Christians of Iraq, Syria and Palestine, and the Maronites of Lebanon) populations, the creation of these novel political units created many dilemmas which remain unresolved to the present. As for Husayn himself, following Ataturk's abolishment of the caliphate in 1924, Husayn made an effort to revive his *da'wa* by declaring himself caliph, but this failed to gain traction. In 1925, 'Abd al-Aziz b. Sa'ud captured Mecca and Medina – cities the Saudis have held ever since – and Husayn was forced into exile. He died in 1931.

A second colonial-era development in the Arab Fertile Crescent with important implications for worldwide *da'wa* was the emergence of Zionism (Jewish nationalism) in the late nineteenth century. The Zionist movement – which called for a national homeland for the Jews – was sparked by the historical Jewish experience of anti-Semitism around the world. Although Zionist leaders discussed several possible locations, they eventually settled on the biblical Promised Land or the land of Palestine as the object of their ambitions. As of the turn of the twentieth century, the vast majority of the inhabitants of Palestine were Arab Muslims and Christians. Nevertheless, Zionists began to encourage Jewish migration to and settlement of Palestine. In a sign that that the Zionist movement was gaining momentum in the first two decades of the twentieth century, in 1917 Britain issued the Balfour Declaration. It proclaimed that Britain would 'view with favour the establishment in Palestine of a national home for the Jewish people' and would 'use their best endeavours to facilitate the achievement of this object'. The Declaration also stated that 'nothing shall be done which may prejudice the civil and religious rights of existing non-Jewish communities in Palestine'.[96] However, as history would show, this caveat was easier to say than to carry out. After 1917, Jewish migration and settlement accelerated. Where there had been 24,000 Jews in Palestine in 1881, by 1939 there were almost half a million.[97] The stage was set for conflict. Throughout the 1920s, as the Arabs of Palestine joined in opposition to Britain's policies,[98] a 'Palestinian' national consciousness emerged which would be channelled into several streams of activism. Like Arab Christians elsewhere and some Palestinian secularists, Palestinian Christians favoured secular approaches to the Zionist threat and nation-building. At the same time, numerous Palestinian Muslims sought to frame the anti-Zionist struggle as an Islamic cause. For instance, Amin al-Husayni (1897–1974), the *mufti* of Jerusalem and president of the Supreme Muslim Council of Mandatory Palestine (established by the British in 1922), tried to rally Muslims worldwide in support of the Muslims of Palestine. In 1931, he organised a conference in Jerusalem in which more than 150 Muslim scholars supported a resolution on the sanctity of Jerusalem and the importance of Palestine to all Muslims.[99] Meanwhile, other groups were calling for armed *jihad*. A significant figure in this stream of activism was Shaykh 'Izz al-Din al-Qassam (1882–1935), the Imam of Haifa and a leader in the Young Men's Muslim Association (founded in 1927, see above), who preached a *da'wa* of radical reform to go along with his anti-British and anti-Zionist activism. He gained a large following and played a major role in the Arab revolt in Palestine of 1936–9. Husayni also lent his leadership to the 1936–9 revolt, before being forced to flee Palestine in 1937.[100]

Into the 1940s and throughout World War II, the British tried to appease both Jews and Arabs. This period, however, was marked by continuing Arab and Jewish restlessness, including the use of terrorist tactics by radical Zionist groups. In 1947, the British declared that they would leave Palestine in early 1948. That year, the United Nations partitioned Palestine, and Israel declared independent statehood, a move that was famously supported by US President Harry Truman against the objections of his own State Department.[101] This set off a dramatic chain of events. With the western powers either ambivalent (in the case of Britain) or supportive (in the case of the United States), Israel decisively prevailed in the 1948–9 Arab–Israeli War (or Israel's 'War of Independence') against a collation of armies sent by Egypt, Syria, Saudi Arabia, Transjordan and Lebanon, along with fighters from groups like the Muslim Brotherhood. The war itself, along with Israel's efforts to forcibly remove Palestinians from the new Jewish state, resulted in the displacement of more than 700,000 Arabs.[102] We will return to the post-1948 history of Palestine and Israel in Chapter 7. For now, we may note that, true to Husayni's and al-Qassam's visions, the 'Palestine issue' would indeed become a rallying point for Muslims around the world. Concern for the Palestinians, a desire to protect the holy places of Islamic Jerusalem and anger at Israel, the West and the Arab states which had been defeated by Israel would mobilise Muslims for several kinds of activism, including *da'wa*.

Iran

Iran in the colonial era provides additional revealing and unique glimpses at the first phase of modern *da'wa*. In contrast to most of our examples so far, *da'wa* in modern Iran has generally been carried out on behalf of (Twelver) Shi'ite Islam. Shi'ite Islam, it will be recalled, became the primary religion of Iran and much of today's Iraq during the period of Safavid rule (*circa* 1501–1722), through the Safavids' aggressive pro-Shi'ite *da'wa* (see Chapter 4). Iran never came under direct colonial rule; however, like Turkey, Iran was no less affected by the onslaught of colonial modernity. In the period covered in this chapter, with the exception of a 'constitutional' period from 1905 to 1911, the major powers in Iran were the Qajar dynasty (r. *circa* 1779–1925) and the Pahlavi dynasty (r. 1925–79). Although we have seen pre-modern examples of Shi'ite religio-political *da'was* leading to great empires (for example, the Fatimids and Safavids), there has long been a significant strand of quietism in Shi'ite thought. This is owing, in part, to the Shi'ites' historical experience of living under Sunni domination in *dar al-Islam*. From the time of the sixth Shi'ite Imam, Ja'far (d. 765), the Shi'ites had learned how to survive and propagate their version(s) of Islam through what this book has been calling Meccan styles of *da'wa*.[103]

Towards the late nineteenth century, European and Russian encroachment on Iran – the Russians from Central Asia, the British from India via Afghanistan – and the perceived failure of the Qajars to respond adequately, along with Qajar attempts to modernise the country, ran afoul of many *'ulama*. As a result, some took up oppositional political activism. Moreover, as in other parts of the Muslim world, Islamic modernism and secularism were becoming popular among new classes of western-educated Iranians. It is in this turbulent context that several new Shi'ite-inspired religious movements arose – movements which were committed to missionary *da'wa*. The yearning for the return of the Twelfth Imam (whom Shi'ites believe went into hiding or 'occultation' in the year 948 and whom they believe will return as an end-times deliverer) and a longing for the restoration of better days lay behind the preaching, first, of Sayyid 'Ali Muhammad (d. 1850), who proclaimed himself 'the Bab', or doorway, to the Hidden Imam. Sayyid 'Ali also denounced the traditional Iranian *'ulama* as too corrupt and incompetent to lead the Muslims in a time of rapid change. In part because of the political rebellions that Sayyid 'Ali's message inspired and in part because the movement was crushed in 1850, the major successor to the movement turned more fully towards quietist *da'wa*. Mirza Husayn 'Ali Nuri, or Baha Allah (d. 1892), claimed to be the coming one allegedly prophesied by 'the Bab' before the latter's death. Developing a unique understanding of religious history, he proclaimed a peaceful *jihad* of *da'wa*, even going so far as to send letters of *da'wa* to the rulers of various nations. His religious movement, which would later be known as the Baha'i Faith, was severely persecuted in Iran and elsewhere, but still managed to spread. Today, it is estimated that there are over seven million Baha'is in dozens of countries worldwide. Despite the fact that most observers today consider Baha'i to be an independent religion (and most Muslims consider it a heresy), there is no question that, like the Ahmadiyya movement discussed above, the emergence of the Baha'i *da'wa* belongs in this chapter. Like the Ahmadiyya, the Baha'i movement serves as a uniquely Iranian example of the rise of creative, quietist *da'wa*s in the conditions of colonial modernity.

As Iran moved into the Pahlavi period (after 1925), the Iranian religious establishment continued to exhibit both quietist and politically activist tendencies. What changed the equation was that the authoritarian Pahlavis, like the regime of Ataturk in Turkey, aggressively pushed the country towards secular-nationalism and westernisation. Reza Shah (r. 1925–41), in fact, deliberately modelled his modernisation program on that of Ataturk. Education and the courts were westernised and brought under state control. The University of Tehran, founded in 1935, was modelled on European universities and became the first in a nationwide system. With the spread of western-style education in Iran, religious schools all over the country declined or felt threatened. In addition, the discovery of oil in Iran (in the early twentieth century) seemed primarily to benefit the European powers who had helped discover the oil. Over time, the Pahlavis became increasingly dependent on western support, particularly from the United States. Iranian history after 1950 will be taken up in Chapter 7, but suffice it to say that the stage was set for the dramatic developments in which some Shi'ite *'ulama*, most notably Ayatollah Ruhollah Khomeini (1902–89), would abandon quietism altogether and engage in a novel, and highly consequential, revolutionary *da'wa*.[104]

Arabia

Turning finally to Arabia, we have already discussed (in Chapter 5) the eighteenth-century beginnings of the Wahhabi movement and *da'wa*, and the early alliance formed between the Wahhabis and the Sa'ud family. Although the religio-political *da'wa* of the Wahhabi-Saudi alliance yielded some early fruit in terms of territorial conquest (they took Riyadh in 1773 and Mecca and Medina in 1803), this first iteration of the Saudi state was soundly defeated by the largely autonomous Ottoman governor of Egypt, Muhammad (or Mehmet) 'Ali, in 1818. Given their stated purpose of crushing both Saudi political power and the 'despised' Wahhabi sect, the Ottoman-Egyptian expedition against the Wahhabis failed in the long term. The Saudi-Wahhabi experiment may have been diminished, but it was not destroyed.[105] From 1818 until the dawn of the twentieth century, the embattled movement survived in the interior of the peninsula. In 1902, however, a new Saudi leader, 'Abd al-Aziz Ibn Sa'ud

(d. 1953), re-took Riyadh, reinvigorated the Wahhabi movement, unified the Arabian tribes under his leadership and through wars of expansion and the use of a religio-political *da'wa* (not unlike that employed by the early Saudi-Wahhabi movement in the eighteenth century) established what are still the international borders of Saudi Arabia to this day. Especially noteworthy is that he re-took the holy cities of Mecca and Medina in 1925. In 1932, he officially declared the establishment of the Kingdom of Saudi Arabia (KSA) as an independent state (see Map 7.1). An important instrument in this second major rise of the Saudi-Wahhabi movement[106] were the Ikhwan (Brothers or Brotherhood), a corps of men devoted to the project of spreading both Saudi rule and Wahhabism. The origins of the Ikhwan are to be found in early-twentieth-century Saudi agricultural settlements known as *hijras*, where nomadic tribesmen were encouraged (or forced) to embrace a settled life. Wahhabi *'ulama* were sent as missionaries to the *hijras* in order to instruct the nomads in 'true' Islam. The Ikhwan, who resulted from these efforts, were among the most zealous missionary-warriors for Wahhabism into the 1920s. We will have more to say about the Ikhwan in a moment, but for now attention should be drawn to two further developments within Saudi Arabia up to 1950 which are relevant to the theme of *da'wa*.

First, the Saudis consolidated the system of government and rule which generally stands in Arabia to the present. In this system, the descendants of 'Abd al-Aziz are authoritarian monarchs who depend on an army of loyal tribesmen to maintain their power. Their rule is also characterised by an uneasy symbiosis with the Wahhabi *'ulama* who make up the country's religious establishment. In the name of 'commanding the right and forbidding the wrong', the religious establishment, through Saudi Arabia's religious police, *shari'a* courts and state-run schools, has enforced compliance with Wahhabi norms. As seen in the venerable Islamic cemeteries of Medina – cemeteries once studded by domed monuments and mausoleums to the great Muslims of the past, but now reduced to blank fields with simple stone markers – they have also destroyed or driven underground most remnants of Sufism in their domain. The Saudis' establishment of the Wahhabi *da'wa* has therefore involved the effective disestablishment of all rival forms of Islam.[107] Since 1925, the Saudis' role as custodians of the holy cities of Mecca and Medina has given them tremendous status around the Muslim world. Yet for all that, the rulers of modern Saudi Arabia have had to make many compromises with regard to Wahhabi orthodoxy in order to build a functioning modern state. The Saudi state has embraced, for instance, modern technologies and a pragmatic foreign policy which partners with 'infidels' and rejects global *jihad* as unrealistic. Over the years, Saudi rulers increasingly have had to 'puncture the seal' which strict Wahhabism (and Salafism more generally) presupposes between the realm of true belief and the realm of falsehood and infidelity.[108] These facts have frequently injected an element of strain into the relationship between the rulers and the *'ulama*.

We may illustrate this by returning to the Ikhwan. In building the new nation, Ibn Sa'ud had to toe the line between maintaining Wahhabi doctrinal purity and adjusting to the demands of modern geopolitics. As an example of the latter, he recognised international boundaries and British supremacy to his north and east and gradually introduced modern technologies into the kingdom. When in the 1920s the Ikhwan, who were 'motivated more by ideal-ism than allegiance to Ibn Sa'ud', expressed their unhappiness about the ruler's compromises, Ibn Sa'ud 'crushed them and in so doing reasserted dynastic power over the religious mission'.[109] This episode taught the Wahhabi *'ulama* an important lesson: their job was to show loyalty to the ruler by accepting his prerogative to do what was politically necessary to build the state. In exchange for the *'ulama*'s quietism and loyalty, the rulers would give them a free hand to develop the state's religious institutions and policies. Still, this tension – between the demands of ruling a modern state, on the one hand, and the purist ideal-ism of Wahhabi belief, on the other – has never been adequately resolved. The tension has manifested itself throughout Saudi history in a series of 'true believers' movements' which have risen up to chastise and sometimes violently oppose the ruling family (and collaborating *'ulama*) for its alleged failures to live up to 'true Islam'.[110] In general, however, the system in which the Wahhabi *'ulama* maintain a quietist stance in exchange for financial backing and religious influence has proven fairly durable.

The second major development was the discovery of massive reserves of oil in eastern Arabia the 1930s. Today, it is thought that more than one-fourth of the world's oil reserves are in (or under) Saudi territory. American-Saudi partnership in discovering and extracting the oil led to the creation of the Arab American Oil Company, or Aramco. It also contributed to the formation of the sometimes uneasy, unofficial United States–Saudi Arabia alliance that persists to this day. The Saudi regime's welcome of American companies and workers, and the regime's decision to start sending Saudis abroad for technical training accelerated the country's integration into global markets and the global political system. Oil production began in earnest after World War II, and serious oil wealth began to flow into the kingdom from the 1970s onwards. Today, Aramco (which was nationalised in the 1980s and renamed 'Saudi Aramco') is one of the highest valued companies on earth. Already in Ibn Sa'ud's time new oil-generated wealth created dilemmas for piety-minded Wahhabis, including the king himself. Ibn Sa'ud 'lived to see corruption and licentiousness spread among his courtiers and even some of his sons, wounding his conscience and affront-ing his morals [. . .] Palaces sprang up around Riyadh in imitation of what the Saudis had seen in Paris, London, and Hollywood. And camels gave way to Cadillacs'.[111] If Ibn Sa'ud was alive today, we could expect him to be distressed by the even more blatant profligacy of his descendants, but perhaps he and his allies among the *'ulama* would have taken some comfort in knowing just how much oil revenue would be earmarked for Salafi-Wahhabi *da'wa* around the world. In Chapter 7, we will have more to say about the stunning implications of these two developments from *circa* 1950 to 2020.[112]

Muslim minority populations

An important theme of Chapters 5 and 6 has been the rise of situations in the colonial era in which, regardless of whether they constituted demographic majorities within traditional *dar al-Islam* or not, Muslims around the world were subjected to a kind of *felt* minority experience, or experiential 'minoritisation', prompted by foreign domination, disestablishment and heightened religious competition. Our focus here, however, is not on this general trend towards minoritisation, but on the experience of actual Muslim minorities. Muslim minority populations in the colonial era were of several types. First, in some places – such as parts of Europe, sub-Saharan Africa and China – Muslims had lived as minorities from before the colonial period. Such populations exhibited various strategies for navigating these situations: from 'passing' as non-Muslims in contexts of anti-Islamic hostility (as among some Muslims in post-Reconquista Spain), to blending into a non-Muslim majority without losing their religious identity (as among some Hui Muslims in Han-dominated China), to engaging in separatist activities (as among some Turkic Muslims in western China/eastern Central Asia).[113] A more general trend in such situations, however, has been for Muslim minorities to focus on quietly maintaining their faith and traditions (as among Central Asia's Muslims under the Russians and Soviets, as mentioned above). Second, there were several instances in which Muslims who had already been demographic minorities, but under Muslim rule, rather suddenly found themselves under non-Muslim rule. This was the case, for instance, for India's Muslims as British power tightened on the subcontinent, as well as for Muslims in areas of southeastern Europe which were lost by the Ottomans in the nineteenth century. Finally, as noted earlier, the colonial period engendered waves of Muslim migration to destinations outside traditional *dar al-Islam*. This led to the creation of newer Muslim communities in places like South Africa, Britain, France, Germany, Canada and the United States. It is especially after 1950 that these communities came into their own in terms of *da'wa*, and we will have more to say about them in Chapter 7.

In Part I of this book, we saw that classical Islamic law tends to assume situations in which Islam is 'established' to some degree. Although pre-modern Muslim scholars sometimes grappled with the existence of non-Muslim minorities or non-Muslim powers *within dar al-Islam* (as Ibn Taymiyya did in the thirteenth and fourteenth centuries after the Mongol invasions),[114] situations in which Muslims were permanently living as minorities *outside dar al-Islam* were rarely contemplated.[115] As noted in Chapter 3, since classical Islamic law assumes that one can truly practise Islam only in an Islamic polity or society, it tended to prescribe *hijra* (migration) to *dar al-Islam* for Muslims who found themselves living in *dar al-harb*. In addition, the pre-modern Islamic tradition scarcely develops a concept of Muslims taking up residence outside *dar al-Islam* for the express purpose of missionary outreach.[116] Needless to say, each of these dynamics – limited Muslim reflection on the status of Muslim minorities and the lack of a theology of relocating outside *dar al-Islam* for missionary purposes – began to change in the colonial period.

Among some prominent colonial-era scholars, there was a growing acceptance of the idea that Muslims could and should live in non-Muslim societies under non-Muslim rule, provided they were free to publicly practise Islam. Even among scholars who insisted on using '*dar al-harb*' for formerly Muslim territories which had fallen under the Europeans, there was often a pragmatic willingness to encourage Muslims to get on with life. Such was the case, for instance, with Shah 'Abd al-Aziz (d. 1823, the son of Shah Wali Allah) who famously declared India under the British to be *dar al-harb*, but who nevertheless encouraged Muslims to try to live peacefully under British rule.[117] A similar position to that of 'Abd al-Aziz was taken by Rashid Rida (d. 1935); when asked about Bosnian Muslims under non-Muslim rule (Bosnia had come under the Austro-Hungarian Empire in 1878), he issued a series of *fatwa*s (published in *al-Manar*) stating that Muslims were permitted to live under non-Muslim rule so long as they could still observe Islamic rituals freely.[118] Although rarely explicit, one can detect an underlying orientation towards *da'wa* in these writings. A key concern of thinkers such as 'Abd al-Aziz and Rida was not only to help Muslims be at ease wherever they found themselves, but also to maintain their faith and identity in minority situations. This in turn would ensure that an Islamic presence and witness was maintained.[119] Building on what is implicit among these thinkers from the first phase of modern *da'wa*, thinkers in the second phase (after 1950) would develop a new field of Islamic jurisprudence, *fiqh al-aqaliyyāt* or minorities' jurisprudence. Rida's rulings on minorities, in fact, have been called a 'prelude' to the emergence of full-blown Islamic minorities' jurisprudence.[120] A fuller discussion of this significant development in Islamic thought must wait until Chapter 7.

Summary and conclusions

This chapter has surveyed what we are calling the *first phase* of modern *da'wa*. Moving from region to region, it provided snapshots of representative *da'wa*-oriented thinkers and movements up to roughly 1950. Our use of the term '*da'wa*-oriented' in this chapter has been intentional. While a good number of thinkers and movements did in fact use the words '*da'wa*' and/or '*tabligh*', others exhibited an orientation towards *da'wa* without necessarily using the terminology. Along the way, the chapter also highlighted certain key developments, such as the establishment of modern Saudi Arabia, the Partition of British India, the founding of the modern state of Israel and the growth of Muslim minority communities in various places. Each of these, while not instances of missionary *da'wa* as such, are crucial for understanding modern *da'wa*'s first and second phases. By way of concluding this chapter, let us draw out some key characteristics and themes of the first phase of modern *da'wa*.

First, we have seen ample evidence to support this book's argument that, in many contexts during the first phase, *da'wa* emerged with a decidedly 'Meccan' flavour, or undergirded by (explicit or implicit) Meccan *da'wa*logies. Responding to the rise of the colonial powers, widespread disestablishment and minoritisation, and the prominence of religious marketplace mentalities (see Chapter 5), Muslims across the globe embraced quietist styles of mission which were oriented towards grassroots preaching, education and renewal. They accepted *de facto*, if not necessarily *de jure*, the typically modern arrangement whereby religion operates chiefly in the realms of personal piety and voluntary choice.[121] Faced with rising religious competition, particularly from missionary Christianity, they took up the very tools and techniques of the missionaries – the non-state mission society or 'faith mission', the printing press, pamphlets and periodicals, modern schools and styles of training, the convening of international conferences and so on. None of this is to suggest that Muslims like India's Muhammad Ilyas, Egypt's (Syria-born) Rashid Rida, Indonesia's Ahmad Dahlan, West Africa's Ahmadu Bamba, Turkey's Said Nursi, Algeria's 'Abd al-Hamid Ben Badis, Egypt's Zaynab al-Ghazali, or figures like Mawdudi and al-Banna rejected politics altogether. Far from it. When conditions proved conducive, several of these thinkers or movements took up political activism. Other leaders or parties, such as the Muslim League in India, Husayni and al-Qassam in Palestine, and the Saudi-Wahhabi alliance in Arabia had explicit political goals from the start. Furthermore, movements which have remained steadfastly apolitical, like the Tablighi Jama'at (TJ), have still sometimes cherished what might be called 'political dreams' – hopes that Muslims will rule the world someday. Of the movements surveyed above, perhaps those which most fully embraced quietist Meccan *da'wa*logies in the first phase were the newer *da'wa*-oriented sectarian movements covered in this chapter: the Ahmadiyya movement and the Baha'i faith. In light of contemporary western and media obsession with political or militant Islam, this chapter's focus on the widespread emergence of peaceful, preaching-oriented *da'wa* provides a useful corrective.

Second, this chapter has illustrated the diversification of Muslims and of Islamic activism in the period from *circa* 1850 to 1950. Facing external threats to their faith and way of life, many Muslims found common cause through *da'wa*. At the same time, *da'wa* quickly became an arena of vigorous internal diversity and debate. Not only were there *da'wa*s for competing sects of Islam, there were *da'wa*s emerging on behalf of alternative Muslim visions of the future: modernism, reformism, Islamism, secularism and so on. Indeed, there were even '*da'wa*s' directed to Muslims on behalf of various nationalisms. In short, *da'wa* in this period not only provided a basis for Muslim accord and mobilisation, it was also implicated in the emerging battle for Muslim minds, a battle in which a myriad of 'projects for recruiting and attuning the ear' were directed towards Muslim populations.[122] This trend has not abated up to the present.

Third, although we have seen some instances of *external da'wa* (for example, in sub-Saharan Africa), Islamic mission in this period was largely a matter of *internal da'wa*. This trend was fuelled, in part, by a 'turn to the masses' on the part of Muslim leaders around the world. For reasons stated throughout Chapters 5 and 6, everywhere in the former Muslim ecumene, there was a new urgency to revive, instruct and put Islamic resources into the hands of ordinary Muslims. Included in this broader trend was a turn towards Muslim women. On the one hand, some colonial officials and Muslim secularists were pushing for greater freedoms for Muslim women, while nationalists tended to see women as the bearers of authentic (Turkish, Arab, Egyptian) nationhood. On the other hand, since Muslim wives and mothers were seen as the first religious teachers of Islam's future generations and since they were sometimes viewed as particularly prone to passing on 'incorrect' practices, groups like the TJ (along with activists like al-Banna, Mawdudi, Zaynab al-Ghazali and others) sought to instruct Muslim women in 'true' Islam and to mobilise them to reach children and other women. The most important point is that, in the first phase, the expectations made of laypeople, including women, *vis-à-vis* the preservation and propagation of Islam increased markedly from pre-modern times. Each of these trends, powered in part by *da'wa*, would only accelerate after 1950.

Notes

1. Kuiper 2018a; see also Metcalf 1982, p. 63.
2. On the 'firsts' of India's Muslims, see Kuiper 2018a, pp. 6–7. India's Muslims had never been a majority, but they had been ruled by Muslim empires for centuries. Also, South Asian Muslims have constituted a growing proportion of all Muslims worldwide in modern times. Today, 40 percent of all Muslims are South Asian.
3. Along with a 1852 conversion scare at Delhi College, schools set up by missionaries Alexander Duff, John Wilson and John Anderson witnessed some notable conversions to Christianity. Frykenberg 2008, pp. 314–27. Kuiper 2018a, pp. 119–20.
4. See Powell 1993. See also Kuiper 2018a, pp. 184–7.
5. Kairanawi apparently took part in the uprising. Malik remarks that, in 1857, he 'transformed himself from a fighter with the pen to a fighter with the sword'. Malik 2008, p. 272.
6. Schirrmacher 1999, pp. 270–9.
7. Robinson 2000b, pp. 66–104. See also Gelvin and Green 2014a.
8. Robinson 2000b, p. 67.

9. Green 2015a, ch. 2. Green goes so far as to speak of the 'evangelical midwifery' of Muslim printing (p. 97).
10. Kuiper 2018a, pp. 123–7.
11. In fact, Ilyas also drew analogies between his situation and that of the Prophet in Medina, but he transposed these Medinan stories into a Meccan key.
12. This followed Deobandi scholar Ashraf 'Ali Thanawi (d. 1943), who wrote a very popular late-nineteenth-century reformist handbook for Muslim women, *Bihishti Zewar* (Heavenly Ornaments). See Metcalf 1999.
13. For an overview, see Reetz 2006, ch. 2; see also Masud 2000, p. lii. Masud lists seven such movements which all emerged around the 1920s.
14. The Deobandis' main Sunni rivals are the Salafi Ahl-i Hadith (people of hadith) and the Barelvis. Both also emerged in the late nineteenth century and had their associated institutions and *da'was*. All three consider themselves to be bearers of Shah Wali Allah's legacy. The Indian Ahl-i Hadith has not only been influenced by Wahhabism, but the movement has also influenced Muslims in Arabia and Salafi movements elsewhere. See Lacroix 2009, pp. 58–80. See also Inayatullah (1960–2007), pp. 259–60. As for the Barelvis, they have promoted India's traditional Sunni Islam, including Shrine Sufism. See Sanyal 2005.
15. Lelyveld 2004, pp. 30–2. See Ahmad, Mirza Ghulam 2006.
16. Moore 2014.
17. Robinson 2000b.
18. The Jama'at 'encourages the reformation of society through education and conversion rather than by coercion'. See Oxford Islamic Studies Online [n. d.]. Like al-Banna and the Brotherhood, Mawdudi and the Jama'at spoke of Islam as a total 'system', a system which they contrasted sharply with godless 'western' systems. See, for example, Mawdudi 1994.
19. For a nuanced portrayal of the shifting stances of the JI since Partition, see Ahmad 2011.
20. The term 'new religious intellectuals' comes from Eickelman and Piscatori 1996, p. 13.
21. On 'Abduh, see Haddad 1994, pp. 30–63.
22. It disseminated 'Salafi' ideas. It is important to distinguish between 'modernist Salafis' in the tradition of 'Abduh and Rida and today's purist Salafis who look to Ibn Taymiyya and resemble Wahhabis. See Lauziere 2010, pp. 369–89.
23. Excerpts of the journal devoted to answering Christian missionaries were later published as a book entitled *Shubuhāt al-Naṣārā wa Ḥujaj al-Islām* (Criticisms of the Christians and Proofs of Islam). See Rida 2009.
24. 'Although most Islamic bookstores will not sell copies of the Bible, many will sell a work known as the Gospel of Barnabas . . . which tells the story of Jesus from an Islamic perspective'. Reynolds 2012, p. 123.
25. Sharkey 2005, pp. 43–60.
26. Sharkey 2008, p. 143.
27. Ibid., pp. 144–5; Ryad 2006, pp. 283–7.
28. Baron 2013, pp. 121–6.
29. See Ende 1960–2007.
30. Stanley 2009.
31. The 1911 conference followed the 1910 conference in Edinburgh. The proceedings reveal that Protestants were actively seeking Muslim converts. See Wherry, Mylrea and Zwemer 1911.
32. Kramer 1986, p. ix.
33. Ibid., pp. 9, 166–7.
34. Haykal 1976.
35. See, for instance, Newby 2009, p. 117.

36. Haykal 1976, pp. xlvii–li.
37. Mitchell 1969, p. 2, quoted in Wickham 2013, p. 21.
38. Poston 1992, p. 65f.
39. Delanoue 1960–2007, pp. 1068–71.
40. *Majjalat al-Ikhwān al-Muslimūn.*
41. Ryad 2006, pp. 303–4.
42. Sharkey 2005, pp. 49–50.
43. Wickham 2013, p. 25.
44. See Kuiper 2018a, pp. 82–3.
45. Mahmood 2005, p. 65.
46. Mahmood 2005, pp. 64–73; Hoffman-Ladd 2009a, pp. 337–44; Hoffman-Ladd 2009b, pp. 316–18. Another movement in Egypt which has successfully mobilised women is al-Jam'iyya al-Shar'iyya, founded in 1912. Mahmood 2005, p. 72.
47. Reid 2009, pp. 265–70.
48. From the traditional, more informal approach of Islamic knowledge transmission, it embraced the trappings of modern (western) education: admission procedures, classrooms, fixed curricula, course requirements, a regular faculty, academic departments, modern non-religious subjects and so on.
49. I thank Umar Ryad for this information. See also Skovgaard-Petersen 2007, pp. 185–8.
50. However, there was a faculty of *Usul al-Din* (foundations of religion) and *Da'wa*, as well as a Deptartment of Preaching as of the 1930s. Ryad 2006, p. 283.
51. Sharkey 2005, p. 47.
52. Ryad 2006, pp. 281–307.
53. The story is complicated. Russia was the primary antagonist of the empire, and the Ottomans lost significant territory to the tsarist regime over the eighteenth and nineteenth centuries. Britain and France, fearing Russian expansionism and in rivalry with one another, sometimes defended the Ottomans, sometimes undermined them.
54. As we will see below, in the same time span, Arab nationalism was emerging in the Ottomans' Arab territories.
55. Lapidus 2014, p. 537.
56. Weismann 2007, p. 156.
57. Turgay 2004, p. 513.
58. Turam 2004, p. 512.
59. Kuspinar 2009, pp. 260–2.
60. Sayilgan 2019, pp. 103–12.
61. Ibid., p. 105.
62. Green 2012, pp. 218, 226–8.
63. Nursi's legacy has also been felt in 'science in the Qur'an' discourse. See Chapter 7 below; Edis 2007, pp. 86–93.
64. This was also true, although to a lesser extent, in 'protectorates' such as Bukhara, where the Russians left the Muslim emir in power. Khalid 2007, pp. 39–40.
65. Khalid 2007, p. 42. For more on Gasprinski, including his interactions with Rashid Rida among others, see Kramer 1986, pp. 36–54.
66. To forestall pan-Turkic or pan-Islamic sentiments, the Soviets reinforced the incipient ethnic divisions of Muslim peoples, by dividing them into 'autonomous' republics. This laid the foundation for today's Central Asian states.
67. Olcott 2012, pp. 51–3.
68. Lapidus 2014, p. 678.
69. Yemelianova 2019, ch. 3.

70. This vision 'had little place for the toleration of local particularities that had marked the tsarist regime'. Khalid 2007, p. 51.
71. Olcott 2012, p. 49.
72. 'For the first time in history, one empire ruled the . . . archipelago. Thus the Dutch laid the foundation for the modern nation-state of Indonesia'. Lapidus 2014, p. 729.
73. Peacock and Trent Grunkmeyer 2009, p. 124.
74. Recalling the role of trade in the pre-modern Islamisation of the region (see Chapter 4), Dahlan (a batik merchant) often made journeys during which he combined *da'wa* and trade.
75. *Pesantren* boarding schools 'first appeared in the region in the eighteenth century . . . The institution became commonplace in Java, Sumatra, southern Thailand, and the Malay peninsula only a full century later . . . The advent of boarding schools for the study of the Islamic sciences coincided with the rise of modern varieties of Islamic reform in the Middle East and an expansion of Southeast Asian Muslim pilgrimage to Arabia'. Hefner 2007.
76. On Dahlan and the Muhammadiyya, see Lapidus 2014, p. 737; Hefner 2004, p. 487; Peacock and Trent Grunkmeyer 2009, pp. 124–5.
77. Qibtiyah, 'Muslimat NU', pp. 190–1.
78. On NU, see Lapidus 2014, pp. 737–8; van Doorn-Harder 2004, pp. 499–500; Kafrawi and Nakamura 2009, pp. 206–12.
79. Levtzion and Pouwels 2000, pp. 13–15.
80. Lapidus 2014, p. 798.
81. Ibid., p. 758.
82. Launay 2011, p. 258.
83. Sanneh 2008, p. 186.
84. Green 2012, p. 191f.
85. East African examples include the Sammaniyya (which spawned the Mahdist movement), the Khatmiyya, the Usuwiyya, the Shadhilyya and others. The colonial situation led to a new competitiveness between the brotherhoods. In earlier times, it had been normal for people to participate in several Sufi orders at once, but in the colonial period some began to make exclusive demands. This was true, for instance, of the Tijaniyya order, founded in 1782. See Launay 2011, pp. 257–8; Lapidus 2014, pp. 770–1, 780–97.
86. See Kollman 2005.
87. Lapidus 2014, p. 766.
88. Isichei 1995, pp. 284–6; Shank 1986, pp. 170–6.
89. On Bamba and the Muridiyya, see Green 2012, p. 202 (and endnotes); Robinson 2009, pp. 142–3; Chande 2004, pp. 19–24; Creevey2004, p. 104; Lapidus 2014, pp. 766–7.
90. Lapidus 2014, pp. 648–50.
91. Shorter 2006, p. xxi.
92. Gazzini 2004, p. 747.
93. McDougall 2007; Shahin 2009b; Lapidus 2014, pp. 632–3.
94. The proposal for Kawakibi's imagined missionary organisation came in his fictional account of a pan-Islamic congress he portrayed as having been held in 1898, entitled *Umm al-qura*. This 'Society for the Teaching of the Keepers of Tawhid' would rejuvenate Islam through 'publications, educational programs, and missionary activities'. Kramer 1986, pp. 31–3. See also Shahin 2009b, pp. 303–4.
95. Iqbal 1999, p. 159, quoted in Brown 2017, p. 294.
96. Quoted in Goldschmidt and Davidson 2006, p. 278.
97. Lapidus 2014, p. 599; Abed 2009, p. 173.
98. In fact, British policies were ambiguous. In the international arena, they tended to back

Zionist aims, while in Palestine itself British officials often favoured Arabs. Goldschmidt and Davidson 2006, p. 279.

99. Abed 2009, p. 174.
100. The remaining years of Husayni's life were full of intrigue and tragedy. Yet, he remains a hero among Palestinians to this day. Goldschmidt and Davidson 2006, p. 282.
101. Goldschmidt and Davidson 2006, pp. 289, 293.
102. Ibid., p. 291.
103. On Shiʻite strategies for surviving under Sunni dominance, see Stewart 1998.
104. On Iran up to 1950, see Keddie2003, chs 2–5. See also Lapidus 2014, pp. 544–52.
105. Commins 2006, pp. 41–3.
106. In fact, there were three Saudi emirates; the first began in the time of ʻAnd al-Wahhab and Ibn Saʻud and lasted until 1818, the second lasted from the 1820s to the 1880s, and the third from 1902 to the present. See Farquhar 2017, pp. 45–6, Commins 2006, chs 1–3.
107. This means, for instance, that Saudi Arabia's Shiʻite minority community (mostly concentrated in the country's eastern regions) has had to practise its faith in a disestablishment setting since 1932.
108. Commins 2006, p. 103.
109. Ibid., p. 80.
110. On which, see Mandaville 2007a, pp. 159–68.
111. Goldschmidt and Davidson 2006, p. 247.
112. On Saudi Arabia up to 1950, see Commins 2006, chs 1–3. See also Lapidus 2014, pp. 611–17; Doumato and Kechichian 2009, pp. 60–8.
113. Like Jews in medieval Europe, or Coptic Christians under the Mamluks in Egypt, minorities might keep a low profile or even feign conversion to the dominant religion, a strategy seen in post-Reconquista (sixteenth-century) Spain. While the Hui Muslims of China have assimilated to the dominant Han culture to a greater degree, ethnically Turkic Muslims of Xinjiang have faced greater difficulties.
114. For example, Verskin 2012.
115. Nevertheless, that it was contemplated to some extent has been shown by Abou El Fadl 1994, pp. 141–87.
116. Closely related to this, Bonner and Hagen note that pre-modern Muslim writings on non-Muslim societies were 'not part of the accepted canon of Islamic knowledge, and . . . [they were] often . . . neglected or ignored'. Bonner and Hagen 2010, p. 474.
117. Verskin 2012, pp. 53–5, 58–64. Many subsequent Indian Muslims came to similar conclusions, with some declaring British India to be, in fact, *dar al-Islam*. Jumping forward in time, it is interesting that in 1947, while many Muslims did in fact 'migrate' to the new Pakistan, most of India's Muslims remained in non-Muslim India.
118. Ibid., pp. 113–27.
119. For instance, there was a concern in the late nineteenth century that Bosnia might lose its Muslim presence altogether.
120. Ryad 2009.
121. A development which may be compared to the widespread embrace of voluntarist, non-coercive approaches to mission by most Christian denominations – including the Catholic Church – in the last 250 years, as the old European 'Christendom' gave way before secular, nationalist European states.
122. Kepel 2006; Hirschkind 2006.

CHAPTER 7

The second phase of modern *da'wa*, *circa* 1950–2020: a survey

This chapter surveys the *second phase* of modern *da'wa*, a phase which coincides with post-colonial or late modern Islamic history (*circa* 1950–2020). Just as Chapter 5 provided background and context for Chapter 6 ('Contextualising modern *da'wa* 1 and 2'), this chapter begins by exploring some important features of the history of Muslim societies in post-colonial times – features which gave further stimulus to *da'wa* and shaped it in new and dynamic ways. The greater part of Chapter 7, however, is dedicated to a global survey of *da'wa* actors, movements and developments from *circa* 1950 to 2020. Like Chapter 6 *vis-à-vis* the first phase of modern *da'wa*, Chapter 7 concludes with summarising reflections on modern *da'wa*'s second phase and a brief conclusion to the book as a whole. The afterword to Chapter 7 discusses the COVID-19 pandemic in relation to *da'wa*.

Contextualising modern *da'wa* 3: post-colonial times to the present

The colonial era was not to last, but its effects would linger. Decolonisation, which began in earnest after World War II and continued up to the 1990s, may have ended the formal political control of western powers, but it did not signal an end to the processes of change that the colonial period had unleashed. In other words, if pious Muslims hoped that the end of colonial rule would restore some idealised vision of 'the good old days', they were, in most cases, destined for disappointment. To begin with, from the 1920s (and especially from around 1950) to the 1990s, departing foreign powers and collaborating indigenous elites drew up new and sometimes arbitrary boundaries for the former Muslim ecumene, producing new entities such as 'Turkey', 'Iraq', 'Syria', 'Pakistan', 'Indonesia', 'Nigeria', 'Mali', 'Algeria', 'Kazakhstan' and so on (see Map 7.1).[1] These entities bore the trappings of modern statehood (parliaments, armies and police, massive bureaucracies and so on), but they enshrined and institutionalised divisions between Muslim peoples, making the fulfillment of colonial-era pan-Islamic hopes (see Chapter 6) that much more elusive. Moreover, the baton of power was often passed to indigenous leaders who had internalised western mentalities about the nation-state, education and governance. In a surprisingly

Map 7.1 Post-colonial North and Central Africa, the Middle East and Central, South and Southeast Asia.

large number of instances, the founding leaders of post-colonial Muslim states were secular-nationalist or socialist in their orientations to nation-building. Although independence movements might have used the symbolism of Islam, they were mainly concerned with forming states capable of joining the modern family of nations. The peoples of these nations were to be mobilised, educated and disciplined by the state, not for religious ends, but for seemingly secular projects of national development.[2]

The westernising Turkish reforms of the 1920s, 1930s and 1940s under the leadership of Mustafa Kemal Ataturk (discussed in Chapter 6) provide perhaps the most dramatic example of this tendency. For his part, Pakistan's founding father, Muhammad 'Ali Jinnah, might have spoken of drawing on 'Islamic' principles to guide the state's development, but in fact he envisioned Pakistan as a more or less secular state. A state *for Muslims*, that is, was not the same thing as an *Islamic state*.[3] Similar dynamics can be seen in the efforts of the rulers of post-1952 Egypt. In 1952, the nationalist 'Free Officers' seized power in Egypt and leadership soon passed to the towering figure of Gamal 'Abd al-Nasser (d. 1970). Under Nasser and subsequent rulers, such as Sadat and Mubarak, the state sought to bring religion under government purview and to keep a watchful eye on Muslim groups (such as the MB) which wanted to transform Egypt into an Islamic state.[4] As noted in Chapter 6, the early post-colonial rulers of Iraq, Syria, Tunisia, Algeria, Indonesia and numerous other Muslim majority states were also secularist in their orientations. As for the Palestinians, the organisation which emerged as their main voice in the 1960s, the Fatah wing of the Palestine Liberation Organization (PLO), acted on a mostly secular-nationalist platform in order to mobilise both Muslim and Christian Palestinians. In post-colonial West Africa, the new ruling elites tended to 'accept Islam as a "personal religion" . . . not necessarily relevant to the political order'.[5] Even in cases where the leaders were not specifically committed to an ideology of secularism, many adopted versions of secular nationalism by default.[6] In Uzbekistan, a country whose post-colonial history only began in 1991, the state has promoted Uzbek ethnicity and moderate Islam, along with the memory of the medieval conqueror Timur as national rallying points. To put it simply, post-colonial Muslim-majority states appealed to a range of symbols and myths to forge national loyalties, and while 'Islam' was sometimes included in such efforts, this rarely amounted to much in practice.[7] Although there were exceptions, such as Saudi Arabia, and although Muslim countries were not monolithic in terms of how they included or excluded 'Islam' in national life, it is still reasonable to follow Hefner in characterising the 1950s and 1960s as 'the secularist interregnum'.[8]

It is noteworthy, however, that independence did change the dynamics of the religious marketplace in Muslim majority nations in several significant ways. For starters, the relative freedom that foreign missionaries had enjoyed under colonialism mostly disappeared in the new states. The post-colonial rulers were often anxious to win the support of Muslim populations who expected their rulers, however secular, to serve as protectors of Islam. Across the post-colonial Muslim world, then, doors closed 'in the face of missionaries – though this was the case not only in the . . . the wider Islamic world . . . but also in places such as China and North Korea where communist regimes took hold'.[9] In many contexts, therefore, 'post-colonial' also meant 'post-missionary',[10] a fact that has had ambiguous consequences for indigenous Christian communities in Muslim countries.[11] In assessing this trend, it is important to remember that the colonial legacy left a bitter aftertaste in much of the Muslim world. Among other things, this led some Muslims to contest western understandings of 'religious freedom', such as that which seems to be implied in Article 18 of the 1948 United Nations Universal Declaration on Human Rights (UDHR).[12] For many in the West, religious freedom meant the unfettered right of *individuals* to convert into or out of any religion, as well as the right of religious actors to seek converts through non-coercive means.[13] By contrast, some Muslim thinkers have argued that 'freedom of religion' can also be taken to mean the right of *collective groups* (or societies) to be free *from* unwelcome religious activity (such as proselytising).[14] Thus, although most Muslim countries endorsed the UDHR – only Saudi Arabia abstained when the UDHR was ratified – a good number have nevertheless maintained or passed laws prohibiting not only non-Muslim missionary outreach, but also conversion from Islam.

It is also important to note that restrictions like these constitute but one aspect of a broader pattern – namely, that many post-colonial Muslim states have taken an assertive role in regulating religion within their borders. While pious Muslims may have cheered the curtailing of Christian evangelism (and the outlawing of 'heretical' groups such as the Ahmadiyya and Baha'i), they would soon come face to face with state interference in mainstream Islamic religious life. Indeed, as we will see, many independent Muslim-majority states have established sprawling government bureaus of religious affairs, in part to keep religion under their watchful gaze. The key point for now is this: While foreign missionary activity played a major role in prompting Muslims to organise for *da'wa* in colonial times (see Chapters 5 and 6), that threat was somewhat mitigated in many areas of the Muslim world in post-colonial times. Nevertheless, under widespread secular-nationalist rule and owing to other factors, Muslims have continued to face what we have been calling situations of disestablishment and to operate with religious marketplace mentalities. Indeed, inter-religious competition has continued to play a major role in the second phase of modern *da'wa*, not least among Muslim minority populations. Even in Muslim majority areas, post-colonial states and Muslim organisations have continued to appeal rhetorically to non-Muslim missionary competition as a way of mobilising Muslim populations for *da'wa*.[15]

Another important caveat regarding the so-called secularist interregnum is that it was 'built on a Muslim substrate'.[16] In many places, that is, neither top-down efforts at secularisation, nor varieties of secularism-by-default seriously disturbed the Islamic loyalties of the masses. Ataturk's 'People's Houses' may have had some impact in the major cities of Turkey, for instance, but the towns and countryside remained solidly religious. Popular society remained 'thick with religious associations and values';[17] indeed, many of the organisations we discussed in Chapter 6 – for instance, the MB, TJ, Nurcu, Muhammadiyah, Muridiyya and so on – continued their vigorous programs of renewal through-out the middle decades of the twentieth century and beyond. Ironically, then, in many places during the secularist interregnum, populations were becoming more, not less, identified with Islam. Meanwhile, massive urbanisation and population growth throughout the Muslim world, along with rising literacy rates and the new availability of information technology, created critical publics that were increasingly aware of the failings of post-colonial states. Newly urbanised populations were simultaneously uprooted from traditional life pathways and exposed to glaring inequalities in the mushrooming cities.[18] As a result of all this, Muslim populations grew increasingly disillusioned with the nationalist modernisation projects of post-colonial states.

The continuing geopolitical and cultural domination of the Muslim world by the West added another layer of disillusionment. In the decades after World War II, many Muslim-majority states found themselves entangled in the Cold War. While some, such as the socialist or Baathist states of the Middle East, aligned with the Soviet Union, others aligned with the United States in exchange for military and development aid. Still others, like Sukarno's Indonesia or Nasser's Egypt, attempted to maintain non-aligned stances.[19] Muslims in Central Asia were in a unique situation: They remained under Soviet rule until the early 1990s. As noted in Chapter 6, a particularly important event in the mid-twen-tieth century was the establishment of the state of Israel in 1948, an event that was followed nearly twenty years later by Israel's stunning victory in the 'Six Day War' of 1967. Israel's victory enabled it to occupy – illegally, according to the United Nations – the Golan Heights, parts of the West Bank and Gaza, as well as the Sinai Peninsula. This tarnished the reputation of secular-socialist leaders such as the once wildly-popular Gamal 'Abd al-Nasser of Egypt, thus creating an opening for other powers, such as Saudi Arabia, to emerge as the voice of Palestinian liberation.[20] 'For many Muslims the injustices meted out to the Palestinians symbolise both the injustices many experience in their own lives and their own impotence in the face of overwhelming power'.[21] Indeed, foreign powers demonstrated their raw strength by meddling in Muslim countries' affairs seemingly at will. This may be illustrated by the 1953 CIA-orchestrated coup against the government of Muhammad Mossadeq in Iran and the 1979 Soviet occupation of Afghanistan.

With the collapse of the Soviet Union in the 1980s and 1990s, the United

States became 'the hegemonic power' in the Muslim world.[22] The United States has remained steadfast in its support of Israel, even as it has engaged in costly interventions in the Middle East and elsewhere, such as the 1991 campaign to oust Saddam Hussein from Kuwait (and protect its ally, Saudi Arabia), the air campaign to end the ethnic cleansing of Bosnian Muslims by the Serbs, the post-9/11 invasion of Afghanistan, the 2003 invasion of Iraq, the air campaign against the Islamic State or ISIS which began in 2014 and the use of targeted drone assassinations in Muslim territories (for instance, the killing of Qasem Sulaimani in January 2020). More subtly, American/western foreign policy has propped up dictators and often remained silent in the face of widespread corruption and human rights abuses, as long as the rulers of Muslim states served western interests. Just as in colonial times, western influence in the post-colonial Muslim world has also taken cultural dimensions, for instance, in the flooding of the airwaves and internet with western entertainment, much of it offensive to pious Muslim sensibilities. Many have also been alarmed by the impact of western individualism and materialism on Muslim youth, as well as by the seeming invasion of western sexual mores and feminist ideas into their societies.

In sum, a host of factors in the secularist interregnum and beyond – including migration to the cities, unequal distribution of wealth and power, the collapse of old ways of life in the face of rapid change, the 1967 war with Israel and the Palestinian problem, the authoritarianism of many post-colonial governments and the continuing domination of the Muslim world by the West – combined to produce a great deal of soul-searching and analysis among Muslims, not unlike the soul-searching that had accompanied the onset of European colonialism a century earlier.[23] This led many to reject, or at least question, the nationalist projects of the secularist interregnum and to return to 'Islam' as the answer to the world's problems. 'Frustrated in their attempts to realise nationalist dreams of equality and prosperity', many Muslims turned to newly emerging mosques, *madrasa*s, NGO-like Muslim welfare associations, or other 'informal social networks' which evaded the state's controls in a variety of ways.[24] Of course, they also turned to organisations which had been established in the colonial period, such as the MB.[25] Along with new organisations and movements, Islamic printing skyrocketed, so that inexpensive books, magazines and pamphlets flooded the market. These were soon joined by audio and video cassettes, radio and television programmes and, later, the internet. Muslim preachers criticised post-colonial states and, like Muslims under colonialism, argued that the problems of the Muslim world were traceable in part to the failure of Muslims to follow 'true' Islam. That is to say, the 'Muslim substrate' now broke out into the open across the Muslim world. Scholars have called this, appropriately, the 'Islamic revival' or 'Islamic resurgence'.[26] This phenomenon, which became most noticeable in the 1970s and 1980s, has had dramatic effects. While all Muslim orientations to modernity – modernist, reformist, Islamist – have participated in and benefited from the revival, the growing popularity of Salafism (defined in the Introduction to Part II) has proven to be a particularly prominent outcome.

It is pertinent to stress that this 'revival' did not come out of nowhere, nor was it *sui generis*. For starters, adherents of other world religions have experienced analogous patterns of revival and movement formation throughout the twentieth century. As noted in the Introduction to Part II, modernity has not led to the once-widely-expected triumph of secularisation and the decline of religions (at least, not yet), but rather to a widespread religious resurgence in most regions of the world. One might call to mind, for instance, religious awakenings among Evangelical, Pentecostal and Charismatic Christians around the world, along with the birth of revivalist and religious-nationalist movements among Hindus and Buddhists in various places. Indeed, as stressed throughout Part II, the missionary endeavours of religious competitors, both internal and external to Islam, have played a significant part in prompting Muslims to take up *da'wa* in modern times. In addition, one might see the Islamic revival of the later twentieth century as but one more instance of Islam's long-term disposition towards renewal (*tajdid*) and reform (*islah*). In fact, the late-twentieth-century Islamic revival is directly linked, through shared ideas and lineages, to the renewal/*da'wa* movements of the eighteenth, nineteenth and early twentieth centuries, as examined in Chapters 5 and 6. That is, although the recent Islamic resurgence is unprecedented in terms of its reach and effects, there is much continuity with earlier Islamic revivals.[27] Although some observers suggest that the Muslim world has entered or may soon enter a post-revivalist phase somewhat akin to the 'post-Christian' ethos which has come to characterise parts of western Europe, it must be said that this Islamic revival is still going strong. Most important for our purposes is that the revival gave birth to a new wave of *da'wa*-oriented movements and reinvigorated older ones. Trends noted in Chapter 6, such as the democratisation and diversification of *da'wa*, the involvement of women and the use of new technologies, have accelerated. Not surprisingly, then, as Muslims under colonialism found *da'wa* to be a relevant and vital resource, so too have Muslims in the post-colonial situation.

However, if Chapter 6 stressed the rise and preponderance of 'Meccan' styles of *da'wa* in the circumstances of colonial modernity, it must be said that in the circumstances of post-colonial modernity, religio-political 'Medinan' *da'was* have made something of a comeback. That is, if the conditions of colonial modernity generally favoured quietist, preaching-oriented Meccan *da'wa*logies, then the conditions of post-colonial modernity, while continuing to favour Meccan *da'wa* in many respects, have also opened spaces for Medinan *da'was*. In other words, we cannot adequately deal with the second phase of modern *da'wa* without dealing with the (re)politicisation of *da'wa* in some quarters.[28] In very general terms, where Muslims live as minorities or where state power is perceived to be strong, quietist and/or gradualist versions of *da'wa* continue to thrive as the outlet of choice for many activist Muslims. By contrast, in Muslim-majority contexts where the state is perceived as weak, vulnerable, or astray from Islam, religio-political or Islamist *da'was* have become prominent. In many cases, of course, the two coexist side-by-side or within the same movement, regardless of context. Furthermore, religio-political movements have come in many varieties and have sometimes pursued their political goals in pragmatic fashions. And in general, although politically-active movements attract a great deal of media attention, it is still the case that far more Muslims around the world are involved in quietist Meccan *da'wa*.[29] We conclude this section by highlighting four political developments which have had important consequences for *da'wa* in the second phase.

First, two important Islamic organisations which had been founded in the colonial period, the MB and the JI, moved in explicitly political directions in the post-colonial period. It will be recalled that in Chapter 6, we saw that each of these movements began with a focus on grassroots *da'wa* in their colonial settings. However, post-colonial conditions and the Islamic revival provided the context for both movements to put the political blueprints of their founders, al-Banna and Mawdudi, into action by openly seeking to actualise Islam as a 'total system'.[30] Flowing particularly from the Islamist thought of the MB's Sayyid Qutb (d. 1966), *da'wa* became increasingly implicated in politics and militant *jihad*, not only within the MB itself, but within Islamist (and jihadist) movements the world over. For Qutb, *da'wa* and *jihad* were two sides of the same coin – both preaching/persuasion and militant struggle against '*jahiliyya*' (meaning non-Muslim states *and* Muslim states which failed to implement Islam as a total system) were necessary.[31] The MB and the JI spread around the world in the second half of the twentieth century, making the thought and ethos of these groups globally relevant. Yet, it is important to add that, where Muslims live as minorities (see below), JI and MB activists have mostly confined themselves to quietist *da'wa* and education over the past half-century.[32] Even in Egypt, the MB has tended towards pragmatic gradualism, a fact that contributed to the emergence of more radical 'Qutbist' alternatives to the MB, such as Islamic Jihad (the group which assassinated President Anwar Sadat in 1981) and Takfir w'al-Hijra.[33] It is important, finally, to add that in the post-colonial scramble for influence, even predominantly quietist groups like the Muhammadiyah and Nahdlatul Ulama in Indonesia, the Deobandis and Tablighis in South Asia, and the Muridiyya in West Africa have found it difficult to stay out of politics altogether.

Second, in response to western, particularly American, support for Israel in the October 1973 war (the 'Yom Kippur War' between Israel, Egypt and Syria), the Organization of Petroleum Exporting Countries (OPEC) imposed an embargo on oil exports to many western countries. They demanded that Israel withdraw from the territories it had occupied in 1967 and that it recognise the national rights of the Palestinians. Not only did this move cause fuel shortages and raise western anxieties, it also brought untold new wealth to countries like Kuwait, the UAE, Iraq, Iran, Libya and especially Saudi Arabia. By the time the embargo ended in March 1974, the price of a barrel of oil had nearly quadrupled, as had Saudi oil revenues. In turn, several of these countries used their 'petrodollars' to embark on ambitious development programs at home and to increase their standing abroad. Saudi Arabia, for instance, stepped up assistance to poorer Muslim countries, like Pakistan and the countries of sub-Saharan Africa, some of which was earmarked for *da'wa*. By standing up to the West, the countries which launched the embargo also earned new credibility. Libya's Mu'ammar al-Qaddhafi, for instance, who had come to power in 1969, became a symbol of muscular Muslim defiance of the West.

A third political development with important ramifications for *da'wa* was the 1979 Soviet occupation of Afghanistan. In this case, petrodollars, along with US military aid, went to support the self-described 'Mujahideen', or volunteer Muslim warriors, who were fighting against the Soviets. These groups of Mujahideen were made up both of Afghans (of various tribal and regional loyalties) and of Muslim youth from around the world who rallied to the cause. US aid flowed through the 'middleman' of Pakistan, which had its own strategic interests in mind in partnering with the US, the Saudis and others. In fact, under its military ruler, General Zia ul-Haqq (in office 1978–88), Pakistan was also at the time pursuing a state-directed program of Islamisation, or '*shari'a*-isation' at home, a program which allowed Pakistan's conservative *'ulama* and the JI an unprecedented level of influence in government. Returning to Afghanistan, in their foreign-abetted struggle against the Soviets, the Mujahideen would learn the skills of political propaganda and guerrilla insurgency which would later be deployed for jihadist causes in global settings, for instance, by al-Qaeda and ISIS. Although the Soviets finally quit Afghanistan in 1989, the effects of the anti-Soviet *jihad* are still a major factor in modern Islam.

Fourth, the Iranian Revolution of 1979 represents the most stunning example of successful resistance to western domination fuelled by (Shi'ite) Islamic revivalism. As noted in Chapter 6, the background to the Islamic Revolution were the decades of secularising rule by the Pahlavi dynasty. Following the 1953 CIA-supported coup, the Shah became increasingly repressive, even as he relied heavily on the United States and other western powers. From exile, Ayatollah Khomeini began to use the tools of modern *da'wa* – books, cassette sermons and so on – to spread a message of Shi'ite Islamic revival as well as the need to overthrow the Shah.[34] By 1970, he had published a series of influential lectures, known as *Wilayat al-Faqih*, or Government of the Islamic Jurist. In *Wilayat al-Faqih*, Khomeini laid out his view that a truly Islamic state should be governed by the religious scholars or *'ulama*. Although Iranian liberals, communists and others also worked to overthrow the Shah, Khomeini outmanoeuvred these rivals, and once the Shah was deposed, positioned himself as the Supreme Leader of the new Islamic Republic.[35] The effects of Iran's Islamic Revolution have been as dramatic as they have been ambiguous. Islamists around the world – both Sunnis and Shi'ites – saw in the Islamic Revolution a model of a successful Islamist takeover of a modern state. For their part, the existing governments of Muslim countries feared the revolution and its implications for their own holds on power. All of this shows that, if anything is true of post-colonial Islamic societies, it is that they have not been static. The situation within and between countries and regions has been a moving target, constantly changing depending on many factors. With this review of the context of post-colonial times in place, we are now ready to survey modern *da'wa*'s second phase.

Surveying the second phase of modern *da'wa*

If we were to try to say something about every *da'wa*-oriented movement which has gained any amount of traction over the past seventy years, this chapter would have to be the length of an entire book in its own right, and it would be of limited analytical value. The challenge, then, is to avoid compiling a mere list and instead to highlight cases which are revealing of broader trends. Whereas a geographical arrangement made sense for our discussion of modern *da'wa*'s first phase (Chapter 6), here we are dealing with movements which very often transcend boundaries. In other words, although the process began in the first phase, the second phase has witnessed an accelerating globalisation or transnationalisation of *da'wa* movements, actors and discourses. *Da'wa* is increasingly polycentric and multi-directional. For instance, while the inspirational home of the world's largest *da'wa* movement, the TJ, is still India, the movement no longer really 'belongs' to India, but is now active in over 150 nations. Another caveat is that the realm of *da'wa* has become extremely fluid in the second phase. Like dot-com companies in the 1990s, *da'wa* organisations and initiatives – not to mention *da'wa* websites – are constantly springing up and disappearing. Consequently, this section generally prioritises movements that have had some staying power. In the remainder of this chapter, we survey *da'wa*'s second phase under three headings: (1) *da'wa* initiatives undertaken by non-state actors and organisations, (2) *da'wa* initiatives undertaken by state-sponsored actors and organisations, and (3) migration and the *da'wa* initiatives of Muslim minorities.

Non-state initiatives and actors in *da'wa*

It will be recalled that the nineteenth and early twentieth centuries witnessed a dramatic rise in voluntary associations and organisations around the world and that Protestant Christians were among the pioneers in forming such associations, in using the printing press, in holding missionary congresses and so on. All of this served as a challenge to and model for Muslims who, as we saw in

Chapter 6, generated new *da'wa*-oriented 'firms, products, and communities' of their own.[36] In contrast to the generally *ad hoc da'wa* initiatives of pre-modern times (see Chapters 1 to 4), this trend of organising and institutionalising *da'wa* has picked up considerable speed in the second phase of modern *da'wa*. Here, we survey this phenomenon in terms of non-state or private *da'wa* initiatives and organisations. 'Non-state' refers to voluntary organisations formed by committed individuals generally independent of the state.

Among the earliest non-state, voluntary *da'wa* organisations were the Ahmadiyya, the TJ, the MB and the JI. Chapter 6 profiled the early histories of these movements and others, most of which are still going strong today. The MB and JI, for instance, remain active and have affiliates and imitators in many countries. As for the TJ, under its second and subsequent leaders after the death of Muhammad Ilyas in 1944, the movement has spread across the globe. While it has generally maintained its *modus operandi* of non-political preaching and education geared towards reviving Muslim piety, the movement has also contextualised itself to new contexts, from the jungles of Papua New Guinea to secular France.[37] Owing in part to the success of the TJ, numerous organisations have emerged, which imitate the TJ's approach, although often for alternative versions of Islam (the TJ, it will be recalled, propagates Deobandi Sunni Islam). One such imitator is Da'wat-i Islami (the *Da'wa* of Islam), founded in 1981 as the 'Barelvi version of the TJ'. Barelvi Islam is a South Asian Sunni orientation which contrasts with the reformist Deobandi and Salafi Ahl-i Hadith movements in supporting the traditional Sufi-oriented Islam of South Asia.[38] Gugler writes: 'While Da'wat-i Islami copies the structure and activities of TJ, their members differ from them in appearance mainly because of their green turban. The green colour of the turban . . . is regarded as their trade mark . . . and has led to their popular label "*jannat ke tūte*," parrots of paradise'.[39] As the TJ has made mass missionary conferences (known is *ijtima's*) one of its hallmarks, so too has Da'wat-i Islami.[40] Although Da'wat-i Islami was founded (in Pakistan) decades after the TJ, it has also established a global presence, with centres of the movement throughout South Asia, as well as in Europe and the United States. In 1992, the Indian branch of Da'wat-i Islami split off to form another TJ imitator, Sunni Da'wat-i Islami.[41] Stories such as these (of imitation in modern *da'wa* leading to new *da'wa* initiatives) could be repeated many times over.

Along with imitation, sectarian or ideological dissension and division has also been a major source of new non-state *da'wa* movements. The Ahmadiyya, for instance, split into two factions in the early twentieth century; both groups ('the Qadianis' and 'the Lahoris'), despite the persecution they have faced, have been active in *da'wa* around the world ever since.[42] Decades later and on the other side of the world, we could point to the splintering of the African American Nation of Islam movement during the 1960s and 1970s.[43] We have already mentioned the tendency of the MB to spin off new movements, such as radical 'Qutbist' groups like Islamic Jihad and Takfir w'al-Hijra in Egypt. In Arabia and beyond, several new movements have separated themselves from the 'official' Wahhabi Islam of the Saudi religious establishment and engaged in *da'wa* and political activism on behalf of what they consider to be purer forms of the religion: for instance, the millenarian movement of Juhayman al-'Utaybi (d. 1980), which seized the Grand Mosque of Mecca in 1979 (before he was captured and executed by the Saudis), and the anti-Saudi (but still theologically Wahhabi) *da'wa* and activism of al-Qaeda beginning in the late 1980s. More will be said about militant groups and their *da'wa*s below. Given its central belief that there is only one true 'saved' sect in Islam, Salafism in general has been highly prone to splits and divisions. As with the historical fissiparousness of Protestant Christianity, the same tendency in Salafism has arguably led to more, not less, Salafi *da'wa*.[44]

Although we will return to Muslim migrant communities below, for now it is worth noting that migration has served as yet another major modality by which new non-state *da'wa* movements have been born in the second phase. Indian migrants, for instance, have transplanted Deobandi, Barelvi and Ahl-i Hadith versions of Islam and their associated organisations to new places, as Indonesian migrants have done for movements like the Muhammadiyah and Nahdlatul Ulama, and as West African migrants have done for movements like the Muridiyya. In turn, such movements have had to adjust to new sociopolitical contexts. This also has led to the formation of new *da'wa* organisations. Once again, the MB and JI are good examples. While both of these movements have tended theoretically to reject the 'western' separation of religion and state which renders Islam but one option in a religious marketplace, in many contexts Brotherhood- or Jama'at-inspired organisations have had little choice but to function as quietist *da'wa* movements. For example, a leading *da'wa* organisation in Britain, the Islamic Foundation (founded 1973), has strong ideological connections with the JI, but functions pragmatically as a bottom-up *da'wa* movement in the secular British context.[45] Similar are the Muslim Student Association of North America, founded in 1963, and the Islamic Society of North America (ISNA), founded in 1982, both of which were started by men with ties to the JI and the MB. Both function as quietist *da'wa* and advocacy organisations in the setting of disestablishment America.[46] A contrasting case may be seen in Saudi Arabia, which gave refuge to persecuted members of the MB from neighbouring secularist states (such as Nasser's Egypt) in the 1950s and 1960s. In this case, Brotherhood ideas fed into radical Salafi movements – such as that of the above-mentioned 'Utaybi – which sought to overthrow the Saudi regime.[47]

Yet another leading cause of the founding of new non-state *da'wa* organisations (and one on which we will dwell a bit longer) has consisted of the activities of charismatic Muslim preachers and superstar *da'i*s. In Chapter 6, we observed that technologies such as the printing press and steam-powered travel facilitated the rise of new kinds of Muslim spokespersons who did *da'wa*, started organisations and fashioned Islamic modernities in the colonial age. This trend has continued and expanded in the post-colonial age, still driven by print, but now enhanced by technologies such as the airplane, microphone, audio and video cassettes, DVDs, satellite television and the internet (see Text Box 7.1). A few examples of leading late-modern non-state *da'wa* preachers who have facilitated the institutionalisation of *da'wa* are provided here, but the reader should keep in mind that there are scores of others. In fact, there are countless individuals, 'ordinary' Muslim men and women, who have preached *da'wa* under the radar, so to speak. Some such individuals and the movements they represent have been studied by Antoun (Jordan),[48] Gaffney, Hirschkind, Mahmood and al-Arian (Egypt),[49] Millie (Indonesia),[50] Ahmad (Kuwait),[51] Ahmad (East Africa)[52] and others.

For our purposes, we begin with Fethullah Gulen (b. 1941, see Figure 7.1), a Muslim preacher who founded Turkey's most important pietistic *da'wa* movement in the later decades of the twentieth century. A prolific author of many books and a popular preacher who has used video and audio technologies and the internet to broadcast his messages, Gulen built on the work of Said Nursi discussed in Chapter 6, and his movement is usually considered to be an offshoot of the Nurcu movement. Like Nursi, he combines a belief in modern science and education with Sufi-inflected Islam. His messages have appealed to members of the modern-educated middle class in Turkey, and with their support his movement has built an impressive empire of educational, publishing and even banking operations.[53] As with the Nurcu, the Gulen movement functions as a modern Sufi movement, with Gulen serving as the supreme shaykh or teacher.

Figure 7.1 Fethullah Gulen (b. 1941), founder of the Gulen movement. Photo: EFE from Wikimedia Commons, CC BY-SA.

Having run afoul of the Turkish government in the late 1990s, Gulen took up residence in the state of Pennsylvania, where he has lived ever since. Though Gulenists had initially been supportive of Erdogan's Justice and Virtue Party (AKP), following the 2016 attempted coup in Turkey, the Gulen movement was subject to a severe government crackdown and was banned as a terrorist organisation, a designation the movement rejects.

Another example of a *da'wa* organisation founded to support the missionary preaching of a superstar *da'i* was the Islamic Propagation Centre International (IPCI) founded by the late Ahmad Deedat (d. 2005) in South Africa in 1982. Deedat, who felt his own calling to *da'wa* when he read about the nineteenth-century efforts of Rehmatullah Kairanawi (see Chapter 6), primarily focused on inter-religious polemics, or what he called 'comparative religion'. He wanted to move South Africa's

7.1 Electronic media and *da'wa*

If the nineteenth century witnessed the print revolution in the Muslim world, the twentieth and twenty-first have witnessed a second revolution: an electronic-media revolution. The twentieth century witnessed the rise of numerous preachers who made names for themselves through audio and video cassettes. The late twentieth and early twenty-first centuries have witnessed the migration of such voices to satellite television and the internet. Virtually any Muslim who knows how to set up a website or blog can become a spokesperson for Islam, and evidence suggests that this is precisely what is happening. Sufis, *'ulama* and newer self-trained spokespersons for Islam are engaged in this field. Abundant examples of non-state and state-sponsored *da'wa* can be seen online, but it may be that the medium itself has relativised the control of the state. The internet is characteristically open, democratic and consumer-oriented. If 'disestablishment' refers to situations in which no religion enjoys official favour or special privileges, the internet is clearly a disestablishment space. This makes it inevitably a competitive space in which personal choice and agency are maximised. Governments which try to restrict internet access or block websites find their efforts only partially effective.

Although public debate and dialogue are nothing new in the Muslim world (see Part I of this book), they have never been seen on this scale. Because of the internet, Muslims are more conscious than ever of the global *umma* and the threats it faces. But they are also simultaneously aware of the *umma*'s internal divisions. 'While the Internet technology helps to unify Muslims by compressing distance and time between them, it also serves as a mirror through which Muslims . . . realize how diverse they are' (El Nawawy and Khamis 2009, p. 163) In short, today's resurgence in *da'wa* has served to widen the playing field and bring Muslims together from diverse backgrounds, but it has simultaneously served to heighten their differences. Muslims' plural responses to the predicaments of modernity and their varied efforts to forge Islamic modernities are on full display in the world of digital *da'wa* (Sources: Kuiper 2018a, pp. 94–5, and notes; Eickelman and Anderson 2003; Bunt 2006; Larsson 2011; El-Nawawy and Khamis 2009).

Muslim minority community away from a defensive posture towards Christian missionary efforts (he called South Africa a threatening 'ocean of Christianity') and towards an aggressive posture of openly attacking the Bible and Christian beliefs. For instance, in his booklet 'Combat Kit Against Bible Thumpers', he laid out his own proven strategies for silencing Christian missionaries 'who harass Muslims in their own homes'.[54] As he travelled the world speaking to Muslim audiences and debating prominent Christians, Deedat quickly attained a global profile. The year 1986 marked the high point of Deedat's career; in that year, he debated the Pentecostal preacher Jimmy Swaggart in Louisiana (see Figure 7.2) and won the Saudi King Faisal Prize for Service to Islam. Deedat was a pioneer in using audio and video cassettes, along with cheap, copyright-free literature, to broadcast his *da'wa* efforts to wider and wider audiences.[55] In this regard, Deedat's career parallels that of the Egyptian preacher Shaykh 'Abd al-Hamid Kishk, who also gained widespread popularity through the distribution of his sermons on audio cassettes in the 1970s and 1980s.[56] Although Deedat had no formal Islamic training, he has had many imitators; perhaps the most famous is Dr Zakir Naik, the Mumbai-based founder of the Islamic Research Foundation (banned by India in 2016) and of the *da'wa*-oriented satellite television channel Peace TV. Naik, in fact, was personally trained

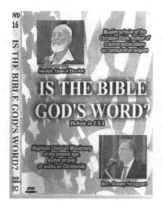

by Deedat (see Text Box 7.2). After a stroke incapacitated him in 1996, Deedat passed the mantle of his *da'wa* to Naik who, like his mentor, went on to travel the world doing *da'wa* through 'comparative religion'. An avowed quietist Salafi, Naik has nonetheless recently been accused by India's Hindu nationalist BJP government of laundering money and inspiring terrorism.[57]

Under the same general pattern exemplified by Gulen, Deedat and Naik are *da'wa* organisations which support the work of *da'i*s such as the wildly popular Amr Khaled of Egypt (b. 1967), a televangelist who preaches a positive message of Islamic faith, everyday piety and Islam-based social development.[58] Like Zakir Naik and Aa Gym (see below), Khaled has been included in the Royal Ahl al-Bayt Institute for Islamic Thought's 500 Most Influential Muslims list for several years running. In its write-up on Khaled, the Institute notes:

Figure 7.2 The cover of one of Ahmed Deedat's blockbuster video cassettes/DVDs – the IPCI recording of his 'Great [1986] Debate' with Jimmy Swaggart, characterised as 'one of the mightiest Christian missionaries of the present age'. No copyright.

Amr Khaled has been a televangelist to the Islamic world since 1998. He communicates through his TV shows and web campaigns using Islamic ethics

7.2 A modern *da'wa* lineage or *silsila*

In Islamic thought, a *silsila* (or *isnād*) is a lineage or chain of authority. Scholars and Sufis both trace their lineages to the great scholars and Sufis of the past, and even back to Prophet Muhammad. Knowledge, authority and charisma (spiritual power) can be passed down through such lineages. Historically, scholars and Sufis have made journeys (*riḥla*s) in order to study with renowned shaykhs (teachers or Sufi masters). Doing so could earn them an *ijāza*, a certificate certifying the student's participation in a particular lineage and authorisation to speak for Islam. The modern age has given rise to new, distinctly modern *silsila*s. One modern *silsila* which is related both to the rising popularity of *da'wa* and to the democratisation of Islamic religious authority in modernity is the '*silsila*' of Kairanawi, Deedat and Naik. Rehmatullah Kairanawi (see Chapter 6) was a pioneer in doing *da'wa* through 'comparative religion' (although he did not use that term). In turn, Ahmed Deedat picked up Kairanawi's mantle in the mid-twentieth century. Deedat's *riḥla*, of course, was not literal but figurative; yet, Deedat himself claimed to have been inspired to enter the field of *da'wa* and to do verbal battle against Christianity through the influence of Kairanawi. Zakir Naik made several literal *riḥla*s to South Africa in the last decades of the twentieth century to study from Deedat, whom he called his 'shaykh'. In addition, Naik studied Deedat's video cassettes before he ever met Deedat in person. That Naik studied under Deedat both personally and virtually draws attention to the fact that Muslims, using new media technologies, can now seek out Islamic knowledge from a shaykh of their own choosing without ever leaving home. Naik frequently draws attention to a plaque Deedat presented to him in 2000. On the plaque, which may be seen as Naik's *ijāza*, Deedat called Naik 'son' and affirmed his *da'wa* ministry (Source: Kuiper 2018a, pp. 224–5).

as a way to inspire, foster community development, tolerance and intercultural relations. He holds a degree in accounting, and has no formal religious education; wears suits and ties, and has a clean-shaven face except for a trimmed moustache . . . His website is translated from Arabic into nearly twenty languages and it rivals Oprah Winfrey's in terms of traffic. His videos have racked up over 90 million views on YouTube.

We might also highlight Abdullah Gymnastiar, or Aa Gym, of Indonesia, a popular preacher who has attracted a modern-educated Muslim audience by blending Sufism, pop psychology and management theory, and by preaching in an engaging, humorous style.[59] Interestingly, as with televangelists in other religions, controversy has sometimes hounded such figures, whether related to Gulen's role in Turkish politics, Aa Gym's polygamy, Amr Khaled's wealth, or Zakir Naik's alleged inspiration of terrorism. In addition, although these figures are certainly examples of non-state *da'wa*, superstar Muslim preachers have often been courted by politicians and/or have made forays into politics. Other popular Muslim preachers who have founded non-state *da'wa* organisations include Bilal Philips, Abdur Raheem Green, Yusuf Estes, Jamal Badawi and many others. This is a trend that looks set to continue and increase in the years to come. After all, with its new technologies and religious marketplace assumptions, late modernity has proven to be a fertile time for the emergence of new spokespersons and personalities in most religions.[60]

A final example, Yusuf al-Qaradawi (b. 1926; see Figure 7.3), presents a distinctive case. While many prominent *da'is* of the second phase of modern *da'wa* have been 'new religious intellectuals' (self-taught preachers and activists lacking formal Islamic seminary or *madrasa* training), al-Qaradawi is a leading member of the *'ulama* (the traditional guild of Islamic scholars, see Chapter 4). This al-Azhar-trained 'global mufti' was catapulted to fame through his television show 'Shari'a and Life' (*al-shari'a wa'l-haya*) on the Qatar-based network Al-Jazeera, as well as through his role in founding the website IslamOnline.net.[61] Al-Qaradawi was also instrumental in the founding of the European Council for Fatwa and Research (ECFR) and the International Union of Muslim Scholars (IUMS). Along with his media presence and institution-building activities, Qaradawi represents an important kind of *da'wa* in the period under discussion here: internal *da'wa* through the dissemination of *fatwas* (or Islamic legal advice). As seen on his TV show and on IslamOnline, he largely earned his reputation by answering Muslims' questions about how to be faithful Muslims in the modern world. Today there are numerous websites and television preachers which, like al-Qaradawi, offer *fatwas* to ordinary Muslims. The above-mentioned Deoband movement, while sometimes wary of modern technology, also runs a popular *fatwa* website (darulifta-deoband.com) with thousands of *fatwas* in English and Urdu. Another is the popular Salafi *fatwa* website, IslamQA (islamqa.info). Besides English and Arabic, IslamQA features *fatwas* translated into thirteen other languages. Websites which contain religious advice specifically for Shi'ite Muslims include Ahlulbayt Global Information Center (al-shia.org) and Ahlulbayt Islamic Mission (aimislam.com). Even non-*'ulama* preachers, such as Zakir Naik, have functioned as quasi-*muftis* (givers of *fatwas*). Naik performs this role in the Q and A sessions which are a trademark of his public lectures (as they had been for his mentor, Ahmed Deedat).[62] This proliferation of *fatwas* within the realm of *da'wa* certainly reflects what we have been calling the spread of religious marketplace mentalities in modernity. Those offering the *fatwas* generally have no power to compel obedience, but must rely on their reputations, charisma and the power of persuasion. Similarly, in the media age, individual Muslims have been empowered to pick and choose which *fatwa* 'provider' they will pay attention to, if any.

Flowing from the patterns highlighted so far – the continuation and imitation of older *da'wa* movements, sectarian division, Muslim migration, adaptations to new contexts and the rise of superstar *da'is* – as well as from other patterns, hundreds of non-state, voluntary Islamic associations, large and small, have been founded

Figure 7.3 Yusuf al-Qaradawi (b. 1926), a pioneer in disseminating Islamic religious rulings and advice through television and the internet. Photo: Ebong abd from Wikimedia Commons, CC BY-SA.

around the world since 1950.[63] Countless Islamic storefronts, reading rooms, community centres, bookshops, medical clinics, schools and the like now exist all over the world. Noting their parallels to Christian voluntary societies or 'parachurch' organisations, Poston speaks of a burgeoning of Islamic 'para-mosque' organisations in the later twentieth century.[64] Indeed, just as Christian 'mission' is an umbrella term that covers activities as diverse as evangelism, the building of churches, education, the provision of humanitarian aid, healthcare initiatives, poverty alleviation, agricultural training, orphan sponsorship and so on, so the work of *da'wa* has been diversified in this second phase.

In fact, the addition of humanitarian and social-welfare concerns to *da'wa* is a relatively recent phenomenon, prompted in part by the example of (and competition from) Christian missions. Masud writes: 'Until recently, modern Muslim writers on Christian missionary activities strongly criticised the use of educational institutions, and other welfare provided by Christian missionaries as exploitative'.[65] In spite of this, since the early twentieth century, Muslim *da'wa* organisations have taken up relief and social welfare activities energetically. Examples of this include the educational and social welfare activities initiated by groups such as the MB, JI, HAMAS, Hezbollah, the Muhammadiyah, Muridiyya and others. Since the 1970s and 1980s, Muslim-initiated humanitarian programs have proliferated.[66] Some organisations have been formed specifically for the purpose of social welfare, while many existing *da'wa* organisations have added humanitarian relief to their agendas. The Muslim World League (discussed below) 'adopted social welfare in its *da'wa* programs in 1974 . . . in 1988 a World Islamic Committee for Da'wa and Relief was formed. Education and medicine are also the concerns of *da'wa* movements like . . . World Assembly of Muslim Youth (WAMY) . . ., Jama'at Nasr al-Islam and Ansar al-Islam in Nigeria, Muslim Youth Movement of Malaysia, and Diwan Dawat al-Islam in Indonesia'.[67] Further examples of such 'Islamic NGOs' include Islamic World Relief and Muslim Aid, both founded by British Muslims in the 1980s. Functioning in ways that are analogous to Christian agencies such as World Vision or Catholic Relief Services, these organisations 'cite a religious basis and inspiration for . . . providing humanitarian assistance, but generally operate along the same lines . . . as "secular" relief organisations'.[68] Nevertheless, there should be little doubt that *da'wa* concerns lie at the heart of many such efforts. Even if assistance is offered with no strings attached, those doing the offering are still acting in the name of Islam, with the hope of making Islam attractive to a watching world. In some cases, humanitarian or development work may serve as the public face of an organisation, while *da'wa* is in fact a major goal. For instance, the Shaykh Eid Foundation (which works in dozens of countries and is supported by the Qatari royal family) presents itself online as an Islamic relief agency,[69] yet much of the organisation's work in, say, Indonesia has focused on spreading Salafi *da'wa* through building and funding Salafi schools and mosques.[70]

Modern heirs of the Isma'ili movement provide a particularly interesting example of Muslims who have given a central place to humanitarian efforts in their *da'wa*. It will be recalled that the Isma'ili *da'wa* of the ninth through twelfth centuries was a restorationist religio-political *da'wa* (see Chapter 3). Several groups of Isma'ilis have survived to modern times, particularly in India, where a Nizari community known as the Khojas has flourished under the leadership of the Aga Khan.[71] Despite their medieval legacy of militancy, the Isma'ili Khojas today represent an approach to *da'wa* that is modern, sophisticated and peaceful. Under the current Aga Khan, whom Isma'ili Khojas believe is the forty-ninth Imam in direct succession from the Prophet Muhammad, Khoja *da'wa* efforts are channeled into an extensive network of development projects, particularly in the poorer regions of South Asia and East Africa. The Aga Khan Development Network (AKDN), the umbrella organisation which coordinates this humanitarian empire, works in over thirty countries; as of 2020, it has some 80,000 employees and an operating budget of $950 million.[72] This money supports education (for instance, Aga Khan University, with branches in several countries), healthcare (for instance, Aga Khan hospitals in Afghanistan, India, Kenya, Pakistan and Tanzania), economic development (through the Aga Khan Fund for Economic Development) and the preservation of the cultural heritage of Islam (through the Aga Khan Trust for Culture which 'has restored and rehabilitated over 350 monuments and historic sites').[73] While Isma'ili Khoja development projects such as these generally have little to do with proselytising, they still clearly constitute one way the Khoja community projects its *da'wa* to the world.

Another project of the Isma'ili community – which provides a segue to another type of non-state *da'wa* – is the London-based Institute of Isma'ili Studies (IIS), an academic unit that produces scholarship on Islam generally, but which also has a special mission of preserving 'the heritage of the Ismaili communities'.[74] The IIS is representative of a broader trend: Islamic study centres and institutes along these lines have popped up around the world in the second phase. As noted in Chapter 6, *tarbiyya* (education, training) is a central concept in the lexicon of modern *da'wa*. Most of the organisations and preachers discussed in these chapters make use of the concept (see Text Box 7.3). Another example of an Islamic study centre is the International Institute of Islamic Thought (IIIT), founded in the United States in 1981 by the Palestinian-American scholar Isma'il al-Faruqi (d. 1986). Even though al-Faruqi was a renowned scholar of religion with a faculty post at Temple University, he often exhibited the heart of a Muslim missionary. Faruqi's zest for *da'wa* can be seen in his writings, particularly his essay 'On the Nature of Islamic Da'wah'. Drawing mainly from the Qur'an, Faruqi presents a vision of a persuasion-oriented ('Meccan') *da'wa* which is rational, non-coercive and obligatory for all Muslims. *Da'wa* recalls non-Muslims to the true, natural religion of humanity (Islam) and dignifies man as God's partner in creating a better world.[75] While he was a participant in inter-faith dialogues and spent part of his career studying Christianity, Faruqi was a thoroughgoing exclusivist in his theology.[76] The IIIT has continued to reflect the hybrid life's work of its founder. On the one hand, it is a scholarly, academic organisation. It is what one might call an Islamic 'think tank'.[77] On the other hand, the activities of the IIIT have an orientation towards *da'wa* – advocating for Islam among its western detractors, encouraging Muslims to celebrate Islam's intellectual tradition and promoting Islamic thought in the modern age.[78] A final example is the Abul Hasan Ali Nadwi Center for Research, Dawah and Islamic Thought, based in Lucknow, India. 'Ali Nadwi (d. 1999) was one of the greatest twentieth-century Muslim theologians of *da'wa*; the center founded in his memory carries on his legacy by publishing a journal, maintaining a library and organising *da'wa* training programs.[79]

7.3 The how-to of *da'wa*: contemporary *da'wa* manuals

Among *da'wa* preachers and theologians, there is an almost universal effort to convince every Muslim that *da'wa* is his or her individual responsibility – that it is, in terms borrowed from Islamic legal thought, a *farḍ al-ʿayn* or 'individual obligation', rather than a *farḍ al-kifaya* or 'collective obligation'. For instance, in his *Words of Advice Regarding Da'wah*, the former grand *mufti* of Saudi Arabia, 'Abd al-Aziz b. Baz (d. 1999) wrote: *'Da'wah* is an obligation upon every [Muslim] who has the ability'. This concern has spawned a flourishing industry of *da'wa* manuals meant to help ordinary Muslims carry out the task of *da'wa*. One can often discern 'Meccan' assumptions in this literature: namely, that, like the Prophet in Mecca, Muslims must be prepared in situations of religious pluralism to use persuasion and example to encourage conversions to Islam. *Da'wa* manuals usually begin by saying something about the character of the *da'i*, that he or she should be a 'good' Muslim whose lifestyle will be attractive. They usually then quote several standard qur'anic proof texts, such as Q 3:104 and 16:125 (see Chapter 1), which are said to enjoin *da'wa* upon all Muslims. Modern *da'wa* manuals frequently use the Qur'an and hadith, not only to justify *da'wa*, but also to deduce principles on how *da'wa* should be carried out. This can be seen in *Inviting to the Way of Allah* by Abu'l-Hasan 'Ali Nadwi. Based on his study of the Qur'an, Nadwi argues that the *da'wa* of all the Qur'an's prophets was perfectly suited to their hearers, and that each prophet knew just the moment to turn the conversation to *tawhid* (the oneness of God). According to Nadwi, the prophets also had answers ready for typical objections, and used their 'profound knowledge of human psychology' to make persuasive arguments.

Another *da'wa* manual is Yahya Emerick's *How to Tell Others About Islam*. In this easy-to-read guide written for Muslims in America, Emerick begins by quoting the above-mentioned qur'anic proof texts along with hadith reports meant to prove to the reader that he or she should actively preach Islam to Americans of every kind. He includes a chapter on what he calls '*da'wa* to Muslims', in which he provides step-by-step guidelines on how to help wayward Muslims back onto the right path. From that point onwards, each chapter is devoted to a different demographic group of the American population or realm of society. He has chapters, for instance, on '*Da'wa* to Jews', '*Da'wa* to Christians' (one of Emerick's longest chapters complete with detailed arguments against the Christian Bible and doctrine of the Trinity), '*Da'wa* on Campus', '*Da'wa* at work' and '*Da'wa* in Prison'. Subsequent chapters give tips on how to share Islam with 'Latinos', 'Asians', 'Native Americans', 'The African American', 'The Caucasian', 'The Elderly', 'The Poor' and so on. The book concludes with appendices regarding Emerick's favorite *da'wa* literature, recommended reading and useful websites (Sources: Baz 1998; Emerick 2010; Nadwi 1996; Kuiper 2018a, pp. 90–2 and notes)

For yet further examples of non-state *da'wa* organisations, we might look briefly at a few specific regions of the world. While we cannot comment on every region, the examples given here, from Southeast Asia and sub-Saharan Africa, may be taken as indicative of trends across the Muslim world. Since the 1950s, Indonesia has witnessed the rise of numerous home-grown non-state *da'wa* initiatives. Alongside the older and still very active Muhammadiyah and Nahdlatul Ulama (see Chapter 6), mention might be made of the Lembaga Dakwah Islam Indonesia (Indonesia Institute of Islamic Dawah) or LDII, founded in 1972, a conservative Sunni group that sends missionaries throughout the archipelago and operates a *da'wa* television channel. Also significant is the Dewan Dakwah Islamiyah Indonesia (DDII, the Indonesian Islamic Da'wa Council), an organisation founded in 1967 by Mohammad Natsir, an Indonesian religious leader and politician. The DDII has been a major promoter of Salafi *da'wa* in Indonesia, and it has served as a local partner organisation for the Saudi-led Muslim World League. In fact, according to Wahid, the DDII has been a major conduit of Saudi (and other Gulf countries') *da'wa* funds and influence in Indonesia.[80] Neighbouring Malaysia has also seen the rise of mass *da'wa* movements since the 1960s. PERKIM (All Malaysia Muslim Welfare Association), for instance, was founded in 1960 by Tunku Abdul Rahman, independent Malaysia's first Prime Minister. From its founding, PERKIM has engaged in *da'wa* and social welfare projects. Capitalising on the international contacts and political cachet of its founder, PERKIM benefited from Saudi funding through the Muslim World League as well as the Organisation of Islamic Conference.[81] Yet another influential *da'wa* organisation is the Youth Movement of Malaysia (ABIM), which was founded in 1971. Looking briefly to neighbouring Singapore, although Muslims constitute only about 14 percent of the population, they have founded a number of organisations to advocate for Muslims and Islam in Singaporean society. One example is the Muslim Converts' Association of Singapore, an organisation founded in 1979, which seeks to spread Islam and provide guidance for new converts to Islam.[82]

Turning to sub-Saharan Africa: Chapter 5 examined the eighteenth-century establishment of the Sokoto Caliphate through the religio-political *da'wa* of 'Uthman Dan Fodio (d. 1817). In more recent times, northern Nigeria has witnessed the rise of mass *da'wa* movements, such as the *Jama'at Izalat al-Bid'a wa Iqamat as-Sunna* or Yan Izala (JIBWIS), founded in 1978 by Shaykh Ismaila Idris (d. 2000). Another important figure in the organisation's founding was Abubakr Gumi (d. 1992), a member of the *'ulama* who made savvy use of both political contacts and new media (like television) to spread the movement's message. The name of the organisation literally means 'Society for the Removal of Innovation and the Restoration of the Sunna' and is taken from the title of a treatise by none other than dan Fodio. The organisation has benefited from Saudi sponsorship;[83] along with promoting Salafi *da'wa*, it has been a major advocate for pro-*shari'a* initiatives in northern Nigeria.[84] In line with its Salafi theology and Saudi patronage, JIBWIS is anti-Sufi. The activities of JIBWIS, along with those of groups like Boko Haram (see below) have not only exacerbated intra-religious, but also inter-religious tensions in Nigeria, as the country's population is split almost evenly, with a predominantly Muslim north and a predominantly Christian south. According to Commins, the Saudi-sponsored Muslim World League

> ... sent missionaries to West Africa, where it funded schools, distributed religious literature and gave scholarships to attend Saudi religious universities. These efforts bore fruit in Nigeria's Muslim northern region with the creation of a movement (the Izala Society) dedicated to wiping out ritual innovations. Essential texts for members of the Izala Society are Muhammad ibn Abd al-Wahhab's treatise on God's unity [*Kitab al-Tawhid*].

The Saudis funded similar efforts in Ghana, the Ivory Coast, Guinea and Mali. Nevertheless, Sufi *da'wa*, such as that spearheaded by the Tijaniyya, Muridiyya, Qadiriyya and other Sufi groups, remains active and popular throughout the continent.

The East African countries of Kenya and Tanzania, where Muslims are a minority of each country's total population, provide additional glimpses into contemporary non-state *da'wa*. Chanfi Ahmed notes how a 'habitus of competition' in a 'market of religious conversion'[85] has led to the emergence of several 'Preachers of Islam' movements, sometimes also called 'Muslim Preachers of the Bible'. Most of these preachers are laymen (non-*'ulama*), and some are converts to Islam from Christian backgrounds. They preach, not in the mosque, but in marketplaces, bus stops and football stadiums. A major aspect of their approach is using the Bible to attack Christianity and make arguments for Islam. Ahmed shows the complex local and global influences which shape this unique form of *da'wa* in East Africa: the missionary efforts of the Ahmadiyya movement in East Africa by members who had arrived there in the late nineteenth and early twentieth centuries; the rising prominence among Muslims of the *Gospel of Barnabas*, which had been disseminated to East Africa following Rida's popularisation of the text in the early twentieth century (see Chapter 6); the polemical discourses of Ahmed Deedat who visited East Africa in the 1980s and whose books and tapes became popular from that time onward; and the influence of local Pentecostal Christians who serve as the 'main opponent and a role model to be imitated when it comes to methods ... of conversion'. Ahmed also shows how Salafi currents have impacted these preachers' movements. While they have faced the criticism of other Muslim organisations, these East African preachers' movements provide a telling case study of the multifaceted currents of influence which feed into contemporary manifestations of *da'wa*.[86]

Non-state religio-political or militant da'was

While most modern non-state Islamic organisations, including those highlighted above, generally exemplify quietist, 'Meccan' approaches to Islamic outreach, it is important to conclude this section by mentioning several 'Medinan' styles of non-state activism. We are referring to Muslim movements and organisations which are explicitly political in their methods and goals and/or which may embrace militant *jihad* (sometimes including the use of 'terrorist' tactics) among their strategies. For many movements of this kind, the modern disestablishment of Islam and its relegation to the realm of individual choice is a travesty. Islam is destined to rule. Just as the Prophet took up politics and the sword alongside *da'wa*, in order to establish a truly Islamic state in Medina, so Muslims are called to do so today. The movements which embrace such thinking are diverse and often at odds with one another, as are the strategies they adopt. As such, care must be taken not to lump them all together.

We have already spoken of the MB and JI as the paradigmatic modern organisations which, over time, pioneered 'Islamist' thinking. Another organisation which follows an Islamist ideology and which employs a religio-political *da'wa* is Hizb ut Tahrir (HT, Islamic Liberation Party), founded in 1952 by the Palestinian scholar-activist Taqiuddin al-Nabhani. HT longs to unite Muslims under a global caliphate, for which the group has drawn up detailed plans and even a 'constitution'. HT does not hide the fact that its goals are political or that it opposes current governments: 'HT is a political party whose ideology is Islam . . . Its purpose [is] to revive the Islamic Ummah from . . . severe decline . . . and to liberate it from the . . . domination and influence of the Kufr (unbelieving) states'.[87] As for the *modus operandi* of the organisation, HT engages in *da'wa* to persuade Muslims of the need for an Islamic caliphate. Drawing on Q 3:104 and 3:110 (see Chapter 1), HT asserts that it is only within a caliphate that Muslims can fulfill their calling to be 'the best community'. While HT thinkers and activists foresee a time when it may be necessary to take up arms, their strategy for now is generally non-violent and gradualist. For this reason, it is better to classify HT as 'khilafist' (working for a caliphate) than 'jihadist'.[88] In fact, HT's program resembles the *da'was* of the eighth-century 'Abbasids and ninth-century Fatimids, as discussed in Chapter 3. In both cases, a period of (clandestine) *da'wa* preceded the actual taking up of arms and establishment of new empires. So too, the HT today operates in over fifty countries. When conditions are right, the HT's supreme leader (or Amir) will declare that the time for 'seeking power' has arrived. Because of the group's political goals and its critique of current governments, it has been banned and persecuted in multiple Muslim-majority states, while it operates relatively freely in others. On HT's website, a section called 'Da'wa News' (*akhbār al-da'wa*) highlights HT's religio-political missionary activities – including conferences, book publications and street protests.[89] We may note in passing that another 'Medinan' *da'wa* of the second phase which resembled the pre-modern *da'wa*s of the 'Abbasids and Fatimids was the Islamic Revolution in Iran. In focusing on the climactic events of 1979, when Khomeini's movement overthrew the Shah and established an Islamic state, one can easily forget that these events were preceded by a preparatory non-state religio-political *da'wa*.

Other non-state religio-political movements with associated *da'wa*s in the second phase include Hizb al-Da'wa in Iraq ('Party of Da'wa', Shi'ite, founded 1957), the Taliban in Afghanistan ('Students', Sunni, founded in the early 1990s) and many others. HAMAS in the Palestinian Territories ('Movement of Islamic Resistance', Sunni, founded 1987) and Hezbollah in Lebanon ('Party of God', Shi'ite, founded 1970s–80s) have generally operated as non-state movements, but have also taken on governing powers in recent times. This brings us to Sunni 'Jihadi-Salafi' movements,[90] such as the Lashkar-i Tayyiba in South Asia (LeT, 'Army of the Pure', founded in 1987) and its political/social wing Jama'at al-Da'wa (JuD, 'Congregation of Da'wa'), Jamaah Islamiyah in Southeast Asia ('Congregation of Islam', founded in the early 1980s), the Abu Sayyaf Group of the Philippines (ASG, founded in 1991), the Islamic Movement of Uzbekistan (IMU, founded in 1997), the Harakat al-Shabab al-Mujahideen in Somalia (or al-Shabab, 'The Youth', founded in 2002) and numerous others.[91] Perhaps the best-known Jihadi-Salafi groups are al-Qaeda ('The Base', present globally, founded in 1988), Boko Haram ('Western Education is Forbidden', primarily in Nigeria and surrounding areas, later affiliated with the Islamic State, founded in 2003) and ISIS (or the Islamic State, IS, or ISIL, focused on Syria and Iraq, but with global ambitions and affiliates in numerous places, founded in 2004).

As we turn to this subject, it is important to keep in mind that, despite Salafism's theological narrowness and blatant disdain for non-Salafis, the dominant streams of the modern Salafi movement tend to be quietist (see Introduction to Part II). By contrast, Jihadi-Salafis consider militant *jihad* against the realm of godless *jahiliyya* to be an urgent duty binding on all Muslims. Blending Salafi-Wahhabi theology and the radical Islamist thought of Sayyid Qutb (see above), and inspired by the anti-Soviet *jihad* in Afghanistan from 1979 to 1989, these groups have engaged in acts of horrific violence and terrorism, against both 'near enemies' (when they pursue local political goals, say, in Nigeria or Syria) and 'far enemies' (when they turn to 'global *jihad*' against the 'the West'). Yet, all of these groups also use *da'wa* as means of recruiting Muslims and of spreading their Salafi-Wahhabi versions of Islam around the world.

This can be seen, for instance, in the public communications of al-Qaeda, both before and after 9/11 – for instance, in bin Laden's and al-Zawahiri's 1998 call for 'Jihad against Zionists and Crusaders'. It should also be understood that the atrocities of 9/11 were not only heinous acts of terrorism, but were also intended by their perpetrators as spectacles of *da'wa*. The attacks, that is, were not only intended to terrorise the West, but also to 'summon' Muslims to al-

Qaeda's cause. For its part, before it lost much of its territory between 2017 and 2019 and before its 'caliph', Abu Bakr al-Baghdadi, was killed in October 2019, ISIS made savvy use of visual media and the internet to broadcast its *da'wa* (often appalling in its content) to a global audience.[92] An analysis of the Islamic State's online magazine *Dabiq*, later renamed *Rumiyah*, shows the repeated use of the word '*da'wa*'. For instance, the Ramadan 1438 (Spring 2017) edition of *Rumiyah* states: 'The Islamic State was only established to spread *tawhid*, and . . . its *da'wa* is merely an extension of the *da'wa* of the Prophets and Messengers [and] that of the righteous Salaf . . . It was [also] established upon the same principles as the blessed Najdi *da'wa* state founded by the followers of . . . Muhammad Ibn 'Abd al-Wahhab'.[93] Even though Saudi Arabia and most Wahhabi scholars have distanced themselves from ISIS, it is interesting that the militant group sees itself as fulfilling the eighteenth-century Najdi *da'wa* of 'Abd al-Wahhab (see Chapter 5). In an earlier issue, *Rumiyah* highlighted the anti-Sufi *da'wa* efforts of ISIS's 'Da'wa Center' in its erstwhile territories. Alongside a photo of a Sufi 'soothsayer' about to be beheaded by an ISIS executioner, the magazine states, 'the soldiers of the Islamic State implement *shari'a* programs for giving *da'wa* to the people and teaching them the religion . . . We also print and disseminate *da'wa* booklets and pamphlets . . . and hold *da'wa* expeditions in which we focus on strengthening the *tawhid* of Muslim commoners and warning them against all forms of shirk [idolatry] and apostasy'.[94] Although the majority of the world's Muslims have rejected ISIS,[95] it cannot be denied that the group's *da'wa* has had some success in recruiting Muslims from around the world.[96]

The important points for our purpose are that Islamist and Jihadi-Salafi groups have been highly organised, have operated independently of and in opposition to existing states, and have engaged in *da'wa* among other activities. Although radical Islamist and Jihadi-Salafi organisations clearly act in the name of Islam and deploy Islamic rationales to justify their actions, they represent a small minority of all Muslims. To repeat a central point: In light of modern conditions, most non-state *da'wa* actors and organisations – whatever their ultimate political dreams – have embraced the assumptions of the religious marketplace and have found 'Meccan' styles of *da'wa* to be more practical and realistic than 'Medinan' approaches. This observation also holds for most groups that fall under the 'Salafi' umbrella (see Text Box 7.4). It is also important to stress that Islamist and Jihadi projects have had very limited real-world success. When examined from the perspective of their utopian goals, one might go even further and say that these movements have been abject failures.[97] Consequently, some scholars argue that recent decades have witnessed the rise of a phenomenon they call 'post-Islamism'.[98] This refers to one-time Islamists and Jihadis (and their sympathisers) who, coming to grips with their movements' failures, have set aside explicit political activism in favour of the bottom-up renewal of Muslim devotion and the missionary propagation of Islam through peaceful means.

According to this thinking, one can still engage in *jihad*, but it is now the *jihad* of education and *da'wa*. Post-Islamism may also be taken to refer to Muslim communities which have suffered the effects of Islamist and Jihadi violence and have therefore become weary and wary of such approaches. Whether or not 'post-Islamism' has anything to do with it,[99] the fact is that today Meccan styles of *da'wa* are generally more popular among Muslims than Medinan alternatives, and we can expect for this trend to continue. Still, we should not expect religio-political and militant approaches to disappear entirely.[100]

7.4 Mainstream Salafi *da'walogy*

Despite the high-profile actions of Jihadi-Salafi groups, the fact is that much of what falls under the umbrella of 'Salafism' today is quietist in its orientation. Indeed, major Salafi thinkers explicitly embrace what this book has been calling Meccan *da'walogies*. Wiktorowicz explains the views of the major twentieth-century Salafi theologians Nasir al-Din al-Albani (d. 1999) and 'Abd al-Aziz Ibn Baz (d. 1999) in the following way:

> *The proper method for implementing the [Salafi] creed is . . . propagation* (da'wa)*, purification* (tazkiyya)*, and religious education . . .* (tarbiya)*. This is based on an analogy to the Meccan period, when the Prophet first began his mission. During this period, the Prophet and his followers . . . preferred propagation and advice to leaders rather than rebellion and overt opposition . . . Jihad during this period meant peaceful struggle in the effort to promote Islam, not uprisings and dissent. As Nasir al-Din al-Albani argues, '. . . Everybody claims that the Prophet is their role model. Our Prophet spent the first half of his message [in Mecca] making* da'wa*, and he did not start it with* jihad*' . . . When asked about the proper response to the [1991 Algerian government crackdown on Islamist groups] . . . Abd al-Aziz Bin Baz (d. 1999) . . . referred back to the Meccan period: 'They did not use to call the people to the sword. They used to call the people with the aayaat [verses] of the Qur'an, good speech and good manners, because this was more effective in . . . causing others to accept the truth'* (Source: Wiktorowicz 2006, p. 217, emphasis added).

State-sponsored *da'wa* initiatives

An important theme of Part II has been the disestablishment of Islam and the related (and remarkable) rise of voluntary, non-state and often 'Meccan' *da'wa* activism in modernity. It is important at this point, however, to stress that post-colonial conditions have paved the way for the limited re-establishment of Islam in multiple contexts. As noted, no matter how secular they may have been, post-colonial Muslim states have still attempted to play the part of pro-tectors of Islam in a variety of ways. As the secularist interregnum passed into the Islamic revival, moreover, many governments initiated or stepped up pro-Islamic policies. That is to say, in response to the Islamic revival, in consequence of geopolitical rivalries and following in some instances from the alarm caused by the 1979 Iranian Revolution (or all of the above), the governments of many Muslim-majority states got in the game of *da'wa*. Particularly from the 1970s onwards, appearing to defend and extend 'Islam' or promote '*shari'a*' became a central way for governments to try to bolster their legitimacy, outmanoeuvre Islamist opposition and forestall revolutionary fervour.[101] Pakistan, as we have seen, passed a raft of legislation during the regime of Zia ul-Haqq, intended to make Pakistan more thoroughly Islamic. This included the country's notorious blasphemy law, which is still in effect. In Egypt of the 1970s, Sadat tried to rally Muslim support to his regime by adopting a more pro-religious stance than had been the norm under Nasser. In Turkey, explicitly Islamic political parties made gains throughout the 1980s and took power in the 1990s, which allowed them to roll back aspects of Ataturk-era secularism. In Palestine, the largely secular-nationalist PLO found itself challenged by HAMAS, an organisation that frames its struggle in explicitly Islamic terms. Bangladesh, Malaysia and Indonesia have all witnessed gains by Muslim parties and government concessions to Islamic initiatives. However, such moves towards the re-establishment of Islam have had a limited impact in terms of mitigating the overall disestablishment conditions and religious marketplace mentalities which have become so integral to global culture in modernity. In this section we survey, first, state-sponsored *da'wa* within states' domestic or internal affairs and, second, state-sponsored *da'wa* as part of their foreign policies or external affairs.

State-sponsored da'wa *as domestic policy*
First, as noted above, nearly all post-colonial Muslim states have set up bureaus or ministries of religious affairs, which have attempted not only to regulate and control Islam, but also to promote it to some extent. When governments adopt pro-Islamic or *shari'a* policies, it often falls to state bureaus of religious affairs to implement them. In a statement that could be applied to most Muslim-majority countries today, Nathan Brown writes: 'All Arab states have large official Muslim religious establishments that give governments a major role in [domestic] religious life ... Through them the state has a say over religious education, mosques, and religious broadcasting'.[102] From the 'enforced tolerance' of the Ibadi (a sect of Islam that is neither strictly Sunni nor Shi'ite) Omani Ministry of Endowments and Religious Affairs,[103] to the powerful and centralised pro-monarchy Ministry of Religious Affairs in Morocco,[104] to the Ministry of Religious Affairs and Inter-Faith Harmony in Pakistan,[105] state bureaus of religious affairs fulfill similar functions in modern Islamic societies, but are far from uniform in terms of their local influence. Speaking generally, along with education, mosques and religious broadcasting, such bureaus tend to

oversee religious endowments and charitable giving, offer state-approved *fatwas*, provide guidance for mosque sermons, apply some version of Islamic family law (legal provisions regarding marriage, divorce, inheritance and so on) and facilitate their citizens' participation in the *hajj*. Some states also have national *muftis*, religious courts and Islamic judges (or *qadis*). Most also have some sort of *da'wa* mandate. Given governments' predilection for maintaining peace and order, it is not surprising that many religious affairs bureaus have been tasked with doing *da'wa* for peaceful versions of Islam and against oppositional and/or militant versions. For instance, despite a brief period of MB rule between 2012 and 2013 following the Arab Spring in Egypt, the post-colonial Egyptian state has generally used its state apparatuses to promote a quietist, pro-regime Islam and to suppress the MB and other political *da'was*.

The history of Turkey's Directorate of Religious Affairs (Diyanet İşleri Bakanlığı) illustrates how the role of such institutions may change and evolve towards *da'wa* over time. In its early history, the Diyanet was tasked with carrying out Ataturk's secularisation policies and ensuring that religion would not threaten the secularism of the state. Since the early 2000s, however, under the pro-Islamic governments of Erdogan and his allies, the Diyanet has taken on an orientation towards *da'wa*. The agency actively promotes mainstream Sunni (Hanafi) Islam and seeks to make the population more (not less) Muslim. The Diyanet also provides religious support to Turks in other countries, for instance, by building mosques in places like Germany and the United States. After the 2016 coup attempt in Turkey, the government has attempted to use the Diyanet to oppose the Gulen movement (which the government now calls Fethullahist Terrorist Organisation or FETO).[106] The Diyanet today has a budget of roughly $2 billion, oversees some 85,000 mosques in Turkey, certifies that food producers comply with Islamic *halal* regulations, runs a 24–hour religious television channel and operates a *fatwa* hotline.[107] Comparing Turkey's Diyanet and Indonesia's Ministry of Religious Affairs (MORA), van Bruinessen notes: 'The budgets of [the two countries'] religious establishments have kept increasing over time and are of comparable magnitude with the military establishments of those countries'.[108]

Not surprisingly, Saudi Arabia is a distinctive case. There are several government agencies engaged in activities one could loosely classify as *da'wa*, for instance, the Ministries of Education and Information, and the Ministry of Islamic Affairs, Dawah and Guidance (*da'wa wa'l-irshād*).[109] While the state-sponsored religious establishment propagates a quietist version of Salafi Wahhabism through its control of education, broadcasting and religious enforcement (see below), history has shown that Salafi theology, with its sharp exclusivism and utopian dispositions, tends to produce oppositional movements that refuse to remain quietist. When governments, such as the Saudi royal regime, are perceived as having strayed from the pure Islam of the Prophet and Companions,

Salafi-Wahhabi opposition has tended to break out in political or militant form. Such movements, in turn, have tended to see government-supported religious establishments as hopelessly compromised by their support of and by the state. Teitelbaum discusses another way in which the Saudi authorities' control over religious affairs has been tenuous: Since the introduction of the internet into the kingdom in the 1990s, the rulers have struggled to maintain the state's monopoly on the flow of information, religious or otherwise.[110] This dilemma has been seen across the Muslim world since the 1990s.

We will return to Saudi Arabia and its *da'wa*-infused 'religious foreign policy' below,[111] but for now mention should also be made of Saudi Arabia's Islamic University of Medina (IUM). Serving the kingdom's domestic and foreign policy goals, the university, founded in 1961 as a royal project to 'champion the fortunes of Muslims in the East and in the West' through *da'wa*, has been a major player in training *da'wa* functionaries who graduate, at least in theory, sympathetic to Salafi-Wahhabi Islam.[112] Although Saudi citizens are welcome at IUM, regulations stipulate that 75 percent of the all-male student body must come from abroad. The strategy of taking in (and subsidising) students from across the Muslim world, training them at IUM and sending them back to their countries as *da'is* holds obvious advantages for Saudi Arabia and the brand of Islam it sponsors. The president of the university is usually a leading member of the Saudi-Wahhabi *'ulama*. For instance, 'Abd al-Aziz b. Baz was president of the university from 1969 to 1975. At the same time, it should be acknowledged that IUM has striven to present a pan-Sunni face, and not only in terms of its student body. On the founding Advisory Committee of IUM were non-Salafi (reformist Sunni) personages such as 'Ali Nadwi and Mawdudi from South Asia, as well as a number of leading *'ulama* from other parts of the Middle East.[113]

The issue of the credibility (or lack thereof) of 'official Islam' is observable throughout the Muslim world. Many state-supported religious officials, for instance, may give voice to quietism and openly oppose violent extremism.[114] When they do so, however, they may be regarded, especially by younger generations, as 'co-opted, ineffective . . . and authoritarian'. Holding a post of government-sponsored religious authority, in other words, does 'not confer doctrinal or moral authority' on the street.[115] Indeed, the search for 'authentic' religious authority has led many to turn away from state-supported religious officials and instead towards the kinds of private or non-state actors and movements highlighted in the previous section. In this competitive scenario, according to Brown, official religious bureaus attempt to gain credibility in several ways. First, they may take up new technologies or offer services (such as community development projects or marriage counseling) which are deemed to be relevant to their target populations. Second, sometimes with tacit regime support, they may seek to create some distance – or the appearance of distance – between themselves and the governments that support them. They may try, in other words, to show that they are not mechanical mouthpieces of the regime but speak for Islam. To these, however, a third strategy should be added: that of taking up *da'wa*.

In the decades since independence and the emergence of the Islamic revival, the religious affairs ministries of Muslim-majority states have funded *da'wa* departments in Islamic universities, started new schools and institutes devoted to *da'wa*, sponsored *da'wa* websites and built countless mosques, *madrasas* and Islamic study centres. Given the rising salience of *da'wa* as a discourse of activism among Muslims in general, this has been a shrewd move on the part of state-sponsored Islam. In Pakistan, for instance, the state supports the Da'wah Academy of the International Islamic University, Islamabad (IIUI), as it does the university in general (see Text Box 7.5).[116]

7.5 On *da'wa*, from the Da'wah Academy of the International Islamic University, Islamabad

Da'wah i.e. inviting people to the right path . . . is an Islamic obligation. The Quran and the Sunnah make it explicit that Muslims are individually as well as collectively, responsible for amr-bil-ma'ruf *(2:145), i.e. for enjoining good, and for tabligh . . . This noble task has been taken up by various Muslim groups throughout the ages . . . However, the present era poses a formidable challenge perhaps never experienced before . . . An integrated and comprehensive approach and methodology which fully utilizes disciplines such as communication, comparative religion, cross-cultural studies and social psychology has to be developed in order to disseminate the message of Islam in an effective manner. Unfortunately, [such an] institution . . . rarely exists in the entire Muslim world . . .*

In compliance with the directive of the President of Pakistan (No. 952 of 1981), the International Islamic University, Islamabad . . . set up a Da'wah Project (1983–5). Later on in March 1985 . . . an Academy for Da'wah and training of Imams was established . . . within the International Islamic University . . . in order to develop Da'wah-oriented training, research and publication programs for the Pakistani people in general and for overseas Muslim communities in particular (Source: Da'wah Academy [n. d.]).

Among many others, an example of a successful *da'wa* website sponsored by a state's religious agency is the Kuwait-based website DawahSkills.com.[117] Even more prominent is IslamWeb.net, a popular *da'wa* and fatwa website operated by the government of Qatar. Along with thousands of fatwas, the website has dozens of articles on *da'wa*, available in Arabic, English, French, German and Spanish. Titles include: 'Calling to Islam – the duty of every Muslim', 'The *da'wa* of the prophets', 'Women in *da'wa*', 'The use of the internet to propagate Islam' and many others.[118] Trumpeting its own achievement, the website of Qatar's Ministry of Endowments and Religious Affairs notes: '[T]he Ministry . . . flew high in the sky with its *da'wa* . . . by launching "Islamweb.net" website, which is a distinguished site that has won many international and regional awards, thanks to its excellence in its presentation of the noble meanings of Islam through the Internet' (see Text Box 7.6). In addition to these examples, official religious bureaus sometimes support or find common cause with private *da'wa* actors and organisations of which they approve. Examples of the latter include the support the TJ has enjoyed – owing to its quietism and popularity

---

7.6 Excerpt from IslamWeb.net's article 'Women in *Da'wa*'

This short excerpt of a longer article is characteristic of contemporary (reformist/conservative) *da'wa* discourse regarding the need to mobilise women for *da'wa* and regarding the roles women should play in *da'wa*:

From the very beginning of the Islamic history, Muslim women have played vital roles in the propagation of the Divine Message (Islam) . . . Unfortunately, during our present times, the Islamic revival suffers from weaknesses in its properly qualified personnel, which . . . restricts the da'wa work to an elite group of activists, with finite and limited efforts of da'wa and tarbiyah (education) being focused on women . . . The reasons women's participation in da'wa is important are various and diverse:

Women are more capable than men are in communicating with other women. Women are usually more affected by word, deed, and conduct of other women, more so than by men . . .

Women can better comprehend the direction in which women's da'wa should be geared . . .

The need of education with women is greater than that with men . . . If they are not allowed to share in the da'wa efforts of their husbands, a lot of the much-needed results may not be attained.

Women have a great effect on their husbands. If they have strong Eeman (faith) and character, they have a very good chance at helping their husbands become strong as well . . .

It is time that Muslims who profess to follow the Sunnah . . . of Prophet Muhammad (pbuh) rethink the issue of da'wa among women and by women. We should remember . . . many Muslim women throughout our history, and . . . learn from [them]. We also have to realize that mere talk . . . [is] useless. We need to do something about our immediate situation now. Education, preparation, and qualification of women will be the key to our future success (Source: IslamWeb 2018a, and IslamWeb 2019).

– from Muslim governments the world over, as well as the private *da'wa* actors who have been feted by Saudi Arabia with the King Faisal Prize.

In earlier chapters, we saw that, historically, *da'wa* has been closely related to the qur'anic duty of commanding the right and forbidding the wrong and that state power was often thought to be necessary for its fulfillment. In the midst of the many non-state actors and organisations which have taken up variations of commanding and forbidding, the governments of many Muslim-majority countries have also sought to fulfill this duty. Sometimes, they have done so under the banner of '*shari'a*', as for instance in Pakistan or the states of northern Nigeria.[119] A minority of Muslim countries even have religious police forces (*muṭawwi'īn*), for instance, Saudi Arabia, Malaysia, Sudan, Iran and (under the Taliban until 2001) Afghanistan.[120] Deployed on the basis of the notions of commanding and forbidding, as well as *hisba* (enforcement of moral behaviour, specifically related to commercial transactions),[121] such religious police forces are often integrated in their countries' law enforcement systems and have tended to limit their activities to public spaces. For instance, both Iran's 'Guidance Patrol' (*gasht-i irshād*, in Farsi) and Saudi Arabia's Committee for the Promotion of Virtue and the Prevention of Vice (*hay'at al-amr b'il-ma'rūf wa nahī 'an al-munkar*, in Arabic) have enforced proper Islamic dress or head coverings for women and have discouraged the mixing of the sexes in public places, as well as the celebration of 'un-Islamic' festivals like Valentine's Day. More seriously, these groups may bring charges of apostasy or blasphemy, which, at least in Saudi Arabia and pre-2001 Afghanistan, were/are punishable by death. In Malaysia, a less formal system of 'religious officers' encourages Muslims to fast during Ramadan or attend Friday prayers. In recent times, along with criticism that religious police forces have seemed preoccupied with the behaviour of women, there are also complaints that they have become overly intrusive. Some countries have responded by trying to rein in their religious police.[122]

In sum, the phenomena of state-sponsored domestic *da'wa* add yet more complexity to our already crowded and competitive picture of *da'wa* activism in the second phase. While their credibility is frequently challenged, state religious agencies and their *da'wa* initiatives nevertheless play a major role – directly and indirectly – in the lives of millions of Muslims around the world. While state-supported initiatives are often housed in 'sprawling bureaucracies' which are 'difficult to steer in any particular direction', they remain relevant to the religious (and political) life of Muslim societies in modernity.[123] Their efforts to establish officially approved versions of Islam, however, always remain imperfect and incomplete. Individual Muslim agency has been enhanced in modernity, and as such, the realm of private, non-state *da'wa* remains vibrant and highly attractive.

State-sponsored da'wa *as foreign policy*

Second, as for state-sponsored *da'wa* as an aspect of Muslim countries' foreign policies or external affairs: although we have already seen instances in which *da'wa*-as-domestic-policy and *da'wa*-as-foreign-policy overlap (as in Turkey's building of mosques abroad or Saudi Arabia's Islamic University of Medina), here we look at several emblematic *da'wa*-infused foreign policy initiatives undertaken by Muslim-majority states, either independently or in concert with one another. A watershed event in the globalisation of state-sponsored *da'wa* was the decision by then crown prince of Saudi Arabia, Faisal, to steer his country towards an 'Islamic foreign policy' in the early 1960s. This was done partially in response to the secularising winds which were blowing through the Arab world at the time. Nasser posed a particular challenge: After World War II, Gamal 'Abd al-Nasser 'built up a *da'wa* network . . . [and] championed the cause of Islamic socialism and pan-Arabism . . .' This style of '*da'wa*' was represented by the Arab League, founded in 1945.[124] In response, 'Other Muslim leaders . . . took recourse to a more classic [Islamic] understanding of *da'wa*. Most notably, Saudi Arabia's King Faisal . . . stress[ed] the ideal of . . . Muslim solidarity based on Islam, not Arabism'.[125] Hence, Faisal (who reigned as king from 1964 to 1975) developed 'Saudi Arabia's Islamic policy . . . in response to Nasser's adoption of socialism and intervention in Yemen's civil war' (*circa* 1962–70). 'The policy's formal birth took place at a May 1962 conference that the Saudis organised to discuss ways to combat secularism and socialism'.[126] The conference resulted in a milestone event in modern *da'wa*, the establishment of the Muslim World League (MWL, in Arabic *rabiṭat al-ʿālam al-Islāmī*). Since its 1962 founding, the MWL has played a major role in *da'wa* around the world. While the league has not exclusively supported or partnered with Salafis, it is always headed by a Saudi, and it has generally functioned as 'an instrument for exporting the Najdi doctrine' globally.[127] Through their control of the holy cities of Mecca and Medina, and of institutions such as the Muslim World League, 'Saudi officials [have] sought to portray the Kingdom as possessing the purest, most unadulterated form of Islam'.[128] In this, they have been strikingly successful.[129]

It is not easy to access detailed information on the MWL's finances or to enumerate its many activities. Earlier, we drew attention to some MWL-sponsored efforts in Africa and Southeast Asia. We could also point to Pakistan, where Saudi support for state Islamisation programs and Sunni movements like the Ahl-i Hadith and Deobandis has been widely reported. In fact, it is no secret that since the 1970s significant amounts of money, 'well in the billions of dollars, though there is no clear tally of the total', have flowed from Saudi Arabia to Pakistan, sometimes mediated by the MWL. Symbolic of this relationship is Pakistan's largest mosque, appropriately named the Shah (or King) Faisal Mosque in Islamabad, 'built with a $120 million grant from the Kingdom of Saudi Arabia. For a few years after its completion in 1986, it was the largest

Figure 7.4 The Shah Faisal Mosque in Islamabad, Pakistan. Photo: M. Ali Mir from Wikimedia Commons, CC BY-SA.

mosque in the world. It quickly became one of Pakistan's best-known structures, surpassing many centuries-old buildings of historic significance' (see Figure 7.4).[130] Other examples come from neighbouring India, where Zaman has traced patterns of Saudi/MWL funding for Salafi and other of Sunni reformist *da'was*. Zaman highlights, for instance, a *madrasa* in the city of Varanasi (a *madrasa* I have visited on several occasions), the Jamia-tus-Salafiah (Congregation of the Salaf) where Ahl-i Hadith preachers are trained.[131] According to its website, 'Al-Jamia-tus-Salafiah Varanasi, India is a central institution of education . . . It is the outcome of the dreams and blessings of the . . . Jama'at Ahl-i Hadith. This education centre was founded in 1963 by the honourable ambassador of Saudi Arabia'.[132] Similar stories – of lavish Saudi patronage of Islamic institutions and *da'wa* efforts – could be told from nearly every part of the Muslim world. Through the MWL and other mechanisms, billions of dollars of Saudi oil wealth have been pumped into global *da'wa*. In pointing this out, we are not implying that funding equals allegiance or dependency in any linear sense. What sponsors intend and what recipients actually do are not always one and the same.[133]

More accessible than data on finances is information on the MWL's convening of conferences and formation of subsidiary organisations. For instance, in 1975, one year after Evangelical Christians convened the Lausanne Congress for World Evangelization, the League held the Mosque Message Conference, an international conference which discussed how local mosques could better carry out *da'wa*. As a reult of this meeting, the World Supreme Council for Mosques was formed, an organisation which 'aims at reactivating the mission of the Mosque as a vital focal point of the religious as well as the temporal life of the Muslim'.[134] The idea of promoting Islamic cooperation through a Council of Mosques was perhaps inspired by the founding not only of the Lausanne movement, but also of the World Council of Churches in 1948. As noted earlier, the League has made significant investments in Islamic relief work, in part through its subsidiary, the International Organization for Relief, Welfare and Development.[135] The MWL has also attempted to coordinate the work of Islamic legal scholars through its Islamic Fiqh Council, an organisation which is mandated to prove 'the supremacy of Islamic Fiqh over man-made laws' and to show 'the comprehensive nature of Fiqh and its ability to provide solutions to problems facing the Muslim Ummah at any time and place'.[136] Through its International Organization for the Holy Quran and Immaculate Sunnah, the league funds programs meant to help Muslims around the world memorise the Qur'an.[137] The league has additionaly proven to be a champion of the use of media in *da'wa*. At a 1977 conference, 'all delegates criticized the poor quality of Islamic media . . . In order to solve the problem the League organized an international media conference in Jakarta in September 1980, during which the delegates drafted a Covenant on Islamic Media'.[138] This led to the founding of the International Islamic Organization of Media.

Similar to the ways in which it seeks to harness modern media for *da'wa* is the MWL's appeal to 'science'. In 1984, the league organised the International Commission on Scientific Signs in Qur'an and Sunna. Over the years, this commission has organised numerous conferences, publications, films and so on, which have promoted the idea that qur'anic verses and certain hadith anticipate the findings of modern science and thus are 'proven' to be divine in origin. According to its one-time official website, the commission considers 'the field of scientific signs . . . a form of effective assistance to the other branches of *da'wa* in . . . the age of science . . . [M]any disbelievers . . . start their journey to the truth [of Islam] from the scientific signs in the Ever-Glorious Qur'an and the Sunnah'.[139] The discovery of 'scientific signs' in the Qur'an and the use of these 'signs' in *da'wa* is a truly unprecedented development in Islamic history, one that is only explainable in light of the challenges that modern science has posed to religion in general, and western modernity to Islam in particular.[140] The idea that qur'anic verses anticipate the findings of modern science is known by academics as 'Bucailleism', because this line of thinking originated with the French medical doctor Maurice Bucaille (1920–98). In his 1976 book, *La Bible, La Coran, et La Science*,[141] translated into English as *The Bible, the Qur'an and Science* in 1978,[142] Bucaille promoted the idea that 'the Qur'an conforms exactly to modern science and imparts knowledge that was unknown during the

Figure 7.5 The notion that the Qur'an anticipates modern scientific discoveries is known by scholars as 'Bucailleism' because of the role of Dr Maurice Bucaille's 1976 book (and subsequent translations) in popularising the idea. The concepts of Buccailleism are prominent in much contemporary *da'wa* discourse and have been promoted by the Muslim World League and numerous state-sponsored and non-state *da'wa* organisations.

lifetime of the Prophet (see Figure 7.5)'.[143] Closely related was Bucaille's critique of the Christian Bible, which he believed was shot through with 'scientific' inaccuracies. Bucaille's ideas were later showcased in a *da'wa* film – produced with financial backing from Malaysia, Egypt and Saudi Arabia – called *The Book of Signs*.[144] The MWL's Commission on Scientific Signs also recruited some western scientists and subsidised their participation in lavish conferences, in order to enlist (and video record) their support for the ideas of Bucailleism.[145] In the 1980s, it even published a Bucailleism-informed version of the embryology textbook of Professor Keith Moore (d. 2019).[146] Subsequently and continuing up to the present, the concepts of Bucailleism have been repeated by countless non-state and state-sponsored activists.

Along with its leadership and sponsorship of the MWL, Saudi Arabia has also sponsored the World Assembly of Muslim Youth (WAMY), which seeks to mobilise young Muslims by organising conferences and youth-oriented *da'wa* activities around the world. Additionally, since 1977, Saudi Arabia has sponsored the King Faisal Prize for 'service to Islam'. Appropriately, given the major role that King Faisal played in building up a global *da'wa* infrastructure, several prominent modern *da'is* have been awarded the prize since its inception, including Mawdudi, 'Ali Nadwi, Deedat, Khurshid Ahmad and Zakir Naik.[147]

Another carrier of state-sponsored *da'wa* in the realm of foreign affairs is the Organisation of Islamic Cooperation (OIC).[148] This transnational body of 57 Muslim majority states, founded in 1969, today constitutes the second-largest inter-governmental organisation in the world after the United Nations, and is the only one founded on the basis of shared religion. That is, there is no comparable intergovernmental organisation representing Christian-, Hindu- or Buddhist-majority nation states. To some extent, then, the OIC represents a fulfillment of the pan-Islamic sentiments of the late nineteenth and early twentieth centuries (associated with thinkers like Afghani, Abduh and Rida, as discussed in Chapter 6). Indeed, the formation and continuation of the OIC, which claims to be 'the collective voice of the Muslim world',[149] has been a monumental achievement. Nevertheless, if earlier pan-Islamists could return today, they would likely be somewhat disappointed by the OIC. For one thing, many observers note that the OIC, like the Arab League, has been relatively toothless in fostering real-world political results. The OIC charter itself makes it clear that the organisation exists, not to work towards actual Muslim political unity, but to preserve the national sovereignty of the various member states.[150] In spite of this, several areas in which the OIC has been effective are those of education and *da'wa*.

Although not a *da'wa* organisation as such, the OIC charter contains many clauses which show an orientation towards missionary propagation. Sections 11 and 12 of Article 1, for instance, state that the OIC exists '[t]o disseminate, promote and preserve the Islamic teachings and values . . .' and '[t]o protect and defend the true image of Islam, to combat defamation of Islam and encourage dialogue among civilisations and religions'.[151] While the OIC may be less than effective in bringing about political results, it has recognised 'Islamic *da'wa*' as 'a fundamental pillar . . . of joint Islamic action'. Out of this conviction, the OIC has formed a Committee for the Coordination of Joint Islamic Action in the Field of Da'wa.[152] In the fifty years since its founding, the OIC has also founded and funded several Islamic universities, including the Islamic University of Technology in Bangladesh, the Islamic University in Uganda, Islamic University Niger and the International Islamic University Malaysia (IIUM). The OIC has also launched the Islamic Development Bank and promoted the achievements of Islamic civilisation through the Islamic Educational, Scientific and Cultural Organization (ISESCO). Through another of its wings, the Islamic Broadcasting Union (IBU, founded in 1975), the OIC seeks '[t]o propagate the principles of the Islamic Da'wa, and teach the Arabic language . . . to explain and fight for Islamic causes, to strengthen the spirit of brotherhood among the Muslim peoples . . . '[153] In recent years, in light of the 'rise of attacks on Islam and Muslims', the OIC launched an 'Islamophobia Observatory' which calls attention to the mistreatment of Muslims around the world and 'reaffirm[s] that Islam is a religion of moderation'.[154]

The idea that Islamophobia is rampant around the world (for which there exists plenty of evidence) is a recurring theme in global Islamic discourse,[155] and this idea has provided a powerful motivation for *da'wa*. Countless state and non-state *da'wa* initiatives, publications, websites and so on devote significant space to 'correcting misconceptions' or 'overcoming misunderstandings' about Islam and Muslims. In western cities and university campuses, *da'wa*-minded Muslims occasionally set up 'Ask a Muslim' displays, while *da'wa*-minded mosques and community centres organise open houses where they put out literature on the 'true' nature of Islam.[156] As for the OIC, at its 2013 Islamic Summit meeting in Cairo, the OIC commended the founding of the King Abdullah Bin Abdulaziz International Center for Interreligious and Intercultural Dialogue (KAICIID) in Vienna, an 'intergovernmental organisation whose mandate is to promote the use of dialogue globally to prevent and resolve conflict, to enhance understanding and cooperation'.[157] This focus on 'dialogue' also represents an important recent trend in *da'wa*. In the official statements of leading bodies such as the OIC and MWL, as well as of local and national Muslim advocacy and *da'wa* organisations, one hears less and less about *da'wa* (which may be negatively associated with proselytising) and more and more about 'dialogue' (which usually has a positive connotation).[158] The OIC, in short, is not only a diplomatic organisation pursuing political goals; it also has specifically religious, even missionary, objectives. To take in just how distinctive this is from a global, and particularly from a western perspective, the reader might imagine a scenario in which another inter-governmental organisation, for example, the contemporary European Union, formed a standing committee to promote a generally conservative version of Christianity and to combat 'misinformation' about Christianity and the Bible.

Although common concerns such as combating Islamophobia and promoting Islam as a religion of peace have brought state actors together in organisations like the MWL and OIC, such forums also reveal fissures in the worldwide *umma*. Not surprisingly, in response to Saudi initiatives in *da'wa*, which are seen as ultimately promoting Saudi political interests, other countries founded *da'wa* organisations of their own. For instance, beginning in 1964, Egypt's Nasser responded to Saudi initiatives by organising congresses of Egyptian and foreign *'ulama* under the auspices of al-Azhar's Academy of Islamic Research.[159] Many other Muslim majority countries followed suit, although it must be said that none have proven as successful as the MWL and OIC.[160] Worthy of special mention in this context is the World Islamic Call Society (WICS), established in 1982 by the Libyan regime of Mu'ammar al-Qaddhafi. Like Saudi-sponsored organisations, the WICS has used Libyan oil revenues to engage vigorously in garden-variety *da'wa* activities, such as distributing literature and copies of the Qur'an, building schools and mosques, sponsoring education for Muslim students and so on, particularly in sub-Saharan Africa. In 1974, it opened the Islamic Call College in order to train full-time missionaries for Islam. As of 2004, the college had awarded 'Islamic Mission Licenses' and other degrees to some 3,000 students representing 65 countries.[161] Although well-funded as long as Qaddhafi was in power and although generally well-received by those who benefited from its largesse, the impact of the WICS was limited by several factors. First, alongside aspects of mainstream Sunni Islam (the Qur'an, prayer, fasting and so on), the WICS also promoted Qaddhafi's idiosyncratic interpretation of Islam.[162] Second, the organisation remained under Qaddhafi's personal control and was used as an instrument of Libyan foreign policy. Throughout its history, behind the front of missionary work, the WICS was suspected of engaging in more nefarious activities.[163] Since the demise of Qaddhafi in October 2011, the future of the WICS has been somewhat unclear. The organisation still exists, but according to reports, efforts have been made to 'purge' the organisation of its 'Qaddhafian' ideology and to operate it strictly as a non-political missionary organisation.[164]

Another development with significant implications for state sponsorship of *da'wa* was the 1979 Revolution in Iran. If Khomeini and his allies employed a non-state religio-political *da'wa* before 1979 to prepare the way for revolution, after 1979 the Islamic Republic began to actively engage in state-sponsored *da'wa* as an element of its domestic and foreign policy. Along with state agencies that oversee *da'wa* within Iran, such as the Ministry of Education and the above-mentioned Guidance Patrols, Iran's Ministry of Culture and Islamic Guidance[165] and Islamic Culture and Religious Organization[166] are among the agencies that use *da'wa* (under the umbrella of the Ministry of Foreign Affairs) to advocate abroad for Shi'ite Islam and the ideology of the Revolution (see Text Box 7.7). Like the Saudis, the Iranian regime claims to speak for all Muslims and has called many conferences of its own. According to Kramer, '[t]he OIC . . . remained . . . biased in favour of Saudi policies. For this reason, the existence of the OIC did not prevent several of its members from independently organizing . . . Islamic congresses and organizations'. After 1979, 'Iran virtually ignored the OIC, and convened frequent conferences of its own . . . '[167] This competitive and inflammatory situation is once again somewhat reminiscent of the 'Abbasid and Fatimid concept of *da'wa*: *da'wa* as religio-political summons on behalf of particular parties or regimes which claim the mantle of 'true' Islam against their rivals. In short, it is not only geopolitical issues that divide today's Saudi Arabia and Iran, but competing religio-political *da'was* as well.

Non-state and state-sponsored *da'wa* organisations: conclusions

One of the truly striking features of modern Islamic history is the extent to which Muslims have *organised* themselves for *da'wa* on the local, regional and international levels. While this has resulted in a discernible 'standardisation' of *da'wa* in certain respects,[168] it still is the case that multiple and sometimes crisscrossing *da'wa*logies – Meccan and Medinan, non-state and state-sponsored, bottom-up and top-down – lie behind these efforts. The preceding two sections have surveyed *da'wa* actors and initiatives during the second phase (*circa* 1950–2020) under the categories of (1) non-state and (2) state-sponsored *da'wa*. However, it should now be obvious that this categorisation is not airtight. For one thing, state initiatives often support or endorse non-state actors, as seen in the Saudi King Faisal Prize and the work of the MWL. For another thing, non-state movements or actors (like Islamists and Jihadis) may be motivated by the desire to (immediately or eventually) establish an Islamic state of their own. It should also be clear from our discussion that non-state does not necessarily mean 'Meccan' or non-political; nor does state-sponsored necessarily signal an explicit 'Medinan' political agenda. The state-sponsored initiatives we have discussed often favour

7.7 The 'aims' of Iran's Islamic Culture and Religious Organization (ICRO) and Ministry of Culture and Islamic Guidance (MCIG)

[T]he ICRO is to pursue the following aims and objectives: 1. Revival and dissemination of Islamic tenets . . . with a view to reaching the true message of Islam to the people of the world; 2. Creating awareness among the people of the world as regards the principles . . . of the Islamic Revolution of Iran . . .; 3. Expansion of cultural relations with various nations and communities in general; and the Muslims and the oppressed, in particular; 4. Strengthening and regulating the existing cultural relations between the Islamic Republic of Iran and other countries of the world . . .; 5. Appropriate presentation of the Iranian culture and civilization . . .; 6. Preparation of the necessary grounds for the unity among Muslims . . . on the basis of the indisputable principles of Islam; 7. Scholarly debates and confrontations with anti-religion, anti-Islam, and anti-Revolutionary cultures with a view to awakening the [world's] Muslims . . .

As for the MCIG, among its aims are to introduce . . .

. . . the fundamentals, characteristics and objectives of the Islamic Revolution to people of the world by making use of audio-visual media, books and other publications, holding of cultural gatherings and other means within the country and abroad through coordination with Ministry of Foreign Affairs . . .'

Other goals include:

Research and study works on propaganda of foreign media . . . and taking appropriate measure to confront them if necessary . . . Establishment, expansion and operation of all Iranian cultural missions abroad and appointing cultural and press attaches and supervising their activities (Islamic Culture and Religious Organization, 'Aims'; Ministry of Culture and Islamic Guidance [n. d.]).

quietist, voluntary styles of *da'wa* because they are not seen as a threat to the *status quo*. By contrast, militant non-state *da'wa* movements explicitly seek to overthrow existing governments. A further complication is the fact that even the most quietist movements may have unforeseen political consequences. There is much more to the 'political', after all, than dynamics related to state power and its capture and maintenance.

Migration and the *da'wa* initiatives of Muslim minority populations
While much of our focus in the preceding pages of this chapter has been on Muslim-majority contexts, we have nevertheless encountered Muslim minority communities in India, East Africa and several western contexts. Although we have argued that disestablishment and minoritisation have been felt across

the Muslim world in the colonial and post-colonial periods, it is obvious that Muslim minority communities have experienced these dynamics in particularly acute ways. Because of their experiences and contexts, such communities, as noted in Chapter 6, have often anticipated or pioneered styles of *da'wa* activism (particularly 'Meccan' styles) well-suited to modern religious marketplace conditions. Here, we pick up the discussion from the end of Chapter 6, by drawing attention to a few key contributions that Muslim minority populations, particularly those in the West, have made to *da'wa* thought and activism in the second phase.

From the time of the Arab-Islamic conquests (see Chapter 3), Muslim 'diasporas' have been a constant feature of Islamic history. This feature, as noted in Part I, has contributed to inter-religious contact between Muslims and others, as well as to the spread of Islam. We spoke, for instance, of 'merchant diasporas' which helped spread Islam to new places in medieval times. As noted in Chapter 6, the colonial period engendered waves of Muslim migration to, and settlement in, destinations outside traditional *dar al-Islam*, such as South Africa, Britain, France, Germany, Canada and the United States. In the post-colonial situation, from the mid-twentieth century, the process of decolonisation and the two World Wars caused massive *involuntary* migration. One can think, for instance, of the mass relocations (and horrific violence) sparked by the Partition of British India in 1947, or the migrations of Palestinian Arabs following the creation of Israel in 1948 and the Six Day War in 1967. Skipping ahead to the present, we might call to mind the desperate plight of uprooted Syrian, Iraqi and Afghan refugees and other migrants, many of whom are Muslim. Moreover, in recent years groups like the Rohingya Muslims of Myanmar, the Uighur (and other Turkic) Muslims of western China and the Muslims of India have been uprooted and subjected to extreme cases of minoritisation resulting from religious-nationalist prejudice and anti-Muslim government policies. Shifting our perspective to *voluntary* migration, from around the mid-twentieth century onwards, increasing numbers of Muslims chose to relocate from North Africa, Turkey, the Middle East and South Asia to European countries such as France, Germany and Britain. Many of these migrants were blue-collar workers.[169] The United States also began to see a steady increase in the numbers of Muslim migrants arriving in the US after the passage of the Immigration and Nationality Act of 1965.[170] In contrast to the European situation, US policy has tended to prefer migrants with professional backgrounds. In addition to Muslims in Europe and North America who came as migrants, or who are the children and grandchildren of migrants, there has been a steady trickle of conversions to Islam among Americans and Europeans from non-Muslim backgrounds. The black 'pilgrimage to Islam' in America has been particularly noteworthy.[171]

Before we address the contributions that Muslim communities in the West have made to global *da'wa*, a few caveats are in order. First, it must be emphasised that the position of Muslims in society varies significantly from country to country, and that there is a great deal of internal diversity among western Muslims themselves. Indeed, Muslims in the West promote and are objects of the whole panoply of *da'wa*s that we have examined in Part II. In addition, Muslim communities in western contexts such as the US are very heterogeneous in terms of ethnicity and language. Second, Muslims of the West are active participants in global Islamic networks. As such, they are aware of and may draw on Islamic and *da'wa* resources developed in India, Malaysia, Senegal, Saudi Arabia, Qatar and other places. Moreover, the governments of countries like Turkey or Saudi Arabia may take an interest in the Muslims of America, France, or Germany and seek to resource them in various ways. Of course, *da'wa* websites can be hosted and accessed from almost anywhere. Among the consequences of all this are multi-directional influence and networking. Western Muslims (like Muslims elsewhere), therefore, participate in a global *da'wa* ecosystem. Third, although 'Islamophobia' refers to diverse phenomena and is not unique to the West (consider the status of the above-mentioned Muslims of China, Myanmar and India, or of non-conforming Muslims, like the Ahmadiyya, in Pakistan), Muslim communities in the West have certainly been subject to anti-Muslim hostility and bias, especially since 9/11. The experience of Islamophobia cannot but impact the ways Muslims in the West engage in *da'wa*. Fourth, perhaps most importantly for our purposes, despite their relatively small numbers *vis-à-vis* the total populations of countries such as Britain and the United States, Muslims in the West have exercised a larger and larger footprint within the global Muslim community because of their generally greater wealth, access to education and roles in serving as religio-cultural mediators between the West and the rest of the Muslim world. Indeed, in contrast to the largely negative 'Occidentalism' (viewing the West as the godless, anti-Islamic 'other' of the Muslim world) which can be seen in the writings of many *da'wa* activists,[172] some western Muslims have developed more nuanced approaches to the West. Although Muslim preachers continue to warn of the dangers of an essentially alien 'West', others have argued for authentically European or American Islams.[173] Muslim minorities in the West and their *da'wa* initiatives have been shaped by all of these factors and others. What, then, can be said about western Muslims' *da'wa* initiatives?

Prior to the 1950s, Muslims in the West, particularly in the United States, tended to quietly blend in or assimilate. After 1950, and especially after 1965, there has been a trend towards organising for common action, especially and not surprisingly in the realm of *da'wa*. As a result, countless Muslim advocacy organisations have been founded in western countries, not only to defend the rights of Muslims, but also to engage in missionary outreach. Like the models of activism developed by Muslims in colonial India (see Chapter 6), *da'wa*-minded Muslims in the West have overwhelmingly tended towards 'Meccan' *da'wa*logies. This has followed from a pragmatic acknowledgement that, in the face of western systems of disestablishment and the religious marketplaces that flow from them, *da'wa* has to be carried out in a bottom-up fashion, even if for some the ultimate goal is the far-off dream of the restoration of Islamic dominance. The realities of minoritisation in western contexts perhaps also help to explain the rising prominence of the discourse of 'dialogue' over '*da'wa*' among some western Muslims in recent years.[174] Taking just the United States, some major organisations which engage in *da'wa*, dialogue and other activities include the Ahmadiyya movement in Islam USA, the Muslim Student Association (MSA), the Islamic Society of North America (ISNA), the Council on American–Islamic Relations (CAIR), the Fiqh Council of North America, the Islamic Circle of North America, Islamic Relief USA, Muslims for Progressive Values, the American Muslim Council, the Institute of Islamic Information and Education, As-Sunnah Foundation of America and many others. To these may be added countless mosques, Qur'an schools, Islamic cultural centres and the like, which have sprung up over the past several decades.[175]

The Muslim Community Center (MCC) of Chicago provides an example of a mosque/community centre with a significant local impact.[176] The MCC provides a range of services to Chicago's Sunni Muslims, but also fulfills a *da'wa* mandate to represent Islam in Chicago. The current Imam of the mosque (as of mid-2020), interestingly, was born and raised in the United States and has a degree from none other than the Islamic University of Medina (IUM, see above). I have visited the MCC on several occasions, and on one of these I met Eddie Redzovik, the host of the YouTube *da'wa* program, *The Deen Show*.[177] For a British example, we might look to the Islamic Foundation (IF). The first two directors of the IF in Britain were Khurshid Ahmad and Khurram Murad, both of whom had been disciples of Mawdudi and active in the JI.[178] Ahmad and Murad were particularly attuned to the problems facing Muslim minorities in Britain and through their tireless activism helped to contextualise Islam for a British audience. This effort involved, as with Faruqi in the US (see above), an assumption that Muslims should justify their presence in the West by energetically engaging in *da'wa*. The Islamic Foundation has developed initiatives on Islamic finance, outreach to non-Muslims and an 'inter-faith unit' that pursues dialogues with people of other faiths.[179] For other case studies of *da'wa* in the West, readers may consult a growing body of scholarship.[180]

This brings us to a crucial development which has fed into, and been fed by, the growing involvement of western Muslims in *da'wa*. It will be recalled that colonial-era scholars such as Shah 'Abd al-Aziz and Rashid Rida supported the idea that Muslims could live in non-Muslim societies under non-Muslim rule, provided they were free to publicly practise Islam. Building on these ideas from the first phase of modern *da'wa* and responding to the fact of continuing – and seemingly permanent – Muslim migration to western

7.8 Women and *da'wa*: the contrasting *da'wa*s of Maryam Jameelah and Amina Wadud

Part II has spoken much of the modern democratisation of *da'wa*. This has included efforts by both non-state and state-sponsored groups to mobilise women for *da'wa*. In contrast to pre-modern times, it is now almost universally accepted that Muslim women should be instructed in Islam and should see themselves as missionaries for Islam. However, even if modern *da'wa* has empowered women in some ways, most modern *da'wa* initiatives continue to be male-dominated. Moreover, *da'wa* movements and manuals generally instruct women to limit their *da'wa* to 'appropriate' spheres – the home, or among other women. Here, two Muslim women with powerful, but quite different *da'wa*s are compared.

Maryam Jameelah (1934–2012) was an American Jewish convert to Islam from New York who, after her conversion, moved to Pakistan in 1962. There, she lived with the family of Mawdudi for a time and eventually married a full-time worker in Mawdudi's JI. While raising her family alongside her husband, her zeal for *da'wa* and her incisive intellect drove her to write many books and tracts. Like Mawdudi, Jameelah was strongly critical of 'the West' and saw the 'total system' of Islam as the solution to the world's problems. Jameelah called on Muslim women to reject western ideas about women's liberation and to instead follow traditional Islamic teachings on polygamy, divorce and veiling. For Jameelah, true happiness is to be found in obeying one's husband and father and in fulfilling the duties of wife and mother, as traditionally understood in Islam. What Muslim women need is not western feminism, but a radical commitment to God's will, no matter what western critics might say. Jameelah represents a significant trend among *da'wa*-minded Muslim women today, that of defying what are thought to be 'western' ideas about women and instead calling on women to self-consciously embrace traditional Islamic patriarchy (male leadership in the family and mosque, and male domination of public roles and spaces) as normative and ultimately liberative for women.

Amina Wadud, an African-American convert to and scholar of Islam, has written several seminal books and is a sought-after speaker. In 2005, Wadud made headlines around the world (and won enemies among some conservative Muslims) by serving as the imam (prayer leader, a position traditionally reserved for men) in a mixed-gender Islamic prayer (*salah*) service in New York. In several of her books, *Qur'an and Woman* and *Inside the Gender Jihad*, Wadud argues that the spirit of the Qur'an and life of Muhammad need to be separated from the later male-dominated exegetical tradition of classical Islam. The former, for Wadud, communicates a message of equality between the genders and of empowerment for women, while the latter has been the historical basis for patriarchal attitudes and the oppression of women in Islamic societies. Like Jameelah, then, Wadud draws directly from the early sources, but reaches a different conclusion. Her *da'wa* (or *jihad*, as she calls it in her 2006 book) is for an 'Islamic feminism' which seeks the emancipation of Muslim women, not in secular, but in Islamic terms. She thus rejects both what she calls the 'Islamist women's movement', represented by Jameelah and many others, and what she calls 'Muslim secular feminism'. In between these two options is a third way, 'Islamic feminism'. For Wadud, Islamic feminism is a call both to Islam as a religious way of life (although without patriarchy) *and* human rights (Sources: Jameelah 1976; Esposito and Voll 2001, ch. 3; Wadud 1999; Wadud 2006; Wadud 2012).

countries in the second phase, major Sunni thinkers like 'Ali Nadwi, Yusuf al-Qaradawi, al-Faruqi and Taha al-Alwani developed a new field of Islamic jurisprudence, *fiqh al-aqaliyyāt* or minorities' jurisprudence.[181] *Fatwa*s based on this kind of *fiqh* utilise the Islamic legal principle of *ḍarūra* (necessity) in order to facilitate Muslim life in non-Muslim societies.[182] Embedded in minorities' jurisprudence is both concern and hope. The *concern* is that the 'glittering lights' of the 'immoral' West will seduce Muslims from their faithfulness to Islam and render them fruitless in their witness. The *hope* is that, with proper guidance, Muslims in the West may not only be at ease, but also demonstrate a truly godly life in the West. This is the animating concern, for instance, in Qaradawi's well-known *fiqh* manual *al-ḥarām wa'l-halāl fi'l-Islām* (*The Lawful and the Prohibited in Islam*).[183]

In fact, woven into most versions of *fiqh al-aqaliyyāt* is the idea that Muslims are to live faithfully in the West precisely for the sake of *da'wa*. Muslims in the West, that is, are thought to be ideally situated to bring about the Islamisation of the West. According to this view, western societies (or non-Muslim societies in general) are no longer conceived of as *dar al-harb*, but rather as *dar al-da'wa* (the abode of missionary propagation). Tariq Ramadan has used a similar concept when he calls the West *dar al-shahada* (the abode of Islamic witness).[184] In a significant reversal of major strands of pre-modern Islamic legal thought (see Chapter 3), '[t]he concept of the "missionary migrant" . . . suggests that it is permissible, and even desirable, for Muslims to reside in the West so long as they manage to preserve their Islamic identity . . . and contribute to spreading . . . Islam' (see Text Box 7.9).[185] Closely related to this is a shift we have noted across the Muslim world throughout Part II: the shift from seeing the missionary propagation of Islam as an obligation of some Muslims (*'ulama*, Sufis, Muslim rulers and so on) on behalf of the entire community, to seeing it as a duty of every individual Muslim.[186]

7.9 A sermon to Muslims in the West

The following excerpt is taken from Abu'l-Hasan 'Ali Nadwi's (d. 1999) book *Muslims in the West: The Message and Mission* (1983). It illustrates what we might call *dar al-da'wa* thinking. The book's publication information speaks to the interconnected, polycentric nature of *da'wa* in the second phase – it was edited and translated into English by Khurram Murad, a British Muslim disciple of Mawdudi who headed the Islamic Foundation of Britain. Chapter 8 of the book (from which the excerpt below is taken) is based on a sermon that Nadwi (who was visiting from India) delivered at the Muslim Community Center (MCC, see above) in Chicago in 1977:

You are Muslims. I would therefore start by impressing upon you not to be overwhelmed by western civilization. You are the fruit of the tree of Prophethood. Live here, but keep away from slavish imitation of the West. Derive as much benefit as you can from your stay, but do not be swayed by crude and vulgar materialism. Remember the message of Islam and . . . [do] not feel ashamed of your faith and culture . . . Your stay here is correct; not only justified, but an act of worship if it is a source of preaching and propagation of faith. *But if not, then I have great misgivings . . . [If] you do not take full care to safeguard your religious life and arrange for the religious education and upbringing of your children and make sure that your future generations remain true to Islam, then your living in this country is a sin and you are in grave danger . . . For us Muslims it is permitted to live only in a country where we can live with our distinctive qualities and observe our duties. If it is not possible in this environment or you feel you can't carry out your religious obligations, it is not permissible for you to stay. It is your duty to see that you live here distinctly as Muslims* (emphasis added).

Summary and conclusions

This chapter has surveyed the second phase of modern *da'wa* (*circa* 1950–2020). We began with some major features of the post-colonial context which shaped *da'wa* in new and dynamic ways ('Contextualising Modern *Da'wa* 3'). Then, we turned to a survey of *da'wa* in the second phase under three headings: (1) Non-state initiatives and actors in *da'wa*, (2) State-sponsored initiatives and actors in *da'wa*, and (3) Migration and the *da'wa* initiatives of Muslim-minority populations. Along the way, we encountered an incredibly diverse array of *da'wa* movements and actors: from the non-state 'Meccan' *da'wa*s of the TJ and its imitators to superstar Muslim televangelists and purveyors of *fatwa*s; from the non-state 'Medinan' *da'wa*s of groups like Hizb ut-Tahrir and ISIS to peaceful *da'wa*-oriented humanitarian and development projects such as those sponsored by the Aga Khan; from initiatives sponsored by Muslim-majority states within and outside their borders to the missionary efforts of large organisations like the MWL and OIC; from the continuing *da'wa* impacts of groups like the MB and JI to the diverse efforts of Muslim minority populations in the West. In addition to all this, we have observed *styles* of *da'wa* that range from the use of Islamic pamphlets, websites and science in the Qur'an arguments all the way to the deployment of religious police forces.

In short, it is hoped that this chapter has brought to life the twin facts that *da'wa* is both incredibly widespread and extremely diverse in the modern world. Researching and writing this chapter has certainly made these facts clearer than ever to me. The ubiquity and diversity of *da'wa* also made writing this chapter quite challenging. For every movement, organisation, preacher, website, *da'wa* manual and theologian covered here, many had to be left out. In some cases, movements and actors of great complexity could only be mentioned in passing. Today, *da'wa* movements and organisations (not to mention *da'wa* websites) number not in the dozens or even hundreds, but in the thousands. If we speak of *da'wa* actors, they number not in the thousands, but in the millions – from full-time preachers to the countless Muslim laypeople who do *da'wa* in the course of their everyday lives. Despite these unavoidable limitations, it is hoped that this chapter, when taken in the context of the book as a whole, provides the reader with a useful introduction to the highly significant, vibrant and multifaceted – yet still overlooked and understudied – world of contemporary *da'wa*.

Notes

1. 'In the early twentieth century, there were only fifty or so sovereign states in the world. By the end of decolonisation that number had more than tripled'. Mandaville 2007a, p. 49.
2. Hefner 2011b, pp. 21–2.
3. See also Mandaville 2007a, pp. 148–9.
4. Hirschkind 2006, pp. 44–50.
5. Lapidus 2014, p. 758.
6. Brown 2017, p. 298.
7. Many Muslim-majority states 'retained a modest Islamic façade, incorporating some reference to Islam in their constitutions such as that . . . Shari'a was a source of law, even when it was not'. Esposito 2000, p. 3.
8. Hefner 2011b, p. 20.
9. Sharkey 2005, p. 48. 'Eager . . . to appease Muslim populations and to perform expected

roles as Islam's protectors, [nationalist leaders] set about curtailing Christian evangelization'. See also Sharkey 2013b, pp. 219–20.

10. Sharkey 2013a, p. 14.
11. While the absence of missionaries might have allowed indigenous Christian communities to stand on their own and thrive, they still had to fight the stigma of being associated with missionary Christianity and, by extension, with colonialism.
12. United Nations 1948.
13. Sharkey 2008, pp. 143–7.
14. See, for example, Hackett 2008, pp. 1–14 and notes.
15. For examples, see Shortt 2012, pp. 48, 100–1. See also Goddard 2001, pp. 134–6.
16. Lapidus 2014, p. 522.
17. Hefner 2011b, p. 24.
18. 'Overwhelmingly rural in 1950, by 1990 most Muslim majority countries had 35 to 55 percent of their people crowded into cities . . . suffering the usual ill-effects of pollution, crime and unemployment'. Hefner 2011b, p. 25.
19. Robinson 2008, pp. 259–60.
20. The collapse of the short-lived United Arab Republic (1958–61) was another disappointment.
21. Robinson 2011, p. 6.
22. Ibid., pp. 4–5.
23. Rippin 1993, vol. 2, p. 15.
24. Wiktorowicz 2004, pp. 12–13.
25. Hefner 2011b, p. 25.
26. Wiktorowicz critiques an over-reliance on 'lists of strains and grievances' to explain the Islamic revival. There is, however, no conflict between describing the strains of post-colonial contexts *and* viewing resulting movements as 'as rational, organized manifestations of collective action'. Wiktorowicz 2004, pp. 6–10.
27. A point also made by Mandaville 2007a, pp. 58, 89.
28. These two periods, while similar, still opened up different kinds of 'opportunity structures' for Muslim activism.
29. 'In most countries during its early years, the [Islamic revival] was not . . . primarily political . . . [but] it was inevitable that some actors would . . . redirect [the revival's] energies towards . . . political ends'. Hefner 2011b, p. 31.
30. Particularly in the case of the JI, the movement's popularity and influence (not to mention the global popularisation of Mawdudi's writings) are post-colonial phenomena, more than they had been colonial ones.
31. Mandaville 2007a, pp. 79–83.
32. Weismann 2015, pp. 146–69.
33. Mandaville 2007a, pp. 83–4, 203–4.
34. Khomeini 1981.
35. See the relevant chapters in Keddie 2003.
36. See Green 2015a, pp. 281–8.
37. See, for instance, Gaborieau 2000, pp. 121–38; Flower 2015, pp. 55–82. For a full bibliography on the TJ's international expansion, see Kuiper 2018b.
38. See Chapter 6.
39. Gugler 2010, pp. 99–122.
40. See Dawat-i Islami [n. d.].
41. See Sunni Dawat-i Islami [n. d.].
42. Friedmann 2009, p. 82.

43. In 1964, Malcolm X left the Nation of Islam and began to promote orthodox Sunni Islam. Later, Warith Deen Muhammad moved the Nation of Islam in a more 'orthodox' direction in the 1970s. This prompted Louis Farrakhan to revive the organisation's black nationalist ideas. Mamiya 2009, pp. 235–7.

44. Countless non-state Salafi organisations have been founded around the world in the later twentieth and early twenty-first centuries, many as a result of Salafi splits. For examples, see Meijer 2009.

45. Janson 2003 provides a detailed study of the Islamic Foundation.

46. Poston 1992, p. 78f.

47. Commins 2006, pp. 4–5, 163–71.

48. Antoun 1989.

49. Gaffney 1994; Hirschkind 2006; Mahmood 2005; al-Arian 2014.

50. Millie 2017.

51. Ahmad 2017.

52. Ahmed 2018. See also the general overview in Millie 2007.

53. There are hundreds of Gulen-affiliated schools throughout the world, for instance, in Central Asia and the United States.

54. Deedat 1992.

55. Deedat seems to have borrowed his methods in part from Christian televangelists. On Deedat, see Kuiper 2018a, pp. 187–91; Larkin 2008; Vahed 2009; Sadouni 2011.

56. Kishk's sermons were initially distributed in an *ad hoc* fashion. For Deedat, the use of cassettes was deliberate. See Hirschkind 2006, pp. 58–9; see also Jansen 2009, pp. 354–5.

57. 'The best jihad today', Naik has declared, 'is the *jihad* of *da'wa* . . . conveying the message of Allah to the non-Muslims' On Naik, see Kuiper 2018a, chs 6–7 (for the quote, see p. 238). For Naik's troubles with the Indian government since 2016, see pp. 239–42; see also Kuiper 2017.

58. Olsson 2015; Rock-Singer 2010, pp. 15–37.

59. Hoesterey 2016; Watson 2005, pp. 773–92.

60. One might consider missionary organisations built around Christian evangelists like Billy Graham, Benny Hinn, D. G. S. Dhinakaran, Joyce Meyer and others. Hindu gurus with their own organisations include Sri Sri Ravi Shankar, Asaram Bapu, Baba Ramdev and others.

61. Gräf and Skovgaard-Petersen 2009; Zaman 2012; Tammam 2009; Rock-Singer 2016; Hermansen 2013, pp. 301–18.

62. Kuiper 2018a, p. 219. On *mufti*s in general, see Masud, Messick and Powers 1996.

63. For another example, see Olsson 2014.

64. Poston 1992, ch. 6. See, for example, ISNA, 'Mission and Vision'.

65. Masud 1995a, pp. 352–3.

66. Benthall 2007. For additional examples, see Tugal 2017.

67. Masud 1995a, p. 353.

68. Mandaville 2007a, p. 286.

69. Eid Charity [n. d.].

70. Wahid 2014.

71. Peterson 2009, pp. 200–1.

72. AKDN, 'What We Do'.

73. Aga Khan Hospitals, 'What We Do'; Aga Khan Development Network, 'Trust for Culture'; see also Ismaili Community, [n. d.].

74. Institute of Ismaili Studies [n. d.].

75. Faruqi 1982, p. 42.

76. For him, Islam was the only true religion; all other religions were fatally flawed. He engaged in several dialogues with Christians, including the Chambesy (Switzerland) Dialogue of 1976. See Esposito and Voll 2001, ch. 1.
77. Mandaville 2007a, p. 286.
78. International Institute of Islamic Thought [n. d.].
79. See Abul Hasan Ali Nadwi Center [n. d.]. For more on Nadwi, see Kuiper 2018a, pp. 90–1, 129–31; Hartung 2005; 2004.
80. Wahid 2014, also points to Kuwaiti and Qatari funding and influence in spreading Salafi *da'wa* in Indonesia, for example, through the Kuwait-based Jam'iyyat Ihya' al-Turath al-Islami and the Qatar-based Eid Charity.
81. See Nagata 2009, pp. 436–47.
82. The Association is also known as Darul Arqam (not related to a Malaysian movement of the same name). Interestingly Arqam 'was an early convert to Islam during the first three years of Prophet Muhammad's ministry in Mecca who allowed for his house to be used for the learning and propagation of Islam'. See Muslim Converts' Association of Singapore [n. d.].
83. Commins 2006, pp. 152–3.
84. Lubeck 2011, p. 255.
85. Ahmed 2008a, p. vii.
86. Ahmed 2008b, pp. 3–18.
87. See Hizb ut Tahrir, 'Hizb ut Tahrir', and Hizb ut Tahrir, 'The Reasons'.
88. Mandaville 2007a, p. 266.
89. Ḥizb al-Taḥrīr, Arabic Homepage. On HT in general, see Mandaville 2007a, pp. 265–71.
90. On the origins of the terms 'Salafi-Jihadi' and 'Jihadi-Salafi', see Hegghammer 2009, pp. 251–7.
91. For a longer list, see Jones 2014, pp. 64–5.
92. Kovensky 2014. See also Melhem 2015, pp. 148–53.
93. AlHayat Media (2017b), p. 12.
94. AlHayat Media (2017a), pp. 14–15.
95. See, for example, the 'Letter to Baghdadi' initiative homepage in which diverse Muslims united to repudiate the ideas of ISIS.
96. As to the specific attractions of these kinds of movements, see Mandaville 2007a, pp. 261–5.
97. David Cook writes: 'Does waging militant *jihad* have a future . . . in Islam? I think that it does not . . . the reality is that *jihad* during the past two centuries has been a dismal failure . . . It is difficult to see situations . . . at the present . . . where *jihad* is likely to gain the Muslim community anything . . .' Cook 2005, p. 164.
98. 'Post-Islamism' was coined by Asef Bayat. See also Roy 2004. Shavit 2014 speaks of a comparable shift among '*wasaṭi* (middle way) Islamists': 'Faced with his movement's failures to capture power, the mainstream (*wasaṭi*) Islamist . . . shifted from political revolutionary activism to . . . populist . . . advocacy'. See also Mandaville 2007a, pp. 343–8.
99. Mandaville 2014.
100. 'While I do not think that *jihad* has a future . . . I also do not think that there is any doubt that it will continue . . . simply because it is too well attested in the Arabic Muslim sources'. Cook 2005, p. 165.
101. This is not to suggest that governments have been driven merely by cynical and never by pious motives.
102. N. Brown 2017, pp. 1–2.
103. Sheline 2017.

104. Engelcke 2017.
105. See Pakistan Ministry of Religious Affairs [n. d.].
106. See, for instance, Putz 2019.
107. Lepeska 2015.
108. Van Bruinessen 2018.
109. See Saudi Arabia, Government of [n. d.].
110. Teitelbaum 2002, pp. 222–39.
111. Commins 2006, pp. 152–3.
112. Farquhar 2017; Commins 2006, pp. 126–9.
113. Farquhar 2017, pp. 87–8.
114. Examples include the Amman Message of 2004 sponsored by the Jordanian monarchy and the Marrakesh Declaration of 2016 sponsored by the king of Morocco.
115. N. Brown 2017, pp. 24–5.
116. See International Islamic University, Islamabad [n. d.].
117. Run by the government-sponsored Al-Najat Charity, dawahskills provides practical tips and tools to help Muslims preach Islam effectively. See Dawahskills [n. d.].
118. IslamWeb [n. d.].
119. For case studies, see Hefner 2011a.
120. For a journalistic overview, BBC Monitoring 2016.
121. Thielmann 2017.
122. See, for example, Salvá 2017.
123. Brown 2017, p. 3.
124. See Campo 2016, pp. 57–9.
125. Hedin, Janson and Westerlund 2004, p. 173.
126. Commins 2006, p. 152.
127. Ibid., pp. 152–3.
128. Teitelbaum 2002, p. 226.
129. By the time of King Faisal's assassination in March 1975, 'he had put Saudi Arabia at the center of a robust set of pan-Islamic institutions . . . [and] made Saudi Arabia a significant player in . . . international affairs'. Commins 2006, p. 153.
130. Afzal 2019, p. 2.
131. Zaman 2002, p. 175.
132. Jamia Tus Salafiah [n. d.].
133. See Bonnefoy 2009, pp. 332–3.
134. See Muslim World League (hereafter MWL), 'World Supreme Council for Mosques'.
135. MWL, 'International Organization for Relief'.
136. MWL, 'Islamic Fiqh Council'.
137. MWL, 'International Organization for the Holy Quran and Immaculate Sunnah'.
138. Schulze 1995, p. 349.
139. See International Commission on Scientific Signs in Qur'an and Sunna, [n. d.]
140. If Muslim leaders cannot deny the political might of the West and the dominance of western science, then at least they can assert that the Qur'an and classical Islamic civilisation anticipated the West's accomplishments.
141. Bucaille 1976.
142. Bucaille 1978.
143. This quote is taken from This is Truth [n. d.] As for Bucaille's popularity, Ahmad Dallal writes, 'Bucaille's book . . . has been extremely popular and has inspired an almost cultic following among large numbers of Muslims all over the world'. Dallal 2001, pp. 552–3.
144. On Bucaille, see Bigliardi 2012, pp. 248–63; Sternberg 1996; Dallal 2001, pp. 554–5.

145. See Golden 2002. Golden looks at how the Commission brought western scientists to con-ferences and videotaped them making statements about the Qur'an's scientific accuracy. Several of these non-Muslim scientists later claimed that their comments were taken out of context. See also Ibrahim 1997, a *da'wa* booklet that contains quotes from these very scientists. Pervez Hoodhbhoy, a scientist and critic of Bucailleism, writes sarcastically: 'Provided one learns one's Arabic properly, and does a correct exegesis of the *Quran*, then out will pop the Big Bang Theory, black holes, quantum mechanics, DNA . . . and whatever your heart desires. Dozens of conferences have had this message . . . but perhaps none can rival the grand First International Conference on Scientific Miracles of The Holy Quran and Sunnah . . . [held] in Islamabad in 1987'. Hoodhbhoy 2005, pp. 215–19.

146. This special edition, which was co-written by 'Abul Majid al-Zindani, alternates chapters of standard science written by Moore with Zindani's 'Islamic additions' on the Qur'an. Moore and Zindani 1983.

147. King Faisal Prize [n. d.].

148. For a general introduction, see Choudhury and Khan 2009, pp. 267–75; Darwich 2016, pp. 824–5.

149. Organization of Islamic Cooperation (hereafter OIC), 'History'.

150. The Preamble commits each member 'to respect, safeguard and defend the national sover-eignty, independence and territorial integrity of all Member States'. OIC, 'Charter'.

151. OIC, 'Charter'. Further statements indicate that the OIC is committed 'to inculcate in [Muslim youth] Islamic values' and 'to assist Muslim minorities . . . to preserve their dignity . . . and religious identity'.

152. OIC, 'Dawa Activities'.

153. OIC, 'Specialized Organs'. Another organisation of the OIC is the humanitarian Islamic Committee of the International Crescent (ICIC).

154. At its 2013 summit in Cairo, the OIC commended the Observatory. See OIC, 'Cairo Final Communique', sections 97–112.

155. For useful definitions and discussion, see Shryock 2010.

156. See, for instance, Islamic Pamphlets [n. d.]; see also Naik 2009.

157. KAICIID Dialogue Centre [n. d.].

158. In official OIC documents from the 1970s and 1980s, the word *da'wa* occurs frequently. In recent years, by contrast, 'dialogue' seems to have replaced *da'wa*. Janson notes a similar phenomenon in the Islamic Foundation in Britain after 2000. Janson 2003, pp. 169–70, ch. 8.

159. Kramer 1995, p. 309.

160. Schulze 1995, p. 348.

161. Mattes 2009, pp. 7–8.

162. For details, see Amoretti 2009, pp. 438–9.

163. In its heyday, '[t]he WICS sent staffers out to build mosques and provide humanitarian relief. It gave poor students a free university education . . . Its missionaries traversed Africa preaching a moderate . . . version of Islam as an alternative to the strict Wahhabism that Saudi Arabia was spreading . . . The Vatican counted it among its partners in Christian-Muslim dialogue . . . But the Society had a darker side that occasionally flashed into view. In Africa, rumors abounded for years of Society staffers paying off . . . politicians or supporting insurgent[s] . . . In 2011, Canada stripped the local Society office of its charity status after it found the director had diverted Society money to a radical group . . .' Heneghan 2012.

164. 'Rather than scrap the Society as a Gaddafi-tainted institution, the government is pursuing a modest purge'. Heneghan 2012.

165. See Ministry of Culture and Islamic Guidance [n. d.].
166. Islamic Culture and Religious Organization, Homepage.
167. Kramer 1995, pp. 310–11.
168. Malik 2018, p. 243.
169. On Muslim migration to Europe, particularly Britain, see Janson, *Your Cradle*, ch. 5. See also University of Minnesota Immigration History Research Center (2015).
170. The Immigration and Nationality Act of 1965 (or Hart-Celler Act) established a policy based on skilled labour. On Muslims in America, see Curtis 2009.
171. Dannin 2002. In this classic study, Dannin explores the phenomena of black American conversion to Islam and asks why African-Americans would 'fashion themselves into a double minority by converting to Islam' (p. 4).
172. Some of this is traceable to thinkers like Sayyid Qutb who harboured particular hostility toward the West. Thanks in part to the influence of Mawdudi and ʿAli Nadwi, Qutb equated the West with *jahiliyya* (ignorance) after he spent time in the US in the 1940s. See Qutb 2000.
173. For example, Tariq Ramadan. See Voll 2016, pp. 1250–53.
174. Kuiper 2018a, pp. 25, 87, 104, 106; also Weismann 2019.
175. See Moore 2013.
176. Muslim Community Center [n. d.].
177. Deen Show [n. d.].
178. See Esposito and Voll 2001, ch. 2. See also, Poston 1992, ch. 5, and Janson 2003, ch. 6.
179. Although the Islamic Foundation uses 'dialogue' for its inter-faith work, the predominant concern seems to be preaching Islam. Janson 2003, ch. 6. Similar dynamics can be observed in American Muslim organisations. See Poston 1992, ch. 6
180. See, for instance, Gerholm and Lithman 1988; Haddad and Smith 1993; Hamid 2016; Janson 2003; Metcalf 1996; Ortega and Peter 2014; Poston 1992; Reetz 2007; Shavit 2014; Wiedl 2015; Howe 2018; Howe 2019. For scholarship on the TJ in the West, see Kuiper 2018b.
181. Al-Alwani 2003.
182. Such concessions, for instance, give Muslims in the West latitude with respect to banking, food and other areas.
183. al-Qaradawi 1994.
184. Ramadan 2004.
185. Shavit 2014, pp. 139, 145.
186. In Islamic legal terms, the shift is from 'collective obligation' or *farḍ al-kifaya* to 'individual obligation' or *farḍ al-ʿayn*.

Conclusion

This book began with the claim that there is a discernible (if non-linear and incredibly complex) story of *da'wa* in Islam from the Qur'an to the present. Although so much of modern *da'wa*, as surveyed in Chapters 5 through 7, can be interpreted as representing a transformation of, or break with, Islam's pre-modern missionary patterns and precedents, there is still significant continuity to be observed. However modern they are and however novel their missionary strategies may be in the context of Islamic missionary history as a whole, *da'wa*-minded Muslims over the past century and a half have been very self-conscious about rooting their practices in the Qur'an and *sunna* of the Prophet Muhammad and other canonical Islamic sources.

In many other instances in which modern Muslims have not drawn explicitly on pre-modern *da'wa* precedents, we have seen how history has nevertheless repeated itself in interesting ways (for instance, the ways the 'Abbasid and Fatimid pattern of *da'wa*, or Chapter 4's 'agents and patterns' have been reprised in modernity). Although the scale and diversity of *da'wa* today is truly unprecedented, the Islamic call to submit to the One God and to heed his Prophet continues to flow in 'Meccan' channels (*da'wa* as missionary invitation) and 'Medinan' channels (*da'wa* as religio-political summons), to involve Muslim governments and non-state actors, to constitute an arena of both internal and external outreach, to involve debate and dialogue with other religious paths, and ultimately to aim for the realisation of God's will on earth – just as it is remembered to have been carried out in time of the Prophet himself and, with many twists and turns, in subsequent Islamic history. From a historical perspective, then, and certainly in the religious imagination of many Muslims today, it seems evident that, whatever the future may hold in the ongoing story of *da'wa*, today's *da'wa* movements and actors, for all their diversity, should be seen as bearers of Islam's missionary legacy and participants in the missionary drama which began in Mecca fourteen hundred years ago.

Epilogue
COVID-19 and *da'wa*

Such was the final paragraph of this book as of early spring 2020. Then came the COVID-19 pandemic. It is worth adding a few a few final comments on Muslim responses to COVID-19, insofar as they underscore several of the observations made in the previous paragraphs and throughout Part II of this book. To start with, it should be stressed that there has been no one Muslim experience of, or response to the pandemic. As this book has repeatedly demonstrated, the world's Muslims are incredibly diverse. They reside in every region of the world, in both urban and rural settings, speak hundreds of languages, are divided on theological and sectarian grounds, and exemplify a variety of orientations towards modernity. There are destitute Muslims and fabulously rich Muslims and Muslims of every socio-economic status in between. While there are many who have had the luxury of reflecting on COVID-19 while 'sheltering in place' in relative safety, many others have had no such luxury. For the millions of Muslim refugees around the world today, particularly those living in crowded camps, COVID-19 has been an immediate and existential threat.

For those Muslims in a position to reflect and take action, however, there has been no shortage of responses to the crisis. Both non-state and state-sponsored Islamic organisations on the local, national and global levels – including many of those discussed in Chapters 6 and 7 – have issued guidance in the form of *fatwa*s, articles and sermons to help Muslims stay safe, overcome loneliness and face anxiety with trust in God.[1] They have even offered tips on educating one's children or getting along with one's relatives when homebound. Islamic relief organisations have appealed for 'Coronavirus aid', *da'wa*-oriented websites have published articles on keeping the faith in trying times, Muslim preachers have delivered online sermons on the spiritual meaning of the pandemic,[2] and *da'wa* groups like Indonesia's Muslimat NU (see Ch. 6) have taken to the streets to distribute masks free of charge.[3] While some *da'wa* groups such as the TJ,[4] and some mosque leaders around the world[5] have been criticised for carrying on with their gatherings and activities regardless of governments' social distancing orders,[6] a consensus seems to have developed among many Muslim organisations and leaders regarding the priority that Islamic law places on the preservation of human life and thus on the permissibility of Muslims staying home and performing legally acceptable alternatives to gathering with fellow Muslims for Friday prayer or breaking the daily fast of Ramadan (which began on 23 April 2020). Interestingly, the latter have drawn on the Qur'an and hadith, particularly on hadith reports dealing with plagues from the time of the Prophet and Companions, to make their arguments. It remains undecided (as of the time of writing) whether the *hajj*, scheduled for late July 2020, will be called off in light of these considerations.[7] In any event, these developments show once again the adaptability of Islamic legal and ethical thinking in the face of new circumstances – something this book has emphasised in several places.

Among the concerns which have informed this pandemic-prompted out-pouring of Islamic reflection and guidance has been the desire to help Muslims continue to fulfill God's commands under these circumstances, *including* God's command to engage in *da'wa*. Indeed, a number of Muslim groups have argued that the pandemic provides an opportunity for what this book has called internal and external *da'wa*, insofar as Muslims and non-Muslims may be more inclined to think about death, heaven and hell, and their standing before God. Similarly, COVID-19 has been interpreted as a test from God to make Muslims more pious and committed to living out and sharing their faith, and as a 'wake-up call' to non-Muslims. Among many examples,[8] we might draw special attention to 'A Message to Humanity: COVID19'. Written and undersigned by an inter-national team of Muslim scholars and *da'wa* luminaries, such as Yasir Qadhi (USA), Taqi Usmani (Pakistan), Zakir Naik (India/Malaysia), Hussein Yee (Malaysia), Abdur Raheem Green (UK), Shadi Alsuleiman (Australia), Ibrahim Saleh Alhussaini (Nigeria) and others, this 'Message' constitutes a stirring call (or *da'wa*) to believe in the One God and his last Prophet, Muhammad.[9] According to the authors, COVID-19 has shown humanity how frail we are, and the pan-demic should have the effect of directing our thoughts to God, death and final accountability. Just as we are dependent on 'trustworthy' experts in science to instruct us during the pandemic, humans should look to 'trustworthy' guides in ultimate matters of faith. For the authors, the greatest expert in that realm is the Prophet Muhammad. With frequent reference to verses from the Qur'an and ocassional swipes at 'polytheism' and 'atheism', the authors argue: 'The choice is ours. We can accept the fact that God is the only deity worthy of worship and that Prophet Muhammad (may God's peace and blessings be upon him) is His final messenger, or we can reject the truth and by virtue of that risk punishment from God . . . Now is the time to believe'. 'A Message to Humanity: COVID19' is available in ten major languages, and its website, amessagetohumanity.com, directs curious readers to explicit *da'wa* websites such as gainpeace.org and why-islam.org. In the midst of intitiatives like these, some militant Islamist groups have suggested that the pandemic is God's punishment on the West, or perhaps God's punishment on wayward Muslims; in any case, it provides a fresh oppor-tunity for *da'wa* or recruitment to their causes.[10]

This recent global challenge, in other words, has prompted Muslims of diverse orientations to engage with Islamic scripture, tradition and law the way they always have: with creativity and diversity. In the midst of all this, it will come as no surprise to readers of this book that *da'wa* is once again proving to be an attractive resource to contemporary Muslims, whatever their background or religious orientation. In short, Muslims have faced COVID-19 as they have faced challenges throughout the modern period: as diverse stewards of the scriptural, legal *and missionary* heritage of Islam.

Notes

1. For numerous examples of Coronavirus *fatwa*s and religious guidance, see the useful database developed by Freidenreich 2020. See also Fiqh Council of North America 2020, IslamQA 2020. For MWL and OIC responses, see MWL, 'Corona'; OIC, 'Extraordinary videoconference'.
2. See, for example, Islamic Relief Worldwide [n. d.]; Muslim Aid [n. d.], Aga Khan Development Network: 'COVID-19'.
3. NU Online 2020.
4. See BBC News 2020. As a transnational organisation, the TJ has had no singular response to COVID-19. The response of TJ groups in different parts of the world is evolving.
5. Abi Habib and ur-Rehman 2020.
6. Indeed, in certain locations, Muslim minorities have had to respond to Islamophobic insinuations that they are to blame for the outbreak. See, for instance, Frayer 2020.
7. See Moosa 2020.
8. Of many online articles on this theme, see, for example, Alasry 2020; Husain 2020.
9. See Various Authors 2020.
10. See Burke 2020.

Bibliography

Abed, Shukri (2009), 'Arab-Israeli Conflict', in John Esposito (ed.), *The Oxford Encyclopedia of the Islamic World*, Oxford: Oxford University Press, vol. 1, pp. 173–84.

Abi Habib, Maria and Zia ur-Rehman (2020), 'Imams Overrule Pakistan's Coronavirus Lockdown as Ramadan Nears', *The New York Times*, 23 April, available at: https://www.nytimes.com/2020/04/23/world/asia/pakistan-coronavirus-ramadan.html?action=click&module=Top%20Stories&pgtype=Homepage, last accessed 25 April 2020.

Abou El Fadl, Khaled (1994), 'Islamic Law and Muslim Minorities: The Juristic Discourse on Muslim Minorities from the Second/Eighth to the Eleventh/Seventeenth Centuries', *Islamic Law and Society* 1(2): 141–87.

Abou Ramadan, Moussa (2018), 'Muslim Jurists Criteria for the Division of the World into Dar al-Harb and Dar al-Islam', in M. Koskenniemi, M. Garcia-Salmones Rovira and P. Amorosa (eds), *International Law and Religion: Historical and Contemporary Perspectives*, Oxford: Oxford University Press, pp. 219–35.

Abū Dāwūd (2008), *Sunan Abū Dāwud: English-Arabic Text*, trans. Mohammad Mahdi al-Sharif, Beirut: Dār al-Kutub al-ʿIlmiyya.

Abu-Lughod, Janet (1991), *Before European Hegemony: The World System A.D. 1250–1350*, Oxford: Oxford University Press.

Abul Hasan Ali Nadwi Center for Research, Dawah, and Islamic Thought [n. d.], Homepage, available at: https://abulhasanalinadwi.org/, last accessed 18 December 2019.

Abun-Nasr, Jamil (2007), *Muslim Communities of Grace: The Sufi Brotherhoods in Islamic Religious Life*, New York: Columbia University Press.

Aflākī, Shams al-Dīn Aḥmad-e (2002), *Manāqeb al-ʿArefīn: Feats of the Knowers of God*, trans., John O'Kane, Leiden: Brill.

Afzal, Madiha (2019), 'Saudi Arabia's Hold on Pakistan', Brookings Institution Policy Reports, May, available at: https://www.brookings.edu/research/saudi-arabias-hold-on-pakistan/, last accessed 8 January 2020.

Aga Khan Hospitals, 'What We Do', available at: https://www.agakhanhospitals.org/Home/AboutUs, last accessed 14 December 2019.

Aga Khan Development Network, 'About the Aga Khan Trust for Culture', available at: https://www.akdn.org/our-agencies/aga-khan-trust-culture, last accessed 14 December 2019.

Aga Khan Development Network, 'AKDN updates: COVID-19', available at: https://
www.akdn.org/akdn-updates-covid-19, last accessed 27 April 2020.

Aga Khan Development Network, 'What We Do', available at: https://www.akdn.org/
about-us/organisation-information, last accessed 14 December 2019.

Ahmad, Atiya (2017), *Everyday Conversions: Islam, Domestic Work and South Asian Migrant
Women in Kuwait*, Durham: Duke University Press.

Ahmad, Irfan (2011), *Islamism and Democracy in India: The Transformation of Jamaat-e-Islami*,
Princeton: Princeton University Press.

Ahmad, Mumtaz (1991), 'Islamic Fundamentalism in South Asia: The Jamaat-Islami
and the Tablighi Jama'at of South Asia', in Martin Marty and Scott Appleby
(eds), *Fundamentalisms Observed*, Chicago: University of Chicago Press, pp.
457–530.

Ahmad, Mirza Ghulam (2006), *Government Angrezi aur Jihad*, translated by T. S. Ahmad.
Islamabad: Islam International.

Ahmed, Chanfi (2008a), 'Introduction to Special Issue: Performing Islamic Revival in
Africa', *Africa Today* 54(4): vii–xiii.

Ahmed, Chanfi (2008b), 'The Wahuburi wa Kislamu (Preachers of Islam) in East
Africa', *Africa Today* 54(4): 3–18.

Ahmed, Chanfi (2018), *Preaching Islamic Revival in East Africa*, Newcastle: Cambridge
Scholars Publishing.

Alasry, Hana (2020), 'How Muslims Should Behave During COVID-19 Outbreak',
AboutIslam.net, 26 March, available at: https://aboutislam.net/shariah/refine-
your-heart/advice/how-muslim-should-behave-during-covid-19–outbreak/, last
accessed 25 April 2020.

Algar, Hamid (1988/2000), 'Barda and Barda-dāri: Regulations Governing Slavery
in Islamic Jurisprudence', *Encyclopaedia Iranica*, vol. III/7, pp. 776–9, available at:
http://www.iranicaonline.org/articles/barda-vi, last accessed 14 June 2019.

Algar, Hamid (1993/2011), 'Dār al-Ḥarb', *Enclopaedia Iranica*, vol. VI/6, pp. 668–9,
available at: http://www.iranicaonline.org/articles/dar-al-harb-the-realm-of-war-
lands-not-under-islamic-rule-a-juridical-term-for-certain-non-muslim-territory-
though-of, last accessed 16 April 2019.

Algar, Hamid (1960–2007), 'Naḳshband', in P. Bearman, T. Bianquis, C. E. Bosworth,
E. van Donzel and W. P. Heinrichs (eds), *Encyclopaedia of Islam, Second Edition*, Leiden:
Brill, vol. 7, pp. 933–4.

AlHayat Media Center (2017a), *Rumiyah* 5 (Rabi' al-Akhir 1438/Winter 2017).

AlHayat Media Center 2017b, *Rumiyah* 10 (Ramadan 1438/Spring 2017).

Al-Jazeera English (2020), 'China emerges as coronavirus scapegoat in US election
campaign', 7 April 2020, available at: https://www.msn.com/en-us/news/world/
china-emerges-as-coronavirus-scapegoat-in-us-election-campaign/ar-BB12NpmZ,
last accessed 27 April 2020.

'Ali, 'Abdullah Yusuf (1989), *The Meaning of the Holy Qur'an*, translated with commentary
by 'Abdullah Yusuf 'Ali, Maryland: Amana Corp.

Ali, Kecia (2014), *The Lives of Muhammad*, Cambridge, MA: Harvard University Press.

Alim.org [n. d.], 'Khalifa Abu Bakr - Before and After Conversion to Islam', available at: http://www.alim.org/library/biography/khalifa/content/KAB/1/2, last accessed 1 November 2018.

Allsen, Thomas (2009), 'Mongols as Vectors for Cultural Transmission', in Nicola di Cosmo, Allen Frank and Peter Golden (eds), *The Cambridge History of Inner Asia: The Chinggisid Age*, Cambridge: Cambridge University Press, pp. 135–54.

Al-Alwānī, Taha (2003), *Towards a Fiqh for Minorities: Some Basic Reflections*, Washington, DC: International Institute of Islamic Thought.

Amoretti, Biancamaria (2009), 'Qadhdhāfī, Muʿammar Al-', in John Esposito (ed.), *The Oxford Encyclopedia of the Islamic World*, Oxford: Oxford University Press, vol. 4, pp 437–9.

Anderson, Benedict (1991), *Imagined Communities: Reflections on the Origin and Spread of Nationalism*, New York: Verso.

Antoun, Richard (1989), *Muslim Preacher in the Modern World: A Jordanian Case Study in Comparative Perspective*, Princeton: Princeton University Press.

al-Arian, Abdullah (2014), *Answering the Call: Popular Islamic Activism in Sadat's Egypt*, New York: Oxford University Press.

Arnold, Thomas (1896/1913/2012), *The Preaching of Islam: A History of the Propagation of the Muslim Faith*, New York: Scribners (1st ed., 1896); London: Constable (2nd ed., 1913); New Delhi: Adam Publishers (2012 reprint of 2nd ed.).

Ayalon, David (1999), 'The Mamluks: The Mainstay of Islam's Military Might', in Shaun Marmon (ed.), *Slavery in the Islamic Middle East*, Princeton: Marcus Wiener, pp. 89–117.

Baron, Beth (2013), 'The Port Said Orphan Scandal of 1933: Colonialism, Islamism, and the Egyptian Welfare State', in Heather Sharkey (ed.), *Cultural Conversions: Unexpected Consequences of Christian Missionary Encounters in the Middle East, Africa, and South Asia*, Syracuse: Syracuse University Press, pp. 121–38.

Bartholomew, Robert (2020), 'The Coronavirus and the Search for Scapegoats', *Psychology Today*, 6 February, available at: https://www.psychologytoday.com/us/blog/its-catching/202002/the-coronavirus-and-the-search-scapegoats, last accessed 27 April 2020.

Bates, Crispin (2007), *Subalterns and the Raj: South Asia since 1600*, London: Routledge.

Bauman, Zygmunt (2000), *Liquid Modernity*, Malden: Blackwell.

Bayly, C. A. (2004), *The Birth of the Modern World, 1780–1914: Global Connections and Comparisons*, Oxford: Blackwell.

Bāz, ʿAbd al-Azīz b. (1998), *Words of Advice Regarding Daʿwah*, trans. Bint Feroz Deen and Bint ʿAbd al-Ghafoor, Birmingham: Al-Hidaya.

BBC Monitoring (2016), 'Who are the Islamic 'Morality Police'?' BBC News, 22 April, available at: https://www.bbc.com/news/world-middle-east-36101150, last accessed 2 January 2020.

BBC News (2020), 'Tablighi Jamaat: the group blamed for new COVID-19 outbreak in India', 2 April, https://www.bbc.com/news/world-asia-india-52131338, last accessed 25 April 2020.

Benthall, Jonathan (2007), 'Charity since 1900', in Kate Fleet, Gudrun Krämer, Denis Matringe, John Nawas and Everett Rowson (eds), *Encyclopaedia of Islam, Three*, Leiden: Brill, available at: http://dx.doi.org.proxy.library.nd.edu/10.1163/1573–3912_ei3_COM_27603, first published online, 2016, last accessed 23 May 2019.

Berend, Nora, ed. (2007), *Christianization and the Rise of Christian Monarchy: Scandinavia, Central Europe and Rus' c. 900–1200*, Cambridge: Cambridge University Press.

Berger, Peter (1969), *The Sacred Canopy: Elements of a Sociological Theory of Religion*, New York: Anchor.

Berger, Peter (1977), *Facing up to Modernity*, New York: Basic Books.

Berger, Peter (2008), 'Secularization Falsified', *First Things*, February, available at: http://www.firstthings.com/article/2008/02/002–secularization-falsified, last accessed 28 January 2020.

Berkey, Jonathan (2001), *Popular Preaching and Religious Authority in the Medieval Islamic Near East*, Seattle: University of Washington Press.

Berkey, Jonathan (2003), *The Formation of Islam: Religion and Society in the Near East, 600–1800*, New York: Cambridge University Press.

Berkey, Jonathan (2004), 'Education', in Richard C. Martin (ed.), *Encyclopedia of Islam and the Muslim World*, New York: Macmillan, vol. 1, pp. 202–6.

Berkwitz, Stephen (2008), 'Religious Conflict and the Politics of Conversion in Sri Lanka', in Rosalind Hackett (ed.), *Proselytization Revisited: Rights, Free Markets, and Culture Wars*, London: Equinox, pp. 199–230.

Beyer, Peter (2005), 'Globalization and Religion', in Lindsay Jones (ed.), *Encyclopedia of Religion*, 2nd ed., Detroit: Macmillan.

Bigliardi, Stephano (2012), 'The Strange Case of Dr. Bucaille: Notes for a Re-examination', *The Muslim World* 102: 248–63.

Biran, Michael (2016), 'The Islamisation of Hülegü: Imaginary Conversion in the Ilkhanate', *Journal of the Royal Asiatic Society* 3(26): 79–88.

Blankenship, Khalid (1994), T*he End of the Jihad State: The Reign of Hisham Ibn 'Abd al-Malik and the Collapse of the Umayyads*, Albany: State University of New York Press.

Bonnefoy, Laurent (2009), 'How Transnational is Salafism in Yemen?' in Roel Meijer (ed.), *Global Salafism: Islam's New Religious Movement*, New York: Columbia University Press, pp. 321–41.

Bonner, Michael and Gottfried Hagen (2010), 'Muslim Accounts of the Dār al-Ḥarb', *The New Cambridge History of Islam, Vol. 4*, Cambridge: Cambridge University Press, pp. 474–94.

Bosworth, C., W. Heffening and M. Shatzmiller (1960–2007), 'Tidjāra', in P. Bearman, T. Bianquis, C. E. Bosworth, E. van Donzel and W. P. Heinrichs (eds), *Encyclopaedia of Islam, Second Edition*, Leiden: Brill, vol. 10, pp. 466–75.

Bosworth, C. E. (1996), *The New Islamic Dynasties*, New York: Columbia University Press.

Bro, Thyge (2004), 'Travel and Travellers', in Richard C. Martin (ed.),

Encyclopedia of Islam and the Muslim World, New York: Macmillan, vol. 2, 698–9.

Brockopp, Jonathan (2001), 'Slaves and Slavery', in Jane McAuliffe (ed.), *Encyclopedia of the Qur'an*, Leiden: Brill, vol. 5, pp. 56–60.

Brockopp, Jonathan, ed. (2010), *The Cambridge Companion to Muḥammad*, Cambridge: Cambridge University Press.

Brown, Daniel (1999), *Rethinking Tradition in Modern Islamic Thought*, Cambridge: Cambridge University Press.

Brown, Daniel (2017), *A New Introduction to Islam*, 3rd ed., Oxford: Wiley.

Brown, Nathan (2017), *Official Islam in the Arab World: The Contest for Religious Authority*, Washington DC: Carnegie Endowment for International Peace, available at: https://carnegieendowment.org/files/CP306_Brown_Religious_Institutions_Final_Web1.pdf, last accessed 29 December 2019.

Brown, Peter (1981), *The Cult of the Saints: Its Rise and Function in Latin Christianity*, Chicago: University of Chicago Press.

Browne, Lawrence E. (1933), *The Eclipse of Christianity in Asia from the Time of Muhammad till the Fourteenth Century*, Cambridge: Cambridge University Press.

Bruce, Steve (1990), *Pray TV: Televangelism in America*, London: Routledge.

Brunschvig, R. (1960–2007), '"Abd', in P. Bearman, T. Bianquis, C. E. Bosworth, E. van Donzel and W. P. Heinrichs (eds), *Encyclopaedia of Islam, Second Edition*, Leiden: Brill, vol. 1, pp. 24–40.

Bucaille, Maurice (1976), *La Bible, La Coran, et La Science*, Paris: Seghers.

Bucaille, Maurice (1978), *The Bible, The Qur'an and Science*, Paris: Seghers.

al-Bukhārī, Muhammad (1420/1999), *Ṣaḥīḥ* Beirut: Dār al-Kutub al-'Ilmiyya. English translation: Muhammad Muhsin Khan, Riyadh: Darussalam, 1997.

Bulliet, Richard W. (1979), *Conversion to Islam in the Medieval Period: An Essay in Quantitative History*, Cambridge, MA: Harvard University Press.

Bulliet, Richard W. (2010), 'Conversion to Islam', in David Morgan and Anthony Reid (eds), *The New Cambridge History of Islam, Vol. 3*, Cambridge: Cambridge University Press, pp. 529–38.

Bunt, Gary (2006), 'Towards an Islamic Information Revolution?' in Liz Poole and John Richardson (eds), *Muslims in the News Media*, London: I. B. Tauris, pp. 153–64.

Burke, Jason (2020), 'Opportunity or threat? How Islamic extremists are reacting to coronavirus', *The Guardian*, 16 April, available at: https://www.theguardian.com/world/2020/apr/16/opportunity-or-threat-how-islamic-extremists-reacting-coronavirus, last accessed 25 April 2020.

Campo, Juan (2016), 'Arab League', in Richard C. Martin (ed.), *Encyclopedia of Islam and the Muslim World*, 2nd ed., New York: Macmillan, vol. 1, pp. 57–9.

Canard, M. (1960–2007), '*Da'wa*', P. Bearman, T. Bianquis, C. E. Bosworth, E. van Donzel and W. P. Heinrichs (eds), *Encyclopaedia of Islam, Second Edition*, Leiden: Brill, vol. 2, pp. 168–70.

Chabbi, Jacqueline (1960–2007), 'Khānḳāh', in P. Bearman, T. Bianquis, C. E.

Bosworth, E. van Donzel and W. P. Heinrichs (eds), *Encyclopaedia of Islam, Second Edition*, Leiden: Brill, vol. 4, pp. 1025–6.

Chabbi, Jacqueline (2007), '"Abd al-Qādir al-Jīlānī', in Kate Fleet, Gudrun Krämer, Denis Matringe, John Nawas and Everett Rowson (eds), *Encyclopedia of Islam, Three*, Leiden: Brill, available at: http://dx.doi.org.proxy.library.nd.edu/10.1163/1573-3912_ei3_COM_22592, last accessed 24 May 2019.

Chande, Abdin (2004), 'African Culture and Islam', in Richard C. Martin (ed.), *Encyclopedia of Islam and the Muslim World*, New York: Macmillan, vol. 1, pp. 19–24.

Chatterjee, Partha (1993), 'Whose Imagined Community?' in *The Nation and Its Fragments: Colonial and Postcolonial Histories*, Princeton: Princeton University Press, pp. 3–13.

Chaumont, E. (1960–2007), 'Al-Salaf wa'l-Khalaf', in P. Bearman, T. Bianquis, C. E. Bosworth, E. van Donzel and W. P. Heinrichs (eds), *Encyclopaedia of Islam, Second Edition*, Leiden: Brill, vol. 8, p. 900.

Chittick, William (2009), 'Sufism: Sufi Thought and Practice', in John Esposito (ed.), *The Oxford Encyclopedia of the Islamic World*, Oxford: Oxford University Press, vol. 5, pp. 207–16.

Choudhury, Golam and Saad Khan (2009), 'Organization of the Islamic Conference', in John Esposito (ed.), *The Oxford Encyclopedia of the Islamic World*, Oxford: Oxford University Press, vol. 4, pp. 267–75.

Christian Mission and Islamic Da'wa: Proceedings of the Chambesy Dialogue Consultation, Leicester: The Islamic Foundation, 1982.

Chrysostomides, Anna (2017), ' "There is no god but God": Religious Code-Switching, Eighth to Tenth Centuries', in A. C. S. Peacock (ed.), *Islamisation: Comparative Perspectives from History*, Edinburgh: Edinburgh University Press, pp. 118–33.

Commins, David (2006), *The Wahhabi Mission and Saudi Arabia*, London: I. B. Tauris.

Constable, Olivia (2010), 'Muslim Trade in the Medieval Mediterranean', in Manibel Fierro (ed.), *The New Cambridge History of Islam, Vol. 2*, Cambridge: Cambridge University Press, pp. 633–47.

Cook, David (2005), *Understanding Jihad*, Berkeley: University of California Press.

Cook, Michael (2000), *Commanding Right and Forbidding Wrong in Islamic Thought*, Cambridge: Cambridge University Press.

Cox, Jeffrey (2002), *Imperial Fault Lines: Christianity and Colonial Power in India, 1818–1940*, Stanford: Stanford University Press.

Crawford, M. J. (2011), 'The Da'wa of Ibn 'Abd al-Wahhāb before the Al Sa'ūd', *Journal of Arabian Studies* 1(2): 147–61.

Creevey, Lucy (2004), 'Bamba, Ahmad', in Richard C. Martin (ed.), *Encyclopedia of Islam and the Muslim World*, New York: Macmillan, vol. 1, p. 104.

Crollius, Roest (1978), 'Mission and Morality: Al-amr bi-l-maruf as Expression of the Communitarian and Missionary Dimensions of Qur'anic Ethics', *Studia Missionalia* 27: 257–83.

Crone, Patricia (1960–2007), 'Mawla', in P. Bearman, T. Bianquis, C. E. Bosworth, E.

van Donzel and W. P. Heinrichs (eds), *Encyclopaedia of Islam, Second Edition*, Leiden: Brill, vol. 6, pp. 874–82.

Crone, Patricia (1980), *Slaves on Horses: The Evolution of the Islamic Polity*, Cambridge: Cambridge University Press.

Crone, Patricia (1987), *Meccan Trade and the Rise of Islam*, Princeton: Princeton University Press.

Crone, Patricia (1994), 'The First-Century Concept of 'Hiǧra', *Arabica* 41: 352–87.

Crone, Patricia (2004), *God's Rule: Government and Islam*, New York: Columbia University Press.

Crone, Patricia and Michael Cook (1976), *Hagarism: The Making of the Islamic World*, New York: Cambridge University Press.

Crone, Patricia and Martin Hinds (1986), *God's Caliph: Religious Authority in the First Centuries of Islam*, Cambridge: Cambridge University Press.

Cunningham, Lawrence (2005), *A Brief History of Saints*, Malden: Blackwell.

Curtis, Edward (2009), *Muslims in America: A Short History*, New York: Oxford.

Daftary, Farhad (1995), *The Isma'ilis: Their History and Doctrines*, Cambridge: Cambridge University Press.

Daftary, Farhad (1998), *A Short History of the Ismailis*, Edinburgh: Edinburgh University Press.

Dallal, Ahmad (1993), 'Origins and Objectives of Islamic Revivalist Thought, 1750–1850', *Journal of the American Oriental Society* 113(3): 341–59.

Dallal, Ahmad (2001), 'Science and the Qur'an', in Jane McAuliffe (ed.), *Encyclopedia of the Qur'an*, Leiden: Brill, vol. 4, pp. 540–58.

Daniel, Elton (2007), ''Abbāsid Revolotion', in Kate Fleet, Gudrun Krämer, Denis Matringe, John Nawas and Everett Rowson (eds), *Encyclopaedia of Islam, Three*, Leiden: Brill, available at: http://dx.doi.org.proxy.library.nd.edu/10.1163/1573-3912_ei3_COM_0025, last accessed 23 May 2019.

Dannin, Robert (2002), *Black Pilgrimage to Islam*, Oxford: Oxford University Press.

Darwich, May (2016), 'Organisation of Islamic Cooperation', in Richard C. Martin (ed.), *Encyclopedia of Islam and the Muslim World*, 2nd ed., New York: Macmillan, vol. 2, pp. 824–5.

Daryābādī, 'Abd al-Mājid (1957/1991), *Tafsīr-ul-Qur'an, Volumes 1–4*, Karachi: Darul Ishaat.

Da'wah Academy [n. d.], 'Background and History', available at: https://dawah.iiu.edu.pk/about-us/background-history/, last accessed 3 January 2020.

Dawah Institute [n. d.], 'Strategic Steps in Dawah and Dialogue', available at: https://dawahinstitute.org/strategic-steps-in-dawah-and-dialogue/, last accessed 8 November 2018.

Dawat-i Islami [n. d.], Homepage, available at: https://www.dawateislami.net/, last accessed 13 December 2019.

Dawahskills [n. d.], Homepage, available at: https://www.dawahskills.com/, last accessed 3 January 2020.

268 *Da'wa*

Deedat, Ahmed (1992), *Combat Kit Against Bible Thumpers,* Durban: IPCI.

Deen Show [n. d.], 'Eddie Redzovic', available at: https://www.thedeenshow.com/author/eddie_redzovic/, last accessed 9 January 2020.

Delanoue, G. (1960–2007), 'al-Ikhwān al-Muslimūn', in P. Bearman, T. Bianquis, C. E. Bosworth, E. van Donzel and W. P. Heinrichs (eds), *Encyclopaedia of Islam, Second Edition,* Leiden: Brill, vol. 3, pp. 1068–71.

DeLong-Bas, Natana (2004), *Wahhabi Islam: From Revival and Reform to Global Jihad,* Oxford: Oxford University Press.

DeWeese, Devin (1994), *Islamization and Native Religion in the Golden Horde,* University Park: Pennsylvania State University Press.

DeWeese, Devin (1999), 'Sayyid 'Alī Hamadānī and Kubrāwī Hagiographical Traditions', in Leonard Lewisohn and David Morgan (ed.), *The Heritage of Sufism, Vol. II: The Legacy of Medieval Persian Sufism (1150–1500),* Oxford: Oneworld, pp. 121–58.

DeWeese, Devin (2009), 'Islamization in the Mongol Empire', in Nicola Di Cosmo, Allen Frank and Peter Golden (eds), *The Cambridge History of Inner Asia: The Chinggisid Age,* Cambridge: Cambridge University Press, pp. 120–34.

DeWeese, Devin (2017), 'Khwaja Ahmad Yasavi as an Islamising Saint: Rethinking the Role of Sufis in the Islamisation of Central Asia', in A. C. S. Peacock (ed.), *Islamisation: Comparative Perspectives from History,* Edinburgh: Edinburgh University Press, pp. 336–52.

Donner, Fred M. (1981), *The Early Islamic Conquests,* Princeton: Princeton University Press.

Donner, Fred M. (2004), 'Expansion', in Richard C. Martin (ed.), *Encyclopedia of Islam and the Muslim World,* New York: Macmillan, vol. 2, pp. 239–45.

Donner, Fred M., ed. (2008), *The Expansion of the Early Islamic State,* Aldershot: Ashgate.

Doumato, Eleanor A. and Joseph A. Kechichian (2009), 'Saudi Arabia', in *The Oxford Encyclopedia of the Islamic World,* Oxford: Oxford University Press, 2009, vol. 5, pp. 60–8.

Eaton, Richard (1993), *The Rise of Islam and the Bengal Frontier, 1204–1760,* Berkeley: University of California Press.

Eaton, Richard (2001), *Essays on Islam and Indian History,* Oxford: Oxford University Press.

Edis, Taner [n. d.], "'Quran-science': Scientific Miracles from the 7th century?' available at: http://edis.sites.truman.edu/quran-science-scientific-miracles-from-the-7th-century/, last accessed 30 January 2020.

Edis, Taner (2007), *An Illusion of Harmony: Science and Religion in Islam,* Amherst: Prometheus Books.

Editorial Staff (2018), 'Tufayl ibn Amr Ad-Dawsi: Prophet Muhammad as I Knew Him', available at: http://www.the-faith.com/prophet-muhammad/tufayl-ibn-amr-ad-dawsi-prophet-muhammad-as-i-knew-him/, last accessed 12 December 2018.

Eickelman, Dale and James Piscatori, eds (1990), *Muslim Travelers: Pilgrimage, Migration, and the Religious Imagination,* Berkeley: University of California Press.

Eickelman, Dale and James Piscatori (1996), *Muslim Politics*, Princeton: Princeton University Press.

Eickelman, Dale and Jon Anderson, eds (2003), *New Media in the Muslim World: The Emerging Public Sphere*, Bloomington: Indiana University Press.

Eid Charity [n. d.], 'Who We Are', available at: https://www.eidcharity.net/en/index.php?page=article&id=2337, last accessed 13 January 2020.

Eisenstadt, S. N. (2000), 'Multiple Modernities', *Daedalus*, 129(1): 1–29.

Elias, Abu Amina (2012), 'Lessons from the *Da'wa* Journey of Muadh Ibn Jabal to Yemen', available at: https://abuaminaelias.com/lessons-from-the-journey-of-muadh-ibn-jabal-to-yemen/, last accessed 17 December 2018.

Emerick, Yahya (2010), *How to Tell Others About Islam*, Islamic Foundation of North America.

Ende, W. (1960–2007), 'Rashīd Riḍā', in P. Bearman, T. Bianquis, C. E. Bosworth, E. van Donzel and W. P. Heinrichs (eds), *Encyclopaedia of Islam, Second Edition*, Leiden: Brill, vol. 8, pp. 446–8.

Engelcke, Dorthe (2017), 'Reasserting State Control Over Official Islam in Morocco', in Nathan Brown (ed.), *Official Islam in the Arab World: The Contest for Religious Authority*, Washington DC: Carnegie Endowment for International Peace, pp. 13–15.

Ernst, Carl (1997), *The Shambhala Guide to Sufism*, Boston: Shambhala.

Ernst, Carl (2004), *Eternal Garden: Mysticism, History and Politics and a South Asian Sufi Center*, Oxford: Oxford University Press.

Esposito, John, Yvonne Haddad and John Voll, eds (1991), *The Contemporary Islamic Revival: A Critical Survey and Bibliography*. Westport: Greenwood Press.

Esposito, John (2000), 'Introduction: Islam and Secularism', in John Esposito and Azzam Tamimi (eds), *Islam and Secularism in the Middle East*, New York: NYU Press, pp. 1–12.

Esposito, John and John Voll (2001), *Makers of Contemporary Islam*, New York: Oxford University Press.

Euben, Roxanne and Muhammad Qasim Zaman, eds (2009), *Princeton Readings in Islamist Thought*, Princeton: Princeton University Press.

Farquhar, Michael (2017), *Circuits of Faith: Migration, Education, and the Wahhabi Mission*, Stanford: Stanford University Press.

al-Faruqi, Isma'il (1982), 'On the Nature of Islamic Da'wah', in *Christian Mission and Islamic Da'wa: Proceedings of the Chambesy Dialogue Consultation*, Leicester: The Islamic Foundation, pp. 33–51.

Featherstone, Mike (2002), 'Islam Encountering Globalization: An Introduction', in 'Alī Mohammadi (ed.), *Islam Encountering Globalization*, London: RoutledgeCurzon, pp. 1–13.

Fiazer, Rizwi and Andrew Rippin (2011), 'Introduction', in Rizwi Faizer, Amal Ismail and Abdulkader Tayob (eds), *The Life of Muhammad: Al-Waqidi's Kitab al-Maghāzī*, London: Routlege, pp. xi–xviii.

Fierro, Maribel (2010a), 'Introduction', in Maribel Fierro (ed.), *The New Cambridge History of Islam, Vol. 2*, Cambridge: Cambridge University Press, pp. 1–18.

Fierro, Maribel (2010b), 'The Almohads and Hafsids', in Maribel Fierro (ed.), *The New Cambridge History of Islam, Vol. 2*, Cambridge: Cambridge University Press, pp. 66–105.

Findley, Carter (2005), *The Turks in World History*, Oxford: Oxford University Press.

Fiqh Council of North America (2020), 'Prayer and Funeral Issues Pertaining to COVID-19', *Christian Mission and Islamic Da'wa* http://fiqhcouncil.org/prayer-and-funeral-issues-pertaining-to-covid-19/, last accessed 27 April 2020.

al-Fiqī, Muhammad Ḥāmid (1358/1935), *Āthār al-da'wa al-wahhābiyya*, Cairo [n. p.].

Fisk, Robert (2020), 'Iran's coronavirus outbreak is bizarrely reminiscent of the Black Death', *The Independent*, 27 February, available at: https://www.independent.co.uk/voices/coronavirus-covid19–iran-middle-east-virus-hajj-black-death-a9362731.html, last accessed 27 April 2020.

Fletcher, Joseph (1986), 'The Mongols: Ecological and Social Perspectives', *Harvard Journal of Asiatic Studies* 46(1): 11–50.

Flower, Scott (2015), 'Conversion to Islam in Papua New Guinea: Preserving Traditional Culture against Modernity's Cargo-Cult Mentality', *Nova Religio: The Journal of Alternative and Emergent Religions* 18(4): 55–82.

Frayer, Lauren (2020), 'Blamed for Coronavirus Outbreak, Muslims in India Come Under Attack', NPR, 23 April, available at: https://www.npr.org/2020/04/23/839980029/blamed-for-coronavirus-outbreak-muslims-in-india-come-under-attack, last accessed 25 April 2020.

Freidenreich, David, ed. (2020), 'Corona Guidance: Religious Norms for Navigating the COVID-19 Pandemic: A database for comparative study', available at: http://web.colby.edu/coronaguidance/, last accessed 25 April 2020.

Friedmann, Yohannan (2003), *Tolerance and Coercion in Islam: Interfaith Relations in the Muslim Tradition*, Cambridge: Cambridge University Press.

Friedmann, Yohannan (2009), 'Aḥmadīyah', in John Esposito (ed.), *The Oxford Encyclopedia of the Islamic World*, Oxford: Oxford University Press, vol. 1, pp. 81–5.

Friedmann, Yohannan (2017), 'Dār al-Islām and Dār al-Ḥarb in Modern Indian Muslim Thought', in C. Calasso and G. Lancioni (eds), *Dar al-Islam / Dar al-Harb: Territories, People, Identities*, Leiden: Brill, pp. 341–80.

Frykenberg, Robert (2008), *Christianity in India: From Beginnings to the Present*, Oxford: Oxford University Press.

Gaborieau, Marc (1960–2007), 'Tablīghī Djamā'at', in P. Bearman, T. Bianquis, C. E. Bosworth, E. van Donzel and W. P. Heinrichs (eds), *Encyclopaedia of Islam, Second Edition*, Leiden: Brill, vol. 10, pp. 38–9.

Gaborieau, Marc (2000), 'The Transformation of the Tablighi Jama'at into a Transnational Movement', in Muhammad Khalid Masud (ed.), *Travellers in Faith: Studies of the Tablighi Jama'at as a Transnational Islamic Movement for Faith Renewal*, Leiden: Brill, pp. 121–38.

Gaborieau, Marc (2006), 'What is left of Sufism in the Tablighi Jama'at?' *Archives de sciences sociales des religions* 51(135): 53–72.

Gaborieau, Marc (2009), 'South Asian Muslim Diasporas and Transnational Movements: Tablighi Jama'at and Jama'at-i Islami', *South African Historical Journal* 61(1): 8–20.

Gaborieau, Marc (2011), 'Préface', in Samadia Sadouni, *La controverse islamo-chrétienne en Afrique du Sud: Ahmed Deedat et les nouvelles formes de débat*, Aix-en-Provence: Presses universitaires de Provence, pp. 5–8.

Gade, Anna M. (2009), 'Sunan Ampel of the Javanese Wali Songo', in John Renard (ed.), *Tales of God's Friends*, Berkeley: University of California Press, pp. 341–58.

Gaffney, Patrick (1994), *The Prophet's Pulpit: Islamic Preaching in Contemporary Egypt*, Berkeley: University of California Press.

Gaffney, Patrick (2004), 'Khutba', in Richard C. Martin (ed.), *Encyclopedia of Islam and the Muslim World*, New York: Macmillan, vol. 1, pp. 394–6.

Galal, Ehab (2009), 'Yusuf al-Qaradawi and the New Islamic TV', in Bettina Gräf and Jakob Skovgaard-Petersen (eds), *Global Mufti: The Phenomenon of Yusuf al-Qaradawi*, New York: Columbia University Press, pp. 149–80.

Garcia-Arenal, Mercedes (2010), 'Conversion to Islam: from the "age of conversions" to the millet system', in Maribel Fierro (ed.), *The New Cambridge History of Islam, Vol. 2*, Cambridge: Cambridge University Press, pp. 586–606.

Gardet, L. (1960–2007), ''Ilm al-Kalām', in P. Bearman, T. Bianquis, C. E. Bosworth, E. van Donzel and W. P. Heinrichs (eds), *Encyclopaedia of Islam, Second Edition*, Leiden: Brill, vol. 3, pp. 1141–50.

Gazzini, Claudia (2004), 'Zaytuna', in Richard C. Martin (ed.), *Encyclopedia of Islam and the Muslim World*, New York: Macmillan, vol. 2, p. 747.

Georgeon, François (2007), 'Abdülhamid II', in Kate Fleet, Gudrun Krämer, Denis Matringe, John Nawas and Everett Rowson (eds), *Encyclopaedia of Islam, Three*, Leiden: Brill.

Gelvin, James and Nile Green, eds (2014a), *Global Muslims in the Age of Steam and Print*, Berkeley: University of California Press.

Gelvin, James and Nile Green (2014b), 'Introduction', in James Gelvin and Nile Green (eds), *Global Muslims in the Age of Steam and Print*, Berkeley: University of California Press, pp. 1–23.

Gerholm, Tomas and Yngve Georg Lithman, eds (1988), *The New Islamic Presence in Europe*, London: Mansell.

Gift2Sufis (2011), 'Ibn Alawi Al-Maliki (from Makkah) – A Chief Innovator: The Amr Ibn Luhayy of our Time', available at: https://gift2sufis.wordpress.com/2011/10/19/ibn-alawi-al-maliki-from-makkah-the-amr-ibn-luhayy-of-our-time/, last accessed 28 January 2020.

Gilliand, Dean (1979), 'Religious Change Among the Hausa, 1000–1800: A Hermeneutic of the "Kano Chronicle,"' *Journal of Asian and African Studies* 14(3): 241–57.

Giroux, S. and J. Nealon (2012), *The Theory Toolbox: Critical Concepts for the Humanities, Arts, and Social Sciences*, New York: Rowman and Littlefield.

Gleave, R. M. (1960–2007), 'Maḳāṣid al-Sharīʿa', in P. Bearman, T. Bianquis, C. E.

Bosworth, E. van Donzel and W. P. Heinrichs (eds), *Encyclopaedia of Islam, Second Edition*, Leiden: Brill, vol. 12, pp. 569–70.

Gobillot, G. (1960–2007), 'Zuhd', in P. Bearman, T. Bianquis, C. E. Bosworth, E. van Donzel and W.P. Heinrichs (eds), *Encyclopaedia of Islam, Second Edition*, Leiden: Brill, vol. 11, pp. 559–62.

Goddard, Hugh (2001), *A History of Christian-Muslim Relations*, Chicago: New Amsterdam.

Golden, Daniel (2002), 'Strange Bedfellows: Western Scholars Play Key Role in Touting "Science" of the Qur'an', *Wall Street Journal*, 23 January.

Golden, Peter (1992), *An Introduction to the History of the Turkic Peoples*, Wiesbaden: Harrassowitz.

Golden, Peter (2011), *Central Asia in World History*, Oxford: Oxford University Press.

Goldschmidt, Arthur and Lawrence Davidson (2006), *A Concise History of the Middle East*, 8th ed., Boulder: Westview.

Goldziher, Ignaz (1981), *Introduction to Islamic Theology and Law*, Princeton: Princeton University Press.

Gräf, Bettina and Jakob Skovgaard-Petersen, eds (2009), *Global Mufti: The Phenomenon of Yūsuf al-Qaradawi*, New York: Columbia.

Graham, William (1993), 'Traditionalism in Islam: An Essay in Interpretation', *Journal of Interdisciplinary History* 23(3): 495–522.

Green, Nile (2011), *Bombay Islam: The Religious Economy of the West Indian Ocean, 1840–1915*, Cambridge: Cambridge University Press.

Green, Nile (2012), *Sufism: A Global History*, Malden: Wiley-Blackwell.

Green, Nile (2015a), *Terrains of Exchange: Religious Economies of Global Islam*, Oxford: Oxford University Press.

Green, Nile (2015b), 'Islam in the Early Modern World', in J. Bentley, S. Subrahmanyam and M. Wiesner-Hanks (eds), *The Cambridge World History, Vol. 6*, Cambridge: Cambridge University Press, pp. 358–86.

Griffith, Sidney (2008), *The Church in the Shadow of the Mosque*, Princeton: Princeton University Press.

Gugler, Thomas (2010), 'Public Religiosity, Parrots of Paradise and the Symbols of the Super-Muslim', in Mushirul Hasan (ed.), *Islam in a Globalized World: Negotiating Faultlines*, Gurugram, India: ImprintOne, pp. 99–122.

Guillaume, Alfred (1955/2012), 'Introduction', in *The Life of Muhammad: A Translation of Ishaq's Sirat Rasal Allah*, New York: Oxford University Press, pp. xiii–xlvii.

Hackenburg, Clint (2009), 'An Arabic-to-English Translation of the Religious Debate between the Nestorian Patriarch Timothy I and the 'Abbasid Caliph al-Mahdī', Master's Thesis, The Ohio State University.

Hackett, Rosalind (2008), 'Revisiting Proselytization in the Twenty-first Century', in Rosalind Hackett (ed.), *Proselytization Revisited: Rights, Free Markets, and Culture Wars*, London: Equinox, pp. 1–14.

Haddad, Yvonne (1991), 'The Revivalist Literature and the Literature on Revival: An Introduction', in John Esposito, Yvonne Haddad and John Voll (eds), *The*

Contemporary Islamic Revival: A Critical Survey and Bibliography, New York: Greenwood, pp. 3–22.

Haddad, Yvonne (1994), 'Muhammad 'Abduh: Pioneer of Islamic Reform', in 'Ali Rahnema (ed.), *Pioneers of Islamic Revival*, London: Zed Books, pp. 30–63.

Haddad, Yvonne and Jane I. Smith (1993), *Mission to America: Five Islamic Sectarian Communities in North America*, Gainesville: University Press of Florida.

Halm, Heinz (1991), *Shi'ism*, Edinburgh: Edinburgh University Press.

Halm, Heinz (2005), *The Shi'ites: A Short History*, Princeton: Marcus Wiener.

Hamid, Sadek (2016), *Sufis, Salafis and Islamists: The Contested Ground of British Islamic Activism*, London: I. B. Tauris.

Hardy, Peter (1972), *The Muslims of British India*, Cambridge: Cambridge University Press.

Hartung, Jan-Peter (2004), 'Ulama of Contemporary South Asia: Globalizing the Local by Localizing the Global', *Oriente Moderno* 84(1): 83–101.

Hartung, Jan-Peter (2005), *Viele Wege und ein Ziel: Leben und Wirken von Sayyid Abū l-Ḥasan 'Alī Ḥasanī Nadwī*, Würzburg: Ergon.

Hatch, Nathan (1989), *The Democratization of American Christianity*, New Haven: Yale University Press.

Hawting, G. R. (1960–2007), 'Umayyads', in P. Bearman, T. Bianquis, C. E. Bosworth, E. van Donzel and W. P. Heinrichs (eds), *Encyclopaedia of Islam, Second Edition*, Leiden: Brill, vol. 10, pp. 840–7.

Hawting, G. R. (1987), *The First Dynasty of Islam: The Umayyad Caliphate A.D. 661–750*, Carbondale: Southern Illinois University Press.

Hawting, G. R. (1999), *The Idea of Idolatry and the Emergence of Islam: From Polemic to History*, Cambridge: Cambridge University Press.

Haykal, Muhammad Husayn (1976), *The Life of Muhammad*, trans. Isma'il al-Faruqi, [n. p.]: North American Trust.

Haykal, Bernard (2009), 'On the Nature of Salafi Thought and Action', in Roel Meijer (ed.), *Global Salafism: Islam's New Religious Movement*, New York: Columbia University Press, pp. 33–50.

Hegghammer, Thomas (2009), 'Jihadi-Salafis or Revolutionaries: On Religion and Politics in the Study of Militant Islamism', in Roel Meijer (ed.), *Global Salafism: Islam's New Religious Movement*, New York: Columbia University Press, pp. 244–66.

Hedin, Christer, Torsten Janson and David Westerlund (2004), '*Da'wa*', in Richard C. Martin (ed.), *Encyclopedia of Islam and the Muslim World*, New York: Macmillan, vol. 1, pp. 170–4.

Hefner, Robert (1998), 'Multiple Modernities: Christianity, Islam, and Hinduism in a Globalizing Age', *Annual Review of Anthropology* 27: 83–104.

Hefner, Robert (2004), 'Muhammadiyya', in Richard C. Martin (ed.), *Encyclopedia of Islam and the Muslim World*, New York: Macmillan, vol. 2, p. 487.

Hefner, Robert, ed. (2005), *Remaking Muslim Politics: Pluralism, Contestation, Democratization*, Princeton: Princeton University Press.

Hefner, Robert (2007), 'Education in Muslim Southeast Asia', in Kate Fleet, Gudrun Krämer, Denis Matringe, John Nawas and Everett Rowson (eds), *Encyclopaedia of Islam, Three*, Leiden: Brill.

Hefner, Robert, ed. (2011a), *Shari'a Politics: Islamic Law and Society in the Modern World*, Bloomington: Indiana University Press.

Hefner, Robert (2011b), 'Introduction: Muslims and Modernity: Culture and Society in an Age of Contest and Plurality', in Robert Hefner (ed.), *The New Cambridge History of Islam, Vol. 6: Muslims and Modernity: Culture and Society since 1800*, Cambridge: Cambridge University Press, pp. 1–36.

Heneghan, Tom (2012), 'Special Report: Gaddafi's Secret Missionaries', *Reuters*, 29 March 29, available at: https://in.reuters.com/article/us-libya-missionary/special-report-gaddafis-secret-missionaries-idINBRE82S07T20120329, last accessed 5 January 2020.

Hermansen, Marcia (2004), 'Rahman, Fazlur (1919–1988)', in Richard C. Martin (ed.), *Encyclopedia of Islam and the Muslim World*, New York: Macmillan, vol. 2, pp. 571–2.

Hermansen, Marcia (2013), 'The Emergence of Media Preachers: Yusuf al-Qaradawi', in Jeffrey Kenney and Ebrahim Moosa (eds), *Islam in the Modern World*, London: Routledge, pp. 301–18.

Hermansen, Marcia (2014), 'Conversion to Islam in Theological and Historical Perspectives', in Lewis Rambo and Charles Farhadian (eds), *The Oxford Handbook of Religious Conversion*, Oxford: Oxford University Press, pp. 632–66.

Hillenbrand, R. (1960–2007), 'Madrasa', in P. Bearman, T. Bianquis, C. E. Bosworth, E. van Donzel and W. P. Heinrichs (eds), *Encyclopaedia of Islam, Second Edition*, Leiden: Brill, vol. 5, pp. 1123–54.

Hinds, Martin (1960–2007), 'Miḥna', in P. Bearman, T. Bianquis, C. E. Bosworth, E. van Donzel and W. P. Heinrichs (eds), *Encyclopaedia of Islam, Second Edition*, Leiden: Brill, vol. 7, pp. 2–6.

Hinds, Martin (1983), '*Maghāzī* and *Sīra* in Early Islamic Scholarship', in *La vie du Prophete Mahomet*, Paris: Presses Universitaires de France, pp. 57–66.

Hirschkind, Charles (2006), *The Ethical Soundscape: Cassette Sermons and Islamic Counterpublics*, New York: Columbia University Press.

Hiskett, M. (1960–2007), 'Kano', in P. Bearman, T. Bianquis, C. E. Bosworth, E. van Donzel and W. P. Heinrichs (eds), *Encyclopaedia of Islam, Second Edition*, Leiden: Brill, vol. 4, pp. 548–49.

Ḥizb al-Taḥrīr, Arabic Homepage, available at: http://www.hizb-ut-tahrir.info/ar/index.php/, last accessed 18 December 2019.

Hizb ut-Tahrir, 'Hizb ut-Tahrir', available at: http://www.hizb-ut-tahrir.info/en/index.php/multimedia/item/7980–hizb-ut-tahrir, last accessed 18 December 2019.

Hizb ut-Tahrir, 'The Reasons for the Establishment of Hizb ut-Tahrir', available at: http://www.hizb-ut-tahrir.info/en/index.php/definition-of-ht/item/7981–the-reasons-for-the-establishment-of-hizb-ut-tahrir, last accessed 18 December 2019.

Hodgson, Marshall G. S. (1960–2007), 'Dāʿī', in P. Bearman, T. Bianquis, C. E. Bosworth, E. van Donzel and W. P. Heinrichs (eds), *Encyclopaedia of Islam, Second Edition*, Leiden: Brill, vol. 2, pp. 97–8.

Hodgson, Marshall G. S. (1974), *The Venture of Islam: Conscience and History in World Civilization*, vols. 1–2, Chicago: University of Chicago Press.

Hoesterey, James (2016), *Rebranding Islam: Piety, Prosperity, and a Self-Help Guru*, Stanford: Stanford University Press.

Hoffman-Ladd, Valerie (2009a), 'Women's Religious Observances', in John Esposito (ed.), *The Oxford Encyclopedia of the Islamic World*, Oxford: Oxford University Press, vol. 5, pp. 537–44.

Hoffman-Ladd, Valerie (2009b), 'Ghazali, Zaynab Al-', in John Esposito (ed.), *The Oxford Encyclopedia of the Islamic World*, Oxford: Oxford University Press, vol. 2, pp. 316–18.

Hoodhbhoy, Pervez (2005), 'When Teaching Science Becomes a Subversive Activity', in Noretta Koertge (ed.), *Scientific Values and Civic Virtues*, Oxford: Oxford University Press, pp. 215–19.

Hourani, Albert (1962/1983), *Arabic Thought in the Liberal Age*, Cambridge: Cambridge University Press.

Hourani, Albert (1991), 'How Should We Write the History of the Middle East', *International Journal of Middle East Studies* 23: 125–36.

Howe, Justine (2018), *Suburban Islam*, New York: Oxford University Press.

Howe, Justine (2019), 'Daʿwa in the Neighborhood: Female-Authored Muslim Students Association Publications, 1963–1980', *Religion and American Culture* 29(3): 291–325.

Hoyland, Robert (2004), 'Introduction', in Robert Hoyland (ed.), *Muslims and Others in Early Islamic Society*, Aldershot: Ashgate.

Hoyland, Robert (2007), 'Writing the Biography of the Prophet Muḥammad: Problems and Solutions', *History Compass* 5: 1–22.

Hoyland, Robert (2012), 'Early Islam as a Late Antique Religion', in *The Oxford Handbook of Late Antiquity*, Oxford: Oxford University Press, pp. 1053–77.

Hoyland, Robert (2015), *In God's Path: The Arab Conquests and the Creation of an Islamic Empire*, Oxford: Oxford University Press.

Hudson, Winthrop (1973), *Religion in America*, 2nd ed., New York: Scribner's.

Humphreys, R. Stephen (1991), *Islamic History: A Framework for Inquiry*, Princeton: Princeton University Press.

Hunwick, John O. (1960–2007), 'Al-Maghīlī', in P. Bearman, T. Bianquis, C. E. Bosworth, E. van Donzel and W. P. Heinrichs (eds), *Encyclopaedia of Islam, Second Edition*, Leiden: Brill, vol. 5, pp. 1165–6.

Hunwick, John O., ed. and trans. (1985), *Shariʾa in Songhay: The Replies of al-Maghili to the Questions of Askia al-Hajj Muhammad*, Oxford: Oxford University Press for the British Academy.

Husain, Habeeba (2020), 'Reframing the Challenges of COVID-19', WhyIslam.org, 7 April, available at: https://www.whyislam.org/spiritual-journeys/reframing-covid19/, last accessed 25 April 2020.

Ibn Baṭṭūṭa (2010), *The Travels of Ibn Baṭṭūṭa*, 5 volumes, trans. H. A. R. Gibb, Burlington: Ashgate.

Ibn Hisham (1858–60), *Sīrat Rasūl Allāh*, ed. F. Wüstenfeld, Göttingen: Dieterich.

Ibn Ishaq (1955/2012), *The Life of Muhammad: A Translation of Ibn Ishaq's Sirat Rasul Allah*, trans. Alfred Guillaume, New York: Oxford University Press.

Ibn Khaldūn (1958), *The Muqaddimah: An Introduction to History*, trans., Franz Rozenthal, New York: Pantheon.

Ibn Saʿd (1986), *Ibn Saʿd's Kitab al-Tabaqat al-Kabir*, vol. II, trans. S Moinul Haq, New Delhi: Kitab Bhavan.

Ibrahim, Ayman (2018), *The Stated Motivations for the Early Islamic Expansion (622–641)*, New York: Peter Lang.

Ibrahim, I. A. (1997), *A Brief Illustrated Guide to Understanding Islam*, Houston: Darussalam.

Inayatullah, Sh. (1960–2007), 'Ahl-i Ḥadīth', in P. Bearman, T. Bianquis, C. E. Bosworth, E. van Donzel and W. P. Heinrichs (eds), *Encyclopaedia of Islam, Second Edition*, Leiden: Brill, vol. 1, pp. 259–60.

Ingram, Brannon (2011), 'Deobandis Abroad: Sufism, Ethics and Polemics in a Global Islamic Movement', PhD Dissertation, University of North Carolina.

Ingram, Brannon (2018), *Revival from Below: The Deoband Movement and Global Islam*, Berkeley: University of California Press.

Institute of Ismaili Studies [n. d.], 'About Us', available at: https://iis.ac.uk/about-us, last accessed 18 December 2019.

International Commission on Scientific Signs in Qur'an and Sunna [n. d.], 'The General Secretary Word', available at: http://www.eajaz.org/eajaz/index.php?option=com-content&view=article&id=75&Itemid=65&lang=en, last accessed 5 May 2015. Archived: https://web.archive.org/web/20101225034036/http://www.eajaz.org/eajaz/index.php?option=com_content&view=article&id=75&Itemid=65&lang=en, last accessed 6 January 2020.

International Institute of Islamic Thought [n. d.], 'About Us', available at: https://iiit.org/en/about-us/, last accessed 18 December 2019.

International Islamic University, Islamabad [n. d.], 'Dawah Academy', available at: https://dawah.iiu.edu.pk/, last accessed 3 January 2020.

Iqbal, Muhammad (1999), *The Reconstruction of Religious Thought in Islam*, Lahore: Sheikh Muhammad Ashraf.

Irwin, Robert (2011), 'Introduction', in Robert Irwin (ed.), *The New Cambridge History of Islam, Vol. 4*, Cambridge: Cambridge University Press, pp. 1–16.

Isichei, Elizabeth (1995), *A History of Christianity in Africa*, Grand Rapids: Eerdmans.

Islamic Culture and Religious Organization (Iran), 'Aims', available at: https://en.icro.ir/index.aspx?fkeyid=&siteid=257&pageid=9641, last accessed 7 January 2020.

Islamic Culture and Religious Organization (Iran), Homepage, available at: https://en.icro.ir/, last accessed 7 January 2020.

Islamic Pamphlets [n. d.], 'Misconceptions about Islam: What do you really know?', available at: http://islamicpamphlets.com/, last accessed 7 January 2020.

Islamic Relief Worldwide [n. d.], 'Coronavirus Appeal', available at: https://www.islamic-relief.org/category/appeals/emergencies/coronavirus-appeal/, last accessed 27 April 2020.

Islamic Society of North America [n. d.], 'ISNA Mission and Vision', available at: http://www.isna.net/mission-and-vision/, last accessed 16 January 2020.

IslamQA (2020), 'Is the one who dies of the coronavirus (Covid-19) a martyr?', available at: https://islamqa.info/ en/ answers/ 334078/ is-the-one-who-dies-of-the-coronavirus-covid-19-a-martyr, last accessed 25 April 2020.

IslamWeb [n. d.], 'Articles: Dawah', available at: https://www.islamweb.net/en/articles/100/dawah, last accessed 9 January 2020.

IslamWeb (2018a), 'Women in Da'wah I', available at: https://www.islamweb.net/en/article/156479/women-in-dawah-call-to-islam-i, last accessed 9 January 2020.

IslamWeb (2018b), 'Women in Da'wah – II', available at: http://www.islamweb.net/en/article/156480/, last accessed 1 November 2018.

IslamWeb (2019), 'Women in Dawah – III', available at: https://www.islamweb.net/en/article/156481/women-in-dawah-iii, last accessed 9 January 2020.

Ismaili Community [n. d.], Homepage, available at: https://the.ismaili, last accessed 18 December 2019.

Jackson, Peter (2009), 'Mongols', in John Esposito (ed.), *The Oxford Encyclopedia of the Islamic World*, Oxford: Oxford University Press, vol. 4, pp. 40–6.

Jalāl al-Dīn al-Maḥallī and Jalāl al-Dīn al-Suyūṭī (1410/1995), *Tafsīr al-Jalālayn*, ed. Marwān Siwār, Beirut: Dār al-Jīl. English translation: Feras Hamza, Amman: Royal Ahl al-Bayt Institute for Islamic Thought, 2009.

Jameelah, Maryam (1976), *Islam and the Muslim Woman Today*, Lahore, Pakistan: Mohammad Yusuf Khan.

Jamia Tus Salafiah [n. d.], Homepage, available at: http://aljamiatussalafiah.org/, last accessed 7 January 2020.

Jansen, Johannes (2009), 'Kishk, 'Abd al-Ḥamīd', in John Esposito (ed.), *The Oxford Encyclopedia of the Islamic World*, Oxford: Oxford University Press, vol. 3, pp. 354–5.

Janson, Torsten [n. d.], *Invitation to Islam: A History of Da'wa*, Uppsala: Swedish Science Press.

Janson, Torsten (2001), 'Da'wa: Islamic Missiology in Discourse and History', *Swedish Missiological Themes* 89(3): 355–415.

Janson, Torsten (2003), *Your Cradle is Green: The Islamic Foundation and the Call to Islam in Children's Literature*, Stockholm: Almqvist and Wiksell.

Jenkins, Philip (2009), *The Lost History of Christianity: The Thousand Year Golden Age of the Church in the Middle East, Africa and Asia – and How it Died*, New York: HarperOne.

Johnstone, D. (2004), 'Ikhwan al-Muslimin', in Richard C. Martin (ed.), *Encyclopedia of Islam and the Muslim World*, New York: Macmillan, vol. 1, pp. 345–8.

Jones, J. M. B. (1983), 'The *Maghāzī* Literature', in A. F. L. Beeston, T. M. Johnstone,

R. B. Serjeant and G. R. Smith, *The Cambridge History of Arabic Literature: Arabic Literature to the End of the Umayyad Period*, Cambridge: Cambridge University Press, pp. 344–51.

Jones, Kenneth (1989/2007), *Socio-Religious Reform Movements in British India*, Cambridge: Cambridge University Press.

Jones, Kenneth, ed. (1992), *Religious Controversy in British India: Dialogues in South Asian History*, Albany: State University of New York Press.

Journal of the International Qur'anic Studies Association, 'JIQSA Guidelines and Style Sheet', available at: https://iqsaweb.files.wordpress.com/2014/10/jiqsa-guide lines-and-style-sheet.pdf, last accessed 21 January 2020.

Jones, Seth (2014), *A Persistent Threat: The Evolution of al Qa'ida and Other Salafi Jihadists*, Washington, DC: Rand Corp.

Juynboll, G. H. A. (1960–2007), 'Sunna', in P. Bearman, T. Bianquis, C. E. Bosworth, E. van Donzel and W. P. Heinrichs (eds), *Encyclopaedia of Islam, Second Edition*, Leiden: Brill, vol. 9, pp. 878–81.

Kafrawi, Shalahudin and Mitsuo Nakamura (2009), 'Nahdatul Ulama', in John Esposito (ed.), *The Oxford Encyclopedia of the Islamic World*, Oxford: Oxford University Press, vol. 4, pp. 206–12.

KAICIID Dialogue Centre [n. d.], 'Who We Are', available at: http://www.kaiciid.org/who-we-are, last accessed 7 January 2020.

Karkainnen, Veli-Matti (2003), *An Introduction to the Theology of Religions*, Downers Grove: IVP.

Kearney, M. (1995), 'The Local and the Global: The Anthropology of Globalization and Transnationalism', *Annual Review of Anthropology* 24: 547–65.

Keddie, Nikki (2003), *Modern Iran: Roots and Results of Revolution*, New Haven: Yale University Press.

Keddie, Nikki (2007), *Women in the Middle East: Past and Present*, Princeton: Princeton University Press.

Kendall, Diana (2000), *Sociology in Our Times*, 2nd ed., California: Wadsworth.

Kennedy, Hugh (2007), *The Great Arab Conquests*, Philadelphia: Da Capo Press.

Kenney, Jeffrey and Ebrahim Moosa, eds. (2013), *Islam in the Modern World*, London: Routledge.

Kepel, Gilles (2006), *The War for Muslim Minds: Islam and the West*, Cambridge, MA: Harvard University Press.

Kerr, David (2000), 'Islamic Da'wa and Christian Mission: Toward a Comparative Analysis', *International Review of Mission* 89(353): 150–71.

Kersten, Carool and Susanne Olsen, eds. (2013), *Alternative Islamic Discourses and Religious Authority*, Burlington: Ashgate.

Khadduri, Majid (1966), *The Islamic Law of Nations: Shaybānī's Siyar*, Baltimore: The Johns Hopkins Press.

Khadduri, Majid (1955), *War and Peace in the Law of Islam*, Baltimore: The Johns Hopkins Press.

Khalid, Adeeb (2007), *Islam after Communism: Religion and Politics in Central Asia*, Berkeley: University of California Press.

Khalidi, Tarif (2009), *Images of Muhammad: Narratives of the Prophet in Islam Across the Centuries*, New York: Doubleday.

Khalidi, Tarif (2013), 'Islam and Literature', in F. B. Brown (ed.), *The Oxford Handbook of Religion and the Arts*, Oxford: Oxford University Press, pp. 302–9.

Khomeini, Ruhallah (1981), *Islam and Revolution I: Writings and Declarations of Imam Khomeini (1941–1980)*, trans. Hamid Algar, Berkeley: Mizan.

al-Kindī, *Apology*, English translation in Arnold, *Preaching*, 428–435; J. Monferrer Sala, B. Roggema and D. Thomas (2009), *Christian Muslim Relations: A Bibliographical History*, Vol. 1, Leiden: Brill, pp. 587–94.

King Faisal Prize [n. d.], 'Service to Islam', available at: https://kingfaisalprize.org/service-to-islam/, last accessed 7 January 2020.

Kirk, J. Andrew (2010), ' "God is on Our Side": The Anatomy of an Ideology', *Transformation* 27(4), 239–47.

Kister, M. J. (1983), 'The *Sīrah* Literature', in A. F. L. Beeston, T. M. Johnstone, R. B. Serjeant and G. R. Smith (eds), *The Cambridge History of Arabic Literature: Arabic Literature to the End of the Umayyad Period*, Cambridge: Cambridge University Press, pp. [352–67.

Kollman, Paul (2005), *The Evangelization of Slaves and Catholic Origins in East Africa*, Maryknoll: Orbis.

Koser, Khalid (2007), *International Migration: A Very Short Introduction*, New York: Oxford.

Kovensky, Josh (2014), 'ISIS's New Mag Looks Like a New York Glossy – With Pictures of Mutilated Bodies', *New Republic*, 25 August.

Krämer, Gudrun (2006), 'Drawing Boundaries: Yusuf al-Qaradawi on Apostasy', in Gudrun Krämer and Sabine Schmidtke (eds), *Speaking for Islam: Religious Authorities in Muslim Societies*, Leiden: Brill.

Krämer, Gudrun and Sabine Schmidtke, eds (2006), *Speaking for Islam: Religious Authorities in Muslim Societies*, Leiden: Brill.

Kramer, Martin (1986), *Islam Assembled: The Advent of Muslim Congresses*, New York: Columbia University Press.

Kramer, Martin (1995), 'Congresses', in John Esposito (ed.), *The Oxford Encyclopedia of the Modern Islamic World*, New York: Oxford University Press, vol. 1, pp. 308–11.

Kuiper, Matthew J. (2014), 'The Roots and Achievements of the Early Proto-Sunni Movement: A Profile and Interpretation', *The Muslim World* 104(1): 71–88.

Kuiper, Matthew J. (2016), 'Indian Muslims, Other Religions and the Modern Resurgence of Da'wa: The Tablīghī Jamā'at and Zakir Naik's Islamic Research Foundation', PhD Dissertation, University of Notre Dame.

Kuiper, Matthew J. (2017), 'Zakir Naik: A Different Kind of Jihadist', *Open Magazine*, 7 July, available at: https://openthemagazine.com/columns/comment/zakir-naik-a-different-kind-of-jihadist/, last accessed 28 December 2019.

Kuiper, Matthew J. (2018a), *Da'wa and Other Religions: Indian Muslims and the Modern Resurgence of Global Islamic Activism*, London and New York: Routledge.

Kuiper, Matthew J. (2018b), 'Tablighi Jama'at', in John O. Voll (ed.), *Oxford Bibliographies in Islamic Studies*, New York: Oxford University Press, available at: https://www.oxfordbibliographies.com/view/document/obo-9780195390155/obo-9780195390155–0250.xml?rskey=1zDckx&result=202, last accessed 13 December 2019.

Kuiper, Matthew J. (2018c), 'Da'wa', in John O. Voll (ed.), *Oxford Bibliographies in Islamic Studies*, New York: Oxford University Press, available at: http://www.oxfordbibliographies.com/view/document/obo-9780195390155/obo-9780195390155–0252.xml, last accessed 24 October 2019.

Kuspinar, Bilal (2009), 'Nursī, Said', in John Esposito (ed.), *The Oxford Encyclopedia of the Islamic World*, Oxford: Oxford University Press, vol. 4, pp. 260–2.

Lacroix, Stéphane (2009), 'Between Revolution and Apoliticism: Nasir al-Din al-Albani and His Impact on the Shaping of Contemporary Salafism', in Roel Meijer (ed.), *Global Salafism: Islam's New Religious Movement*, New York: Columbia University Press, pp. 58–80.

Lane E. W. (1867/1997), *An Arabic-English Lexicon*, Beirut: Libraire du Liban.

Laoust, H. (1960–2007), 'Ibn 'Abd al-Wahhāb', in P. Bearman, T. Bianquis, C. E. Bosworth, E. van Donzel and W. P. Heinrichs (eds), *Encyclopaedia of Islam, Second Edition*, Leiden: Brill, vol. 3, pp. 677–9.

Lapidus, Ira (1975), 'Separation of State and Religion in the Development of Early Islamic Society', *International Journal of Middle East Studies* 6(4): 363–85.

Lapidus, Ira (1988), *A History of Islamic Societies*, Cambridge: Cambridge University Press.

Lapidus, Ira (2002), *A History of Islamic Societies*, 2nd ed., Cambridge: Cambridge University Press.

Lapidus, Ira (2014), *A History of Islamic Societies*, 3rd ed., Cambridge: Cambridge University Press.

Larkin, Brian (2008), 'Ahmed Deedat and the Form of Islamic Evangelism', *Social Text* 26(3): 101–21.

Larsson, G. (2011), *Muslims and the New Media*, Burlington: Ashgate.

Last, D. M. (1960–2007), ''Uthmān b. Fūdī', in P. Bearman, T. Bianquis, C. E. Bosworth, E. van Donzel and W. P. Heinrichs (eds), *Encyclopaedia of Islam, Second Edition*, Leiden: Brill, vol. 10, pp. 949–51.

Last, Murray (2008), 'The Search for Security in Muslim Northern Nigeria', *Africa* 78(1): 41–63.

Latourette, Kenneth Scott (1937–45), *A History of the Expansion of Christianity*, New York: Harper and Brothers.

Launay, Robert (2011), 'New Frontiers and Conversion', in Robert Hefner (ed.), *The New Cambridge History of Islam, Vol. 6: Muslims and Modernity: Culture and Society since 1800*, Cambridge: Cambridge University Press, pp. 254–67.

Lauziere, Henri (2010), 'The Construction of Salafiyya', *International Journal of Middle East Studies* 42(3): 369–89.

Lawrence, Bruce (1982/2011), ''Abd-Al-Qader Jilani', *Encyclopaedia Iranica*, vol. I/2, pp. 132–3, available at: http://www.iranicaonline.org/articles/abd-al-qader-jilani, last accessed 3 June 2019.

Lawrence, Bruce (1983/2011), 'Abū Esḥāq Kāzārūnī', *Encyclopaedia Iranica*, vol. I/3, pp. 274–5, available at: http://www.iranicaonline.org/articles/abu-eshaq-ebrahim-b-2, last accessed 3 June 2019.

Lechner, Frank (2007), 'Religion', in Roland Robertson and Jan Aart Scholte (eds), *Encyclopedia of Globalization*, New York: Routledge, pp. 1024–26.

Lecker, Michael (2010), 'Glimpses of Muhammad's Medinan Decade', in Jonathan Brockropp (ed.), *The Cambridge Companion to Muḥammad*, Cambridge: Cambridge University Press, pp. 61–79.

el-Leithy, Tamer (2005), 'Coptic Culture and Conversion in Medieval Cairo, 1293–1524 A.D.', PhD Dissertation, Princeton University.

Lelyveld, D. (2004), 'Ahmadiyya', in Richard C. Martin (ed.), *Encyclopedia of Islam and the Muslim World*, New York: Macmillan, vol. 1, pp. 30–2.

Lepeska, David (2015), 'Turkey Casts the Diyanet', *Foreign Affairs*, 17 May, available at: https://www.foreignaffairs.com/articles/turkey/2015-05-17/turkey-casts-diyanet, last accessed 2 January 2020.

'Letter to Baghdadi' [n. d.], Homepage, available at: http://www.lettertobaghdadi.com/, last accessed 15 January 2020.

Levi, Scott (2010), 'Commercial Structures', in David Morgan and Anthony Reid (eds), *The New Cambridge History of Islam, Vol. 3*, Cambridge: Cambridge University Press, pp. 561–81.

Levi, Scott and Ron Sela, eds (2010), *Islamic Central Asia: An Anthology of Historical Sources*, Bloomington: Indiana University Press.

Levtzion, Nehemiah, ed. (1979a), *Conversion to Islam*, London: Holmes and Meier.

Levtzion, Nehemiah (1979b), 'Patterns of Islamization in West Africa', in Nehemiah Levtzion (ed.), *Conversion to Islam*, London: Holmes and Meier, pp. 207–16.

Levtzion, Nehemiah (1979c), 'Toward a Comparative Study of Islamization', in Nehemiah Levtzion (ed.), *Conversion to Islam*, London: Holmes and Meier, pp. 1–23.

Levtzion, Nehemiah (1985), 'Slavery and Islamization in Africa: A Comparative Study', in John Ralph Willis (ed.), *Slaves and Slavery in Muslim Africa, Vol. 1*, London: Frank Cass, pp. 182–98.

Levtzion, Nehemiah and Randall Pouwels (2000), 'Introduction: Patterns of Islamization and Varieties of Religious Experience among Muslims of Africa', in Nehemiah Levtzion and Randall Pouwels (eds), *The History of Islam in Africa*, Athens: Ohio University Press, pp. 1–20.

Lewis, B. (1960–2007), "Abbāsids', in P. Bearman, T. Bianquis, C. E. Bosworth, E. van Donzel and W. P. Heinrichs (eds), *Encyclopaedia of Islam, Second Edition*, Leiden: Brill, vol. 1, pp. 5–7.

Lewis, Bernard (1990), *Race and Slavery in the Middle East: An Historical Inquiry*, Oxford: Oxford University Press.

Loimeier, Roman (2005), 'Is There Something like 'Protestant Islam?' *Die Welt des Islams* 45(2): 216–54.

Lubeck, Paul (2011), 'Nigeria: Mapping a Shari'a Restorationist Movement', in Robert Hefner (ed.), *Shari'a Politics: Islamic Law and Society in the Modern World*, Bloomington: Indiana University Press, pp. 244–79.

Ludwig, Frieder (2008), 'Christian-Muslim Relations in Northern Nigeria since the Introduction of Shari'ah in 1999', *Journal of the American Academy of Religion* 76(3): 602–37.

Lynch, Gordon (2010), 'Religion, Media and Cultures of Everyday Life', in John Hinnels (ed.), *The Routledge Companion to the Study of Religion*, New York: Routledge, pp. 543–57.

Madelung, Wilfred (1997), *The Succession to Muhammad: A Study in the Early Caliphate*, Cambridge: Cambridge University Press.

Mahmood, Saba (2005), *Politics of Piety: The Islamic Revival and the Feminist Subject*, Princeton: Princeton University Press.

Malik, Jamal (2008), *Islam in South Asia: A Short History*, Leiden: Brill.

Malik, Jamal (2018), 'Fiqh al-*Da'wa*: The Emerging Standardization of Islamic Proselytism', *Die Welt Des Islams* 58: 206–43.

Mamiya, Lawrence (2009), 'Nation of Islam', in John Esposito (ed.), *The Oxford Encyclopedia of the Islamic World*, Oxford: Oxford University Press, vol. 4, pp. 233–38.

Mandaville, Peter (2007a), *Global Political Islam*, London: Routledge.

Mandaville, Peter (2007b), 'Globalization and the Politics of Religious Knowledge: Pluralizing Authority in the Muslim World', *Theory, Culture and Society* 24(2): 101–15.

Mandaville, Peter (2014), 'Is the Post-Islamism Thesis Still Valid?' Project on Middle East Political Science, February, available at: https://pomeps.org/wp-content/uploads/2014/02/POMEPS_BriefBooklet24–_Rethinking_web.pdf, last accessed 20 January 2020.

Manz, Beatrice F. (2010), 'The Rule of the Infidels: The Mongols and the Islamic World', in David Morgan and Anthony Reid (eds), *The New Cambridge History of Islam, Vol. 3*, Cambridge: Cambridge University Press, pp. 128–68.

al-Marghīnānī, Burhān al-Dīn (1720), *Kitāb al-Hidāyah*, Erzurum.

al-Marghīnānī, Burhān al-Dīn (2006), *Al Hidaya: The Guidance, Volumes 1 and 2*, trans. Imran Ahsan Khan Nyazee, Bristol: Amal Press.

Marin, Manuela (2010), 'The *'Ulama*', in Maribel Fierro (ed.), *The New Cambridge History of Islam, Vol. 2*, Cambridge: Cambridge University Press, pp. 679–704.

Marmon, Shaun (1999), 'Domestic Slavery in the Mamluk Empire: A Preliminary Sketch', in Shaun Marmon (ed.), *Slavery in the Islamic Middle East*, Princeton: Marcus Wiener, pp. 1–8.

Martin, David (2005), *On Secularization: Towards a Revised General Theory*, Aldershot: Ashgate.

Masud, Muhammad Khalid (1995a), 'Da'wah: Modern Usage', in John Esposito (ed.),

The Oxford Encyclopedia of the Modern Islamic World, Oxford: Oxford University Press, vol. 1, pp. 350–3.

Masud, Muhammad Khalid (1995b), 'Tablīgh', in John Esposito (ed.), *The Oxford Encyclopedia of the Modern Islamic World*, Oxford: Oxford University Press, vol, 4, pp. 162–5.

Masud, Muhammad Khalid (2000), 'Introduction', in Muhammad Khalid Masud (ed.), *Travelers in Faith: Studies of the Tablighi Jama'at as a Transnational Islamic Movement for Faith Renewal*, Leiden: Brill, pp. xiii–lx.

Masud, Muhammad Khalid (2009), 'Tablīgh', in John Esposito (ed.), *The Oxford Encyclopedia of the Islamic World*, Oxford: Oxford University Press, vol. 5, pp. 289–92.

Masud, Muhammad Khalid, Brinkley Messick and David Powers (1996), 'Muftis, Fatwas, and Islamic Legal Interpretation', in Muhammad Khalid Masud, Brinkley Messick and David Powers (eds), *Islamic Legal Interpretation: Muftis and their Fatwas*, Cambridge, MA: Harvard University Press, pp. 3–32.

Masud, Muhammad Khalid, Armando Salvatore and Martin van Bruinessen, eds (2009), *Islam and Modernity: Key Issues and Debates*. Edinburgh: Edinburgh University Press.

Mattes, Hanspeter (2009), 'World Islamic Call Society', in John Esposito (ed.), *The Oxford Encyclopedia of the Islamic World*, Oxford: Oxford University Press, vol. 6, pp. 7–8.

Mawdūdī, Abul A'lā (1994), *Salāmati Kā Rāsta (The Road to Peace and Salvation)*, UK Islamic Centre.

Mayaram, Shail (1997), *Resisting Regimes: Myth Memory and the Shaping of a Muslim Identity*, New Delhi: Oxford University Press.

Mayaram, Shail (2004), 'Hindu and Islamic Transnational Religious Movements', *Economic and Political Weekly*, 3 January.

McDougall, James (2007), 'Ben Bādīs, ʿAbd al-Ḥamīd', in Kate Fleet, Gudrun Krämer, Denis Matringe, John Nawas and Everett Rowson (eds), *Encyclopaedia of Islam, Three*, Leiden: Brill, available at: https://www.academia.edu/9033383/Abd_al-Hamid_Ben_Badis_entry_for_EI3_, last accessed 18 December 2019.

McLeod, Hugh (2007), *The Religious Crisis of the 1960s*, Oxford: Oxford University Press.

McLoughlin, Sean (2010), 'Religion and Diaspora', in John Hinnels (ed.), *The Routledge Companion to the Study of Religion*, New York: Routledge, pp. 558–80.

Meijer, Roel, ed. (2009), *Global Salafism: Islam's New Religious Movement*, New York: Columbia University Press.

Melchert, Christopher (1996), 'The Transition from Asceticism to Mysticism at the Middle of the Ninth Century C.E.', *Studia Islamica* 83: 51–70.

Melchert, Christopher (1997), *The Formation of the Sunni Schools of Law, 9th–10th Centuries C.E.*, Leiden: Brill.

Melchert, Christopher (2002a), 'Early Renunciants as Hadith Transmitters', *The Muslim World* 92: 407–18.

Melchert, Christopher (2002b), 'The Piety of the Hadith Folk', *International Journal of Middle East Studies* 34(3): 425–39.

Melchert, Christopher (2003), 'The Early History of Islamic Law', in Herbert Berg (ed.), *Method and Theory in the Study of Islamic Origins*, Leiden: Brill, pp. 293–324.

Melchert, Christopher (2006), *Ahmad Ibn Hanbal*, Oxford: Oneworld.

Melhem, Hisham (2015), 'Keeping Up with the Caliphate: An Islamic State for the Internet Age', *Foreign Affairs* 94(6): 148–53.

Melville, Charles (1990), 'Pādshāh-i Islām: The Conversion of Sultan Maḥmūd Ghāzān Khān', *Pembroke Papers* 1: 159–77.

Metcalf, Barbara (1982), *Islamic Revival in British India: Deoband 1860–1900*, Oxford: Oxford University Press.

Metcalf, Barbara (1990), *Perfecting Women: Maulana Ashraf 'Ali Thanawi's Bihishti Zewar*, Oxford: Oxford University Press.

Metcalf, Barbara (1992), 'Imagining Community: Polemical Debates in Colonial India', in Kenneth Jones (ed.), *Religious Controversy in British India*, New York: State University Press.

Metcalf, Barbara, ed. (1996), *Making Muslim Space in North America and Europe*, Berkeley: University of California Press.

Metcalf, Barbara (2004), *Islamic Contestations: Essays on the Muslims of India and Pakistan*, Oxford: Oxford University Press.

Millie, Julian (2007), 'Da'wa, Modern Practices', in Kate Fleet, Gudrun Krämer, Denis Matringe, John Nawas and Everett Rowson (eds), *Encyclopaedia of Islam, Three*, Leiden: Brill, pp. 51–4.

Millie, Julian (2017), *Hearing Allah's Call: Preaching and Performance in Indonesian Islam*, Ithaca: Cornell University Press.

Mingana, Alphonse (1928), 'Timothy's Apology for Christianity', *Woodbrooke Studies: Christian Documents in Syriac, Arabic, and Garshuni*, Cambridge: Heffer and Sons, vol. 2, pp. 1–162.

Ministry of Culture and Islamic Guidance (Iran) [n. d.], Homepage, available at: https://www.farhang.gov.ir/en/home, last accessed 7 January 2020.

Mitchell, Richard (1969), *The Society of Muslim Brothers*, New York: Oxford University Press.

Moffett, Samuel H. (1992/2009), *A History of Christianity in Asia, Vol. 1*, Maryknoll: Orbis.

Mohammadi, 'Alī, ed. (2002), *Islam Encountering Globalization*, London: RoutledgeCurzon.

Mojaddedi, Jawid (2003), 'Getting Drunk with Abū Yazīd or Staying Sober with Junayd', *Bulletin of the School of Oriental and African Studies* 66(1): 1–13.

Mondschein, Ken (2020), 'The Coronavirus is not the Black Death', Medievalists.net, March, available at: https://www.medievalists.net/2020/03/coronavirus-black-death/, last accessed 27 April 2020.

Monferrer Sala, J., B. Roggema and D. Thomas (2009), *Christian Muslim Relations: A Bibliographical History*, Leiden: Brill.

Moore, Kathleen M. (2013), 'Muslim Advocacy in America', in Jeffrey Kenney and Ebrahim Moosa (eds), *Islam in the Modern World*, London: Routledge, pp. 370–88.

Moore, Kathleen M. (2014), '*Da'wa* in the United States', in Yvonne Haddad and Jane Smith (eds), *The Oxford Handbook of American Islam*, Oxford: Oxford University Press, pp. 268–85.

Moore, Keith L. and A. Zindani (1983), *The Developing Human: Clinically Oriented Embryology, 3rd Edition, With Islamic Additions: Correlation Studies with Qur'an and Hadith*, Jeddah: Dar al-Qiblah for Islamic Literature.

Moore, Keith L., T. V. N. Persaud and M. G. Torchia (2015), *The Developing Human: Clinically Oriented Embryology*, 10th ed., Philadelphia: Saunders.

Moore, R. I. (2004), 'Forward', in C. A. Bayly, *The Birth of the Modern World, 1780–1914: Global Connections and Comparisons*, Oxford: Blackwell.

Moosa, Ebrahim (2020), 'Saudi Arabia Must Suspend the Hajj', *The New York Times*, 27 April, available at: https://www.nytimes.com/2020/04/27/opinion/coronavirus-hajj-pilgrimage.html, last accessed 27 April 2020.

Morewedge, Parviz (2009), 'Theology', in John Esposito (ed.), *The Oxford Encyclopedia of the Islamic World*, Oxford: Oxford University Press, vol. 5, pp. 354–76.

Morgan, David and Anthony Reid (2010), 'Introduction: Islam in a Plural Asia', in David Morgan and Anthony Reid (eds), *The New Cambridge History of Islam, Vol. 3*, Cambridge: Cambridge University Press, pp. 1–17.

Morony, Michael (2004), 'Religious Communities in Late Sasanian and Early Muslim Iraq', in Robert Hoyland (ed.), *Muslims and Others in Early Islamic Society*, Aldershot: Ashgate, pp. 1–23.

Moscati, S. (1960–2007a), 'Abū Muslim', in P. Bearman, T. Bianquis, C. E. Bosworth, E. van Donzel and W. P. Heinrichs (eds), *Encyclopaedia of Islam, Second Edition*, Leiden: Brill, vol. 1, p. 141.

Moscati, S. (1960–2007b), 'Abū Salama', P. Bearman, T. Bianquis, C. E. Bosworth, E. van Donzel and W. P. Heinrichs (eds), *Encyclopaedia of Islam, Second Edition*, Leiden: Brill, vol. 1, p. 149.

Mufti, Amir (2007), *Enlightenment in the Colony: The Jewish Question and the Crisis of Postcolonial Culture*, Princeton: Princeton University Press.

Muranyi, M. (1960–2007), 'Ṣaḥāba', in P. Bearman, T. Bianquis, C. E. Bosworth, E. van Donzel and W. P. Heinrichs (eds), *Encyclopaedia of Islam, Second Edition*, Leiden: Brill, vol. 8, pp. 827–29.

Muslim Aid [n. d.], 'Coronavirus Emergency', available at: https://www.muslimaid.org/appeals/covid19/, last accessed 27 April 2020.

Muslim Community Center of Chicago [n. d.], Homepage, available at: https://mcc-chicago.org/, last accessed 9 January 2020.

Muslim Converts' Association of Singapore [n. d.], Homepage, available at: https://www.darul-arqam.org.sg/, last accessed 7 December 2019.

Muslim ibn al-Hajjāj (1433/2012), *Ṣaḥīḥ Muslim*, Beirut: Dār al-Ma'rafa; English translation: 'Abdul Ḥamīd Ṣiddīqī, Islamic Book Service, 2005.

Muslim World League, 'Corona immediate pandemic response plan', available at: https://www.themwl.org/en/node/37227, last accessed 27 April 2020.

Muslim World League, International Organization for Relief, Welfare and Development, available at: https://en.themwl.org/international-organization-relief-welfare-development, last accessed 7 January 2020.

Muslim World League, Islamic Fiqh Council, available at: http://www.en.themwl.org/islamic-fiqh-council, last accessed 7 January 2020.

Muslim World League, International Organization for the Holy Quran and Immaculate Sunnah, available at: https://en.themwl.org/content/International%20Organization%20for%20the%20Holy%20Quran-%20Immaculate%20Sunnah, last accessed 7 January 2020.

Muslim World League, 'World Supreme Council for Mosques', available at: http://en.themwl.org/node/46, last accessed 6 January 2020.

Nadwi, Sayyid Abul Ḥasan 'Ali [n. d.], *Haḍrat Mawlānā Muḥammad Ilyās aur Unkī Dīnī Da'wat*, Delhi: Idārah Ishā'at Dīniyyāt; English translation: *Life and Mission of Maulana Mohammad Ilyās*, Lucknow: Academy of Islamic Research.

Nadwi, Sayyid Abul Ḥasan 'Ali (1957/1991), 'Introduction', in Daryābādī, *Tafsīr-ul-Qur'an*, Karachi: Darul Ishaat.

Nadwi, Sayyid Abul Ḥasan 'Ali (1977), *Islam and the World* (English translation of *Mādhā khasir al-ʿālam b'inḥiṭāṭ al-muslimīn*), trans. Mohammad Asif Kidawi, Beirut: The Holy Qur'an Publishing House.

Nadwi, Sayyid Abul Ḥasan 'Ali (1983), *Muslims in the West: The Message and Mission*, Leicester: The Islamic Foundation.

Nadwi, Sayyid Abul Ḥasan 'Ali (1992), *Dawah in the West: The Qur'anic Paradigm*, trans. M. A. Kidawi, Leicester: Islamic Foundation.

Nadwi, Sayyid Abul Ḥasan 'Ali (1993), *Muhammad The Last Prophet: A Model for All Time*, Leicester: UK Islamic Academy.

Nadwi, Sayyid Abul Ḥasan 'Ali (1996), *Inviting to the Way of Allah*, London: Ta-Ha.

Nagata, Judith (2009), 'PERKIM', in John Esposito (ed.), *The Oxford Encyclopedia of the Islamic World*, Oxford: Oxford University Press, vol. 4, pp. 436–47.

Naik, Zakir (2009), "Misconceptions about Islam," PeaceTV video of a lecture given in Dubai, 28 August, posted 26 October 2012, available at: www.youtube.com/watch?v=BdXDJlWY_Os, last accessed 20 February 2020.

El-Nawawy, Mohammed, and Sahar Khamis (2009), *Islam Dot Com: Contemporary Islamic Discourses in Cyberspace*, New York, NY: Palgrave Macmillan.

Neill, Stephen (1991), *A History of Christian Missions*, 2nd ed., London: Penguin.

Neuwirth, Angelika (2003), 'Qur'an and History – A Disputed Relationship', *Journal of Qur'anic Studies* 5: 1–18.

Newby, Gordon (2009), 'Muhammad: Biographies', in John Esposito (ed.), *The Oxford Encyclopedia of the Islamic World*, Oxford: Oxford University Press, vol. 4, pp. 113–16.

Nicholson, Oliver, ed. (2018), *The Oxford Dictionary of Late Antiquity*, Oxford: Oxford University Press.

Nicholson, R. A. (1989), *The Mystics of Islam*, London: Arkana.

Nizami, K. A. (1960–2007), 'Cishtiyya', in P. Bearman, T. Bianquis, C. E. Bosworth, E. van Donzel and W. P. Heinrichs (eds), *Encyclopaedia of Islam, Second Edition*, Leiden: Brill, vol. 2, pp. 50–6.

Noll, Mark (2009), *The New Shape of World Christianity: How American Experience Reflects Global Faith*, Downers Grove: IVP Academic.

Norton, Anne (2004), *95 Theses on Politics, Culture and Method*, New Haven: Yale University Press.

NU Online (2020), 'Muslimat NU Tegal Bagikan 10 Ribu Masker kepada Pedagang Pasar Tradisional', 6 April, available at: https://www.nu.or.id/post/read/118782/muslimat-nu-tegal-bagikan-10–ribu-masker-kepada-pedagang-pasar-tradisional, last accessed 25 May 2020.

Oddie, Geoffrey, ed. (1997), *Religious Conversion Movements in South Asia: Continuities and Change, 1800–1900*, London: Curzon.

Olcott, Martha Brill (2012), *In the Whirlwind of Jihād*, Washington DC: Carnegie Endowment for International Peace.

Olsson, Susanne (2014), 'Proselytizing Islam — Problematizing 'Salafism'', *The Muslim World* 104(1–2): 171–97.

Olsson, Susanne (2015), *Preaching Islamic Revival: Amr Khaled, Mass Media and Social Change in Egypt*, London: I. B. Tauris.

Omar, Farouk (1974), 'The Nature of Iranian Revolts in the Early Abbasid Period', *Islamic Culture* 48: 1–9.

Organisation of Islamic Cooperation, 'Cairo Final Communique of the 12th Session of the Islamic Summit Conference', Sections 97–112, available at: http://www.oic-oci.org/oicv2/page/?p_id=67&p_ref=36&lan=en, last accessed 11 April 2015.

Organisation of Islamic Cooperation, 'Charter', available at: https://www.oic-oci.org/upload/documents/charter/en/oic_charter_2018_en.pdf, last accessed 7 January 2020.

Organisation of Islamic Cooperation, 'Dawa Activities', available at: https://www.oic-oci.org/page/?p_id=215&p_ref=67&lan=en, last accessed 7 January 2020.

Organisation of Islamic Cooperation, 'Final Communique Extraordinary Videoconference of the OIC Executive Committee at the Level of Foreign Ministers on the Consequences of the Novel Coronavirus Disease (COVID-19) Pandemic and Joint Response', available at: https://www.oic-oci.org/topic/?t_id=23348&t_ref=13988&lan=en, last accessed 27 April 2020.

Organisation of Islamic Cooperation, 'History', available at: https://www.oic-oci.org/page/?p_id=52&p_ref=26&lan=en, last accessed 6 January 2020.

Organisation of Islamic Cooperation, 'Islamic Committee of the International Crescent', available at: http://www.icic-oic.org/, last accessed 7 January 2020.

Organisation of Islamic Cooperation, 'Specialized Organs', available at: https://www.oic-oci.org/page/?p_id=65&p_ref=34&lan=en#ibu, last accessed 7 January 2020.

Ortega, Rafael and Frank Peter, eds (2014), *Islamic Movements of Europe: Public Religion and Islamophobia in the Modern World*, London: I. B. Tauris.

Oxford Islamic Studies Online, 'Jamaat-i Islami', available at: http://www.oxfordis-lamicstudies.com/article/opr/t125/e1167, last accessed 30 October 2019.

Paden, William (2005), 'Comparative Religion', in Lindsay Jones (ed.), *Encyclopedia of Religion*, 2nd ed., Detroit: Macmillan, pp. 1877–81.

Pakistan Ministry of Religious Affairs and Inter-Faith Harmony [n. d.], Homepage, available at: http://www.mora.gov.pk/, last accessed 3 January 2020.

Palmer, H. R., trans. (1908), 'The Kano Chronicle', *The Journal of the Royal Anthropological Institute of Great Britain and Ireland* 38: 58–98.

Parker, Charles (2015), 'Entrepreneurs, Families, and Companies', in J. Bentley, S. Subrahmanyam and M. Wiesner-Hanks (eds), *The Cambridge World History, Vol. 6*, Cambridge: Cambridge University Press, pp. 190–212.

Peacock, A. C. S., ed. (2017a), *Islamisation: Comparative Perspectives from History*, Edinburgh: Edinburgh University Press.

Peacock, A. C. S. (2017b), 'Introduction', in A. C. S. Peacock (ed.), *Islamisation: Comparative Perspectives from History*, Edinburgh: Edinburgh University Press, pp. 1–20.

Peacock, A. C. S. (2017c), 'Islamisation in Medieval Anatolia', in A. C. S. Peaock (ed.), *Islamisation: Comparative Perspectives from History*, Edinburgh: Edinburgh University Press, pp. 134–55.

Peacock, James (1981), 'The Third Stream: Weber, Parsons, Geertz', *Journal of the Anthropological Society of Oxford* 7: 122–9.

Peacock, James, and Marilyn Trent Grunkmeyer (2009), 'Muhammadiyya', in John Esposito (ed.), *The Oxford Encyclopedia of the Islamic World*, Oxford: Oxford University Press, vol. 4, pp. 124–5.

Peters, F. E. (1994), *Muhammad and the Origins of Islam*, Albany: State University of New York Press.

Peters, R. (2009), 'Dār al-Islām', in John Esposito (ed.), *The Oxford Encyclopedia of the Islamic World*, Oxford: Oxford University Press, vol. 2, pp. 27–8.

Peterson, Daniel (2009), 'Ismāʿīlīyah', in John Esposito (ed.), *The Oxford Encyclopedia of the Islamic World*, Oxford: Oxford University Press, vol. 3, pp. 200–1.

Pew Research Center (2015), 'The Future of World Religions', available at: http://www.pewforum.org/2015/04/02/religious-projections-2010–2050/, last accessed 11 September 2018.

Philips, Bilal [n. d.], 'Introduction to *Da'wa*', available at: http://bilalphilips.com/port-folio/dawah-course-manual/, last accessed 18 February 2020.

Picken, Gavin (2011), 'General Introduction', in Gavin Picken (ed.), *Islamic Law: Critical Concepts in Islamic Studies*, London: Routledge, pp. 1–29.

Poston, Larry (1992), *Islamic Da'wah in the West*, New York: Oxford University Press.

Powell, Avril (1992), 'Muslim-Christian Conflagration: Dr. Wazir Khan in Nineteenth-Century Agra', in Kenneth W. Jones (ed.), *Religious Controversy in British India: Dialogues in South Asian History*, Albany: State University of New York Press, pp. 77–92.

Powell, Avril (1993), *Muslims and Missionaries in Pre-Mutiny India*, London: Curzon.

Pratt, Mary Louise (1991), 'Arts of the Contact Zone', *Profession* [n. vol.]: 33–40.

Pregill, Michael (2018), 'Editor's Introduction: Eastern Perspectives on Late Antiquity', *Mizan: Journal for the Study of Muslim Societies and Civilizations* 3(1), available at: http://www.mizanproject.org/journal-post/editors-introduction-eastern-perspectives-on-late-antiquity/, last accessed 4 April 2019.

Putz, Catherine (2019), 'Turkey Seeks Extradition of 2 Gulen School Employees from Kyrgyzstan', *The Diplomat*, 31 December, available at: https://thediplomat.com/2019/12/turkey-seeks-extradition-of-2-gulen-school-employees-from-kyrgyzstan/, last accessed 3 January 2020.

Qadhi, Yasir (2014), 'On Salafi Islam', available at: http://muslimmatters.org/2014/04/22/on-salafi-islam-dr-yasir-qadhi/, last accessed 14 January 2020.

al-Qaraḍāwī, Yūsuf (1994), *Al-halāl wa'l ḥarām fi'l-Islam*, English translation: *The Lawful and the Prohibited in Islam*, Plainfield: American Trust.

Qassem, Hamzah [n. d.], 'Abu Bakr as-Siddiq', available at: http://sunnahonline.com/library/history-of-islam/305–abu-bakr-as-siddiq, last accessed 1 November 2018.

Qibtiyah, Alimatul (2015), 'Muslimat NU', in Jesudas Athyal (ed.), *Religion in Southeast Asia: An Encyclopedia of Faiths and Cultures*, Santa Barbara: ABC-CLIO, pp. 190–191.

Quli Qara'i, 'Ali (2011), *The Qur'an: With a Phrase by Phrase English Translation*, 2nd ed., New York: Tahrike Tarsile Qur'an, Inc.

Qutb, Sayyid (2000), 'The America That I have Seen: In the Scale of Human Values', trans., Tarek Masoud and Ammar Fakeeh, in Kamal Abdel Malek (ed.), *America in an Arab Mirror: Images of America in Arabic Travel Literature: An Anthology*, New York: Palgrave Macmillan, pp. 9–28.

Racius, Egdunas (2004), *The Multiple Nature of the Islamic Da'wa*, PhD Diss., University of Helsinki.

Rahman, Fazlur (1994), *Major Themes of the Qur'an*, Minneapolis: Bibliotheca Islamica.

Ramadan, Tariq (2004), *Western Muslims and Future of Islam*, Oxford: Oxford University Press, 2004.

Raven, W. (1960–2007), 'Sīra', in P. Bearman, T. Bianquis, C. E. Bosworth, E. van Donzel and W. P. Heinrichs (eds), *Encyclopaedia of Islam, Second Edition*, Leiden: Brill, vol. 9, pp. 660–3.

Reetz, Dietrich (2006), *Islam in the Public Sphere: Religious Groups in India, 1900–1947*, Oxford: Oxford University Press.

Reetz, Dietrich (2007), 'Islamische Missionsbewegungen in Europa', in Ruth Heidrich-Blaha, Michael Ley and Rüdiger Lohlker (eds), *Islam in Europa*, Vienna: Diplomatic Academy of Vienna, pp. 117–36.

Reetz, Dietrich (2009), 'Tablīghī Jamā'at', in John Esposito (ed.), *The Oxford Encyclopedia of the Islamic World*, Oxford: Oxford University Press, vol. 5, pp. 293–9.

Reetz, Dietrich (2010), 'From Madrasa to University: The Challenges and Formats of Islamic Education', in Abar Ahmad and Tamara Sonn (eds), *The Sage Handbook of Islamic Studies*, London: Sage, pp. 106–39.

Reid, Donald (2009), 'Azhar, Al-', in John Esposito (ed.), *The Oxford Encyclopedia of the Islamic World*, Oxford: Oxford University Press, vol. 1, pp. 265–70.

Renard, John (2005), *Historical Dictionary of Sufism*, Oxford: The Scarecrow Press.

Renard, John (2008), *Friends of God: Islamic Images of Piety Commitment, and Servanthood*, Berkeley: University of California Press.

Renard, John, ed. (2009), *Tales of God's Friends*, Berkeley: University of California Press.

Reynolds, Gabriel Said (2004), *A Muslim Theologian in the Sectarian Milieu: 'Abd al-Jabbār and the Critique of Christian Origins*, Leiden: Brill.

Reynolds, Gabriel Said (2011), 'Remembering Muhammad', *Numen* 58(2/3): 188–206.

Reynolds, Gabriel Said (2012), *The Emergence of Islam*, Minneapolis: Fortress.

Richards, John (2007), *The Mughal Empire*, New Delhi: Cambridge University Press.

Riḍā, Muḥammad Rashīd (2009), *Christian Criticisms, Islamic Proofs: Rashīd Riḍā's Modernist Defense of Islam*, trans. Simon Wood, Oxford: Oneworld.

Ridgeon, Lloyd (2001), 'Christianity as Portrayed by Jalāl al-Dīn Rūmī', in Lloyd Ridgeon (ed.), *Islamic Interpretations of Christianity*, Richmond: Curzon, pp. 99–126.

Riesebrodt, Martin (2010), *The Promise of Salvation: A Theory of Religion*, Chicago: University of Chicago Press.

Rippin, Andrew (1993), *Muslims: Their Religious Beliefs and Practices, Vol. 2: The Contemporary Period*, London: Routledge.

Rippin, Andrew (2000), 'Muhammad in the Qur'an: Reading Scripture in the 21st Century', in H. Motzki (ed.), *The Biography of the Prophet Muhammad: The Issue of the Sources*, Leiden: Brill, pp. 298–309.

Robert, Dana (2009), *Christian Mission: How Christianity Became a World Religion*, Malden: Wiley-Blackwell.

Robinson, Chase (2003), *Islamic Historiography*, Cambridge: Cambridge University Press.

Robinson, Chase (2005), *'Abd Al-Malik*, Oxford: Oneworld.

Robinson, David (2009), 'Murīdīyah', in John Esposito (ed.), *The Oxford Encyclopedia of the Islamic World*, Oxford: Oxford University Press, vol. 4, pp. 142–3.

Robinson, Francis (1960–2007), 'Mawdūdī,', in P. Bearman, T. Bianquis, C. E. Bosworth, E. van Donzel and W. P. Heinrichs (eds), *Encyclopaedia of Islam, Second Edition*, Leiden: Brill, vol. 6, pp. 872–4.

Robinson, Francis (1999), 'Religious Change and the Self in Muslim South Asia Since 1800', *South Asia* 22: 13–27.

Robinson, Francis (2000a), 'Islam and Muslim Society in South Asia', in Francis Robinson (ed.), *Islam and Muslim History in South Asia*, Oxford: Oxford University Press, pp. 44–65.

Robinson, Francis (2000b), 'Islam and the Impact of Print in South Asia', in Francis Robinson (ed.), *Islam and Muslim History in South Asia*, Oxford: Oxford University Press, pp. 66–104.

Robinson, Francis (2008), 'Islamic Reform and Modernities in South Asia', *Modern Asian Studies* 42(2/3), pp. 259–81.

Robinson, Francis (2011), 'Introduction', in Francis Robinson (ed.), *New Cambridge History of Islam, Vol. 5: The Islamic World in the Age of Western Dominance*, Cambridge: Cambridge University Press, pp. 1–28.

Rock-Singer, Aaron (2010), 'Amr Khaled: From Da'wa to Political and Religious Leadership', *British Journal of Middle Eastern Studies* 37(1): 15–37.

Rock-Singer, Aaron (2016), 'Scholarly Authority and Lay Mobilization: Yusuf al-Qaradawi's Vision of Da'wa, 1976–1984', *Muslim World* 106(3): 588–604.

Rowe, T. Jack (2007), 'Kubraviyya', in Kate Fleet, Gudrun Krämer, Denis Matringe, John Nawas and Everett Rowson (eds), *Encyclopaedia of Islam, Three*, Leiden: Brill, available at: http://dx.doi.org.proxy.library.nd.edu/10.1163/1573–3912_ei3_COM_35697, last accessed 24 May 2019.

Roy, Olivier (2004), *Globalized Islam: The Search for a New Ummah*, New York: Columbia University Press.

Rubin, Uri (1995), *The Eye of the Beholder: The Life of Muhammad as Viewed by the Early Muslims*, Princeton: Darwin Press.

Rubin, Uri (2001a), 'Prophets and Prophethood', in Jane McAuliffe (ed.), *Encyclopedia of the Qur'an*, Leiden: Brill, vol. 4, pp. 289–306.

Rubin, Uri (2001b), 'Muhammad', in Jane McAuliffe (ed.), *Encyclopedia of the Qur'an*, Leiden: Brill, vol. 3, pp. 440–57.

Rubin, Uri (2010), 'Muḥammad's Message in Mecca: Warnings, Signs, and Miracles', in Jonathan Brockropp (ed.), *The Cambridge Companion to Muḥammad*, Cambridge: Cambridge University Press, pp. 39–60.

Rubin, Uri (2016), ''Amr b. Luḥayy', in Kate Fleet, Gudrun Krämer, Denis Matringe, John Nawas and Everett Rowson (eds), *The Encyclopedia of Islam, Three*, Brill Online, available at: http://referenceworks.brillonline.com.proxy.library.nd.edu/entries/encyclopaedia-of-islam-3/amr-b-luhayy-SIM_0327, last accessed 23 May 2016.

Ryad, Umar (2006), 'Muslim Response to Missionary Activities in Egypt: With a Special Reference to the Al-Azhar High Corps of *'Ulama* (1925–1935)', in H. L. Murre-van den Berg (ed.), *New Faith in Ancient Lands : Western Missions in the Middle East in the Nineteenth and Early Twentieth Centuries*, Leiden: Brill, pp. 281–307.

Ryad, Umar (2009), 'A Prelude to Fiqh al-Aqaliyyāt: Rashid Rida's Fatwas to Muslims under Non-Muslim Rule', in Christiane Timmerman, Johan Leman, Hannelore Roos and Barbara Segaert (eds), *In-Between Spaces: Christian and Muslim Minorities in Transition in Europe and the Middle East*, Brussels: Peter Lang, pp. 239–70.

Sadouni, Samadia (2011), *La controverse islamo-chrétienne en Afrique du Sud: Ahmed Deedat et les nouvelles formes de débat*, Aix-en-Provence: Presses universitaires de Provence.

Sadouni, Samadia (2013), 'Ahmed Deedat, Internationalization, and Transformations of Islamic Polemic', *Journal of Religion in Africa* 43: 53–73.

Saleh, Walid (2010), 'The Arabian Context of Muḥammad's Life', in Jonathan Brockropp (ed.), *The Cambridge Companion to Muḥammad*, Cambridge: Cambridge University Press, pp. 21–38.

Saleh, Walid (2018), 'The Preacher of the Meccan Qur'an: Deuteronomistic History and Confessionalism in Muḥammad's Early Preaching', *Journal of Qur'anic Studies* 20(2): 74–111.

Salvá, Ana (2017), 'Here Come the Malaysian Morality Police', *The Diplomat*, 22

February, available at: https://thediplomat.com/2017/02/here-come-the-malay sian-morality-police/, last accessed 2 January 2020.

Salvatore, Armando (2009), 'Tradition and Modernity within Islamic Civilization and the West', in Muhammad Khalid Masud, Armando Salvatore and Martin van Bruinessen (eds), *Islam and Modernity: Key Issues and Debates*, Edinburgh: University of Edinburgh Press, pp. 3–35.

Sanneh, Lamin (1994), 'Translatability in Islam and Christianity in Africa: A Thematic Approach', in T. D. Blakely (ed.), *Religion in Africa: Experience & Expression*, London: Curry, pp. 22–45.

Sanneh, Lamin (2003), 'Shari'a Sanctions as Secular Grace? A Nigerian Islamic Debate and an Intellectual Response', *Transformation* 20(4): 232–44.

Sanneh, Lamin (2008), *Disciples of All Nations: Pillars of World Christianity*, New York: Oxford.

Sanneh, Lamin (2009), *Translating the Message: The Missionary Impact on Culture*, Maryknoll: Orbis.

Sanyal, Usha (1996), *Devotional Islam and Politics in British India: Ahmad Riza Khan Barelwi and his Movement, 1870–1920*, Oxford: Oxford University Press.

Sanyal, Usha (2005), *Ahmad Riza Khan Barelwi: In the Path of the Prophet*, Oxford: Oneworld.

Saudi Arabia, Government of [n. d.], '*wizārat al-shu'ūn al-Islāmiyya wa'l-da'wa wa'l-irshād*', available at: https://www.my.gov.sa/wps/portal/snp/pages/agencies/agencyDe tails/AC172, last accessed 6 January 2020.

Sayilgan, Salih (2019), *An Islamic Jihād of Non-Violence: Said Nursi's Model*, Eugene: Cascade.

Schacht, J. (1960–2007), 'Fiḳh', in P. Bearman, T. Bianquis, C. E. Bosworth, E. van Donzel and W. P. Heinrichs (eds), *Encyclopaedia of Islam, Second Edition*, Leiden: Brill, vol. 2, pp. 886–91.

Schacht, J. (1977), 'Law and Justice', in P. M. Holt, A. K. S Lambton and B. Lewis (eds), *Cambridge History of Islam, Vol. 2B: Islamic Society and Civilization*, Cambridge: Cambridge University Press, pp. 539–68.

Schimmel, Annemarie (1975), *Mystical Dimensions of Islam*, Chapel Hill: University of North Carolina Press.

Schirrmacher, Christine (1999), 'The Influence of Higher Bible Criticism on Muslim Apologetics in the Nineteenth Century', in J. Waardenburg (ed.), *Muslim Perceptions of Other Religions*, Oxford: Oxford University Press, pp. 270–9.

Schulze, Reinhard (1995), 'Da'wah: Institutionalization', in John Esposito (ed.), *The Oxford Encyclopedia of the Modern Islamic World*, Oxford: Oxford University Press, vol. 1, pp. 346–50.

Schulze, Reinhard (2000), 'Is There an Islamic Modernity?' in Kai Hafez (ed.), *The Islamic World and the West*, Leiden: Brill, pp. 21–32.

Sedgwick, Mark (2007), 'Jihad, Modernity, and Sectarianism', *Nova Religio: Journal of Alternative and Emergent Religions* 11(2): 6–27.

Serjeant, R. B. (1983), 'Early Arabic Prose', in A. F. L. Beeston, T. M. Johnstone, R.

B. Serjeant and G. R. Smith (eds), *The Cambridge History of Arabic Literature: Arabic Literature to the End of the Umayyad Period*, Cambridge: Cambridge University Press, pp. 114–53.

Shaban, M. (1979), 'Conversion to Early Islam', in Nehemiah Levtzion (ed.), *Conversion to Islam*, New York: Holmes and Meier, pp. 24–9.

Shah, Zia (2012), 'The Constitution of Medina: A Symbol of Pluralism in Islam', 11 November, available at: https://themuslimtimes.info/2012/11/09/the-constitution-of-medina-a-symbol-of-pluralism-in-islam/, last accessed 6 November 2018.

Shahin, Emad Eldin (2009a), 'Kawākibī, 'Abd al-Raḥmān Al-', in John Esposito (ed.), *The Oxford Encyclopedia of the Islamic World*, Oxford: Oxford University Press, vol. 3, pp. 303–4.

Shahin, Emad Eldin (2009b), 'Ibn Bādīs, ʿAbd al-Ḥamīd', in John Esposito (ed.), *The Oxford Encyclopedia of the Islamic World*, Oxford: Oxford University Press, vol. 2, pp. 484–5.

Shank, David (1986), 'The Legacy of William Wadé Harris', *International Bulletin of Missionary Research* 10(4): 170–76.

Sharkey, Heather (2005), 'Empire and Muslim Conversion: Historical Reflections on Christian Missions in Egypt', *Islam and Christian-Muslim Relations* 16(1): 43–60.

Sharkey, Heather (2008), 'Muslim Apostasy, Christian Conversion, and Religious Freedom in Egypt: A Study of American Missionaries, Western Imperialism, and Human Rights Agendas', in Rosalind Hackett (ed.), *Proselytization Revisited: Rights, Free Markets, and Culture Wars*, London: Equinox, pp. 139–66.

Sharkey, Heather (2013a), 'Introduction: The Unexpected Consequences of Christian Missionary Encounters', in Heather Sharkey (ed.), *Cultural Conversions: Unexpected Consequences of Christian Missionary Encounters in the Middle East, Africa, and South Asia*, Syracuse: Syracuse University Press, pp. 1–14.

Sharkey, Heather (2013b), 'The Gospel in Arabic Tongues: British Bible Distribution, Evangelical Mission, and Language Politics in North Africa', in Heather Sharkey (ed.), *Cultural Conversions: Unexpected Consequences of Christian Missionary Encounters in the Middle East, Africa, and South Asia*, Syracuse: Syracuse University Press, pp. 203–24.

Sharma, Arvind (2011), 'Religions: Missionary and Non-missionary', in Arvind Sharma (ed.), *Problematizing Religious Freedom*, New York: Springer, pp. 175–96.

Sharon, Moshe (1983), *Black Banners from the East*, Leiden: Brill.

Sharon, Moshe (1991), 'The Umayyads as Ahl al-Bayt', *Jerusalem Studies in Arabic and Islam* 14: 115–52.

Shavit, Uriya and Frederick Weisenbach (2009), 'Muslim Strategies to Convert Western Christians', *Middle East Quarterly* 16(2): 3–14.

Shavit, Uriya (2014), *Islamism and the West: From Cultural Attack to Missionary Migrant*, New York: Routledge.

Sheline, Anelle (2017), 'The Uncertainty of Enforced Tolerance in Oman', in Nathan

Brown (ed.), *Official Islam in the Arab World: The Contest for Religious Authority*, Washington DC: Carnegie Endowment for International Peace, pp. 22–3.

Shepard, William (1987), 'Islam and Ideology: Towards a Typology', *International Journal of Middle East Studies* 19: 307–36.

Shepard, William (2004), 'The Diversity of Islamic Thought: Towards a Typology', in S. Taji-Farouki (ed.), *Islamic Thought in the Twentieth Century*, London: I. B. Tauris, pp. 61–103.

Shepard, William (2013), 'Militant Movements', in Jeffrey Kenney and Ebrahim Moosa (eds), *Islam in the Modern World*, London: Routledge, pp. 00-00.

Shorter, Aylward (2006), *Cross and Flag in Africa: The 'White Fathers' during the Colonial Scramble (1892–1914)*, Maryknoll: Orbis.

Shortt, Rupert (2012), *Christianophobia: A Faith Under Attack*, Grand Rapids: Eerdmans.

Shryock, Andrew, ed. (2010), *Islamophobia/Islamophilia: Beyond the Politics of Enemy and Friend*, Bloomington: Indiana University Press.

Sikand, Yoginder (2002), *The Origins and Development of the Tablighi Jama'at: 1920–2000*, Hyderabad: Orient Longman.

Silvers, Laury (2015), 'Early Pious, Mystic Sufi Women', in Lloyd Ridgeon (ed.), *Cambridge Companion to Sufism*, Cambridge: Cambridge University Press, pp. 24–52.

Sinai, Nicolai (2017), *The Qur'an: A Historical-Critical Introduction*, Edinburgh: Edinburgh University Press.

Sirry, Mun'im (2014), *Scriptural Polemics: The Qur'an and Other Religions*, Oxford: Oxford University Press.

Skovgaard-Petersen, Jacob (2007), 'al-Azhar, Modern Period', in Kate Fleet, Gudrun Krämer, Denis Matringe, John Nawas and Everett Rowson (eds), *Encyclopaedia of Islam, Three*, Leiden: Brill, pp. 185–8.

Skreslet, Stanley (2012), *Comprehending Mission: The Questions, Methods, Themes, Problems, and Prospects of Missiology*, Marknoll: Orbis.

Smith, M. G. (1983), 'The Kano Chronicle as History', in Bawuro M. Barkindo (ed.), *Studies in the History of Kano*, Nigeria: Heinemann Books for Department of History, Bayero University, pp. 31–58.

Soucek, Svat (2000), *A History of Inner Asia*, Cambridge: Cambridge University Press.

Stanley, Brian (2009), *The World Missionary Conference: Edinburgh 1910*, Grand Rapids: Eerdmans.

Stark, Rodney and Roger Finke (2000), *Acts of Faith: Explaining the Human Side of Religion*, Berkeley: University of California Press.

Starr, Frederick (2013), *Lost Enlightenment: Central Asia's Golden Age from the Arab Conquest to Tamerlane*, Princeton: Princeton University Press.

Sternberg, Leif (1996), *The Islamization of Science: Four Muslim Positions Developing an Islamic Modernity*, New York: Coronet Books.

Stewart, Devin (1998), *Islamic Legal Orthodoxy: Twelve Shiite Responses to the Sunni Legal System*, Salt Lake City: University of Utah Press.

Storrs, W. T. (1884), 'Henry William Shackell', *The Church Missionary Intelligencer and Record* 35.

Strathern, Alan (2017), 'Global Patterns of Ruler Conversion to Islam and the Logic of Empirical Religiosity', in A. C. S. Peacock (ed.), *Islamisation: Comparative Perspectives from History*, Edinburgh: Edinburgh University Press, pp. 21–55.

Sunni Dawat-i Islami [n. d.], Homepage, available at: http://www.sunnidawateislami. net/, last accessed 13 December 2019.

Tammam, Husam (2009), 'Yusuf al-Qaradawi and the Muslim Brothers: The Nature of a Special Relationship', in Bettina Gräf and Jakob Skovgaard-Petersen (eds), *Global Mufti: The Phenomenon of Yusuf al-Qaradawi*, New York: Columbia University Press, pp. 55–83.

Tareen, SherAli (2012), 'The Polemic of Shahjahanpur: Religion, Miracles and History', *Islamic Studies* 51(1): 49–67.

Tayob, Abdulkader (1999), *Islam in South Africa: Mosques, Imams, and Sermons*, Gainsville: University Press of Florida.

Teitelbaum, Joshua (2002), 'Dueling for 'Da'wa': State vs. Society on the Saudi Internet', *Middle East Journal* 56(2): 222–39.

Thielmann, Jörn (2017), 'Ḥisba (Modern Times)', in Kate Fleet, Gudrun Krämer, Denis Matringe, John Nawas and Everett Rowson (eds), *Encyclopaedia of Islam, Three*, Leiden: Brill, available at: http://dx.doi.org.proxy.library.nd.edu/10.1163/1573–3912_ei3_COM_30485, last accessed 27 December 2019.

This is Truth [n. d.], 'Scientific Facts', available at: http://thisistruth.org/truth.php?f= ScientificFacts, last accessed 6 January 2020.

Thomas, David (2008), *Christian Doctrines in Islamic Theology*, Leiden: Brill.

Trimingham, J. S. (1971), *The Sufi Orders in Islam*, Oxford: Clarendon.

Trix, Frances (2009), 'Bektāshīyah', in John Esposito (ed.), *The Oxford Encyclopedia of the Islamic World*, Oxford: Oxford University Press, vol. 1, pp. 332–4.

Troll, Christian W. (1994), 'New Light on the Christian-Muslim Controversy of the 19th and 20th Century', *Die Welt Des Islams* 34: 85–8.

Troll, Christian W. (1998), 'Jesus Christ and Christianity in Abdullah Yusuf Ali's English Interpretation of the Qur'an', *Islamochristiana* 24: 77–101.

Tugal, Cihan (2017), *Caring for the Poor: Islamic and Christian Benevolence in a Liberal World*, New York: Routledge.

Turam, Berna (2004), 'Nur Movement', in Richard C. Martin (ed.), *Encyclopedia of Islam and the Muslim World*, New York: Macmillan, pp. 512–13.

Turan, Osman (1959), 'L'Islamisation dans la Turquie du Moyen Âge', *Studia Islamica* 10: 137–52.

Turgay, A. Under (2004), 'Nursi, Said', in Richard C. Martin (ed.), *Encyclopedia of Islam and the Muslim World*, New York: Macmillan, p. 513.

al-Ṭūsi, Abū Ja'far (2008), *Al-Nihayah: A Concise Description of Islamic Law and Legal Opinions*, trans., A. Ezzati, London: ICAS Press.

Tweed, Thomas (2006), *Crossing and Dwelling: A Theory of Religion*, Cambridge, MA: Harvard University Press.

Tweed, Thomas (2012), 'Tracing Modernity's Flows: Buddhist Currents in the Pacific World', *The Eastern Buddhist* 43(1–2): 35–56.

University of Minnesota Immigration History Research Center (2015), 'Muslim Migration to Europe', available at: http://cla.umn.edu/ihrc/news-events/other/muslim-migration-europe, last accessed 16 January 2020.

United Nations (1948), Office of the High Commissioner on Human Rights, *Universal Declaration of Human Rights*, available at: www.ohchr.org/EN/UDHR/, last accessed 7 November 2019.

Vahed, Goolam (2009), 'Ahmed Deedat and Muslim-Christian Relations at the Cape, c. 1960–1980', *Journal for Islamic Studies* 29(1): 2–32.

Vajda, G., I. Goldziher and S. Bonebakker (1960–2007), 'Idjāza', in P. Bearman, T. Bianquis, C. E. Bosworth, E. van Donzel and W. P. Heinrichs (eds), *Encyclopaedia of Islam, Second Edition*, Leiden: Brill, vol. 3, pp. 1020–2.

Van Bruinessen, Martin (2007), 'Jumadil Kubra', in Kate Fleet, Gudrun Krämer, Denis Matringe, John Nawas and Everett Rowson (eds), *Encyclopaedia of Islam, Three*, Leiden: Brill, available at: http://dx.doi.org.proxy.library.nd.edu/10.1163/1573-3912_ei3_COM_32870, last accessed 24 May 2019.

Van Bruinessen, Martin (2018), 'Comparing the Governance of Islam in Turkey and Indonesia: Diyanet and the Ministry of Religious Affairs', *RSIS Working Papers* No. 312, pp. 1–19.

Van der Veer, Peter (1994), *Religious Nationalism: Hindus and Muslims in India*, Berkeley: University of California Press.

Van der Veer, Peter (2002), 'Religion in South Asia', *Annual Review of Anthropology* 31: 173–87.

van Doorn-Harder, Nelly (2004), 'Nahdlatul Ulama', in Richard C. Martin (ed.), *Encyclopedia of Islam and the Muslim World*, New York: Macmillan, vol. 2, pp. 499–500.

Various Authors (2020), 'A Message to Humanity: COVID19', available at: https://www.amessagetohumanity.com/, last accessed 7 May 2020.

Verskin, Alan (2012), *Oppressed in the Land: Fatwas on Muslims Living under Non-Muslim Rule from the Middle Ages to the Present*, Princeton: Wiener.

Viguera-Molins, Maria Jesus (2010), 'Al-Andalus and the Maghrib', in Maribel Fierro (ed.), *The New Cambridge History of Islam, Vol. 2*, Cambridge: Cambridge University Press, pp. 19–47.

Voll, John (1983), 'Renewal and Reform in Islamic History: *Tajdid* and *Islah*', in John Esposito (ed.), *Voices of Resurgent Islam*, New York: Oxford University Press, pp. 00-00.

Voll, John (2004a), 'Salafiyya', in Richard C. Martin (ed.), *Encyclopedia of Islam and the Muslim World*, New York: Macmillan, vol. 2, pp. 608–10.

Voll, John (2004b), 'Tajdīd', in Richard C. Martin (ed.), *Encyclopedia of Islam and the Muslim World*, New York: Macmillan, vol. 2, pp. 675–6.

Voll, John (2010), 'Islam as a Community of Discourse and a World System', in Akbar Ahmed and Tamara Sonn (eds), *The Sage Handbook of Islamic Studies*, London: Sage, pp. 3–16.

Voll, John (2016), 'West, Conceptions of', in Richard C. Martin (ed.), *Encyclopedia of Islam and the Muslim World*, 2nd ed., New York: Macmillan, vol. 2, pp. 1250–3.

Vryonis, Speros (1971), *The Decline of Medieval Hellenism and the Process of Islamization from the Eleventh to the Fifteenth Century*, Berkeley: University of California Press.

Waardenburg, Jacques, ed. (1999), *Muslim Perceptions of Other Religions: A Historical Survey*, New York: Oxford University Press.

Wadud, Amina (2012), 'Amina Wadud on Feminism in Islam', YouTube video posted 8 March 2012, available at: https://www.youtube.com/watch?v=WGH-01KQB_A, last accessed 10 January 2020.

Wadud, Amina (2006), *Inside the Gender Jihad: Women's Reform in Islam*, Oxford: Oneworld.

Wadud, Amina (1999), *Qur'an and Woman: Re-Reading the Sacred Text from a Woman's Perspective*, Oxford: Oxford University Press.

Wagner, E. (1960–2007), 'Munāẓara', in P. Bearman, T. Bianquis, C. E. Bosworth, E. van Donzel and W. P. Heinrichs (eds), *Encyclopaedia of Islam, Second Edition*, Leiden: Brill, vol. 7, pp. 565–8.

Wahid, Din (2014), 'Nurturing the Salafi Manhaj: A Study of Salafi Pesantrans in Contemporary Indonesia', PhD Dissertation, Utrecht University.

Wain, Alexander (2017), 'China and the Rise of Islam on Java', in A. C. S. Peacock (ed.), *Islamisation: Comparative Perspectives from History*, Edinburgh: Edinburgh University Press, pp. 419–43.

Waines, David (2002), 'Islam', in Linda Woodhead (ed.), *Religions in the Modern World*, London: Routledge, pp. 182–203.

Walker, Paul (1995), 'Da'wah: Qur'anic Concepts', in John Esposito (ed.), *The Oxford Encyclopedia of the Modern Islamic World*, New York: Oxford University Press, vol. 3, pp. 343–6.

Walker, Paul (1998), 'The Isma'ili Da'wa and the Fatimid Caliphate', in Carl Petry (ed.), *The Cambridge History of Egypt, Vol. 1*, Cambridge: Cambridge University Press, pp. 120–50.

Walls, Andrew (1997), 'Christianity', in John Hinnels (ed.), *A New Handbook of Living Religions*, New York: Penguin, pp. 55–161.

Walls, Andrew (2002), 'Christianity in the Non-Western World', in Andrew Walls (ed.), *The Cross-Cultural Process in Christian History*, Maryknoll: Orbis, pp. 27–48.

Wansbrough, John (2004), *Qur'anic Studies: Sources and Methods of Scriptural Interpretation*, New York: Prometheus Books.

Wansbrough, John (1978), *Sectarian Milieu: Content and Composition of Islamic Salvation History*, New York: Oxford University.

Watson, William (2005), 'A Popular Indonesian Preacher: The Significance of Aa Gymnastiar', *Journal of the Royal Anthropological Institute* 11: 773–92.

Watt, Katherine (2002), 'Thomas Walker Arnold and the Re-Evaluation of Islam, 1864–1930', *Modern Asian Studies* 36(1): 1–98.

Watt, W. M. (1953), *Muhammad at Mecca*, Oxford: Oxford University Press.

Watt, W. M. (1956), *Muhammad at Medina*, Oxford: Oxford University Press.

Watt, W. M. (1967), 'The Christianity Criticized in the Qur'an', *The Muslim World* 57(3): 197–201.

Weber, Max (1963), *The Sociology of Religion*, trans. E. Fischoff, Boston: Beacon Press.

Weismann, Itzchak (2007), *The Naqshbandiyya: Orthodoxy and Innovation in the Worldwide Sufi Tradition*, New York: Routledge.

Weismann, Itzchak (2015), 'Framing a Modern Umma: The Muslim Brothers' Evolving Project of *Da'wa*', *Sociology of Islam* 3(3–4): 146–69.

Weismann, Itzchak (2019), 'Between *Da'wa* and Dialogue: Religious Engagement in Muslim-minority Environments', *Islam and Christian-Muslim Relations* 30(4), 505–22.

Wellhausen, Julius (1927), *The Arab Kingdom and its Fall*, trans. Margaret Weir, Calcutta: University of Calcutta.

Wellhausen, Julius (1975), *The Religio-Political Factions of Early Islam*, trans. R. C. Ostel et al., Amsterdam: North Holland.

Westerlund, David (2003), 'Ahmed Deedat's Theology of Religion: Apologetics Through Polemics', *Journal of Religion in Africa* 33(3): 263–78.

Wherry, E. M., C. G. Mylrea and S. M. Zwemer, eds (1911), *Lucknow, 1911*, Madras: Christian Literature Society.

Wickham, Carrie (2013), *The Muslim Brotherhood: Evolution of an Islamist Movement*, Princeton: Princeton University Press.

Wiedl, Nina (2015), 'Contemporary Calls to Islam – Salafi Da'wa in Germany, 2002–2011', PhD Dissertation, Ben-Gurion University of the Negev.

Wiktorowicz, Quintan (2004), 'Introduction: Islamic Activism and Social Movement Theory', in Quintan Wiktorowicz (ed.), *Islamic Activism: A Social Movement Theory Approach*, Bloomington: Indiana University Press, pp. 1–33.

Wiktorowicz, Quintan (2006), 'Anatomy of the Salafi Movement', *Studies in Conflict & Terrorism* 29(3): 207–39.

Willis, John (1985), 'Preface', in John Ralph Willis (ed.), *Slaves and Slavery in Muslim Africa*, *Vol. 1*, London: Frank Cass.

Wink, André (2010), 'The Early Expansion of Islam in India', in David Morgan and Anthony Reid (eds), *The New Cambridge History of Islam, Vol. 3*, Cambridge: Cambridge University Press, pp. 78–99.

Woodhead, Linda (2002), 'Introduction', in Linda Woodhead (ed.), *Religions in the Modern World*, London: Routledge, pp. 1–12.

Wright, Christopher (2006), *The Mission of God*, Downers Grove: IVP.

Yemelianova, Galina M. (2019), *Muslims of Central Asia: An Introduction*, Edinburgh: Edinburg University Press.

Zahniser, A. H. Mathias (2001), 'Invitation', in Jane McAuliffe (ed.), *Encyclopedia of the Qur'an*, Leiden: Brill, vol. 2, pp. 557–8.

Zakariyya, Muḥammad [n. d.], *Faḍāʾil-i-Aʿmāl*, Delhi: Yaseen Book Depot; English translation: *Teachings of Islam*, translated by Abul Rashid Arshad et. al., Des Plaines: Library of Islam, [n. d.].

Zaman, Muhammad Qasim (1997), *Religion and Politics under the Early Abbasids: The Emergence of the Proto-Sunni Elite*, Leiden: Brill.

Zaman, Muhammad Qasim (2002), *The Ulama in Contemporary Islam: Custodians of Change*, Princeton: Princeton University Press.

Zaman, Muhammad Qasim (2006), 'Consensus and Religious Authority in Modern Islam', in Gudrun Krämer and Sabine Schmidtke (eds), *Speaking for Islam: Religious Authorities in Muslim Societies*, Leiden: Brill, pp. 00-00.

Zaman, Muhammad Qasim (2010), 'Transmitters of Authority and Ideas across Cultural Boundaries, Eleventh to Eighteenth Centuries', in David Morgan and Anthony Reid (eds), *The New Cambridge History of Islam, Vol. 3*, Cambridge: Cambridge University Press, pp. 582–610.

Zaman, Muhammad Qasim (2012), *Modern Islamic Thought in a Radical Age: Religious Authority and Internal Criticism*, Cambridge: Cambridge University Press.

Zebiri, Kate (1997), *Muslims and Christians Face to Face*, Oxford: Oneworld.

Zebiri, Kate (2001), 'Polemic and Polemical Language', in Jane McAuliffe (ed.), *Encyclopedia of the Qurʾan*, Leiden: Brill, vol. 4, pp. 114–25.

Zebiri, Kate (2004), 'Argumentation', in Andrew Rippin (ed.), *The Blackwell Companion to the Qurʾan*, Oxford: Blackwell, pp. 266–81.

Ze'evi, Dror (2009), 'Slavery', in John Esposito (ed.), *The Oxford Encyclopedia of the Islamic World*, Oxford: Oxford University Press, vol. 5, pp. 172–4.

Index

Note: *italic* indicates figure, n indicates endnote

Aa Gym *see* Gymnastiar, Abdullah
al-'Abbas (Muhammad's uncle), 54, 80
'Abbasids, 54, 74–5, 76, 77–8, 84, 85, 86n4, 87n24, 105, 144, 157, 226, 227, 242, 257
'Abd al-Aziz, Shah, 196, 246
'Abd al-Aziz (Ottoman Sultan), 165
'Abd al-'Aziz b. Baz, 137–8, 142n20, 223, 229, 232
'Abd al-Aziz b. Sa'ud (Ibn Saud), 145, 146, 189, 192–3
'Abd al-Malik, Caliph, 71
'Abd al-Nasser, President Gamal, 205, 207, 230, 236, 241
'Abd al-Qader, 157
'Abd al-Wahhab, Muhammad b. *see* Ibn 'Abd al-Wahhab, Muhammad
'Abduh, Muhammad, 137, 162n69, 172, 180, 186, 187, 188
Abdulhamid II, Sultan, 157
'Abdullah, King of Transjordan, 189
Abraham (The Prophet Ibrahim), 27, 37n40, 42
Abu Bakr (Companion, Caliph), 1, 44, 45, 52, 55, 61n40, 62n54, 74, 75
Abu Lahab (Muhammad's uncle), 43–4
Abu Musa (Companion), 56–7
Abu Sufyan b. Harb, 54, 63n80, 63n85
Abu Sufyan b. al-Harith (Muhammad's cousin), 54, 63n85
Abu Talib (Muhammad's uncle), 45, 48, 62n55
Abyssinia (Axum; Ethiopia), 23, 47
  Negus of, 46–7, 58
  see also Ethiopia
acculturation *see* indigenisation
Aceh (Indonesia), 92, 157
al-Afghani, Jamal al-Din, 157, 162n69, 172, 239
Afghanistan, 67 (map), 68, 85, 104 (map), 112

(map), 150–1, 152 (map), 166, 204 (map), 207, 208, 211, 227, 235; *see also* Ghazna
Aflaki, Shams al-Din Ahmad, 113, 128n109
Africa, 120, 184
  colonial period, 150, 152 (map), 153, 154, 157
  da'wa c. 1850–1950, 181–5, 186–7, 188, 195, 197–8
  da'wa c. 1950–present, 214, 215, 217, 218, 221, 224–5, 236, 241, 243, 244
  North Africa, 2, 68, 72, 82, 88n51, 91, 98, 102, 119, 150, 157, 186–7
  post-colonial, 204 (map), 205, 210, 211
  reform movements, 147
  Society of Missionaries of Africa ('White Fathers'), 155, 186
  sub-Saharan Africa, 91, 98, 101, 116, 153, 181–5, 205, 215, 221, 225, 243
  see also individual African country names; Bamba, Ahmadu; Deedat, Ahmed; Gumi, Abubakr; *Jama'at Izalat al-Bid'a wa Iqamat as-Sunna; Kano Chronicle*; Muridiyya Sufi order; Uthman Dan Fodio; World Islamic Call Society (WICS)
African Americans, 213, 223, 247, 256n171; *see also* Nation of Islam; United States; Wadud, Amina
Aga Khan, 221, 250
Aga Khan Development Network, 221–2
Age of Exploration, 141n6
agents (of *da'wa* and Islamisation), 5, 11, 46, 53, 55–8, 59, 63n95, 69, 74, 99, 107, 111, 116, 121–3, 146, 151, 257; *see also* envoys
Ahl-i Hadith (followers of Shami Damullah), 179
Ahl-i Hadith (India), 137, 142n20, 167, 199n14, 213, 214, 237
Ahmad, Khurshid, 239, 246
Ahmad b. Idris, 147

Ahmad Khan, Sir Sayyid, 163n69, 168–9, 178
Ahmadiyya movement, 133, 166, 167–8, 197, 206, 213, 225, 245, 246; *see also* Ghulam Ahmad, Mirza; India
Ahmed, Chanfi, 225
'Aisha (Muhammad's wife), 107
Ajmer (India): Shrine (*dargah*) of Mu'inuddin Chishti, 113, *114*
al-Albani, Shaykh Nasir al-Din, 137, 142n20, 229
Albania, 115; *see also* Balkans
Algar, Hamid, 89n80, 90n83
Algeria, 103, 157, 186–7, 203, 205, 229
    Young Algerians, 186
    see also 'Abd al-Qader; France
Ali, Kecia, 60n13
'Ali, Yusuf, 171
'Ali b. Abu Talib (Muhammad's cousin and son in law, fourth Caliph), 1, 44, 52, 61n37, 73, 74, 75–6, 78
Almohads, 75, 88n51, 102
Almoravids, 88n51, 102
al-Alwani, Taha, 248
amirs (emirs), 75, 226
'Amr b. al-'As, 50
'Amr b. Luhayy, 42
'Amr b. Ma'dikarib, 55
Anas, Malik b. *see* Ibn Anas, Malik
Anatolia, 2, 68, 91, 94, 102, 113, 115
Anderson, Benedict, 162n61
Andijan uprising (1898), 157
Ansar (helpers), 45–6, 48, 49, 52, 56
Ansar al-Islam (Nigeria), 221
apostasy, 55, 82, 86, 228, 235
'Aqaba pledges, 46, 48, 49
Arab American Oil Company (Aramco, later Saudi Aramco), 194
Arab Fertile Crescent (colonial era), 187–90
Arab-Islamic conquests, 40–1, 66–72, 67 (map), 72–3, 80, 85, 92, 97–8, 105, 116, 119, 120, 122, 244
Arab-Israeli war (1948–9), 190
Arab League, 236
Arab nationalism, 174, 188–9
Arabia
    conversion to Islam, 55–6, 67 (map)
    da'wa c. 1850–1950, 192–5
    independence of in colonial period, 150–1
    Muslim Brotherhood (MB) in, 214
    pre-Islamic, 23, 42
    see also Mecca; Medina; Muhammad; Najran; Quraysh; Saudi Arabia; Tabuk; Ta'if

Arabisation, 10, 66, 71, 119
argumentation and debate, 26, 28, 29–30, 35, 38n43, 59, 84–5, 90n95, 106, 164–5, 216, 217, 223, 225, 257; *see also* polemics
Armenia, 68, 125n59
Arnold, Thomas, 5, 9, 19–20, 39, 62n61, 173
Arya Samaj, 166
Ash'arites, 84
Asia
    colonial period, 152 (map)
    Gunpowder empires, 104 (map)
    Inner Asia, 93, 94, 98, 124n11
    Mongol period, 95 (map)
    post-colonial, 204 (map)
    trade, 121
    see also Central Asia; China; India; Southeast Asia
Ataturk, Mustafa Kemal, 177, 205
'Attab b. Asid, 55
Attar, Farid al-Din, 111, 113, 117
Aurangzeb, Emperor, 147
Austro-Hungarians, 150, 176, 196
Axum *see* Abyssinia
al-Azhar (mosque and *madrasa*), 77, 175–6, 179, 187, 219

Baba Tukles, 100, 127n98
Badawi, Jamal, 219
Badawiyya Sufi order, 110
Baghdad, 77, 86n4, 94
al-Baghdadi, Abu Bakr, 228
Baha Allah (Nuri, Mirza Husayn 'Ali), 191
Baha'i Faith, 191–2, 197, 206
Bahira (Christian monk), 42
al-Bakharzi, Sayf al-Din, 100
al-Baladhuri, Ahmad ibn Yahya, 62n60, 68
Balfour Declaration (1917) 189–90
Balkans, 91, 101, 115, 116, 150, 158; *see also* Albania; Bektashi brotherhood; Bosnia; Ottoman Empire: *devshirme*
Balkh, 68
Bamba, Ahmadu, 184–5, *185*, 197
Bangladesh, 167, 170, 230
    Islamic University of Technology, 240
al-Banna, Hasan, 174–5, 176, 197, 198, 210; *see also* Muslim Brotherhood (MB)
Barelvi movement, 133, 167, 199n14, 213, 214
Barnabas, Gospel of *see* Gospel of Barnabas
Battle of Badr (624 CE), 52
Battle of Hunayn (630 CE), 52, 53
Battle of Khaybar (628 CE), 52
Battle of Mu'ta (629 CE), 52
Battle of Qadisiyya (c. 637 CE), 66
Battle of Talas (751 CE), 68

Battle of the Trench (627 CE), 52, 63n75
Battle of Yarmuk (636 CE), 66
Baybars, Sultan, 102
Bektash Wali, Haji, 113
Bektashi Sufi order (Bektashiyya), 113, 115, 177
Ben Badis ('Abd al-Hamid b. Badis), 186–7, 197
Bengal, 116
    Fara'idi movement, 146
Berbers, 75, 87n29, 121
Berger, Peter, 138
Berke Khan, 100
Berkey, Jonathan, 89n63, 118, 129n140
Bhopal (India), 167
Bible, 37n19, 123, 155, 199n24, 223, 241
    and Daryabadi's *Tafsir-ul-Qur'an*, 171
    da'wa manuals and, 223
    Muslim critiques of, 164–5, 217, 238–9
    Muslim Preachers (East Africa) and, 225
    New Testament: Matthew 28:18–20, 38n49; Acts 2, 63n95; 1 Peter 2:9–10, 32
    Old Testament: Exodus 19:5–6, 32
    Sayyid Ahmad Khan's commentary on, 169
    see also Bucaille, Maurice; Deedat, Ahmed; Gospel of Barnabas; Kairanawi, Rehmatullah
Bilal (Companion), 48
bin Laden, Osama *see* Osama b. Laden
Black Death, 102
blasphemy, 230, 235
Bosnia, 196
Bosnian Muslims, 196, 208
Bosworth, C. E., 92
boundaries/borders, 68, 71, 78, 82, 96, 98, 103, 116, 120, 121, 162n61, 193, 195, 203, 206, 212, 250
Britain
    Balfour Declaration (1917), 189–90
    colonialism, 150, 152 (map), 154–5, 156, 164, 167, 169, 172–3, 176, 180, 181–2, 187, 191, 195, 197
    decolonization, 203, 204 (map), 205
    East India Company, 153; *see also* India
    Islamic Foundation (IF), 214, 246, 255n158
    minority Muslim population, 195
    Sykes-Picot Agreement (1916), 189
    uprisings against, 157, 164
    see also India; Iraq; Malaysia; Palestine; Transjordan
Brown, Nathan, 230, 232
Brown, Peter, 110
Bucaille, Maurice, 238–9
Bucailleism, 238–9

Buddhists/Buddhism, 2, 82, 91, 99, 111, 114, 161n49, 209, 239
Buddhist missionaries 111, 117, 155
Bughra Khan, 99
Bukhara, 68, 90n84, 96, 97, 98, 154, 200n64
al-Bukhari, Muhammad (hadith compiler), 40, 53, 59, 62n62, 62n71
Bulliet, Richard W., 14n21
Byzantine Empire, 23, 66, 71, 94

Cairo
    Dar al-Da'wa wa'l Irshad (House of *Da'wa* and Guidance), 173
    Dar al-'Ilm (House of Knowledge), 77
    Islamic Summit meeting (2013), 240–1
    Salafiyya bookstore, 142n19
    see also al-Azhar; Egypt
caliphs/caliphate, 45, 53, 60n3, 69, 71, 73, 74, 75, 76, 77, 84, 86n4, 92, 94, 103, 105, 119, 123n8, 138, 140, 147, 157, 177, 188, 189, 226, 228
caravanserais, 116, 119
Carey, William, 155, 162n62
Catherine the Great (Russia), 154
Catholic Church *see* Christians/Christianity
Caucasus, 150, 154, 157, 158, 162n58, 179
cemeteries *see* tombs/cemeteries
Central Asia (Transoxania)
    Cold War, 207
    conquest of 67 (map), 68, 71, 72
    da'wa c.1850–1950, 178–9
    independence (of post-Soviet states), 204 (map)
    Russian/Soviet control of, 94, 150, 152 (map), 154, 156, 161n36, 178–9, 191, 196, 207
    separatism, 195
    slave trade, 98
    spread of Islam to, 2, 71, 72, 82, 91, 94, 96, 113, 115, 146–7, 154
    trade, 119
    Turkic peoples and, 93, 94, 196
    see also Bukhara; Khiva; Mongol Khanates; Mongols; Naqshbandiyya Sufi order; Qarakhanids; Samakand; Uzbekistan
Chicago, 246, 249
children, 90n84, 133
China
    communism, 206
    minorities, 195, 202n113
    missionaries (Christian), 155, 206
    Mongols, 94, 96
    People's Republic, 150
    Qing Empire, 150

spread of Islam, 2, 91, 120–1
T'ang dynasty, 68
Uighurs, 202n113, 244
Xinjiang, 150, 156, 161n36, 195, 202n113, 244
see also Battle of Talas; Kashgar
Chinggis Khan *see* Ghengis Khan
Chishti, Mu'inuddin, 113
  shrine, *114*
Chishtiyya Sufi order, 110, 113, 116
Christians/Christianity, 8, 11, 32, 68, 91, 96, 98, 111, 117, 118, 122, 171, 185, 206, 221, 223, 225, 239
  Abyssinian, 23, 47
  Arab, 23, 76, 188, 189, 190, 205
  Catholics/Catholic Church, 102, 117, 155, 186, 221, 255n163
  Christendom, 87n28, 150, 153, 154, 161n34, 202n121
  Christianisation, 96, 99, 161n49, 183, 186
  and colonialism, 153–6,162n60, 180
  conversion to Christianity, 96, 99, 183
  conversions to Islam, 2, 44, 70, 94, 113, 115
  Coptic, 102, 172, 202n113
  eclipse of in Middle East, 101–2
  Edict of Toleration (313 CE), 54
  Evangelical, 162n63, 199n9, 209, 237
  missio Dei, 24
  missionaries, 111, 117, 151, 153, 154–5, 156, 159, 164–6, 167, 168, 169, 170, 172–3, 174, 175, 176, 180, 183, 184, 186, 202n121, 206, 217, 220
  and the life of Muhammad, 38n43, 42, 44, 46–7, 48, 57, 61n25, 62n69
  Muslim debates with, 21, 29–30, 76, 82, 84, 164–5, 217
  Pentecostal/Charismatic, 209, 225
  persecution of, 102, 125n61
  in pre-Islamic context, 23, 41, 42, 82
  Protestant, 10, 149, 155, 212, 214
  and the Qur'an, 21, 23, 31, 38n43, 38n55
  and Sufism 109–10, 113, 114, 115
  voluntary societies (or associations), 155, 212, 220
  Yemen, 57
  see also Bible; Bucaille, Maurice; churches; Deedat, Ahmed; Kairanawi, Rehmatullah; Reformation, Protestant; Rida, Rashid
Chrysostomides, Anna, 14n23, 87n24
churches, 23, 54, 155, 161n34, 186, 202n121, 220
  World Council of Churches, 238; *see also* Christians/Christianity

cities, 66, 68, 69, 76, 82, 119, 120, 145, 207, 208, 240, 251n18
Cold War, 207
colonialism, 117, 120, 136, 141n9, 143, 144, 148–57, 152 (map), 158–9, 161n48, 162n60, 180, 251n11
  colonial modernity, 136, 139 (definition)
  da'wa initiated under, 164–98
  da'wa initiated in post-colonial times, 203–50
  post-colonial/post-colonial modernity, 136, 140 (definition), 204 (map)
  see also Africa; Asia; Britain, Christians/Christianity: and colonialism; decolonisation, France; Dutch Empire; Middle East; Ottoman Empire; Russia
commanding and forbidding (*al-amr bi'l-ma'ruf*), 8, 33–5, 53, 56, 83, 106, 193, 235
Commins, David, 225, 254n129
common people (ordinary/lay Muslims), 4, 27–8, 35, 73, 94, 97, 107, 111, 115, 117–19, 122, 123, 139, 140, 147, 148, 156, 159, 166, 170, 171, 174, 176, 177, 184, 198, 215, 219, 223
  'turn to the masses', 107, 156, 198
  see also democratisation; laicisation
communication, 14n14, 26, 135, 155, 180, 208, 233; *see also* internet; newspapers; travel
Companions of the Prophet (*ṣaḥāba*), 1, 19, 39, 41, 44, 45, 46, 49, 50, 52, 53, 55, 56–7, 62n54, 63n95, 74, 86n12, 89n64, 117, 119, 144, 149, 168, 231, 259
Confucianism, 91
Constantine, Emperor, 54
Constantinople, 68, 94
convents *see* Sufis/Sufism: convents, *khanqah*s
conversion: definition, 10–11, 13; *see also* Christianity: conversion to; Islam: conversion to; Islamisation; 'reversion'
Cook, David, 253n97, 253n100
Cook, Michael, 38n53
courts, 105, 192, 193, 231
COVID-19 pandemic, 102, 258–60
Crimea, 150
Crusades/Crusaders, 77, 94, 102, 151

Dabiq (IS online magazine) *see Rumiyah*
Dahlan, Ahmad, 163n69, 180–1, 197
*da'i*s (missionary preachers), 13, 24, 25, 29, 31, 34, 39, 45, 46, 53, 57, 74, 77, 111–12, 133, 220, 223, 232, 239; *see also* names of individual preachers

Dallal, Ahmad, 254n143
Damascus, 66, 86n4
Damullah, Shami, 179
Dannin, Robert, 256n171
Daoism, 91
Dar al-Da'wa wa'l Irshad (House of *Da'wa* and Guidance), 173; *see also* Cairo; education; Rida, Rashid
dar al-harb ('the house of war'), 51, 80, 81, 120, 195–6
dar al-Islam ('the house of Islam'), 51, 80, 81–2, 92, 93, 111, 120, 121, 153, 195–6; *see also* Muslim ecumene; Islamdom
Dargah Quli Khan, 128n121
Daryabadi, 'Abd al-Majid, 171
da'wa
    as missionary invitation, 9, 13, 79, 81, 133–4, 159
    as religio-political summons, 9, 46, 49, 51, 54, 56–7, 59–60, 74–5, 78, 188–9, 193, 210, 226–9, 242
    centrifugal, 14n14, 47, 57, 59, 71, 117, 120, 122
    centripetal, 14n14, 47, 55, 57, 59, 71, 97, 117, 120, 122
    as collective obligation or individual obligation (*fard al-kifaya* or *fard al-'ayn*) 38n50, 133, 222–3, 256n186
    definition and variants of, 4, 8–10, 12, 13
    democratisation of *see* common people; separate entry below
    external, 8, 13, 30, 73, 76, 83, 84, 106, 117, 122, 134, 135, 182, 198, 259
    false, 25, 27, 34, 42, 47, 55
    initiated in colonial period, 164–98
    initiated in post-colonial times, 203–50
    internal, 8, 13, 21, 30, 65, 73, 74–8, 83, 84, 103, 106–7, 117, 122, 135, 137, 182, 198, 219, 257, 259
    intra-Muslim competition in, 4, 11, 74–8, 85, 103, 137, 176, 197, 209, 216
    Meccan, 10, 13, 42–8, 49, 59, 134, 139, 168, 172, 176, 191, 197, 209, 210, 222, 223, 228, 229, 244, 245–6, 250, 257
    Medinan, 10, 13, 46, 48–59, 69, 78, 81, 85, 134, 139, 146, 197, 209, 226–7, 228, 229, 250, 257
    'Najdi *da'wa*', 137, 145–6, 228
    non-state and state-sponsored organisations, 242–3
    non-state initiatives and actors, 212–29
    opposition to, 47–8, 50–1
    polycentric/multidirectional nature of, 212
    in prophetic *sira* and hadith, 39–60; *see also* Muhammad
    in the Qur'an *see under* Qur'an
    standardisation of, 242
    state-sponsored as domestic policy, 230–5
    state-sponsored as foreign policy, 236–42
    training manuals, 222–3
    use of term, 9–10, 75, 78
    writings on, 5–6
DawahSkills.com, 233
da'walogy/da'walogies, 14n15, 19–35, 39, 41, 45, 59, 84, 148, 167, 178, 197, 209, 229, 242, 245–6
    definition, 5, 8–9, 13
    see also da'wa: Meccan; *da'wa*: Medinan; missiology; Qur'an: *da'walogy* of
Da'wat-i Islami (the *Da'wa* of Islam), 213
Day of Judgment, 1, 24, 31, 34, 35
debate *see* argumentation and debate
decolonisation, 203, 244, 250n1; *see also* colonialism
Deedat, Ahmed, 165, 215, 217, 218, 219, 225, 239
    Islamic Propagation Centre International (IPCI), 215
Delhi, 147, 198n3
DeLong-Bas, Natana, 160n13, 160n16
democratisation, 4, 123, 134, 139, 140, 209, 218, 247; *see also* laicisation
Deobandis/Deoband movement, 133, 138, 166–7, 199n14, 210, 213, 214, 219, 236
    Deobandi *da'wa*, 166, 168
    see also Ilyas, Muhammad; India; Tablighi Jama'at; Zakariyya, Muhammad
devotionalism, 109; *see also* Sufis/Sufism
DeWeese, Devin, 63n89, 127n96
Dhu Nuwas, 42
dialogue, 30, 52, 59, 76, 160n16, 171, 216, 222, 240–41, 246, 253n76
Dimam b. Tha'laba, 57–8
disestablishment
    definition, 138–9, 140, 161n48
    and the internet, 216
    of Islam, 151, 153–5, 164–5, 167, 170, 176–8, 179, 180, 186, 193, 206, 226, 229, 230
    Muslim minorities and, 214, 243, 246
Donner, Fred M., 56, 61n34, 123n1, 124n10
Dukchi Ishan, Shaykh (Ihsan Madali), 157
Dutch Empire, 150, 152 (map), 153–4, 179–80
    decolonisation, 203, 204 (map), 205

East Indies *see* Indonesia
East Syrian church *see* churches
economic development, 135, 151, 221; *see also* modernity
ecumene: definition, 123n2
education (*tarbiyya*, training), 105–7, 166, 173, 178, 180–1, 192, 210, 213, 220–1, 222, 234, 240, 249; *see also madrasas*; schools; universities
Egypt, 58, 92, 157, 166, 183, 188, 190, 198
al-Azhar's Academy of Islamic Research, 241
    Arab conquest of, 66, 69, 77
    British colonialism in, 150, 153, 173
    Cold War, 207
    Coptic Christians, 102
    da'wa c. 1850–1950, 172–6
    Fatimid Empire, 75–8, 144, 157, 175, 191, 226, 227, 242, 257
    Egyptian Feminist Union, 175
    Mamluk Sultanate, 98, 102
    Muslim Brotherhood (MB), 170, 174–5, 176, 210, 231
    Muslim Women's Association, 175
    Napoleon's colonisation of, 143
    post-1952, 205, 207, 214, 215, 231, 239, 241
    religious communities (pre-Islamic), 23
    Salafi Association, 142n19
    state-sponsored *da'wa* initiatives, 230
    Takfir w'al-Hijra, 210, 214
    see also 'Abd al-Nasser, President Gamal; al-Azhar; Cairo; al-Ghazali, Zaynab; Khaled, Amr; Kishk, Shaykh 'Abd al-Hamid; Muhammad (Mehmet) 'Ali; Muslim Brotherhood; Sadat, President Anwar
Elijah (The Prophet Ilyas), 27
elites, 69, 123, 151, 177, 203
Emerick, Yahya, 223
emirs *see* amirs
Enlightenment, the, 141n6, 150, 151
envoys *see* agents
Erdogan, President Recep Tayyip, 231
Esposito, John, 250n7
Estes, Yusuf, 219
Ethiopia, 125n59, 183; *see also* Abyssinia
Euben, Roxanne, 14n20
Europe, 2, 9, 68, 91, 92, 98, 120, 123, 161n33, 165
    Christianisation of, 96, 99, 117
    colonialism, 136, 143, 147, 148–57, 152 (map), 173, 176, 182, 186, 187, 191, 192, 195, 208

Islam/Muslims/*da'wa* in, 113, 167, 195, 197, 213, 244–5
    nationalism, 150, 162n61
    post-Christian, 209
    see also Balkans; Britain; colonialism; France
European Council for Fatwa and Research (ECFR), 220
European Union, 241
exclusivism, 31, 35, 38n54, 59, 82, 87n36, 116, 171, 222, 231; *see also* inclusivism

Faisal, King of Iraq, 189
Faisal b. 'Abd al-Aziz Al Sa'ud, King of Saudi Arabia, 236
    King Faisal Prize for Service to Islam, 217, 235, 239, 242
Fall, Shaykh Ibrahima, 184
al-Farabi, 84
Farrakhan, Louis, 252n43
al-Faruqi, Isma'il, 222, 248
fasting, 32, 49, 92, 235, 241, 259
Fatimids, 91, 144, 157, 175, 191, 226, 227, 242, 257
    Isma'ili/Fatimid *da'wa*, 75–8, 85, 125n56
fatwas (Islamic legal advice)/*muftis*, 90n84, 101, 106, 166, 176, 190, 196, 219–20, 223, 248, 250, 258
Faymiyun (Christian holy man), 42
feminism, 175, 208, 247–8
Findley, Carter, 128n117
fiqh *see* jurisprudence
al-Fiqī, Muhammad Ḥāmid, 160n10
Fletcher, Joseph, 96
France
    colonialism, 150, 152 (map), 153, 154, 155, 156, 172, 181–2, 184, 186–7, 189
    decolonisation, 203, 204 (map), 205
    French Revolution, 150
    minority Muslim population, 195, 213, 244, 245
    Sykes-Picot Agreement (1916), 189
    see also Africa; Algeria; Lebanon; Morocco; Syria
Franks, 68, 99
Friedmann, Yohannan, 82, 89n70
Frykenberg, Robert, 162n51

Gaborieau, Marc, 162n64
Gambia, 147, 183, 184, 185
Gabriel, Angel, 20, 43, 126n81
Gangohi, Rashid Ahmad, 162n69; *see also* Deobandis/Deoband movement
Gasprinski, Isma'il, 178
gender equality *see* feminism

Genghis (Chinggis) Khan, 94, 96, 100
Georgia, 125n59
Ghana, 183, 185, 225
Ghassanids, 23
al-Ghazali, Abu Hamid, 110
al-Ghazali, Zaynab, 175, 197, 198
Ghazan Khan, 100–1
Ghazi Muhammad, 157
Ghazna (Afghanistan), 98
Ghengis (Chinggis) Khan, 94
Ghulam Ahmad, Mirza, 167–8, *169; see also*
    Ahmadiyya movement
global marketplace, 138–9, 140, 195
globalisation, 141n8, 212, 236, 239
Gnostics, 23
God
    *da'wa*s to and of in the Qur'an, 22–5, 29, 35
    nature of, 21
    sovereign will of, 25
    tawhid (God's Oneness), 75, 145, 223, 228
    as the ultimate *da'i*, 31, 34
Golden, Daniel, 255n145
Golden, Peter, 100
Golden Horde, 96, 100
Goldziher, Ignaz, 6, 87n33, 165
Gospel of Barnabas, 172, 225; *see also*
    argumentation and debate; Rida, Rashid
gradualism, 30, 35, 54, 59, 71–2, 73, 82, 85,
    115, 209–10, 226; *see also* indigenisation
Green, Nile, 14n23, 114–15, 126n83,
    128n122, 142n24, 163n77, 166
Green, Abdur Raheem, 219
Griffith, Sidney, 87n26
Gugler, Thomas, 213
Guinea, 225
Gulen, Fethullah, 215, *215,* 219
Gumi, Abubakr, 224; *see also* Africa; *Jama'at
    Izalat al-Bid'a wa Iqamat as-Sunna;* Nigeria
Gymnastiar, Abdullah (Aa Gym), 218–19;
    see also Indonesia; preachers/preaching;
    televangelists

hadith, 7, 20, 36, 39, 40–1, 43, 44, 49, 50,
    52, 54, 58, 59, 79, 80, 82, 87n33, 105–7,
    109, 110, 115, 126n81, 137, 144, 145,
    148, 223, 238, 259; *see also* Ahl-i Hadith;
    Muhammad
hagiographies, 111, 113, 114, 146
Hamadani, Shaykh Sayyid 'Ali, 113
Hanafis, 80, 89n66, 166, 178, 231
Haram b. Milhan, 51
Harris, William Wade, 185
Hasafiyya Sufi order, 174; *see also* al-Banna,
    Hasan; Egypt

al-Hashimi (ninth-century scholar), 76
Hausaland, 101, 107–8, 147
Haykal, Muhammad Husayn, 163n69, 173–4;
    see also Egypt; modernism
healthcare, 102, 220, 221; *see also*
    humanitarian programmes
Hefner, Robert, 161n40, 205, 251n18,
    251n29
helpers *see* Ansar
Heraclius, Emperor (Byzantium), 58, 59
heresies/heretics, 84–5, 86, 90n84, 168, 192,
    206
heresiography, 84
Hezbollah *see* under Lebanon
hijra, 38n54, 40, 48–9, 50, 59, 81
    'first *hijra*' to Abyssinia (c. 615 CE), 47
    migration to *dar al-Islam*, 81, 126n74,
        160n26, 196
    Saudi agricultural settlements, 193
    see also migration; travel
Hindus/Hinduism, 2, 78, 91, 114, 126n61,
    147, 153, 161n49, 162n50, 167, 170,
    171, 209, 217, 239
    Hindu missionaries, 155, 164, 166, 167,
        252n60
Hiskett, M., 108
Hizb ut Tahrir (HT, Islamic Liberation
    Party), 226–7
Hodgson, Marshall G. S., 87n28, 123n8
Hoodhbhoy, Pervez, 255n145
hospitals, 155, 174, 221; *see also* healthcare
Hourani, Albert, 143–4, 159n2
Hoyland, Robert, 14n20, 86n7, 87n20
Hud (Prophet), 27, 37n31
Hujwiri, Abu'l-Hasan 'Ali, 113
Hulegu Khan, 94, 125n48
humanitarian programmes, 155, 220–2,
    255n153, 255n163, 250; *see also* welfare
    associations and initiatives
Hurgronje, Christiaan Snouck, 154, 157; *see
    also* Dutch Empire; Indonesia
al-Husayni, Amin (*mufti* of Jerusalem), 190, 197

Ibadi sect, 230
Ibn 'Abd al-Wahhab, Muhammad b., 137,
    145–6, 160n10, 228; *see also* Wahhabis/
    Wahhabism
Ibn Anas, Malik, 40
Ibn al-Athir, 'Ali 'Izz al-Din, 99
Ibn Baz *see* 'Abd al-'Aziz b. Baz
Ibn Battuta, 92
Ibn Hanbal, Ahmad, 40, 126n65
Ibn Hisham, Abu Muhammad 'Abd al-Malik,
    40

Ibn 'Idhari, Abu al-Abbas Ahmad, 87n29
Ibn Idris, Ahmad, 147
Ibn Ishaq, Muhammad, 40, 42, 43, 45, 46,
    47–8, 49, 50, 51, 53–4, 56
Ibn Khaldun, Abu Zayd ar-Rahman ibn
    Muhammad, 75, 87n29, 124n13
Ibn Sa'd, Abu Abd Allah Muhammad, 40, 53,
    62n60, 62n72
Ibn Taymiyya, Taqi ad-Din Ahmad, 84,
    89n75, 101, 102, 118, 137, 144, 145, 195
Ibn Tumart, Abu Abd Allah Muhammad, 75
Ibrahim (Prophet) see Abraham
Ibrahim, Ayman, 86n8, 86n10, 87n15
Ibrahim, I. A., 255n145
iconoclasm, 50, 53–5
idols/idolatry, 36n14, 42, 53, 56, 63n80, 80,
    145, 228
Idris, Shaykh Ismaila, 224
Idrisiyya Sufi order see Muhammadiyya Sufi
    order
Ihsan Madali see Dukchi Ishan, Shaykh
Ikhwan (Brothers, Saudi Arabia) see under
    Saudi Arabia
Ilkhanate, 95 (map), 96, 100, 101
illiteracy, 116, 174; see also literacy
Ilyas see Elijah
Ilyas, Muhammad, 166–7, 168, 178, 180, 197,
    213; see also Tablighi Jama'at
Imamiyya (Imamis; Twelvers), 76–7, 103,
    104, 133, 191
Imams/imams, 74, 75, 76, 78, 106, 190, 191,
    221, 233, 246
immigration see migration
inclusivism, 30–1, 35, 116
independence movements, 158, 180, 182,
    187, 205
India, 2, 3 (map), 82, 91, 95 (map), 98, 101,
    104 (map), 121, 172, 177, 198n2, 217
    Aligarh Muslim University, 168
    BJP (Bhartiya Janata Party), 217
    census (1871), 156
    colonialism, 150, 152 (map), 153–4, 155,
        157, 164–71, 179, 191, 195, 204 (map)
    da'wa c. 1850–1950, 164–71
    da'wa since 1950, 212–13, 217, 221, 222,
        237, 243, 245, 249
    as dar al-harb, 196
    Da'wat-i Islami, 213
    Deoband see Deobandis/Deoband
        movement
    jihad of Sayyid Ahmad of Bareilly, 157
    Khojas, 221; see also Aga Khan
    minority Muslim population, 158, 195
    Partition, 16, 170, 197, 244

spread of Islam, 91, 96, 101, 120, 173
Sufis/Sufism in, 113, 114, 115, 116, 117
    (map), 183
Taj Mahal, 96, 97
see also Ahl-i Hadith; Ahmad Khan, Sir
    Sayyid; Bangladesh; Bhopal; Britain;
    Hindus/Hinduism; Lucknow; Mughal
    Empire; Naik, Zaikr; Pakistan; Sirhindi,
    Shaykh
Ahmad; Tablighi Jama'at; Varanasi; Wali
    Allah, Shah of Delhi
Indian Muslim League, 170–1, 197
Indian Ocean, 98, 161n43
Indian subcontinent see Bangladesh; India;
    Pakistan
Indian Uprising ("Mutiny") (1857), 157
indigenisation, 12, 13, 72, 93, 113, 114, 115,
    116
Indo-Malaysia, 7, 91, 101; see also Indonesia;
    Malaysia
Indonesia, 3 (map), 117 (map), 150, 152
    (map), 153–4, 180, 203, 204 (map)
    Cold War, 207
    colonialism see Dutch Empire; Indo-
        Malaysia; Southeast Asia
    da'wa c. 1850–1950, 178–81, 183
    da'wa since 1950, 215, 218–19, 221, 224
    Dewan Dakwah Islamiyah Indonesia
        (DDII, the Indonesian Islamic Da'wa
        Council), 224
    Diwan Dawat al-Islam, 221
    Jam'iyyat Ihya' al-Turath al-Islami, 253n80
    Lembaga Dakwah Islam Indonesia
        (Indonesia Institute of Islamic Dawah)
        (LDII), 224
    Ministry of Religious Affairs (MORA), 231
    Muhammadiyah movement, 180–1,
        207, 210, 214, 220; Aisyiyah (women's
        branch), 181
    Muslimat NU, 181, 182, 258
    Nahdlatul Ulama (NU), 181
    post-colonial, 180, 203, 207, 210, 230
    re-establishment of Islam, 230
    secularism, 205
    see also Aceh; Dahlan, Ahmad; Dutch
        Empire; Jakarta; Java; Sukarno; Sumatra
industrialisation/Industrial Revolution, 135, 150
information technology, 141n8, 207, 216,
    232; see also communication; internet;
    technologies
International Institute of Islamic Thought
    (IIIT), 222
International Organization for the Holy
    Quran and Immaculate Sunnah, 238

International Union of Muslim Scholars
    (IUMS), 220
internet, 78, 166, 208, 216, 220, 228,
    232, 234; *see also* communication;
    technologies; websites; YouTube
inter-religious relations, 5, 21, 22, 23, 28,
    29–30, 41, 44, 71, 78, 79, 106, 115, 120,
    176, 206, 215–16, 222, 225, 240, 244,
    246
    definition, 11–12, 13, 14n25
    see also da'wa: external
intra-religious relations, 4, 22, 23, 30, 73, 74,
    78, 85, 103, 106, 117, 137, 151, 176,
    197–8, 216
    definition, 11–12, 13
    see also da'wa: internal
Iqbal, Muhammad, 161n45, 163n69, 188
Iran
    colonial period, 150–1, 152 (map)
    conversion to Islam, 42, 66, 67 (map), 71,
        72, 91, 113, 117 (map)
    conversion to Shi'ite Islam, 103, 191
    coup (1953), 207
    da'wa c. 1850–1950, 191–2
    da'wa since 1950, 211–12, 227, 235, 242,
        243
    Islamic Culture and Religious Organisation
        (ICRO), 242, 243
    Ministry of Culture and Islamic Guidance
        (MCIG), 242, 243
    oil, 192, 211
    Pahlavi dynasty, 191, 192, 211–12
    Qajar dynasty, 191
    religious police, 235
    Revolution (1979), 211–12, 227, 230, 242
    see also Kazarun; Khomeini, Ayatollah
        Ruhollah; Khurasan; Persia; Reza Shah;
        Safavid Empire
Iraq, 67 (map), 113, 203, 205, 227, 244
    'Abbasid *da'wa* in, 74–5
    Arab-Islamic conquest, 66, 69
    colonialism, 150, 152 (map), 187, 189, 204
        (map); *see also* Arab Fertile Crescent
    Hizb al-Da'wa in Iraq ('Party of Da'wa'),
        227
    invasion of (2003), 208
    oil wealth, 211
    post-colonial, 203, 205
    Second Fitna (680–92 CE),74
    see also Baghdad
'Isa *see* Jesus
Ishmael (The Prophet Isma'il), 27, 42
ISIS (Islamic State; IS; ISIL), 73, 208, 211,
    227, 228; *see also* Jihadis/Jihadism

Iskandar Shah, 101
Islam
    centrifugal impulse of, 120, 122; *see also*
        da'wa: centrifugal
    centripetal pull of, 97, 117, 120, 122; *see also*
        da'wa: centripetal
    conversion to, 1, 2, 8, 10–11, 13 (definition),
        14n23, 26, 30, 42, 44–6, 46–7, 48, 50,
        51, 52, 54–5, 56, 58, 62n69, 63n89,
        69, 70, 71–3, 78, 79, 80, 81–3, 85, 91,
        93, 94, 96, 97, 98, 99, 100, 101–3,
        105, 107, 111, 113, 115, 116–17, 121,
        122, 128n122, 146, 161n45, 182, 183,
        223, 225, 244, 247, 256n171; *see also*
        Islamisation
    conversion from *see* apostasy
    'courtly-cosmopolitan', 161n47
    cultural diversity of, 72, 91–2
    disestablishment of *see* separate entry
        above
    expansion of, 58, 66, 70, 80, 91
    'in relay' transmission of, 121; *see also*
        Islamisation
    as a missionary religion, 1, 2, 4, 11, 12, 29,
        70, 72, 99
    qur'anic/early Islam, 38n48
    reform/reformism *see* separate entry below
    renewal *see tajdid* (renewal) movements
    revival, 146, 170, 174, 188, 208–9, 211,
        230, 243; *see also* Islamic revival
    as a tribal religion, 70
    universality of, 1, 2, 29, 59, 70, 84–5
    as a world religion, 2, 92, 138–9, 156
    see also Islamists/Islamism; Muslims
Islamabad (Pakistan)
    First International Conference on Scientific
        Miracles of The Holy Quran and
        Sunnah (1987), 255n145
    International Islamic University, Islamabad
        (IIUI), 233
    Shah Faisal Mosque, 236–7, *237*
Islamdom, 71, 72, 94, 96; *see also dar al-Islam*;
    Muslim ecumene
Islamic Broadcasting Union (IBU), 240
Islamic Call College, 241
Islamic civilisation, 14n20, 72, 116, 122, 169
Islamic Development Bank, 240
Islamic Educational, Scientific and Cultural
    Organization (ISESCO), 240
Islamic Jihad group, 210, 214
Islamic law, 52, 68, 78–83, 85–6, 102, 105,
    134, 195–6, 258
    dhimmi regulations, 102–3
    international, 79, 81

schools, 79, 83, 88n59, 89n66, 138, 181, 188
maqāṣid al-sharī'a (the purposes of the law), 83
shari'a, 5, 79, 83, 116, 228, 230, 235
see also courts; *fatwas; 'ulama*
Islamic Liberation Party *see* Hizb ut Tahrir
Islamic Propagation Centre International (IPCI), 215
Islamic Research Foundation, 216
Islamic revival (Islamic resurgence), 149, 208–9, 229–30, 233, 234, 251n26
Islamic Society of North America (ISNA), 214, 246
Islamic State *see* ISIS
Islamic World Relief, 221
Islamisation, 4, 7, 9, 66, 83, 91, 122, 124n10, 134, 148, 151–2
  agents and patterns of c. 1100–1700 CE, 91–123
  Arab-Islamic conquests and, 66–72, 85
  colonial powers and, 182–3
  definition, 10–11, 13
  gradual, 30, 71–2, 73, 82, 85, 93, 94, 96, 99, 114–16, 122, 209, 210; *see also* gradualism
  through in-migration, 93–9
  and Muslim diaspora, 71, 248
  through popularisation, 117–19
  processes, 10, 13, 71–2, 99
  rulers/ruler-converts and, 99–103
  slavery and, 97–9
  state-supported, 211, 236
  Sufis' role, 109–17, 144–5
  traders and, 119–21
  the *'ulama* and, 105–8
Islamists/Islamism, 5, 9, 14n17, 133, 137–8, 140, 166, 169, 175, 186, 198, 210, 212, 226, 227–8, 230, 242, 248
  post-Islamism, 228–9, 253n98
Islamophobia, 5, 240–1, 245, 260n6
  'Islamophobia Observatory', 240
IslamQA (website), 220
IslamWeb.net, 233–5
Isma'il I, Shah (Safavid), 103
Isma'il (Prophet) *see* Ishmael
Isma'il (son of Imam Ja'far), 77
Isma'ilis, 133
  Institute of Isma'ili Studies (IIS), 221, 222
  Isma'ili Fatimid movement and *da'wa*, 75–8, 85, 125n56
  Isma'ili Khojas, 221–2
  see also Aga Khan; Fatimid Empire, Nizaris; Qarmatis

isnad see silsilas
Israel, modern state of, 197, 208, 244
  formation of, 190, 207, 244
  'Six Day War' (1967), 207, 208
  'Yom Kippur War' (1973), 210–11
  see also Jerusalem; Jews; Palestine; Palestinians; Zionism
Ivory Coast, 183, 185, 225

Jabbar b. Salma, 51
Jadidism, 178
Ja'far, Imam, 77, 191
Ja'far b. Abu Talib, 47
jahiliyya, 42, 145, 210, 227, 256n172
Jakarta, 238
al-Jalalayn (Qur'an commentary), 38n50, 38n51
Jama'at Izalat al-Bid'a wa Iqamat as-Sunna (Yan Izala; JIBWIS), 224–5
Jama'at-i Islami (JI), 170, 180, 175, 199n18, 210, 211, 213, 214, 220, 226, 246, 247, 250; *see also* Mawdudi, Abul A'la; Pakistan
Jameelah, Maryam, 247–8
Jam'iyya al-Shar'iyya movement, 200n46
Janissaries, 115, 177; *see also* Ottoman Empire: *devshirme*
Janson, Torsten, 89n61, 141n1, 255n158
Java, 101, 114, 120–1, 157, 180, 182, 201n75
Jenkins, Philip, 125n61
Jerusalem, 44, 66, 77, 190
  Dome of the Rock, 71
Jesus, 27, 38n49, 44, 47, 63n95, 172
Jews, 2, 21, 23, 31, 34, 38n43, 38n55, 41, 42, 44, 84
  da'wa to/conversion to Islam, 50, 57, 70, 84, 103, 108, 113, 223, 247
  migration to Palestine, 189–90
  nationalism, 189; *see also* Zionism
  persecution of, 102–3, 108, 125n61, 202n113
  see also Israel; Judaism
JIBWIS *see Jama'at Izalat al-Bid'a wa Iqamat as-Sunna*
jihad
  anti-colonial, 157, 183
  anti-Soviet (Afghanistan), 211, 227
  classical concepts of, 5, 8, 72, 134
  'Fulani *jihad*', 147, 183
  'gender jihad', 247–8
  against Ghazan Khan, 101
  global, 193, 227

jihad (*cont.*)
and Islamic law, 79–81, 82
jihad al-akbar (the 'greater jihad'), 52, 116, 184
jihad al-asghar (the 'lesser jihad'), 52, 116; *see also* military below
jihad-as-da'wa, 159, 164, 167, 178, 180, 183, 184, 191, 210, 229, 252n57
and martyrdom, 51
meaning of, 51–2, 229
military, 68, 145–6, 157, 158–9, 167, 190, 210, 226
in Muhammad's life, 50, 51–2, 62n71
and post-Islamism, 229, 253n98
in the Qur'an, 30, 32, 34, 37n30
Sufis and, 116
Jihadis/Jihadism, 51, 73, 166, 211, 226, 228, 229, 242
failure of, 229–30, 253n97
Jihadi-Salafism, 138, 140, 227–8, 229; *see also* Islamic Jihad group; Islamists/Islamism; al-Qaeda
Jilani, 'Abd al-Qadir, 113
Jinnah, Muhammad 'Ali, 205
Jordan, modern state of, 189, 254n114
Joseph (The Prophet Yusuf), 27
Judaism, 23, 42, 60n2, 91, 96, 114, 171; *see also* Jews
jurisprudence (*fiqh*)
and *da'wa*, 78–83
definition, 79
fiqh al-da'wa, 4, 9
Fiqh Council of North America, 246
Hanafi school, 80
Islamic Fiqh Council, 238
minorities' (*fiqh al-aqaliyyāt*), 196, 248–9
and Sunna, 79

Kairanawi, Rehmatullah, 162n69, 164–5, 171, 172, 174, 218
kalām see theology (Islamic)
Kano Chronicle, 107–8, 147
Kashgar (China), 96, 99
Kashmir, 113
al-Kawakibi, 'Abd al-Rahman, 188
Kazakhstan, 203; *see also* Central Asia
al-Kazaruni, Ibrahim, 111–13
Kazaruniyya Sufi order, 111
Kenya, 150, 183, 221, 225
Khadija (Muhammad's wife), 1, 42, 44, 45, 48
Khaled, Amr, 217–18, 219
Khalid, Adeeb, 178, 179
Khalid b. al-Walid (Companion), 50–1, 52, 53, 63n80, 86n12
Khalidi, Tarif, 40

Khalwatiyya Sufi order, 160n32
Kharijites (Khawarij), 73, 74, 84
Khatmiyya Sufi order, 201n85
Khiva, 98, 154
Khomeini, Ayatollah Ruhollah, 192, 211–12, 226–7, 242; *see also* Iran; Islamists/Islamism; Shi'ites
Khurasan, 74, 90n84, 106, 128n109; *see also* Central Asia; Iran
al-Kindi, 76
King Abdullah Bin Abdulaziz International Center for Interreligious and Intercultural Dialogue (KAICIID), 240–1
King Faisal Prize for Service to Islam, 217, 235, 239, 242
Kishk, Shaykh 'Abd al-Hamid, 216; *see also* preachers/preaching; televangelists
Kramer, Martin, 173, 242
Kubrawiyya Sufi order, 110, 113
Kurds, 71, 189
Kuwait, 208, 211, 215, 233, 253n80
Kuyper, Abraham, 153–4

Lacroix, Stephane, 142n20
Lahore: Data Darbar shrine, 113
laicisation, 139, 140; *see also* democratisation
Lakhmids, 23
Lapidus, Ira, 126n67, 126n85, 129n148, 160n26, 161n47, 201n72
Lavigerie, Cardinal Charles, 155, 186; *see also* Africa: Society of Missionaries of Africa
law *see* Islamic law; jurisprudence
Lebanon, 150, 166, 187, 188, 189, 190
Hezbollah, 220, 227
Lecker, Michael, 61n35
Levant, the, 102
Levtzion, Nehemiah, 87n29
Libya, 186, 211, 241
World Islamic Call Society (WICS), 241–2
literacy, 107, 139, 149, 207; *see also* illiteracy
Luqman (Prophet), 33

madrasas, 4, 77, 92, 96, 97, 106–7, 117, 118, 175–6, 179, 187, 208, 219, 233, 237
madrasa-khanqahs, 113
see also education; schools
al-Maghili, 'Abd al-Karim ibn Muhammad, 103, 108
al-Mahdi, Caliph, 76, 90n95
Malaysia, 2, 91, 101
colonialism, 150, 152 (map), 180
International Islamic University Malaysia (IIUM), 240

Muslim Youth Movement of Malaysia, 221
PERKIM (All Malaysia Muslim Welfare Association), 224
religious police, 235
Youth Movement of Malaysia (ABIM), 224
see also Indo-Malaysia; Indonesia; Southeast Asia
Malcolm X, 252n43
Mali, 101, 108, 120, 203, 225; see also Timbuktu
Malik, Jamal, 9, 198n5
Malik al-Salih, 101
Malinke people, 121
mamluks/Mamluk sultanate, 98, 102, 125n56, 202n113
al-Ma'mun, Caliph, 76, 84, 90n95, 105
al-Manar (journal), 172, 174, 197; see also Rida, Rashid
Manichaeism, 2, 23, 41, 82
Mansa Musa (ruler of Mali, d. 1337), 120
Marcionites, 23
al-Marghinani, Burhan al-Din, 79, 80
Maronites, 189
martyrs/martyrdom, 69, 110
  da'wa through, 51, 59
Mary, mother of Jesus, 47
al-Massabiki, Niqula, 166
Masud, Muhammad Khalid, 220
Mawdudi, Abul A'la, 169–70, 175, 197, 198, 199n18, 210, 232, 239, 246, 247
Mawlawiyya (Mevleviyya) Sufi order, 110, 112 (map), 113
Mazdakism, 23
Mecca, 9, 23, 29, 37n42, 40, 41, 43, 45, 46, 47–8, 49, 53, 54–5, 59, 116, 126n74, 142n19, 145, 159, 163n73, 180, 189, 192, 193, 223, 229, 236
  Grand Mosque, 214
  Muhammad's da'wa in, 42–8
  see also da'wa: Meccan; hajj; hijra; Qur'an: 'Meccan' and 'Medinan' chapters
media, 10, 46, 58, 141n3, 197, 210, 228
  Covenant on Islamic Media, 238
  electronic, 216, 218, 219–20, 224, 243; see also internet
  international media conference (Jakarta, September 1980), 238
  see also communication; information technology; internet; newspapers; technologies
medicine, 115, 221

Medina, 9, 23, 29, 31, 40, 45–6, 48–50, 52, 53, 59, 62n61, 66, 80, 86n4, 108, 145, 159, 173, 189, 192, 193, 226, 236
  'Constitution of Medina', 62n63
  Islamic University of Medina (IUM), 232, 246
  Mosque of the Prophet Muhammad, 57
  Muhammad's da'wa in, 48–58
  see also da'wa: Medinan; hijra; Mecca; Qur'an: 'Meccan' and 'Medinan' chapters
Mehmet 'Ali see Muhammad (Mehmet) 'Ali
merchants see Islamisation: traders and; traders/trade
Mesopotamia, 102; see also Iraq
Mevleviyya Sufi order see Mawlawiyya (Mevleviyya) Sufi order
Middle East, 2, 22, 23, 40, 41, 66, 70, 71, 72, 82, 91, 101–2, 114, 119, 146, 172, 207, 208, 232, 244
  Arab-Islamic conquests, 67 (map)
  colonial, 152 (map)
  Gunpowder empires, 104 (map)
  Mongol period, 95 (map)
  post-colonial, 204 (map)
  pre-Islamic, 23, 42
migration 2, 182
  and birth of da'wa movements, 81, 214, 220
  and colonialism, 135, 150, 195
  forced, 97–9, 150
  Jewish, 189–90
  in-migration, 93–9
  minority Muslim populations, 195–6, 243–9
  Muslim since 1950, 208, 214, 220, 243–9
  to towns, 51, 119, 182
  see also hijra; jurisprudence: minorities'; Muslim 'diaspora'; travel
minoritisation, 139 (definition), 136, 150, 158, 164, 170, 179, 195, 244
miracles, 43–4, 45, 109, 113
missiology, 8, 87n31; see also da'walogy/ da'walogies
missionaries
  Muslim, 11, 155–6, 159, 167, 174, 193, 213, 225, 241, 248–9; see also da'is; da'wa; preachers/preaching; Sufis/Sufism: as missionaries
  'post-missionary', 206
  see also under Buddhists/Buddhism; Christians/Christianity; Hindus/ Hinduism
modernism, 133, 136–7, 140, 168, 172, 173–4, 178, 181, 186, 187, 188, 191, 208

modernity, 5, 7, 65, 104, 107, 123
  colonial, 136, 139, 148–57, 158, 176, 177,
    180, 184, 187, 191, 192, 209
  definition, 135–6, 139, 141n9
  and disestablishment, 138, 140, 219, 229–30
  early modern, 135–6, 139, 141n6
  high modern, 135, 136, 139, 141n7, 155
  late modern, 135, 136, 137, 139, 141n8, 219
  multiple modernities, 136–7, 140, 215, 216
  post-colonial, 136, 140, 209, 219, 238
  responses to, 143–4, 158–9, 208–9, 216,
    229, 235, 238, 257
  and secularisation, 136, 138–9, 209
monasticism, 23, 109, 110
Mongol Khanates, 95 (map), 96, 100
Mongols, 2, 71, 91, 94–6, 97, 99, 100–1, 102,
  115, 119, 122, 151, 195
monotheists/monotheism, 1, 26, 35, 42, 79,
  84, 96, 144; see also tawhid
Moore, Prof. Keith, 239
Moore, R. I., 141n9, 161n46
Morocco, 7, 186, 230, 254n114
Moses (The Prophet Musa), 27, 44
mosques, 1, 4, 47, 92, 96, 103, 106, 108, 113,
  116, 117, 123, 166, 175, 179, 208, 221,
  230–1, 233, 236, 240, 246
  al-Azhar mosque, Cairo, 77
  call to prayer, 1–2, 12n1, 92
  Chaqchan Mosque, Pakistan, 123n4
  Djinguereber Mosque, Timbuktu, 123n4
  Grand Mosque, Mecca, 214
  Mosque Message Conference (1975), 237–8
  mosque of the Prophet Muhammad,
    Medina, 57
  Muslim Community Center, Chicago, 246,
    249
  'paramosque' organisations, 220
  Shah Faisal Mosque, Islamabad, 236–7,
    237
  World Supreme Council for Mosques,
    237–8
Mourides see Muridiyya Sufi order
Mu'adh b. Jabal (Companion), 55, 56–7,
  89n64
Mu'awiyya (founder of the Umayyad
  Dynasty), 54
Mubarak, President Hosni, 205
muftis see fatwas
Mughal Empire, 92, 103, 104 (map), 126n61,
  147, 150
Muhammad
  and the Angel Gabriel, 20, 42–3, 126n81
  battles of, 51–3; see also names of individual
    battles

conquest of Mecca, 53
converts, 1, 44–6, 50–1, 54, 55
da'wa of, 28–31, 33, 35, 39–60
al-Hashimi on, 76
hijra (migration), 40, 47, 48, 49, 50, 59
  as inspiration, 5, 19, 39
  letter-writing, 58, 59
  life of, 20, 21, 23, 40–1, 173–4; see also sira
  miracles of, 43–4
  as a missionary preacher, 1, 2, 6, 9, 29, 39,
    41, 42–3, 47, 48, 80
  as missionary strategist, 43, 45, 46–7, 54–7,
    58–60
  and Sufism, 109
  titles in the Qur'an, 29
  'Year of Delegations', 54–6
  see also da'wa: Meccan; da'wa: Medinan;
    Mecca; Medina; Qur'an
Muhammad, Warith Deen, 252n43
Muhammad (Mehmet) 'Ali (Ottoman
  governor of Egypt), 192
Muhammad b. Sa'ud, 145
Muhammadiyah movement (Indonesia),
  180–1, 207, 210, 214, 220
  Aisyiyah (women's branch), 181
Muhammadiyya (Sufi order), 147
mujaddids ('renewers'), 144, 146–7; see also tajdid
Al-Muntaqid (The Critic) (newspaper), 187
Murad, Khurram, 246, 249
Muridiyya Sufi order, 133, 184–5, 207, 210,
  214, 220, 225; see also Bamba, Ahmadu
Murji'ites, 73, 84
Musa (the prophet) see Moses
Musa (son of Imam Ja'far), 77
Mus'ab b. 'Umayr (Companion), 46
Musaylima b. Habib al-Hanafi, 55
Muslim Aid, 221
Muslim b. al-Hajjaj, 40, 43
Muslim Brotherhood (MB), 170, 174–5, 176,
  180, 190, 205, 207, 208, 210, 213, 214,
  220, 226, 231, 250; see also al-Banna,
  Hasan
Muslim 'diaspora', 71, 120, 150, 185, 244
Muslim ecumene, 91–2, 93, 94, 97–8, 103,
  105, 106, 107, 110–11, 112, 119, 120,
  121, 152 (map), 154, 156, 198, 203; see
  also dar al-Islam; Islamdom
Muslim laypeople see common people
Muslim minority populations, 158, 161n36,
  183, 195–6, 206, 215–16, 225, 243–9; see
  also minoritisation
Muslim population (global, 2020), 3 (map)
Muslim Preachers of the Bible, 225; see also
  preachers/preaching

Muslim Sisters Group, 175; *see also* Muslim
    Brotherhood
Muslim Women's Association (Egypt), 175
Muslim World League (MWL), 220, 224, 225,
    236, 237–8, 241, 242, 250
    Commission on Scientific Signs, 239
    International Organization for Relief,
        Welfare and Development, 238
    Islamic Fiqh Council, 238
    Mosque Message Conference (1975), 237–8
Mu'tazilites, 84; *see also* theology (Islamic)
mysticism, 109, 126n85; *see also* Sufis/Sufism

al-Nabhani, Taqiuddin, 226
Nadir Shah, 160n24
Nadwi, Abu'l-Hasan 'Ali, 56, 96, 124n13,
    167, 171, 222, 223, 232, 239, 248, 249
    Abul Hasan Ali Nadwi Center for
        Research, Dawah and Islamic Thought
        (Lucknow, India), 222
Nahdlatul Ulama (NU), 180, 181, 182, 210,
    214; *see also* Indonesia; Muslimat NU
Naik, Zakir, 165, 216, 218, 219, 239, 259
Najran (Arabia), 42, 62n69
Nanautawi, Muhammad Qasim, 162n69
Naqshbandiyya Sufi order, 110, 116, 146–7,
    157, 162n58, 177
Nasser, Gamal *see* 'Abd al-Nasser, Gamal
Nation of Islam, 133, 213
nationalism, 198
    Arab, 174, 188–9
    European, 150, 162n61
    Indian, 170
    Jewish *see* Zionism
Natsir, Mohammad, 224
Neill, Stephen, 54
new religious intellectuals, 170, 219; *see also*
    common people; democratisation
newspapers, 163n73, 174, 178, 187; *see also*
    printing
Niger, 147
Nigeria
    Ansar al-Islam, 221
    Boko Haram, 225, 227
    colonialism, 150, 152 (map), 153
    intra- and inter-religious tensions, 225
    Izala Society *see Jama'at Izalat al-Bid'a wa
        Iqamat as-Sunna*
    Jama'at Nasr al-Islam, 221
    Kano Chronicle, 107–8
    missionaries (Christian) in, 182–3
    post-colonial, 203, 221, 224, 225, 235, 259
    shari'a initiatives, 235
    Sokoto Caliphate, 147

see also Africa: sub-Saharan Africa;
    Hausaland; 'Uthman Dan Fodio
Nizaris, 88n60; *see also* Isma'ilis
Noah (prophet), 27, 28, 37n31
Nock, A. D., 73, 88n36
nomads, 51, 69, 96, 119–20, 193
    late modern nomadism, 141n8
non-Muslims *see* Buddhists/Buddhism;
    Christians/Christianity; conversion;
    Hindus/Hinduism; inter-religious
    relations; Islam: conversion to;
    Islamisation; Jews: *da'wa* to; protected/
    tolerated peoples (*dhimmis*); religious
    tolerance; taxation

North Korea, 206
Nubia, 98, 125n59
Nur al-Islam (Light of Islam) (periodical), 176
Nur (Nurcu) movement, 178, 180, 207, 215;
    see also Said Nursi, Bediuzzaman
Nuri, Mirza Husayn 'Ali *see* Baha Allah

'occidentalism', 245
oil, 146, 192, 194–5, 210–11, 237, 241
Omani Ministry of Endowments and
    Religious Affairs, 230
ordinary Muslims *see* common people
Organisation of Islamic Cooperation (OIC),
    224, 239–41, 242, 250
Organization of Petroleum Exporting
    Countries (OPEC), 210–11
orientalists/orientalism, 9, 151, 154, 171, 173
orphans/orphanages, 36n9, 155, 181, 186,
    220
Osama b. Laden, 227; *see also* Jihadis/
    Jihadism; al-Qaeda
Ottoman Empire, 92, 94, 102, 103, 104
    (map), 115, 116, 145, 147, 165, 173, 186,
    187, 188, 189, 192
    collapse of, 150, 157, 163n73, 176–7, 196,
        210n53
    devshirme system, 98
    as an Islamic Empire, 154
    Tanzimat reforms, 157
    Young Ottomans, 178

pagans/paganism, 21, 42, 44, 56, 79, 82, 83,
    115, 171; *see also* polytheists/polytheism
Pahlavis, 191, 192; *see also* Iran
Pakistan, 77, 164, 166, 167, 168, 169, 170,
    188, 202n117, 213, 221, 233, 236–7,
    245, 247
    and Afghanistan, 211
    founding/formation of, 170, 188, 203, 205

Pakistan (*cont.*)
  Ministry of Religious Affairs and Inter-
    Faith Harmony, 230
  shari'a law, 211, 230, 235
  Sufi shrines, 113
  see also Ahmadiyya movement; India;
    Islamabad; Jama'at-i Islami; Jinnah,
    Muhammad 'Ali; Raiwind
Palestine
  colonial era, 150, 152 (map), 156, 187–90,
    197
  HAMAS, 220, 227, 230
  post-World War II, 207
  pre-Islamic, 23
  Supreme Muslim Council of Mandatory
    Palestine, 190
  Sykes-Picot Agreement (1916), 189
  see also Palestinians
Palestine Liberation Organization (PLO), 205,
  230
Palestinians, 190, 202n100, 205, 207, 208,
  211, 222, 226, 244
pan-Islamism, 163, 188, 203, 239
People of the Book, 21, 29, 30–1, 32, 33,
  38n43, 57, 59, 79, 80, 82; *see also*
  Christians/Christianity; Jews; Judaism
persecution, 43, 47, 48, 66, 73, 101–3,
  125n61, 148,168, 191–2, 213, 226, 227
Persia, 2, 42, 71, 91, 103, 113, 121, 147; *see*
  also Iran
Persian language, 94, 109, 115, 119
Persianisation, 72, 94, 119
Pfander, Karl, 164–5
Philips, Bilal, 219
pilgrimage, 109, 113, 114
  hajj (pilgrimage to Mecca), 107, 126n74,
    180, 259
  'pilgrimage to Islam' (United States), 244
  see also hijra; travel
polemics, 6, 35, 58, 85, 118, 148, 169,
  215–16; *see also* argumentation and
  debate
police, religious, 193, 235, 250; *see also*
  commanding and forbidding
polytheists/polytheism, 21, 23, 26, 27, 31,
  38n43, 38n55, 79, 259
Portugal, 120
post-colonial *see under* colonialism
Poston, Larry, 87n31, 220
poverty, 36n9, 220
prayers, 22, 24, 27, 34, 45, 48, 49, 51, 57, 99,
  106, 108, 235, 247, 259
  Islamic call to (*adhān*), 1–2, 62n54, 92
  see also mosques

preachers/preaching, 4, 7, 8, 9, 23, 27, 45,
  47, 55, 58, 68, 75, 83, 96, 106, 111–14,
  117–19, 144, 147, 148, 157, 166, 168,
  174, 178, 179, 185, 191, 198, 208, 209,
  213, 214–19, 222, 225, 237, 245, 249,
  258
  democratisation of in modernity, 133, 175,
    216, 219, 223, 249
  Islam as 'preacher's religion', 1, 2, 117
  preaching in/of the Qur'an, 1, 21, 24, 25,
    26, 29, 30, 34, 36n4, 70
  Muhammad as preacher, 1, 6, 39, 43, 44,
    48, 49, 53, 59, 62n61, 70, 109
  The Preaching of Islam see Arnold, Thomas
  see also televangelists
printing, 78, 107, 136, 142n19, 151, 155,
  157, 162n61, 165–6, 170, 173, 178,
  197, 208, 212, 214; *see also* newspapers;
  technologies
prophets, 25, 26–8, 30, 35, 223
  monoprophetism, 27
  see also names of individual prophets;
    Muhammad
proselytisation, 78, 80, 99, 120, 160n13, 166,
  167, 172–3
  counter-proselytism, 155, 156
protected/tolerated peoples (*dhimmis*), 71, 79,
  81–2, 102–3

al-Qaddhafi, Mu'ammar, 211, 241; *see also*
  Libya
Qadianism, *see* Ahmadiyya movement
Qadiriyya Sufi order, 103, 110, 113, 184, 225;
  see also Jilani, 'Abd al-Qadir
al-Qaeda, 211, 214, 227–8; *see also* Jihadis/
  Jihadism
Qajars, 191; *see also* Iran
al-Qaradawi, Yusuf, 219, *220*, 248
Qarakhanids, 94, 99
Qarmatis, 88n54
al-Qassam, 'Izz al-Din, 190, 197
Qatar, 219, 221, 233–4, 245, 253n80
quietism, 49, 135, 159, 172, 177, 178, 179,
  185, 191, 192, 194, 197, 209–10, 214,
  226, 231, 232, 234, 243
  Salafi, 138, 140, 217, 227, 229
  see also da'wa: Meccan
Qur'an, *33*
  and *da'wa*, 19–36
  da'wa of God's prophets in, 25–8
  da'wa of Muhammad in, 28–31
  da'wa to and of God in, 22–5
  *da'wa*logy of, 9, 19–28, 34–5, 39
  disputation in, 30

as first *da'wa* of Islam, 21
International Organization for the Holy
    Quran and Immaculate Sunnah, 238
inter-religious context, 23, 29
'Meccan' and 'Medinan' chapters, 29, 31
messengers, 27–8, 35
as a miracle, 44
missionary character of, 26, 33
recitation of, 46–7
revelatory nature of, 20–1
scientific signs in, 238–9; *see also* Bucailleism
Sufi view of, 109
translations of, 4, 20, 155, 171
verses (with 3 or more mentions in the text):
    Q 3:104, 32, 33, 38n50, 50, 168, 223; Q
    3:110, 32, 33, 37n22, 38n50, 50; Q 9:33,
    29, 31, 76; Q 14:44, 24, 25, 38n46; Q
    16:125, 1, 29, 32, 33, 223; Q 30:25, 24,
    37n18, 38n46
Quraysh tribe, 43, 44, 45, 49, 50, 53, 54,
    56
Qutb, Sayyid, 210, 227, 256n172

Rabi'a al-'Adawiyya, 117
Racius, Egdunas, 37n42, 38n44
Rahman, Fazlur, 21, 87n32
Rahman, Tunku Abdul, 224
Raiwind (Pakistan), 167
Ramadan, 92, 235, 259
Ramadan, Tariq, 248–9
Raniri, Nur al-Din, 92
Rashid al-Din, 100
Redzovik, Eddie, 246
reform/reformism, Islamic, 5, 73, 75, 116,
    134, 137, 138, 140 (definition), 143–8,
    149, 154, 159, 165, 166, 168, 172, 175,
    177, 178, 180, 181, 183, 186, 187, 188,
    190, 209, 213, 232, 234, 237
Reformation, Protestant, 123, 141n6, 149
refugees, 47, 244, 258
religion/religions
    comparative religion, 215–16, 218, 233
    concept of 'religion', 12, 14n3, 15n29
    missionary, 1, 2, 11, 12, 29, 55, 70, 84–5
    'prophetic', 73
    reception of, 13
    transmission of, 13
    world, 138–9
    see also Baha'i Faith; Buddhists/Buddhism;
        Christians/Christianity; Confucianism;
        Hindus/Hinduism; Islam; Judaism;
        Zoroastrians/Zoroastrianism
Religious Affairs bureaus, 177, 206, 230–5; *see
    also* police, religious

religious diversity/pluralism, 11, 21–2, 23,
    41, 70, 91, 100, 153, 165, 188, 198, 216,
    223, 245; *see also* inter-religious relations;
    intra-religious relations
religious freedom, 30, 62n63, 179, 206
    Universal Declaration on Human Rights
        (UDHR), 206
religious marketplaces, 138–9, 140 (definition),
    156, 159, 165, 166, 167, 197, 205–6,
    214, 219–20, 228, 230, 244, 246
religious tolerance, 70, 71, 101, 230
Renaissance, the, 141n6, 149
renewers *see mujaddids*
'reversion', 11
Reynolds, Gabriel Said, 36n4
Reza Shah (Pahlavi), 192
Rida, Rashid, 137, 163n69, 165, 172, *172*,
    173, 174, 196, 197, 246
Riesebrodt, Martin, 11–12
Rifa'iyya Sufi order, 110
Rimfa (Rumfa) (Hausa chief), 108
Riyadh (Saudi Arabia), 192, 194
Robinson, Francis, 149, 161n38, 165
Royal Ahl al-Bayt Institute for Islamic
    Thought, 217–18
Rumfa (Hausa chief) *see* Rimfa
Rumi (Sufi master, poet), 113, 115, 116
Rumiyah (later *Dabiq*, ISIS online magazine)
    228
Russia, 94, 150, 152 (map), 154, 156, 157,
    176, 177, 178–9, 191, 195, 204 (map)
    Vladimir ('Baptiser of Russia'), 99
    see also Soviet Union

Sa'd b. Abu Waqqas (Companion), 45
Sadat, President Anwar, 205, 210, 230
Saddam Hussein, 208
Sadr al-Din, Shaykh, 100–1
Safavid Empire, 92, 103, 104 (map), 126n70,
    150, 191
Safwan b. Umayya, 54
Said Nursi, Bediuzzaman, 177–8, 180, 197,
    215
saints, 23, 103, 109, 110, 111, 113, 114, 118,
    181; *see also* Sufis/Sufism
Saladin, 77
Salafis/Salafism, 19, 36n1, 133, 144, 145,
    148, 166, 193, 213, 214, 219, 221, 224–5
    definition, 137–8, 140
    divisions, 138, 140, 214
    Indonesia, 224
    Islamic Revival and, 208–9
    Jihadi-Salafis, 138, 140, 227–8, 229, 231–2
    mainstream *da'wa*logy of, 229

Salafis/Salafism (*cont.*)
   and Muslim World League, 236–7
   and quietism, 138, 140, 217, 227, 229,
      231
   spread of, 221
   and Sufism, 161n45
   and Wahhabism, 137, 140, 146, 193, 195,
      231–2
Salih (Prophet), 27, 37n31
Salih, Mirza, 166
Saljuq (Oghuz chieftain), 99–100
Saljuqs, 77, 94, 100
Salman the Persian, 42
Samarkand, 68, 96, 98
   The Registan, *97*
Sanussiyya Sufi order, 157
Sassanian Empire, 23, 66
Satan, 25
Sa'ud family, 192; *see also* 'Abd al-Aziz b.
      Sa'ud; Faisal bin Abdulaziz Al Saud;
      Muhammad b. Sa'ud
Saudi Arabia, 145, 189, 193
   da'wa policy, 231–2, 224–5
   emirates, 202n106
   foreign policy, 207, 236–7
   Ikhwan (Brothers or Brotherhood), 193,
      194
   and ISIS, 228
   Ministry of Islamic Affairs, Dawah and
      Guidance, 231
   oil wealth, 194, 211
   and religious freedom, 206
   religious police, 235
   Salafism, 138
   Wahhabism, 146, 192, 193
   and World Assembly of Muslim Youth
      (WAMY), 239
   see also Muslim World League; Medina:
      Islamic University of Medina
Saudi Aramco, 194, 195
Sayyid Ahmad of Bareilly, 157
Sayyid 'Ali Muhammad, 191
scholars *see 'ulama*
schools, 151, 155, 166, 173, 174, 176, 180,
      181, 186, 187, 193, 197, 221, 225, 233,
      241, 246; *see also* education; Islamic law:
      schools; *madrasas*; theology (Islamic)
science (modern), 102, 135, 137, 139, 140,
      149–50, 151, 173, 177, 180, 250, 259
   appeal to in modern *da'wa*, 4, 238–9, 250;
      see also Bucailleism
   International Commission on Scientific
      Signs in Qur'an and Sunna, 238
scripturalism, 36n1, 58

secularism, 153, 171, 174, 177, 178, 182,
      186–7, 190, 192, 198, 205, 206–7, 208,
      211, 214, 231, 236
   'secularist interregnum', 205–8, 229
secularisation, 136, 138, 209
Senegal, 3, 91, 150, 183, 184–5, 245; *see also*
      Bamba, Ahmadu; Gambia; Muridiyya;
      Touba
Serbs, 208
Shadhilyya Sufi order, 201n85
al-Shafi'i, 40
shamans/'Shamanism', 93, 100, 115,
      128n117
Shamil, Imam, 157, 162n58
Sha'rawi, Huda, 175
Shariatullah, Haji, 146
Sharkey, Heather, 162n50, 250n9
Sharon, Moshe, 88n43
al-Shaybani, 79
Shaybanids, 94
Shaykh Eid Foundation, 221
Sheba, Queen of, 58
al-Shidyak, Ahmad Faris, 166
Shi'ites, 4, 74, 75–8, 79, 84, 106, 133, 167,
      227
   Iran, 103, 191–2, 211–12, 242
   Saudi Arabia, 202n107
   and Sufism, 128n112, 147
   Twelver, 76–7, 103, 104, 133, 191
   websites for, 220
   see also Imamiyya (Imamis); Isma'ilis;
      Safavids; Zaydiyya (Zaydis)
shrines, 103, 111, 115, 116, 117, 126n61
   'Shrine Sufism', 110, 148, 156
   tomb-shrines, 109, 110, 111, 113, 114,
      127n96, 185
Shu'ayb (Prophet), 27, 37n31
Silk Road, 68, 117, 161n43
*silsila*s (lineage; chain of authority), 109,
      218
Singapore: Muslim Converts' Association of
      Singapore (Darul Arqam), 224
sira (traditional biography of the Prophet
      Muhammad), 35–6, 39, 40–1, 42–3,
      44–5, 49, 58, 59
Sirhindi, Shaykh Ahmad, 146–8
'Six Day War' (1967), 207, 208
Al-Siyasa (newspaper), 174
slaves and slavery, 48, 71, 79, 80, 82–3, 93,
      97–9, 115, 116, 120, 151, 184
Society for the Defense of Islam, 176
Solomon (Sulayman), King, 27, 58
Songhay (West Africa), 101
Soninke people, 121

South Africa, 150, 165, 196, 215, 217, 218,
    244
Southeast Asia, 91, 101, 113–14, 115, 178–81;
    see also Aceh, Dutch Empire; Indo-
    Malaysia; Indonesia; Java; Malaysia;
    Singapore; Sumatra
Soviet Union, 94, 150, 152 (map), 154, 157,
    178–9, 196, 204 (map), 207, 211, 227; see
    also Russia
Spain, 66, 68, 75, 82, 91, 101, 102, 120, 150,
    161n41, 195, 202n113
storytellers, 115, 117–18
Sudan, 157, 235
Sufis/Sufism, 62n71, 89n61, 92, 93, 100, 103,
    107, 118, 122, 133, 144–5, 147, 149,
    151, 154, 157, 168, 174, 178, 181, 186,
    187, 213, 216, 218, 225, 249
    convents, 92, 109, 117
    critique/rejection of (early modern and
        modern), 144–5, 147, 148, 177, 179, 188,
        193, 225, 228
    da'wa of (pre-modern), 107–8, 109–17, 119,
        122
    da'wa of (in modernity), 166, 178, 181,
        183–4, 213, 215, 216, 218, 225
    definition of, 109
    khanqahs (lodges), 109, 113, 117, 127n99,
        128n122
    orders or brotherhoods, 103, 110, 111, 112
        (map), 113, 116, 146–7, 157, 160n32,
        162n58, 174, 177, 184–5, 201n85, 207,
        210, 214, 220, 225; see also names of
        individual orders
    Saudi Arabia, 193
    Shari'a-Sufism, 110, 146, 166
    Shrine-Sufism, 110, 148, 156
    spread of, 112 (map), 114–17
    and 'ulama, 105–6
    'Visionary Sufism', 110
Suhrawardiyya Sufi order, 110
Sukarno, President of Indonesia, 180
Sulaimani, Qasem, 208
Sulayman, King see Solomon, King
Sumatra, 101, 180, 201n75
    Padri movement, 146, 157
Sunna (of the Prophet Muhammad), 35–6, 39,
    60n2, 79, 137, 140, 233, 257
    jurisprudence and, 79
    scientific signs in, 238
Sunnis, 4, 11, 69, 73, 74, 77, 78, 79, 83, 84,
    93, 94, 100, 103, 104, 117–18, 133, 137,
    138, 140, 166, 167, 175–6, 179, 191,
    199n14, 212, 213, 224, 227, 231, 232,
    236, 237, 241, 246, 248

Sykes-Picot Agreement (1916), 189
Syria, 66, 69, 74, 102, 150, 179, 187–90, 203,
    205, 210, 227, 244
    religious communities, 23
    see also Damascus; Umayyads

al-Tabari, 40, 63n95, 68, 87n27
tabligh (conveying, communicating, or
    preaching Islam), 8, 13, 14n14, 26, 133,
    164, 167, 168, 196, 233
Tablighi Jama'at (TJ), 8, 45, 133, 138, 166–7,
    168, 174, 197, 198, 207, 210 212, 213,
    258
    ijtima's (congregations, missionary
        conferences), 167, 213
Tabuk (Arabia), 53
Ta'if (Arabia), 48, 52, 53
tajdid (renewal) movements, 144, 209; see also
    reform/reformism, Islamic
takfir (labelling others kafirs or unbelievers), 73,
    148
Takfir w'al-Hijra group, 210, 214
Talha b. 'Ubaydallah (Companion), 45
Tanzania, 183, 221, 225
tarbiyya see education
Tarjuman al-Qur'an (journal), 170
Tatars, 98, 125n49
taxation, 56, 70, 76, 79, 80
Taylor, Hudson, 155
technologies, 78, 133, 135, 149, 151, 158,
    163n78, 165–6, 177, 193, 194, 207, 209,
    209, 214–15, 216, 218, 219, 232
Teitelbaum, Joshua, 232
televangelists, 5, 119, 214–19, 250; see also
    preachers/preaching
terrorism, 46, 190, 215, 217, 219, 226, 227
Thanawi, Ashraf 'Ali, 199n12
theology (Islamic), 83–4
al-Tijani, Ahmad, 147
Tijaniyya Sufi order, 147, 201n85, 225
Timbuktu (Mali): Djinguereber Mosque,
    123n4
Timothy I, Patriarch, 76
Timur, 94, 96, 205
tombs/cemeteries, 185, 193
    tomb-shrines, 109, 110, 111, 113, 114, 185
Tongi (Bangladesh), 167
Touba (Senegal), 184; see also Bamba,
    Ahmadu
traders/trade, 4, 7, 91, 101, 107–8, 116, 117,
    119–21, 129n147, 161n43, 182, 183,
    201n74, 244
training (for da'wa) see education
Transjordan, 189

translation, 4, 12, 20, 107, 155, 165, 171, 172, 218, 219, 238, 239, 249
transnationalisation *see* globalisation
Transoxania *see* Central Asia
travel, 78, 106, 107, 113, 116, 122, 126n74, 135, 151, 155, 163n73, 214, 217; *see also* communication; migration; Muslim minority populations; pilgrimage
Treaty of Hudaybiyya, 50, 63n77
Truman, President Harry, 190
al-Tufayl (Companion), 45, 46
Tunisia, 186, 205
  Young Tunisians, 186
Turkey, 91, 163n73, 178, 191, 192, 197, 203, 205, 230, 244, 245
  da'wa c. 1850–1950, 176–8
  Directorate of Religious Affairs (Diyanet), 231, 236
  establishment of, 157
  Gulen movement, 133, 178, 215, 217, 219, 231
  Justice and Virtue Party (AKP), 215
  'People's Houses', 177, 207
  Young Turks, 177
  see also Anatolia; Ataturk, Mustafa Kemal; Ottoman Empire; Turks/Turkic peoples
Turkification, 72, 94, 100
Turks/Turkic peoples, 2, 71, 72, 93–4, 96, 97, 98, 99, 100, 101, 113, 115, 122; *see also* Turkey
al-Tusi, Nasir al-Din, 80
Tuwat (Algeria), 103
Twelvers *see under* Shi'ites

'Ubaydallah al-Mahdi (founder of Fatimid Empire), 77
Uganda, 183, 240
'ulama (Muslim scholars), 92, 103, 105–8, 109, 115, 116, 117, 119, 120, 122, 133, 147, 149, 151, 166, 170, 176, 177, 178, 181, 186, 187, 191, 192, 193, 194, 211, 211, 216, 219, 224, 232, 241, 249
'Umar (Companion, Caliph), 45, 46, 52
'Umar II, Caliph, 71
Umayyads, 54, 70, 71, 74, 75, 77, 86n4, 92
United Arab Emirates (UAE), 211
United Arab Republic, 251n20
United Nations, 190, 207, 239
United Nations Universal Declaration on Human Rights (UDHR), 206
United States, 150, 155, 176, 214, 223
  9/11 attacks, 227–8
  and Afghanistan, 211

African Americans, 213, 223, 244, 247, 256n171
Cold War, 207
da'wa manuals for, 223
'hegemonic power' of, 207–8
Immigration and Nationality Act (1965), 244
and Iran, 192
and Israel, 190, 210
mosques, 231
Muslim Student Association of North America (ISNA), 214, 246
Muslims in, 195, 213, 222, 223, 231, 244, 245, 246, 247, 249
Nation of Islam movement, 213
and Saudi Arabia, 194
see also Islamic Society of North America
universities, 192, 221, 232, 233, 240
urbanisation, 207
al-'Utaybi, Juhayman, 214
'Uthman (Companion, Caliph), 45
'Uthman Dan Fodio ('Uthman b. Fudi), 147, 148
Uzbek Khan, 100
Uzbekistan, 97, 205; *see also* Central Asia; Khiva; Samarkand
  Islamic Movement of Uzbekistan, 227
Uzbeks, 94, 100, 125n49, 205

Van Bruinessen, Martin, 231
Varanasi (India): Jamia-tus-Salafiah *madrasa*, 237
vernacularisation, 114–15; *see also* indigenisation
violence, 66, 73, 101, 148, 227; *see also* persecution
voluntary societies/associations, 4, 155, 162n61, 180–1, 212–13, 220, 229
  'age of the voluntary society', 155
Vryonis, Speros, 127n107

Wadud, Amina, 247–8
Wahhabis/Wahhabism, 75, 133, 138, 140, 145–6, 147, 148, 192–5, 197, 214, 227–8, 231, 232; *see also* Ibn 'Abd al-Wahhab, Muhammad; Salafis/Salafism; Saudi Arabia
Wahid, Din, 224
Wali Allah, Shah of Delhi, 146, 147, 148, 199n14
Wali Songo ('Nine Saints'), 114, 121
Walker, Paul, 36n15
Walls, Andrew, 162n60
Wansbrough, John, 21

Waraqa b. Naufal, 42
Watt, W. M., 56
Weber, Max, 141n4
welfare associations and initiatives, 180,
    208, 220–1, 238; *see also* humanitarian
    programmes
West, the, 135, 136, 143, 145, 155, 158, 171,
    172, 177, 190, 206, 207, 208, 211, 227
  Muslims/*da'wa* in 47, 232, 243–9
westernisation, 136, 157, 177, 192, 205
Wiktorowicz, Quintan, 142n18, 229, 251n26
women 5, 98, 151
  and *da'wa*, 34, 44, 107, 123, 133, 167, 168,
      170, 175, 181, *182*, 198, 209, 215, 234,
      247–8
  and education, 107, 181
  as popular preachers, 118, 215
  and religious police, 235
  and Sufism, 117
  see also common people; *da'wa*: as collective
      obligation or individual obligation;
      democratisation; laicisation
World Assembly of Muslim Youth (WAMY),
    221, 239
World Islamic Call Society (WICS), 241–2
World Islamic Committee for Da'wa and
    Relief, 220

Yahya, al-Hadi ila al-Haqq, 75
Yaji (Hausa chief), 107, 108

Yasawi, Shaykh Ahmad, 110
Yav Izala *see Jama'at Izalat al-Bid'a wa Iqamat
    as-Sunna*
Yasawi, Shaykh Ahmad, 110
Yasawiyya Sufi order, 110, 113, 115
Year of Delegations, 52, 54, 55–6
Yemen, 23, 56, 75, 150–1
'Yom Kippur War', 210
Young Men's Muslim Association (YMMA),
    175, 190
youth movements, 211, 221, 224, 239
YouTube, 218, 246
Yusuf *see* Joseph

Zaite, Abdurahaman, 108
Zakariyya, Muhammad, 162n69, 168
Zaman, Muhammad Qasim, 14n17, 237
al-Zawahiri, Ayman, 227; *see also* al-Qaeda
Zayd (Companion), 44
Zaydiyya (Zaydis), 76
Zebiri, Kate, 26, 38n44
Zia ul-Haqq, President Muhammad, 211,
    230
al-Zindani, 'Abul Majid, 255n146
Zionism, 189, 190, 227; *see also* Israel; Jews;
    Judaism
Zoroastrians/Zoroastrianism, 2, 23, 41, 42,
    96, 113
al-Zubayr (Companion), 45
Zwemer, Samuel, 176

CPSIA information can be obtained
at www.ICGtesting.com
Printed in the USA
LVHW080859040321
680413LV00001B/1

9 781474 451536